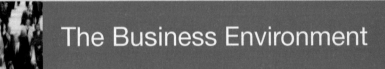

The Business Environment

fourth edition

The Business Environment

Ian Worthington and Chris Britton

Leicester Business School, De Monfort University, Leicester

FT Prentice Hall
FINANCIAL TIMES

An imprint of **Pearson Education**
Harlow, England • London • New York • Boston • San Francisco • Toronto • Sydney • Singapore • Hong Kong
Tokyo • Seoul • Taipei • New Delhi • Cape Town • Madrid • Mexico City • Amsterdam • Munich • Paris • Milan

Pearson Education Limited

Edinburgh Gate
Harlow
Essex CM20 2JE
United Kingdom

and Associated Companies throughout the world

Visit us on the World Wide Web at:
www.pearsoned.co.uk

_____

First published in Great Britain in 1994
Second edition 1997
Third edition 2000
Fourth edition 2003

© Ian Worthington and Chris Britton 1994, 1997, 2000, 2003

ISBN 0 273 678272

British Library Cataloguing-in-Publication Data
A catalogue record for this book is available from the British Library.

10 9 8 7 6 5 4
09 08 07 06 05 04

Typeset in 9.5/13pt Stone Serif by 30.
Printed and bound by Mateu Cromo Artes Graficas, Madrid, Spain

The publisher's policy is to use paper manufactured from sustainable forests.

For Lindsey, Tom and Georgina and for
Rachael, Philip, Nick and Megan, with our love

Brief contents

Brief contents

Full contents

Part One INTRODUCTION

Part Two CONTEXTS

3 The political environment   41

Ian Worthington

4 The macroeconomic environment   80

Ian Worthington

Part Three FIRMS

Part Five ISSUES

Contributors

Authors

Ian Worthington, BA (Hons), PhD, is Principal Lecturer in the Department of Strategy and Management, Leicester Business School, De Montfort University, where he specialises in business environment and greening business. He has published both in Britain and the USA and is co-author of a recent book on economics.

Chris Britton, BA (Hons), MSc, is Principal Lecturer in the Department of Strategy and Management, Leicester Business School, De Montfort University. Her teaching and research interests lie in the field of industrial economics and labour markets, where she has contributed to several publications, including co-authorship of a book on executive recruitment for *The Economist*. With Ian Worthington and Andy Rees she has recently completed a book on Business Economics.

Contributors

Diane Belfitt, BA (Hons), Diploma in Welfare Law, has taught law at a number of institutions, including Leicester Polytechnic, Leicester University and Charles Keene College in Leicester. She has examined for a number of Examination Boards.

Zena Cumberpatch, BA (Hons), MSc, is Senior Lecturer at Nene College, Northampton. Her main research interests include teaching and learning strategies and gender issues; she has given conference papers on these topics. She is currently engaged in doctoral research in this area.

Martyn Kendrick, BA (Hons), FCII, Chartered Insurance Practitioner, is Principal Lecturer and Deputy Head in the Department of Strategy and Management, Leicester Business School, De Montfort University. His main teaching and research interests lie in the fields of business ethics, corporate responsibility and E-Business.

Dean Patton, BA (Hons), Ph.D, PGCE, is Principal Lecturer in the Department of Strategy and Management, Leicester Business School, De Montfort University. His teaching and research interests centre on small firms and environmental policies within business. He has published in both these areas.

Preface to the first edition

Interest in business studies has never been greater; witness, for example, the spectacular growth in the number of business schools in British universities and institutes of higher education over the last ten years and the rapidly increasing number of courses at degree and sub-degree level in which business is an important, and frequently dominant, element. Accompanying this growth in institutional provision has been an equally impressive growth in the number of books and journals devoted to the various aspects of business – including texts on management principles and practice, organisation theory, strategic management, marketing, human resource management, business economics, accounting and finance, and so on. While such contributions have invariably been welcomed and have augmented our knowledge of the business world, the overwhelming preoccupation of scholars with the internal aspects of organisational life has tended to mean that the external influences on business activity have received little attention. This book is an attempt to redress the balance.

It should be stated at the outset that our central aim is to provide a study of business, rather than a study for business – a text for students rather than practitioners, although hopefully the latter will find much of the material useful and informative. In embarking on this study, we recognise that our perspective has been conditioned by years of teaching students on business studies courses in a variety of institutions, as well as our own interests and specialisms, and consequently the choice of subject matter and the ordering of material will not suit all tutors teaching on Business Environment courses. We have, however, attempted to discuss all the mainstream areas found on degree and HND-level courses in the large number of institutions with which we are familiar, as well as exploring some newer topics which are beginning to receive prominence in a growing number of business schools (e.g. corporate responsibility). In addition, whilst adopting a UK perspective, we have also drawn a substantial amount of our material from European and international sources – something often promised but not always delivered!

Each chapter in the book follows a common format, which includes objectives, a case study, review questions and assignments, and a guide to further reading. A comprehensive review of data and information sources is included in Chapter 16 (now Chapter 17) and we would strongly encourage students to make regular use of these sources, particularly the quality newspapers and journals which contain a wealth of information and analysis on the changing business environment.

In carrying out this study, we have received considerable help from numerous organisations to whom we extend our thanks. These have included the Department of Trade and Industry, the Department of the Environment, the Cabinet Office, the Monopolies and Mergers Commission, the European Commission, the European Information Centre (Leicester City Council), Business in the Community, and the Confederation of British Industry.

Our gratitude also goes to the students and staff of Leicester Business School who have unwittingly helped us to gather information and to formulate our ideas over more years than we would care to mention. In particular we would like to acknowledge the considerable help and encouragement given to us by Gary Cook, Andy Rees, Professor Derrick Ball, Professor John Coyne and the staff of De Montfort University Library. To Janice Cox, who typed the majority of the script under demanding circumstances, goes our special thanks and admiration – she never once complained and always met the deadlines.

We would also like to acknowledge the considerable help, support and encouragement given to us by Dr Penelope Woolf of Pitman Publishing who has retained faith in us throughout the project. To her go our special thanks.

Our greatest debt, however, is owed to our families who have paid the highest price in terms of lost time, boring conversations, tetchiness and a general lack of consideration. Despite all this they have remained encouraging, supportive and loving. It is to them that we rightly dedicate this book.

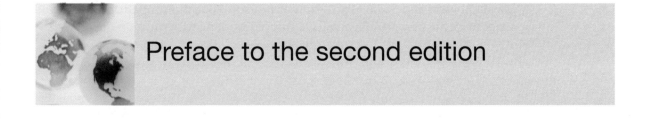

Preface to the second edition

Reactions to the first edition were very favourable and we were encouraged by this fact. In the new edition, we have updated the facts and figures from the original book, and added some new information and a number of new case studies which have contemporary relevance. Each chapter now contains additional case material in the form of mini cases which are used to highlight specific aspects of the text. As ever we remain grateful to our colleagues and to our students for their continuing support and encouragement, and to the large number of organisations that have kindly provided us with material. We would also like to thank Beth Barber of Pitman Publishing for her support and guidance.

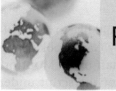 # Preface to the third edition

While retaining the successful format of previous editions, we have taken the opportunity to make a number of changes in the third edition, most notably in Chapters 3 and 15. Chapter 3 now provides a more generic view of the political environment, which is useful for cross-national comparisons; Chapter 15 looks in more detail at the concept of corporate social responsibility. In addition, facts, figures and tables from the previous edition have been updated and there is some new information and a number of new case studies and mini cases reflecting recent developments in the business environment.

We continue to be grateful to our colleagues and students for their encouragement and support and would like to thank in particular Jo Webb, Bharat, Rebecca Coleman, Michael Edwards and Nikos Karaoularis of De Montfort University Library for their help and advice with part of Chapter 16. Special thanks, too, must go to Magda Robson and Sadie McClelland at Pearson Education for all their help and support; we are very grateful and have enjoyed working with them on the project.

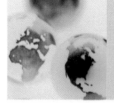# Preface to the fourth edition

In writing the fourth edition of the book we have been guided by the very helpful observations of our reviewers and by our own feelings on how we could build upon the well-received format of previous editions. Apart from updating the facts and figures to reflect recent developments, we have added a new chapter on technology (Chapter 15), additional material in a number of other chapters and a variety of new, topical case studies and mini cases, many of which have an international focus. Added to this all chapters now include key terms, a summary of key learning points and numerous **weblinks** which students can use to research an organisation or issue in more detail. A complete glossary of terms and their definitions can be found at the end of the book.

As in the past a number of individuals have contributed significantly to this project, particularly Jo Webb and Carol Keddie of De Montfort University Library and the team at Pearson Education who guided us through the process of assembling this edition. To them, and to our colleagues and students who have encouraged and supported us over the years, we would like to give our special thanks.

Ian Worthington
Chris Britton
November 2002

In some instances we have been unable to trace the owners of copyright material, and we would appreciate any information that would enable us to do so.

Guided tour of the book

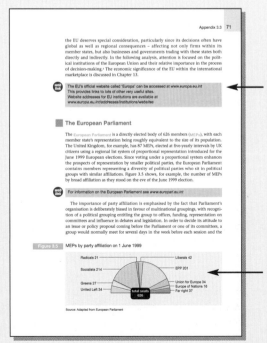

Learning Objectives highlight core coverage in terms of expected learning outcomes after completing each chapter, to help students focus their learning and evaluate their progress.

Key Terms are drawn out at the start of every chapter and are emboldened the first time they appear in the text to enable students to locate information quickly. A full **Glossary** appears at the end of the book.

Links to relevant web pages are highlighted throughout the text and repeated on the website *www.booksites.net/worthington* to help direct students' research.

Where possible colourful **figures** and **diagrams** are used to illustrate concepts and provide memorable learning aids.

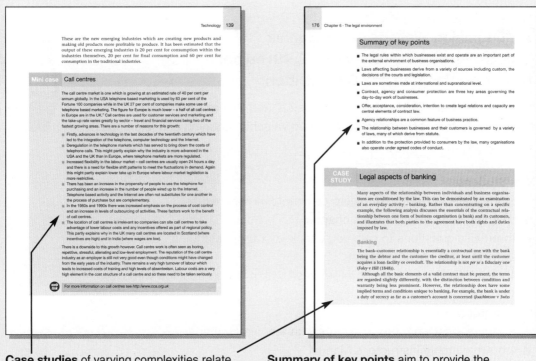

Case studies of varying complexities relate the theory represented in the chapter to real life situations in a range of diverse organisations.

Summary of key points aim to provide the student with a useful revision aid.

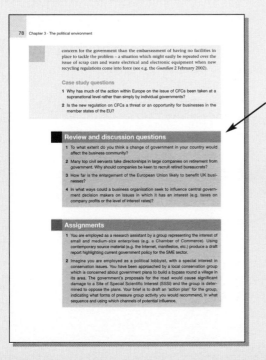

Questions and **assignments** provide engaging activities for students and lecturers in and out of the classroom situation. Further questions on the website help to evaluate their progress.

Also available with this text is access to integrated, easy-to-use online course content for use with Course Compass, Blackboard or Web CT. It contains 40 hours of interactive learning and assessment material. For further information visit: *www.booksites.net/cms_uk_book/busmang/0273641638.htm*

Part One

INTRODUCTION

1

Business organisations: the external environment

Ian Worthington

Business organisations differ in many ways, but they also have a common feature: the transformation of inputs into output. This transformation process takes place against a background of external influences which affect the firm and its activities. This external environment is complex, volatile and interactive, but it cannot be ignored in any meaningful analysis of business activity.

Objectives

- To understand the basic features of business activity.

- To portray the business organisation as a system interacting with its environment.

- To recognise the range and complexity of the external influences on business activity.

- To survey the central themes inherent in the study of the business environment.

Key terms

Environmental change	Immediate (or Operational)	Outputs
External environment	environment	PESTLE analysis
General (or Contextual)	Inputs	Transformation system
environment	Open system	

Introduction

Business activity is a fundamental and universal feature of human existence and yet the concept of 'business' is difficult to define with any degree of precision. Dictionary definitions tend to describe it as being concerned with buying and selling or with trade and commerce, or the concern of profit-making organisations, and clearly all of these would come within the accepted view of business. Such a restricted view, however, would exclude large parts of the work of government and its agencies and the activities of non-profit-making organisations – a perspective it would be hard to sustain in a climate in which business methods, skills, attitudes and objectives are being increasingly adopted by these organisations. It is this broader view of business and its activities which is adopted below and which forms the focus of an investigation into the business environment.

The business organisation and its environment

A model of business activity

Most business activity takes place within an organisational context and even a cursory investigation of the business world reveals the wide variety of organisations involved, ranging from the small local supplier of a single good or service to the multibillion dollar international or multinational corporation producing and trading on a global scale. Given this rich organisational diversity, most observers of the business scene tend to differentiate between organisations in terms of their size, type of product and/or market, methods of finance, scale of operations, legal status and so on. Nissan, for example, would be characterised as a major multinational car producer and distributor trading on world markets, while a local builder is likely to be seen as a small business operating at a local level with a limited market and relatively restricted turnover.

web link   Further information on Nissan is available at *www.nissanmotors.com*
The Nissan UK website address is *www.nissanco.uk*

While such distinctions are both legitimate and informative, they can conceal the fact that all business organisations are ultimately involved in the same basic activity, namely, the transformation of inputs (resources) into outputs (goods or services). This process is illustrated in Figure 1.1.

In essence, all organisations acquire resources – including labour, premises, technology, finance, materials – and transform these resources into the goods or services required by their customers. While the type, amount and combination of resources will vary according to the needs of each organisation and may also vary over time, the simple process described above is common to all types of business organisation and provides a useful starting-point for investigating business activity and the environment in which it takes place.

A more detailed analysis of business resources and those internal aspects of organisations which help to transform inputs into output can be found in Chapters 2, 5 and 15 below. The need, here, is simply to appreciate the idea of the firm as a transformation

Figure 1.1   The business organisation as a transformation system

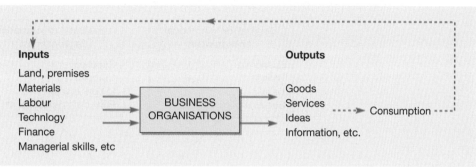

system and to recognise that in producing and selling output most organisations hope to earn sufficient revenue to allow them to maintain and replenish their resources, thus permitting them to produce further output which in turn produces further inputs. In short, inputs help to create output and output creates inputs. Moreover, the output of one organisation may represent an input for another, as in the case of the firm producing capital equipment or basic materials or information or ideas. This interrelationship between business organisations is just one example of the complex and integrated nature of business activity and it helps to highlight the fact that the fortunes of any single business organisation are invariably linked with those of another or others – a point clearly illustrated in many of the examples cited in the text.

The firm in its environment

The simple model of business activity described above is based on the systems approach to management (see Chapter 2). One of the benefits of this approach is that it stresses that organisations are entities made up of interrelated parts which are intertwined with the outside world – the 'external environment' in systems language. This environment comprises a wide range of influences – economic, demographic, social, political, legal, technological, etc. – which affect business activity in a variety of ways and which can impinge not only on the transformation process itself, but also on the process of resource acquisition and on the creation and consumption of output. This idea of the firm in its environment is illustrated in Figure 1.2.

Figure 1.2   The firm in its environment

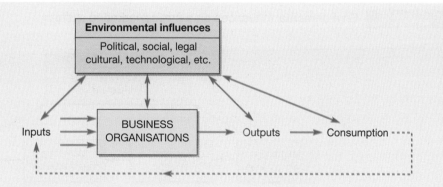

Figure 1.3	Two levels of environment

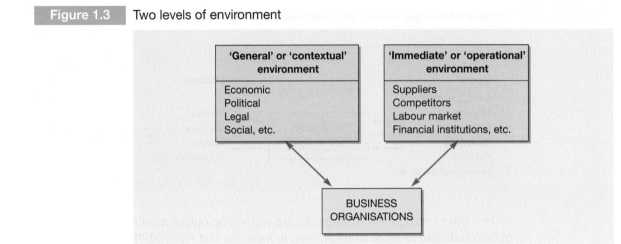

In examining the business environment, a useful distinction can be made between those external factors which tend to have a more immediate effect on the day-to-day operations of a firm and those which tend to have a more general influence. Figure 1.3 makes this distinction.

The immediate or operational environment for most firms includes suppliers, competitors, labour markets, financial institutions and customers, and may also include trading organisations, trade unions and possibly a parent company. In contrast the general or contextual environment comprises those macroenvironmental factors such as economic, political, socio-cultural, technological and legal influences on business which affect a wide variety of businesses and which can emanate not only from local and national sources but also from international and supranational developments.

This type of analysis can also be extended to the different functional areas of an organisation's activities such as marketing or personnel or production or finance, as illustrated in Figure 1.4. Such an analysis can be seen to be useful in at least two ways. First, it emphasises the influence of external factors on specific activities within the firm and in doing so underlines the importance of the interface between the internal and external environments. Second, by drawing attention to this interface, it highlights the fact that, while business organisations are often able to exercise some degree of control over their internal activities and processes, it is often very difficult, if not impossible, to control the external environment in which they operate.

Figure 1.4	Environmental influences on a firm's marketing system

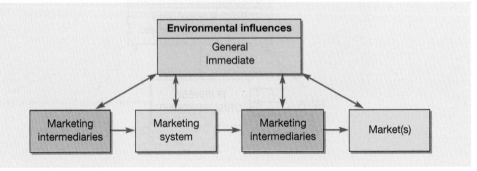

The general or contextual environment

While the external factors referred to above form the subject-matter of the rest of the book, it is useful at this point to gain an overview of the business environment by highlighting some of the key environmental influences on business activity. In keeping with the distinction made between general and more immediate influences, these are discussed separately below. In this section we examine what are frequently referred to as the 'PESTLE' factors (i.e. political, economic, socio-cultural, technological, legal and ethical influences). A 'PESTLE' (or 'PEST') analysis can be used to analyse a firm's current and future environment as part of the strategic management process (*see* Chapter 17).

The political environment

A number of aspects of the political environment clearly impinge on business activity. These range from general questions concerning the nature of the political system and its institutions and processes (Chapter 3), to the more specific questions relating to government involvement in the working of the economy (Chapter 4) and its attempts to influence market structure and behaviour (Chapters 8, 12, 14). Government activities, both directly and indirectly, influence business activity and government can be seen as the biggest business enterprise at national or local level (Chapter 10). Given the trend towards the globalisation of markets and the existence of international trading organisations and blocs, international politico-economic influences on business activity represent one key feature of the business environment (Chapters 3, 5, 13). Another is the influence of public, as well as political, opinion in areas such as environmental policy and corporate responsibility (Chapter 16).

The economic environment

The distinction made between the political and economic environment – and, for that matter, the legal environment – is somewhat arbitrary. Government, as indicated above, plays a major role in the economy at both national and local level (Chapters 4 and 10) and its activities help to influence both the demand and supply side (e.g. see Chapter 11). Nevertheless there are a number of other economic aspects related to business activity which are worthy of consideration. These include various structural aspects of both firms and markets (Chapters 7, 8, 9, 12) and a comparison of economic theory and practice (e.g. Chapters 11, 12, 13).

Mini case　Cars off the shelf

Proposed changes by the European Commission to the way in which new cars are to be sold in Europe after September 2002 (*see* Case Study in Chapter 14) have opened up some interesting possibilities for enterprising businesses. Colruyt, the Belgian supermarket chain, has indicated that it intends to market and sell a limited number of new vehicles at prices up to 25 per cent lower than licensed dealers in Belgium, which is already one of Europe's cheapest countries for cars. The company plans to buy its vehicles in southern Europe, where prices are lower than in Belgium, and then resell them through a limited number of stores. If the experiment is successful Colruyt seems destined to extend the project to other stores and possibly other models of car. It is unlikely to be long before other companies follow suit, thereby paving the way for major European supermarket chains to gain a slice of the lucrative car market and to offer a new product range alongside their traditional offering.

The socio-cultural environment

Both demand and supply are influenced by social and cultural factors. Cultural factors, for example, may affect the type of products being produced or sold, the markets they are sold in, the price at which they are sold and a range of other variables. People are a key organisational resource and a fundamental part of the market for goods and services. Accordingly, socio-cultural influences and developments have an important effect on business operations, as do demographic changes (Chapter 5).

The technological environment

Technology is both an input and an output of business organisations as well as being an environmental influence on them. Investment in technology and innovation is frequently seen as a key to the success of an enterprise and has been used to explain differences in the relative competitiveness of different countries (Chapter 5). It has also been responsible for significant developments in the internal organisation of businesses in the markets for economic resources (Chapter 15).

The legal environment

Businesses operate within a framework of law which has a significant impact on various aspects of their existence. Laws usually govern, among other things, the status of the organisation (Chapter 7), its relationship with its customers and suppliers and certain internal procedures and activities (Chapter 6). They may also influence market structures and behaviour (e.g. Chapter 12). Since laws emanate from government (including supranational governments) and from the judgments of the courts, some understanding of the relevant institutions and processes is desirable (e.g. Chapters 3 and 6).

The ethical environment

Ethical considerations have become an increasingly important influence on business behaviour, particularly among the larger, more high profile companies. One area where this has been manifest is in the demand for firms to act in a more socially responsible way and to consider the impact they might have on people, their communities and the natural environment (Chapter 16).

The immediate or operational environment

Resources and resource markets

An organisation's need for resources makes it dependent to a large degree on the suppliers of those resources, some of whom operate in markets which are structured to a considerable extent (e.g. Chapter 5). Some aspects of the operation of resource markets or indeed the activities of an individual supplier can have a fundamental impact on an organisation's success and upon the way in which it structures its internal procedures and processes. By the same token, the success of suppliers is often intimately connected with the decisions and/or fortunes of their customers. While some organisations may seek to gain an advantage in price, quality or delivery by purchasing resources from overseas, such a decision can engender a degree of uncertainty, particularly where exchange rates are free rather than fixed (Chapter 13). Equally, organisations may face uncertainty and change in the domestic markets for resources as a result of factors as varied as technological change, government intervention or public opinion (e.g. conservation issues).

Customers

Customers are vital to all organisations and the ability both to identify and to meet consumer needs is seen as one of the keys to organisational survival and prosperity – a point not overlooked by politicians, who are increasingly using business techniques to attract the support of the electorate. This idea of consumer sovereignty – where resources are allocated to produce output to satisfy customer demands – is a central tenet of the market economy (Chapter 4) and is part of an ideology whose influence has become all pervasive in recent years. Understanding the many factors affecting both individual and market demand, and the ways in which firms organise themselves to satisfy that demand is a vital component of a business environment that is increasingly market led.

Competitors

Competition – both direct and indirect – is an important part of the context in which many firms operate and is a factor equally applicable to the input as well as the output side of business. The effects of competition, whether from domestic organisations or from overseas firms (e.g. *see* Chapter 13), is significant at the macro as well as the micro level and its influence can be seen in the changing structures of many advanced industrial economies (Chapter 9). How firms respond to these competitive challenges (e.g. Chapter 8) and the attitudes of governments to anti-competitive practices (Chapter 14) is a legitimate area of concern for students of business.

Analysing the business environment

In a subject as all encompassing as the business environment it is possible to identify numerous approaches to the organisation of the material. One obvious solution
would be to examine the various factors mentioned above, devoting separate chapters to each of the environmental influences and discussing their impact on
business organisations. While this solution has much to recommend it – not least
of which is its simplicity – the approach adopted below is based on the grouping of
environmental influences into four main areas, in the belief that this helps to focus
attention on key aspects of the business world, notably contexts, firms and their
markets and issues of significance to entrepreneurs and to society as a whole.

Mini case   ## Levi Strauss: jean therapy?

Levi Strauss is a privately owned company based in San Francisco in the United States.
For much of the latter half of the twentieth century its traditional blue riveted '501' denim
jeans – worn originally by gold-miners and cowboys – had been the world's favourite pair
of trousers. As a global brand name the 501 was almost without equal and had been
popularised by cult movie stars such as James Dean, Marilyn Monroe and Marlon
Brando. Its image had always been that of a sexy and youthful product worn by the
rebellious; this had helped to make 501s popular with people of all ages in all countries.

As one of the last major American clothing companies to maintain a significant
manufacturing base in the United States, Levi Strauss had been an important contributor
to the US economy in symbolic as well as economic terms. Its announcement in February
1999 that it was to close half of its North American plants with the loss of around 6000
jobs (about one-third of its workforce) represented a blow to an industry which had been
in decline for some time in the face of overseas competition. Coming on the back of the
7500 jobs shed the previous year by the company, the new redundancies had a
significant impact in those areas of the United States and Canada where Levi factories
were located.

The turnaround in Levi's fortunes provides a good illustration of how an evolving business
environment can impact on an organisation, particularly if it fails to recognise and
respond to changing external circumstances. In this case the problem seems to be that
the company was slow to recognise changes in fashion tastes; in effect it appears to
have taken its market for granted and forgotten about the importance of the needs and
wants of its customers, many of whom were switching to alternative products such as
combat, cargo and utility trousers. For those buyers who still remained loyal to jeans,
competition from imported Japanese products and designer brands such as Tommy
Hilfiger and Calvin Klein had further eroded Levi's formerly dominant position. In 1997,
for example, Levi faced a 4 per cent cut in sales; in 1998 this increased to 13 per cent.

Press speculation at the time suggested that Levi might respond to the competitive
challenge by moving its manufacturing facilities overseas in order to reduce its costs.

 Information on Levi Strauss can be obtained at *www.levistrauss.com*

In Part Two consideration is given to the political, economic and legal contexts within which businesses function. In addition to examining the influence of political and economic systems, institutions and processes on the conduct of business, this section focuses on the macroeconomic environment and on influences affecting key organisational resources, particularly labour, technology and raw materials. The legal system and the influence of law in a number of critical areas of business activity is also a primary concern and one which has links with Part 3.

In Part Three, attention is focused on three central structural aspects: legal structure, size structure and industrial structure. The chapter on legal structure examines the impact of different legal definitions on a firm's operations and considers possible variations in organisational goals based on legal and other influences. The focus then shifts to how differences in size can affect the organisation (e.g. access to capital, economies of scale) and to an examination of how changes in scale and/or direction can occur, including the role of government in assisting small-business development and growth. One of the consequences of changes in the component elements of the economy is its effect on the overall structure of industry and commerce – a subject which helps to highlight the impact of international competition on the economic structure of many advanced industrial economies. Since government is a key actor in the economy, the section concludes with an analysis of government involvement in business and in particular its influence on the supply as well as the demand side of the economy at both national and local level.

In Part Four, the aim is to compare theory with practice by examining issues such as pricing, market structure and foreign trade. The analysis of price theory illustrates the degree to which the theoretical models of economists shed light on the operation of business in the 'real' world. Similarly, by analysing basic models of market structure, it is possible to gain an understanding of the effects of competition on a firm's behaviour and to appreciate the significance of both price and non-price decisions in the operation of markets.

The analysis continues with an examination of external markets and the role of government in influencing both the structure and operation of the marketplace. The chapter on international markets looks at the theoretical basis of trade and the development of overseas markets in practice, particularly in the context of recent institutional and financial developments (e.g. the Single Market, the Euro). The section concludes with an investigation of the rationale for government intervention in markets and a review of government action in three areas, namely, privatisation and deregulation, competition policy and the operation of the labour market.

Finally, in Part Five, consideration is given to three aspects of business which are highly topical. One of these – corporate responsibility towards the natural environment – raises fundamental questions about the moral dimension of business activity, a subject often overlooked by writers and commentators on the business scene. A second, on the subject of technology, looks in detail at the impact of new technology on organisations and on market development and examines the increasingly important issue of 'E-Business'.

The concluding chapter in this section – and appropriately, in the book as a whole – emphasises the continuing need for organisations to monitor change in the business environment and examines a number of frameworks through which such an analysis can take place. In seeking to make sense of their environment, businesses need access to a wide range of information, much of which is available from published material, including government sources. Some of the major types of information available to students of business and to business organisations – including statistical and other forms of information – are considered in the final part of this chapter.

Central themes

A number of themes run through the text and it is useful to draw attention to these at this point.

Interaction with the environment

Viewed as an open system, the business organisation is in constant interaction with its environment. Changes in the environment can cause changes in inputs, in the transformation process and in outputs and these in turn may engender further changes in the organisation's environment. The internal and external environments should be seen as interrelated and interdependent, not as separate entities.

Interaction between environmental variables

In addition to the interaction between the internal and external environments, the various external influences affecting business organisations are also frequently interrelated. Changes in interest rates, for example, may affect consumer confidence and this can have an important bearing on business activity. Subsequent attempts by government to influence the level of demand could exacerbate the situation and this may lead to changes in general economic conditions, causing further problems for firms. The combined effect of these factors could be to create a turbulent environment which could result in uncertainty in the minds of managers. Failure to respond to the challenges (or opportunities) presented by such changes could signal the demise of the organisation or at best a significant decline in its potential performance.

The complexity of the environment

The environmental factors identified above are only some of the potential variables faced by all organisations. These external influences are almost infinite in number and variety and no study could hope to consider them all. For students of business and for managers alike, the requirement is to recognise the complexity of the external environment and to pay greater attention to those influences which appear the most pertinent and pressing for the organisation in question, rather than to attempt to consider all possible contingencies.

Environmental volatility and change

The organisation's external environment is further complicated by the tendency towards environmental change. This volatility may be particularly prevalent in some areas (e.g. technology) or in some markets or in some types of industry or organisation. As indicated above, a highly volatile environment causes uncertainty for the organisation (or for its sub-units) and this makes decision making more difficult (*see* Case study: A shock to the system).

Environmental uniqueness

Implicit in the remarks above is the notion that each organisation has to some degree a unique environment in which it operates and which will affect it in a unique way. Thus, while it is possible to make generalisations about the impact of the external environment on the firm, it is necessary to recognise the existence of this uniqueness and where appropriate to take into account exceptions to the general rule.

Different spatial levels of analysis

External influences operate at different spatial levels – local, regional, national, supranational, international. There are few businesses, if any, today which could justifiably claim to be unaffected by influences outside their immediate market(s).

Two-way flow of influence

As a final point, it is important to recognise that the flow of influence between the organisation and its environment operates in both directions. The external environment influences firms, but by the same token firms can influence their environment and this is an acceptable feature of business in a democratic society which is operating through a market-based economic system. This idea of democracy and its relationship with the market economy is considered in Chapters 3 and 4.

Synopsis

In the process of transforming inputs into output, business organisations operate in a multifaceted environment which affects and is affected by their activities. This environment tends to be complex and volatile and comprises influences which are of both a general and an immediate kind and which operate at different spatial levels. Understanding this environment and its effects on business operations is of vital importance to the study and practice of business.

Summary of key points

- Business activity is essentially concerned with transforming inputs into outputs for consumption purposes.

- All businesses operate within an external environment which shapes their operations and decisions.

- This environment comprises influences which are both operational and general.

- The operational environment of business is concerned with such factors as customers, suppliers, creditors and competitors.

- The general environment focuses on what are known as the PESTLE factors.

- In analysing a firm's external environment attention needs to be paid to the interaction between the different environmental variables, environmental complexity, volatility and change and to the spatial influences.

- While all firms are affected by the environment in which they exist and operate, at times they help to shape that environment by their activities and behaviour.

CASE STUDY   A shock to the system

For the most part changes in a firm's (or industry's or sector's) external environment tend to be relatively predictable and this can aid business planning. Economic indicators, for example, usually signal the onset of a recession (or recovery) well before it occurs and this provides businesses with time to consider not only how they are likely to be affected by economic change, but also what steps they can take to minimise any potential threat to the organisation (or maximise any opportunity). On occasions, however, the business environment can change dramatically and unexpectedly for the worse, leaving some firms to face rapidly deteriorating trading conditions often without any contingency plans in place.

Such a situation occurred on Tuesday 11 September 2001 when terrorist attacks on the World Trade Centre and the US Department of Defense rapidly sent shock waves through the global economic system, engulfing a wide range of firms and industries in all countries. The most immediate and obvious manifestation of the crisis was seen in the airline industry where the major airline operators suddenly found people unwilling to fly, thereby significantly exacerbating the problems already being experienced as a result of increased competition and recession in some of their markets. In the United States carriers such as United, Delta and Continental announced tens of thousands of redundancies and further job losses were announced by British Airways, Virgin and Air Canada. Elsewhere in Europe both Swissair and Sabena went into receivership and other operators signalled a period of retrenchment (*see also* case study in Chapter 12).

The knock-on effect of the reduction in air travel also impacted on two allied industries: aircraft manufacturing and tourism. Again this found expression in falling demand and the inevitable loss of jobs. Companies such as Airbus Industrie, Boeing and Bombardier slimmed down their workforces and additional job losses occurred in supplier organisations including Rolls-Royce and in travel, tourism and allied industries such as hotels, catering and car hire. For a company such as Disney, for instance, the impact on visitor numbers at its theme parks in America and Europe was immediately felt and numerous other organisations and holiday destinations rapidly experienced the effect of the decline in overseas tourists in the immediate aftermath of the attack. (*See* Case Study in Chapter 9.)

While it was suggested at the time by a number of observers that some businesses might have been taking advantage of the crisis to slim down their workforces, there seems little doubt that the attack had a significant economic as well as human and psychological impact. Mercifully such shocks to the system tend to be few and far between and even when they occur some enterprising firms will find they provide unexpected business opportunities.

Case study questions

1 Can you think of any other examples of major unanticipated events in your own country that have had a serious adverse effect on businesses?

2 Can you think of any businesses which may have benefited commercially from the events of September 11?

There is a great deal of commentary on September 11 and its aftermath. You should try typing 'September 11 and Business' in *Google*. There is also an archive of material at *September11.archive.org*

Review and discussion questions

1 In what senses could a college or university be described as a business organisation? How would you characterise its 'inputs' and 'output'?

2 Taking examples from a range of quality newspapers, illustrate ways in which business organisations are affected by their external environment.

3 Give examples of the ways in which business organisations can affect the external environment in which they operate.

4 With regard to the Mini Case, to what extent do you think that moving its manufacturing overseas would help to solve Levi's problems?

Assignments

1 Assume you are a trainee in a firm of management consultants. As part of your induction process you have been asked to collect a file of information on an organisation of your choice. This file should contain information not only on the structure of the organisation and on its products, but also on the key external influences which have affected its operations in recent years.

2 For a firm or industry of your choice, undertake a 'PESTLE' analysis indicating the likely major environmental influences to be faced by the firm/industry in the next five to ten years.

Further reading

Brooks, I. and Weatherston, J., *The Business Environment: Challenges and Changes*, 2nd edition Financial Times Management, 2000.

Daniels, J. D. and Radebough, L. H., *International Business: Environments and Operations*, 9th edition, Prentice Hall, 2001.

Morris, H. and Willey, B., *The Corporate Environment*, Financial Times/Prentice Hall, 1996.

Steiner, G. A. and Steiner, J. F., *Business, Government and Society: A Managerial Perspective*, 7th edition, McGraw-Hill, 1994.

Web links and further questions are available on the website at:
www.booksites.net/worthington

2

Business organisations: the internal environment

Ian Worthington and Zena Cumberpatch

The systems approach to the study of business organisations stresses the interaction between a firm's internal and external environments. Key aspects of the internal context of business include the organisation's structure and functions and the way they are configured in pursuit of specified organisational objectives. If the enterprise is to remain successful, constant attention needs to be paid to balancing the different influences on the organisation and to the requirement to adapt to new external circumstances. This responsibility lies essentially with the organisation's management, which has the task of blending people, technologies, structures and environments.

Objectives

- To outline the broad approaches to organisation and management, paying particular attention to the systems approach.

- To examine alternative organisation structures used by business organisations.

- To discuss major aspects of the functional management of firms.

- To illustrate the interaction between a firm's internal and external environments.

Key terms

Bureaucracy
Classical theories of
    organisation
Contingency approaches
Divisional structure
Downsizing
Formal structures
Functional organisation
Functional specialisation
Hierarchy of needs

Holding company
Human relations approach
Human resource
    management
Management
Marketing
Marketing concept
Marketing mix
Matrix structure
Organisation by product

Organisation chart
Profit centre
Project team
Re-engineering
Scientific management
Sub-systems
Systems approach
Theory X and Theory Y
Theory Z
Virtual organisation

Introduction

The internal features of business organisations have received considerable attention by scholars of organisation and management, and a large number of texts have been devoted to this aspect of business studies.[1] In the discussion below, the aim is to focus on three areas of the internal organisation that relate directly to a study of the business environment: approaches to understanding organisations, organisation structures, and key functions within the enterprise. Further insight into these aspects and into management and organisational behaviour generally can be gained by consulting the many specialist books in this field, a number of which are mentioned at the end of this chapter.

A central theme running through any analysis of the internal environment is the idea of 'management', which has been subjected to a wide variety of definitions. As used in this context, management is seen both as a system of roles fulfilled by individuals who manage the organisation (e.g. entrepreneur, resource manager, co-ordinator, leader, motivator, organiser) and as a process which enables an organisation to achieve its objectives. The essential point is that management should be seen as a function of organisations, rather than as a controlling element, and its task is to enable the organisation to identify and achieve its objectives and to adapt to change. Managers need to integrate the various influences on the organisation – including people, technology, systems and the environment – in a manner best designed to meet the needs of the enterprise at the time in question and be prepared to institute change as and when circumstances dictate.

The *Financial Times* has produced a very useful source of material on management ideas. This is available at *www.business-minds.com/goto/mastering*

Approaches to organisation and management

An important insight into the principles which are felt to underlie the process of management can be gained by a brief examination of organisational theories. These theories or approaches – some of which date back to the late nineteenth century – represent the views of both practising managers and academics as to the factors that determine organisational effectiveness and the influences on individuals and groups within the work environment. Broadly speaking, these approaches can be broken down into three main categories: the classical approach, the human relations approach, and the systems approach.[2] Since the last of these encompasses the model presented in Chapter 1, particular attention is paid to this perspective.

The classical approach

Classical theories of organisation and management mostly date from the first half of the twentieth century and are associated with the work of writers such as Taylor, Fayol, Urwick and Brech. In essence, the classicists basically viewed organisations as formal structures established to achieve a particular number of objectives under the direction of management. By identifying a set of principles to guide managers in the design of the organisational structure, the proponents of the classical view believed that organisations would be able to achieve their objectives more effectively. Fayol, for example, identified fourteen principles which included the division of work, the scalar chain, centralisation and the unity of command – features which also found expression in Weber's notion of 'bureaucracy'. Urwick's rules or principles similarly emphasised aspects of organisation structure and operations – such as specialisation, co-ordination, authority, responsibility and the span of control – and were presented essentially as a code of good management practice.

Within the classical approach special attention is often given to two important sub-groupings, known as 'scientific management' and 'bureaucracy'. The former is associated with the pioneering work of F. W. Taylor (1856–1915) who believed that scientific methods could be attached to the design of work so that productivity could be increased. For Taylor, the systematic analysis of jobs (e.g. using some form of work study technique) was seen as the key to finding the best way to perform a particular task and thereby of achieving significant productivity gains from individuals which would earn them increased financial rewards. In Taylor's view, the responsibility for the institution of a scientific approach lay with management, under whose control and direction the workers would operate to the mutual benefit of all concerned.

The second sub-group, bureaucracy, draws heavily on the work of Max Weber (1864–1920) whose studies of authority structures highlighted the importance of 'office' and 'rules' in the operation of organisations. According to Weber, bureaucracy – with its system of rules and procedures, specified spheres of competence, hierarchical organisation of offices, appointment based on merit, high level of specialisation and impersonality – possessed a degree of technical superiority over other forms of organisation, and this explained why an increasing number of enterprises were becoming bureaucratic in structure. Over 50 years after Weber's studies were first published in English, bureaucratic organisation remains a key feature of many enterprises throughout the world and is clearly linked to increasing organisational size and complexity. Notwithstanding the many valid criticisms of Weber's work, it is difficult to imagine how it could be otherwise.

The human relations approach

Whereas the classical approach focuses largely on structure and on the formal organisation, the human relations approach to management emphasises the importance of people in the work situation and the influence of social and psychological factors in shaping organisational behaviour. Human relations theorists have primarily been concerned with issues such as individual motivation, leadership, communications and group dynamics and have stressed the significance of the informal pattern of relationships which exist within the formal structure. The factors influencing human behaviour have accordingly been portrayed as a key to achieving greater organisational effectiveness, thus elevating the 'management of people' to a prime position in the determination of managerial strategies.

The early work in this field is associated with Elton Mayo (1880–1949) and with the famous Hawthorne Experiments, conducted at the Western Electric Company (USA) between 1924 and 1932. What these experiments basically showed was that individuals at work were members of informal (i.e. unofficial) as well as formal groups and that group influences were fundamental to explaining individual behaviour. Later work by writers such as Maslow, McGregor, Argyris, Likert and Herzberg continued to stress the importance of the human factor in determining organisational effectiveness, but tended to adopt a more psychological orientation, as exemplified by Maslow's 'hierarchy of needs' and McGregor's 'Theory X and Theory Y'. Maslow's central proposition was that individuals seek to satisfy specific groups of needs, ranging from basic physiological requirements (e.g. food, sleep, sex), through safety, love and esteem, to self-actualisation (i.e. self-fulfilment); progressing systematically up the hierarchy as each lower-level need is satisfied (*see* Figure 2.1). To McGregor individuals at work were seen by management as either inherently lazy (Theory X) or committed to the organisation's objectives and often actively seeking responsibility (Theory Y). These perceptions consequently provided the basis for different styles of management, which ranged from the coercive to the supportive.

McGregor's concern with management styles is reflected in later studies, including Ouichi's notion of 'Theory Z'.[3] According to Ouichi one of the key factors in the success of Japanese manufacturing industries was their approach to the management of people. Theory Z organisations were those which offered workers long-term (often lifetime) employment, a share in decision making, opportunities for training, development and promotion, and a number of other advantages which gave them a positive orientation towards the organisation. For Ouichi, the key to organisational effectiveness lay in the development of a Japanese-style Theory Z environment, adapted to western requirements.

Figure 2.1 A hierarchy of needs

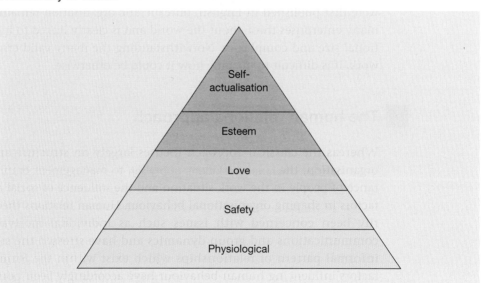

The systems approach

More recent approaches to organisation and management have helped to integrate previous work on structures, people and technology, by portraying organisations as socio-technical systems interacting with their environment. Under this approach – which became popular in the 1960s – organisations were seen as complex systems of people, tasks and technologies that were part of and interacted with a larger environment, comprising a wide range of influences (*see* Chapter 1). This environment was frequently subject to fluctuations, which on occasions could become turbulent (i.e. involving rapid and often unpredictable change). For organisations to survive and prosper, adaptation to environmental demands was seen as a necessary requirement and one which was central to the process of management.

The essence of the systems approach has been described in Chapter 1, but is worth repeating here. Organisations, including those involved in business, are open systems, interacting with their environment as they convert inputs into output. Inputs include people, finance, materials and information, provided by the environment in which the organisation exists and operates. Output comprises such items as goods and services, information, ideas and waste, discharged into the environment for consumption by 'end' or 'intermediate' users and in some cases representing inputs used by other organisations.

Systems invariably comprise a number of sub-systems through which the process of conversion or transformation occurs. Business organisations, for example, usually have sub-systems which deal with activities such as production, marketing, accounting and human resource management and each of these in turn may involve smaller sub-systems (e.g. sales, quality control, training) which collectively constitute the whole. Just as the organisation as a system interacts with its environment, so do the sub-systems and their component elements, which also interact with each other. In the case of the latter, the boundary between sub-systems is usually known as an 'interface'.

While the obvious complexities of the systems approach need not be discussed, it is important to emphasise that most modern views of organisations draw heavily on the work in this area, paying particular attention to the interactions between people, technology, structure and environment and to the key role of management in directing the organisation's activities towards the achievement of its goals. Broadly speaking, management is seen as a critical sub-system within the total organisation, responsible for the co-ordination of the other sub-systems and for ensuring that internal and external relationships are managed effectively. As changes occur in one part of the system these will induce changes elsewhere and this will require a management response that will have implications for the organisation and for its sub-systems. Such changes may be either the cause or effect of changes in the relationship between the organisation and its environment, and the requirement for managers is to adapt to the new conditions without reducing the organisation's effectiveness.

Given the complex nature of organisations and the environments in which they operate, a number of writers have suggested a 'contingency approach' to organisational design and management (e.g. Lawrence and Lorsch, Woodward, Perrow, Burns and Stalker).[4] In essence, this approach argues that there is no single form of organisation best suited to all situations and that the most appropriate organisational structure and system of management is dependent upon the contingencies of the situation (e.g. size, technology, environment) for each organisation. In some cases a bureaucratic structure might be the best way to operate, while in others much looser and more organic methods of organisation might be more effective. In short, issues of organisational design and management depend on choosing the best combination in the light of the relevant situational variables; this might mean different structures and styles coexisting within an organisation.

Organisation structures

Apart from the very simplest form of enterprise in which one individual carries out all tasks and responsibilities, business organisations are characterised by a division of labour which allows employees to specialise in particular roles and to occupy designated positions in pursuit of the organisation's objectives. The resulting pattern of relationships between individuals and roles constitutes what is known as the organisation's structure and represents the means by which the purpose and work of the enterprise is carried out. It also provides a framework through which communications can occur and within which the processes of management can be applied.

Responsibility for establishing the formal structure of the organisation lies with management and a variety of options is available. Whatever form is chosen, the basic need is to identify a structure which will best sustain the success of the enterprise and will permit the achievement of a number of important objectives. Through its structure an organisation should be able to:

■ achieve efficiency in the utilisation of resources;
■ provide opportunities for monitoring organisational performance;
■ ensure the accountability of individuals;
■ guarantee co-ordination between the different parts of the enterprise;
■ provide an efficient and effective means of organisational communication;
■ create job satisfaction, including opportunities for progression; and
■ adapt to changing circumstances brought about by internal or external developments.

In short, structure is not an end in itself, but a means to an end and should ideally reflect the needs of the organisation within its existing context and taking into account its future requirements.

Mini case   Change at Deutsche Bank?

On 17 January 2002 the *Financial Times* carried a report that one of Europe's biggest banks, Deutsche Bank, was poised to announce a change to its management structure. This change would involve a move away from the traditional consensus-driven German board model towards an executive style of management along US lines. According to the *FT*, the incoming head of the bank, Josef Ackermann, intended to create a powerful new executive committee to run the bank's operations and to install a strong chief executive with full control over bank strategy. The executive committee would bring together 'global product heads' from the bank's two divisions and would be chaired by Ackermann himself. Ackermann would also chair a slimmed-down *Vorstand* (management board) which under national law retains the final say on business matters and is collectively responsible for decision-making.

 You can access the website for the Deutsche Bank at *www.deutsche-bank.com*

The essence of structure is the division of work between individuals and the formal organisational relationships that are created between them. These relationships will be reflected not only in individual job descriptions, but also in the overall organisation chart which designates the formal pattern of role relationships, and the interactions between roles and the individuals occupying those roles. Individual authority relationships can be classified as line, staff, functional and lateral and arise from the defined pattern of responsibilities, as follows:

- *Line relationships* occur when authority flows vertically downward through the structure from superior to subordinate (e.g. managers–section leader–staff).
- *Staff relationships* are created when senior personnel appoint assistants who normally have no authority over other staff but act as an extension of their superior.
- *Functional relationships* are those between specialists (or advisers) and line managers and their subordinates (e.g. when a specialist provides a common service throughout the organisation but has no authority over the users of the service). The personnel or computing function may be one such service that creates a functional relationship. (Note that specialists have line relationships with their own subordinates.)
- *Lateral relationships* exist across the organisation, particularly between individuals occupying equivalent positions within different departments or sections (e.g. committees, heads of departments, section leaders).

With regard to the division of work and the grouping of organisational activities, this can occur in a variety of ways. These include:

- *By function or major purpose*, associated particularly with departmental structures.
- *By product or service*, where individuals responsible for a particular product or service are grouped together.
- *By location*, based on geographical criteria.
- *By common processes* (e.g. particular skills or methods of operation).
- *By client group* (e.g. children, the disabled, the elderly).

In some organisations a particular method of grouping will predominate; in others there will tend to be a variety of types and each has its own particular advantages and disadvantages. In the discussion below, attention is focused on five main methods of grouping activities in business organisations. Students should attempt to discover what types of structure exist within their own educational institution and the logic (if any) which underlies the choices made.

Figure 2.2   A functional organisation structure

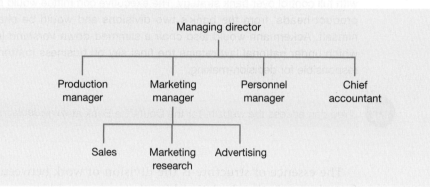

Functional organisation

The functional approach to organisation is depicted in Figure 2.2. As its name indicates, in this type of structure activities are clustered together by common purpose or function. All marketing activities, for example, are grouped together as a common function, typically within a marketing department. Similarly, other areas of activity, such as production, finance, personnel and research and development, have their own specialised sections or departments, responsible for all the tasks required of that function.

Apart from its obvious simplicity, the functional organisation structure allows individuals to be grouped together on the basis of their specialisms and technical expertise, and this can facilitate the development of the function they offer as well as providing a recognised path for promotion and career development. On the downside, functional specialisation, particularly through departments, is likely to create sectional interests which may operate to the disadvantage of the organisation as a whole, particularly where inequalities in resource allocation between functions become a cause for interfunction rivalry. It could also be argued that this form of structure is most suited to single-product firms and that it becomes less appropriate as organisations diversify their products and/or markets. In such circumstances, the tendency will be for businesses to look for the benefits which can arise from specialisation by product or from the divisionalisation of the enterprise.

Organisation by product or service

In this case the division of work and the grouping of activities is dictated by the product or service provided (*see* Figure 2.3), such that each group responsible for a particular part of the output of the organisation may have its own specialist in the different functional areas (e.g. marketing, finance, personnel). One advantage of this type of structure is that it allows an organisation to offer a diversified range of products, as exemplified by the different services available in National Health Service hospitals (e.g. maternity, orthopaedic, geriatric, and so forth). Its main disadvantage is the danger that the separate units or divisions within the enterprise may attempt to become too autonomous, even at the expense of other parts of the organisation, and this can present management with problems of co-ordination and control.

Figure 2.3   A product-based structure

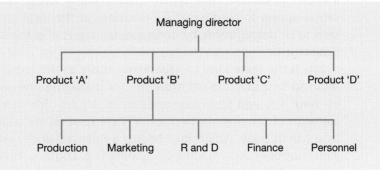

The divisional structure

As firms diversify their products and/or markets – often as a result of merger or takeover – a structure is needed to co-ordinate and control the different parts of the organisation. This structure is likely to be the divisional (or 'multi-divisional') company.

A *divisionalised structure* is formed when an organisation is split up into a number of self-contained business units, each of which operates as a profit centre. Such a division may occur on the basis of product or market or a combination of the two, with each unit tending to operate along functional or product lines, but with certain key functions (e.g. finance, personnel, corporate planning) provided centrally, usually at company headquarters (*see* Figure 2.4).

The main benefit of the multi-divisional company is that it allows each part of what can be a very diverse organisation to operate semi-independently in producing and marketing its products, thus permitting each division to design its offering to suit local market conditions – a factor of prime importance where the firm operates on a multinational basis. The dual existence of divisional *profit centres* and a

Figure 2.4   A divisional structure

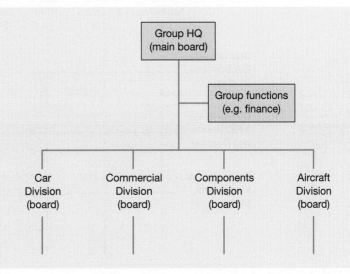

central unit responsible for establishing strategy at a global level can, however, be a source of considerable tension, particularly where the needs and aims of the centre appear to conflict with operations at the local level or to impose burdens seen to be unreasonable by divisional managers (e.g. the allocation of central overhead costs).

Much the same kind of arguments apply to the holding company, though this tends to be a much looser structure for managing diverse organisations, favoured by both UK and Japanese companies. Under this arrangement, the different elements of the organisation (usually companies) are co-ordinated and controlled by a parent body, which may be just a financial entity established to maintain or gain control of other trading companies (e.g. Lonrho). Holding companies are associated with the growth of firms by acquisition which gives rise to a high degree of product or market diversification. They are also a popular means of operating a multinational organisation.

Matrix structures

A matrix is an arrangement for combining functional specialisation (e.g. through departments) with structures built around products, projects or programmes (*see* Figure 2.5). The resulting grid (or matrix) has a two-way flow of authority and responsibility. Within the functional elements, the flow is vertically down the line from superior to subordinate and this creates a degree of stability and certainty for the individuals located within the department or unit. Simultaneously, as a member of a project group or product team, an individual is normally answerable

Figure 2.5   A matrix structure in a business school

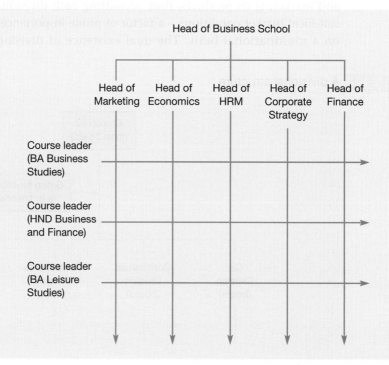

horizontally to the project manager whose responsibility is to oversee the successful completion of the project, which in some cases may be of very limited duration.

Matrix structures offer various advantages, most notably flexibility, opportunities for staff development, an enhanced sense of ownership of a project or programme, customer orientation and the co-ordination of information and expertise. On the negative side, difficulties can include problems of co-ordination and control, conflicting loyalties for staff and uncertain lines of authority. It is not uncommon in an organisation designed on matrix lines for project or programme leaders to be unsure of their authority over the staff from the contributing departments. Nor is it unknown for functional managers to withdraw their co-operation and/or support for projects located outside their immediate sphere of influence.

Project teams

Despite its flexibility, the matrix often has a degree of permanence; in contrast, the project team is essentially a temporary structure established as a means of carrying out a particular task, often in a highly unstable environment. Once the task is complete, the team is disbanded and individuals return to their usual departments or are assigned to a new project.

Fashioned around technical expertise rather than managerial rank and often operating closely with clients, project teams are increasingly common in high-technology firms, construction companies and in some types of service industry, especially management consultancies and advertising. Rather than being a replacement for the existing structure, they operate alongside it and utilise in-house staff (and in some cases, outside specialists) on a project-by-project basis. While this can present logistical and scheduling problems and may involve some duplication of resources, it can assist an organisation in adapting to change and uncertainty and in providing products to the customer's specifications. Project teams tend to be at their most effective when objectives and tasks are well defined, when the client is clear as to the desired outcome and when the team is chosen with care.

Mini case Royal Dutch Shell

In March 1995 the multinational Anglo-Dutch oil giant, Royal Dutch Shell, announced its intention to radically change its long-admired matrix organisation (*see*, for example, the *Financial Times*, 30 March 1995). For historical reasons, Shell had developed a structure based on geographically defined operating companies. These operating companies had executives representing national or regional units, business sectors (or divisions) and functions such as finance. Within this three-dimensional matrix, powerful individuals were able to influence the organisation's policies at regional level and a considerable bureaucracy was required to 'police' the matrix and to co-ordinate decisions between the different elements of the structure.

Faced with growing global competition and shareholder pressure for improved performance, Shell decided to restructure the organisation by attacking problems of overstaffing and bureaucracy and by eliminating many of the regional fiefdoms through which the company had come to run its worldwide empire. Its plan involved shaping the group around five business organisations covering its main activities (e.g. exploration and production, refining and marketing, etc.), with each operating company reporting to and receiving its strategic targets from whichever of the five organisations were relevant to its activities. A new system of business committees was given responsibility for strategic and investment decisions within the different organisations, although executive authority rested with the operating companies. Through this arrangement Shell hoped to retain the sensitivity to local market needs that had traditionally been part of its organisational creed.

In a further effort to improve the company's performance, Shell subsequently indicated that more restructuring needed to take place (see, for example, The *Guardian*, 15 December 1998). Part of its blueprint for reshaping itself for the twenty-first century included additional streamlining of its management structure, away from committee-based decision making and towards a system based on American-style chief executives.

 The website address for Royal Dutch Shell is *www.Shell.com*

The virtual organisation

As indicated above traditional organisations have structures which are designed to facilitate the transformation of inputs into output. Increasingly as the business environment changes, relationships both within and between organisations have needed to become more flexible and this has given rise to such developments as the growth in teleworking and the establishment of dynamic broker/agent networks involving considerable outsourcing of sub-tasks to 'agents' (e.g. manufacturing, distribution) by the core organisation (the 'broker'). It is fair to say that this demand for greater flexibility has been driven partly by the market and partly by cost considerations and the process of change has been facilitated by relatively rapid developments in information technology (*see* e.g. Chapter 15). One area currently exciting the interest of writers on management and organisation is the concept of the virtual organisation, arguably the ultimate form of organisational flexibility (*see* also Chapter 8 for a further discussion).

In essence a virtual organisation or firm signifies an extremely loose web of essentially freelance individuals or businesses who organise themselves to produce a specific customer product (e.g. an individual holiday package with particular features unique to the customer). Without any permanent structure or hierarchy this so-called firm can constantly change its shape and, despite existing across space and time, tends to appear edgeless, with its inputs, outputs and employees increasingly dispersed across the linked world of information systems. Given modern forms of communication, the potential exists for a totally electronic-based organisation trading in expertise and information with no real-world physical identity. This stands in stark contrast to the traditional view of the firm as an arrangement which adds value by transforming basic economic inputs (e.g. land, labour capital) into physical outputs or services.

Useful articles on virtual organisation can be found at:
www.comp.lancs.ac.uk/sociolog/VSOC/virtual
virtualsociety.sbs.ox.uk/projects/hughes
www.stratege.com.au/virtual_organisation

Structural change

Internal change is an important feature of the modern business organisation. In order to remain competitive and meet stakeholder needs, a firm may have to find ways to restructure its organisation as the environment in which it operates changes. Solutions can range from a partial or wholesale shift in the organisation's structural form to strategies for reducing the overall size and shape of the company (e.g. 'downsizing') or a radical redesign of business processes (e.g. 're-engineering').

Whereas business re-engineering normally connotes a root-and-branch reform of the way in which the business operates, downsizing essentially involves shrinking the organisation to make it 'leaner' and 'fitter' and hopefully more 'flexible' in its response to the marketplace. For some companies this means little more than reducing the size of the workforce through natural wastage and/or redundancies, as and when opportunities arise; for others it involves 'delayering' the organisation by removing a tier, or tiers, of management, thus effectively flattening the organisation's hierarchy and helping it to reduce its unit costs of production.

In its most systematic and long-term form, downsizing can be used as a vehicle for cultural change through which an organisation's employees are encouraged to embrace notions of continuous improvement and innovation, and to accept that structural reform is a permanent and natural state of affairs. Under such an approach, retraining and reskilling become vital tools in implementing the chosen strategy and in shaping the organisation to meet the demands of its changing environment. The danger is, however, that a firm may become too concerned with restructuring as a cure for all its problems, when the real cause of its difficulties lies in its marketplace. Cutting the number of employees, in such a situation, is unlikely to make unattractive products attractive; nor is it likely to boost morale within the organisation.

Aspects of functional management

Most organisation structures reflect a degree of functional specialisation, with individuals occupying roles in departments, units or sections which have titles such as Production, Finance, Marketing, Personnel and Research and Development. These functional areas of the internal organisation, and the individuals who are allocated to them, are central to the process of transforming organisational inputs into output. The management of these functions and of the relationships between them will be a key factor in the success of the enterprise and in its ability to respond to external demands for change.

The interdependence of the internal functions can be demonstrated by a simple example. Providing goods and services to meet the market's needs often involves research and development which necessitates a financial input, usually from the capital market or the organisation's own resources. It also requires, as do all the other functions, the recruitment of staff of the right quality, a task which is more often than not the responsibility of the Personnel department. If research and development activities lead to a good idea which the Marketing department is able to sell, then the Production department is required to produce it in the right quantities, to the right specifications and at the time the market needs it. This depends not only on internal scheduling procedures within the Production department, but also on having the right kind of materials supplied on time by the Purchasing department, an appropriate system of quality control and work monitoring, machinery that is working and regularly serviced, the finished items packed, despatched and delivered and a multitude of other activities, all operating towards the same end.

The extent to which all of these requirements can be met simultaneously depends not only on internal factors, many of which are controllable, but also on a host of external influences, the majority of which tend to be beyond the organisation's control. To demonstrate this interface between the internal and external environments, two key areas of functional management are discussed briefly below – marketing and human resource management. An examination of the other functions within the organisation would yield very similar findings.

Human resource management (HRM)

People are the key organisational resource; without them organisations would not exist or function. All businesses need to plan for and manage the people they employ if they are to use this resource effectively and efficiently in pursuit of their objectives. In modern and forward-looking organisations this implies a proactive approach to the management of people which goes beyond the bounds of traditional personnel management and involves the establishment of systems for planning, monitoring, appraisal and evaluation, training and development and for integrating the internal needs of the organisation with the external demands of the marketplace. Such an approach is associated with the idea of human resource management.

As in other areas of management, HRM involves a wide variety of activities related to the formulation and implementation of appropriate organisational policies, the provision of opportunities for monitoring, evaluation and change, and the application of resources to the fulfilment of organisational ends. Key aspects of 'people management' include:

- recruitment and selection;
- working conditions;
- training and career development;
- job evaluation;
- employee relations;
- manpower planning; and
- legal aspects of employment.

In most, if not all, cases these will be affected by both internal and external influences (e.g. size of the firm, management style, competition, economic and political developments), some of which will vary over time as well as between organisations.

The provision of these activities within an organisation can occur in a variety of ways and to different degrees of sophistication. Some very small firms may have little in the way of a recognisable HRM function, being concerned primarily with questions of hiring and firing, pay and other working conditions, but not with notions of career development, staff appraisal or job enrichment. In contrast, very large companies may have a specialist HRM or Personnel department, often organised on functional lines and responsible for the formulation and implementation of personnel policies throughout the organisation. Such centralisation provides not only some economies of scale, but also a degree of standardisation and consistency across departments. To allow for flexibility, centralised systems are often combined with an element of decentralisation which permits individual departments or sections to exercise some influence in matters such as the recruitment and selection of staff, working conditions, training and career development.

To illustrate how the different aspects of HRM are influenced by external factors, one part of this function – recruitment and selection of staff – has been chosen. This is the activity within the organisation which seeks to ensure that it has the right quantity and quality of labour in the right place and at the right time to meet its requirements at all levels. To achieve this aim, the organisation initially needs to consider a large number of factors, including possible changes in the demand for labour, the need for new skills and likely labour turnover, before the processes of recruitment and selection can begin. These aspects in turn will be conditioned by a variety of factors such as changes in the demand for the product, the introduction of new technology and social, economic and demographic changes, some of which may not be anticipated or expected by strategic planners.

Once recruitment and selection is ready to begin, a further raft of influences will impinge upon the process, some of which emanate from external sources. In drawing up a job specification, for example, attention will normally need to be paid to the state of the local labour market, including skill availability, competition from other employers, wage rates in comparable jobs and/or organisations, and socio-demographic trends. If the quality of labour required is in short supply, an organisation may find itself having to offer improved pay and working conditions simply to attract a sufficient number of applicants to fill the vacancies on offer. Equally, in fashioning its job advertisements and in drawing up the material it sends out to potential applicants, a firm will need to pay due attention to the needs of current legislation in areas such as equal opportunities, race discrimination and employment protection, if it is not to infringe the law.

Among the other external factors the enterprise may need to take into consideration in recruiting and selecting staff will be:

- the relative cost and effectiveness of the different advertising media;
- existing relationships with external sources of recruitment (e.g. job centres, schools, colleges, universities);
- commitments to the local community;
- relationships with employee organisations (e.g. trade unions, staff associations); and
- opportunities for staff training and development in local training and educational institutions.

Ideally, it should also pay some attention to possible future changes in the technology of the workplace, in order to recruit individuals either with appropriate skills or who can be retrained relatively easily with a minimum amount of disruption and expense to the organisation.

The marketing function

The processes of human resource management provide a good illustration of the interactions between a firm's internal and external environments. An even better example is provided by an examination of its marketing activities, which are directed primarily, though not exclusively, towards what is happening outside the organisation.

Like 'management', the term 'marketing' has been defined in a wide variety of ways, ranging from Kotler's essentially economic notion of an activity directed at satisfying human needs and wants through exchange processes, to the more managerial definitions associated with bodies like the Chartered Institute of Marketing.[5] A common thread running through many of these definitions is the idea that marketing is concerned with meeting the needs of the consumer in a way which is profitable to the enterprise. Hence, strategic marketing management is normally characterised as the process of ensuring a good fit between the opportunities afforded by the marketplace and the abilities and resources of an organisation operating in it.

 web link Information about the Chartered Institute of Marketing is available at *www.cim.co.uk*

This notion of marketing as an integrative function within the organisation – linking the needs of the consumer with the various functional areas of the firm – is central to modern definitions of the term and lies at the heart of what is known as the 'marketing concept'. This is the idea that the customer is of prime importance to the organisation and that the most significant managerial task in any enterprise is first to identify the needs and wants of the consumer and then to ensure that its operations are geared to meeting these requirements profitably. Though it would be true to say that not all organisations subscribe to this view, it is generally accepted that the successful businesses are predominantly those with a customer rather than a production or sales orientation. Equally, the evidence suggests that the need to adopt such a customer-centred approach applies not only to private sector trading organisations, but also increasingly to public sector enterprises and to bodies not established for the pursuit of profits but for other purposes (e.g. charities, political parties, trade unions).

When viewed from a customer perspective, marketing can be seen to comprise a range of activities that go beyond the simple production of an item for sale. These include:

- Identifying the needs of consumers (e.g. through marketing research).
- Designing different 'offerings' to meet the needs of different types of customers (e.g. through market segmentation).
- Choosing products, prices, promotional techniques and distribution channels that are appropriate to a particular market (i.e. designing a 'marketing mix' strategy).
- Undertaking market and product planning.

■ Deciding on brand names, types of packages, and methods of communicating with the customer.
■ Creating a marketing information system.

As already indicated, in carrying out these activities the firm is brought into contact with a range of external influences of both an immediate and indirect kind. This external marketing environment can have a fundamental impact on the degree to which the firm is able to develop and maintain successful transactions with its customers and hence on its profitability and chances of survival.

To illustrate how a firm's marketing effort can be influenced by external factors, the following brief discussion focuses on 'pricing', which is one of the key elements of the 'marketing mix', that is, the set of controllable variables which a business can use to influence the buyer's response, namely, product, price, promotion and place – the 4Ps. Of all the mix elements, price is the only one which generates revenue, while the others result in expenditure. It is therefore a prime determinant of a firm's turnover and profitability and can have a considerable influence on the demand for its products and frequently for those of its competitors (*see* Chapter 11).

web link You can find a useful discussion of the Marketing Mix in the Business Open Learning Archive at *sol.brunel.ac.uk/~jarvis/bola/marketing/mix.html*

Leaving aside the broader question of a firm's pricing goals and the fact that prices will tend to vary according to the stage a product has reached in its life cycle, price determination can be said to be influenced by a number of factors. Of these, the costs of production, the prices charged by one's competitors and the price sensitivity of consumers tend to be the most significant.

In the case of cost-based pricing, this occurs when a firm relates its price to the cost of buying or producing the product, adding a profit margin or 'mark-up' to arrive at the final selling price. Such an approach tends to be common amongst smaller enterprises (e.g. builders, corner shops) where costs are often easier to estimate and where likely consumer reactions are given less attention than the need to make an adequate return on the effort involved. The essential point about this form of price determination is that many of the firm's costs are influenced by external organisations – including the suppliers of materials, components and energy – and hence pricing will often vary according to changes in the prices of inputs. Only larger organisations, or a group of small businesses operating together, will generally be able to exercise some influence over input prices and even then not all costs will be controllable by the enterprise.

Organisations which take an essentially cost-based approach to pricing will sometimes be influenced by the prices charged by competitors – particularly in markets where considerable competition exists and where the products are largely homogeneous and a buyer's market is evident (e.g. builders during a recession). The competitive approach to pricing, however, is also found in markets where only a few large firms operate and where the need to increase or maintain market share can give rise to virtually identical prices and to fierce non-price competition between the market leaders (*see* Chapter 12). In Britain, for instance, a big cross-

Channel ferry operator will normally provide the service to customers at the same price as its rivals, differentiating its offering in terms of additional benefits (e.g. on-board entertainment) rather than price. Where this is the case, the external demands of the market rather than costs constitute the primary influence on a firm's decisions, and changes in market conditions (e.g. the actual or potential entry of new firms; changes in a competitor's prices; economic recession) will tend to be reflected in price changes.

This idea of market factors influencing pricing decisions also applies to situations where firms fix their prices according to the actual or anticipated reactions of consumers to the price charged for a product – known in economics as the price elasticity of demand (*see* Chapter 11). In this case, the customer rather than a firm's competitors is the chief influence on price determination, although the two are often interrelated in that consumers are usually more price sensitive in markets where some choice exists. Differential levels of price sensitivity between consumers of a product normally arise when a market has distinct segments based on factors such as differences in income or age or location. In such cases a firm will often fix its prices according to the segment of the market it is serving, a process known as 'price discrimination' and one which is familiar to students claiming concessionary fares on public transport.

While the above discussion has been oversimplified and does not take into account factors such as the price of other products in an organisation's product portfolio (e.g. different models of car), it illustrates quite clearly how even one of the so-called controllable variables in a firm's marketing mix is subject to a range of external influences that are often beyond its ability to control. The same argument applies to the other elements of the marketing function and students could usefully add to their understanding of the internal/external interface by examining how the external environment impinges upon such marketing activities as promotion, distribution or market research.

Synopsis

The internal dimension of business organisations constitutes an extensive field of study and one to which students of business devote a considerable amount of time. In seeking to illustrate how a firm's internal organisation is influenced by its external environment, emphasis has been placed on a selected number of aspects of a firm's internal operations. Of these, its structure and functions were seen to provide a good illustration of the interface between the internal and external environments. Appreciating the existence of this interface is facilitated by adopting a systems approach to organisational analysis.

Summary of key points

- Management is a key aspect of the internal environment of the business organisation.

- Theories of organisation and management basically fall into three categories: classical theories; human relations approaches; systems approaches.

- The systems view of organisations depicts businesses as open systems interacting with their external environment as they convert inputs into outputs.

- The external environment of the organisation affects all aspects of the business including its structures, functions and processes.

- To carry out their tasks businesses can structure themselves in a variety of ways, including functionally, by product/service, by divisions, in a matrix format or via project teams. Each has its advantages and disadvantages.

- Structural change tends to be a feature of large modern organisations.

- Within the organisation the different business functions such as marketing, production, HRM, purchasing and so on are influenced by external factors of both a general and operational kind.

- An examination of the marketing and HRM functions reveals the importance of the wide range of external influences that can impinge upon the day-to-day areas of organisational work.

- Investigations of other functional areas within the organisation would produce a similar picture.

CASE STUDY

Structuring global companies

As the chapter illustrates, to carry out their activities in pursuit of their objectives, virtually all organisations adopt some form of organisational structure. One traditional method of organisation is to group individuals by function or purpose, using a departmental structure to allocate individuals to their specialist areas (e.g. Marketing, HRM and so on). Another is to group activities by product or service, with each product group normally responsible for providing its own functional requirements. A third is to combine the two in the form of a matrix structure with its vertical and horizontal flows of responsibility and authority, a method of organisation much favoured in university Business Schools.

What of companies with a global reach: how do they usually organise themselves?

Writing in the *Financial Times* in November 2000 Julian Birkinshaw, Associate Professor of Strategic and International Management at London Business School, identifies four basic models of global company structure (*www. ftmastering.com*):

■ *The International Division* – an arrangement in which the company establishes a separate division to deal with business outside its own country. The International Division would typically be concerned with tariff and trade issues, foreign agents/partners and other aspects involved in selling overseas. Normally the division does not make anything itself, it is simply responsible for international sales. This arrangement tends to be found in medium-sized companies with limited international sales.

■ *The Global Product Division* – a product-based structure with managers responsible for their product line globally. The company is split into a number of global businesses arranged by product (or service) and usually overseen by their own president. It has been a favoured structure among large global companies such as BP, Siemens and 3M.

■ *The Area Division* – a geographically based structure in which the major line of authority lies with the country (e.g. Germany) or regional (e.g. Europe) manager who is responsible for the different product offerings within her/his geographical area.

■ *The Global Matrix* – as the name suggests a hybrid of the two previous structural types. In the global matrix each business manager reports to two bosses, one responsible for the global product and one for the country/region. As we indicated in the previous edition of this book, this type of structure tends to come into and go out of fashion. Ford, for example, adopted a matrix structure in the later 1990s, while a number of other global companies were either streamlining or dismantling theirs (e.g. Shell, BP, IBM).

As Professor Birkinshaw indicates, ultimately there is no perfect structure and organisations tend to change their approach over time according to changing circumstances, fads, the perceived needs of the senior executives or the predispositions of powerful individuals. This observation is no less true of universities than it is of traditional businesses.

Case study questions

1 Professor Birkinshaw's article identifies the advantages and disadvantages of being a global business. What are his major arguments?

2 In your opinion what are likely to be the key factors determining how a global company will organise itself?

Review and discussion questions

1 In the systems approach to organisations, reference is made to 'feedback'. What is meant by this term and how can feedback influence the process of transforming 'inputs' into 'output'?

2 Should a firm's internal structure be influenced by considerations of management or by the market it serves? Are the two incompatible?

3 Examine ways in which a firm's external environment can influence one of the following functional areas: finance *or* production *or* research and development.

4 Describe the structure of an organisation with which you are familiar (e.g. through employment or work experience), indicating why the organisation is structured in the way it is. Are there any alternative forms of structure the organisation could adopt?

Assignments

1 As a student on a business studies course, you have decided to get some practical experience of the business world by running a small venture with a number of colleagues which you hope will also earn you enough income to support you during your time at college or university. Your idea involves printing and selling customised T-shirts throughout the institution and possibly to a wider market. Design an appropriate organisational structure which you feel will help you achieve your objectives, indicating your rationale for choosing such a structure and the formal pattern of relationships between individuals.

2 In self-selecting groups of three or four, identify an organisation which you feel has a bureaucratic structure. Produce a report indicating:

(a) those features of the organisation's structure, management and operations which best fit the idea of bureaucracy; and

(b) the practical consequences of these features for the working of the organisation.

Give examples to support your comments.

Notes and references

1   *See*, for example, Mullins, L. J., *Management and Organisational Behaviour*, 5th edition, Financial Times/Prentice Hall, 1999; Cole, G. A., *Management: Theory and Practice*, 5th edition, Continuum, 1996.

2   For a more detailed account of the three approaches *see*, *inter alia*, the texts referred to in n. 1.

3   Ouichi, W. G., *Theory Z: How American Business can Meet the Japanese Challenge*, Addison-Wesley, 1981.

4   The contingency approach is discussed in Cole, *op. cit.*,

5   *See*, for example, Kotler, P. and Armstrong, G., *Principles of Marketing*, 8th edition, Prentice Hall, 1999.

Further reading

Campbell, D. J., *Organizations and the Business Environment*, Butterworth-Heinemann, 1997.

Cole, G. A., *Management: Theory and Practice*, 5th edition, Continuum, 1996.

Handy, C., *The Age of Unreason*, Arrow Books, 2nd edition, 1995.

Kotler, P., *Principles of Marketing*, 9th edition, Prentice Hall International, 2001.

Morrison, J. *The International Business Environment: Diversity and the Global Economy*, Palgrave, 2002.

Mullins, L. J., *Management and Organisational Behaviour*, 5th edition, Financial Times/Prentice Hall, 1999.

Pugh, D. S. and Hickson, D. J., *Writers on Organisations*, 5th edition, Penguin, 1996.

Web links and further questions are available on the website at:
www.booksites.net/worthington

Part Two

CONTEXTS

3

The political environment

Ian Worthington

Politics is a universal activity which affects the business world in a variety of ways. Understanding political systems, institutions and processes provides a greater insight into business decisions and into the complexities of the business environment. Given the increasing globalisation of markets, this environment has an international as well as a domestic element and the two are closely interrelated. Appreciating some of the key aspects of this environment and its impact on business organisations is vital for students of business and for managers alike.

Objectives

- To gain an insight into the political context within which business operates.

- To appreciate the relevance of political values to the organisation of business activity.

- To examine key political institutions and processes at a variety of spatial levels.

- To recognise that business organisations can influence, as well as be influenced by, the political environment.

Key terms

Authoritarianism
Backbench MPs
Bureaucrats
Cabinet
Checks and balances
Civil servants
Coalition government
Constitution
Council of Ministers
Decisions
Democracy
Direct (or pure) democracy
Directorates-General
Directives
Electoral system
European Commission

European Council
European Court of Justice
European Parliament
Federal system of government
First-past-the-post system
Government
Government departments
House of Commons
House of Lords
Judiciary
Legislature
Lobbies
Manifesto

MEPs
Ministers
MPs
Parliament
Parliamentary system of government
Plebiscites
Political accountability
Political executive
Political parties
Political sovereignty
Politics
Presidential system of government
Pressure groups
Prime Minister
Professional lobbyist

Proportional representation
Qualified majority vote (qmv)
Recommendations and opinions
Referendums
Regulations
Representative government
Secretary of State
Separation of powers
Sovereignty
Supreme Court
Unitary system of government

Introduction

In the late 1980s, following a period of difficult negotiations, the British government entered into a collaborative agreement with the governments of Germany, Italy and Spain, to develop and produce a European fighter aircraft (EFA), due to come into service in the later 1990s. This agreement, which involved the participants jointly funding research and development costs, was greeted with delight by firms in Britain's aerospace industry and by their suppliers who welcomed the prospects of a large order of aircraft at a time when defence spending was being restrained. For firms such as GEC Ferranti, BAe, Lucas Aerospace, Rolls-Royce and Smiths Industries, the collaborative venture offered the prospects of future profits and the opportunity to retain their technological edge. For the communities in which these firms were based, it promised to sustain and possibly create employment during a period of growing economic uncertainty.

Subsequent indications (in 1992) that the German government would pull out of the venture – on the grounds of escalating costs and a reduced military threat – sent shock waves through the British aerospace industry and threatened to sour relations between the participating governments, the rest of whom wished to continue with the project. In the event, a compromise was reached under which the countries involved agreed to continue with research and development in an effort to produce a cheaper aircraft, to be known as the Eurofighter 2000. Given the problems of German reunification, the German government reserved the right to make a final decision on production at some time in the future. In late 1997 the four countries finally signed an agreement to proceed with production after years of political controversy and delay, thereby triggering a multi-billion-pound contract culminating in delivery of the first aircraft in 2002.

What this simple example illustrates is that business activity takes place both within and across state boundaries and frequently involves governments, whether directly or indirectly. Consequently the political and economic arrangements within the state in which a business is located and/or with which it is trading can have a fundamental impact on its operations – even to the extent of determining whether it is willing or, in some cases able, to trade at all. It is this politico-economic context within which businesses function and the philosophical foundations on which it is based that are the focus of this and the following chapter.

As a prelude to a detailed analysis of the political environment, it is necessary to make a number of general observations regarding political change and uncertainty and its impact on business activity. First, the nature of a country's political system – including its governmental institutions – tends to reflect certain underlying social values and philosophies which help to determine how decisions are made, including decisions about the allocation of resources. Thus, while governments may come and go, the values on which their decisions are based tend to be more enduring and as a result disputes normally centre around 'means' (e.g. sources of revenue), rather than 'ends' (e.g. controlling inflation). While this gives a certain degree of stability to the business environment, this stability cannot be taken for granted, as events in eastern Europe have readily demonstrated. In short, the political environment of business is a dynamic environment, containing elements of both continuity and change, and students and practitioners of business alike need to be constantly aware of developments in this area, if they are to gain a greater insight into the background of business decision making.

Second, changes in the political environment also emanate from a country's institutional arrangements. The tendency in democratic states, for example, to have regular elections, competing political parties offering alternative policies, and a system of pressure groups, all help to generate a degree of discontinuity, which renders predictions about the future more uncertain. For a business, such uncertainty can create not only opportunities but also a degree of risk which will often be an important influence on its decisions. Moreover, given that perceptions of such risks (or opportunities) are also normally reflected in the attitudes and behaviour of a country's financial and other markets, this represents a further variable which at times can be critical for an organisation's future prospects. For many businesses, taking steps to maximise opportunities (or to minimise risk) may ultimately make the difference between short-term failure and long-term survival.

Third, it is important to emphasise that political influences are not restricted to national boundaries – a point emphasised by the increasing importance of international and supranational groupings such as the G7 nations, the European Union and the World Trade Organisation, all of which are discussed below. These external politico-economic influences form part of the environment in which a country's governmental institutions take decisions and their impact on domestic policy and on business activity can often be fundamental. No discussion of the business environment would be complete without an analysis of their role and impact, particularly in shaping international political and economic relationships.

Fourth, the precise impact of political factors on a business tends to vary to some degree according to the type of organisation involved. Multinational corporations – operating on a global scale – will be more concerned with questions such as the stability of overseas political regimes than will the small local firm operating in a localised market, where the primary concern will be with local market conditions. That said, there will undoubtedly be occasions when even locally based enterprises will be affected either directly or indirectly by political developments in other parts of the globe – as in the case of an interruption in supplies or the cancellation of a foreign order in which a small business is involved as a subcontractor. In short, while some broad generalisations can be made about the impact of global (or domestic) political developments on an individual organisation, each case is to some extent unique in both space and time, and observers of the business scene need to be cautious and open-minded in their analysis if they are to avoid the twin dangers of over-simplification and empiricism.

Finally, it needs to be recognised that businesses are not merely reactive to changes in the political environment; they can also help to shape the political context in which they operate and can influence government decision makers, often in a way which is beneficial to their own perceived needs. One of the hallmarks of democracy is the right of individuals and groups to seek to influence government, and businesses – both individually and collectively – have been active in this sphere for centuries. It would be a mistake to underestimate their impact on government policy or on the shaping of values in the established capitalist nations of western Europe and elsewhere.

Political systems

The nature of political activity

All social situations at certain times require decisions to be made between alternative courses of action. Parents may disagree with their offspring about the kind of clothes they wear or how late they stay out at night or how long they grow their hair. Students may challenge lecturers about a particular perspective on an issue or when they should submit a piece of work. The members of the board of directors of a company may have different views about future investment or diversification or the location of a new factory. In all these cases, some solution needs to be found, even if the eventual decision is to do nothing. It is the processes involved in arriving at a solution to a problem, where a conflict of opinion occurs, that are the very essence of political activity.

Politics, in short, is concerned with those processes which help to determine how conflicts are contained, modified, postponed or settled, and as such can be seen as a universal social activity. Hence, individuals often talk of 'office politics' or the 'politics of the board room' or the 'mediating role' played by a parent in the event of a family dispute. For most individuals, however, the term 'politics' tends to be associated with activities at state level, where the resolution of conflict often involves large numbers of people and may even involve individuals in other states. Political activity at this level is clearly qualitatively different from the other social situations mentioned, and given the scale and complexity of the modern state, the problems requiring solutions can often be acute and chronic. Solving those problems tends to be seen, at least in part, as the function of government.

Government as a process is concerned with the pursuit and exercise of power – the power to make decisions which affect the lives of substantial numbers of people, be it at local, regional, national or even international level. Government may also refer to the institutions through which power tends to be formally and legitimately exercised, whether they be cabinets, parliaments, councils, committees or congresses. Whereas the pursuit and exercise of power tends to be an enduring feature of any society, governments are normally transitory, comprising those individuals and/or groups who, at a particular time, have the responsibility for controlling the state, including making laws for 'the good of society'. How governments exercise their power and the ideological foundations on which this is based, helps to indicate the nature of the political system and its likely approaches to the resolution of conflicts.

Authoritarian political systems

Broadly speaking, political systems can be seen to range across two extremes, on the one hand 'authoritarian' and on the other 'democratic'. In an authoritarian political system the disposition is to settle conflicts through the enforcement of rules, regulations and orders by an established authority. This authority may be an individual (e.g. a monarch or other powerful individual) or a group of individuals (e.g. a political party or military junta) who may have assumed political power in a variety of ways (e.g. by birth, election or coup). Once in power, the individual or group will tend to act so as to limit the degree of participation by others in the process of decision making, even to the extent of monopolising the process altogether and permitting no opposition to occur. Where this is the case, a society is often described as being 'totalitarian' and is perhaps best exemplified by Nazi Germany and Stalinist Russia.

Democratic political systems

In contrast, in a democratic political system, the assumption is that as far as possible conflicts should be resolved by rational discussions between the various parties concerned, with the final solution being accepted voluntarily by all participants, even if they disagree. At one extreme, such consultation may involve all individuals, who have – in theory at least – equal influence over the final outcome (e.g. as in referendums or plebiscites). Given the scale and complexity of modern states, however, such examples of 'pure' or 'direct' democracy tend to be rare and it is invariably the case that the democratic solution to conflict resolution is achieved 'indirectly' through a system of political representation and responsibility. Under such a system, the wishes and views of individuals are said to be represented in an established authority (e.g. a government) that has normally been chosen by the people and which is accountable (responsible) to them at regular intervals through a variety of mechanisms, including regular and free elections (*see* Figure 3.1). Implicit in this, of course, is the requirement that individuals are able to change this authority and select another individual or group to represent them. Monopolisation of political power by any one individual or group can only occur, therefore, with the expressed consent of the people.

Figure 3.1   Representative democracy

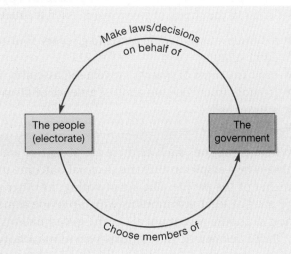

Government in democratic states

Democratic institutions and processes

Democracy means far more than just popular government or a system of regular elections; the democratic approach to government implies the existence of a complex array of institutions and processes through which the wishes of the people are articulated and carried out. While the specific institutional arrangements tend to vary between states, countries which are held to be democratic invariably have a political system which comprises four common and interlocking elements: an electoral system, a party system, a representative assembly and a system for the articulation of sectional interests. The generic roles of these major building blocks of democratic government are discussed below. Location-specific information on how the system operates in a national (i.e. United Kingdom) and a supranational (i.e. European Union) context can be found in the appendices to this chapter. Non-UK readers are encouraged to substitute their own political arrangements for those described in the appendices.

The electoral system

As indicated above, in a representative democracy the electoral system links the people (the electorate) with government; it is through elections that a country's citizens periodically get to choose who will exercise the power to make decisions which will ultimately shape the lives of individuals. Elections, in short, are a vital ingredient of a representative system of government. That said, the fact that elections exist in a particular country is not a sufficient guarantee that it is democratic in the accepted sense of the word.

In order to operate in a way which is normally regarded as democratic, a country's electoral system would need to exhibit a number of features which suggest that the wishes of individual citizens – as expressed through the ballot box – are reasonably reflected in the choice of government. Such features would include:

- a system of regular elections (e.g. every four to five years) based on universal adult suffrage;
- basic freedoms of speech, movement, assembly, etc.;
- freedom from coercion and the absence of illegal electoral practices;
- a secret ballot;
- free media.

Where conditions such as these are absent or are not fully operational, there will always be a suspicion that the electoral outcome may not be a true reflection of the wishes of the people. The act of voting, in other words, needs to be accompanied by a set of legal prescriptions which provide some kind of guarantee that an election to choose part, if not all, of the government is both free and fair.

To be democratic the electoral system must not only be transparent; it must also ensure that the wishes of the majority – as expressed through the number of votes cast – are reflected in the final result. In 'first-past-the-post systems' (e.g. in most current UK elections) a simple majority is sufficient to ensure victory; as a consequence some winning candidates may be elected with fewer than half of the votes cast. Where a system of 'proportional representation' operates (e.g. in many other European countries) a redistribution of votes occurs when there is no outright winner, resulting in a final decision which can be said to more closely represent the wishes of the whole electorate. While the intricacies of different electoral systems are beyond the scope of this book, it is worth observing that the voting system a country uses can have important ramifications for the government elected to office. On the whole, a 'plurality' or 'first-past-the-post system' of voting usually results in majority government, with a single party dominating the organs of decision making and able to pursue its legislative programme relatively free from constraint by the losing side(s). In contrast, where a proportional representation system is used the resulting government is often made up of a coalition of different parties, some of which may hold radically different views from the largest party within the coalition. In effect, coalition government is predominantly a matter of negotiation, accommodation and compromise, an exercise in consensus building and persuasion, as commonly found in most types of organisational setting, including the business world.

The party system

While it is possible to have democratic government in a one-party state, democracy is normally taken to imply that citizens get to choose between alternative candidates when casting their vote at an election. Invariably such candidates tend to represent different political parties and to this extent a vote for a specific candidate can be said to equate to a vote for the party that he or she represents and which is ultimately hoping to form the government.

The existence of political parties, which compete for office at election time, is clearly a convenient – if sometimes questionable – means of organising a system of representative democracy; hence the universality of party systems in democratic states and the relative lack of candidates standing with no party tag at governmental elections at all spatial levels. Parties not only help to choose most of the candidates who compete in these elections, but usually also support and sustain them (e.g. financially) before, during and after the election campaign and help to organise a system of (largely unpaid) volunteers to work to get them elected, as well as providing candidates with a platform of policies on which to stand for office. Whereas some of these activities tend to be the responsibility of the party at national level, others are undertaken at a regional and/or local level, often in the constituency (i.e. geographical area) that a candidate represents. Since questions of organisation, policy making and finance are central to the operation and success of a political party in modern democratic states, party structures have tended to become complex, bureaucratic, multi-layered and increasingly professionalised. As in other types of organisation framework, they also provide an arena in which a substantial degree of in-fighting occurs between individuals of different temperaments, views and ambitions who are seeking to push the party in a particular direction.

From the electors' point of view one of the primary benefits of the party system is that it provides a means of selecting political leaders and the kind of policies they are likely to pursue if the party achieves political office. Describing candidates by a party label (e.g. Democratic, Republican, Socialist, Conservative, Liberal, etc.) allows voters to choose those candidates whose views most closely represent their own, given that parties normally have an identifiable policy stance and produce some form of statement (or manifesto) outlining their policy preferences during an election campaign. Thus, while an individual elector is unlikely to agree with every single policy or proposed piece of legislation that a party puts forward in its attempts to gain office, he/she is at least able to express a preference between alternative approaches to government at the ballot box. To that extent it can be argued that there is likely to be a degree of congruence between the legislative programme of the party democratically elected to form the government and the wishes of the people who elected it, albeit that in some cases the government may have received less than 50 per cent of the popular vote.

It is worth remembering that party labels are not always a good guide to the policy or legislative preferences of individual candidates, since someone described as a 'Democrat' or 'Liberal' in one part of a country may hold radically different views on a range of issues from others of the same title elected to constituencies in other areas. If anything, identifying election candidates in party political terms gives voters a broad indication of the underlying values and beliefs to which an individual subscribes: parties in practice are always destined to be (sometimes fragile) coalitions of groups and individuals representing a range of opinions and preferences under a party banner.

A representative assembly

As previously indicated, one of the key features of democratic government is the existence of a representative decision-making body; a group of individuals chosen by a country's citizens to help make important decisions on their behalf. In the same way that shareholders in a public company elect directors to guide the organisation and to represent their interest, voters at election time choose individuals they wish to represent them in government in the various organs of decision making and policy implementation (see below). While not everyone chosen by the electorate becomes part of the small group of key decision makers (the government or political executive), all normally have some kind of role to play in the decision-making process and usually get an opportunity to scrutinise policy and legislative proposals put forward by the governing element and to vote upon them. The fact that the electorate periodically has the opportunity to express its opinion on the performance of the incumbent decision makers – and where necessary to replace them – provides for a degree of political accountability, a central tenet of a democratic system of government.

As over two centuries of political theory have demonstrated, the concept of 'representation' can have at least two meanings: decision makers may represent the views of their constituents in the literal sense that they articulate them in or to government or they may simply represent them in so far as they have been elected by a majority (simple or otherwise) of voters to be the representative of a geographical area. In practice both these interpretations of representation can be seen to operate at different times, according to the predispositions of individual decision makers and the influences emanating from the prevailing political culture in a country, region or area. For example, in a system of government where national political parties are relatively weak and where an individual's success in elections depends very much on supporting policies which are consistent with those of significant elements in one's electorate (e.g. in the United States), representation tends to be seen in the more literal sense of supporting local views and preferences. In contrast, where there is a strong party system and where individuals are held to be elected on the basis of party affiliation (e.g. the United Kingdom), elected representatives are generally expected to be loyal to the party in a policy sense, even if this results on occasions in a conflict with the views of the majority of one's constituents.

In modern democratic states the model of representative decision making usually operates at all spatial levels. In Europe, for example, voters not only elect their own national governments but also choose decision makers at a local and/or regional level and many European citizens are also able to vote in elections for pan-European institutions (i.e. for the European Parliament – *see* Appendix 3.3). One of the consequences of this arrangement is that on occasions the party (or parties) elected to office at national level may be different from that (or those) in power locally, regionally and/or supranationally. Where this occurs, clashes between decision makers representing different geographical areas tend to be inevitable and can give rise to problems of decision making and policy implementation, thus potentially disrupting the programme on which a government has been elected to office.

In this context a useful distinction can be drawn between 'federal' and 'unitary' systems of government. In the former, sovereignty (i.e. the legitimate power to make decisions) is divided between two levels of government (e.g. national and local/regional), each with independent powers that are usually laid down in a written constitution which is interpreted by the courts. Thus in the United States education is in the hands of the elected government at state (i.e. subnational) level, while defence and foreign affairs are federal (i.e. national) governmental responsibilities. In Germany, the federal government similarly has exclusive jurisdiction over foreign and defence policy and environmental protection, while the Länder (states) control such areas as education and the police.

In contrast, under a unitary system ultimate authority rests with the national government and any powers granted to subnational levels by the central sovereign authority can ultimately be rescinded, including the right of government at subnational level to exist. Under such an arrangement – particularly where it is written down in the form of a constitution – government at national level clearly holds the whip hand and would normally expect its view to prevail where a dispute over an issue or policy occurred between it and a subnational authority. That said, decision makers in democratic states at all levels and under different governmental systems have, on the whole, a tendency to settle such conflicts through negotiation, bargaining and compromise rather than by exerting their power and authority, although this might be used on occasions. This predisposition goes some way to explaining why in democratic systems of government, the policies and legislative programmes of elected governments are much more likely to be incremental than they are to be radical.

Mini case   Action on the environment

The failure of markets to take into account the external costs and benefits of economic behaviour is often put forward as a key justification for government intervention in the economy (*see* Chapter 10). Thus while governments on the whole prefer to allow the market to determine most economic choices, there are circumstances in which the state feels it appropriate to use means such as legislation, regulation and fiscal intervention to shape some of the day-to-day decisions made by individuals and organisations. The environment has increasingly become one such arena of government action.

Writing in the *Guardian* on 2 February 2002, Philip Willan reported that the President of Italy's Lombardy region was planning to ban the sale of new petrol- and diesel-powered cars as part of an ambitious plan to reduce the chronic levels of air pollution being experienced by local citizens in many of the region's large towns and cities. Despite weekend bans on cars in many Italian cities and other restrictions on their use on weekdays, atmospheric pollution in parts of Italy frequently reaches danger levels. In Lombardy, one of the industrial powerhouses of Europe, the problem has proved particularly acute; hence the response by the regional authorities.

In essence the President's plan is to challenge car manufacturers to design alternative 'green' vehicles for introduction from 2005 onwards. The initiative – said to be the first of its kind in Europe – aims to promote the sort of environmental awareness found in California, where the state authorities plan to have around 10 per cent of all cars running on hydrogen by 2004. Given the large measure of support for the proposal from local citizens and from the national government, Lombardy's president is confident the plan is feasible and will form a key part of a multifaceted strategy to tackle environmental pollution in the region. Early indications suggest that some of the major car manufacturers – including Fiat, BMW and Citroen – are responding positively to the proposed initiative.

A system for articulating sectional interests

Elections and a party system provide one way in which the views of an individual can be represented in government; an alternative is via pressure group activity. Like competing political parties, the existence of pressure groups is usually regarded as an important indicator of a democratic system of government. For many citizens in democratic countries, joining such a group is seen as a much more effective way of influencing government than through the party system.

Whereas political parties seek influence by formally contesting political office, pressure groups seek to influence government in other ways, although this distinction is increasingly becoming blurred. In essence pressure groups (or 'lobbies') are collections of like-minded people who have voluntarily joined together to try to influence government thinking and behaviour and to represent the interest of their members. As a sectional interest within society, pressure groups provide a vehicle through which a collective and non-party political view can be articulated in decision-making circles; as such they can be said to operate as kind of safety-valve within a democratic system of government.

Traditionally in pressure group literature, a distinction tends to be drawn between groups which represent 'somebody' and those which represent 'something'. The former are usually referred to as 'interest groups' or 'protective groups' and would include groups representing a particular section of the community, such as trade unions or professional associations. The latter tend to be known as 'cause groups' or 'issue groups', as exemplified by Greenpeace, Amnesty International and the various animal rights groups. In practice, of course, it is often difficult to make such a clear-cut distinction, given that some interest groups such as trade unions often associate themselves with particular causes and may campaign vigorously alongside other groups in support of or against the issue concerned.

 Most large pressure groups have websites which contain useful information. Greenpeace, for example, can be accessed at *www.greenpeace.org*

From a governmental point of view the existence of structures for articulating sectional interests is seen as an aid to efficient and representative decision making. Pressure groups not only provide government with detailed information on specific areas of everyday activity without which rational decision making would be difficult; they also fulfil a number of other important functions in a democratic system. These would include:

- helping to defend minority interests;
- assisting in the implementation of government policy and legislation;
- providing for continuity in communication and consultation between the governors and the governed between elections.

The successful introduction of reforms in a country's health service, for example, is dependent upon support from the various arms of the medical profession and from organisations representing the different interests of health service workers. Similarly the effectiveness of government economic policies, and their subsequent impact on the business community, will be conditioned at least in part by the reactions of groups representing large employers, small and medium enterprises, workers, financial interests, etc., as well as by individual entrepreneurs and consumers (*see* Chapter 10).

This relative interdependence between government and pressure groups under a democratic system is exemplified by the practice of prior consultation; this is the arrangement whereby the elected government actively seeks the views of interested parties during the policy and/or legislative process. Such consultation may be 'formal' (e.g. where a group has representation on an advisory or executive body or where it is invited to offer its views on a proposal) or 'informal' (e.g. off-the-record meetings between representatives of the group and the government) or a mixture of the two; it may also involve a group in hiring the services of a professional lobbyist – often an ex-politician or bureaucrat familiar with the structure of decision making in government and with access to key decision makers. Groups which are regularly consulted and whose opinion is readily sought by government may acquire 'insider status' and may even be incorporated into the formal decision-making process – prizes which are highly valued since they imply that the group has a legitimate right to be consulted by government prior to deciding on a particular course of action or inaction. In comparison, 'outsider groups' often find it difficult to make their voice heard in decision-making circles and for this reason may be forced to resort to different forms of direct action in order to publicise their views in the wider community in the hope of gaining influence through public sympathy and support.

As this discussion of 'insider' and 'outsider groups' illustrates, pressure groups can use a variety of methods to attract support for their cause or to protect and promote the interests of their members. These range from direct lobbying of government to marches, strikes, disruption and other forms of demonstrative action designed to attract media and hence public attention – although frequently such action can have an adverse effect. In addition, some of the larger and better-resourced groups may employ experts to advise on policy issues and/or establish their own research facilities to provide information to strengthen their case (e.g. Greenpeace).

What method(s) a group employs and where it seeks to bring its influence to bear tends to vary from issue to issue and group to group, and generally reflects not only differences in group status and resources but also the structure of decision making within the policy community concerned. In the United States for instance, direct lobbying of Congressmen/women is a common tactic used by pressure groups, given the relative weakness of the party system and the tendency for an individual's electoral fortunes to be tied up with the views of key groups in the constituency. In contrast in the United Kingdom, the pressures of party discipline, the domination of the executive branch of government and the influence of senior civil servants tend to make direct appeals to key actors in government a more effective method of achieving political influence than operating at constituency level.

As a final comment it is worth recalling that decisions in a democracy may be made locally, nationally, supranationally or internationally and often require co-operation between different levels of government and/or between different agencies and arms of government at both the formulation and implementation stages. Accordingly, pressure groups are increasingly to be found operating at the interface between the institutions of government and across the whole range of spatial levels from the local to the global (*see* Mini Case: Supranational lobbying). Given the large number of pressure points where vested interests can bring their influence to bear, it tends to be easier for a group to prevent or limit government action rather than to persuade decision makers to change the direction of policy. To this extent policy formulation and implementation in democratic states is perhaps best portrayed as the 'art of the possible' rather than the 'science of the desirable'.

The three branches or functions of government

In a broad sense the process of governing involves three major activities: making decisions, putting them into effect and adjudicating over them in the event of dispute or non-compliance. Each of these functions or branches of government, as they operate at a national level, is discussed in turn below. A similar form of analysis could, if necessary, be applied at other spatial levels.

The legislative function

Governing, as we have seen, is about making decisions which affect the lives of large numbers of people. Some of these decisions require new laws or changes to existing laws to bring them into effect so that the individuals and/or groups to whom they apply become aware of the government's wishes and requirements. In a democratic system of government this formal power to make the law (i.e. to legislate) is vested in a legislative body (the legislature) which is elected either wholly or partly by the people. As indicated above, this process of choosing a representative decision-making body by popular election is a central feature of the democratic approach to government.

Leaving aside for one moment the relative power of the legislative and executive branches of government, it is possible to identify a number of common features which apply to legislatures and the legislative function in most, if not all, democratic states. These include the following:

- *A bicameral legislature*, that is, a legislature with two chambers: an upper house and a lower house, each with specific powers and roles in the legislative process. In most countries each chamber comprises representatives chosen by a separate electoral process and hence may be dominated by the same party or different parties or by no single party, depending on the electoral outcome. For a legislative proposal to be accepted, the consent of both chambers is normally required. This is one of the many checks and balances normally found in democratic systems of government (*see* below).

- *A multi-stage legislative process* – involving the drafting of a legislative proposal, its discussion and consideration, where necessary amendment, further debate and consideration and ultimate acceptance or rejection by either or both legislative chambers. Debates on the general principles of a proposed piece of legislation would normally involve all members of each chamber, whereas detailed discussion tends to take place in smaller groups or committees.

- *An executive-led process*, that is, one in which most major legislative proposals emanate from the executive branch of government. In a presidential system of government (e.g. the USA) the chief executive (the President) is normally elected separately by the people and is not part of the legislature (in other words there is a 'separation of powers'). In a parliamentary system (e.g. the UK) members of the executive may also be members of the legislative body and hence may be in a position to control the legislative process.

- *Opportunities for legislative initiatives by ordinary representatives*, that is, arrangements which permit ordinary members of the legislative assembly to propose new laws or changes to existing laws. In practice such opportunities tend to be limited and dependent to a large degree for their success on a positive response from the political executive.

- *Opportunities to criticise and censure the government and, in some cases, remove it from office* (e.g. through impeachment) – this is a vital function within a democratic system of government in that it forces decision makers to defend their proposals, explain the logic of their actions and account for any mistakes they may have made. Opposition parties play an important role in this context within the legislative body and through media coverage can attack the government and articulate alternative views to the wider public. Specialist and Standing Committees for scrutinising legislation and the day-to-day work of the executive branch of government also usually exist in democratic regimes.

■ *Control of the purse strings*, that is, the power to grant or deny government the money required to carry out its policies and legislative programme. In theory this is a formidable power, given that no government can operate without funds. In practice the power of the legislature to deny funding to a democratically elected government may be more apparent than real and, where necessary, compromise tends to occur between the executive and legislative branches of government.

As will be evident from the comments above, legislating is a complex and time-consuming process, offering numerous opportunities for individuals and groups both within and outside the legislative body (e.g. pressure groups) to delay and disrupt the passage of legislation. While no government can guarantee to achieve all its legislative aims, there is a cultural expectation in a democracy that, as far as possible, promises made before an election will be put into effect at the earliest opportunity by the democratically elected government. Such an expectation usually provides the incumbent administration with a powerful argument for legislative support on the occasions when it is confronted with intransigence within the legislative assembly or hostility from outside sectional interests.

Mini case   Supranational lobbying

Lobbying government is a key and familiar feature of the political process in democratic states. In seeking to influence government decisions, pressure groups (or 'lobbies') tend to target their activities at those parts of government where they are likely to have the maximum impact on official thinking and action. Where decisions are taken on a supranational (or inter-governmental) basis, it is common to find many of the major vested interests establishing facilities to lobby decision makers at this level.

A good example of such activity is provided by the lobbying of EU governments by a number of groups representing European business organisations. Concerned that the process of structural reform and market liberalisation in the EU was faltering, the European Round Table of Industrialists (ERT), the Association of European Chambers of Commerce and Industry and the EU Banking Federation each produced reports in 2001 urging Member State governments to take more action to achieve the target – set at the Lisbon Summit in March 2000 – of making the EU the world's most competitive economy by 2010. The ERT, representing the 45 leaders of very large European-based companies, called for clearer and more predictable decision making and for an improved democratic process within the EU, including greater use of qualified majority voting and greater policy co-ordination. In contrast the Banking Federation and Chambers of Commerce stressed the need for more flexible labour markets as part of a process of improving the EU's potential for growth and employment.

In a separate report (December 2001) on the functioning of the product and capital markets, the European Commission echoed business concerns about the speed of reform in the post-Lisbon period. The report complained that start-up costs for entrepreneurs were still too high and warned that the process of market integration was beginning to slow down, particularly in the service sector. According to the Commission, the elimination of barriers to cross-border trade in services alone could boost the EU's GDP by between about 1 and 4 per cent.

The executive function

Governing is not only about making decisions, it is also about ensuring that these decisions are put into effect in order to achieve the government's objectives. Implementing governmental decisions is the responsibility of the executive branch of government.

In modern states the term 'the executive' refers to that relatively small group of individuals chosen to decide on policy and to oversee its implementation; some of these individuals will hold political office, others will be career administrators and advisers, although some of the latter may also be political appointees. Together they are part of a complex political and administrative structure designed to carry out the essential work of government and to ensure that those responsible for policy making and implementation are ultimately accountable for their actions.

The policy-making aspect of the executive function is normally the responsibility of a small political executive chosen (wholly or in part) by popular election. Under a presidential system of government, the chief executive or President is usually chosen by separate election for a given period of office and becomes both the nominal and political head of state. He/she subsequently appoints individuals to head the various government departments/ministries/bureaux which are responsible for shaping and implementing government policy. Neither the President nor the heads of departments normally sit in the legislative assembly, although there are sometimes exceptions to this rule (e.g. the Vice-President in the United States).

In contrast, in a parliamentary system the roles of head of state and head of government are separated, with the former usually largely ceremonial and carried out by either a president (e.g. Germany, India) or a monarch (e.g. UK, Japan). The head of government (e.g. Prime Minister), while officially appointed by the head of state, is an elected politician, invariably the head of the party victorious in a general election or at least seen to be capable of forming a government, possibly in coalition with other parties. Once appointed, the head of government chooses other individuals to head the different government departments/ministries and to be part of a collective decision-making body (e.g. a Cabinet) which meets to sanction policy proposals put forward through a system of executive committees and subcommittees (e.g. Cabinet Committees). These individuals, along with the head of government, are not only part of the executive machinery of the state but also usually members of the legislative assembly and both 'individually' and 'collectively' responsible to the legislature for the work of government.

The day-to-day administration of government policy is largely carried out by non-elected government officials (sometimes referred to as **civil servants** or **bureaucrats**) who work for the most part in complex, bureaucratic organisations within the state bureaucracy. Apart from their role in implementing public policy, government officials help to advise ministers on the different policy options and on the political and administrative aspects of particular courses of action. Needless to say, this gives them a potentially critical role in shaping government policy, a role which has been substantially enhanced over the years by the practice of granting officials a significant degree of discretion in deciding on the details of particular policies and/or on how they should be administered.

Whereas politicians in the executive branch of government tend to be transitory figures – who come and go at the whim of the head of government or of the electorate – most, if not all, officials are permanent, professional appointees who may serve a variety of governments of different political complexions and preferences during a long career in public administration. Whatever government is in power, officials are generally expected to operate in a non-partisan (i.e. 'neutral') way when advising their political masters and when overseeing the implementation of government policy. Their loyalty in short is to the current administration in office, a principle which helps to ensure a smooth transition of government and to guarantee that the upheaval caused by a general election does not prevent the business of the state from being carried out 'as usual'.

The judicial function

Governing is not just about making and implementing laws; it is also about ensuring that they are applied and enforced; the latter is essentially the role of the third arm of government, namely the judiciary and the system of courts. Like political institutions, legal structures and processes tend to a degree to be country specific and vary according to a number of influences including history, culture and politics. For example, while some states have a relatively unified legal system, others organised on a federal basis usually have a system of parallel courts adjudicating on federal and state/provincial law, with a Supreme Court arbitrating in the event of a dispute. In some countries a proportion of the judges may be directly or indirectly elected by the public, in others they may be appointed by government and/or co-opted by fellow judges. Business students should make themselves familiar with the legal arrangements within their own country (*see* e.g. Chapter 6, which contains information on the legal system in England and Wales). In this section we look briefly at the judicial function as related to the concept of democracy.

Whereas in totalitarian systems of government the judiciary is essentially the servant of the ruling élite (e.g. the 'party'), in a democracy it is an accepted principle that there should be a separation between the judicial function and the other two branches of government in order to protect the citizen from a too powerful state. This notion of an impartial and independent judiciary, free to challenge the government and to review its decisions, is regarded as one of the hallmarks of a democratic system of government; a further manifestation of the doctrine of the separation of powers.

In practice of course, notions of judicial independence and role within the democratic political process tend to be the subject of certain amount of debate, particularly in countries where senior appointments to the judiciary appear to be in the gift of politicians (e.g. Supreme Court judges in the United States are nominated by the President with the consent of the Senate) or where individuals with judicial powers also have an executive and/or legislative role (e.g. the Lord Chancellor and Home Secretary in Britain). Equally there are questions over the degree to which the courts should have the power to review the constitutionality of decisions made by a democratically elected government. In the United States, for example, the Supreme Court has a long-established right to declare a law void if it conflicts with its own interpretation of the American constitution. In contrast in Britain, the legal sovereignty of Parliament and the absence of a codified written constitution push the judiciary towards trying to interpret the intentions of the framers of government legislation and any legal decision unwelcomed by the government can be reversed by further legislation. That said, it is interesting to note that in recent years there has been an increased willingness on the part of the British judiciary to review administrative decisions, particularly those made by ministers.

Other aspects, too, call into question how far in modern democratic states there is a total separation between the different arms of government (e.g. increasing use of administrative courts/tribunals) and whether it makes sense to rigidly distinguish between rule making and rule adjudication. Certainly some of the past judgments by the United States Supreme Court (e.g. in the area of civil rights) demonstrate that the courts can be influential in shaping decisions on major issues of policy and suggest that the judiciary are susceptible to influences from their own values or to general societal pressures. In short it seems fair to suggest that under current legal arrangements, legal adjudication is not far removed from the world of politics; arguably we may like to perpetuate the myth of an entirely separate and independent judiciary since this is a necessary aspect of the stability of many existing political systems.

Checks and balances in democracies

As will be evident from the analysis above democracy implies the existence of a system of checks and balances, arrangements which serve to curb government action and restrict its influence on the day-to-day lives of its citizens. These restraints on the actions of the state at national level can be divided into two main types: political and social/economic.

Political checks and balances emanate primarily from three main sources:

- *the separation of powers* – particularly the notion that the three arms of government are in separate hands and that decisions require the concurrence of all branches of government;
- *a bicameral legislature* – with legislation having to be accepted by both houses and subject to scrutiny and amendment by opposition parties;
- *the territorial division of powers* – whether under a federal arrangement or through the devolution of power to regional bodies and/or local authorities. Supranationalism is a further development.

The point is not that these arrangements necessarily exist in their most complete form in democratic states, but that – however imperfect in practice – their existence helps to provide time for reflection and delay in the decision-making process and to encourage consultation, negotiation and consensus building: the essence of the democratic approach to conflict resolution.

The notion of social and economic checks and balances refers to those countervailing pressures on the activities of the state and its agencies that derive from the existence of non-state structures and processes which affect the lives of individuals and which ultimately restrict the scope of government influence. These include private business organisations, professional associations, promotional bodies, churches and other groups which help to shape our economic, social and moral environment. As subsequent chapters will demonstrate, the bulk of economic decisions in democratic states are not taken by the government but by private individuals and organisations (i.e. firms) interacting through a market system. This acts as a kind of check and balance on the free activity of the public sector and is a fundamental characteristic of democratic government.

A model of the policy process

It is appropriate to conclude this examination of the political environment with a brief discussion of the process of governmental decision making in democratic systems. Here, the basic model of the organisation in its environment introduced in Chapter 1 serves as a useful analytical tool (*see* Figure 3.2). Governments, like firms, are organisations which transform inputs into output and they do so in an environment largely the same as that which confronts other types of enterprise. Like other organisations, government is a user of resources, especially land, labour, capital, finance and expertise, but in addition all governments face political demands and supports when considering their policy options.

As indicated above, political demands – including those directly or indirectly impinging on business activity – become translated into action through a variety of mechanisms, including the electoral system, party activity, pressure group influence and political communication; hence a government is always keen to point out that electoral victory implies that it has a mandate for its policies. The supports of the political system are those customs, conventions, rules, assumptions and sentiments which provide a basis for the existence of the political community and its constituent parts and thus give legitimacy to the actions and existence of the incumbent government. In democratic systems, the belief in democratic principles, and the doctrines and practices emanating from that belief, are seen as central to the activities of government and its agencies.

Figure 3.2   Government and its environment

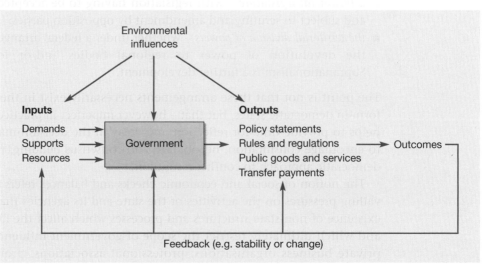

Feedback (e.g. stability or change)

The outputs of the political system vary considerably and range from public goods and services (e.g. healthcare) – provided predominantly from money raised through taxation – to rules and regulations (e.g. legislation, administrative procedures, directives) and transfer payments (i.e. where the government acts as a reallocator of resources, as in the case of the provision of state benefits). Taken together, the nature, range and extent of government output not only tend to make government the single biggest 'business' in a state, they also influence the environment in which other businesses operate and increasingly in which other governments make decisions.

As far as governmental decision making is concerned, this is clearly a highly complex process which in practice does not replicate the simple sequence of events suggested by the model. Certainly governments require 'means' (inputs) to achieve 'ends' (output), but the outputs of the political system normally only emerge after a complex, varied and ongoing process involving a wide range of individuals, groups and agencies. To add further confusion, those involved in the process tend to vary according to the decision under discussion as well as over time, making analysis fraught with difficulties. One possible solution may be to distinguish between the early development of a policy proposal ('initiation') and its subsequent 'formulation' and 'implementation', in the hope that a discernible 'policy community' can be identified at each stage. But even this approach involves a degree of guesswork and arbitrary decision making, not least because of the difficulty of distinguishing precisely between the different stages of policy making and of discerning the influence of individuals and groups at each phase of the process.

Notwithstanding these difficulties, it is important for students of business and for businesses themselves to have some understanding of the structure of decision making and of the underlying values and beliefs which tend to shape governmental action, if they are to appreciate (and possibly 'influence') the political environment in which they exist. In short, studies of political systems, institutions and processes help to provide insight into how and why government decisions are made, who is important in shaping those decisions and how influence can be brought to bear on the decision-making process. As an increasing number of individuals and groups recognise, knowledge of this kind can prove a valuable organisational resource that on occasions is of no less significance than the other inputs into the productive process.

Synopsis

Laws and policies which influence business activity are made by politicians and bureaucrats, operating at a variety of spatial levels. In the United Kingdom, the decisions of local and central government emanate from a complex process of discussion and negotiation involving a range of formal and informal institutions, including political parties and pressure groups, and frequently involving international and supranational bodies. This process is part of the democratic approach to decision making and provides opportunities for individuals and groups to influence government thinking on both the formulation and implementation of policy and legislation. Students of business and managers need to have a broad understanding of this political environment in order to appreciate one of the key influences on a firm's operations.

Summary of key points

- Politics is a universal activity which affects businesses of all types and sizes.

- It occurs at a variety of spatial levels from the local to the global.

- Political systems, structures and processes reflect underlying social values and philosophies and these influence the ways in which major decisions are taken.

- In any democratic system of government the key political institutions are likely to include an electoral system, a party system, a representative decision-making assembly and a system for articulating sectional interests.

- The three key functions of government are legislative, executive and judicial.

- While political institutions, practices and processes tend to vary between countries, democratic government is typified by a system of representative democracy and by political, social and economic checks and balances which act as a constraint on the actions of government.

- Such checks and balances in the system include the activities of pressure groups which seek to influence government through a variety of means and who often play a key role in policy formulation and implementation.

- Business organisations and the bodies which represent them are key pressure groups in democratic societies and an important part of the external environment in which government and its agencies operate.

Appendix 3.1 A democratic political system in action: UK national government

As far as the United Kingdom is concerned, the four interrelated elements of a democratic system of government are illustrated in Figure 3.3.

Through a system of regular elections British citizens (the electorate) vote for candidates of competing political parties who are seeking to form the national government (or to be members of the devolved assemblies in Northern Ireland, Scotland or Wales). Successful candidates at the national elections become Members of Parliament (MPs) and the party with the largest number of MPs is invited by the monarch to form a government, with individuals within the government being allocated specific responsibilities for particular areas of work. The work of government is scrutinised by Parliament (see below) which acts as the people's representative between elections, thereby providing for a measure of public accountability. Equally, between (or during) elections individuals are free to seek to influence government by joining pressure groups or other types of organisation (e.g. political parties) and by making their views known to their elected representatives. The media is free and therefore able to scrutinise the government's performance and to inform the public about political developments.

Figure 3.3   The elected government at Westminster

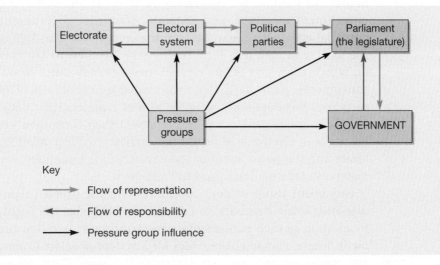

For information on the Scottish Parliament and the Welsh and Northern Ireland Assemblies you can consult:
www.scottish.parliament.uk; www.wales.gov-uk; www.ni-assembly.gov.uk

The legislative branch of government at national level

As indicated above, a directly elected legislature – representative of the people and responsible for making laws – is an important component of a democratic system of government. In the United Kingdom as a whole this function is carried out by Parliament, which currently comprises a non-elected upper chamber (the House of Lords) and an elected lower chamber (the House of Commons) whose members (currently 659 MPs) are elected by universal suffrage by the majority of citizens aged 18 and over. While it is true to say that the Lords still retains some important powers, including the power to delay government legislation, the upper house is currently being reformed and in future is likely to contain an elected element. Whatever happens it seems likely that the House of Commons will remain the most important part of the UK legislature, particularly since it contains key members of the political executive, including the Prime Minister and most of the Cabinet. For this reason the discussion below focuses on the role of the House of Commons.

Website addresses for the UK Parliament include
www.explore.parliament.uk/; www.parliament.uk/

As far as political representation and responsibility are concerned, this is achieved in a number of ways. For a start, Members of Parliament are directly elected by their constituents and one of the MP's main roles is to represent the constituency for the period between general elections. Apart from holding regular surgeries at which individuals (including businessmen and women) can discuss their problems and views with their representative, MPs also speak on constituency matters in Parliament, frequently raise questions which require answers from government ministers, and generally scrutinise government proposals for any potential effects they may have on the constituency, including key groups within the local electorate (e.g. local businesses). Needless to say, there will be occasions on which the views of the elected member may differ from those of his or her constituents, particularly those who voted for candidates of an opposing political party; but this does not negate the idea of representation under the British system of parliamentary democracy. MPs represent their constituents first and foremost by having been elected *by them* and hence they provide a direct link between the electorate and the government of the day, which is essentially drawn from the senior members of the majority party in Parliament.

Parliament also provides opportunities for the people's representatives to scrutinise and, where necessary, to criticise and challenge the decisions of government. In addition to such parliamentary mechanisms as question time and the adjournment debate, Parliament provides for a system of Select Committees of backbench MPs whose primary role is to scrutinise the work of government departments and other state agencies. Such committees – chaired by both government and opposition backbenchers – are able to question ministers and civil servants, call for departmental papers, cross-examine experts from outside government, and generally investigate the work of the executive, prior to reporting to Parliament on their findings. In bringing their views before Parliament and the public generally (especially through the media), Select Committees provide a check on government activity and hence form one of the strands by which governments remain answerable to the electorate in the period between elections.

Another significant strand is provided by the Opposition who represent not only an alternative choice of government, but also a means of scrutinising and criticising the work of the incumbent administration. Fundamental to this role is the ability of opposition MPs to publicise the decisions of government and to present alternative views to the public via party political broadcasts or promotional literature or debates in parliament, or by general media coverage. Such free and open discussion of issues and policies is a necessary condition for democracy and is an important element in the political education of the nation. Even where governments have large majorities – as is currently the case – the role of opposition parties remains a vital component of democracy and helps to provide a curb on unlimited government action.

Turning to its role as a legislative body, there is little doubt that the UK Parliament is largely a legitimising institution, giving formal authority to the wishes of the majority party. Through its control of the process of legislation, the parliamentary timetable, the flow of information and the votes of its members, the government is able to ensure that its legislative proposals not only come before Parliament, but also are almost invariably accepted, even if some delay occurs from time to time in enacting the government's programme. Opportunities for individual MPs to sponsor legislation (e.g. through private members' bills) are few and far between and the outcome of such proposals depends ultimately on government support (or reluctant acquiescence), if the legislation is to get through its various stages in Parliament. Not surprisingly, this effective stranglehold by the government on the legislative process has led some commentators to talk of an 'elective dictatorship' and to question the true extent of democratic decision making, particularly when modern governments are invariably elected by less than 50 per cent of the electorate.

The executive branch of government

Putting laws and policies into effect is formally the work of the executive. In the UK this role is carried out by a wide variety of institutions and agencies that are part of the machinery of government. These include the Cabinet, government departments, local authorities, nationalised industries and a large number of other non-departmental public bodies or quasi-autonomous national government agencies, often referred to as 'quangos'.[1] In the discussion below attention is focused initially on the key institutions at central level since these are fundamental to the process of decision making in Britain. Discussion of some of the other agencies can be found in subsequent sections of this chapter.

Information on non-departmental public bodies (NDPBs) is available at
www.cabinet-office.gov.uk/quango/index/whatis
See also *www.cabinet-office.gov.uk/quango/homepage*

Under the British system of government, the core of the executive is the Cabinet, headed by the Prime Minister, an office of crucial importance given the absence of an elected head of state with effective political powers. British Prime Ministers not only have a number of significant political roles – including leader of the governing party, head of the government and head of the Cabinet – but also have a formidable array of political powers, including the power to:

- choose members of the Cabinet;
- choose other non-Cabinet ministers;
- promote, demote or dismiss ministers;
- appoint individuals to chair Cabinet committees;
- appoint top civil servants;
- confer certain appointments and titles; and
- determine the date of the general election within the five-year term of office.

While the existence of such rights and responsibilities does not infer that Prime Ministers will inevitably be all-powerful, it is clear that holders of the office have a key role to play in the decision-making process and much will depend upon how an individual interprets that role, upon their personality, and upon the constraints they face (both 'real' and 'imagined') in carrying it out. As the Conservative Prime Minister Mrs Thatcher (1979–90) found to her cost, retaining the office of Prime Minister is dependent not only on the electorate, but also on maintaining the support and confidence of parliamentary colleagues in the period between elections.

As indicated above, as head of the Cabinet the Prime Minister chairs the committee of senior ministers that is the overall directing force – or board of management – within British central government. Comprising about 25 to 30 ministers who have been appointed by the Prime Minister to head the various government departments (or to fulfil some other important functions), the Cabinet is responsible for directing and co-ordinating the work of the whole executive machine. Its functions include:

- making decisions on the nature and direction of government policy, including public expenditure, economic policy, defence, foreign relations, industrial policy, and so on;
- overseeing and co-ordinating the administration of government;
- arbitrating in the event of disputes between ministers or departments;
- discussing, deciding and generally directing the government's legislative programme, including laws relating to business.

A large part of this work, of course, is carried out using a system of committees and subcommittees, which are comprised of individuals chosen by the Prime Minister (including the chairperson) and which are supported by a small but powerful secretariat, headed by the Cabinet Secretary (a civil servant). Apart from providing an opportunity for more detailed discussions of issues and policies prior to full consideration by the Cabinet, the committee system has the advantage of allowing non-members of the Cabinet (including non-Cabinet ministers and civil servants) to participate in discussions in which they may have an interest. In this way, the system helps to provide a mechanism for communication and co-ordination between government departments and serves as a training ground for junior ministers, many of whom will subsequently achieve full Cabinet responsibilities. A selected list of Cabinet committees for 2002 is shown in Table 3.1.

Much of the day-to-day work of central government is carried out in vast and complex administrative structures called government departments – a selected list of which is shown in Table 3.2. Most government departments are headed by Cabinet ministers (usually called the Secretaries of State) and include other ministers outside the Cabinet (e.g. Ministers of State, Parliamentary Under Secretaries of State) who have been appointed by the Prime Minister. Together these ministers constitute the political executive. As the head of a department, the Secretary of State has ultimate responsibility for its work and is answerable to Parliament through the various mechanisms referred to above.[2] In addition, he or she is

Table 3.1 Selected Cabinet committees, 2002

Committee name	Designation
Ministerial Committee on Economic Affairs, Productivity and Competitiveness	EAPC
Ministerial Sub-Committee on Employment	EAPC(E)
Ministerial Committee on the Environment	ENV
Ministerial Committee on E-Democracy	MISC17
Ministerial Committee on the Legislative Programme	LP
Ministerial Group on Public Services and Public Expenditure	PSX
Ministerial Committee on Science Policy	SCI
Ministerial Committee on Domestic Affairs	DA
Ministerial Committee on the Nations and the Regions	CNR
Ministerial Sub-Committee on Electronic Service Delivery	PSX(E)

Source: Cabinet Office (*www.cabinet-office.gov.uk/cabsec/index/cabcom/index*).

expected to give overall direction to the work of the department – within the policy of the government as a whole – and to represent its interest in the Cabinet (e.g. over the size and use of its budget), in Parliament (e.g. in steering through legislation) and in the outside world (e.g. in the media). Large areas of this work are delegated to the Ministers of State who assume responsibility for specific areas of departmental work and they in turn will tend to delegate some duties to the department's junior ministers. Such an arrangement not only ensures coverage of the different aspects of a department's responsibilities, but also provides invaluable experience and training for ambitious young MPs appointed to a ministerial post.

Each government department has its own website. Useful addresses currently include
www.dfes.gov.uk (Education and Skills)
www.defra.gov.uk (Environment, Food and Rural Affairs)
www.dtlr.gov.uk (Transport, Local Government and the Regions)
www.hm-treasury.gov.uk (The Treasury)
www.dti.gov.uk (Trade and Industry)

Ministers are assisted in their work by permanent officials, known as **civil servants**, many of whom have spent a large part of their working lives in the government machine and hence are familiar with how it works and how to manipulate it in order to achieve particular objectives. Whereas ministers are politicians, civil servants are administrators vested formally with the task of carrying out the policies of the incumbent government, irrespective of their own political views and preferences. Perhaps not surprisingly, as key advisers to ministers on policy formulation and implementation, senior civil servants can exercise considerable influence over the nature and shape of government policy and legislation – a point amusingly emphasised in a popular British television programme *Yes, Minister*.[3] For this reason, individuals or groups seeking to shape government thinking on an issue or piece of legislation frequently 'target' senior departmental officials in the hope of gaining influence in the policy process.

This potential for influence by senior civil servants is, of course, enhanced by the scope and complexities of modern government and by the fact that government

Table 3.2	Key government departments, 2002

Cabinet Office

HM Treasury

Foreign and Commonwealth Office

Home Office

Environment, Food and Rural Affairs

Education and Skills

Defence

Health

Work and Pensions

Trade and Industry

Culture, Media and Sport

Transport, Local Government and The Regions

ministers have a wide range of non-departmental as well as departmental responsibilities (e.g. as constituency MPs). Ministers consequently rely heavily on their officials for information and advice and civil servants are normally entrusted, under ministers, with the conduct of the whole gamut of government activities, including filling in the details of some legislation. Added to this, the need for policy co-ordination between departments requires regular meetings between senior officials, in groups which mirror the meetings of Cabinet subcommittees. Since these meetings of officials help to provide the groundwork and briefing papers for future discussions by ministers, they permit civil servants to influence the course of events, especially when a particular line or policy option is agreed by the senior officials in a number of departments.

Criticism of the influence of the senior civil service and of its secrecy and reluctance to change has led to a number of inquiries into how to improve its efficiency and *modus operandi*. In 1979, the new Conservative government appointed Sir Derek Rayner of Marks & Spencer to introduce private-sector management methods into the service and this was continued by his successor, Sir Robin Ibbs of ICI, who produced a report called *The Next Steps* (1988). This report led to many civil service responsibilities being 'hived off' to 'executive agencies', which operate semi-independently of government ministers, with their own budgets and performance targets and with a greater degree of independence over pay, financial and staffing matters, despite remaining formally part of the civil service. In the early 1990s the government under John Major introduced 'market testing', under which a proportion of the work of each department and agency had to be put out to competitive tender. There are currently attempts to further modernise the civil service as part of a general overhaul of the machinery of government.

It is perhaps worth noting at this point that, however pervasive its influence, the civil service is not the only source of policy advice for governments. Apart from traditional bureaucratic channels, ministers often turn to specially appointed bodies for help and guidance in making policy choices. Some of these sources are permanent (or relatively permanent) and would include the various advisory bodies set up by past and present governments to assist in the policy process in specific functional areas (e.g. the Arts Council). Others are temporary, having been specially constituted by government to consider a particular problem and to report on their findings prior to going out of existence (e.g. public inquiries, Royal Commissions). While the appointment of these advisory sources does not oblige the government to follow their advice, they can be regarded as useful sources of information, ideas and advice from outside the formal bureaucratic machine. Moreover the fact that they tend to have a membership representing a wide cross-section of interests (including representatives of particular pressure groups, industrialists, trade unionists, MPs, academics and others drawn from the list of 'the great and the good') helps to widen the scope of consultation and thus to enhance the democratic process.

The last generation has also seen governments turning increasingly to special advisers and policy planning units for help with policy development. Whereas advisers are individuals appointed by ministers (including the Prime Minister), usually from outside the civil service, policy planning units and/or research units are groups of individuals generally recruited from and located within the government machine, with the aim of providing a range of policy and programme advice to both policy makers and administrators. Often comprised of young and highly qualified individuals seconded to a unit from a wide range of occupational categories and disciplines (including statisticians, social scientists, economists, and general administrators), policy units are a valuable source of information and advice, and their operation at both central and local government level provides policy makers with detailed research and analysis with which to support their policy judgements.

A further important development has been the increased use of 'focus groups', collections of individual citizens consulted by government on policy proposals prior to legislation and/or implementation. In canvassing the views of individuals affected by government policy, the current government hopes to improve the policy process in a wide range of areas, including the delivery of public services, where it has a programme to provide round-the-clock availability and (ultimately) complete electronic access. While some see citizens' panels or focus groups as nothing more than a gimmick, others regard their use as a move towards a more modern and democratic form of government with increased levels of public accountability and access to information.

web link A useful discussion on focus groups is available at *www.soc.surrey.ac.uk/sru/SRU19*

The judicial branch of government

The third arm of government, the judiciary – comprising the judges and the courts – is formally separate from and independent of Parliament and the government, despite the fact that the head of the judiciary, the Lord Chancellor, is both a member of the government and a member of the House of Lords, where he or she presides as Speaker. In essence the role of the judiciary is to put into effect the laws enacted by Parliament and to keep the government within the limits of its powers as laid down in statutes and in common law, as interpreted by the judiciary. Since 1973, it has also been responsible for interpreting European Union law. Given the complexities of the legal system and its relevance to the world of business, it is important to examine this aspect of government in more detail. This is undertaken in Chapter 6.

Postscript

In Britain as elsewhere, both 'change' and 'continuity' are features of the political system. Apart from the developments mentioned above (e.g. reform of the House of Lords, elections to the new Scottish Parliament, Welsh Assembly and Northern Ireland Assembly, proposed reforms of the civil service), there are proposals to introduce a new voting system (*see*, for example, the Jenkins Report 1998), to reform government policy-making and delivery systems (*see*, for example, the Wilson Report 1998) and to consider regional assemblies in England. Various systems of proportional representation have been used for the elections to the new regional assemblies and for the European elections (in June 1999) and London elected a mayor in the year 2000 (*see* below). Developments such as these clearly have implications for the business environment.

Appendix 3.2   Subnational government : UK local authorities

Democratic government occurs at subnational as well as national level and takes a wide variety of forms. In addition to the local branches of central government departments and public utilities, many states have local agencies for the administration of justice, local special-purpose authorities (e.g. in the health service) and a system of regional and/or local government, whether under a federal or a unitary arrangement. Such decentralisation and deconcentration of political authority is generally seen as beneficial, since it brings the formulation and administration of policy 'nearer to the people' and is said to provide for decisions which are more sensitive to local needs and aspirations. Concomitantly, however, it can raise the question as to the degree of autonomy of local agencies within a centralised system of government and as recent history has demonstrated this is a controversial and perennial source of debate and dispute in many parts of the world.

Within the United Kingdom as a whole, political power is devolved at two main levels: regionally and locally. Scotland, Wales and Northern Ireland now have their own directly elected regional assemblies with differing levels of devolved authority. The Scottish Parliament, for example, essentially took over the role of the Scottish Office in 2000, with responsibilities including education, health and transport and the power to raise income tax in Scotland by up to 3p in the pound. The Welsh Assembly, in contrast, has no fiscal powers and is able to make secondary legislation in areas where executive functions have been transferred to it. The Northern Ireland Assembly has legislative authority in the fields previously administered by the Northern Ireland Departments. Plans for possible new regional assemblies in England are currently under discussion (*see* e.g. the *Guardian* 10 May 2002).

Local government – the focus of this section – has a considerable historical pedigree and remains a key element of the country's system of institutionalised democracy and a major actor in the national as well as the local economy. Given its impact in the business environment, it deserves special attention.

As one form of local administration, local government has a number of distinctive features. For a start it involves self-government by the people of the locality as well as for them, with local authorities exercising considerable discretion in the ways they apply national laws within their areas. In addition, local decision-makers (councillors) are elected to oversee multi-purpose authorities, financed by revenue raised predominantly from local sources – although the proportion from central government has risen in recent years. In short, each local authority constitutes a miniature political and administrative system: each has the institutions and processes of government – including an electoral system, a legislative body (the council), appointed officials (local government officers), party activity, and conflict between individuals and groups within the local community over the allocation of resources and the enforcement of values.

Figure 3.4 illustrates this parallel between the basic operation of government at central and local level. The electorate in each local constituency (e.g. district, county, metropolitan district) periodically choose between candidates who are mostly representing the same parties as those found at national level and the successful candidates in the election are elected to represent their constituency in

Figure 3.4   The local government system

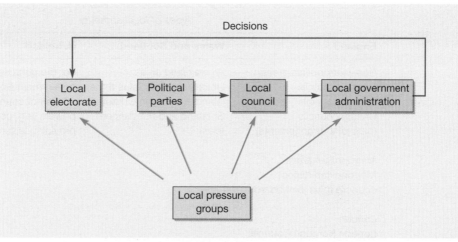

the deliberating body (the council). Senior members of this body are chosen to serve on the various committees and subcommittees, with the leading party on the council having an in-built majority in the committee system, where most decisions have traditionally been made prior to being sanctioned (or not) by the full council. Since the passage of the Local Government Act (2000), councils have been allowed to adopt one of three broad categories of constitution which provide for a separate executive. These three categories are (1) a directly elected mayor with a cabinet selected by the mayor, (2) a cabinet either elected by the council or appointed by its leader, and (3) a directly elected mayor and council manager.

For the most part, senior councillors are the political heads of the various local authority departments and agencies (e.g. housing, social services, education, and so on) that are responsible for providing those services within the local community which national laws require or, in some cases (e.g. sports centres), do not forbid. Much of this work is carried out by local officials who are appointed by the local authority to administer local services and to advise councillors on policy matters. As the local equivalent of civil servants, local government officers exercise consider-able influence over the formulation as well as the implementation of local decisions. For this reason, they too tend to be targeted by local pressure groups which operate at all levels and stages of the political process in their attempts to influence local decision making.

The current structure of local government in the United Kingdom is illustrated in Table 3.3. In England, outside the metropolitan areas, most 'shire' counties have a two-tier structure of county councils and district councils, with the former providing the larger services (e.g. education and social services) while the latter have responsi-bility for a range of other services (such as housing, leisure, refuse collection and local planning). Elsewhere (e.g. Avon, Cleveland, Humberside, Isle of Wight) new 'unitary authorities' either have taken over the functions of the former county and district councils or operate alongside them as all-purpose authorities (e.g. Leicester, York). In the metropolitan areas (including London) the single tier of district councils (or London borough councils) remains unchanged from previous years (*see* below).

Following legislation in 1994, the two-tier structure in Wales and Scotland was abolished and was replaced (on 1 April 1996) with single-tier, all-purpose, unitary

Table 3.3	The structure of UK local government, 2002

Types of local authority		
England	**Wales and Scotland**	**N. Ireland**
Non-metropolitan areas County councils District councils Unitary councils (plus joint arrangements)	*All mainland areas* Unitary councils (plus three island councils in Orkney, Shetland and the Western Isles)	For the purpose of local government Northern Ireland has 26 district councils with limited powers (e.g. collecting rubbish and providing leisure facilities)
Metropolitan areas Metropolitan district councils (plus joint boards)		
London London Borough Councils (plus Corporation of the City of London and joint boards)		

authorities which have inherited the majority of the functions of the previous councils. In Northern Ireland the system of single-tier district councils remains, although these authorities still have limited responsibility for service provision.

Like central government, UK local government has also faced pressures for reform, and a number of important developments have taken place in recent years.

■ London elected its first executive mayor in 2000 and a streamlined assembly (25 members) to control its budget and appointments. The assembly of the Greater London Authority was elected by proportional representation and is responsible for major strategic issues such as transport, economic development, planning and the environment.

■ Compulsory Competitive Tendering has been replaced by 'Best Value' in the delivery of local services.

■ Councils have been asked to consider reform of the decision-making process and to consider alternative models (*see* also White Paper, 'Modern Local Government in Touch with the People', 1998). Some councils have implemented such changes.

As indicated previously, such changes in the political system have implications for the relationship between business and government.

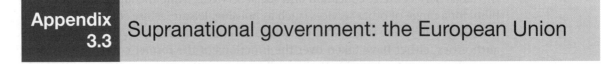

Appendix 3.3   Supranational government: the European Union

Decisions and law affecting business activity are increasingly being made at supranational as well as national and subnational levels. Nowhere is this more evident than in western Europe, where the influence of the European Union is profound. As a significant part of the political environment of the major world economies, the EU deserves special consideration, particularly since its decisions often have global as well as regional consequences – affecting not only firms within its member states, but also businesses and governments trading with these states both directly and indirectly. In the following analysis, attention is focused on the political institutions of the European Union and their relative importance in the process of decision-making.[4] The economic significance of the EU within the international marketplace is discussed in Chapter 13.

> **web link**
>
> The EU's official website called 'Europa' can be accessed at *www.europa.eu.int*
> This provides links to lots of other very useful sites.
> Website addresses for EU institutions are available at
> *www.europa.eu.int/addresses/institutions/websites*

The European Parliament

The European Parliament is a directly elected body of 626 members (MEPs), with each member state's representation being roughly equivalent to the size of its population. The United Kingdom, for example, has 87 MEPs, elected at five-yearly intervals by UK citizens using a regional list system of proportional representation introduced for the June 1999 European elections. Since voting under a proportional system enhances the prospects of representation by smaller political parties, the European Parliament contains members representing a diversity of political parties who sit in political groups with similar affiliations. Figure 3.5 shows, for example, the number of MEPs by broad affiliation as they stood on the eve of the June 1999 election.

> **web link**
>
> For information on the European Parliament see *www.europarl.eu.int*

The importance of party affiliation is emphasised by the fact that Parliament's organisation is deliberately biased in favour of multinational groupings, with recognition of a political grouping entitling the group to offices, funding, representation on committees and influence in debates and legislation. In order to decide its attitude to an issue or policy proposal coming before the Parliament or one of its committees, a group would normally meet for several days in the week before each session and the

Figure 3.5   MEPs by party affiliation on 1 June 1999

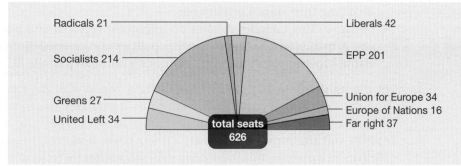

Source: Adapted from European Parliament

issue would be discussed and an agreed line would be decided. As in the case of national parliaments, the attitudes of the political groups have a significant impact on the discussions and decisions within the European Parliament, both in committee and when the House is in full session. Given the number of party groups, however, and the fact that no single group tends to have an absolute majority – unlike in some national parliaments – there is often a need for a group to try to build a coalition of support if it is to achieve its objectives in Parliament. Understandably – and perhaps inevitably – decisions by the European Parliament thus tend to involve compromise between individuals and groups, with the final outcome frequently being a course of action which is 'acceptable' to a majority.

In terms of its role and methods of operation, the European Parliament essentially mirrors national parliaments. Much of its detailed work is handled by specialist committees, meeting mostly in Brussels, which report on and offer recommendations to full sessions of the House which take place in Strasbourg. Membership of each committee is broadly representative of the strengths of the party groupings and the chairmen and women of the permanent committees tend to be influential figures in their own right. In addition to carrying out detailed examination and amendment of draft laws, the committees discuss issues (e.g. women's rights, consumer protection, employment), question officials, hold public hearings at which experts and representatives of specialist organisations give evidence, and generally offer their opinion and advice on issues of concern to the EU. As in the case of national parliaments, detailed discussion in committee prior to debate and decision by the full house provides Parliament with an effective means of carrying out its duties and serves as a mechanism for scrutinising the work of both the Council and the Commission.

With regard to its functions, these predominantly fall into four main areas:

1 *Legislation*. The Parliament's formal approval is required on most proposals before they can be adopted by the Council of Ministers (see below).
2 *The budget*. Along with the Council of Ministers, the Parliament acts as the Community's 'budgetary authority' and can reject the Council's draft budget and may modify expenditure proposals on 'non-compulsory' items. It can question the Commission's management of the budget and call in the Court of Auditors.
3 *Supervision*. The Parliament supervises the Commission, which it has the power to dismiss by a vote of censure and whose work it scrutinises using a variety of mechanisms. Under the Maastricht Treaty (1992) it has the right to be consulted on the appointment of a new Commission and can veto its appointment. The power of democratic supervision has been extended to other EU institutions including the Council of Ministers.
4 *Initiative*. This includes debates on important regional and international issues and demands for changes to existing policies and/or legislation. Parliament must also approve applications from countries wishing to join the EU.

In the legislative field, authority traditionally rested with the Council of Ministers and the Commission, and Parliament's role was largely to sanction proposals put before it. Changes under the Single European Act (1986), the Maastricht Treaty (1992) and the Amsterdam Treaty (1997) have, however, helped to strengthen Parliament's position by establishing new procedures for 'assent', 'co-operating' and 'co-decision'. Thus:

- In certain fields an absolute majority of the European Parliament must vote to approve laws before they are passed (e.g. foreign treaties, accession treaties, the Common Agricultural Policy).
- In specified areas Parliament now has a second reading of proposals and its rejection of such proposals can only be overturned by a unanimous decision of the Council of Ministers (e.g. Single Market laws, trans-European networks).
- Parliament can also reject certain legislation by an absolute majority vote if, after the second reading of a proposal and subsequent conciliation, the Council and Parliament are unable to agree (e.g. education and training, health, consumer protection).

The Amsterdam Treaty extends the co-decision procedure to all areas covered by qualified majority voting.

The Council of Ministers

The Council of Ministers – the Union's ultimate decision-making body – comprises one minister from each of the 15 member states, with participants on the Council varying according to the issue under discussion (e.g. agricultural issues are discussed by Ministers of Agriculture from each state). Meetings of the Council, which are mainly held in Brussels, are chaired by the minister from the country holding the presidency, which rotates on a six-monthly basis (e.g. Spain and Denmark held the presidency in 2002). Along with the meetings of ministers are regular meetings of officials (Council Working Groups), together with the work of the Committee of Permanent Representatives of the Member States (COREPER) whose task is to co-ordinate the groundwork for Union decisions undertaken by the numerous meetings of senior officials. In addition, the Council is serviced by a general secretariat of about 2000, also based in Brussels.

web link   The Council of Ministers website is at *ue.eu.int*

In essence, the role of the Council of Ministers is to make major policy decisions and to respond to legislative proposals put forward mainly by the Commission. In general, major EU decisions require unanimity in the Council but, increasingly, many decisions (especially after the Amsterdam Treaty) are now being taken by a qualified majority vote (qmv) – with France, Germany, Italy and the UK currently having ten votes each; Spain eight; Belgium, Greece, the Netherlands and Portugal five each; Austria and Sweden four each; Denmark, Finland and Ireland three each; and Luxembourg two. For a measure to be adopted by 'qmv' 62 votes are needed (out of a total of 87). In preparation for the enlargement of the EU, the weighting of votes in the council is to be altered in January 2005, under the terms of the Treaty of Nice (2000). This Treaty also sets the number of MEPs that both existing and new member states will have following enlargement.

While the 'right of initiative' under the Treaties rests with the Commission, the ultimate power of decision essentially lies with the Council, which may adopt Commission proposals as drafted, amend them, reject them, or simply take no decision, having consulted the European Parliament and normally a number of other bodies (see below). If adopted, Council of Ministers' decisions have the force of law and are described as regulations, directives, decisions, or recommendations and opinions. Regulations apply directly to all member states and do not have to be confirmed by national parliaments to have binding legal effect. Directives lay down compulsory objectives, but leave it to member states to translate them into national legislation. Decisions are binding on those states, companies or individuals to whom they are addressed, while recommendations and opinions have no binding force, but merely state the view of the institution which issues them.

The Council's power to pass a law – even if the European Parliament disagrees with it – was reduced under the Maastricht Treaty. In specified policy areas, joint approval is now necessary and MEPs have an effective veto if the two sides cannot reach agreement following conciliation. Moreover, following Maastricht a Committee of the Regions has been established to advise the Commission and the Council on issues concerning the European regions – a development which should help to ensure a stronger regional voice at European level. That said, it is still the case that the Council remains responsible for setting general policy within the EU and relies on the Commission to take decisions on the detailed application of legislation or to adapt legislative details to meet changing circumstances. To this extent – and given the Commission's other responsibilities – the ultimate influence over EU decisions is, to say the very least, open to question, as is often the case at national level.

The European Council

The work of the 'specialist' Councils within the Council of Ministers (e.g. Agriculture, Economics and Finance, Employment and Social Affairs) is co-ordinated by the General Affairs Council, comprising the Foreign Ministers of the 15 member states. This Council is also responsible for preparing for the meetings of the European Council which occur two or three times each year. The European Council is attended by the Heads of Government of each member state along with their Foreign Ministers and the President of the Commission, and its work invariably attracts substantial media coverage. Under the chairmanship of the country holding the presidency, the European Council's role is to discuss important policy issues affecting the EU and to propose policy to the Council of Ministers. As the meeting at Maastricht in December 1991 indicated, these 'summits' of Heads of Governments can have a profound effect on the development of the Union and its institutions.

web link The European Council's website address is *ue.eu.int/en/info/eurocouncil/index*

The European Commission

The Commission, which has its headquarters in Brussels and Luxembourg, is the EU's bureaucratic arm, currently comprising 20 Commissioners chosen by their respective governments (the five largest members send two Commissioners, the others send one) and a staff of about 16,000 civil servants drawn from all member states. Headed by a president, and organised into Directorates-General, each with a Commissioner responsible for its work, the European Commission's role is essentially that of initiator, supervisor and executive. More specifically its tasks are:

1 To act as guardian of the Treaties so as to ensure that EU rules and principles are respected.
2 To propose policies and legislation for the Council of Ministers to discuss and, if appropriate, adopt or amend.
3 To implement EU policies and supervise the day-to-day running of these policies, including managing the funds which account for most of the EU budget (e.g. EAGGF, ERDF, ECSC).[5]

You can find further information on the Commision at *europa.eu.int*

In carrying out these duties, the Commissioners are required to act in the interest of the EU as a whole and may not receive instructions from any national government or from any other body (Article 157 of the Treaty of Rome). Moreover, while each Commissioner is responsible for formulating proposals within his or her area of responsibility, the final decision is taken on a collegiate basis and the work is subject to the supervision of the European Parliament. As mentioned above, Parliament is the only body which can force the Commission to resign collectively; interestingly, it has no authority over individual Commissioners, although its endorsement is needed when the President of the Commission and the other Commissioners are appointed.

Much of the undoubted power and influence of the Commission stems from its central involvement in the legislative process. Proposals for consideration by the Council and the Parliament are initially drafted by the Commission, usually following consultation with the Economic and Social Committee (representing the interests of employers, trade unions, farmers, consumers, etc.) and other advisory bodies as appropriate. Moreover EU Treaties specifically give the Commission the power to make regulations, issue directives, take decisions, make recommendations and deliver opinions, as well as to implement policies based on either Council decisions or Treaty provisions. Thus, while legislative power in the EU in general rests with the Council of Ministers, the Commission is also able to legislate in order to implement earlier Council regulations, particularly where technical or routine matters are concerned – a situation which has parallels in the operation of government at national level.

Further powers with regard to specific sectors (e.g. coal and steel) or particular aspects of EU work (e.g. the budget, international agreements) serve to enhance the Commission's influence and to confirm its position as the 'driving force' of the Union. Perhaps understandably, pressure groups seeking to influence the policy process within the European Union regard the Commission as an important institution to target, together with Parliament and the Council of Ministers. Recent and proposed changes in the relationship between these three institutions will undoubtedly have an effect not only on the legislative process, but also on the practice of lobbying within the EU context.

The European Court of Justice

The European Court of Justice, which sits in Luxembourg, comprises fifteen judges who are appointed for a six-year period by consent of the member states and eight advocates-general. The Court's role is:

1 To pass judgment, at the request of a national court, on the interpretation or validity of points of EU law.
2 To quash, at the request of an EU institution, government or individual, any measures adopted by the Commission, the Council or national governments which are judged to be incompatible with the existing treaties.

The Court can also be invited to offer an opinion, which then becomes binding, on agreements the EU proposes to undertake with third countries.

Three aspects of its work are particularly worthy of note:

1 Individuals as well as member states can bring cases to the Court, and its judgments and interpretations apply to all (i.e. EU institutions, member states, national courts and private citizens) and are backed by a system of penalties for non-compliance.
2 Its rulings on matters of European law, which has primacy over national law, are final and its decisions are binding on member countries.
3 The Court has tended to follow the principle that EU Treaties should be interpreted with a degree of flexibility so as to take account of changing conditions and circumstances. This has permitted the Community to legislate in areas where there are no specific Treaty provisions, such as the fight against pollution.

The Court of Justice website can be accessed at *europa.eu.int/cj/index*. You can also try *www.curia.eu.int*

Current developments

A number of countries are currently seeking to join the EU as full members, and accession negotiations began in late 1998 initially with six potential members (Poland, Hungary, Estonia, the Czech Republic, Slovenia and Cyprus) in the first wave of enlargement that could ultimately take the EU from 15 to 26 states and extend its borders to the Black Sea (*see* Case Study Chapter 13). It is accepted that as the number of member states grows, institutional reform will be necessary in order to streamline the decision-making process. This process has already begun under the Nice Treaty (2000).

CASE STUDY

Left out in the cold

We saw in the Mini Case ('Action on the Environment') how governments at subnational level sometimes act to tackle problems of 'market failure'. The same is true at national, supranational and international levels, particularly over cross-border issues such as environmental pollution and degradation which invariably have no simple cause nor solution (see also Chapter 16). When governmental proposals in areas such as this are being formulated, then thought needs to be given by the relevant authorities to how any new policies or laws will be implemented and the implications that such changes may bring for affected groups and individuals. Failure to consider the different dimensions of the implementation process can prove problematic (and frequently embarrassing) for government and/or for its citizens.

The problem of the United Kingdom's 'fridge mountain' illustrates this issue very clearly. As a member of the European Union, the UK helped to shape a new EU regulation which outlawed the traditional method of dumping CFC foam from fridges and freezers into landfill sites because of the danger of it escaping into the atmosphere and causing further damage to the ozone layer. From 1 January 2002 when the new regulation came into effect, it became illegal to send unwanted fridges and freezers to giant metal crushers which prepared them prior to going to landfill. Instead they now have to be crushed in special closed units which capture the CFCs in liquid form so they can be burned and destroyed.

Believing that the new regulation applied only to industrial fridges and freezers, the Department of the Environment was slow to establish a system for dealing with the looming problem of discarded equipment. In particular the government's failure to ensure that the special closed recycling units were in place when the regulation came into force meant that thousands of redundant fridges and freezers began to pile up in warehouses and hangars across the country (or were dumped illegally by the roadside) with no means of disposal. UK stores and suppliers of equipment had stopped taking away old models for free from November 2001 and consequently local authorities have had to be funded by central government to deal with the growing problem of storage until proper means of disposal can be arranged.

While this misreading of the regulations is by no means unique to the UK (e.g. only Germany, Holland and Sweden had new closed units in place by 1 January 2002), it has proved something of a *cause célèbre* in UK political circles and a task force has been set up to tackle the immediate problem of the country's fridge mountain. Ultimately the plan is to send the discarded equipment to new recycling units which will be run by licensed entrepreneurs who are currently collecting and storing fridges from all over the country ready for when the new equipment arrives. Given the commercial opportunities arising from the new regulations, some observers feel that the supply side of the market for this service might ultimately become over-subscribed by the new breed of licensed operators, as has evidently happened in Holland. At the time of writing this is less of a concern for the government than the embarrassment of having no facilities in place to tackle the problem – a situation which might easily be repeated over the issue of scrap cars and waste electrical and electronic equipment when new recycling regulations come into force (see e.g. the *Guardian* 2 February 2002).

Case study questions

1 Why has much of the action within Europe on the issue of CFCs been taken at a supranational level rather than simply by individual governments?

2 Is the new regulation on CFCs a threat or an opportunity for businesses in the member states of the EU?

Review and discussion questions

1 To what extent do you think a change of government in your country would affect the business community?

2 Many top civil servants take directorships in large companies on retirement from government. Why should companies be keen to recruit retired bureaucrats?

3 How far is the enlargement of the European Union likely to benefit UK businesses?

4 In what ways could a business organisation seek to influence central government decision makers on issues in which it has an interest (e.g. taxes on company profits or the level of interest rates)?

Assignments

1 You are employed as a research assistant by a group representing the interest of small and medium-size enterprises (e.g. a Chamber of Commerce). Using contemporary source material (e.g. the Internet, manifestos, etc.) produce a draft report highlighting current government policy for the SME sector.

2 Imagine you are employed as a political lobbyist, with a special interest in conservation issues. You have been approached by a local conservation group which is concerned about government plans to build a bypass round a village in its area. The government's proposals for the road would cause significant damage to a Site of Special Scientific Interest (SSSI) and the group is determined to oppose the plans. Your brief is to draft an 'action plan' for the group, indicating what forms of pressure group activity you would recommend, in what sequence and using which channels of potential influence.

Notes and references

1 See, for example, Barker, A., *Quangos in Britain*, Macmillan, 1982; Ridley, F. F. and Wilson, D. (eds), *The Quango Debate*, OUP/Hansard Society, 1995; www.cabinet-office.gov.uk/quango

2 Individual ministerial responsibility should not be confused with collective Cabinet responsibility, both of which apply to Ministers of the Crown.

3 Senior civil servants who are in a position to influence policy are sometimes called 'mandarins'. This term only applies to a very small percentage of the civil service.

4 Numerous books exist on the EU. Students can also gain information by contacting EU institutions directly, particularly through their national offices or by accessing the numerous websites.

5 European Agriculture Guarantee and Guidance Fund (EAGGF); European Regional Development Fund (ERDF); European Coal and Steel Community (ECSC). See Chapter 10 for a further discussion of EU structural funds.

Further reading

Budd, S. A. and Jones, A., *The European Community: A Guide to the Maze*, 4th edition, Kogan Page, 1994.

Coxall, W. N. and Robins, L., *Contemporary British Politics*, 3rd edition, Macmillan, 1998.

European Commission, *The Institutions and Bodies of the European Union: Who's Who in Europe*, Office of Official Publications of the European Communities, 2001.

Goodman, S. F., *The European Union*, 3rd edition, Macmillan, 1996.

Greenwood, J. and Wilson, D., *Public Administration in Britain Today*, 2nd edition, Unwin Hyman, 1993.

Pedler, R. H (ed.), *European Union Lobbying*, Palgrave, 2002.

Rose, A. and Lawton, A. (eds.), *Public Services Management*, Financial Times/Prentice Hall, 1999.

Wilson, D. and Game, C., *Local Government in the United Kingdom*, 2nd edition, Macmillan, 1998.

Web links and further questions are available on the website at:
www.booksites.net/worthington

4

The macroeconomic environment

Ian Worthington

Business organisations operate in an economic environment which shapes, and is shaped by, their activities. In market-based economies this environment comprises variables which are dynamic, interactive and mobile and which, in part, are affected by government in pursuit of its various roles in the economy. As a vital component in the macroeconomy, government exercises a significant degree of influence over the flow of income and hence over the level and pattern of output by the public and private sectors. Other key influences include a country's financial institutions and the international economic organisations and groupings to which it belongs or subscribes.

Objectives

- To compare alternative economic systems and their underlying principles and to discuss the problems of transition from a centrally planned to a market-based economy.

- To examine flows of income, output and expenditure in a market economy and to account for changes in the level and pattern of economic activity.

- To analyse the role of government in the macroeconomy, including government macroeconomic policies and the objectives on which they are based.

- To consider the role of financial institutions.

- To survey the key international economic institutions and organisations which influence the business environment in open, market economies.

Key terms

Accelerator effect
Aggregate monetary demand
Balance of payments
Capital market
Capitalist economy
Central bank
Centrally planned economy
Circular flow of income model
Consumer sovereignty
Crowding out
Cyclical unemployment
Deindustrialisation
Direct controls
Direct taxation
Economic growth

Economic scarcity
Economics
Exchange rate
Factory gate prices
Financial intermediaries
Fiscal policy
Free-market economy
Full employment
G7 nations
Government spending
Gross domestic product
Headline inflation
Income flows
Indirect taxation
Inflation
Injections

Interest rates
Leakages
Macroeconomic analysis
Macroeconomic environment
Microeconomic analysis
Monetary aggregates
Monetary policies
Money market
Money stock
Multiplier effect
National Debt
Opportunity cost
Public sector net borrowing (PSNB)
Real cost

Real flows
Real interest rates
Real national income
Recession
Retail Price Index (RPI)
State bank
Stock exchange
Structural unemployment
Technological unemployment
Underlying rate of inflation
Wages/prices inflationary spiral
Withdrawals

Introduction

In September 1992, following a period of sustained turbulence on the foreign exchanges, the British government decided to withdraw sterling from what was then known as the Exchange Rate Mechanism (ERM) of the European Monetary System (EMS). As a result, the value of the pound continued to fall against a number of currencies, particularly the Deutschmark (DM) and large-scale speculation against sterling forced its value down to a level well below its previously agreed 'floor' in the ERM. Freed from the constraints of the ERM, the British government announced a series of cuts in interest rates in an effort to boost the British economy, which at the time was in the midst of a substantial recession. These cuts in interest rates – together with the more favourable exporting conditions resulting from a weaker pound – were welcomed by most British businesses, which were struggling to find customers. At the same time, a number of influential commentators from both the academic and the business world warned of the likelihood of increased inflation in the future as a result of dearer import prices and of the uncertainties caused by a free floating currency. Business leaders, in particular, called for a statement of government intentions and for a clear guide to future government economic policy with regard to inflation, recession and membership of the ERM. Some ten years later, Britain still retains a measure of independence in currency matters, having declined to commit itself to adopting the 'Euro' in the first wave of monetary union within the EU (*see* Chapter 13).

What this simple example is designed to demonstrate is the intimate relationship between business activity and the wider economic context in which it takes place, and a glance at any quality newspaper will provide a range of similar illustrations of this interface between business and economics. What is important at this point is not to understand the complexities of exchange rate systems or their effect on businesses (these are discussed in Chapter 13), but to appreciate in broad terms the importance of the macroeconomic environment for business organisations and, in particular, the degree of compatibility between the preoccupations of the entrepreneur and those of the economist. To the economist, for example, a recession is generally marked by falling demand, rising unemployment, a slowing down in economic growth and a fall in investment. To the firm, it usually implies a loss of orders, a likely reduction in the workforce, a decline in output (or a growth in stocks) and a general reluctance to invest in capital equipment and/or new projects.

Much of the detailed discussion of the economic aspects of business can be found in Parts 3 and 4. In this chapter the focus is on the broader question of the economic structure and processes of a market-based economy and on the macroeconomic influences affecting and being affected by business activity in this type of economic system. As suggested in the previous chapter, an understanding of the overall economic context within which businesses operate and its core values and principles is central to any meaningful analysis of the business environment.

Three further points are worth highlighting at this juncture. First, business activity not only is shaped by the economic context in which it takes place, but helps to shape that context; consequently the success or otherwise of government economic policy depends to some degree on the reactions of both the firms and markets (e.g. the stock market) which are affected by government decisions. Second, economic influences operate at a variety of spatial levels – as illustrated by the plight of the pound – and governments can find that circumstances largely or totally beyond their control can affect businesses either favourably or adversely. Third, the economic (and for that matter, political) influence of industry and commerce can be considerable and this ensures that business organisations – both individually and collectively – usually constitute one of the chief pressure groups in democratic states. This political and economic relationship between government and business is discussed more fully in Chapter 10.

Economic systems

The concept of economic scarcity

Like 'politics', the term 'economic' tends to be used in a variety of ways and contexts to describe certain aspects of human behaviour, ranging from activities such as producing, distributing and consuming, to the idea of frugality in the use of a resource (e.g. being 'economical' with the truth). Modern definitions stress how such behaviour, and the institutions in which it takes place (e.g. households, firms, governments, banks), are concerned with the satisfaction of human needs and wants through the transformation of resources into goods and services which are consumed by society. These processes are said to take place under conditions of 'economic scarcity'.

The economist's idea of 'scarcity' centres around the relationship between a society's needs and wants and the resources available to satisfy them. In essence, economists argue that whereas needs and wants tend to be unlimited, the resources which can be used to meet those needs and wants are finite and accordingly no society at any time has the capacity to provide for all its actual or potential requirements. The assumption here is that both individual and collective needs and wants consistently outstrip the means available to satisfy them, as exemplified, for instance, by the inability of governments to provide instant health care, the best roads, education, defence, railways, and so on, at a time and place and of a quality convenient to the user. This being the case, 'choices' have to be made by both individuals and society concerning priorities in the use of resources, and every choice inevitably involves a 'sacrifice' (i.e. forgoing an alternative). Economists describe this sacrifice as the 'opportunity cost' or 'real cost' of the decision that is taken (e.g. every pound spent on the health service is a pound not spent on some other public service) and it is one which is faced by individuals, organisations (including firms), governments and society alike.

From a societal point of view the existence of economic scarcity poses three serious problems concerning the use of resources:

1 What to use the available resources for? That is, what goods and services should be produced (or not produced) with the resources (sometimes described as the 'guns v. butter' argument)?

2 How best to use those resources? For example, in what combinations, using what techniques and what methods?

3 How best to distribute the goods and services produced with them? That is, who gets what, how much and on what basis?

In practice, of course, these problems tend to be solved in a variety of ways, including barter (voluntary, bilateral exchange), price signals and the market, queuing and rationing, government instruction and corruption (e.g. resources allocated in exchange for personal favours), and examples of each of these solutions can be found in most, if not all, societies, at all times. Normally, however, one or other main approach to resource allocation tends to predominate and this allows analytical distinctions to be made between different types of economic system. One important distinction is between those economies which are centrally planned and those which operate predominantly through market forces, with prices forming the integrating mechanism. Understanding this distinction is fundamental to an examination of the way in which business is conducted and represents the foundation on which much of the subsequent analysis is built.

The centrally planned economy

In this type of economic system – associated with the post-Second World War socialist economies of eastern Europe, China, Cuba and elsewhere – most of the key decisions on production are taken by a central planning authority, normally the state and its agencies. Under this arrangement, the state typically:

- owns and/or controls the main economic resources;
- establishes priorities in the use of those resources;
- sets output targets for businesses which are largely under state ownership and/or control;
- directs resources in an effort to achieve these predetermined targets; and
- seeks to co-ordinate production in such a way as to ensure consistency between output and input demands.

The fact that an economy is centrally planned does not necessarily imply that all economic decisions are taken at central level; in many cases decision making may be devolved to subordinate agencies, including local committees and enterprises. Ultimately, however, these agencies are responsible to the centre and it is the latter which retains overall control of the economy and directs the use of scarce productive resources.

The problem of co-ordinating inputs and output in a modern planned economy is, of course, a daunting task and one which invariably involves an array of state planners and a central plan or blueprint normally covering a number of years (e.g. a five-year plan). Under such a plan, the state planners would establish annual output targets for each sector of the economy and for each enterprise within the sector and would identify the inputs of materials, labour and capital needed to achieve the set targets and would allocate resources accordingly. Given that the outputs of some industries (e.g. agricultural machinery) are the inputs of others (e.g. collective farms), it is not difficult to see how the overall effectiveness of the plan would depend in part on a high degree of co-operation and co-ordination between sectors and enterprises, as well as on good judgement, good decisions and a considerable element of good luck. The available evidence from planned economies suggests that none of these can be taken for granted and each is often in short supply.

Even in the most centralised of economies, state planning does not normally extend to telling individuals what they must buy in shops or how to use their labour, although an element of state direction at times may exist (e.g. conscription of the armed forces). Instead, it tends to condition *what* is available for purchase and the *prices* at which exchange takes place, and both of these are essentially the outcome of political choices, rather than a reflection of consumer demands. All too often consumers tend to be faced by queues and 'black markets' for some consumer products and overproduction of others, as state enterprises strive to meet targets frequently unrelated to the needs and wants of consumers. By the same token, businesses which make losses do not have to close down, as the state would normally make additional funds available to cover any difference between sales revenue and costs. This being the case, the emphasis at firm level tends to be more on meeting targets than on achieving efficiency in the use of resources and hence a considerable degree of duplication and wastage tends to occur.

In such an environment, the traditional entrepreneurial skills of efficient resource management, price setting and risk taking have little, if any, scope for development and managers behave essentially as technicians and bureaucrats, administering decisions largely made elsewhere. Firms, in effect, are mainly servants of the state and their activities are conditioned by social and political considerations, rather than by the needs of the market – although some market activity normally occurs in planned economies (especially in agriculture and a number of private services). Accordingly, businesses and their employees are not fully sensitised to the needs of the consumer and as a result quality and choice (where it exists) may suffer, particularly where incentives to improved efficiency and performance are negligible. Equally, the system tends to encourage bribery and corruption and the development of a substantial black market, with differences in income, status and political influence being an important determinant of individual consumption and of living standards.

The free-market economy

The free-market (or capitalist) economy stands in direct contrast to the centrally planned system. Whereas in the latter the state controls most economic decisions, in the former the key economic agencies are private individuals (sometimes called 'households') and firms, and these interact in free markets, through a system of prices, to determine the allocation of resources.

The key features of this type of economic system are as follows:

- Resources are in private ownership and the individuals owning them are free to use them as they wish.
- Firms, also in private ownership, are equally able to make decisions on production, free from state interference.
- No blueprint (or master plan) exists to direct production and consumption.
- Decisions on resource allocation are the result of a decentralised system of markets and prices, in which the decisions of millions of consumers and hundreds of thousands of firms are automatically co-ordinated.
- The consumer is sovereign, i.e. dictates the pattern of supply and hence the pattern of resource allocation.

In short, the three problems of what to produce, how to produce and how to distribute are solved by market forces.

The diagram in Figure 4.1 illustrates the basic operation of a market economy. In essence individuals are owners of resources (e.g. labour) and consumers of products; firms are users of resources and producers of products. What products are produced – and hence how resources are used – depends on consumers, who indicate their demands by purchasing (i.e. paying the price) or not purchasing, and this acts as a signal to producers to acquire the resources necessary (i.e. pay the price) to meet the preferences of consumers. If consumer demands change, for whatever reason, this will cause an automatic reallocation of resources, as firms respond to the new market conditions. Equally, competition between producers seeking to gain or retain customers is said to guarantee that resources are used efficiently and to ensure that the most appropriate production methods (i.e. how to produce) are employed in the pursuit of profits.

The distribution of output is also determined by market forces, in this case operating in the markets for productive services. Individuals supplying a resource (e.g. labour) receive an income (i.e. a price) from the firms using that resource and this allows them to purchase goods and services in the markets for products, which in turn provides an income for firms that can be spent on the purchase of further resources (*see* below). Should the demand for a particular type of productive

 Figure 4.1   The market economy

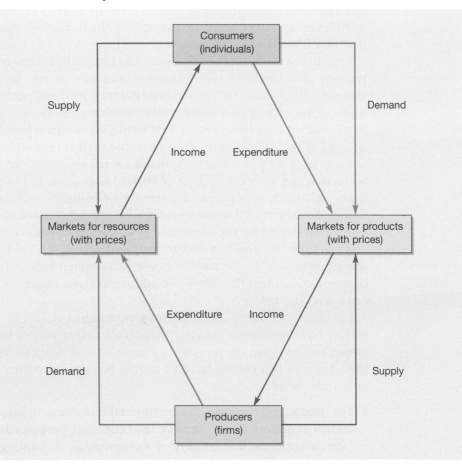

resource increase – say, as a result of an increase in the demand for the product produced by that resource – the price paid to the provider of the resource will tend to rise and hence, other things being equal, allow more output to be purchased. Concomitantly, it is also likely to result in a shift of resources from uses which are relatively less lucrative to those which are relatively more rewarding.

This matching of supply and demand through prices in markets is described in detail in Chapter 11 and the analysis can also be applied to the market for foreign currencies (*see* Chapter 13). In practice, of course, no economy operates entirely in the manner suggested above; firms after all are influenced by costs and supply decisions as well as by demand and generally seek to shape that demand, as well as simply responding to it. Nor for that matter is a market-based economy devoid of government involvement in the process of resource allocation, as evidenced by the existence of a public sector responsible for substantial levels of consumption and output and for helping to shape the conditions under which the private sector operates. In short, any study of the market economy needs to incorporate the role of government and to examine, in particular, its influence on the activities of both firms and households. Such an analysis can be found below in the later sections of this chapter.

Eastern Europe: economies in transition

The political and economic disintegration of eastern Europe in the late 1980s provides an excellent historical example of the difficulties faced by states moving from one form of economic system to another.

Prior to the collapse of the old order, the communist states of eastern Europe had systems of centralised state planning basically of the type described above, although some countries, especially Hungary, were experimenting with various forms of free enterprise. Growing dissatisfaction with the command system, and in particular with its failure to deliver living standards equivalent to those being enjoyed at the time by most citizens in the market economies of western Europe (*see* e.g. Table 4.1), gave rise to demands for reform, and these were translated into political action with the election of Mikhail Gorbachev to the post of Soviet leader in the mid-1980s. Gorbachev's programme of economic reconstruction (*perestroika*) signalled the start of a move towards a more market-based economic system and this was bolstered by his commitment to greater openness (*glasnost*) and democratic reform. By the late 1980s and early 1990s, the old Soviet empire had effectively ceased to exist and the newly independent states, almost without exception, had committed themselves to radical economic change of a kind unthinkable just a few years before.

For states anxious to move from an entrenched system of state planning to a market-based economic system, the obstacles have proved formidable and have helped to slow down the progress of economic (and political) reform in some countries. Among the problems faced by eastern European countries in the transitionary phase have been:

■ The need to create a legal and commercial framework to support the change to a market economy (e.g. company laws, laws on property rights, competition, external trade, the development of an appropriate accounting system).

| Table 4.1 | Comparative economic indicators, 1988 |

	Population (million)	GDP ($ billion)	GDP per capita ($)
East Germany	17	156	9360
Czechoslovakia	16	118	7600
Hungary	11	69	6500
Bulgaria	9	51	5630
Poland	37	207	5540
Romania	23	94	4120
European Union	325	4745	14609
West Germany	61	1202	19575

Source: *The Amex Bank Review*, November 1989.

- The need to establish different forms of free enterprise and to develop financial institutions capable of providing risk and venture capital, at commercial rates of return.
- The need to develop truly competitive markets, free from state control and protection.
- The need to liberalise labour markets and to develop entrepreneurial skills in a workforce traditionally demotivated by the old bureaucratic system.
- The need to allow prices to move to levels determined by market forces, rather than by political decision.
- The need to achieve macroeconomic stability as markets become more open both internally and externally.
- The need to reduce the burden of international debt.
- The need to attract substantial overseas investment to assist in the rebuilding of the collapsed old socialist economies.

Meeting these requirements has not been made any easier by economic collapse and the perceived need on the part of some reformers to bring about rapid economic change whatever the consequences. In Russia, in particular, widespread bribery, corruption and criminal activity have helped to undermine an economy struggling with economic and political instability that appears endemic.

Evidence suggests that, given these and other requirements, the process of systemic change is destined to be long and painful and will be subject to political as well as economic developments, many of which are as yet unpredictable. Central to this process will be the attitude of western countries towards such issues as debt relief, financial assistance, investment and other forms of help, and perhaps understandably the approach thus far has been relatively cautious, particularly given the relative uncertainty that comes from dealing with countries historically perceived to be adversaries. For example, a contemporary analysis by the accountants Ernst & Young in 1992 suggested that the uncertainty was at its greatest in countries such as Russia, Ukraine and Albania and at its least in Hungary, the then Czechoslovakia and Poland, where reforms were often further down the road (*see* Table 4.2). Hungary's high notional score, for instance, was justified by its relative degree of political and economic stability and its favourable attitude to foreign investment, backed by a legal framework to encourage it. In contrast, in Albania – one of the

| Table 4.2 | Eastern Europe: A comparative risk analysis |

	Business opportunities	Political risk	Credit rating	Status of economy	Stability of local economy	Business infrastructure	Total
Hungary	2	1	2	3	2	2	12
Czechoslovakia	2	3	2	3	2	2	14
Poland	2	3	3	3	3	2	16
Baltic States	4	3	3	4	3	3	20
Bulgaria	4	3	4	4	3	3	21
Romania	4	4	4	4	4	3	23
Russia and Ukraine	1	4	5	5	4	4	23
Albania	5	4	4	5	5	4	27

Source: Adapted from the *Daily Telegraph*, 13 May 1992.
Note: Countries are rated on a scale 1 to 5, where low scores are best and high scores worst.

most rigid of the old communist regimes – political and economic instability, limited business opportunities and a reluctance to change were seen as considerable obstacles to involvement on the part of western companies and governments.

With regard to western corporate involvement, in practice this has taken a variety of forms including direct acquisition, joint ventures (which tend to carry tax advantages) and the development of local distribution networks, and much of it has been undertaken by multinational companies seeking to establish market share and to gain low-cost production sites. Coca-Cola, Pepsico, Levi Strauss, Philip Morris, BAT, Mars, Unilever, McDonald's, Procter & Gamble and General Electric are just some of the organisations that have sought to take advantage of the growing demand for western consumer goods, and Hungary, Poland and the former Czechoslovakia have proved the most favourable locations for much of the investment.[1]

How far this interest in eastern Europe will continue in the future is open to question, particularly in view of recent political developments in the Balkans and in the former Soviet Union and because of the severe economic problems arising from the move to a market-based system (e.g. hyperinflation). Some observers believe that in the circumstances a policy of 'wait-and-see' is the best option for western companies looking for market expansion at a time of lower growth in their traditional markets. Others have argued that the risks involved are far outweighed by the potential benefits and that businesses willing to take a long-term view and commitment will come to dominate some of the fastest growing markets of the future, at the expense of competitors who are more cautious or conservative.[2]

One further factor, which will undoubtedly influence corporate attitudes to investment in eastern Europe, will be the process of enlargement within the European Union, with a large number of former Communist states lining up to join the EU in the next five to ten years. While many of the applicant countries – which include Hungary, Poland, Romania, Bulgaria and the Czech Republic – have economies that are growing faster than those of their western counterparts, they also have much lower levels of GDP per capita. (For example, in 1998 the GDP per capita as a percentage of the EU average was estimated as follows: Czech Republic,

63 per cent; Hungary, 47 per cent; Poland, 47 per cent; Romania, 31 per cent; Bulgaria, 23 per cent – see case study in Chapter 13.) The lower GDP is likely to affect both their demand for western products and their relative competitiveness, particularly in manufactured items. In the circumstances, western companies trading and investing in eastern Europe will face both 'opportunities' and 'threats' which are likely to change over time; the net beneficiaries in such an environment are likely to be those organisations that take a long-term strategic view rather than a short-term opportunistic one based on immediate gain.

Politico-economic synthesis

The economic problem of resource allocation, described above, clearly has a political dimension, given its focus on the ownership, control and use of wealth-producing assets within society. This allows links to be made between a country's chosen economic system and its political regime. A useful way of representing possible relationships is illustrated in Figure 4.2. As suggested in Chapter 3, political systems can be characterised as ranging from democratic to authoritarian, depending on the degree of public involvement in decision-making processes. Similarly, economic systems can be seen to range from free market to planned, according to the level of state intervention in the process of resource allocation. This two-dimensional model thus provides for four major combinations of politico-economic systems, ranging from democratic–free-market on the one hand (quadrant 1) to authoritarian–planned on the other (quadrant 3).

In applying this model to specific cases, it is clear that free-market approaches to resource allocation are predominantly associated with democratic states. Such a

Figure 4.2   Politico-economic systems

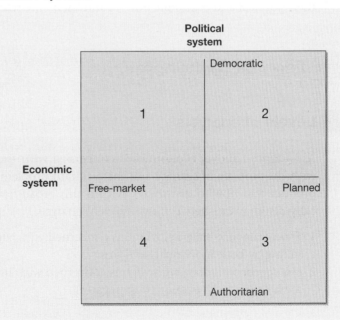

link is not surprising. Democracy, after all, includes the notion of individuals being able to express their preferences through the ballot box and having the opportunity to replace one government with another at periodic intervals. In free markets similar processes are at work, with individuals effectively 'voting' for goods and services through the price system and their expressed preferences being reflected in the pattern of resource allocation.

A link between authoritarian regimes and planned economic systems can equally be rationalised, in that government control over the political system is considerably facilitated if it also directs the economy through the ownership and/or control of the means of production, distribution and exchange. In effect, the relative absence of democratic mechanisms, such as free elections and choice between alternative forms of government, is echoed in the economic sphere by the inability of individuals to exercise any real influence over resource allocation. At the extreme, this could involve a government ban on any forms of free enterprise and total government control of the pattern of output and consumption in an economy which is devoid of effective consumer sovereignty.

In practice, of course, the picture is much more complicated than suggested by this simple dichotomy. Some authoritarian states, for instance, have predominantly capitalist economic systems (quadrant 4), while some democratic countries have a substantial degree of government intervention (i.e. moving them towards quadrant 2), either by choice or from necessity (e.g. wartime). Added to this, even in states where the political or economic system appears to be the same, considerable differences can occur at an operational and/or institutional level and this gives each country a degree of uniqueness not adequately portrayed by the model. That said, it is still the case that the basic congruity between democracy and free-market systems represents a powerful and pervasive influence in the business environment of the world's principal democratic states. The process of economic reform – as in eastern Europe – accordingly tends to be accompanied by corresponding pressures for political change and these are often resisted by regimes not prepared to give up their political and economic powers and their élite status.

The macroeconomy

Levels of analysis

As indicated above, economics is concerned with the study of how society deals with the problem of scarcity and the resultant problems of what to produce, how to produce and how to distribute. Within this broad framework the economist typically distinguishes between two types of analysis:

1 Microeconomic analysis, which is concerned with the study of economic decision taking by both individuals and firms.
2 Macroeconomic analysis, which is concerned with interactions in the economy as a whole (i.e. with economic aggregates).

The microeconomic approach is exemplified by the analysis of markets and prices undertaken in Chapter 11 which shows, for example, how individual consumers in the market for beer might be affected by a price change. This analysis could be extended to an investigation of how the total market might respond to a movement in the price, or how a firm's (or market's) decisions on supply are affected by changes in wage rates or production techniques or some other factor. Note that in these examples, the focus of attention is on decision taking by individuals and firms in a single industry, while interactions between this industry and the rest of the economy are ignored: in short, this is what economists call a 'partial analysis'.

In reality, of course, all sectors of the economy are interrelated to some degree. A pay award, for example, in the beer industry (or in a single firm) may set a new pay norm that workers in other industries take up and these pay increases may subsequently influence employment, production and consumer demand in the economy as a whole, which could also have repercussions on the demand for beer. Sometimes such repercussions may be relatively minor and so effectively can be ignored. In such situations the basic microeconomic approach remains valid.

In contrast, macroeconomics recognises the interdependent nature of markets and studies the interaction in the economy as a whole, dealing with such questions as the overall level of employment, the rate of inflation, the percentage growth of output in the economy and many other economy-wide aggregates – exemplified, for instance, by the analysis of international trade in Chapter 13 and by the macroeconomic model discussed below. It should be pointed out, however, that while the distinction between the micro and macro approaches remains useful for analytical purposes, in many instances the two become intertwined. UK Chancellor Nigel Lawson's decision (in 1988) to cut the top rate of income tax from 60 per cent to 40 per cent was presented at the time as a means of boosting the economy by providing incentives for entrepreneurs – clearly a macroeconomic proposition. However, to investigate the validity of the Chancellor's view, it is necessary to lean heavily on microeconomic analysis to see how lower taxation might influence, say, an individual's preference for work over leisure. Given that macroeconomic phenomena are the result of aggregating the behaviour of individual firms and consumers, this is obviously a common situation and one which is useful to bear in mind in any study of either the firm or the economy as a whole.

The 'flows' of economic activity

Economic activity can be portrayed as a flow of economic resources into firms (i.e. productive organisations), which are used to produce output for consumption, and a corresponding flow of payments from firms to the providers of those resources, who use them primarily to purchase the goods and services produced. These flows of resources, production, income and expenditure accordingly represent the fundamental activities of an economy at work. Figure 4.3 illustrates the flow of resources and of goods and services in the economy – what economists describe as 'real flows'.

In effect, firms use economic resources to produce goods and services, which are consumed by private individuals (private domestic consumption) or government

| Figure 4.3 | 'Real flows' in the economy |

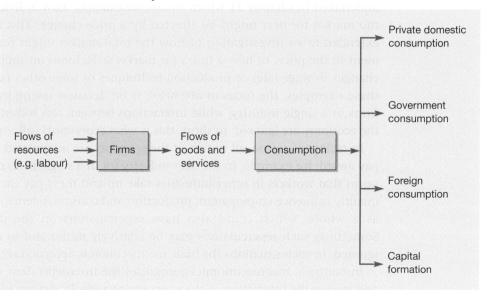

(government consumption) or by overseas purchasers (foreign consumption) or by other firms (capital formation). This consumption gives rise to a flow of expenditures that represents an income for firms, which they use to purchase further resources in order to produce further output for consumption. This flow of income and expenditures is shown in Figure 4.4.

web link The CFI model is also discussed at
www. *bized.ac.uk/stafsup/options/notes/econ210.htm*

| Figure 4.4 | Income flows in the economy |

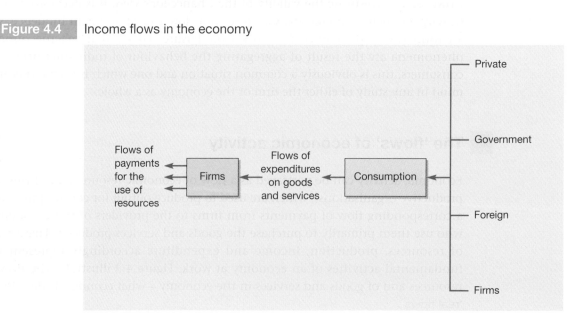

Figure 4.5   A simplified model of real flows and income flows

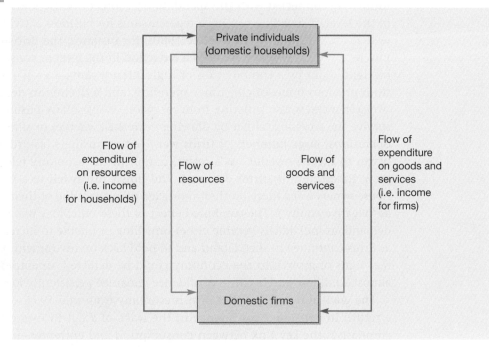

The interrelationship between income flows and real flows can be seen by combining the two diagrams into one, which for the sake of simplification assumes only two groups operate in the economy: firms as producers and users of resources, and private individuals as consumers and providers of those resources (*see* Figure 4.5). Real flows are shown by the arrows moving in an anti-clockwise direction; income flows by the arrows flowing in a clockwise direction.

Despite a degree of over-simplification, the model of the economy illustrated in Figure 4.5 is a useful analytical tool which highlights some vitally important aspects of economic activity which are of direct relevance to the study of business. The model shows, for example, that:

1 Income flows around the economy, passing from households to firms and back to households and on to firms, and so on, and these income flows have corresponding real flows of resources, goods and services.
2 What constitutes an income to one group (e.g. firms) represents an expenditure to another (e.g. households), indicating that income generation in the economy is related to spending on consumption of goods and services and on resources (e.g. the use of labour).
3 The output of firms must be related to expenditure by households on goods and services, which in turn is related to the income the latter receive from supplying resources.
4 The use of resources (including the number of jobs created in the economy) must also be related to expenditure by households on consumption, given that resources are used to produce output for sale to households.
5 Levels of income, output, expenditure and employment in the economy are, in effect, interrelated.

From the point of view of firms, it is clear from the model that their fortunes are intimately connected with the spending decisions of households and any changes in the level of spending can have repercussions for business activity at the micro as well as the macro level. In the late 1980s, for instance, the British economy went into recession, largely as a result of a reduction in the level of consumption that was brought about by a combination of high interest rates, a growing burden of debt from previous bouts of consumer spending, and a decline in demand from some overseas markets also suffering from recession. While many businesses managed to survive the recession, either by drawing from their reserves or slimming down their operations, large numbers of firms went out of business, as orders fell and costs began to exceed revenue. As a result, output in the economy fell, unemployment grew, investment by firms declined, and house prices fell to a point where some houseowners owed more on their mortgage than the value of their property (known as 'negative equity'). The combined effect of these outcomes was to further depress demand, as individuals became either unwilling or unable to increase spending and as firms continued to shed labour and to hold back on investment. By late 1992, few real signs of growth in the economy could be detected, unemployment stood at almost 3 million, and business confidence remained persistently low.

The gradual recovery of the British economy from mid-1993 – brought about by a return in consumer confidence in the wake of a cut in interest rates – further emphasises the key link between consumption and entrepreneurial activity highlighted in the model. Equally, it shows, as did the discussion on the recession, that a variety of factors can affect spending (e.g. government policy on interest rates) and that spending by households is only one type of consumption in the real economy. In order to gain a clearer view of how the economy works and why changes occur over time, it is necessary to refine the basic model by incorporating a number of other key variables influencing economic activity. These variables – which include savings, investment spending, government spending, taxation and overseas trade – are discussed below.

Changes in economic activity

The level of spending by consumers on goods and services produced by indigenous firms is influenced by a variety of factors. For a start, most households pay tax on income earned which has the effect of reducing the level of income available for consumption. Added to this, some consumers prefer to save (i.e. not spend) a proportion of their income or to spend it on imported products, both of which mean that the income of domestic firms is less than it would have been had the income been spent with them. Circumstances such as these represent what economists call a 'leakage' (or 'withdrawal') from the circular flow of income and help to explain why the revenue of businesses can fluctuate over time (*see* Figure 4.6).

At the same time as such 'leakages' are occurring, additional forms of spending in the economy are helping to boost the potential income of domestic firms. Savings by some consumers are often borrowed by firms to spend on investment in capital equipment or plant or premises (known as investment spending) and this generates income for firms producing capital goods. Similarly, governments use

Figure 4.6   The circular flow of income with 'leakages'

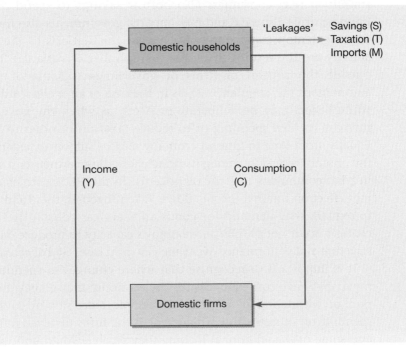

taxation to spend on the provision of public goods and services (public or government expenditure) and overseas buyers purchase products produced by indigenous firms (export spending). Together, these additional forms of spending represent an 'injection' of income into the circular flow (*see* Figure 4.7).

Figure 4.7   The circular flow of income with 'injections' added

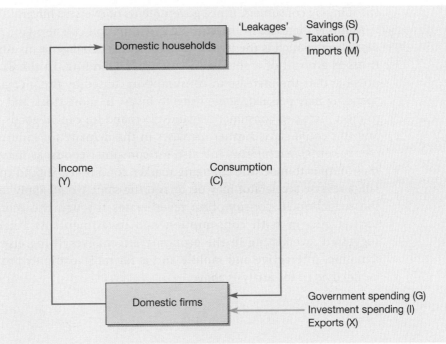

While the revised model of the economy illustrated in Figure 4.7 is still highly simplified (e.g. consumers also borrow savings to spend on consumption or imports; firms also save and buy imports; governments also invest in capital projects), it demonstrates quite clearly that fluctuations in the level of economic activity are the result of changes in a number of variables, many of which are outside the control of firms or governments. Some of these changes are autonomous (i.e. spontaneous), as in the case of an increased demand for imports, while others may be deliberate or overt, as when the government decides to increase its own spending or to reduce taxation in order to stimulate demand. Equally, from time to time an economy may be subject to 'external shocks', such as the onset of recession among its principal trading partners or a significant price rise in a key commodity (e.g. the oil price rise in the 1970s), which can have an important effect on internal income flows. Taken together, these and other changes help to explain why demand for goods and services constantly fluctuates and why changes occur not only in an economy's capacity to produce output, but also in its structure and performance over time (*see* mini case: Global economic crisis).

It is important to recognise that where changes in spending do occur, these invariably have consequences for the economy that go beyond the initial 'injection' or 'withdrawal' of income. For example, a decision by government to increase spending on infrastructure would benefit the firms involved in the various projects and some of the additional income they receive would undoubtedly be spent on hiring labour. The additional workers employed would have more income to spend on consumption and this would boost the income for firms producing consumer goods, which in turn may hire more staff, generating further consumption and so on. In short, the initial increase in spending by government will have additional effects on income and spending in the economy, as the extra spending circulates from households to firms and back again. Economists refer to this as the 'multiplier effect' to emphasise the reverberative consequences of any increase or decrease in spending by consumers, firms, governments or overseas buyers.

Multiple increases in income and consumption can also give rise to an 'accelerator effect', which is the term used to describe a change in investment spending by firms as a result of a change in consumer spending. In the example above it is possible that the increase in consumption caused by the increase in government spending may persuade some firms to invest in more stock and capital equipment to meet increased consumer demands. Demand for capital goods will therefore rise, and this could cause further increases in the demand for industrial products (e.g. components, machinery) and also for consumer goods, as firms seek to increase their output to meet the changing market conditions. Should consumer spending fall, a reverse accelerator may occur and the same would apply to the multiplier as the reduction in consumption reverberates through the economy and causes further cuts in both consumption and investment. As Peter Donaldson has suggested, everything in the economy affects everything else; the economy is dynamic, interactive and mobile and is far more complex than implied by the model used in the analysis above.[3]

| Mini case | Global economic crisis |

Throughout the 1980s and early 1990s the Asian Tiger economies – Indonesia, Hong Kong, Malaysia, Singapore, South Korea, Taiwan and Thailand – were widely regarded as an unqualified success story with their rapid rates of growth and booming stock markets. As exemplars of free-market capitalism, these economies had an enviable reputation in the West and attracted considerable funds from foreign investors. This miracle began to unravel in 1997 with the onset of an economic crisis in the Far East which sent shock waves throughout the world financial system.

The roots of the crisis appear to lie in unregulated investment decisions which ultimately resulted in the inability of the tiger economies to protect their currencies which at the time were pegged against the US dollar. Following the collapse of a number of Thai property companies which had overextended themselves in the boom times and the subsequent withdrawal of loans by an increasing number of foreign investors, the Thai government was forced to let the currency (the baht) float. As the speculators gathered, other currencies came under pressure and were ultimately forced to give up the dollar peg. As currency values collapsed and forced up the size of multibillion-dollar loans, foreign investors rapidly withdrew their funds, resulting in a collapse on Asian stock markets which spread to London, New York and elsewhere, provoking fears of a worldwide recession.

The Asian crisis was followed in 1998 by the collapse of the Russian rouble which also came under speculative attack. The subsequent announcement by the Russian government that it was to devalue the currency and to suspend repaying its foreign debts simply convinced investors that emerging markets were too risky an investment and other countries' currencies came under pressure, particularly Brazil. Understandably the American stock market reacted very unfavourably to the problem in Latin America and share prices plummeted, sparking off similar falls on other stock exchanges across the globe.

Fears that the global economic crisis could plunge the whole world into recession gradually subsided, but we should not underestimate the human cost of the problems in the countries affected by economic collapse, particularly widespread job loss and growing poverty. Nor should we forget that our own economy and its business felt the effect, whether from deferred investment by Far Eastern companies, lost trade, bad debts or reduced overseas earnings for UK multinationals. As economies across the globe become increasingly interlinked, economic collapse in one country or region spreads to other parts of the world. Arguably this makes the role of international institutions such as the IMF and the World Bank (see below) more rather than less relevant in the twenty-first century.

Government and the macroeconomy: objectives

Notwithstanding the complexities of the real economy, the link between business activity and spending is clear to see. This spending, as indicated above, comes from consumers, firms, governments and external sources and collectively can be said to represent total demand in the economy for goods and services. Economists frequently indicate this with the following notation:

Aggregate Monetary Demand = Consumer spending + Investment spending
+ Government spending + Export spending
− Import spending

or   AMD = C + I + G + X − M

Within this equation, consumer spending (C) is regarded as by far the most important factor in determining the level of total demand.

While economists might disagree about what are the most significant influences on the component elements of AMD,[4] it is widely accepted that governments have a crucial role to play in shaping demand, not only in their own sector but also on the market side of the economy. Government policies on spending and taxation or on interest rates clearly have both direct and indirect influences on the behaviour of individuals and firms, which can affect both the demand and supply side of the economy in a variety of ways. Underlying these policies are a number of key objectives which are pursued by government as a prerequisite to a healthy economy and which help to guide the choice of policy options. Understanding the broad choice of policies available to government, and the objectives associated with them, is of prime importance to students of the business environment.

Most governments appear to have a number of key economic objectives, the most important of which are normally the control of inflation, the pursuit of economic growth, a reduction in unemployment, the achievement of an acceptable balance of payments situation, controlling public (i.e. government) borrowing, and a relatively stable exchange rate.

Controlling inflation

Inflation is usually defined as an upward and persistent movement in the general level of prices over a given period of time; it can also be characterised as a fall in the value of money. For governments of all political complexions reducing such movements to a minimum is seen as a primary economic objective (e.g. the current UK government's target for 'underlying inflation' is 2.5 per cent).

Monitoring trends in periodic price movements tends to take a number of forms; in the UK these include:

1 The use of a Retail Price Index (RPI), which measures how an average family's spending on goods and services is affected by price changes. The RPI is the measure used for 'headline inflation' in the UK and includes mortgage interest payments.
2 An examination of the 'underlying rate of inflation', which excludes the effects of mortgage payments (known as RPIX in the UK).
3 Measuring 'factory gate prices', to indicate likely future changes in consumer prices.
4 Comparing domestic inflation rates with those of the United Kingdom's chief overseas competitors, as an indication of the international competitiveness of UK firms.

In addition, changes in monetary aggregates, which measure the amount of money (and therefore potential spending power) in circulation in the economy, and movements of exchange rates (especially a depreciating currency – see Chapter 13) are also seen as a guide to possible future price increases, as their effects work through the economy.

Explanations as to why prices tend to rise over time vary considerably, but broadly speaking fall into two main categories. First, supply-siders tend to focus on rising production costs – particularly wages, energy and imported materials – as a major reason for inflation, with firms passing on increased costs to the consumer in the form of higher wholesale and/or retail prices. Second, demand-siders, in contrast, tend to emphasise the importance of excessive demand in the economy, brought about, for example, by tax cuts, cheaper borrowing or excessive government spending, which encourages firms to take advantage of the consumer's willingness to spend money by increasing their prices. Where indigenous firms are unable to satisfy all the additional demand, the tendency is for imports to increase. This not only may cause further price rises, particularly if imported goods are more expensive or if exchange rate movements become unfavourable, but also can herald a deteriorating balance of payments situation and difficult trading conditions for domestic businesses.

Government concern with inflation – which crosses both party and state boundaries – reflects the fact that rising price levels can have serious consequences for the economy in general and for businesses in particular, especially if a country's domestic inflation rates are significantly higher than those of its main competitors. In markets where price is an important determinant of demand, rising prices may result in some businesses losing sales, and this can affect turnover and may ultimately affect employment if firms reduce their labour force in order to reduce their costs. Added to this, the uncertainty caused by a difficult trading environment may make some businesses unwilling to invest in new plant and equipment, particularly if interest rates are high and if inflation looks unlikely to fall for some time. Such a response, while understandable, is unlikely to improve a firm's future competitiveness or its ability to exploit any possible increases in demand as market conditions change.

Rising prices may also affect businesses by encouraging employees to seek higher wages in order to maintain or increase their living standards. Where firms agree to such wage increases, the temptation, of course, is to pass this on to the consumer in the form of a price rise, especially if demand looks unlikely to be affected to any great extent. Should this process occur generally in the economy, the result may be a wages/prices inflationary spiral, in which wage increases push up prices which push up wage increases which further push up prices and so on. From an international competitive point of view, such an occurrence, if allowed to continue unchecked, could be disastrous for both firms and the economy.

Economic growth

Growth is an objective shared by governments and organisations alike. For governments, the aim is usually to achieve steady and sustained levels of non-inflationary growth, preferably led by exports (i.e. export-led growth). Such growth is normally indicated by annual increases in real national income or gross domestic product (where 'real' = allowing for inflation, and 'gross domestic product (gdp)' = the economy's annual output of goods and services measured in monetary terms).[5] To compensate for changes in the size of the population, growth rates tend to be expressed in terms of real national income per capita (i.e. real gdp divided by population).

Exactly what constitutes desirable levels of growth is difficult to say, except in very broad terms. If given a choice, governments would basically prefer:

- steady levels of real growth (e.g. 3–4 per cent p.a.), rather than annual increases in output which vary widely over the business cycle;
- growth rates higher than those of one's chief competitors; and
- growth based on investment in technology and on increased export sales, rather than on excessive government spending or current consumption.

It is worth remembering that, when measured on a monthly or quarterly basis, increases in output can occur at a declining rate and gdp growth can become negative. In the United Kingdom, for example, a recession is said to exist following two consecutive quarters of negative gdp.

From a business point of view, the fact that increases in output are related to increases in consumption suggests that economic growth is good for business prospects and hence for investment and employment, and by and large this is the case. The rising living standards normally associated with such growth may, however, encourage increased consumption of imported goods and services at the expense of indigenous producers, to a point where some domestic firms are forced out of business and the economy's manufacturing base becomes significantly reduced (often called 'deindustrialisation').[6] Equally, if increased consumption is based largely on excessive state spending, the potential gains for businesses may be offset by the need to increase interest rates to fund that spending (where government borrowing is involved) and by the tendency of government demands for funding to 'crowd out' the private sector's search for investment capital. In such cases, the short-term benefits from government-induced consumption may be more than offset by the medium- and long-term problems for the economy that are likely to arise.

Where growth prospects for the economy look good, business confidence tends to increase, and this is often reflected in increased levels of investment and stock holding and ultimately in levels of employment. In Britain, for example, the monthly and quarterly surveys by the Confederation of British Industry (CBI) provide a good indication of how output, investment and stock levels change at different points of the business cycle and these are generally seen as a good indication of future business trends, as interpreted by entrepreneurs. Other indicators – including the state of the housing market and construction generally – help to provide a guide to the current and future state of the economy, including its prospects for growth in the short and medium term.

web link The CBI's website address is *www.cbi.org.uk*

Reducing unemployment

In most democratic states the goal of 'full employment' is no longer part of the political agenda; instead government pronouncements on employment tend to focus on job creation and maintenance and on developing the skills appropriate to future demands. The consensus seems to be that in technologically advanced market-based economies some unemployment is inevitable and that the basic aim should be to reduce unemployment to a level which is both politically and socially acceptable.

As with growth and inflation, unemployment levels tend to be measured at regular intervals (e.g. monthly, quarterly, annually) and the figures are often adjusted to take into account seasonal influences (e.g. school-leavers entering the job market). In addition, the statistics usually provide information on trends in long-term unemployment, areas of skill shortage and on international comparisons, as well as sectoral changes within the economy. All of these indicators provide clues to the current state of the economy and to the prospects for businesses in the coming months and years, but need to be used with care. Unemployment, for example, tends to continue rising for a time even when a recession is over; equally, it is not uncommon for government definitions of unemployment to change or for international unemployment data to be based on different criteria.

The broader social and economic consequences of high levels of unemployment are well documented: it is a waste of resources, it puts pressure on the public services and on the Exchequer (e.g. by reducing tax yields and increasing public expenditure on welfare provision), and it is frequently linked with growing social and health problems. Its implication for businesses, however, tends to be less clear-cut. On the one hand, a high level of unemployment implies a pool of labour available for firms seeking workers (though not necessarily with the right skills), generally at wage levels lower than when a shortage of labour occurs. On the other hand, it can also give rise to a fall in overall demand for goods and services which could exacerbate any existing deflationary forces in the economy, causing further unemployment and with it further reductions in demand. Where this occurs, economists tend to describe it as cyclical unemployment (i.e. caused by a general deficiency in demand) in order to differentiate it from unemployment caused by a deficiency in demand for the goods produced by a particular industry (structural unemployment) or by the introduction of new technology which replaces labour (technological unemployment).

A favourable balance of payments

A country's balance of payments is essentially the net balance of credits (earnings) and debits (payments) arising from its international trade over a given period of time (see Chapter 13). Where credits exceed debits a balance of payments surplus exists; the opposite is described as a deficit. Understandably governments tend to prefer either equilibrium in the balance of payments or surpluses, rather than deficits. However, it would be fair to say that for some governments facing persistent balance of payments deficits, a sustained reduction in the size of the deficit may be regarded as signifying a 'favourable' balance of payments situation.

Like other economic indicators, the balance of payments statistics come in a variety of forms and at different levels of disaggregation, allowing useful comparisons to be made not only on a country's comparative trading performance, but also on the international competitiveness of particular industries and commodity groups or on the development or decline of specific external markets. Particular emphasis tends to be given to the balance of payments on current account, which measures imports and exports of goods and services and is thus seen as an indicator of the competitiveness of an economy's firms and industries. Sustained current account surpluses tend to suggest favourable trading conditions, which can help to boost growth, increase employment and investment and create a general feeling of confidence amongst the business community. They may also give rise to surpluses which domestic firms can use to finance overseas lending and investment, thus helping to generate higher levels of corporate foreign earnings in future years.

While it does not follow that a sustained current account deficit is inevitably bad for the country concerned, it often implies structural problems in particular sectors of its economy or possibly an exchange rate which favours importers rather than exporters. Many observers believe, for instance, that the progressive decline of Britain's visible trading position after 1983 was an indication of the growing uncompetitiveness of its firms, particularly those producing finished manufactured goods for consumer markets at home and abroad. By the same token, Japan's current account trade surplus of around $120 billion in late 1995 was portrayed as a sign of the cut-throat competition of Japanese firms, particularly those involved in producing cars, electrical and electronic products, and photographic equipment.

Controlling public borrowing

Governments raise large amounts of revenue annually, mainly through taxation, and use this income to spend on a wide variety of public goods and services (see below). Where annual revenue exceeds government spending, a budget surplus occurs and the excess is often used to repay past debt (formerly known in the United Kingdom as the 'public sector debt repayment' or PSDR). The accumulated debt of past and present governments represents a country's National Debt.

In practice, most governments often face annual budget deficits rather than budget surpluses and hence have a 'public sector borrowing requirement' or PSBR (now known in the UK as 'public sector net borrowing' or PSNB). While such deficits are not inevitably a problem, in the same way that a small personal over-draft is not necessarily critical for an individual, large scale and persistent deficits are generally seen as a sign of an economy facing current and future difficulties which require urgent government action. The overriding concern over high levels of public borrowing tends to be focused on:

1 Its impact on interest rates, given that higher interest rates tend to be needed to attract funds from private sector uses to public sector uses.
2 The impact of high interest rates on consumption and investment and hence on the prospects of businesses.
3 The danger of the public sector 'crowding out' the private sector's search for funds for investment.
4 The opportunity cost of debt interest, especially in terms of other forms of public spending.
5 The general lack of confidence in the markets about the government's ability to control the economy and the likely effect this might have on inflation, growth and the balance of payments.
6 The need to meet the 'convergence criteria' laid down at Maastricht for entry to the single currency (e.g. central government debt no higher than 3 per cent of GDP).

The consensus seems to be that controlling public borrowing is best tackled by restraining the rate of growth of public spending rather than by increasing revenue through changes in taxation, since the latter could depress demand.

A stable exchange rate

A country's currency has two values: an internal value and an external value. Internally, its value is expressed in terms of the goods and services it can buy and hence it is affected by changes in domestic prices. Externally, its value is expressed as an 'exchange rate' which governs how much of another country's currency it can purchase (e.g. £1 = $1.50 or £1 = €1.63). Since foreign trade normally involves an exchange of currencies, fluctuations in the external value of a currency will influence the price of imports and exports and hence can affect the trading prospects for business, as well as a country's balance of payments and its rate of inflation (*see* Chapter 13).

On the whole, governments and businesses involved in international trade tend to prefer exchange rates to remain relatively stable, because of the greater degree of certainty this brings to the trading environment; it also tends to make overseas investors more confident that their funds are likely to hold their value. To this extent, schemes which seek to fix exchange rates within predetermined levels (e.g. the ERM), or which encourage the use of a common currency (e.g. the 'Euro'), tend to have the support of the business community, which prefers predictability to uncertainty where trading conditions are concerned.

Mini case   Indicators of success

Government success in managing the macroeconomy tends to be measured in terms of certain key economic indicators: most notably 'inflation', 'growth', 'unemployment' and 'international trade'. In mid-1996, for example, the Paris-based Organisation for Economic Co-operation and Development (OECD) reported that the prospects for the British economy in the short to medium term were very bright, thanks to an anticipated combination of the low inflation, falling unemployment and robust growth. Much of the UK's 'success' was attributed to the policy of labour market deregulation pursued by successive Conservative administrations. According to the OECD, labour market reforms had been responsible for creating a more conducive environment for employment than in many continental European countries and this was felt to be responsible for helping the UK to become more competitive in international markets.

Broader measures of performance can often paint a different picture. One such measure – produced by the International Institute for Management Development (IMD) – has examined the relative competitiveness of the leading world economies, using a wide range of indicators to assess an economy's strengths and weaknesses. Apart from standard measures such as GDP growth and export performance, the IMD survey took into account aspects as varied as investment in training, retaining and technology, management quality and public trust in bankers. Using these and other criteria, the 1996 IMD survey ranked the UK as 19th on the international scoreboard, compared to 15th in 1995 and 11th in 1989. By these measures Britain was becoming relatively less competitive and was clearly trailing the Asian 'Tiger' economies and many of its main European rivals (e.g. in 1996 Singapore was ranked 2nd; Hong Kong 3rd; Japan 4th; Denmark 5th; Luxembourg 8th; Germany 10th; Sweden 14th; Austria 16th; Belgium 17th; Taiwan 18th).

At the time the IMD defined competitiveness as being concerned with 'the ability of a country to create added value and . . . increase national wealth by managing assets and processes, attractiveness and aggressiveness, globality and proximity, and by integrating these relationships into an economic and social model'. A much simpler definition suggested by the World Economic Forum (WEF) related competitiveness to a country's ability to achieve sustained high rates of growth in GDP per capita. Under the WEF approach, countries were ranked according to around 150 criteria which were selected for their reliability and correlation with growth rates (e.g. tax levels, savings rates, human capital), with the different factors being weighted in relation to their perceived contribution to GDP growth. Thus the Forum's 1996 index* ranked the UK as 15th, well behind Singapore (1st), Hong Kong (2nd), Malaysia (10th) and the 'rising star' New Zealand (3rd). Interestingly, under the WEF index countries such as Germany (22nd) and Japan (13th) fared less well than under the IMD survey. In Germany's case, this seems to have reflected the additional weighting given by the Forum to relative labour market inflexibility and the impact on growth of a substantial welfare state. It probably also helps to explain why under the Forum's index the UK was rated higher relative to the rest of the EU than under the IMD report.

Since the last edition was published both the IMD and WEF measures of competitiveness have become more finely-tuned. WEF, for instance, has enlisted staff from Harvard University – including Professor Michael Porter – to produce enhanced measures of global competitiveness based on two indices : one for 'current competitiveness' and one for 'growth competitiveness'. The former examines what underpins high current productivity and economic performance. The latter looks at the factors that contribute to the future growth of an economy, measured as the rate of change of GDP per person.

*WEF and IMD were originally partners in producing their annual world competitiveness report. They are now competitors!

You can obtain further information from *www.weforum.org/* and *www.imd.ch/wcy*

Government and the macroeconomy: policies

Governments throughout Europe and beyond play various key roles in their respective economies. These include the following functions:

■ consumer of resources (e.g. employer, landowner);
■ supplier of resources (e.g. infrastructure, information);
■ consumer of goods and services (e.g. government spending);
■ supplier of goods and services (e.g. nationalised industries);
■ regulator of business activity (e.g. employment laws, consumer laws);
■ regulator of the economy (e.g. fiscal and monetary policies); and
■ redistributor of income and wealth (e.g. taxation system).

The extent of these roles, and their impact on the economy in general and on business in particular, varies from country to country as well as over time.

Despite the economic significance of these roles, in most market-based economies democratically elected governments prefer levels and patterns of production and consumption to be determined largely by market forces, with a minimum of government interference. This approach is exemplified by the philosophical stance of the UK and US governments in the 1980s, that became colloquially known as 'Thatcherism' (UK) and 'Reaganomics' (USA). At the same time, the recognition that market forces alone are unable to guarantee that an economy will automatically achieve the objectives established by governments has meant that state intervention – to curb inflation, encourage growth, reduce unemployment, correct a balance of payments or budgetary problem or restore currency stability – invariably occurs to some degree in all countries. In broad terms, this intervention usually takes three main forms, described as fiscal policy, monetary policy and direct controls. These policy instruments – or 'instrumental variables' – and their effects on the business community are discussed below.

Fiscal policy

As indicated above, each year governments raise and spend huge amounts of money. The UK government's estimates for 2002/3, for example, suggest that government spending will be about £418 billion and is to be allocated in the manner illustrated in Figure 4.8. This spending will be funded mainly from taxation (direct and indirect), and national insurance contributions (*see* Figure 4.9). The PSNB is estimated at £11 billion.

Fiscal policy involves the use of changes in government spending and taxation to influence the level and composition of aggregate demand in the economy and, given the amounts involved, this clearly has important implications for business. Elementary circular flow analysis suggests, for instance, that reductions in taxation and/or increases in government spending will inject additional income into the economy and will, via the multiplier effect, increase the demand for goods and services, with favourable consequences for business. Reductions in government spending and/or increases in taxation will have the opposite effect, depressing business prospects and probably discouraging investment and causing a rise in unemployment.

Apart from their overall impact on aggregate demand, fiscal changes can be used to achieve specific objectives, some of which will be of direct or indirect benefit to the business community. Reductions in taxes on company profits and/or increases in tax allowances for investment in capital equipment can be used to encourage business to increase investment spending, hence boosting the income of firms producing industrial products and causing some additional spending on consumption. Similarly, increased government spending targeted at firms involved in exporting, or at the creation of new business, will encourage increased business activity and additionally may lead to more output and employment in the economy.

In considering the use of fiscal policy to achieve their objectives, governments tend to be faced with a large number of practical problems that generally limit their room for manoeuvre. Boosting the economy through increases in spending or reductions in taxation could cause inflationary pressures, as well as encouraging an inflow of imports and increasing the public sector deficit, none of which would be particularly welcomed by entrepreneurs or by the financial markets. By the same token, fiscal attempts to restrain demand in order to reduce inflation will

Figure 4.8	The allocation of UK government spending, 2002/3

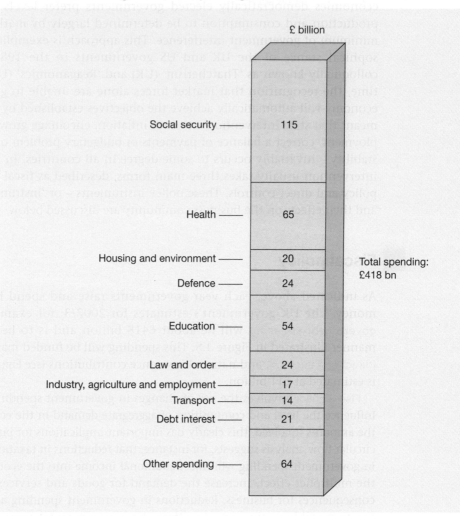

Source: Adapted from Budget Statement, 2002

generally depress the economy, causing a fall in output and employment and encouraging firms to abandon or defer investment projects until business prospects improve.

Added to this, it should not be forgotten that government decision makers are politicians who need to consider the political as well as the economic implications of their chosen courses of action. Thus while cuts in taxation may receive public approval, increases may not, and, if implemented, the latter may encourage higher wage demands. Similarly, the redistribution of government spending from one programme area to another is likely to give rise to widespread protests from those on the receiving end of any cuts; so much so that governments tend to be restricted for the most part to changes at the margin, rather than undertaking a radical reallocation of resources and may be tempted to fix budgetary allocations for a number of years ahead (e.g. the Comprehensive Spending Review in the UK).

Figure 4.9   Sources of government revenue, 2002/3

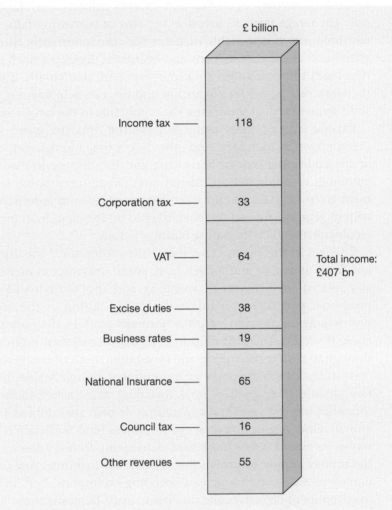

£ billion

Income tax ——	118
Corporation tax ——	33
VAT ——	64
Excise duties ——	38
Business rates ——	19
National Insurance ——	65
Council tax ——	16
Other revenues ——	55

Total income:
£407 bn

Source: Adapted from Budget Statement, 2002

Other factors too – including changes in economic thinking, self-imposed fiscal rules, external constraints on borrowing and international agreements – can also play their part in restraining the use of fiscal policy as an instrument of demand management, whatever a government's preferred course of action may be. Simple prescriptions to boost the economy through large-scale cuts in taxation or increases in government spending often fail to take into account the political and economic realities of the situation faced by most governments.

Monetary policy

Monetary policy seeks to influence monetary variables such as the money supply or rates of interest in order to regulate the economy. While the supply of money and interest rates (i.e. the cost of borrowing) are interrelated, it is convenient to consider them separately.

As far as changes in interest rates are concerned, these clearly have implications for business activity, as circular flow analysis demonstrates. Lower interest rates not only encourage firms to invest as the cost of borrowing falls, but also encourage consumption as disposable incomes rise (predominantly through the mortgage effect) and as the cost of loans and overdrafts decreases. Such increased consumption tends to be an added spur to investment, particularly if inflation rates (and, therefore 'real' interest rates) are low and this can help to boost the economy in the short term, as well as improving the supply side in the longer term.[7]

Raising interest rates tends to have the opposite effect – causing a fall in consumption as mortgages and other prices rise, and deferring investment because of the additional cost of borrowing and the decline in business confidence as consumer spending falls. If interest rates remain persistently high, the encouragement given to savers and the discouragement given to borrowers and spenders may help to generate a recession, characterised by falling output, income, spending and employment and by increasing business failure.

Changes in the money stock (especially credit) affect the capacity of individuals and firms to borrow and, therefore, to spend. Increases in money supply are generally related to increases in spending and this tends to be good for business prospects, particularly if interest rates are falling as the money supply rises. Restrictions on monetary growth normally work in the opposite direction, especially if such restrictions help to generate increases in interest rates which feed through to both consumption and investment, both of which will tend to decline.

As in the case of fiscal policy, government is usually able to manipulate monetary variables in a variety of ways, including taking action in the money markets to influence interest rates and controlling its own spending to influence monetary growth. Once again, however, circumstances tend to dictate how far and in what way government is free to operate. Attempting to boost the economy by allowing the money supply to grow substantially, for instance, threatens to cause inflationary pressures and to increase spending on imports, both of which run counter to government objectives and do little to assist domestic firms. Similarly, policies to boost consumption and investment through lower interest rates, while welcomed generally by industry, offer no guarantee that any additional spending will be on domestically produced goods and services, and also tend to make the financial markets nervous about government commitments to control inflation in the longer term (see below, 'The role of the central bank').

This nervousness among market dealers reflects the fact that in modern market economies a government's policies on interest rates and monetary growth cannot be taken in isolation from those of its major trading partners and this operates as an important constraint on government action. The fact is that a reduction in interest rates to boost output and growth in an economy also tends to be reflected in the exchange rate; this usually falls as foreign exchange dealers move funds into those currencies which yield a better return and which also appear a safer investment if the market believes a government is abandoning its counterinflationary policy. As the UK government found in the early 1990s, persistently high rates of interest in Germany severely restricted its room for manoeuvre on interest rates for fear of the consequences for sterling if relative interest rates got too far out of line.

Direct controls

Fiscal and monetary policies currently represent the chief policy instruments used in modern market economies and hence they have been discussed in some detail. Governments, however, also use a number of other weapons from time to time in their attempts to achieve their macroeconomic objectives. Such weapons, which are designed essentially to achieve a specific objective – such as limiting imports or controlling wage increases – tend to be known as direct controls. Examples of such policies include:

- *Incomes policies*, which seek to control inflationary pressures by influencing the rate at which wages and salaries rise.
- *Import controls*, which attempt to improve a country's balance of payments situation, by reducing either the supply of, or the demand for, imported goods and services (see Chapter 13).
- *Regional and urban policies*, which are aimed at alleviating urban and regional problems, particularly differences in income, output, employment, and local and regional decline (see Chapter 10).

A brief discussion of some of these policy instruments is found at various points in the text below. Students wishing to study these in more detail are recommended to consult the books referred to at the end of this chapter.

The role of financial institutions

Interactions in the macroeconomy between governments, businesses and consumers take place within an institutional environment that includes a large number of financial intermediaries. These range from banks and building societies to pension funds, insurance companies, investment trusts and issuing houses, all of which provide a number of services of both direct and indirect benefit to businesses. As part of the financial system within a market-based economy, these institutions fulfil a vital role in channelling funds from those able and willing to lend, to those individuals and organisations wishing to borrow in order to consume or invest. It is appropriate to consider briefly this role of financial intermediation and the supervision exercised over the financial system by the central bank, before concluding the chapter with a review of important international economic institutions.

Elements of the financial system

A financial system tends to have three main elements:

1 *Lenders and borrowers* – these may be individuals, organisations or governments.
2 *Financial institutions*, of various kinds, which act as intermediaries between lenders and borrowers and which manage their own asset portfolios in the interest of their shareholders and/or depositors.
3 *Financial markets*, in which lending and borrowing takes place through the transfer of money and/or other types of asset, including paper assets such as shares and stock.

Financial institutions, as indicated above, comprise a wide variety of organisations, many of which are public companies with shareholders. Markets include the markets for short-term funds of various types (usually termed 'money markets') and those for long-term finance for both the private and public sectors (usually called the 'capital market'). Stock exchanges normally lie at the centre of the latter, and constitute an important market for existing securities issued by both companies and government.

The vital role played by financial intermediaries in the operation of the financial system is illustrated in Figure 4.10 and reflects the various benefits which derive from using an intermediary rather than lending direct to a borrower (e.g. creating a large pool of savings; spreading risk; transferring short-term lending into longer-term borrowing; providing various types of funds transfer services). Lenders on the whole prefer low risk, high returns, flexibility and liquidity; while borrowers prefer to minimise the cost of borrowing and to use the funds in a way that is best suited to their needs. Companies, for example, may borrow to finance stock or work-in-progress or to meet short-term debts and such borrowing may need to be as flexible as possible. Alternatively, they may wish to borrow in order to replace plant and equipment or to buy new premises – borrowing which needs to be over a much longer term and which hopefully will yield a rate of return which makes the use of the funds and the cost of borrowing worthwhile.

The process of channelling funds from lenders to borrowers often gives rise to paper claims, which are generated either by the financial intermediary issuing a claim to the lender (e.g. when a bank borrows by issuing a certificate of deposit) or by the borrower issuing a claim to the financial intermediary (e.g. when government sells stock to a financial institution). These paper claims represent a liability to the issuer and an asset to the holder and can be traded on a secondary market (i.e. a market for existing securities), according to the needs of the individual or organisation holding

Figure 4.10 The role of financial intermediaries

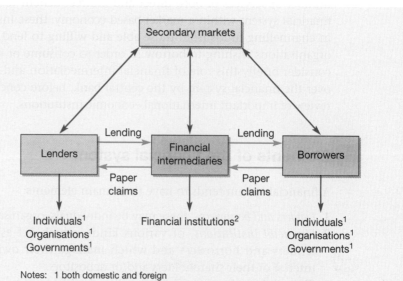

Notes: 1 both domestic and foreign
2 including retail and wholesale banks, building societies, overseas banks, pension funds, and so on.

the paper claim. At any point, financial intermediaries tend to hold a wide range of such assets (claims on borrowers), which they buy or sell ('manage') in order to yield a profit and/or improve their liquidity position. Decisions of this kind, taken on a daily basis, invariably affect the position of investors (e.g. shareholders) and customers (e.g. depositors) and can, under certain circumstances, have serious consequences for the financial intermediary and its stakeholders (e.g. the bad debts faced by western banks in the late 1980s and early 1990s).

Given the element of risk, it is perhaps not surprising that some financial institutions tend to be conservative in their attitude towards lending on funds deposited with them, especially in view of their responsibilities to their various stakeholders. UK retail banks, for instance, have a long-standing preference for financing industry's working capital rather than investment spending, and hence the latter has tended to be financed largely by internally generated funds (e.g. retained profits) or by share issues. In comparison, banks in Germany, France, the United States and Japan tend to be more ready to meet industry's medium- and longer-term needs and are often directly involved in regular discussions with their clients concerning corporate strategy, in contrast to the arm's length approach favoured by many of their UK counterparts.[8]

The role of the central bank

A critical element in a country's financial system is its central or state bank; in the United Kingdom this is the Bank of England. Like most of its overseas counterparts, the Bank of England exercises overall supervision over the banking sector, and its activities have a significant influence in the financial markets (especially the foreign exchange market, the gilts market and the sterling money market). These activities include the following roles:

- banker to the government;
- banker to the clearing banks;
- manager of the country's foreign reserves;
- manager of the national debt;
- manager of the issue of notes and coins;
- supervisor of the monetary sector; and
- implementer of the government's monetary policy.

In the last case, the Bank's powers were significantly enhanced following the decision by the new Labour government (1997) to grant it 'operational independence' to set interest rates and to conduct other aspects of monetary policy free from Treasury interference. This historic decision has given the Bank the kind of independence experienced by the US Federal Reserve and the Deutsche Bundesbank and has been designed to ensure that monetary policy is conducted according to the needs of the economy overall, particularly the need to control inflation.

For further information on the Bank of England you should consult
www.bankofengland.co.uk

International economic institutions and organisations

Given that external factors constrain the ability of governments to regulate their economy, it is appropriate to conclude this analysis of the macroeconomic context of business with a brief review of a number of important international economic institutions and organisations which affect the trading environment. Foremost among these is the European Union, which is examined at length in Chapters 3 and 13. In the discussions below, attention is focused on the International Monetary Fund (IMF), the Organisation for Economic Co-operation and Development (OECD), the European Bank for Reconstruction and Development (EBRD), the World Trade Organisation (WTO) and the World Bank (IBRD).

The International Monetary Fund (IMF)

The IMF came into being in 1946 following discussions at Bretton Woods in the USA which sought to agree a world financial order for the post-Second World War period that would avoid the problems associated with the worldwide depression in the inter-war years. In essence, the original role of the institution – which today incorporates most countries in the world – was to provide a pool of foreign currencies from its member states that would be used to smooth out trade imbalances between countries, thereby promoting a structured growth in world trade and encouraging exchange rate stability. In this way, the architects of the Fund believed that the danger of international protectionism would be reduced and that all countries would consequently benefit from the boost given to world trade and the greater stability of the international trading environment.

> **web link** The IMF's website is *www.imf.org*

While this role as international 'lender of last resort' still exists, the IMF's focus in recent years has tended to switch towards helping the developing economies with their mounting debt problems and assisting eastern Europe with reconstruction, following the break-up of the Soviet empire.[9] It has also been recently involved in trying to restore international stability following the global economic turmoil in Asia and elsewhere (see mini case earlier in this chapter). To some extent its role as an international decision-making body has been diminished by the tendency of the world's leading economic countries to deal with global economic problems outside the IMF's institutional framework. The United States, Japan, Germany, France, Italy, Canada and Britain now meet regularly as the 'Group of Seven' (G7) leading industrial economies to discuss issues of mutual interest (e.g. the environment, eastern Europe). These world economic summits, as they are frequently called, have tended to supersede discussions in the IMF and as a result normally attract greater media attention.

The Organisation for Economic Co-operation and Development (OECD)

The OECD came into being in 1961, but its roots go back to 1948 when the Organisation for European Economic Co-operation (OEEC) was established to co-ordinate the distribution of Marshall Aid to the war-torn economies of western Europe. Today it comprises around 30 members, drawn from the rich industrial countries and including the G7 nations, Australia, New Zealand and most other European states. Collectively, these countries account for less than 20 per cent of the world's population, but produce around two-thirds of its output – hence the tendency of commentators to refer to the OECD as the 'rich man's club'. Not surprisingly other countries are keen to join the organisation and a number have recently been allowed to attend part of its annual ministerial meeting for the first time (e.g. Russia, China and India in 1999).

 web link   You can access the OECD's website at *www.oecd.org*

In essence the OECD is the main forum in which the governments of the world's leading industrial economies meet to discuss economic matters, particularly questions concerned with promoting stable growth and freer trade and with supporting development in poorer non-member countries. Through its council and committees, and backed by an independent secretariat, the organisation is able to take decisions which set out an agreed view and/or course of action on important social and economic issues of common concern. While it does not have the authority to impose ideas, its influence lies in its capacity for intellectual persuasion, particularly its ability through discussion to promote convergent thinking on international economic problems. To assist in the task, the OECD provides a wide variety of economic data on member countries, using standardised measures for national accounting, unemployment and purchasing-power parities. It is for these data – and especially its economic forecasts and surveys – that the organisation is perhaps best known.

The European Bank for Reconstruction and Development (EBRD)

The aims of the EBRD, which was inaugurated in April 1991, are to facilitate the transformation of the states of central and eastern Europe from centrally planned to free-market economies and to promote political and economic democracy, respect for human rights and respect for the environment. It is particularly involved with the privatisation process, technical assistance, training and investment in upgrading of the infrastructure and in facilitating economic, legal and financial restructuring. It works in co-operation with its members, private companies and organisations such as the IMF, OECD, the World Bank and the United Nations.

web link   Information on the EBRD can be obtained at *www.ebrd.com*

The World Trade Organisation (WTO)

The World Trade Organisation, which came into being on 1 January 1995, superseded the General Agreement on Tariffs and Trade (the GATT), which dated back to 1947. Like the IMF and the International Bank for Reconstruction and Development (see below), which were established at the same time, the GATT was part of an attempt to reconstruct the international politico-economic environment in the period after the end of the Second World War. Its replacement by the WTO can be said to mark an attempt to put the question of liberalising world trade higher up the international political agenda.

 The WTO can be accessed at *www.wto.org*

With a membership of over 130 states, and which now includes China, the WTO is a permanent international organisation charged with the task of liberalising world trade within an agreed legal and institutional framework. In addition it administers and implements a number of multilateral agreements in fields such as agriculture, textiles and services and is responsible for dealing with disputes arising from the Uruguay Round Final Act. It also provides a forum for the debate, negotiation and adjudication of trade problems and in the latter context is said to have a much stronger and quicker trade compliance and enforcement mechanism than existed under the GATT.

The World Bank (IBRD)

Established in 1945, the World Bank (more formally known as the International Bank for Reconstruction and Development or IBRD) is a specialised agency of the United Nations, set up to encourage economic growth in developing countries through the provision of loans and technical assistance. The IBRD currently has around 180 members.

 The IBRD can be accessed at *www.worldbank.org* and *web.worldbank.org*

The European Investment Bank (EIB)

The European Investment Bank was created in 1958 under the Treaty of Rome and is the financing institution of the European Union. Its main task is to contribute to the integration, balanced development and the economic and social cohesion of EU Member States. Using funds raised on the markets, it finances capital projects which support EU objectives within the European Union and elsewhere.

 For further information on the EIB see *www.eib.org*

Synopsis

Business and economics are inextricably linked. Economics is concerned with the problem of allocating scarce productive resources to alternative uses – a fundamental aspect of business activity. In market-based economies, this problem of resource allocation is largely solved through the operation of free markets, in which price is a vital ingredient. The existence of such markets tends to be associated primarily, though not exclusively, with democratic political regimes.

In all democratic states, government is a key component of the market economy and exercises considerable influence over the level and pattern of business activity – a point illustrated by the use of elementary circular flow analysis. A government's aims for the economy help to shape the policies it uses and these policies have both direct and indirect consequences for business organisations of all kinds.

In examining the economic context in which firms exist, due attention needs to be paid to the influence of a wide range of institutions and organisations, some of which operate at international level. Equally, as markets become more open and business becomes more global, the fortunes of firms in trading economies become increasingly connected and hence subject to fluctuations that go beyond the boundaries of any individual state.

Summary of key points

■ Business activity exists in and is affected by the broader macroeconomic environment; it also helps to shape that environment.

■ Economics is concerned with how societies allocate scarce economic resources to alternative uses and the 'real costs' of the choices that are made.

■ Broadly speaking two main approaches to the problem of resource allocation exist: state planning and the market.

■ Most economies in the world are market-based economies which operate through a price mechanism. Within such economies the state also plays a key role in some allocative decisions.

■ In market economies economic activity essentially involves 'real flows' and corresponding flows of income and expenditure between producers and consumers.

■ Combining these flows into a simple model of the macroeconomy illustrates that income basically flows round the economy in a circular motion.

■ Levels of income in the economy are related to levels of output, expenditure and employment.

■ Changes in the level of economic activity can be explained by examining changes in one or more of the key economic variables such as consumer spending, saving, government decisions on state spending/taxation and external trade.

- Within the macroeconomy governments often play a key role in influencing both the levels and patterns of demand in pursuit of their macroeconomic objectives.

- Key government objectives usually include controlling inflation, promoting economic growth, reducing unemployment, and creating a stable macroeconomic environment.

- To pursue these objectives governments use a range of policies, most notably fiscal and monetary policies.

- Government policy decisions take place within a broader economic and financial framework which includes the influence of financial institutions and markets and the requirements which accrue from membership of different supranational and international organisations.

CASE STUDY · Toyota UK

Toyota's origins can be traced back to the early twentieth century when the inventor of Japan's first automatic loom, Sakidu Toyoda, established a spinning and weaving company. By the 1930s, using funds from selling patent rights to a British machine maker, the company had begun to invest in automotive technology research and soon produced its first prototype passenger vehicle. In August 1937, Kiichiro Toyoda, the son of the original owner, established the Toyota Motor Company, beginning mass production at its Koromo plant in 1938, just before the outbreak of the Second World War.

Despite experiencing considerable difficulties in the post-war period, Toyota recommenced production and began to build up a sales network to market its vehicles. In 1950, the company was split into two parts – production and sales – with the Toyota Motor Company the manufacturing arm of the organisation. Using techniques which have subsequently been emulated by other large companies (e.g. total quality control, just-in-time), Toyota began to increase its output and sales and was beginning to make significant inroads into overseas markets by the mid-1960s. By 1982, when the sales and manufacturing arms of the organisation merged to form the Toyota Motor Corporation, export sales of vehicles had exceeded domestic registrations and Toyota had grown into a large multinational corporation with a range of interests in various parts of the world.

For much of the early post-war period, Toyota focused its attention on the American market and established sales facilities in California in 1957, to be followed by a design base in 1973 and a joint production venture with General Motors in 1984. Less than two years later, the Corporation established its first wholly owned production plant at Georgetown in Kentucky, from which the first of many US-built Toyotas emerged in 1988.

Toyota's development in post-war Europe proceeded along broadly similar lines, with the company establishing local sales and distribution networks, followed by design and production facilities. Initially, production took place under licence (e.g. in Portugal in 1968) or through joint ventures (e.g. with Volkswagen in 1989) and was restricted to commercial vehicles and fork-lift trucks. By the late 1980s, however, the company had signalled its intention of establishing a passenger vehicle manufacturing facility in Europe, as part of its programme of overseas market development. This plant was opened in mid-1992 at Burnaston near Derby and was followed by the opening of an engine plant at Deeside, North Wales, some months later.

Toyota's decision to establish production facilities in Europe is best understood against the political and economic realities of the period. Japan's post-war success in export markets had, by the 1980s, given rise to a huge Japanese balance of payments surplus that was bitterly resented by US and European governments and became the focus of attention in numerous meetings of the G7 countries. As part of this success, the Japanese car industry was under pressure from US and European car manufacturers and their governments to restrain exports, and this ultimately culminated in a system of agreed voluntary restraints (known as VERs) by Japanese car producers, for fear of more draconian measures. Since these restraints did not apply to vehicles produced by Japanese factories overseas ('transplants'), establishing a manufacturing presence outside Japan made sound commercial and political sense. This was particularly true in western Europe, where the EU's Common External Tariff made cars imported from Japan more expensive to consumers and hence relatively less competitive than locally produced vehicles.

The EU's decision to establish a 'single market' within the Union added a further impetus to the decision by Japanese car manufacturers (and others) to seek a European presence. The fact that the United Kingdom was a favoured location for Toyota – and for many other Japanese companies – is not difficult to explain. Apart from providing direct access to the largest single market for motor vehicles in the world, the United Kingdom had a substantial market in its own right and a developed vehicle manufacturing industry with a significant parts and component sector. Added to this, the favourable response given to direct foreign investment by United Kingdom national and local government – including the use of financial and other inducements – made the United Kingdom an attractive proposition and a location of minimal risk for investing multinational corporations.

As far as the choice of Burnaston was concerned, this seems to have been dictated by economic and commercial rather than political factors, although Derbyshire County Council actively lobbied the parent company and offered it a number of inducements to locate in the Midlands. Being centrally placed in Britain and close to the M1, Burnaston offered direct access to all parts of the country and a relatively quick route to the Continent, via the ports and the Channel Tunnel. It also boasted a highly skilled local workforce, a developed infrastructure and a large site with room for further expansion.

There is no doubt that the multi-million Toyota development in Derbyshire has had a considerable impact on the local economy. Apart from the jobs created in building and operating the car plant, further employment has been created directly among local component suppliers and indirectly amongst those involved in providing services and materials and from the extra spending resulting from the growth of jobs. The area has also benefited from the prestige

▶

of having attracted a famous company to invest and this is expected to encourage investment by other overseas organisations. How far these gains will ultimately be at the expense of the other car-producing areas of Britain still remains to be seen, but economic analysis suggests they may prove significant.

Case study questions

1 What do you think are the key factors which have made the UK an attractive location for direct foreign investment?

2 To what extent do you think the expansion of the European Union will affect future inward investment decisions?

Review and discussion questions

1 To what extent do you agree with the proposition that the market economy is the 'best' form of economic system? Do you have any reservations?

2 Explain how interest rates could be used to boost the economy. Why, then, do governments frequently hesitate to take such steps?

3 Using circular flow analysis, suggest why a large programme of capital expenditure by government (e.g. on new motorways, roads, railways) will benefit businesses. How could such a programme be financed?

4 Which businesses are likely to benefit from a recovery in a country's housing market?

5 How are the Japanese and Korean economies likely to benefit from the 2002 football World Cup?

Assignments

1 Imagine you work in the economic development unit of a local authority. Produce a draft report outlining the benefits to the local economy of encouraging direct inward investment. Indicate any disadvantages.

2 You are a trainee journalist on a regional or national newspaper. As part of your first big assignment, you have been asked to provide information on the 'privatisation' of eastern European economies. Using journals and newspapers, provide a scrapbook of information indicating the different ways in which western companies have sought to exploit business opportunities in eastern Europe.

Notes and references

1 See, for example, *Creditanstalt/EIU Vienna 1992*, Eastern Investment Survey.

2 *Financial Times*, 2 March 1992.

3 Donaldson, P. and Farquhar, J., *Understanding the British Economy*, Penguin, 1988, p. 84.

4 See, for example, Griffiths, A. and Wall, S. (eds), *Applied Economics*, 9th edition, Financial Times/Prentice Hall, 2001.

5 See, for example, Morris, H. and Willey, B., *op. cit.*, pp. 117–22.

6 See, for example, Griffiths and Wall, *op. cit.*, ch. 1.

7 Real interest rates allow for inflation.

8 See, for example, Neale, A. and Haslam, C., *Economics in a Business Contex*t, Chapman & Hall, 1991, p. 141.

9 The role of assisting reconstruction in eastern Europe is also undertaken by the European Bank for Reconstruction and Development (EBRD). See text below.

Further reading

Donaldson, P. and Farquhar, J., *Understanding the British Economy*, Penguin, 1988.

Ferguson, K., *Essential Economics: A Guide for Business Students*, Palgrave, 2002.

Griffiths, A. and Wall, S. (eds), *Applied Economics*, 9th edition, Financial Times/Prentice Hall, 2001.

Macdonald, N. T., *Macroeconomics and Business: An Interactive Approach*, International Thomson Publishing, 1999.

Mulhearn, C., Vane, H.R. and Eden, J., *Economics for Business*, Palgrave, 2001.

Neale, A., Haslam, C. and Johal, S., *Economics in a Business Context*, Thomson Learning, 3rd edition, 2000.

Worthington, I., Britton, C. and Rees, A., *Economics for Business: Blending Theory and Practice*, Financial Times/Prentice Hall, 2001.

 Web links and further questions are available on the website at: ***www.booksites.net/worthington***

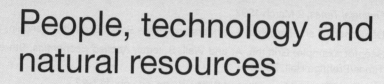

5

People, technology and natural resources

Chris Britton

Businesses carry out a variety of activities, but their main activity is to produce goods and services to be sold on the market. In the production process inputs are turned into outputs. Key inputs into the production process are people, technology and natural resources.

Objectives

- To be aware of the importance of people, technology and natural resources to business.

- To understand what determines the quantity and quality of labour in the economy.

- To recognise the effect of technological change on business.

- To understand the main issues affecting natural resources.

Key terms

Age structure	Land	Resources
Ageing population	Minimum wage	Sex distribution of
Capital	Natural resources	population
Computer-aided design	Negademand	Social capital
(CAD)	Net investment	Stock
Demographic time bomb	Non-renewable resources	Technological change
Derived demand	NVQs	Technological
Educated workforce	Occupational immobility	unemployment
Factor of production	Occupational structure	Technology
Fixed capital	Participation rate	Trade union
Geographical immobility	People	Wage rate
Gross investment	Process innovation	Wages
Immobility of labour	Product innovation	Workforce
Information technology	Quantity of people	Working capital
Infrastructure	Renewable resources	Working week
Innovation	Replacement investment	
Investment	Research and development	

Introduction

The main aim of business is to produce goods and services that people want. This production cannot take place without people, technology and natural resources. In economics these three are called the factors of production and are categorised under the headings of labour, capital and land. This chapter will consider each of these in turn. Resources can be renewable or non-renewable. Renewable resources would include labour, water, fishing stocks, soil, air and solar power even though many of these might not be renewable for a long period of time. Non-renewable resources would be most minerals including oil, iron ore and coal, agricultural land, forests and electricity (in so far as most electricity is derived from minerals).

People

People are important in the economy as both producers and consumers of goods and services. For most products that are produced people are the most important input into the production process. Therefore the quantity and quality of the people available in an economy will have a considerable impact upon the economy's ability to produce.

The quantity of people available for work depends upon a variety of factors:

- the size of the total population;
- the age structure of the population;
- the working population;
- the length of the working week; and
- the wage level.

As well as the quantity of labour, productivity will be affected by its quality. This in turn depends upon:

- education and training;
- working conditions;
- welfare services (e.g. national insurance schemes which cover sickness pay, the NHS which maintains the health of workers; also many firms provide their own welfare services like private pension plans, and so on);
- motivation; and
- the quality of the other factors of production.

Most of these factors will be considered in some detail in the next sections of this chapter.

The population of the UK

The UK population was estimated to be 59.8 million in mid 2000 and forecast to be 62.3 million in 2031.[1] This makes it the second largest country by population in western Europe after Germany. Figure 5.1 shows population size for selected years in the United Kingdom since 1851. Population size and the growth of population depend on many things, but the main determinants are the birth rate, the death rate and the net migration rate.

| Figure 5.1 | Population of the UK (thousands) |

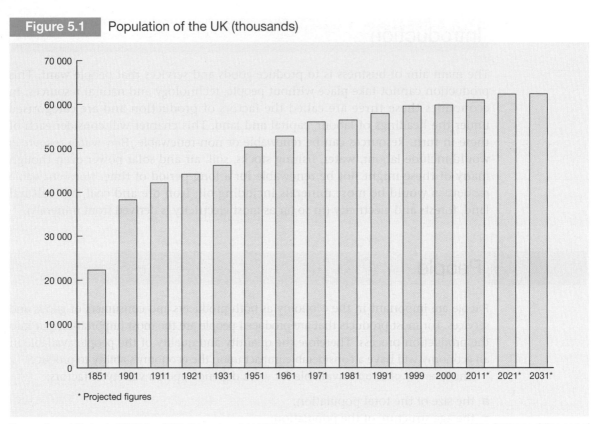

* Projected figures

Source: *Annual Abstract of Statistics*, 2001. Crown copyright 2001. Reproduced by permission of the Controller of The Stationery Office and of the Office for National Statistics, UK.

 ## The birth rate

The birth rate is the number of live births per thousand of the population in a given year. In 2000 the birth rate in the United Kingdom was 11.4, which was lower than the EU average of 13. Table 5.1 shows the UK birth rates for selected time periods since the turn of the century.

The picture is one of steady decline in the birth rate since 1900. There are many reasons for this:

■ There has been a trend towards smaller families as people become better off and as health improves and the death rate falls. This is evident from comparisons of birth rates between the developed and less developed countries. In less developed countries, where mortality is higher, family size also tends to be higher as insurance against loss of children.

■ The availability of contraception has had a dramatic effect on the birth rate, as people now have much greater control over family size than previously.

■ Both men and women are marrying later (between 1961 and 1999 the average age of first marriage rose from 26 to 34.4 for men and from 23.5 to 31.8 for women)[2] and either choosing not to have children or to have them later in life. Fertility rates for women aged between 35 years and 39 years have doubled since 1981, while fertility rates for younger women have declined. The average age at

Table 5.1   Birth rates in the UK (number of births per 1000 population)

Year	Number
1900–2	28.6
1910–12	24.6
1920–2	23.1
1930–2	16.3
1940–2	15.0
1950–2	16.0
1960–2	17.9
1970–2	15.8
1980–2	13.0
2000	11.4

Source: *Annual Abstract of Statistics*, 2001. Crown copyright 2001. Reproduced by permission of the Controller of The Stationary Office and Office for National Statistics, UK.

which mothers give birth rose from 26.4 years in 1971 to 29.3 years in 1993.[3] This was forecast to continue to rise to the year 2000 then gradually fall back again to 28 by the year 2026. The average number of children born per woman in the UK fell from 2.4 in 1970 to 1.5 in 2000. There has been a similar trend in other EU countries and fertility rates are converging.

■ There has also been a change in the attitude towards women and work; a higher proportion of women work now than ever before and for women to work is much more acceptable in society than it was in the past.

Although the trend since the beginning of the century is downward, Table 5.1 shows that the trend is not smooth. Variations in the birth rate occur; Figure 5.2 shows the UK birth rate from 1981 to 2000 and illustrates this point.

It can be seen that the UK birth rate continued its downward path in the early 1980s but then rose again up to 1990 when it resumed its downward path. This is in part due to the 'baby boom' of the 1960s.

The death rate

This is the number of deaths per thousand of a population in a given year. Over the last 100 years there has been a dramatic fall in the death rate in the United Kingdom, although over the past 20 years it has been fairly stable. It stood at 10.6 per thousand population in 1999, exactly the same as the EU average. In 1998 the life expectancy of a man in the United Kingdom was 75 years and for a woman was 80 years. The death rate is forecast to decline further and the average life expectancy is therefore forecast to rise. By 2021 the life expectancy of men is estimated to rise to 78.7 years and for women to 82.7 years. The death rate has fallen because of the following factors:

■ increased medical knowledge;
■ more health care;
■ better food, housing and clothing;
■ better-educated population;

| Figure 5.2 | Birth rates in the UK, 1981–2000 (number of births per 1000 population) |

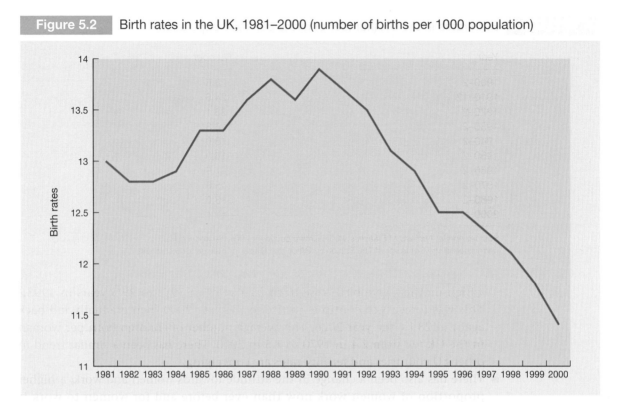

Source: *Annual Abstract of Statistics*, 2001. Crown copyright 2001. Reproduced by permission of the Controller of The Stationary Office and of the Office for National Statistics, UK.

- better working conditions;
- better sanitation; and
- a decline in infant mortality due to better antenatal and postnatal care. (In 2000 the number of infant mortalities per thousand live births in the United Kingdom was 5; substantially below the EU average of 12.)

If the birth rate is greater than the death rate there is a process of natural population growth.

Migration

People leave (or emigrate from) a country and others enter (or immigrate into) a country. The balance between these will be the level of net migration. If more are entering than leaving there will be net immigration and population size will be increasing. If more are leaving than entering there will be net emigration and population size will be falling. In the United Kingdom the level of net migration has been small and insignificant in recent years, sometimes positive and sometimes negative. In 2000 there was a net outflow of British citizens to the EU of 3300, but a net inflow from the rest of the world of 95 900.

Population change

The total population in a country changes as a result of changes in the birth rate, death rate and the level of migration. The death rate is now fairly stable, but expected to continue to fall gradually into the future. The birth rate is slightly more variable and dependent on external factors but again has stabilised, as has migration. This means that the UK population is now fairly stable. The forecast growth rate in population up to 2025 is 4.2 per cent.

The age distribution of the population of the UK

The most important factors which have influenced the age structure of the population are the decline in the death rate, which has resulted in a greater number of old people in the population, and changes in the birth rate. As Table 5.1 and Figure 5.3 show, there have been quite marked changes in birth rates, which have affected the age structure of the population. There was a sharp decline in the number of births during the Second World War and immediately afterwards a post-war baby boom. These two changes are shown by the low numbers of 60-year-olds and the relatively high numbers of 50-year-olds. The post-war baby boom in turn led to a further baby boom in the 1960s, as the females of the first boom reached child-bearing age.

Figure 5.3   The age structure of the UK population, 2000

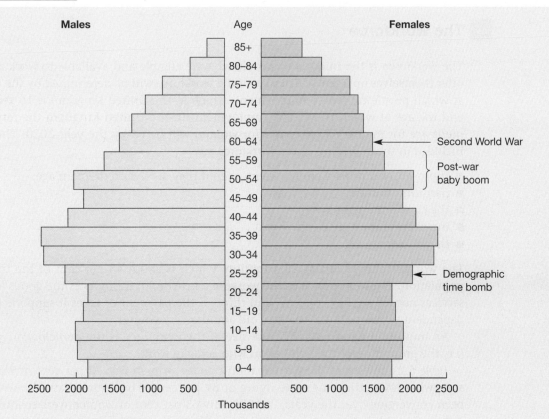

This is shown by the large numbers of the population in the 35-year age group. Since the 1960s there has been a fairly rapid decline in the birth rate, and this has been referred to as the 'demographic time bomb', because of the possible problems of labour shortage that it might create. Again the diagram shows the low numbers of 20-year-olds born in the 1970s who are entering the labour force.

The 'bulge' in the number of 5–14-year-olds reflects the increasing birth rate in the 1980s mentioned earlier.

Because of the falling birth rate and falling death rate the population in the United Kingdom is 'ageing', and thus the average age is increasing. This has a number of implications for the economy. (*See* case study at end of chapter.)

The sex distribution of the population

There are more women than men in the UK population. The 1991 census records 28.2 million men and 29.4 million women. There are more men in the younger age groups than women because there are a greater number of male births. And there are more women in the older age groups because the death rate amongst women is now lower. The sex distribution of the population has important implications for the make-up of the working population because of the differing activity rates of the sexes.

For information on population in the UK see *www.statistics.gov.uk*
For information on world population see *www.undp.org/popin/popin.htm*

The workforce

The workforce is the number of people who are eligible and available to work and offer themselves up as such. The size of the workforce will be determined by the age at which people can enter employment, which in the United Kingdom is 16 years, and the age at which they leave employment. In the United Kingdom the retirement age for men is 65 years and for women will be 65 by the year 2020. Those included in the definition of the workforce are:

- those working in paid employment, even if they are over retirement age;
- part-time workers;
- the claimant unemployed;
- members of the armed forces; and
- the self-employed.

The workforce in 1998 was 28.4 million, which is about 48 per cent of the total population. The importance of the workforce is twofold: it produces the goods and services needed in the economy; and through the payment of taxes it supports the dependent population (i.e. the very old and the very young).

An important determinant of the size of the workforce is the participation rate (i.e. the proportion of the population who actually work).

Table 5.2 shows that the participation rate for women was 72 per cent in 2000; somewhat lower than the male figure of 84 per cent. The figures have, however, been converging over the years. In 1979 only 63 per cent of women were economically active, while the corresponding figure for men was 91 per cent. Activity rates were higher for married than for unmarried women.

| Table 5.2 | Economic activity by gender and marital status of women (%), 2000; persons of working age (16 to 59-64 years) |

	Men	Women		
		All	Married/ cohabiting	Not married/ cohabiting
Economically active	84	72	75	67
In employment	79	69	73	61
Unemployed	5	3	2	6
Economically inactive	16	28	25	32

Source: Adapted from Table 4.8 and 4.2, *Social Trends*, 2001 Office for National Statistics, UK

The trend has been for increased participation rates for women over time as families have become smaller and because of the changing role of women in society as a whole, labour-saving devices in the home and government legislation to promote equal pay and treatment. Also important in this process are the changes in industrial structure which have led to more part-time service jobs (*see* Chapter 9).

The participation rates for both married and unmarried women have moved in a cyclical way, both dipping during the recession of the early 1980s. The general trend, however, is quite different. The participation rate of unmarried women fell between 1973 and 1998 (74 per cent to 66 per cent). The participation rate for married women increased dramatically over the same period, from 55 per cent in 1973 to 74 per cent in 1998.

Table 5.3 gives some comparisons with other EU countries. The United Kingdom has the second-highest activity rates for men after Denmark and the fourth-highest activity rates for women after Denmark, Finland and Sweden in the EU. There are marked differences in the activity rates for women across the EU, but in every country they were lower than the male activity rate.

For information on labour markets see *www.dti.gov.uk*, *http://europa.eu.int/comm/eurostat* and *www.oecd.org*

| Table 5.3 | Economic activity rates* by sex for selected EU countries, 2000 (%) |

	Males	Females	All
UK	84.1	68.4	76.3
France	75.5	62.2	68.8
Germany (incl. new Länder)	79.3	62.9	71.2
Belgium	73.0	56.0	64.6
Italy	73.7	45.6	59.6
Denmark	85.0	76.1	80.6
EU average	78.1	59.2	68.6

Note: *As a percentage of the working-age population.
Source: Adapted from Table 4.7, *Social Trends*, 2001, Office for National Statistics, UK.

The length of the working week

The average length of time for which people work is also a significant determinant of the quantity of labour that is available in an economy. Generally, the shorter the working week, the less labour there is available. There has been, over the last hundred years, a gradual reduction in the length of the working week; 40 hours is now the norm, with a gradual increase in the number of holidays that people take. More recently this trend has been reversed in the UK: the average working week for men was 42.3 hours in 1983, 43.4 hours in 1992 and 45.2 in 2000.[4] Table 5.4 shows the length of the average working week in selected EU countries.

Both men and women in the UK work a longer week than men and women in all other EU countries.

Wages

It is clear that wages will affect how much people are willing to work and therefore the overall supply of labour in the economy. The analysis here will use the basic tools of demand and supply described in Chapter 11. It is advisable to review that chapter before proceeding. The market for labour can be likened to the market for any other commodity, in that there will be a demand for and a supply of labour. The demand for labour will come from the firm which wishes to produce goods and services that can be sold in the market. The demand for labour is a 'derived demand' as its demand is derived from the demand that exists for what it produces. The demand curve can be assumed to be a normal downward-sloping demand curve which indicates that – everything else being equal – as the wage rate goes up the demand for labour goes down.[5] The supply of labour comes from people. It is equally likely that the total supply curve has the normal upward slope, indicating that as the wage rate increases the supply of labour increases. It is argued that as the wage rate increases past a certain level people would prefer to substitute leisure for wages. The individual supply curve will therefore bend backwards at that wage rate.

Table 5.4	Average hours worked per week by gender for selected EU countries, 2000	
	Males	*Females*
UK	45.2	40.7
France	40.2	38.6
Germany	40.5	39.4
Belgium	39.1	36.9
Italy	39.7	36.3
Denmark	39.6	37.9
Netherlands	39.1	36.9
EU average	41.2	39.0

Source: Adapted from Table 4.18, *Social Trends*, 2001. Office for National Statistics, UK.

Figure 5.4   The market for labour

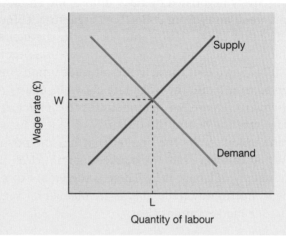

The total supply curve, however, will be upward sloping, indicating that those not working will be encouraged to offer their services and that those already working might be encouraged to work overtime.

Assuming for the time being that the labour market is a totally free market, the wage rate and the amount of labour being used will be determined by the forces of demand and supply, as in Figure 5.4. The equilibrium wage rate is £W and the equilibrium quantity of labour is L. If there is a change in the level of demand or supply, there will be a corresponding change in the wages and quantity of labour.

Trade unions and wages

There are four different types of trade union:

1 *Craft unions*. They represent one particular craft or skill, like the Boilermakers Union, which was formed in 1834 and was the longest-lived craft union in the TUC when it merged with the GMB in 1982. These were the earliest type of union.
2 *Industrial unions*. They have members doing different jobs but in the same industry. Industrial unions are more common in other countries but some UK unions come close to this type; for example, the National Union of Miners.
3 *General unions*. They contain members doing different jobs in different industries, like the Transport and General Workers Union.
4 *White collar unions*. They represent the non-manual workers like teachers, social workers, and so forth. An example is UNISON.

web link   For information on trade unions in the UK see *www.tuc.org.uk*

One of the main aims for all types of union has been to counteract, and protect their members from, the power of the employer. As far as wages are concerned, this has been achieved through collective bargaining. Over the years a situation has been reached where hardly any wage contracts are negotiated individually. Rather, they are collectively negotiated by trade unions and employers. Although there does seem to be a trend away from collective bargaining, coinciding with the anti-trade union legislation of the 1980s and decline in the membership and power of the trade unions, the majority of wage increases are still negotiated by trade unions.

It is argued that the activities of trade unions through collective bargaining have served to increase the wage rate above its equilibrium level and thus cause unemployment. Figure 5.5 demonstrates this effect. Assume that the market clearing wage rate is £W and the quantity of labour being used is L. Assume now that a trade union enters the market that has the power to enforce a wage increase to £W_1. At this wage rate the market does not clear, the demand for labour is L_1 while the supply of labour is L_2. There is therefore excess supply of labour, or unemployment. In this way trade unions are blamed for keeping wages at too high a level so that the market cannot clear.

Figure 5.5 The effect of trade unions on the labour market

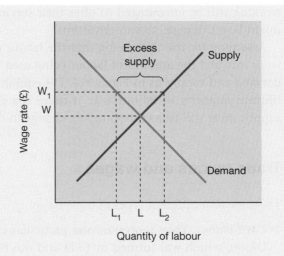

Figure 5.5 can be used to illustrate the argument of those who oppose the setting of a minimum wage. (*See* mini case on the minimum wage.) Although this argument seems plausible enough, it is not quite as simple as it seems. There are other market imperfections which prevent the market from operating as smoothly as suggested and which contribute towards creating unemployment. There are some industries which have only one or two employers who can exercise a great deal of power over the market. The arguments over the minimum wage are also more complicated and centre on much wider economic and social issues. There are additional factors which may prevent people moving easily and smoothly between jobs. For example, people may not easily be able to change jobs if they are geographically or occupationally immobile.

Mini case   The minimum wage

The UK government introduced a minimum wage in April 1999. In October 2002 the minimum wage stands at £4.20 per hour for workers over the age of 22 years, and £3.50 per hour for workers between the ages of 18 and 21 years. It is estimated to affect 1.3 million people

What are the arguments for and against a minimum wage?

1 It will create unemployment – this can be illustrated using Figure 5.5. The market clearing wage rate is £0W per hour. If a minimum wage is set above this level (£0W$_1$) there will be excess supply of labour or unemployment. The minimum wage is a rigidity introduced into the market which is preventing the market from clearing

   But Figure 5.5 tells us little about the effect of a particular minimum wage. For some occupations a minimum wage of £4.20 per hour will be well below the market clearing rate of £0W and therefore will have no impact on the market at all. It will only affect the low paid occupations. The actual effect of a minimum wage will depend upon the shapes of the demand and supply curves shown in Figure 5.5 – there may be other factors like the elasticity of demand which will influence the impact of the minimum wage. If the very low paid receive an increase in their wages, they will have greater spending power and so the demand for goods and services will rise. As the demand for labour is a derived demand, there will be a corresponding increase in the demand for labour – thus using up the excess supply of labour. A study in 2002[6] found that the introduction of the minimum wage had had no significant adverse effects on the level of employment.

2 It will increase costs to the employers who will pass these increased costs on to the consumer in the form of higher prices. It was estimated that a minimum wage of £3.60 (when it was first introduced) would add around 0.75 per cent to the national wage bill, and about 1 per cent to the annual rate of inflation.

   But there is no evidence that this happened. Employers are faced with a choice – instead of increasing prices to consumers they could accept lower profits or attempt to increase productivity in line with wage increases. In fact a minimum wage might reduce costs of recruiting and training if it reduces labour turnover.

3 A minimum wage might encourage employers to cut back spending on training.

   But one way of increasing the productivity of workers so that the minimum wage does not have inflationary consequences is to train workers, so the minimum wage might actually increase the provision of training.

There is no evidence that the introduction of the minimum wage in the UK had any of the negative effects claimed by dissenters. The minimum wage in 2001 in the UK ($6 per hour) was higher than the average for the EU ($5 per hour) and the USA ($5.20). There were considerable differences between countries within the EU, for example the minimum wage in Luxembourg in 2001 was $8.50 per hour while in Spain it stood at $1.70. These do not measure purchasing power however.

Immobility of labour

People are geographically immobile for a variety of reasons:

- The cost of moving. It is an expensive business to move to another part of the country, particularly to areas where housing costs are high, like London.
- There may be shortages of housing in certain areas, or it may be difficult or even impossible to sell a house in other areas.
- There will be many social ties in the form of family and friends that people may be reluctant to leave.
- For people with children, schooling will be important. For example, parents are reluctant to relocate when their children are working for GCSE or A-level examinations.

People are also immobile occupationally for the following reasons:

- Some jobs require some natural ability that an individual might not possess (e.g. entertainers, footballers, and so on).
- Training is required by many occupations (e.g. doctors, engineers). Without this training an individual could not do the job and the length of training might be a deterrent.
- To enter some occupations (like starting up your own business), a certain amount of capital is required. In some cases the amount of capital needed will be very high (dry cleaning, for example, where the machines are expensive to purchase), and for many this might prove to be a barrier to mobility.

In order to help people to be more mobile so that the labour market works more smoothly, the government over the years has evolved a variety of policies. Job centres and the like attempt to overcome the lack of knowledge of jobs that are available. Training schemes are offered so that people can retrain, and relocation allowances can be paid to alleviate the cost of moving. Government policy in this area is considered more fully in Chapter 14.

These are some of the factors that determine the number of people who are available in an economy for producing goods and services. However, it is not just the quantity of labour but also its quality that is important. The quality of the workforce is determined by many factors already mentioned, but most importantly by the level of education and training of the workforce.

The level of education and training of the workforce

An educated workforce is necessary for an advanced industrial nation, in terms of both general qualifications and specific job-related training. The United Kingdom does not fare well in either of these areas compared with other countries. Table 5.5 shows the situation with regard to school qualifications, and although there has been a dramatic improvement over the period shown, it is still true that in 2000 more than 20 per cent of school leavers in the United Kingdom left school with no formal qualifications.

Table 5.5 Percentage leaving school with different educational qualifications

Qualifications	1977/78	1980/81	1983/84	1987/88	1991/92	1996/97*	1999/00*
One or more A-levels	16.8	17.8	18.9	20.6	29.6	18.8	25.9
One or more GCSEs	35.2	35.7	37.0	38.5	39.4	58.9	53.6
No qualification	48.0	46.6	44.1	41.0	31.0	22.3	20.4

Source: Adapted from Table 6.5 *Annual Abstract of Statistics*, 2001, Office for National Statistics, UK.
Note: *Figures exclude sixth form colleges in England which were reclassified as FE Colleges in 1993.

Government policies through the 1960s were designed to increase the proportion of those staying on at school after the statutory minimum leaving age. And although the staying-on rate at school has improved in the United Kingdom it still remains low internationally. More recently the thrust of policy has been towards vocational courses for the over-16s. There have been many initiatives in this area in recent years. Table 5.6 gives a summary of a few of the more recent ones.

National Vocational Qualifications (NVQs) are qualifications that cover a specific skill, like plumbing or carpentry, while General National Vocational Qualifications (GNVQs) are more general and indicate a broad knowledge of an area like the built environment. NVQ level 2 equates to GNVQ intermediate level and is equivalent to 5 GCSE grades A* to C. NVQ level 3 equates to GNVQ advanced level and is equivalent to 2 GCE A-levels, and level 4 equates to a degree or higher level vocational qualification.

In 1991 the National Targets for Education and Training were started following an initiative from the CBI. These were supported by the government, and the National Advisory Council for Education and Training Targets (NACETT) was constituted in 1993. Targets have been set for national learning in England (*see* Table 5.7). Wales and Scotland have set their own targets.

For information on training and targets see *www. NACETT.org.uk*

Table 5.6 Examples of vocational courses for over-16s

Year	Scheme	Description
1983	Youth Training Scheme	Provided work-related training for 16-and 17-year olds, both on and off the job. Largely introduced to fill the gap left by the demise of the traditional apprenticeships.
1985	Certificate of Pre-vocational Education	Full time vocational courses for over-16s containing an element of work experience.
1992	National Vocational Qualifications (NVQs), General National Vocational Qualifications (GNVQs)	A comprehensive system of vocational qualifications at four levels of achievement.
1998	Work-based Training for Young People	This replaced the Youth Training Scheme with the aim of ensuring that young people have access to post-compulsory education or training.

Table 5.7	National learning targets for England for 2002	

Age	Target	Progress towards target end 2000
11-year olds	■ 80% to achieve the expected standard for their age in literacy	75%
	■ 75% for mathematics	72%
16-year olds	■ 50% of 16-year olds getting 5 higher grade GCSEs	49.2%
	■ 95% getting at least 1 GCSE	94.4%
Young people	■ 85% of 19-year olds to be qualified to NVQ level 2 or its equivalent	75.3%
	■ 60% of 21-year olds to be qualified to NVQ level 3 or its equivalent	53.7%
Adults	■ 50% of adults to be qualified to NVQ level 3 or its equivalent	47.2%
	■ 28% of adults to be qualified to level 4 or its equivalent	27.2%
	■ a 7% reduction in non-learners (the Learning Participation Target)	
Organisations	■ 45% of organisations with 50 employees or more to be recognised as Investors in People	32%
	■ 10,000 organisations with 10 to 49 employees to be recognised as Investors in People	6,147

Table 5.7 also shows the progress towards these targets by the end of 2000. It is clear that although achievement is close to the targets, further progress is required to meet these targets. In order to aid this many policies have been implemented, including:

- the National Literacy and Numeracy Strategy launched in 1998 which provide for a dedicated literacy hour and one mathematics lesson every day for primary school children;
- the use of Education Action Zones in areas of educational disadvantage;
- the introduction of the Education Maintenance Allowance which offers financial incentives to young people from low income homes to remain in education;
- an increased number of Modern Advanced Apprenticeships;
- the ill-fated Individual Learning Accounts, which aimed to provide financial aid to those returning to learning. The scheme had to be suspended in November 2001 due to alleged large-scale fraud.

In the UK approximately 27 per cent of young people drop out of education at the age of 16. This is fairly high on international comparisons, the comparable figures are given in brackets for Sweden (4 per cent), Germany (8 per cent), Japan (9 per cent), France (10 per cent) and the USA (17 per cent). In an attempt to improve this situation, new vocational courses are to be introduced to run alongside GCSEs and which will feed into the vocational A-levels to provide a new educational spine from 14 years up to 19 years. These measures are also designed to help overcome the 'snobbery' about academic subjects over vocational courses. It is estimated that 65 per cent of young people in Germany obtain an apprenticeship certificate, while in the UK the figure is less than 20 per cent.

As well as school and higher education, job-related training is important in improving the quality of the workforce. Training at work can be of two types: on-the-job training and off-the-job training. There has been the development of a competence-based approach to training, which partly stems from the introduction of **NVQs**. The system is designed to be easily understood and to provide workers with the skills that are needed by industry. It is designed to unify what is a very diverse system of qualifications existing in the United Kingdom at present.

The government sponsors training programmes in the UK for adults, aimed at long-term unemployed or disadvantaged adults. Successful completion of these programmes has increased over time, and the proportion still unemployed after the scheme has fallen from 53 per cent in 1990–1 to 48 per cent in 1999/2000.

The government also sponsors training for young people through the Work-based Training for Young People scheme. This includes Foundation Modern Apprenticeships and Advanced Modern Apprenticeships. These schemes are designed for the 16–25-year age group and aim to provide training leading to recognised vocational qualifications – Foundation Modern Apprenticeships at NVQ level 2 and Advanced Modern Apprenticeships at NVQ level 3. In March 2001, there were 266 000 young people on work-based training schemes in England.

The Investors in People initiative has had an impact upon training as it is based on four principles:

■ top-level commitment to develop all employees;
■ regular reviews of training and development of all employees;
■ action to train and develop employees throughout their employment; and
■ evaluation of the outcome of training as a basis for continuous improvement.

By January 2002, 24,259 UK organisations had achieved recognition under the standard, representing 24 per cent of the UK workforce.

The number of women receiving job-related training has increased over the last twenty years relative to men, and there has been a gradual increase for both sexes over the time period. There are significant differences between industries, with, for example, the service sector having a much higher level of training than agriculture, forestry and fishing, and between occupations.

Training is an important issue not just for school leavers and the unemployed but for all employees. As Table 5.8 shows, 61 per cent of employers in England reported that an increase in skills was necessary in their workforce in 2000 – only marginally better than for 1999. The skills which were most deficient were technical and practical, communication, customer handling and team working. About half of the companies surveyed felt that these skills shortages were at least partly their fault because of lack of training. What is encouraging from Table 5.8 is that the percentage of companies both with training plans and budgets has increased since 1999, as has the percentage of companies providing off-the-job training.

| Table 5.8 | Changes in skill needs and employers' commitment to training, England |

	Reporting an increase in skills needed in an average employee	*With a training plan*	*With a training budget*	*Providing off-the-job training in the last 12 months*
1999	62	32	25	34
2000	61	39	27	41

Source: Adapted from Table 3.26, *Social Trends*, 2000 and 2001, Office for National Statistics, UK.

For information on training schemes see
www.dfes.gov.uk
www.warwick.ac.uk/ier (Institute for Employment Research)
www.nfer.ac.uk (National Foundation for Employment Research)

Occupational structure of the population

There will be changes in the occupational structure of the population over time. These will be caused by changes in industrial structure and technological change. There has been an increase in the number of non-manufacturing jobs at the same time as a fall in the number of manufacturing jobs. There are more women in the workforce now because there has been an increase in demand for the types of goods that have been produced by women. There has also been an increase in the availability and quality of labour-saving devices in the home, which has released women into the workforce. There has been a decrease in the average family size so that if women leave the workforce to look after their children they now do so for a shorter period of time. There has also been a change in attitude towards women working.

Figure 5.6 shows the structure of occupations in the UK by gender. There is a higher percentage of men than women in the professional/managerial occupations and there are more men working in craft-related occupations than women. Women are clearly concentrated in clerical/selling-type occupations.

There has been a fundamental change in the nature of working life throughout the 1980s and on into the 1990s, and this has to do with the notion of 'flexibility'. There has been an increase in the incidence of part-time working, for both men and women, and an increased use of temporary contract and flexible working patterns. In 2000 6.9 million people worked part time in the UK; this represents about a fifth of the workforce. Approximately 3.1 million people were self-employed. It is estimated that by the year 2003, 45 per cent of all employees will be working part time (*see* mini case on call centres).

| Figure 5.6 | Occupational structure of UK workforce by gender, 2000 |

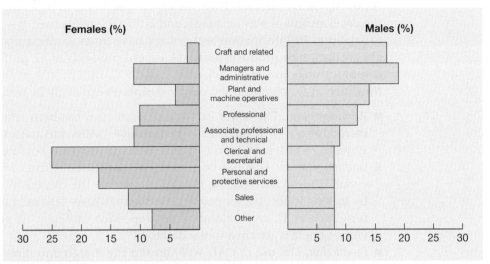

Source: Adapted form Table 4.12, *Social Trends*, 2001, Office for National Statistics, UK

Technology

Technology is defined as 'the sum of knowledge of the means and methods of producing goods and services' (*Penguin Dictionary of Economics*). It is increasingly science based, encompassing things like chemistry, physics and electronics, and refers to the organisation of production as well as the actual techniques of production itself. Technological change leads to the introduction of new products, changes in the methods and organisation of production, changes in the quality of resources and products, new ways of distributing the product and new ways of storing and disseminating information. Technology has a very big impact upon the world of business in all of these areas and has an important effect on the level and type of investment that takes place in an economy and therefore the rate of economic growth (for a fuller discussion of technology, *see* Chapter 15 below).

Technological change

There have been massive changes in technology in the past ten years. This section will consider a few of these and assess their impact upon business and the economy.

Information technology

Developments in information technology have had the effect of transforming existing business activities as well as creating entirely new ones, involving the collection, handling, analysis and transmission of information. There has been a massive increase in the demand for information, and, on the supply side, continued advances in the miniaturisation of components. These will continue even when the capabilities of the silicon chip have been exhausted, with the development of super-conductors and optronics. There are also the advances in the computing area such as the development of new languages and artificial intelligence.

Advances in information technology have many impacts upon business. They are creating new products and making old products more profitable to produce through things like **computer-aided design (CAD)**. The effects they are having on the different functions carried out by businesses can easily be seen:

■ *Administration*. The administration of businesses has been revolutionised by the introduction of information technology. Most businesses have computer systems, records have been computerised and filing has become unnecessary.
■ *Communication*. This has been eased by the introduction of fax machines and e-mail. Video conferencing has contributed to the change in working practices by making it possible for people to work anywhere. Telecommunications companies, such as BT, are working on desktop video conferencing systems, where the video camera is attached to the desktop PC.
■ *Production*. The use of CAD will shorten the design and planning phase of the product and shorten the life cycle of the product. Japan applied this very early on in the field of consumer electronics and many of the products are withdrawn from sale and redesigned within a very short period of time.
■ *Storage and distribution*. The computerisation of stock control has had implications for the storage requirements of firms. It has made implementation of the just-in-time method of stock control possible. This is easily seen in the case of supermarkets where the use of bar-codes on products makes it possible to carry out a stock check of a whole supermarket in a matter of hours. The shelves can then be loaded up as the stock check continues. Similarly, the use of bar-codes with Electronic Point of Sale (EPOS) makes stock control simpler.
■ *Electronic Funds Transfer at Point of Sale (EFTPOS)*. This system has also had a revolutionary effect in the area of retailing. Most shops now accept credit cards or Switch cards where funds are immediately transferred from bank accounts to the supermarkets.
■ *The Internet*. The potential for the Internet is enormous although it is still in its infancy. In February 2002 there were an estimated 544.2 million people wired to the Internet, 165 million in the USA. Japan had 50 million users, Germany 30 million and the UK 33 million.

Other technological developments

■ *New materials*. There are two main developments in this area: the development of materials in the high-tech industries like technical ceramics and the upgrading of materials used in lower-range products like coated sheet metal.
■ *Biotechnology*. This is expected to have wide-ranging effects on many fields. The development of new products like computers that can imitate the activity of the brain can shorten the development process for certain products by speeding up existing processes.
■ *Energy*. The kind of developments that can take place in this field are the use of superconductors to transport electricity and research which might make solar energy a viable source of energy.

These are the new emerging industries which are creating new products and making old products more profitable to produce. It has been estimated that the output of these emerging industries is 20 per cent for consumption within the industries themselves, 20 per cent for final consumption and 60 per cent for consumption in the traditional industries.

Mini case   Call centres

The call centre market is one which is growing at an estimated rate of 40 per cent per annum globally. In the USA telephone based marketing is used by 83 per cent of the Fortune 100 companies while in the UK 27 per cent of companies make some use of telephone based marketing. The figure for Europe is much lower – a half of all call centres in Europe are in the UK.[7] Call centres are used for customer services and marketing and the take-up rate varies greatly by sector – travel and financial services being two of the fastest growing areas. There are a number of reasons for this growth:

- Firstly, advances in technology in the last decades of the twentieth century which have led to the integration of the telephone, computer technology and the Internet.
- Deregulation in the telephone markets which has served to bring down the costs of telephone calls. This might partly explain why the industry is more advanced in the USA and the UK than in Europe, where telephone markets are more regulated.
- Increased flexibility in the labour market – call centres are usually open 24 hours a day and there is a need for flexible shift patterns to meet the fluctuations in demand. Again this might partly explain lower take up in Europe where labour market legislation is more restrictive.
- There has been an increase in the propensity of people to use the telephone for purchasing and an increase in the number of people wired up to the Internet. Telephone based activity and the Internet are often not substitutes for one another in the process of purchase but are complementary.
- In the 1980s and 1990s there was increased emphasis on the process of cost control and an increase in levels of outsourcing of activities. These factors work to the benefit of call centres.
- The location of call centres is irrelevant so companies can site call centres to take advantage of lower labour costs and any incentives offered as part of regional policy. This partly explains why in the UK many call centres are located in Scotland (where incentives are high) and in India (where wages are low).

There is a downside to this growth however. Call centre work is often seen as boring, repetitive, stressful, alienating and low-level employment. The reputation of the call centre industry as an employer is still not very good even though conditions might have changed from the early years of the industry. There remains a very high turnover of labour which leads to increased costs of training and high levels of absenteeism. Labour costs are a very high element in the cost structure of a call centre and so these need to be taken seriously.

For more information on call centres see *http:/www.cca.org.uk*

Technology and investment

The second input into the production process after people is capital. In economics, capital has a special meaning; it refers to all man-made resources which are used in production. Capital is usually divided into working capital and fixed capital. Working capital consists of the stocks of raw materials and components used in producing things. Fixed capital consists of buildings, plant and machinery. The main difference between the two is that fixed capital gives a flow of services over a long period of time, while working capital needs to be replaced on a regular basis. Because of its nature, working capital is much more mobile than fixed capital (i.e. it can be used for other purposes much more easily). Capital is a 'stock' of goods used in the production process, a stock which is continually being used and therefore needing to be replaced. This stock provides a flow of services for the production process.

Capital includes a wide diversity of items, including factory premises, machinery, raw materials in stock, transport vehicles and partly finished goods. As well as these, there is what is often called 'social capital', which refers to capital that is owned by the community such as schools and hospitals. There is also spending on the infrastructure, which is important to all businesses rather than being linked to one particular business. The main components of this are transport, energy, water and information. The transportation system is obviously very important to a developed economy. Road, rail, air and water are used to transport goods, services and raw materials. The capital stock in transport in the UK was £124.9 billion in 2000 (in 1995 prices). The same is true for energy and water; both are used by industry in great quantities, and a good infrastructure in these is essential. The information distribution system is also part of the infrastructure and would include telephone systems and the post.

| Table 5.9 | Gross capital stock in 1996 and 2000 by industry at 1995 replacement cost (£ billion) |

Industry	1996	2000	% change
Agriculture, forestry and fishing	46.6	44.6	−4.3
Mining and quarrying	83.9	76.7	−8.6
Manufacturing	371.2	380.2	+2.4
Electricity, gas and water supply	187.9	193.0	+2.7
Construction	23.2	25.4	+9.5
Wholesale and retail; repairs; hotels and restaurants	177.6	221.2	+24.5
Transport and storage	106.1	124.9	+17.7
Post and telecommunications	77.5	104.9	+35.4
Finance intermediation, real estate and business activities/services	258.4	331.7	+28.4
Other services	485.1	527.2	+8.7
Dwellings	1030.2	1102.9	+7.1
Total			+10.0

Source: Adapted from Table 9.10 UK National Accounts, 2001, Office for National Statistics, UK.

Table 5.9 shows the capital stock of the United Kingdom in 1996 and 2000 by industry. The level of capital stock increased over the period by 10.0 per cent, but there are marked differences between industries, ranging from a growth of 35.4 per cent in post and telecommunications to a fall of minus 8.6 per cent in mining and quarrying.

The increase in the stock of capital over time is called investment. Investment will serve to increase the productive potential of the firm and the economy. Investment usually refers to the purchase of new assets, as the purchase of second-hand assets merely represents a change in ownership and therefore does not represent a change in productive potential. Investment is important for the firm as it is a mechanism for growth; it is an integral part of the innovation process and can have disastrous results for a firm if an investment goes wrong. Generally the higher the level of investment in a country the higher will be the level of economic growth.[8]

Total or gross investment can be broken down into replacement investment, which is investment to replace obsolete or worn-out machines, and new invest-ment, which is any investment over and above this. This includes investment by firms, individuals (in dwellings mainly) and governments. It can be seen that the level of investment is affected by the state of the economy. There was a fall in the level of investment in the early 1980s and again in the early 1990s, both of these as a result of the recession in the economy (*see* Figure 5.8). The level of investment in 2000 represented 20 per cent of GDP.

There is an important relationship between investment and technological change which runs in both directions. Investment can form the basis for improve-ments in technology while improved technology which brings about new ways of producing goods will lead to greater investment. For private firms the main deter-minants of the level of investment will be the rate of technological change and the scope for extra profit as a result of these changes.

Figure 5.7   Categories of investment in the UK in 2000

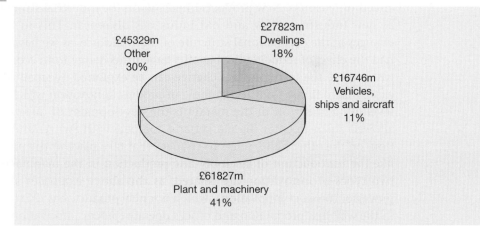

Source: Adapted from Table 15.20, *Annual Abstract of Statistics*, 2001, Office for National Statistics, UK.

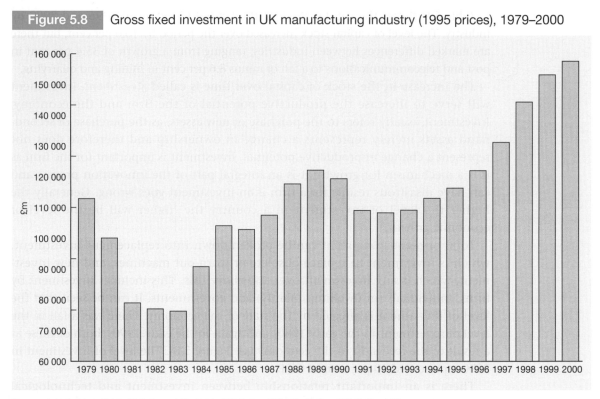

Figure 5.8 Gross fixed investment in UK manufacturing industry (1995 prices), 1979–2000

Source: Adapted from Table 15.2, *Annual Abstract of Statistics*, Office for National Statistics, UK.

Innovation and technology

There are two types of innovation that can occur as a result of technological change: **product innovation** and **process innovation**. Product innovation is the development of new products, like the microprocessor, which will have far-reaching effects on business. New products impact upon the industrial structure of a country, as new industries grow and old industries disappear. This in turn will lead to changes in the occupational structure of the workforce, as we have seen. It has even had the effect of reducing the benefits large firms derive from economies of scale in cases where the technological change can be exploited by small firms as well as it can by large firms. Another example of product innovation which has affected the level of competition in the market is the development of quartz watches, which allowed Japan to enter the market and compete with Switzerland. Process innovation, on the other hand, refers to changes that take place in the production process, like the introduction of assembly-line production in the manufacture of cars. The two types of innovation are related, as the above examples show. The microprocessor (product innovation), which is a new product, has led to massive changes in the way that production and offices operate (process innovation).

Not all innovation is technological in nature; for example, changes in fashion in clothing are not technological. Innovative activity is important for all industry whether manufacturing or non-manufacturing. In some industries (e.g. pharmaceuticals, computers), innovation is essential if firms wish to remain competitive. A recent CBI survey of 408 companies in the UK found that the innovation activities of 84 per cent of the sample had been adversely affected by the economic slow-down post-September 11.[9]

For further information on research by the CBI see
www.cbi.org.uk (Confederation of British Industry)

Research and development

Most, but not all, technological changes have occurred through the process of research and development (R&D). 'Research' can be theoretical or applied, and 'development' refers to the using of the research in the production process. Most research and development carried out by private companies is directed towards applied research and development. It is designed to develop new products and production processes which will render production more profitable. It is also aimed at improving existing products and processes. Most basic theoretical research carried out in the United Kingdom is financed from public sources and is undertaken in places like the universities.

Table 5.10 shows that the level of research and development expenditure in the UK in 2000 was £9405 million, which represents around 2 per cent of GDP. It can be seen that there are wide differences in expenditure between industries, with manufacturing involved in a great deal more research and development spending than non-manufacturing. Even within the broad category of manufacturing there are wide differences, with chemicals accounting for more than a quarter of the expenditure. Table 5.11 shows the sources from which R&D is financed. As can be seen the majority of R&D is financed by companies themselves. If R&D is split into civil and defence spending, it is clear that the government finances the majority of defence R&D, as would be expected.

For information on R&D see *www.oecd.org* or *http://europa.eu.int/comm.eurostat*

Table 5.10 Spending on R & D (£ million) in 2000 (1995 prices)

Product group	£ million	% of total
All product groups	9405	100
All products of manufacturing industry	7236	77
Chemicals industries	2690	29
Mechanical engineering	671	7
Electrical machinery	1213	13
Aerospace	955	10
Transport	904	10
Other manufactured products	803	8
Non-manufactured products	2169	23

Source: Adapted from Table 19.4, *Annual Abstract of Statistics*, 2001, Office for National Statistics, UK.

| Table 5.11 | Sources of funds for R&D within industry in the UK, 1985, 1989, 1990, 1993, 1996 and 1999 (1995 prices) |

	1985	*1989*	*1990*	*1993*	*1996*	*1999*
Total (£ million)	5121.6	7649.8	8082.4	9069.0	9362.0	10231.0
Government funds (%)	23	17	17	12	10	12
Overseas funds (%)	11	13	15	15	22	22
Mainly own funds (%)	66	69	68	72	69	66

Source: Adapted from Table 19.4 *Annual Abstract of Statistics*, 2001, Office for National Statistics, UK.

Figure 5.9 shows that the UK fares badly in international comparisons of research and development spending.

In an attempt to increase the level of R&D spending, the UK government introduced R&D tax credits for small companies in the 2000 budget. This scheme was extended to all companies in 2002. The tax credits bring tax relief for R&D spending, but as yet the take-up rate has been very low.

Limits to technological change

Technological change has many effects on the economy and the environment and if uncontrolled can lead to problems, like high levels of unemployment or the exhaustion of natural resources. One area of concern is energy. The world's stock of

| Figure 5.9 | R&D spending as a percentage of GDP, all sectors, selected countries, 2000 |

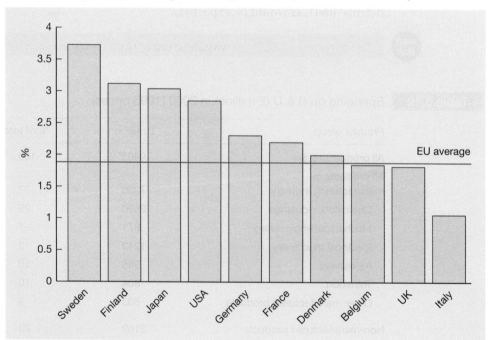

Source: *Eurostat Yearbook*, 2001.

energy is finite and we are still heavily dependent upon fuel which was formed millions of years ago. The development of nuclear power again represents a finite source of energy, and also carries with it other problems like the disposal of nuclear waste and the possibility of accidents. For these and other reasons the scale of technological change needs to be controlled.

It is also the case that technological change can lead to high levels of unemployment in industries that are in decline. This type of unemployment often takes on a regional bias as the older traditional industries tend to be located in particular parts of the country. Technological unemployment is in some respects inevitable as in a changing world it would be expected that new industries would emerge and old industries die. The problem can be tackled by the government and industry through retraining, but what is also needed is a new and more flexible view of work where less time is spent working and more on leisure. Technological change can also give rise to the opposite problem of skill shortage in new industries, where particular skills are required. Technological change has not led to the massive increase in unemployment predicted by many in the 1970s and 1980s.

Natural resources

In economics, natural resources are put under the heading of land as a factor of production. It would include all natural resources like the soil, minerals, oil, forests, fish, water, the sun, and so on. The uneven distribution of natural resources throughout the world means that they can be used as economic and political weapons.

Although the area of land in a country is fixed, land as a factor of production is not completely fixed in supply as more land can be made available through land reclamation schemes and better irrigation. The productivity of agricultural land can be increased by the use of fertilisers. It is true, however, that our natural resources are in finite supply. And often their true extent is not known with certainty.

It is in the area of natural resources that the distinction between renewable and non-renewable resources is most important. Natural resources can be either. Land can often be used for more than one purpose – for example, agricultural land can be used to grow one crop one year and another the next – but oil, once it is used up, cannot be used again. And even though land can be used for more than one purpose it is still immobile both geographically and between different uses. Land can be used for agriculture or industry, but using it for one purpose makes it more difficult to use it for another. If a factory is built on a piece of land, it would be both expensive and time consuming to clear the land for farming.

Table 5.12 show the changing usage of agricultural land in the UK between 1971 and 2000. There are slight differences between the years, most notably the inclusion of 'set aside' land in the 1993, 1997 and 2000 columns. This is part of EU Common Agricultural Policy where farmers are paid not to use land in an attempt to reduce the overproduction of agricultural goods.

| Table 5.12 | The use of agricultural land in 1971, 1993 and 2000 in the UK (thousand hectares) |

	1971	1993	1997	2000
Crops	4838	4519	4990	4709
Bare fallow	74	47	29	33
Grasses	7240	6770	6687	6767
Rough grazing*	6678	5840	5878	5803
Set aside	–	677	306	572
Woodland and other land on agricultural holdings	285	678	763	789
Total	19 115	18 531	18 653	18 579

* Includes sole right rough grazing and common rough grazing

Source: Adapted from Table 20.3, *Annual Abstract of Statistics*, 2001, Office for National Statistics, UK.

Protection of the environment

Increased knowledge of the effects of depletion of natural resources has led to increased environmental awareness amongst the population. There has been an increased interest in conservation and recycling and the search for alternative forms of energy. A survey by the Department of the Environment recently found that 90 per cent of the adult population in the UK were either 'fairly concerned' or 'very concerned' about the environment. The issues which caused concern included traffic congestion, global warming, air and water pollution and depletion of the ozone layer. This change in public opinion has already had a major impact on the way in which business operates and is likely to have even bigger effects (*see* Chapter 16).

The government in the UK has a variety of targets for environmental protection. For example: it is committed to cutting the emission of carbon dioxide by 20 per cent by 2010 (in line with the Kyoto agreement); it wants 10 per cent of the UK's electricity to come from renewable sources by 2010; local authorities are expected to recycle or compost 30 per cent of household rubbish by 2010; it has a target of 20 per cent of plastic to be recycled by 2006. Progress towards these targets (and others) is variable but the level of recycling in the UK is low by international standards. It is often the case that legislation designed to protect the environment has the opposite effect. In the case of the target for composting, because the government has not set out safety standards for compost local authorities worried that their compost might not meet any standards set have resorted to burning household rubbish instead. EU directives that all fridges and cars should be recycled has led to fridge and car mountains springing up all over the place as people dump them rather than pay the cost of recycling (*see* Chapter 3). A new directive from the EU on waste electronic and electrical equipment coming into force in 2004 which will make it illegal to send computers, mobile phones, TVs and radios to landfill sites will worsen this situation. Producers of these items have predicted that as a result of this directive prices are likely to rise by around 5 per cent. Environmental groups try to counter such arguments by estimating how many jobs could be created by shifting investment from private transport to public transport, boosting recycling and organic farming and schemes to clear up the environment.

web link Pressure groups concerned with the environment include *www.foe.co.uk* (Friends of the Earth) and *www.greenpeace.org*

The UK is not well endowed with high-grade minerals; the main natural resource is energy. There is a good deposit of coal and the discovery of North Sea oil and gas has made the UK self-sufficient in energy supplies. The usage of energy has doubled since 1970 but as Table 5.13 shows there has been a change in the relative importance of the different sources of energy.

Coal has lost its place to oil and gas as the most important sources of energy. The increase in the usage of both oil and gas is due to the discovery of North Sea oil and gas in the UK. The biggest single user of energy in the UK is transport (33 per cent of energy produced), followed by the domestic sector (28 per cent) and industry (20 per cent).

There is great variation in the fuels used for the generation of electricity across Europe as Table 5.14 (overleaf) shows.

The amount of electricity generated by nuclear power has increased by around 6 per cent since 1990 and several EU countries use it as their primary generator of electricity. The use of nuclear power creates lower emissions of greenhouse gases (*see* mini case study on pollution in Chapter 11) but increases the risk of accidental leakage of radioactivity and raises the problem of the disposal of radioactive waste. The use of coal and oil in the generation of electricity has fallen and the use of gas has increased. The biggest change between 1990 and 2000 is in the use of hydraulic and wind generation of electricity. In 1990 this did not feature as a separate category but was included under the heading of 'other', which made up only 8.4 per cent of the generation of electricity.

The OECD predicts that the energy requirements of western Europe will increase; the proportion of this being met from oil will fall, the deficiency being taken up by natural gas. There is not expected to be any growth in nuclear power over the next decade although this may change in the long term, as the non-renewable energy sources are used up. There is a demand for alternative sources of energy. The alternatives of hydro, wind and solar energy sources will also grow in importance. In the UK the government has tried to promote the search for

| Table 5.13 | Primary usage of energy in the UK (heat supplied basis); percentage of total |

	1950	1970	1984	1993	1997	2000
Solid fuel	78.6	30.7	11.7	8.9	6.6	16.2
Gas	5.9	10.7	31.8	31.5	34.5	40.3
Oil	12.2	47.2	42.1	43.4	42.0	32.6
Electricity	3.3	11.4	14.2	16.1	16.9	10.8

Source: Adapted from Table 21.4, *Annual Abstract of Statistics*, various, Office for National Statistics, UK.

| Table 5.14 | Fuel used for electricity generation, selected EU countries, 2000 (%) |

	Nuclear	Coal	Oil	Gas	Hydraulic and wind	Other *
France	76	6	2	1	13	1
Belgium	55	17	3	18	2	5
Sweden	46	1	2	0	47	3
Spain	30	28	9	12	19	2
Germany	29	28	1	35	5	3
UK	28	34	2	32	2	2
The Netherlands	4	27	4	57	1	7
EU average	34	20	8	22	14	3

* Includes geothermal, derived gas and biomass.
Source: *Social Trends*, 2001. Crown copyright 2001. Reproduced by permission of the Controller of HMSO and of the Office for National Statistics.

renewable energy sources through projects like the Non-Fossil Fuel Obligation which requires regional electricity boards to obtain a certain percentage of their electricity from clean sources. It also funds experimental work in the search for new sources of energy.

As well as recycling and searching for new sources of energy there is the concept of 'negademand' where the use of less produces negative demand for those commodities. This concept can be applied to energy and water saving, driving, shopping, etc.

web link

For information on the natural environment in the UK see *www.environment-agency.gov.uk* or *www.the-environment-council.org.uk* or *www.business-in-the-environment.org.uk*
In the EU see *www.eea.eu.int* (The European Environment Agency) or *www.europa.eu.int/comm/environment/index*
In the world see *www.oecd.org*

Synopsis

This chapter looked at the three main inputs into the production process: people, technology and natural resources. It considered each in turn and examined their importance to business and the main factors which determine both the quality and the quantity of these factors of production.

People are important in two ways: they are the producers of goods and services, and also the consumers of goods and services. The quantity of human resources available in an economy depends upon things like total population size, participation rates, length of working week and wages. The quality depends upon such things as the level of health care, education and training. There have been significant changes in the labour market over recent years; the case study below considers some of these.

One of the main features of the last 50 years has been the massive changes in technology that have had an enormous impact upon business, resulting in new products and markets and new methods of production and distribution.

As far as natural resources are concerned, the traditional view was that they were fixed in supply and therefore did not receive much consideration. However, with increased environmental awareness there is growing concern that this is not the case and that many of our natural resources are non-renewable and therefore need to be conserved.

Each of the three inputs into the production process has been considered separately but they are interlinked and difficult to separate in reality. It has already been said that the productivity of people will be affected by the technology at their disposal, and this is also true of natural resources. All of the three inputs are 'stocks', from which streams of resources flow to firms. These flows are crucial to business, as without them production could not take place. Both the quantities and qualities of our stocks of these resources are important, as too is the replacement of the stocks that are being used.

Summary of key points

- Three main resources are used in the production of goods and services – labour, capital and land.

- Population size in a country depends upon the birth rate, the death rate and the migration rate.

- The world's population is ageing and this has important implications for all aspects of business.

- The quantity of labour available depends upon population size, regulations in the labour market, the length of the working week and wage levels.

- The level of education and training determines the quality of available labour.

- The quantity and quality of capital depends on the level and type of investment taking place, the extent of research and development and the level of innovation.

- The quantity and quality of land is an important element in the production process and will depend upon many things, including environmental controls.

| CASE STUDY | The effects of an ageing population |

There is no doubt that the world's population is ageing. In 2000 there were 69 million people in the world over the age of 80 years and this is the fastest growing segment of the population (see Table 5.15). By 2050 it is estimated that this figure will have risen to 379 million, which represents 4 per cent of the world's population. In 2000 many countries already had higher percentages of over 80s, including Sweden (5.1 per cent), Norway and Britain (both 4 per cent). In Japan (the fastest ageing country in the 1990s) it is predicted that by 2015 over 25 per cent of the population will be over 65 years of age.

Table 5.15 shows that in all parts of the world the fastest growing segments are the older ones, for the more developed countries reductions in the size of the 0 to 59 age groups are predicted. The predictions are made on the assumption that present trends in life expectancy and fertility rates continue.[10]

Why is the world population ageing?

There are two main causes – increased life expectancy and lower fertility rates. Figure 5.10 shows the fertility rates and Figure 5.11 shows the life expectancy for the same groups of the world's population between 1950 and 2050.

Fertility rates have fallen dramatically in all parts of the world between 1950 and 2000 and this trend is expected to continue into the future. Conversely life expectancy has risen in all parts of the world and is also expected to continue to do so. Putting these two trends together means that the average age of the world population is increasing. (The factors behind these changes have already been discussed in this chapter.) There are of course wide differences between countries but the general picture is one of convergence.

What are the implications of the ageing population for business?

Production

Demand patterns vary a great deal with age and if the grey population is increasing in size businesses will have to respond to the changing demands. If the American experience is repeated in the rest of the world the grey population will spend more on education and leisure services. Many retirees take the opportunity to return to education to pursue their interests.

| Table 5.15 | Projected growth rates between 2000 and 2050, percentages |

	0–14	*15–59*	*60 +*	*80 +*
World	0.15	0.79	2.35	3.40
More developed countries	−0.34	−0.42	1.07	2.23
Less developed countries	0.21	1.01	2.87	4.22
Least developed countries	1.26	2.38	3.37	4.07

Sources: *World Population Prospects*, United Nations, 2000

Figure 5.10 Projected fertility rates between 1950 to 2050

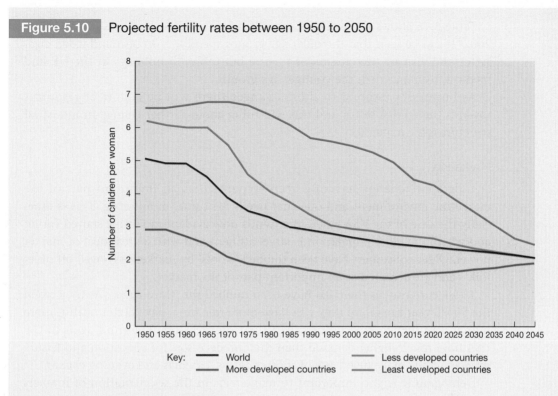

Source: United Nations, 2000

Figure 5.11 Projected life expectancy between 1950 to 2050

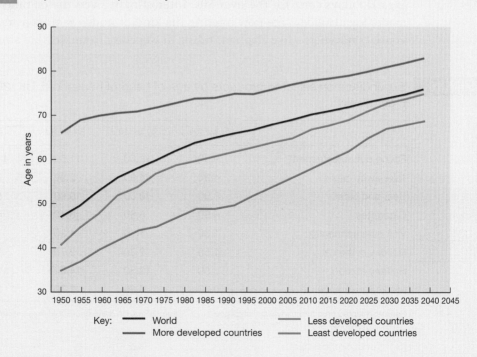

Source: United Nations, 2000

Table 5.16 shows the weekly expenditure on selected products in the UK in 2002. It can be seen that the older age groups spend less on beer and cider, cigarettes and visiting the cinema or theatre but more on holidays in the UK and medical insurance than the younger age groups.

As businesses respond to these changes there will be a shift of resources towards the service sector and this will bring about further change in industrial structure (*see* Chapter 9).

Marketing

Demographic change has long been recognised as an important part of the marketing environment and one that needs continual monitoring. This is especially the case in the USA where the trends now evident in Europe started earlier and where the older population is large, affluent and with a great deal of market power. Older consumers have been dubbed 'woofs' by marketeers – well off older folk – and are accepted as an important part of the market.

Those currently in their 40s have been dubbed the 'third agers'. As they reach the 50–75 year age group they will have more free time, have better health, more money and higher expectations than their predecessors. The third agers in the USA have much higher demand than their predecessors for education and leisure services – they make heavy use of sports centres, cinemas and evening classes.

Demography is also important to marketeers in the segmentation of markets and there are numerous examples of where age is the segregating factor. In recognition of the different needs and wants of the different age groups in the holiday market there is the 18–30 holiday company which caters for young people while Saga Holidays cater for the over 50s. Interestingly given the comments already made, Saga Holidays are now offering the kind of holidays often associated with younger travellers – like elephant riding in Nepal for example.

Table 5.16 Expenditure on selected products by age of head of household, UK, 2002, £ per week

	Under 30	30 to 49	50 to 64	65 +
Eating out at restaurant	9.30	11.60	11.50	11.40
Take away meals	4.90	4.80	2.90	2.20
Beer and cider	9.90	10.60	10.80	5.10
Cigarettes	5.60	6.80	6.10	4.80
Visit cinema/theatre	1.30	1.50	1.30	1.20
Holiday in the UK	1.50	2.30	2.70	5.80
Holiday abroad	5.50	12.50	14.50	11.20
Medical insurance	0.40	0.80	1.70	3.20

Source: Adapted from http://www.statistics.gov.uk/CC1/SearchRes.asp?tem=household+expenditure+age

HRM

A greying population has implications for HR strategies within organisations, especially in those industries which have traditionally employed young people. There will be fewer young people entering the labour market for two reasons: first there are fewer of them and second a higher percentage is now staying on at school. Other sources of labour will need to be found to meet the demand. At the same time people are continuing to retire early, in the USA only a half of men between the ages of 60 and 65 are still working and in some European countries the percentage is much lower. Policies implemented in the 1980s and 1990s by organisations downsizing have created a 'retire early' culture among many, and some pension rules which penalise individuals who wish to work beyond retirement age have worked to exacerbate this. The combination of fewer younger people coming into the workforce and more people leaving early means that employers in many countries are facing a contracting market.

One possibility is the increased participation of older people in the labour force. This means that ageist HRM practices will have to change. Employers often view older workers as more expensive, less flexible and lacking in the required skills, but statistics show that the over 40s age group receives less training than other groups. Many studies in this area have shown that age makes no difference to the ability to acquire new skills with training. It is often the case that older workers are more reliable, are more experienced and have less absenteeism than younger workers. Many employers all around the world are recognising this and are implementing policies which positively encourage older workers.

The employment of older people will call for changes in recruitment practices. The retention of labour will become more important for organisations and therefore training and development will take on greater significance. Work will need to be made more attractive, with more part-time or temporary contracts. This might also overcome the cost implication of having older employees who are higher up incremental pay scales.

From 2006 age discrimination will be banned in the EU under an EU directive but market forces are already making some companies adopt a different approach to older workers. It is likely that the EU will rule in autumn 2002 that retirement age should be abolished for those individuals who wish to continue in work.

Financial

There are financial implications of an ageing population. The Potential Support Ratio (PSR) shows the number of persons aged 15 to 64 years per one person of 65 years and over. It gives an indication of the dependency burden of an ageing population on the working population. This fell from 12:1 to 9:1 between 1950 and 2002 and is forecast to fall further to 4:1 by the year 2050 (*see* Table 5.17).

Again Table 5.17 shows a similar pattern all over the world – there will be an increasing financial burden on people of working age as a result of ageing populations. Within the overall figures there are marked differences. In Japan for

Table 5.17	Projected Potential Support Ratio, 2002 and 2050		
		2002	*2050*
World		9:1	4:1
More developed countries		5:1	2:1
Less developed countries		12:1	5:1
Least developed countries		17:1	10:1

Source: United Nations, 2002

instance, the ratio is forecast to fall from 4:1 in 2002 to 1:1 in 2050. In the USA, where immigration is generally higher (and therefore ageing is less pronounced), the ratio is forecast to fall from 5:1 to 3:1.

This means that a higher proportion of the population will depend upon a smaller proportion of the population for support – in terms of resources for health care and the payment of pensions. Many countries are looking at their pension provisions to try to reduce the cost of dependency. In the UK for example there has been a shift in the burden of pension provision from the state to individuals and many companies have ended their 'final salary' pension schemes. Nevertheless, it is still estimated that to meet the demand for pensions of the ageing population by 2030 the UK needs a 5 per cent annual growth rate in GDP. This is much higher than growth rates have been. In the past in the UK, state pensions have been paid out of current taxation but this is likely to change so that state pensions will be funded from investments. It is also possible that the retirement age will be increased to reduce the cost of dependency.

In addition to the cost of pensions, an increase in the average age of a population has implications for health care and the cost of health care. Although this case study makes the point that the greying population is fitter and healthier than ever before, of course, there are implications for the demand for health care. For example the percentage of 65 year olds in the UK with Altzheimers disease is 5 per cent, and this rises to 20 per cent in the over 80s. Therefore there is a need for greater provision for health care, whether this is done by the state or by individuals.

As well as these major changes the ageing populations will mean changes in:

■ popular culture, which for some time has been dominated by youth
■ crime rates – as most crime is carried out by younger people, crime rates should fall
■ family relationships, with falling birth rates and longer life expectancy the 'beanpole' family structure will become the norm.

It is clear from this discussion that the ageing population being experienced by much of the world has big implications for business in many diverse areas.

Case study questions

1 Think of some examples of goods and services for which demand will rise as a consequence of an ageing population. How should marketeers address this new buyer segment?

2 What type of policies can organisations use to:
 (a) encourage the older worker to stay in employment for longer?
 (b) recruit older workers into the workplace?

web link For information on the ageing population see
www.ARP.org.uk (Association of Retired People over 50)
www.shef.ac.uk/uni/projects/gop/ (Growing Older Programme)
www.ageing.ox.ac.uk (Oxford Institute of Ageing)

Review and discussion questions

1 Why are industries such as electricity 'natural monopolies'? What other examples are there of natural monopolies?

2 Think of one technological advance that has recently been made. What have been the effects of that change on the economy, business and the consumer?

3 In what ways can the general and specific skills of the British workforce be improved?

4 What impact will a much stronger Organisation of Petroleum Exporting Countries (OPEC) have on the market for energy?

5 What impact will increased use of the Internet, both for customer information and purchasing, have on call centres?

Assignments

1 You work in the economic development unit of your local council. The unit is compiling a bid to central government in order to win some resources to improve the basic infrastructure in the locality. Your job is to identify the economic problems that exist in your local town and explain why an increase in resources would overcome the problems. Write a briefing paper to the management committee of the unit on your results.

> **2** You are a member of your local Institute of Personnel and Development branch and have been asked to give a talk on 'Flexibility in Working Practices' to a group of trainee managers from a variety of functional and industrial backgrounds. They are particularly interested in three questions:
> - What is meant by flexibility?
> - Why is flexibility needed?
> - What are the implications of greater flexibility?
>
> (Sources for this would include the second edition of this text and *People Management*, CIPD.)

Notes and references

1 *Annual Abstract of Statistics*, 1999.

2 Series Fm 2, no. 27.

3 *Annual Abstract of Statistics*, 1999.

4 *Social Trends*, 2001.

5 For further reading on this area see Begg, D., Fischer, S. and Dornbusch, R., *Economics*, McGraw-Hill, 1997.

6 See paper entitled 'The impact of the introduction of the minimum wage in UK', by Mark Stewart (www.warwick.ac.uk/res2002/abstracts).

7 See Mintel report on Call Centres (1 October 2001) (www.mintel.co.uk)

8 The relationship between investment and the rate of growth is difficult to prove, but there does seem to be high correlation between the level of investment in a country and its associated level of economic growth. It should be remembered, however, that high correlation does not prove that one thing causes another.

9 *Economic Downturn hits Vital Innovation*, CBI survey, May 2002.

10 For details of the assumptions used in these forecasts and the composition of the groups see World Population Prospects, United Nations, 2000 (www.un.org/esa/population/unpop.htm).

Further reading

Donaldson, P., *Understanding the British Economy*, Penguin, 1991.

Simon, J.L, *The Economics of Population*, Transaction, 1997.

Welford, R. and Starkey, R., *The Earthscan Reader in Business and Sustainable Development*, Earthscan, 2001.

Willaert, D., *World Atlas of Ageing*, WHO, Geneva, 1998.

Worthington, I., Britton, C. and Rees, A., *Economics for Business: Blending Theory and Practice*, Financial Times/Prentice Hall, 2001.

Web links and further questions are available on the website at:
www.booksites.net/worthington

6

The legal environment

Diane Belfitt*

Businesses, like individuals, exist and carry on their activities within a framework of law which derives from custom and practice, from the judicial decisions of the courts and from statutes enacted by governments. This legal environment not only constrains and regulates a firm's operations, but also provides an enabling mechanism through which it is able to pursue its objectives, particularly the achievement of profits through entrepreneurial activity. Like the political and economic environment with which it is intertwined, the legal environment of business is a key influence on the business organisation and an important area of study for students of business. This can be demonstrated by an examination of a number of the fundamental areas in which the law impinges on the operations of an enterprise.

Objectives

■ To gain a broad understanding of the idea of 'law' and the sources from which laws are derived.

■ To examine the court system, including the role of the European Court of Justice.

■ To discuss the basic features of the laws of contract and agency.

■ To analyse the reason for statutory intervention to protect the consumer and some of the principal pieces of legislation in this field.

Key terms

Acceptance	Customs	Principal
Agent	Delegated legislation	Private law
Capacity	Intention to create	Public law
Case law	legal relations	Statute law
Codes of practice	Judicial precedent	Tort
Consideration	Legislation	Trust
Criminal law	Offer	

*We would like to thank Martin Taylor of the School of Law at De Montfort University for his help in updating this chapter.

Introduction

It is almost universally accepted that for a society to exist and function in an ordered way a set of rules is required to regulate human behaviour. Irrespective of whether these rules are laid down in custom or practice or in statute, they constitute a means of regulating and controlling the activities of individuals and groups, and of enforcing minimum standards of conduct – even though they may be ignored or flouted on occasions. This framework of rules and the institutions through which they are formulated and enforced represent what is normally understood as the 'law', which invariably evolves over time in response to changing social, economic and political circumstances (e.g. the influence of pressure groups). As one of the constraining (and enabling) influences on business organisations, this legal environment is an important area of study for students of business, hence the tendency for courses in business-related subjects to have specialist modules or units on different aspects of business law (e.g. contract, agency, property and so on).

The aim of this chapter is not to examine business law in detail or to provide a definitive insight into particular areas of the law as it relates to business organisations. Rather it is to raise the reader's awareness of the legal context within which businesses function and to comment briefly on those aspects of law which regularly impinge on a firm's operations. Students wishing to examine business law in more detail should consult the many specialist texts which have been written in this field, some of which are listed at the end of this chapter.

Classification of law

Laws relating to both individuals and organisations can be classified in a number of ways: international and national, public and private, criminal and civil. In practice there are no hard and fast rules to classification and some categories may overlap (e.g. where a person's behaviour is deemed to infringe different areas of law). Nevertheless, distinguishing laws in these terms serves as an aid to explanation and commentary, as well as helping to explain differences in liabilities and in legal remedies in England and Wales (e.g. a child under the age of 10 cannot be held criminally liable).

Public and private law

Put simply, public law is the law which concerns the state, whether in international agreements or disputes or in the relationship between the state and the individual. Thus public law consists of international treaties and conventions, constitutional law, administrative law and criminal law. In contrast, private law is law governing the relationships between individuals and comprises laws in respect of contract, tort, property, trusts and the family.

Criminal law

Criminal laws relate to a legal wrong (criminal offence) – a breach of a public duty, punishable by the state on behalf of society. Decisions on whether or not to bring a prosecution in a particular instance are taken by the Crown Prosecution Service (in England and Wales) and the matter may or may not involve trial by jury, according to the seriousness of the alleged offence and the plea of the defendant(s). In some cases, the consent of both magistrates and defendants is required for a case to remain in the magistrates' court although this may change in the very near future. Moreover, while the criminal process may also arise from a private prosecution, such prosecutions are rare and, in these cases, the Attorney-General (the government's senior law officer) has the right to intervene if he or she sees fit.

Tort

A **tort** is a civil wrong other than a breach of contract or a breach of trust and is a duty fixed by law on all persons (e.g. road users have a duty in law not to act negligently). The law of tort, therefore, is concerned with those situations where the conduct of one party threatens or causes harm to the interests of another party and the aim of the law is to compensate for this harm. The most common torts are negligence, nuisance, defamation and trespass.

Trusts

A **trust** is generally defined as an 'equitable obligation imposing on one or more persons a duty of dealing with property, over which they have control, for the benefit of other persons who may enforce the obligation'. This property may be in the form of money or stocks and shares or in other types of asset, particularly land, where trusts have become a very common way of permitting persons who are

Mini case   Banking on advice

As the case study at the end of this chapter indicates, banks have duties as well as rights when dealing with the day-to-day affairs of their customers. Failure to discharge these duties, in some circumstances, may be deemed negligent behaviour.

In September 1995 the High Court ruled that Lloyds Bank had been negligent in lending money to two of its customers for use on a speculative property deal which had failed to come off because of a collapse in the property market in the late 1980s. In essence the customers had claimed that the bank owed them a duty of care in advising them on the merits of a loan to invest in property speculation and that it had been in breach of its duty when agreeing to proceed with the loan. In effect the claimants were arguing that they had been badly advised and that this had resulted in a loss which was not only suffered but also reasonably foreseeable.

In finding for the claimants – who were suing Lloyds under the tort of negligence – the judge ruled that the bank manager was in breach of his duty of care in advising them to proceed and that the couple had relied on his advice, including claims made in the bank's promotional literature. While a ruling of this kind sent shock waves through the financial community, it is, as yet, uncertain whether it set a legal precedent. Certainly, this is likely to prove a far more significant question to Lloyds (and other financial institutions) than the £77 000 compensation awarded to the claimants by the High Court.

forbidden to own legal estates in land to enjoy the equitable benefits of ownership. Partnerships, for example, cannot hold property as legal owners, so often several partners will act as trustees for all the partners (as a partnership has no separate corporate identity it cannot own property – see Chapter 7). Similarly, minors may not hold legal estates, so their interests must be protected by a trust, administered by an individual or an institution.

Sources of law

Laws invariably derive from a number of sources including custom, judicial precedent, legislation and international and supranational bodies (e.g. the EU). All of these so-called legal sources of the law can be illustrated by reference to English law, which applies in England and Wales. Where laws made by Parliament are to apply only to Scotland or Northern Ireland the legislation will state this. Similarly, any Act which is to apply to all four home countries will contain a statement to this effect.

Custom

Early societies developed particular forms of behaviour (or 'customs') which came to be accepted as social norms to be followed by the members of the community to which they applied. In England many of these customary rules ultimately became incorporated into a body of legal principles known as the common law. Today customs would be regarded as usage recognised by law, whether by judicial precedent (case law) or through statutory intervention and hence they are largely of historical interest. Occasionally, however, they are recognised by the courts as being of local significance and may be enforced accordingly as exceptions to the general law (e.g. concerning land usage).

Judicial precedent

Much of English law is derived from judicial precedent (previous decisions of the courts). The present system of binding precedent, however, is of fairly recent origin, dating from the latter part of the nineteenth century, when advances in recording legal judgments and a reorganisation of the court structure facilitated its general acceptance.

In essence, judicial precedent is based on the rule that the previous decisions of a higher court must be followed by the lower courts – hence the significance of the court structure. In any judgment will be found a number of reasons, arguments, explanations and cases cited and these must all be considered carefully by judges to determine whether there are material differences in the case before the court and the earlier decision. To reach a decision, the court must find what is termed the *ratio decidendi* of the previous case. Put very simply, the *ratio* of a case are the essential steps in the legal reasoning which led the court to make that particular decision. Anything which cannot be regarded as a *rationes* is termed *obiter dicta* or 'things said by the way'. The whole of a dissenting judgment in a case is regarded as *obiter*. *Obiter dicta* are not binding but may be regarded as persuasive arguments if the facts of the case permit.

Clearly there are times when, perhaps because of the position of a court in the hierarchy, decisions are not to be regarded as binding precedent. However, if the judgment has been delivered by a jurisdiction which has a common law system (e.g. Canada, Australia) or, most importantly, by the Judicial Committee of the Privy Council, then those decisions will be regarded as being of persuasive precedent, and may be used to help the court reach its own decision.

Legislation

A substantial proportion of current law – including laws governing the operations of business organisations – derives from legislation or statute, enacted by the Queen (or King) in Parliament. As Chapter 3 indicated, the initiative in this sphere lies effectively with the government of the day which can virtually guarantee a bill will become law, if it has a working majority in the House of Commons.

Apart from a limited number of bills proposed by backbench MPs (private members' bills), the vast majority of legislation emanates from government and takes the form of Acts of Parliament or delegated legislation. Acts of Parliament are those bills which have formally been enacted by Parliament and have received the Royal Assent and, except where overridden by EU law, they represent the supreme law of the land. In addition to creating new laws (e.g. to protect the consumer), statutes may also be used to change or repeal existing laws. In some instances they may be designed to draw together all existing law (a consolidating Act) or to codify it or to grant authority to individuals or institutions to make regulations for specific purposes (an enabling Act). Under the Consumer Credit Act 1974, for instance, the Secretary of State for Trade and Industry is permitted to make regulations governing the form and content of credit agreements under delegated authority from Parliament.

As its name suggests, delegated legislation is law made by a body or person to which Parliament has given limited powers of law-making – as illustrated by the example above. More often than not, authority will be delegated to a Minister of the Crown, but it may also be conferred on local authorities or other public undertakings, either through the use of a statutory instrument or by some other means of delegation. Since Parliament remains sovereign, such legislation is required to receive parliamentary approval and scrutiny, but time tends to prevent anything other than a cursory glance at a limited proportion of the legislation of this kind. It does, however, remain subject to judicial control, in so far as the body granted authority may be challenged in the courts for exceeding its powers (*ultra vires*).

In addition to these two principal forms of domestic legislation, developments in the law also emanate from Britain's membership of the European Union. Under the Union's main treaties – or those parts to which the British government has agreed – Union legislation becomes part of the law and takes precedence over domestic legislation, although the latter may sometimes be required to implement it. Accordingly, law which is inconsistent with Union law is repealed by implication and British citizens, like their counterparts elsewhere in the EU, become subject to the relevant Union laws (unless an 'opt-out' has been negotiated).[1]

Whereas the provisions of the main treaties represent primary legislation, the regulations, directives and decisions emanating from the Union's institutions are secondary (or subordinate) legislation, made under the authority conferred by the Treaty of Rome (1957) and by subsequent Acts (e.g. the Single European Act 1986, the Maastricht Treaty 1992). As Chapter 3 indicated, regulations are of general application throughout the Member States and confer individual rights and duties which must be recognised by the national courts. Their purpose is to achieve uniformity throughout the EU, as in the requirement for heavy goods vehicles to fit tachographs to control drivers' hours.

Directives, by contrast, are not directly applicable; they are addressed to member states and not individuals, although a directive may create rights enforceable by an individual citizen, as they become directly applicable if a member state fails to implement its provisions within the prescribed time limits. The aim of EU directives is to seek harmonisation or approximation between national laws rather than to achieve uniformity; hence the method of implementation is left to the discretion of the individual state, usually within a given time limit (e.g. the Companies Act of 1981 implemented the Union's fourth directive on company accounts by allowing small and medium-sized companies to reduce the amount of information provided to the Registrar of Companies).

Decisions, too, are binding, but only on the member state, organisation or individual to whom they are addressed and not on the population generally. In practice, EU decisions become effective from the date stated in the decision, which is generally the date of notification, and they are enforceable in national courts if they impose financial obligations.[2]

The legal system: the courts

A country's legal system can be said to have two main functions: to provide an enabling mechanism within which individuals and organisations can exist and operate (e.g. companies are constituted by law) and to provide a means of resolving conflicts and of dealing with those who infringe the accepted standards of behaviour. These functions are carried out by a variety of institutions, including the government and the courts, and a detailed analysis of the legal system within a state would require consideration of the interrelationship between politics and law. Since the political system has been examined in Chapter 3, the focus here is on the courts as a central element of a country's legal system, with responsibility for interpreting the law and administering justice in democratic societies. It is worth remembering, however, that political and governmental activity take place within a framework of law and that framework is itself a product of the political process at a variety of spatial levels.

The English legal system

Under the English legal system, a useful distinction can be made between courts on the basis of their status. The superior courts are the House of Lords, the Court of Appeal and the High Court. Law reports generally emanate from the House of Lords – these cases involve a major point of law of general public interest (e.g. *R v R*, 1991). Inferior courts, in contrast, have limited jurisdiction and are subject to the supervisory jurisdiction of the High Court. The current hierarchy of courts is illustrated in Figure 6.1. For domestic purposes (i.e. not concerning EU legislation), the highest court is the House of Lords, which is the final court of appeal for both civil and criminal cases. Decisions reached by the Law Lords are binding on all other courts, though not necessarily on their Lordships themselves.

Like the House of Lords, the Court of Appeal has only appellate jurisdiction. In the case of the Civil Division of the court, its decisions bind all inferior courts and it is bound by its own previous decisions and by those of the House of Lords. The Criminal Division similarly is bound by the decisions of the Law Lords, but not by

Figure 6.1   The hierarchy of courts

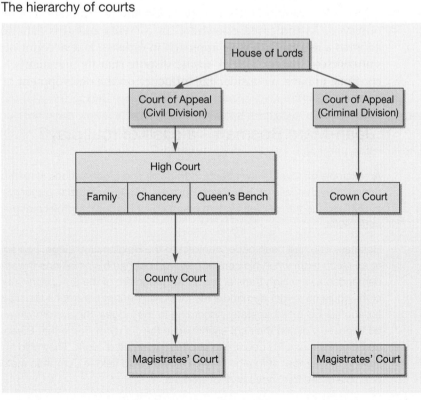

the Court of Appeal's Civil Division; nor is it bound by its own previous decisions where these were against a defendant, as exemplified in a number of celebrated cases in recent years.

The High Court is divided into three separate divisions, Chancery, Queen's Bench and Family, and has virtually unlimited original jurisdiction in civil matters, many of which are of direct relevance to business organisations. The Family court deals with such things as adoption, wardship and contested divorce cases, while the Chancery court deals with cases concerning trusts, property and taxation. Claims in contract and tort are the responsibility of the Queen's Bench division, which has two specialist courts to deal with commercial matters and with ships and aircraft. It also exercises the criminal jurisdiction of the High Court – the latter being entirely appellate in instances referred to it by the magistrates' courts or the Crown Court.

In criminal cases the Crown Court has exclusive original jurisdiction to try all indictable offences and can hear appeals against summary conviction or sentence from magistrates' courts. Broadly speaking, the latter largely deal with less serious offences (especially motoring offences), where trial by judge and jury is not permitted – an issue still under discussion following the publication of the Runciman Report (1993). Whereas magistrates' courts have both criminal and civil jurisdiction – with the emphasis towards the former – the jurisdiction of the county courts is entirely civil and derived solely from statute. Amongst the issues they deal with are conflicts between landlords and tenants and disputes involving small claims (e.g. concerning consumer matters) where a system of arbitration provides for a relatively inexpensive and quick method of resolving problems.

In disputes with a supranational dimension – involving EU member states, institutions, organisations, companies or individuals – ultimate jurisdiction rests with the European Court of Justice. Under Article 164 of the Treaty of Rome, the court is required to ensure that in the application and interpretation of the Treaty the law is observed. As indicated elsewhere, in carrying out this function, the court has adopted a relatively flexible approach in order to take account of changing circumstances (see Chapter 3). Few would dispute that its judgments have had, and will continue to have, a considerable influence on the development of EU law.

Mini case   Jean-Marc Bosman – a case of foul play?

An example of how EU law affects individuals and organisations in member states is provided by the case of Jean-Marc Bosman, a Belgian football player who successfully challenged the transfer fee system operated by Europe's football authorities in the mid-1990s.

Bosman, who had been under contract to the Belgian club Liège, had sought a transfer to a French team when his contract expired but had his ambitions thwarted when Liège demanded a very high transfer fee. In the judgment of the European Court of Justice, clubs could no longer demand a fee for players out of contract if the player was headed for another EU member state. According to the judges, the system allowing for a fee to be imposed violated the right enshrined in the Treaty of Rome that European citizens could go from one EU country to another in pursuit of work. They also held that the rule limiting the number of foreign players a club could field in European matches violated the principle of the free movement of workers.

As a final comment, it is perhaps worth stating that while conflict remains an enduring feature of daily life, many disputes are settled without recourse to the courts, often through direct negotiation between the parties concerned (e.g. Richard Branson's attempts to reach a negotiated settlement with British Airways over its alleged 'dirty tricks' campaign). Moreover even where negotiations fail or where one party declines to negotiate, a dispute will not necessarily result in court action, but may be dealt with in other ways. Disputes over employment contracts, for example, tend to be dealt with by a specialist tribunal, set up by statute to exercise specific functions of a quasi-legal nature. Similarly, complaints concerning maladministration by public (and increasingly private) bodies are generally dealt with by a system of 'ombudsmen', covering areas as diverse as social security benefits, local authority services, banking and insurance.

Business organisations and the law

Business organisations have been described as transformers of inputs into output in the sense that they acquire and use resources to produce goods or services for consumption. As Table 6.1 illustrates, all aspects of this transformation process are influenced by the law.

It is important to emphasise from the outset that the law not only constrains business activity (e.g. by establishing minimum standards of health and safety at work which are enforceable by law), but also assists it (e.g. by providing a means by which a business unit can have an independent existence from its members), and in doing so helps an enterprise to achieve its commercial and other objectives. In short, the legal environment within which businesses operate is an enabling as well as a regulatory environment and one which provides a considerable degree of certainty and stability to the conduct of business both within and between democratic states.

Given the extensive influence of the law on business organisations, it is clearly impossible to examine all aspects of the legal context within which firms function. Accordingly, in the analysis below attention is focused primarily on contract law, agency, and some of the more important statutes enacted to protect the interests of the consumer, since these are areas fundamental to business operations. Laws relating to the establishment of an enterprise and to the operation of markets are discussed in Chapters 7 and 14 respectively.

Table 6.1   Law and the business organisation

Business activity	Examples of legal influences
Establishing the organisation	Company laws, partnerships, business names
Acquiring resources	Planning laws, property laws, contract, agency
Business operations	Employment laws, health and safety laws, contract, agency
Selling output for consumption	Consumer laws, contract, agency

Contract law: the essentials

All businesses enter into contracts, whether with suppliers or employees or financiers or customers, and these contracts will be important – and possibly crucial – to the firm's operations. Such contracts are essentially agreements (oral or written) between two or more persons which are legally enforceable, provided they comprise a number of essential elements. These elements are: offer, acceptance, consideration, intention to create legal relations and capacity.

Offer

An offer is a declaration by the offeror that they intend to be legally bound by the terms stated in the offer if it is accepted by the offeree (e.g. to supply component parts at a particular price within a specified time period). This declaration may be made orally or in writing or by conduct between the parties and must be clear and unambiguous. Furthermore it should not be confused with an 'invitation to treat', which is essentially an invitation to make an offer, as is generally the case with advertisements, auctions and goods on display. Tenders are offers; a request for tenders is merely an invitation for offers to be made.

Termination of an offer can happen in several ways. Clearly an offer is ended when it is accepted but, that apart, an offer may be revoked at any time up to acceptance. It is of no consequence, legally, that an offer may be kept open for a certain time. It is only when some consideration is paid for 'buying the option' that the time factor is important and this 'buying the option' would generally be a separate contract in any case. If an offer is for a certain length of time, then later acceptance is ineffective, and even where there is no specified time limit, the courts will imply a reasonable time. Thus, in *Ramsgate Victoria Hotel v Montefiore* (1866), shares in the hotel were offered for sale. After several months the offer was 'accepted' but the court held that too much time had passed, bearing in mind that the purpose of the shares offer was to raise money.

Another way for an offer to come to an end is by the failure of a condition. Although a genuine offer is always held to be firm and certain, sometimes it may be conditional and not absolute. Thus, should A wish to buy a model car from B, B may agree but impose conditions on the deal, such as stating that A must collect at a specific time on a certain day at a particular place and must pay in cash. This is known as a 'condition precedent' and failure to complete the conditions will nullify the agreement. There is another type of condition, called a 'condition subsequent' where there is a perfectly good contract which runs until something happens. For instance, a garage may have a good contract with an oil company to buy petrol at £x per 1000 litres until the price of oil at Rotterdam reaches $$x per barrel. It is only when oil reaches the stipulated price that the contract ends.

Acceptance

Just as an offer must be firm and certain, the acceptance of an offer by the person(s) to whom it was made must be unequivocal and must not contain any alterations or additions. Accordingly, any attempt to alter the terms of an offer is regarded as a counter-offer and thus a rejection of the original offer, leaving the original offeror free to accept or decline as he or she chooses.

While acceptance of an offer normally occurs either in writing or verbally, it may also be implied by conduct. In the case of *Brogden v Metropolitan Railways Co.* (1877) Mr Brogden had supplied the company for many years without formalities. It was then decided to regularise the position and a draft agreement was sent to him. He inserted a new term, marked the draft 'approved' and returned it to the company where it was placed in a drawer and forgotten about, although both parties traded with each other on the terms of the draft for more than two years. Following a dispute, Mr Brogden claimed there was no contract. The House of Lords decided differently, saying that a contract had been created by conduct.

Inferring the acceptance of an offer by conduct is quite different from assuming that silence on the part of the offeree constitutes acceptance: silence cannot be construed as an acceptance. Equally, while the offeror may prescribe the method of acceptance (although this is regarded as permissive rather than directory), the offeree may not prescribe a method by which he or she will make acceptance. For instance, an offer may be made by fax, thus implying that a fast response is required; therefore a reply accepting the offer which is sent by second-class mail may well be treated as nugatory.

There are some rules about acceptance which are important. Postal acceptance, for example, is a good method of communication and one which is universally used by businesses; but to be valid for contractual purposes a communication must be properly addressed and stamped and then placed into the hands of the duly authorised person (i.e. the post box or over the counter). An acceptance sent to a home address may be nullified if there has been no indication that this is acceptable. Similarly, acceptance of the offer must be effectively received by the offeror where modern, instantaneous methods of communication are used. Thus if a telephone call is muffled by extraneous sound, then the acceptance must be repeated so that the offeror hears it clearly.

Consideration

Together, offer and acceptance constitute the basis of an 'agreement' or meeting of minds, provided the parties are clear as to what they are agreeing about (i.e. a *consensus ad idem* exists). Central to this agreement will be a 'consideration' which has been defined as some right, interest, profit or benefit accruing to one party or some forbearance, detriment, loss or responsibility given, suffered or undertaken by the other. In commercial contracts, the consideration normally takes the form of a cash payment in return for the goods or services provided (i.e. the 'price' in a contract of sale). In contracts involving barter, however, which are sometimes used in international trade, goods are often exchanged for goods or for some other form of non-pecuniary consideration (e.g. information or advice).

Intention to create legal relations

Not every agreement is intended to create a legally binding relationship. For example, most domestic agreements – such as the division of household chores – would not constitute a contract recognised in law. In commercial agreements, however, it is generally accepted that both parties intend to make a legally binding contract and therefore it is unnecessary to include terms to this effect. Should such a presumption be challenged, the burden of proof rests with the person who disputes the presumption.

Capacity

A contract may be valid, voidable or void and one of the factors which determines this is the contractual capacity of the respective parties to the agreement. Normally speaking, an adult may make a contract with another adult which, if entered into freely and without any defects, and which is not contrary to public policy, is binding upon them both (i.e. valid). However, the law provides protection for certain categories of persons deemed not to have full contractual capacity (e.g. minors, drunks and the mentally disordered); hence the practice by firms of excluding people under the age of 18 from offers of goods to be supplied on credit.

Concentrating on minors – those below voting age – the law prescribes that they can only be bound by contracts for 'necessaries' (e.g. food, clothing, lodging) and contracts of employment that are advantageous or beneficial, as in the case of a job which contains an element of training or education. In most other instances, contracts with minors are void or voidable and as such will be either unenforceable or capable of being repudiated by the minor.

In the case of business, legal capacity depends on the firm's legal status. Unincorporated bodies (e.g. sole traders, partnerships) do not have a distinct legal personality and hence the party to the agreement is liable for their part of the bargain. Limited companies, by contrast, have a separate legal identity from their members and hence contractual capacity rests with the company, within the limits laid down in the objects clause of its Memorandum of Association (*see* Chapter 7).

Other factors

To be enforceable at law a contract must be legal (i.e. not forbidden by law or contrary to public policy). Similarly, the agreement must have been reached voluntarily and result in a genuine meeting of minds. Consequently, contracts involving mistakes of fact, misrepresentation of the facts, or undue influence or duress may be void or voidable, depending on the circumstances. In insurance contracts, for instance, the insured is required to disclose all material facts to the insurer (e.g. health record, driving record), otherwise a policy may be invalidated. In this context a 'material fact' is one which would affect the mind of a prudent insurer, even though the materiality may not be appreciated by the insured.

Agency

As business activity has become more specialised and complex, firms have increasingly turned to outside individuals to carry out specialist functions such as freight forwarding, overseas representation, insurance broking and commercial letting. These individuals (known as agents) are authorised by the individual or organisation hiring them (known as the principal) to act on their behalf, thus creating an agency relationship. As in other areas of commercial activity, special rules of law have evolved to regulate the behaviour of the parties involved in such a relationship.

In essence, the function of an agent is to act on behalf of a principal so as to effect a contract between the principal and a third party. The agent may be a 'servant' of the principal (i.e. under their control as in the case of a sales representative) or an 'independent contractor' (i.e. their own master as in the case of an estate agent) and will be operating with the consent of the principal whether by contract or implication. Having established a contractual relationship between the principal and the third party, the agent generally leaves the picture and usually has no rights and duties under the contract thus made.

With regard to an agent's specific obligations under an agency agreement, these are normally expressly stated under the terms of the agreement, although some may also be implied. Traditionally the common law of agency prescribes, however, that agents:

- *Obey the lawful instruction of the principal*, otherwise they may be in breach of contract.
- *Exercise due care and skill*, in order to produce a deal which is to the principal's best advantage.
- *Act personally*, rather than delegate, unless expressly or implicitly authorised to do so.
- *Act in good faith*, thus avoiding conflicts of interest or undisclosed profits and bribes.
- *Keep proper accounts*, which separate the principal's funds from those which belong personally to the agent.

Moreover, in so far as an agent is acting under the principal's authority, the principal is bound to the third party only by acts which are within the agent's authority to make. Consequently *ultra vires* acts only affect the principal if he or she adopts them by ratification and the agent may be liable for the breach of the implied warranty of authority to the third party.

In addition to these common law duties owed by the principal, the Commercial Agents (Council Directive) Regulations 1993 bestow certain duties upon the principal. The Regulations apply when an agent falls within the definition of a commercial agent (Reg. 2(1)). It is clear that these duties overlap to some extent with the common law duties. Regulation 4 specifies the duties:

- to act dutifully and in good faith;
- to provide the commercial agent with the necessary documentation relating to the goods in question;
- to obtain necessary information for the agent. This is a higher standard, perhaps requiring searching for data, than under the common law, where all the principal needs to do is to disclose information in their possession;

- to notify the agent within a reasonable period of time if the usual volume of trade is likely to be significantly reduced;
- to inform the agent within a reasonable period of time of the principal's acceptance, refusal, or non-acceptance of a commercial transaction arranged by the agent.

Law and the consumer

Economic theory tends to suggest that laws to protect the consumer are unnecessary. If individuals are behaving rationally when consuming goods and services, they would arrange their consumption to maximise their satisfaction (or 'utility'), in the words of an economist. Products which because of poor quality or some other factor reduced a consumer's utility would be rejected in favour of those which proved a better alternative and this would act as an incentive to producers (and retailers) to provide the best products. In effect, market forces would ensure that the interest of the consumer was safeguarded as suppliers in a competitive market arranged their production to meet the needs and wants of rational consumers.

The 'ideal' view of how markets work is not always borne out in practice. Apart from the fact that consumers do not always act rationally, they often do not have access to information which might influence their choice of products; in some cases they may not even have a choice of products (e.g. where a monopoly exists) although this situation can change over time (e.g. through privatisation of state monopolies). Also, given the relative resources of producers and consumers, the balance of power in the trading relationship tends to favour producers who can influence consumer choices using a range of persuasive techniques, including advertising.

Taken together, these and other factors call into question the assumption that the consumer is 'sovereign' and hence the extent to which individuals have inherent protection in the marketplace from powerful (and, in some cases, unscrupulous) suppliers. It is in this context that the law is seen to be an important counterbalance in a contractual relationship where the consumer is, or may be, at a disadvantage, and this can be said to provide the basis of legal intervention in this area.

Existing laws to protect consumers are both civil and criminal and the relevant rights, duties and liabilities have been created or imposed by common law (especially contract and tort) or by statute. Significantly, as the examples below illustrate, a large element of current consumer law has resulted from statutory intervention, much of it in the last 30 years. These laws – covering areas as diverse as trade descriptions, the sale of goods and services, and consumer credit and product liability – indicate a growing willingness on the part of governments to respond to the complaints of consumers and their representative organisations and to use legislation to regulate the relationship between business organisations and their customers. As suggested elsewhere, such intervention could reasonably be construed as a political response to some of the socially unacceptable characteristics of a capitalist economy.[3]

The Consumer Affairs Directorate in the DTI is a useful source of reference on consumer law – see *www.dti.gov.uk/CACP/ca/work1* and *work2*

Trade Descriptions Act 1968

The main aim of the Trade Descriptions Act is to protect consumers from traders who deliberately misdescribe goods or give a false description of services in the process of trade. Under the Act – which imposes an obligation on local authorities to enforce its provisions – a trader can be convicted of a criminal offence in three main areas:

1 Making a false trade description of goods.
2 Making a false statement of price.
3 Making a false trade description of services.

The penalty for such offences can be a fine on summary conviction and/or imprisonment following conviction on indictment.

With regard to goods, the Act applies both to goods which have been sold and to those which are offered for sale and to which a false description, or one which is misleading to a material degree, has been applied. It can also apply to advertisements which are 'economical with the truth', such as claims regarding a second-hand car for sale by a local dealer. Similarly, with services it is an offence to make false or misleading statements as to the services offered to consumers and it is possible for an offence to be committed even if the intention to mislead is not deliberate.

In the case of price, the Act outlaws certain false or misleading indications as to the price of goods, such as claims that prices have been reduced from previously higher levels. For this claim to be within the law, a trader needs to show that the goods have been on sale at the higher price for a period of 28 consecutive days during the preceding six months. If not, this must be made quite clear to the consumer when a price reduction is indicated.

The Consumer Credit Act 1974

The Consumer Credit Act, which became fully operational in May 1985, controls transactions between the credit industry and private individuals (including sole traders and business partnerships) up to a limit of £15 000. Under the legislation consumer credit agreement is defined as a personal credit providing the debtor with credit up to the accepted limit. This credit may be in the form of a cash loan or some other type of financial accommodation (e.g. through the use of a credit card). The Act also covers hire purchase agreements (i.e. a contract of hire which gives the hirer the option to purchase the goods), conditional sale agreements for the sale of goods or land, and credit sale agreements, where the property passes to the buyer when the sale is effected.

The main aim of this consumer protection measure is to safeguard the public from trading malpractices where some form of credit is involved. To this end the Act provides, among other things, for a system of licensing controlled by the Director General of Fair Trading (*see* Chapter 14) who must be satisfied that the person seeking a licence is a fit person and the name under which he or she intends to be licensed is neither misleading nor undesirable. Providing credit or acting as a credit broker without a licence is a criminal offence, as is supplying a minor with any document inviting them to borrow money or obtain goods on credit.

A further protection for the consumer comes from the requirements that the debtor be made fully aware of the nature and cost of the agreement and his or her rights and liabilities under it. The Act stipulates that prior to the contract being made the debtor must be supplied with certain information, including the full price of the credit agreement (i.e. the cost of the credit plus the capital sum), the annual rate of the total charge for credit expressed as a percentage (i.e. the annual percentage rate), and the amounts of payments due and to whom they are payable. In addition, the debtor must be informed of all the other terms of the agreement and of their right to cancel if this is applicable. In the case of the latter, this applies to credit agreements drawn up off business premises, and is designed to protect individuals from high-pressure doorstep sellers who offer credit as an incentive to purchase. Some companies, aware of the rights of cancellation on cold calls at home, have adopted a practice of telephoning potential customers, thus any subsequent home visit is not technically a cold call. This practice has raised some concern and is almost certain to be outlawed, either by legislation or under a code of practice.

Sale of Goods Act 1979

Under both the Sale of Goods Act 1979 (as amended by the Sale of Goods and Services Act 1994) and the Unfair Contract Terms Act 1977 consumers are essentially seen as individuals who purchase goods or services for their own personal use from other individuals or organisations selling them in the course of business. A computer sold, for example, to a student is a consumer sale, while the same machine sold to a secretarial agency is not, since it has been acquired for business purposes. This legal definition of a consumer is important in the context of laws designed specifically to provide consumer protection, as in the case of the Sale of Goods Act which governs those agreements whereby a seller agrees to transfer ownership in goods to a consumer in return for a monetary consideration, known as the 'price'. Where such an agreement or contract is deemed to exist the legislation provides consumers with rights in respect of items which are faulty or which do not correspond with the description given to them, by identifying a number of implied conditions to the sale. In the case of contracts for the supply of services (e.g. repair work) or which involve the supply of goods *and* services (e.g. supplying units and fitting them in a bathroom or kitchen), almost identical rights are provided under the Supply of Goods and Services Act 1982 (as amended).

The three main implied conditions of the 1979 Act are relatively well known. Under section 13, goods which are sold by description must match the description given to them and it is of no significance that the goods are selected by the purchaser. This description may be on the article itself or on the packaging or provided in some other way, and will include the price and possibly other information (e.g. washing instructions) which the consumer believes to be true. A shirt described as 100 per cent cotton, for instance, must be just that, otherwise it fails to match the description given to it and the consumer is entitled to choose either a refund or an exchange.

The second condition relates to the quality of the goods provided. Under section 14 of the Act goods had to be of 'merchantable quality', except where any defects are drawn specifically to the attention of the purchaser before the contract is made or where the buyer has examined the goods before contracting and the examination ought to have revealed such defects. As 'merchantable quality' was a matter of some controversy the phrase was amended to 'satisfactory quality' and this is defined in section 1 of the 1994 Act, but the general expectation is that a product should be fit for the purpose or purposes for which it is normally bought, bearing in mind questions of age, price and any other relevant factors (e.g. brand name). A new top-of-the-range car should have no significant defects on purchase, whereas a high-mileage second-hand car sold for a few hundred pounds could not reasonably evoke such expectations in the mind of the consumer. Thus, while the implied condition of 'satisfactory' applies to sale goods and second-hand goods as well as to full-price purchases of new goods, it needs to be judged in light of the contract description and all the circumstances of a particular case, including the consumer's expectations.

The third implied condition also derives from section 14 of the legislation, namely that goods are fit for a particular purpose (i.e. capable of performing the tasks indicated by the seller). Accordingly, if the seller, on request from the purchaser, confirms that goods are suitable for a particular purpose and this proves not to be the case, this would represent a breach of section 14(3). Equally, if the product is unsuitable for its normal purposes, then section 14(2) would also be breached and the consumer would be entitled to a refund of the price.

It is worth noting that 'satisfactory' and 'fitness for a purpose' are closely related and that a breach of one will often include a breach of the other. By the same token, failure in a claim for a breach of section 14(2) is likely to mean that a claim for a breach of section 14(3) will also fail. Moreover, if, on request, a seller disclaims any knowledge of a product's suitability for a particular purpose and the consumer is willing to take a chance, any subsequent unsuitability cannot be regarded as a breach of section 14(3). The same applies if the buyer's reliance on the skill or judgement of the seller is deemed 'unreasonable'.

As a final comment, under the Sale and Supply of Goods and Services Act 1982, section 3, there is an implied condition that a supplier acting in the course of business must carry out the service with reasonable care and skill and within a reasonable time, where a specific deadline is not stated in the contract. Reasonable care and skill tends to be seen as that which might be expected of an ordinary competent person performing the particular task, though this will, of course, depend on the particular circumstances of the case and the nature of the trade or profession. As in the case of the Sale of Goods Act, any attempt to deprive the consumer of any of the implied conditions represents a breach both of the Unfair Contract Terms Act 1977 and the Unfair Terms in Consumer Contracts Regulations 1999.

Exclusion or limitation clauses in consumer contracts are subject to the Unfair Contract Terms Act 1977 and the Unfair Terms in Consumer Contracts Regulations 1999, which operate as a dual regime, giving the consumer the choice of actions. Under the former any clause seeking to exclude or limit liability for personal injury/death is void while all other clauses are subject to the test of reasonableness. Under the latter regulations a term that has not been individually negotiated will be unfair if it is contrary to good faith by causing a significant imbalance between the parties. The situation is a little different in business deals although personal injury/death still cannot be excluded. Thus, where a reference is made on a product or its container or in a related document to a consumer's rights under sections 13 to 15, there must be a clear and accessible notice informing consumers that their statutory rights are not affected when returning an item deemed unsatisfactory. It is an offence under the Fair Trading Act 1974 to display notices stating 'no refunds' or 'no refunds on sale goods'. The aim is to ensure that buyers are made fully aware of their legal rights and are not taken advantage of by unscrupulous traders who seek to deny them the protection afforded by the law.

The Consumer Protection Act 1987

The Consumer Protection Act 1987 came into force in March 1988 as a result of the government's obligation to implement EC directive 85/374 which concerned product liability. In essence the Act provides for a remedy in damages for anyone who suffers personal injury or damage to property as a result of a defective product by imposing a 'strict' liability on the producers of defective goods (including substances, growing crops, ships, aircraft and vehicles). Naturally, the onus is on the plaintiff to prove that any loss was caused by the claimed defect and a claim can be made by anyone, whether damage to property, personal injury or death has occurred. In the case of the latter, for example, a relative or friend could pursue an action and, if American experience is anything to go by, could be awarded very substantial damages if liability can be proven. As far as property is concerned, damage must be to private rather than commercial goods and property and must exceed £275 for claims to be considered.

While the Act is intended to place liability on the producers of defective goods, this liability also extends to anyone putting a name or distinguishing mark on a product which holds that person out as being the producer (e.g. supermarkets' own-brand labels). Similarly, importers of products from outside the EU are also liable for any defects in imported goods, as may be firms involved in supplying components or parts of the process of manufacture of a product. To prevent a firm escaping its liability by a supplier claiming it is unable to identify its own suppliers, the legislation provides a remedy: any supplier unable or unwilling to identify the importing firm or previous supplier becomes liable itself for damages under the Act.

Firms seeking to avoid liability for any claim have a number of defences under section 4 of the Act. Specifically these are:

■ That the defendant did not supply the product in question.
■ That the product was not manufactured or supplied in the course of business (e.g. goods sold at a school bazaar).
■ That the defect did not exist at the time the product was distributed.
■ That where a product has a number of components, the defect is a defect of the finished product or due to compliance with any instructions issued by the manufacturer of the finished product.
■ That the defect is attributable to the requirement to comply with existing laws.
■ That the state of scientific and technical knowledge at the time the product was supplied was not sufficiently advanced for the defect to be recognised.

Of these, the last – the so-called development risks defence – is the most contentious, given that it applies largely to products such as new drugs and new technology where the implications of their usage may not be apparent for some years. As recent cases have shown, manufacturers faced with damages from claimants who appear to have suffered from the use of certain products often decide to settle out of court without accepting liability for their actions.

 The annual Report of the Office of Fair Trading (OFT) contains useful commentary on consumer protection issues, including codes of practice and the powers of the OFT. See *www.oft.gov.uk*

Codes of practice

Alongside the protection provided by the law, consumers may be afforded a further measure of security when the organisation they are dealing with belongs to a trade association which is operating under a **code of practice** (e.g. the Association of British Travel Agents). In essence, codes of practice represent an attempt by trade associations to impose a measure of self-discipline on the behaviour of their members by establishing the standards of service customers should expect to receive and by encouraging acceptable business practices. In addition, such codes of conduct invariably identify how customer complaints should be handled and many offer low-cost or no-cost arbitration schemes to help settle disputes outside the more formal legal process.

While codes of practice do not in themselves have the force of law, they are normally seen as a useful mechanism for regulating the relationship between business organisations and their customers and accordingly they have the support of the Office of Fair Trading, which often advises trade associations on their content. Businesses, too, usually find them useful, particularly if through the establishment of a system of self-regulation they are able to avoid the introduction of restrictions imposed by the law.

Synopsis

All business activities, from the establishment of the organisation through to the sale of the product to the customer, are influenced by the law. This legal environment within which businesses exist and operate evolves over time and is a key influence on firms of all sizes and in all sectors, as illustrated by an examination of some of the main laws governing the relationship between a business and its customers. The majority of consumer laws are of relatively recent origin and derive from the attempts by successive governments to provide individuals with a measure of protection against a minority of firms which behave in ways deemed to be unacceptable. Concomitantly, they also provide reputable organisations with a framework within which to carry out their business and, as such, act as an incentive to entrepreneurial activity in market-based economies.

Summary of key points

- The legal rules within which businesses exist and operate are an important part of the external environment of business organisations.

- Laws affecting businesses derive from a variety of sources including custom, the decisions of the courts and legislation.

- Laws are sometimes made at international and supranational level.

- Contract, agency and consumer protection are three key areas governing the day-to-day work of businesses.

- Offer, acceptance, consideration, intention to create legal relations and capacity are central elements of contract law.

- Agency relationships are a common feature of business practice.

- The relationship between businesses and their customers is governed by a variety of laws, many of which derive from statute.

- In addition to the protection provided to consumers by the law, many organisations also operate under agreed codes of conduct.

CASE STUDY Legal aspects of banking

Many aspects of the relationship between individuals and business organisations are conditioned by the law. This can be demonstrated by an examination of an everyday activity – banking. Rather than concentrating on a specific example, the following analysis discusses the essentials of the contractual relationship between one form of business organisation (a bank) and its customers, and illustrates that both parties to the agreement have both rights and duties imposed by law.

Banking

The bank–customer relationship is essentially a contractual one with the bank being the debtor and the customer the creditor, at least until the customer acquires a loan facility or overdraft. The relationship is not *per se* a fiduciary one (*Foley* v *Hill* (1848)).

Although all the basic elements of a valid contract must be present, the terms are regarded slightly differently, with the distinction between condition and warranty being less prominent. However, the relationship does have some implied terms and conditions unique to banking. For example, the bank is under a duty of secrecy as far as a customer's account is concerned (*Joachimson* v *Swiss*

Bank Corporation (1921)) although the duty has been modified by *Tournier* v *National Provincial and Union Bank of England Ltd* (1924). Disclosure is now justi-fied in the following circumstances:

- Where required by law.
- Where there is a public duty.
- Where the interests of the bank require it.
- Where the customer expressly or impliedly permits it.

Occasionally, the court will order a bank to disclose certain information about a customer's account but may restrict the use of the information so obtained.

Most banks have their own standard-form contracts which, not unnaturally, contain the terms and conditions which the particular bank finds most acceptable and, in the main, these forms are perfectly proper and create no problems for either the bank or the potential customer. Although it usually does not have any great practical significance *when* the contractual relationship begins, it could be important if the bank collects a cheque on behalf of a potential customer. The protection afforded to banks by section 4 of the Cheques Act 1957 cannot be invoked unless the bank collects on behalf of a customer, and if the relationship has not yet been established, the offeror is not yet a customer. Section 4 provides that there is no liability to a true owner of a cheque where the customer has defec-tive title or no title just because the bank has received payment of the cheque. The bank must not act negligently but, because a cheque is not endorsed or is endorsed irregularly that is not evidence of negligence. Many cheque transactions are now A/C payee only, certainly as far as the private customer is concerned. In all other cases, however, the bank must show that it took reasonable care over the transac-tion. Reasonable care is the standard to be expected of an ordinary, competent bank, the criterion being based on current banking practice.

Although in strict law, references are not essential – the bank may already have prior knowledge of the customer, either personally, or through a person the bank considers to be of good standing – the bank must have acted as any reason-able bank would act. Sometimes, good banking practice and the law may be in direct conflict. The Sex Discrimination Act 1975, as amended, makes it unlawful to discriminate against a person solely on the ground of gender; thus questions put to a potential customer who is female regarding marital status and the employment of a spouse should not be asked unless similar questions are asked of male customers. Case law suggests that failure to ask such pertinent questions of this nature where the customer is a married woman might be regarded as not acting reasonably. Many banks appear to evade the problem by not asking such questions of any potential customer; how far the courts would agree that this is reasonable is uncertain.

Any loan facility or overdraft for less than £15 000 falls under the Consumer Credit Act 1974 although the Banking Act 1979, s 38(1) obliges the Director of Fair Trading to exempt banks from all the paperwork required, at least as far as overdrafts are concerned. Periodic statements of account required by section 78(4) may be dispensed with where there is more than one party to an overdraft, to the extent that all such parties need not receive such account (section 185).

Guarantees

Often, when a customer requires a loan facility, even for a fairly short time, a bank may require some form of security for it. Should the customer not possess such security then a guarantor may be required. This means that should the customer default on the loan the guarantor will have to pay the money: if the guarantor has pledged property as the security they stand to lose it. A guarantee must be evidenced by some form of memorandum in writing and is unenforceable if it is not. If a bank is not specifically requested for information about the way in which the borrower's account has been run it need not volunteer the information but, if it does volunteer information, it must be full and frank. Any questions the guarantor asks must be answered clearly and with certainty. The guarantor is entitled to receive information about the indebtedness at any time but is not entitled to inspect, or have details of, the customer's account unless, of course, the customer has agreed to this.

Rights and duties of the bank

A bank has the right to charge its customers reasonable fees for the services it provides. It may charge interest on any loans and, where an account has been permitted an overdraft facility, it may make a repayment on demand call. It is also entitled to be indemnified by a customer for all expenses and liabilities incurred by acting on the customer's behalf. A bank may not exercise a lien over articles left in a safety deposit box for any monies owed the bank (a lien is a right to keep possession of someone else's property in lieu of payment; once payment is made the lien is at an end). A bank also has the right to do as it pleases with any and all monies deposited by a customer just as long as cheques are honoured: such cheques, of course, must be valid ones and the bank has the further right to expect a customer to exercise reasonable care in drawing cheques. One right which banks have, and of which many customers are apparently unaware, is the right to 'set off' accounts. This means that where a customer has more than one account, the bank is permitted and entitled, in the absence of any contrary instruction by the customer, to make a transfer of money from an account in credit to cover any shortfall in an account in debit.

A bank is bound to abide by any express, lawful instruction of a customer, to pay a standing order, for instance. This duty does not arise if there are insufficient funds to meet it. A bank also has the duty to honour properly drawn cheques (on an account in credit or with overdraft facilities); a properly drawn cheque is one which is not 'stale' (most banks regard cheques which have been in circulation for six months or longer as being stale) or overdue. An overdue cheque is one which has been in circulation for an unreasonable length of time. 'Unreasonable' will be interpreted according to the facts and circumstances in each case. If a customer has countermanded ('stopped') a cheque, then a bank must not pay out on it but the countermanding must be done in the proper manner in writing and is not effective unless and until it comes to the attention of the bank (*Curtice* v *London City and Midland Bank Ltd* (1908)). A countermand cannot be made for a cheque made against a cheque guarantee card.

A bank may not make payments from an account where there is a legal bar such as an injunction or a garnishee order. Furthermore if a customer dies or becomes bankrupt or becomes incapable of handling his or her own affairs a bank may not make payments: the bank must know of these things. This is because, in each of the three instances, another party acquires the right to run the account: the Trustee in bankruptcy, the executors/administrators of an estate, or an authorised person for the mentally incapacitated customer. As mentioned earlier, a bank may not disclose information about a customer's account except in certain, defined situations, but all banks have a duty to inform the appropriate authorities where it is suspected that the monies in an account result from drugs or terrorist activities. Clearly, this may prove to be a rather delicate situation. The Drugs Trafficking Offences Act 1986 requires a bank to inspect the deposits into an account and make the necessary enquiries if large, regular and unexplained amounts are paid in – the Act makes it a criminal offence to hold or invest such monies.

Banks must fulfil the normal banking requirements of collecting cheques and other instruments and crediting them to the customer's account while exercising proper skill and care. The duty of skill and care may, of course, go beyond the mere running of an account (see mini case: Banking on advice, p. 159). If a bank acts as an investment adviser, for example, the duty arises (*Woods* v *Martins Bank Ltd* (1959)). Finally, a bank has the right to close an account, even one kept in credit, if it so desires. This sometimes happens when, for instance, the account is used for just one transaction per month. The bank must give the account holder reasonable notice of the intention to close so that the customer may make alternative arrangements. Where the account is a loan account, a breach of the terms of the agreement must be made before the account may be closed. There is no difficulty about closing a debit account since an overdraft is normally payable on demand.

Rights and duties of a customer

Although a bank must keep accurate records of the transactions on the account of a customer, customers do not have a duty to check the statements that are issued and even if the customer does check them that does not prevent a later claim of inaccuracy (*Tai Hing Cotton Mill Ltd* v *Liu Chong Hing Bank Ltd* (1985)) (a Privy Council decision). Naturally, given all the duties of the bank as far as the running of the account is concerned, the customer is under certain duties: to ensure that cheques are properly drawn; to countermand in the proper manner; to keep sufficient funds in the account to meet any standing orders and direct debits as well as any issued cheques.

Over-debit and over-credit of an account

If a bank over-debits an account the money must be reimbursed as soon as the error is found and, if cheques have been dishonoured as a result of the over-debit, the bank must compensate the customer for the injury to credit and reputation – there is no reason why the customer should not also require the bank to write to each recipient of an unpaid cheque stating the position. Such over-debiting may, on occasion, lead to the issuance of a writ for defamation.

Where an account has been over-credited, the bank may not be able to recoup the excess payment if the customer can satisfy three conditions (*United Overseas Bank* v *Jiwani* (1979)):

1 The state of the account must have been misrepresented to the customer by the bank.
2 The customer must have been misled by the misrepresentation (i.e. believed it).
3 The customer must have relied on the misrepresentation to such an extent, changing his or her position in such a way, that it would be inequitable to order him or her to repay.

Case study questions

1 What is the role of the ombudsman with regard to complaints about banking services? (see e.g. www.financial-ombudsman.org.uk)

2 Why have the major banks in the UK been accused of treating their small business customers badly?

Review and discussion questions

1 Why are laws to protect the consumer felt to be necessary? What other means do consumers have of protecting their interest in the marketplace?

2 To what extent does the supranational structure of European Union law infringe the principle of the supremacy of Parliament?

3 Do you think that tobacco companies should be made retrospectively liable for the safety of their product? Justify your answer.

4 Examine the case for and against increased government control over business practices.

Assignments

1 You are a trading standards officer in a local authority trading standards department. You have been asked to talk to a group of school sixth-form students on the Sale of Goods Act 1979. Prepare suitable overhead transparencies outlining the following:
   (a) The main provisions of the 1979 Act.
   (b) The customer's rights in the event of a breach of the implied conditions.
   (c) The sources of help and advice available to an individual with a consumer problem.

2 Imagine you work for a Citizens' Advice Bureau. A large part of your work involves offering advice to individuals with consumer problems. Design a simple leaflet indicating some of the principal pieces of legislation in the field of consumer protection and their main provisions. Your leaflet should also give guidance as to further specialist sources of help and advice.

Notes and references

1 'Opt-outs' may sometimes be negotiated, however. Britain initially opted out of the Social Chapter of the Maastricht Treaty, which includes a provision for a 48-hour maximum working week. Within the Union an attempt was made to treat this issue as a health and safety measure which could then be applicable to British firms by majority (not unanimous) vote of the member states. After the 1997 election, the new Labour government decided to 'opt in' to the Social Chapter. The 48-hour working restrictions are now causing concern in a number of areas, notably transport, deep sea fishing and the health service.

2 Although the UK has been a signatory to the European Convention on Human Rights (ECHR) and there have been many times over the years when the UK government has been taken before the Court, the UK has never been bound by any decision if it chose to ignore it. A Convention is simply a piece of paper until ratified by the government. The ECHR was ratified in May 1999.

3 Beardshaw, J. and Palfreman, D., *The Organisation in its Environment*, 4th edition, Pitman Publishing, 1990, p. 308.

Further reading

Atiyah, P., *The Sale of Goods*, 10th edition, Longman, 2001.

Bradgate, R., *Commercial Law*, 3nd edition, Butterworths, 2000.

Card, R. and James, J., *Law for Accountancy Students*, 7th edition, Butterworths, 2002.

Davies, F. R., *Davies on Contract – Concise Course Texts*, 8th edition, Sweet and Maxwell, 1999.

Web links and further questions are available on the website at:
www.booksites.net/worthington

Part Three

FIRMS

7

Legal structures

Ian Worthington

Market-based economies comprise a rich diversity of business organisations, ranging from the very simple enterprise owned and operated by one person, to the huge multinational corporation with production and distribution facilities spread across the globe. Whatever the nature of these organisations or their scale of operation, their existence is invariably subject to legal definition and this will have consequences for the functioning of the organisation. Viewing the business as a legal structure provides an insight into some of the important influences on business operations in both the private and public sectors.

Objectives

- To examine the legal structure of UK business organisations in both the private and public sectors.

- To compare UK business organisations with those in other parts of Europe.

- To consider the implications of a firm's legal structure for its operations.

- To discuss franchising, licensing and joint ventures.

Key terms

Articles of Association	Golden share	Public corporation
'Black economy'	Joint venture	Public limited company
Company	Licensing	(PLC)
Company directors	Managing director	Public sector organisations
Consortium	Memorandum of Association	Shareholders
Consumer societies	Nationalised industry	Sole trader
Executive directors	Non-executive directors	Stakeholders
Franchising	Partnership	Unlimited personal liability
Gearing	Private limited company	Workers' co-operatives

Introduction

Business organisations can be classified in a variety of ways, including:

- size (e.g. small, medium, large);
- type of industry (e.g. primary, secondary, tertiary);
- sector (e.g. private sector, public sector); and
- legal status (e.g. sole trader, partnership, and so on).

These classifications help to distinguish one type of organisation from another and to focus attention on the implications of such differences for an individual enterprise. In the discussion below, business organisations are examined as legal structures and the consequences of variations in legal status are discussed in some detail. Subsequent chapters in this section investigate alternative structural perspectives in order to highlight how these too have an important bearing on the environment in which businesses operate.

Private sector organisations in the UK

The sole trader

Many individuals aspire to owning and running their own business – being their own boss, making their own decisions. For those who decide to turn their dream into a reality, becoming a sole trader (or sole proprietor) offers the simplest and easiest method of trading.

As the name suggests, a sole trader is a business owned by one individual who is self-employed and who may, in some cases, employ other people on either a full-time or a part-time basis. Normally using personal funds to start the business, the sole trader decides on the type of goods or services to be produced, where the business is to be located, what capital is required, what staff (if any) to employ, what the target market should be and a host of other aspects concerned with the establishment and running of the enterprise. Where the business proves a success, all profits accrue to the owner and it is common for sole traders to reinvest a considerable proportion of these in the business and/or use them to reduce past borrowings. Should losses occur, these too are the responsibility of the sole trader, who has unlimited personal liability for the debts of the business.

Despite this substantial disadvantage, sole proprietorship tends to be the most popular form of business organisation numerically. In the United Kingdom, for example, it is estimated that about 80 per cent of all businesses are sole traders and in some sectors – notably personal services, retailing, building – they tend to be the dominant form of business enterprise. Part of the reason for this numerical dominance is the relative ease with which an individual can establish a business of this type. Apart from minor restrictions concerning the use of a business name – if the name of the proprietor is not used – few other legal formalities are required to set up the enterprise, other than the need to register for Value Added Tax if turnover

exceeds a certain sum (e.g. £55,000 in 2002) and/or to fulfil any special requirements laid down by the local authority prior to trading (e.g. some businesses
require licences). Once established, of course, the sole trader, like other forms of
business, will be subject to a variety of legal requirements (e.g. contract law,
consumer law, employment law) – though not the requirement to file information
about the business in a public place. For some, this ability to keep the affairs of the
enterprise away from public scrutiny provides a further incentive to establishing
this form of business organisation – some of which may operate wholly or partly in
the 'black economy' (i.e. beyond the gaze of the tax authorities).

A further impetus towards sole ownership comes from the ability of the individual to exercise a considerable degree of control over their own destiny. Business
decisions – including the day-to-day operations of the enterprise as well as long-
term plans – are in the hands of the owner and many individuals evidently relish
the risks and potential rewards associated with entrepreneurial activity, preferring
these to the relative 'safety' of employment in another organisation. For others less
fortunate, the 'push' of unemployment rather than the 'pull' of the marketplace
tends to be more of a deciding factor and one which clearly accounts for some of
the growth in the number of small businesses in the United Kingdom in the later
part of the twentieth century.

Ambitions and commitment alone, however, are not necessarily sufficient to
guarantee the survival and success of the enterprise and the high mortality rate
among businesses of this kind, particularly during a recession, is well known and
well documented. Part of the problem may stem from developments largely outside
the control of the enterprise – including bad debts, increased competition, higher
interest rates, falling demand – and factors such as these affect businesses of all
types and all sizes, not just sole traders. Other difficulties, such as lack of funds for
expansion, poor marketing, lack of research of the marketplace and insufficient
management skills are to some extent self-induced and emanate, at least in part,
from the decision to become a sole proprietor rather than some other form of business organisation. Where such constraints exist, the sole trader may be tempted to
look to others to share the burdens and the risks by establishing a partnership or
co-operative or limited company or by seeking a different approach to the business
venture, such as through 'franchising'. These alternative forms of business organisation are discussed in detail below.

The partnership

The Partnership Act 1890 defines a partnership as 'the relation which subsists
between persons carrying on a business in common with a view to profit'. Like the
sole trader, this form of business organisation does not have its own distinct legal
personality and hence the owners – the partners – have unlimited personal liability
both jointly and severally. This means that in the case of debts or bankruptcy of the
partnership, each partner is liable in full for the whole debt and each in turn may
be sued or their assets seized until the debt is satisfied. Alternatively, all the partners
may be joined into the action to recover debts, unless by dint of the Limited
Partnership Act 1907, a partner (or partners) has limited liability. Since it tends to

be much easier to achieve the same ends by establishing a limited company, limited partnerships are not common; nor can all partners in a partnership have limited liability. Hence in the discussion below, attention is focused on the partnership as an unincorporated association, operating in a market where its liability is effectively unlimited.

In essence, a partnership comes into being when two or more people establish a business which they own, finance and run jointly for personal gain, irrespective of the degree of formality involved in the relationship. Such a business can range from a husband and wife running a local shop as joint owners, to a very large firm of accountants or solicitors, with in excess of a hundred partners in offices in various locations. Under the law, most partnerships are limited to 20 or less, but some types of business, particularly in the professions, may have a dispensation from this rule (Companies Act 1985, s 716). This same Act requires businesses which are not exempt from the rule and which have more than 20 partners to register as a company.

While it is not necessary for a partnership to have a formal written agreement, most partnerships tend to be formally enacted in a Deed of Partnership or Articles since this makes it much easier to reduce uncertainty and to ascertain intentions when there is a written document to consult. Where this is not done, the Partnership Act 1890 lays down a minimum code which governs the relationship between partners and which provides, amongst other things, for all partners to share equally in the capital and profits of the business and to contribute equally towards its losses.

In practice, of course, where a Deed or Articles exist, these will invariably reflect differences in the relative status and contribution of individual partners. Senior partners, for example, will often have contributed more financially to the partnership and not unnaturally will expect to receive a higher proportion of the profits. Other arrangements – including membership, action on dissolution of the partnership, management responsibilities and rights, and the basis for allocating salaries – will be outlined in the partnership agreement and as such will provide the legal framework within which the enterprise exists and its co-owners operate.

Unlike the sole trader, where management responsibilities devolve on a single individual, partnerships permit the sharing of responsibilities and tasks and it is common in a partnership for individuals to specialise to some degree in particular aspects of the organisation's work – as in the case of a legal or medical or veterinary practice. Added to this, the fact that more than one person is involved in the ownership of the business tends to increase the amount of finance available to the organisation, thus permitting expansion to take place without the owners losing control of the enterprise. These two factors alone tend to make a partnership an attractive proposition for some would-be entrepreneurs; while for others the rules of their professional body – which often prohibits its members from forming a company – effectively provide for the establishment of this type of organisation.

On the downside, the sharing of decisions and responsibilities may represent a problem, particularly where partners are unable to agree over the direction the partnership should take or the amount to be reinvested in the business, unless such matters are clearly specified in a formal agreement. A more intractable problem is the existence of unlimited personal liability – a factor which may inhibit some individuals from considering this form of organisation, particularly given that the actions of any one partner are invariably binding on the other members of the business. To overcome this problem, many individuals, especially in manufacturing and trading, look to the limited company as the type of organisation which can combine the benefits of joint ownership and limited personal liability – a situation not necessarily always borne out in practice. It is to this type of business organisation that the discussion now turns.

Limited companies

In law a company is a corporate association having a legal identity in its own right (i.e. it is distinct from the people who own it, unlike in the case of a sole trader or partnership). This means that all property and other assets owned by the company belong to the company and not to its members (owners). By the same token, the personal assets of its members (the shareholders) do not normally belong to the business. In the event of insolvency, therefore, an individual's liability is limited to the amount invested in the business, including any amount remaining unpaid on the shares for which they have subscribed.[1] One exception to this would be where a company's owners have given a personal guarantee to cover any loans they have obtained from a bank or other institution – a requirement for many small, private limited companies. Another occurs where a company is limited by guarantee rather than by shares, with its members' liability being limited to the amount they have undertaken to contribute to the assets in the event of the company being wound up. Companies of this type are normally non-profit-making organisations – such as professional, research or trade associations – and are much less common than companies limited by shares. Hence in the discussion below, attention is focused on the latter as the dominant form of business organisation in the corporate sector of business.[2]

Companies are essentially business organisations consisting of two or more individuals who have agreed to embark on a business venture and who have decided to seek corporate status rather than to form a partnership. Such status could derive from an Act of Parliament or a Royal Charter, but is almost always nowadays achieved through 'registration', the terms of which are laid down in the various Companies Acts. Under the legislation – the most recent of which dates from 1985 and 1989 – individuals seeking to form a company are required to file numerous documents, including a Memorandum of Association and Articles of Association, with the Registrar of Companies. If satisfied, the Registrar will issue a Certificate of Incorporation, bringing the company into existence as a legal entity. As an alternative, the participants could buy a ready-formed company 'off the shelf', by approaching a company registration agent who specialises in company formations. In the United Kingdom, advertisements for ready-made companies appear regularly in magazines such as *Exchange and Mart* and *Dalton's Weekly*.

Companies' House has some useful information on topics such as company formation See *Ws5.companies-house.gov-uk/notes/gbfl*

Under British law a distinction is made between public and private companies. **Public limited companies** (PLCs) – not to be confused with public corporations, which in the UK are state-owned businesses (*see* below) – are those limited companies which satisfy the conditions for being a 'PLC'. These conditions require the company to have:

- a minimum of two shareholders;
- at least two directors;
- a minimum (at present) of £50 000 of authorised and allotted share capital;
- the right to offer its shares (and debentures) for sale to the general public;
- a certificate from the Registrar of Companies verifying that the share capital requirements have been met; and
- a memorandum which states it to be a public company.

A company which meets these conditions must include the title 'public limited company' or 'PLC' in its name and is required to make full accounts available for public inspection. Any company unable or unwilling to meet these conditions is therefore, in the eyes of the law, a 'private limited company', normally signified by the term 'Limited' or 'Ltd'.

Like the public limited company, the **private limited company** must have a minimum of two shareholders, but its shares cannot be offered to the public at large, although it can offer them to individuals through its business contacts. This restriction on the sale of shares, and hence on their ability to raise considerable sums of money on the open market, normally ensures that most private companies are either small or medium sized, and are often family businesses operating in a relatively restricted market; there are, however, some notable exceptions to this general rule (e.g. Virgin). In contrast, public companies – many of which began life as private companies prior to 'going public' – often have many thousands, even millions, of owners (shareholders) and normally operate on a national or international scale, producing products as diverse as computers, petro-chemicals, cars and banking services. Despite being outnumbered by their private counterparts, public companies dwarf private companies in terms of their capital and other assets, and their collective influence on output, investment, employment and consumption in the economy is immense.

Both public and private companies act through their **directors**. These are individuals chosen by a company's shareholders to manage its affairs and to make the important decisions concerning the direction the company should take (e.g. investment, market development, mergers and so on). The appointment and powers of directors are outlined in the Articles of Association (the 'internal rules' of the organisation) and so long as the directors do not exceed their powers, the shareholders do not normally have the right to intervene in the day-to-day management of the company. Where a director exceeds his or her authority or fails to indicate clearly that they are acting as an agent for the company, they become personally liable for any contracts they make. Equally, directors become personally liable if they continue to trade when the company is insolvent and they may be dismissed by a court if it considers that an individual is unfit to be a director in view of their past record (Company Directors Disqualification Act 1985).

It is usual for a board of directors to have both a chairperson and a managing director, although many companies choose to appoint one person to both roles.

The chairperson, who is elected by the other members of the board, is usually chosen because of their knowledge and experience of the business and their skill both internally in chairing board meetings and externally in representing the best interest of the organisation. As the public face of the company, the chairperson has an important role to play in establishing and maintaining a good public image and hence many large public companies like to appoint well-known public figures to this important position (e.g. ex-Cabinet ministers). In this case knowledge of the business is less important than the other attributes the individual might possess, most notably public visibility and familiarity, together with a network of contacts in government and in the business world.

The **managing director**, or chief executive, fulfils a pivotal role in the organisation, by forming the link between the board and the management team of senior executives. Central to this role is the need not only to interpret board decisions but to ensure that they are put into effect by establishing an appropriate structure of delegated responsibility and effective systems of reporting and control. This close contact with the day-to-day operations of the company places the appointed individual in a position of considerable authority and they will invariably be able to make important decisions without reference to the full board. This authority is enhanced where the managing director is also the person chairing the board of directors and/or is responsible for recommending individuals to serve as executive directors (i.e. those with functional responsibilities such as production, marketing, finance).

Like the managing director, most, if not all, **executive directors** will be full-time executives of the company, responsible for running a division or functional area within the framework laid down at board level. In contrast, other directors will have a **non-executive** role and are usually part-time appointees, chosen for a variety of reasons, including their knowledge, skills, contacts, influence, independence or previous experience. Sometimes, a company might be required to appoint such a director at the wishes of a third party, such as a merchant bank which has agreed to fund a large capital injection and wishes to have representation on the board. In this case, the individual tends to act in an advisory capacity – particularly on matters of finance – and helps to provide the financing institution with a means of ensuring that any board decisions are in its interests.

In Britain the role of company directors and senior executives in recent years has come under a certain amount of public scrutiny and has culminated in a number of enquiries into issues of power and pay. In the Cadbury Report (1992), a committee, with Sir Adrian Cadbury as chairperson, called for a non-statutory code of practice which it wanted applied to all listed public companies. Under this code the committee recommended:

- a clear division of responsibilities at the head of a company to ensure that no individual had unfettered powers of decision;
- a greater role for non-executive directors;
- regular board meetings;
- restrictions on the contracts of executive directors;
- full disclosure of directors' total enrolments;
- an audit committee dominated by non-executives.

The committee's stress on the important role of non-executive directors was a theme taken up in the Greenbury Report (1995) which investigated the controversial topic of executive salaries in the wake of a number of highly publicised pay rises for senior company directors. Greenbury's recommendations included:

■ full disclosure of directors' pay packages, including pensions;
■ shareholder approval for any long-term bonus scheme;
■ remuneration committees consisting entirely of non-executive directors;
■ greater detail in the annual report on directors' pay, pensions and perks;
■ an end to payments for failure.

Greenbury was followed by a further investigation into corporate governance by a committee under the chairmanship of ICI chairman Ronald Hampel. The Hampel Report (1998) called for greater shareholder responsibility by companies and increased standards of disclosure of information; it supported Cadbury's recommendation that the role of Chairperson and Chief Executive should normally be separated. As might have been anticipated, the Hampel Report advocated self-regulation as the best approach for UK companies. Time will tell how far public companies are prepared to go to implement the various recommendations and whether self-regulation will be sufficient to ensure compliance with the spirit as well as the letter of the different reports.

Mini case   Daimler-Benz under pressure

Public companies have to satisfy the conflicting demands of a range of stakeholder groups (see below), not least their shareholders who expect the organisation to operate in their interest. On the whole, individual shareholders are usually relatively quiescent, leaving the strategic and day-to-day decisions to the organisation's directors and senior executives. As an increasing number of public companies have found, however, many shareholders are becoming more actively involved in corporate decisions which affect their investments and have been willing to voice their feelings at shareholders' meetings and to the media.

Daimler-Benz, Germany's biggest industrial group, is an example of a company which has experienced this rise in shareholder militancy. At its centenary annual meeting held in Stuttgart in May 1996, the company's senior personnel faced around 10 000 shareholders, a significant number of whom expressed concern over record losses, allegations of executive deceit and plans to shed another aerospace subsidiary. Both the board of directors and the supervisory board were accused of failure by small shareholders who had recently experienced no dividends on the back of the largest loss in German corporate history. Claims by board chairperson, Jürgen Schrempp, that he was seeking to turn the situation around and to promote 'shareholder value' did little to placate the critics who were keen to see heads roll.

Apart from allegations of incompetence and abuse of position, the directors were subjected to criticisms from environmentalist shareholders and those campaigning against the company's sales of military hardware. This only serves to demonstrate that within any one stakeholder group there will tend to be a range of different opinions and interests – a fact which can make the task of satisfying stakeholder aspirations considerably more difficult.

Co-operatives

Consumer co-operative societies

Consumer societies are basically 'self-help' organisations which have their roots in the anti-capitalist sentiment which arose in mid-nineteenth-century Britain and which gave rise to a consumer co-operative movement dedicated to the provision of cheap, unadulterated food for its members and a share in its profits. Today this movement boasts a multibillion pound turnover, a membership numbered in millions and an empire which includes thousands of food stores, numerous factories and farms, dairies, travel agencies, opticians, funeral parlours, a bank and an insurance, and property and development business. Taken together, these activities ensure that the Cooperative Group remains a powerful force in British retailing into the early twenty-first century.

The Cooperative Group's website address is *www.co-op.co.uk*
On social enterprises generally see *www.socialenterprises.org.uk*

Although the co-operative societies, like companies, are registered and incorporated bodies – in this case under the Industrial and Provident Societies Act – they are quite distinct trading organisations. These societies belong to their members (i.e. invariably customers who have purchased a share in the society) and each member has one vote at the society's annual meeting, which elects a committee (or board) to take responsibility for running the organisation. This committee appoints managers and staff to run its various stores and offices and any profits from its activities are supposed to benefit the members. Originally this took the form of a cash dividend paid to members in relation to their purchases, but this has largely disappeared, having been replaced either by trading stamps or by investment in areas felt to benefit the consumer (e.g. lower prices, higher-quality products, modern shops and so on) and/or the local community (e.g. charitable donations, sponsorship).

The societies differ in other ways from standard companies. For a start, shares are not quoted on the Stock Exchange and members are restricted in the number of shares they can purchase and in the method of disposal. Not having access to cheap sources of capital on the stock market, co-operatives rely heavily on retained surpluses and on loan finance, and the latter places a heavy burden on the societies when interest rates are high. The movement's democratic principles also impinge on its operations and this has often been a bone of contention as members have complained about their increasing remoteness from decision-making centres. Some societies have responded by encouraging the development of locally elected committees, to act in an advisory or consultative capacity to the society's board of directors and it looks likely that others will be forced to consider similar means of increasing member participation, which still remains very limited.

The Co-operative Commission has put forward numerous proposals for change which are designed to improve the performance of societies. See *www.co-opcommission.org.uk*

The movement's historical links with the British Labour Party are also worth noting and a number of parliamentary candidates are normally sponsored at general elections. These links, however, have tended to become slightly looser in recent years, although the movement still contributes to Labour Party funds and continues to lobby politicians at both national and local level. It is also active in seeking to influence public opinion and, in this, claims to be responding to customer demands for greater social and corporate responsibility. Among its initiatives are the establishment of a customer's charter (by the Co-operative Bank) and the decision to review both its investments and the individuals and organisations it does business with, to ascertain that they are acceptable from an ethical point of view.

Workers' co-operatives

In Britain, workers' co-operatives are found in a wide range of industries, including manufacturing, building and construction, engineering, catering and retailing. They are particularly prevalent in printing, clothing and wholefoods, and some have been in existence for over a century. The majority, however, are of fairly recent origin, having been part of the growth in the number of small firms which occurred in the 1980s.

As the name suggests, a workers' co-operative is a business in which the ownership and control of the assets are in the hands of the people working in it, having agreed to establish the enterprise and to share the risk for mutual benefit. Rather than form a standard partnership, the individuals involved normally register the business as a friendly society under the Industrial and Provident Societies Acts 1965–78, or seek incorporation as a private limited company under the Companies Act 1985. In the case of the former, seven members are required to form a co-operative, while the latter only requires two. In practice, a minimum of three or four members tends to be the norm and some co-operatives may have several hundred participants, frequently people who have been made redundant by their employers and who are keen to keep the business going.

The central principles of the movement – democracy, open membership, social responsibility, mutual co-operation and trust – help to differentiate the co-operative from other forms of business organisation and govern both the formation and operation of this type of enterprise. Every employee may be a member of the organisation and every member owns one share in the business, with every share carrying an equal voting right. Any surpluses are shared by democratic agreement and this is normally done on an equitable basis, reflecting, for example, the amount of time and effort an individual puts into the business. Other decisions, too, are taken jointly by the members and the emphasis tends to be on the quality of goods or services provided and on creating a favourable working environment, rather than on the pursuit of profits – although the latter cannot be ignored if the organisation is to survive. In short, the co-operative tends to focus on people and on the relationship between them, stressing the co-operative and communal traditions associated with its origins, rather than the more conflictual and competitive aspects inherent in other forms of industrial organisation.

Despite these apparent attractions, workers' co-operatives have never been as popular in Britain as in other parts of the world (e.g. France, Italy, Israel), although a substantial increase occurred in the number of co-operatives in the 1980s, largely as a result of growing unemployment, overt support across the political spectrum and the establishment of a system to encourage and promote the co-operative ideal (e.g. Co-operative Development Agencies).[3] More recently, however, their fortunes have tended to decline, as employee shareholding and profit schemes (ESOPs) have grown in popularity. It seems unlikely that workers' co-operatives will ever form the basis of a strong third sector in the British economy, between the profit-oriented firms in the private sector and the nationalised and municipal undertakings in the public sector.

Public sector business organisations in the UK

Public sector organisations come in a variety of forms. These include:

- central government departments (e.g. Department of Trade and Industry);
- local authorities (e.g. Lancashire County Council);
- regional bodies (e.g. the former regional health authorities);
- non-departmental public bodies or quangos (e.g. the Arts Council);
- central government trading organisations (e.g. The Stationery Office); and
- public corporations and nationalised industries (e.g. the BBC).

Some of these were discussed in Chapter 3, which examined the political environment, and numerous other references to the influence of government on business activity can be found throughout the book, most notably in Chapters 4, 8, 10, 12, 13 and 14. In the discussion below, attention is focused on those public sector organisations which most closely approximate businesses in the private sector, namely, public corporations and municipal enterprises. An examination of the transfer of many of these public sector bodies to the private sector – usually termed 'privatisation' – is contained in Chapter 14.

Public corporations

Private sector business organisations are owned by private individuals and groups who have chosen to invest in some form of business enterprise, usually with a view to personal gain. In contrast, in the public sector the state owns assets in various forms, which it uses to provide a range of goods and services felt to be of benefit to its citizens, even if this provision involves the state in a 'loss'. Many of these services are provided directly through government departments (e.g. social security benefits) or through bodies operating under delegated authority from central government (e.g. local authorities, health authorities). Others are the responsibility of state-owned industrial and commercial undertakings, specially created for a variety of reasons and often taking the form of a 'public corporation'. These state corporations are an important part of the public sector of the economy and have contributed significantly to national output, employment and investment. Their numbers, however, have declined substantially following the wide-scale 'privatisation' of state industries which occurred in the 1980s and this process has continued through the 1990s and beyond with the sale of corporations such as British Coal, British Rail and British Energy (see Chapter 14).

Public corporations are statutory bodies, incorporated (predominantly) by special Act of Parliament and, like companies, they have a separate legal identity from the individuals who own them and run them. Under the statute setting up the corporation, reference is made to the powers, duties and responsibilities of the organisation and to its relationship with the government department which oversees its operations. In the past these operations have ranged from providing a variety of national and international postal services (the Post Office), to the provision of entertainment (the BBC), an energy source (British Coal) and a national rail network (British Rail). Where such provision involves the organisation in a considerable degree of direct contact with its customers, from whom it derives most of its revenue, the corporation tends to be called a 'nationalised industry'. In reality, of course, the public corporation is the legal form through which the industry is both owned and run and every corporation is to some degree unique in structure as well as in functions.

As organisations largely financed as well as owned by the state, public corporations are required to be publicly accountable and hence they invariably operate under the purview of a 'sponsoring' government department, the head of which (the Secretary of State) appoints a board of management to run the organisation. This board tends to exercise a considerable degree of autonomy in day-to-day decisions and operates largely free from political interference on most matters of a routine nature. The organisation's strategic objectives, however, and important questions concerning reorganisation or investment, would have to be agreed with the sponsoring department, as would the corporation's performance targets and its external financing limits.

The link between the corporation and its supervising ministry provides the means through which Parliament can oversee the work of the organisation and permits ordinary Members of Parliament to seek information and explanation through question time, through debates and through the select committee system. Additionally, under the Competition Act 1980, nationalised industries can be subject to investigation by the Competition Commission (*see* Chapter 14), and this too presents opportunities for further parliamentary discussion and debate, as well as for government action.

A further opportunity for public scrutiny comes from the establishment of industry-specific Consumers' or Consultative Councils, which consider complaints from customers and advise both the board and the department concerned of public attitudes to the organisation's performance and to other aspects of its operations (e.g. pricing). In a number of cases, including British Rail before privatisation, pressure on government from consumers and from other sources has resulted in the establishment of a 'Customers' Charter', under which the organisation agrees to provide a predetermined level of service or to give information and/or compensation where standards are not achieved. Developments of this kind are already spreading to other parts of the public sector and in future may be used as a means by which governments decide on the allocation of funds to public bodies, as well as providing a vehicle for monitoring organisational achievement.

It is interesting to note that mechanisms for public accountability and state regulation have been retained to some degree even where public utilities have been 'privatised' (i.e. turned into public limited companies). Industries such as gas, electricity, water and telecommunications are watched over by newly created regulatory bodies which are designed to protect the interests of consumers, particularly with regard to pricing and the standard of service provided. Ofgas, for example, which used to regulate British Gas, monitored gas supply charges to ensure that they reasonably reflected input costs and these charges could be altered by the 'regulator' if they were seen to be excessive. Similarly, in the case of non-gas services, such as maintenance, the legislation privatising the industry only allowed prices to be raised to a prescribed maximum, to ensure that the organisation was not able to take full advantage of its monopoly power. The regulator of the gas market is now Ofgem – *see* Chapter 14.)

An additional source of government influence comes from its ownership of a 'golden share' in a privatised state industry which effectively gives the government a veto in certain vital areas of decision making. This notional shareholding – which is written into the privatisation legislation – tends to last for a number of years and can be used to protect a newly privatised business from a hostile takeover, particularly by foreign companies or individuals. Ultimately, however, the expectation is that this veto power will be relinquished and the organisation concerned will become subject to the full effects of the market – a point exemplified by the government's decision to allow Ford to take over Jaguar in 1990, having originally blocked a number of previous takeover bids.

The existence of a 'golden share' should not be equated with the decision by government to retain (or purchase) a significant proportion of issued shares in a privatised (or already private) business organisation, whether as an investment and/or future source of revenue, or as a means of exerting influence in a particular industry or sector. Nor should it be confused with government schemes to attract private funds into existing state enterprises, by allowing them to achieve notional company status in order to overcome Treasury restrictions on borrowing imposed on public bodies. In the latter case, which often involves a limited share issue, government still retains full control of the organisation by owning all (or the vast majority) of the shares – as in the case of Consignia (formerly known as the Post Office). In March 2001 Consignia was incorporated as a government-owned public company. This change in legal status allowed the company more freedom to borrow and invest in the business, to make acquisitions and to enter into joint ventures and to expand internationally.

 web link   Further information on Consignia can be found at *www.consignia.com*

Municipal enterprises

UK local authorities have a long history of involvement in business activity. In part this is a function of their role as central providers of public services (e.g. education, housing, roads, social services) and of their increasing involvement in supporting local economic development initiatives (*see* Chapter 10). But their activities have also traditionally involved the provision of a range of marketable goods and services, not required by law but provided voluntarily by a local authority and often in direct competition with the private sector (e.g. theatres, leisure services, museums). Usually such provision has taken place under the aegis of a local authority department which appoints staff who are answerable to the council and to its committees through the department's chief officer and its elected head. Increasingly, though, local authorities are turning to other organisational arrangements – including the establishment of companies and trusts – in order to separate some of these activities from the rest of their responsibilities and to create a means through which private investment in the enterprise can occur.

One example of such a development can be seen in the case of local authority controlled airports which are normally the responsibility of a number of local authorities who run them through a joint board, representing the interests of the participating district councils (e.g. Manchester Airport). Since the Airports Act 1986, local authorities with airports have been required to create a limited company in which their joint assets are vested and which appoints a board of directors to run the enterprise. Like other limited companies, the organisation can, if appropriate, seek private capital and must publish annual accounts, including a profit and loss statement. It can also be 'privatised' relatively easily if the local authorities involved decide to relinquish ownership (e.g. East Midlands Airport).

Such developments, which have parallels in other parts of the public sector, can be seen to have had at least four benefits:

1 They have provided a degree of autonomy from local authority control that is seen to be beneficial in a competitive trading environment.
2 They have given access to market funds by the establishment of a legal structure that is not fully subject to central government restrictions on local authority borrowing.
3 They helped local authority organisations to compete more effectively under the now defunct system of compulsory competitive tendering (CCT), by removing or reducing charges for departmental overheads that are applied under the normal arrangements.
4 They have provided a vehicle for further private investment and for ultimate privatisation of the service.

Given these benefits and the current fashion for privatisation, there is little doubt that they will become an increasing feature of municipal enterprise in the foreseeable future. That said, local authorities are restricted in their degree of ownership of companies following the passage of the 1990 Local Government and Housing Act.

Business organisations in mainland Europe

Sole traders, partnerships, co-operatives and limited companies are to be found throughout Europe and beyond, and in many cases their legal structure is similar to that of their British counterparts. Where differences occur, these are often a reflection of historical and cultural factors which find expression in custom and practice as well as in law. Examples of some of these differences are contained in the discussion below, which focuses on France, Germany, Denmark and Portugal.

France

Numerically, the French economy is dominated by very small businesses (i.e. fewer than ten employees), the majority of which are sole traders. As in Britain, these are owner-managed-and-operated enterprises, with a husband and wife often assuming joint responsibility for the business. Formal requirements in this type of organisation tend to be few, although individuals as well as companies engaging in a commercial business are required to register before trading officially begins. Since this process is relatively simple and there are no minimum capital requirements nor significant reporting obligations, sole traderships tend to be preferred by the vast majority of individuals seeking to start a business and they are particularly prevalent in the service sector. They carry, however, unlimited personal liability for the owner, whose personal assets are at risk in the event of business failure.

Most of the remaining French business organisations are limited companies, many of which are Petites et Moyennes Entreprises (PMEs) – small and medium enterprises – employing between 10 and 500 employees. These companies come in a variety of legal forms, but two in particular predominate: the Société à Responsabilité Limitée (SARL) and the Société Anonyme (SA). A new company form, the Société Anonyme Simplifée was created by statute in 1994 and combines the legal status of a corporation with the flexibility of a partnership.

The SARL tends to be the form preferred by smaller companies, whose owners wish to retain close control of the organisation; hence many of them are family businesses – an important feature of the private sector in France. This type of enterprise can be established (currently) with a minimum capital of €7500, cannot issue shares to the general public, has restrictions on the transfer of shares and is run by individuals appointed by the shareholders – usually the shareholders themselves and/or relatives. In practice, these various restrictions help to ensure that the owner-managers remain dominant in the organisation and the appointed head of the company will invariably be the most important decision maker. Concomitantly, they help to provide the organisation with a defence against hostile takeover, particularly by overseas companies looking for a French subsidiary in order to avoid the special rules which apply to branches and agencies (e.g. a foreign parent company has unlimited liability for the debts of its branch or agency, since these do not have a separate legal identity).

The SA is the legal form normally chosen by larger companies seeking access to substantial amounts of capital. In the case of a privately owned company, the minimum capital requirement is currently €37 000; if publicly owned the minimum is €225 000 million. Where capital assets are substantial, this tends to ensure that financial institutions are large shareholders in SAs and many of them have interests in a wide range of enterprises which they often manage through a holding company (*see* below). One advantage of this arrangement is that it provides the financial institution with a means of managing its investments and of exerting influence over companies in which it has a large minority stake. Another is that it provides a means of defending French companies from hostile takeovers and hence small and medium enterprises often seek backing from holding companies to help fend off foreign predators.

As in Britain, the legal basis of the SA provides for a clear distinction between the roles of the owners (the shareholders) and the salaried employees, and it is the former who appoint the company's board of directors. In smaller companies, the chairperson and managing director is often the same person and many smaller French companies continue to have extremely strong central control, often by the head of the owning family. In larger companies, the two roles are normally separated, with the managing director assuming responsibility for the day-to-day operations of the enterprise and forming the link between the board and the company's senior executives and managers, some of whom may have considerable delegated authority.

It is worth noting that in companies with more than 50 employees, there is a legal requirement to have elected work councils, and workers' delegates have the right to attend board meetings as observers and to be consulted on matters affecting working conditions. In companies with more than ten employees, workers have the right to elect representatives to look after their interests and regular meetings have to take place between management and workers, over and above the obligation of employers to negotiate annually on pay and conditions. Despite these arrangements and the legal right for unions to organise on a company's premises, trade union membership – outside state-run companies – remains low and hence union influence tends to be limited. Recent steps to encourage local agreements on pay and conditions seem destined to reduce this influence even further – a situation which has parallels in Britain.

Germany

All major forms of business organisation are to be found in Germany, but it is the limited company which is of particular interest. Some of these are of relatively recent origin, having formerly been East German state-owned enterprises which have undergone 'privatisation' following the reunification of the country.

In numerical terms it is the private limited company (*Gesellschaft mit beschränkter Haftung* – GmbH) which predominates and which is the form chosen by most foreign companies seeking to establish an enterprise in Germany. As in Britain, this type of organisation has to be registered with the authorities and its founding members must prepare Articles of Association for signature by a public notary. The Articles include information on the purpose of the business, the amount of capital subscribed, the members' subscriptions and obligations and the company's name and registered address. Once the registration process is complete – usually a matter of a few days – the personal liability of the members becomes limited to the amount invested in the business. Currently, the minimum amount of subscribed share capital required for registration is €25 000, half of which must be paid up by the company itself.

Large numbers of GmbHs are owned and run by German families, with the banks often playing an influential role as guarantors of part of the initial capital and as primary sources of loan finance. As in France, this pattern of ownership makes hostile takeovers less likely, as well as ensuring that the management of the enterprise remains in the hands of the owners. Significantly, the management of a proposed GmbH is subject to quality control, being required to prove that they are qualified for the task prior to trading. This requirement stands in stark contrast to arrangements in Britain, where no such guarantees are needed, other than those implicit in a bank's decisions to help finance a proposed venture on the basis of a business plan.

The procedures for establishing other types of business organisation are similar to those of the GmbH, although in the case of the public limited company (*Aktiengesellschaft* – AG), the current minimum amount of capital required at start-up is €50 000 in negotiable share certificates. Unlike British companies, the AG usually consists of two boards of directors, one of which (the supervisory board) decides on longer-term strategy, while the other (the managing board) concentrates on more immediate policy issues, often of an operational kind. Normally half the members of the supervisory board (*Aufsichtrat*) are elected by shareholders, while the other half are employees elected by the workforce, and it is the responsibility of the board to protect the interests of employees as well as shareholders.

Such worker representation at senior levels is an important element of the German system of business organisation and even in smaller enterprises workers have the right to establish works councils and to be consulted on social and personnel issues and on strategic decisions. Equally, all employees have a constitutional right to belong to a trade union – most of which are organised by industry rather than by craft or occupation, as is largely the case in the United Kingdom. Consequently, German companies typically negotiate with only one union; usually in an atmosphere which stresses consensus and an identity of social and economic interests, rather than conflict and confrontation.

Corporate finance is another area in which German experience differs from that in the United Kingdom, although the situation has changed to some degree in recent years. Historically, in Britain a substantial amount of company finance has been raised through the stock market and this is also the case in the United States and Japan (*see* e.g. Table 7.1). In Germany (and for that matter in France, Italy and Spain), the banks and a number of other special credit institutions play a dominant role, with bank loans far outstripping joint-stock financing as a source of long-term capital. Traditionally, German banks have been willing to take a longer-term view of their investment, even at the expense of short-term profits and dividends, and this has benefited German companies seeking to expand their operations. In return, the banks have tended to exert a considerable amount of influence in the boardrooms of many German companies, usually by providing a substantial number of members of a company's supervisory board, including the chairperson.

Denmark

Denmark, like France, is a country whose economy is dominated by small businesses, many of which are sole traders. As in other countries, there are very few

Table 7.1 Stock market capitalisation (as at 29 December 1989)

Country	Billion ECU	% of GDP
United Kingdom	557	74.1
West Germany	236	21.8
France	182	21.1
Spain	62	18.1
Italy	95	12.1
Japan	2632	102.3
United States	1968	34.8

Source: F. Somers (ed.), *European Economies: A Comparative Study*, Pitman Publishing, 1991.

regulations governing the establishment of this type of enterprise, other than the need to register for VAT if turnover exceeds a predetermined limit and to meet taxation and social security requirements. In keeping with practice throughout Europe and beyond, sole traders have unlimited personal liability and this imposes a considerable burden on the organisation's owner and family, who often run the business jointly. The same conditions also apply in the case of Danish partnerships – whether formal or informal – with the joint owners having full and unlimited liability for all debts accruing to the organisation.

Limited companies in Denmark also reflect practice elsewhere, being required to register under the Companies Act and having a legal existence separate from the owners and employees. Three main types of limited liability company can be distinguished:

1 The *Anpartselskaber* (ApS), which is a private joint-stock company, often run by a family and owned and controlled by a handful of individuals, one of whom may simultaneously occupy the roles of main owner, chairperson and managing director. Many of these companies began life as sole traders, but for reasons of taxation and liability have registered as an ApS.

2 The *Aktieselskaber* (A/S), which is a quoted or (more regularly) unquoted public limited company, subject essentially to the same regulations as the ApS, but having a much larger minimum capital requirement on registration. A large number of A/S companies are still small businesses, run by family members who wish to retain control of the enterprise as an increase in assets occurs.

3 The AMBA is a special kind of limited company – in essence a tax-free co-operative with its own regulations. Many of these companies have grown over the years through merger and acquisition and some of them belong to larger Danish companies and employ a substantial number of workers. They tend to be concentrated in farm-related products, but can also be found in the service sector, especially wholesaling and retailing.

Portugal

A brief look at Portuguese business organisations reveals a range of legal structures which includes sole traders, joint ventures, complementary groups, unlimited companies, limited partnerships and public and private limited companies. In the case of the latter, capital requirements tend to be an important distinguishing feature with the Public Limited Company or Corporation (*Sociedade Anonima* – SA) having a much larger minimum capital requirement than the private company (*Sociedade Por Quotas* or *Limitada* – LDA) as in other countries.

The public sector in mainland Europe

Given the number of countries involved, it is impossible to survey the whole of the public sector in the rest of Europe. Students with an interest in this area are encouraged to read further and to consult the various specialist sources of information covering the countries they wish to investigate. A number of general points, however, are worthy of note:

1 Public sector business organisations can be found in all countries and invariably exist because of the decision by the state to establish a particular organisation under state ownership and control, or to nationalise an existing private business (or industry).
2 In some countries (e.g. France, Greece, Portugal) the state has traditionally played an important role in business and still controls some key sectors of the economy.
3 State involvement in business often includes significant shareholdings in a number of large enterprises, not only by the national government but also by regional and/or local government (e.g. in Germany).
4 State intervention often occurs in organisations or industries which can be deemed 'problematic' (e.g. in Greece).
5 Privatisation of state-owned enterprises has occurred throughout Europe and in other parts of the world. In the former East Germany, for example, most of the state-owned companies have been transferred to private ownership, by turning them initially into trusts which became the vehicle for privatisation and/or joint ventures. Similarly in Portugal, the wholesale nationalisation of the economy after the 1974 Revolution has been reversed and the government is committed to a phased programme of privatisation, involving employees and small investors as well as large national and international organisations.

This latter point serves to re-emphasise that the business environment is subject to change over time and the fashions of today may tomorrow become things of the past. This fluctuating environment is as applicable to the public sector as it is to the private sector of the economy.

Legal structure: some implications

For businesses in the private sector, the choice of legal structure has important implications. Among the factors which the aspiring entrepreneur has to take into account when deciding what form of business enterprise to establish are:

- the degree of personal liability;
- the willingness to share decision-making powers and risks;
- the costs of establishing the business;
- the legal requirements concerning the provision of public information;
- the taxation position;
- commercial needs, including access to capital; and
- business continuity.

For some, retaining personal control will be the main requirement, even at the risk of facing unlimited personal liability and reducing the opportunities for expansion. For others, the desire to limit personal liability and to provide increased capital for growth will dictate that the owner seeks corporate status, even if this necessitates sharing decision-making powers and may ultimately result in a loss of ownership and/or control of the enterprise.

This link between an organisation's legal structure and its subsequent operations can be illustrated by examining three important facets of organisational life: the organisation's objectives, its sources of finance and its stakeholders. As the analysis below illustrates, in each of these areas significant differences occur between alternative forms of business organisation, both *within* the private sector and *between* the state and non-state sectors of the economy. In some cases, these differences can be attributed directly to the restraints (or opportunities) faced by an organisation as a result of its legal status, suggesting that the legal basis of the enterprise conditions its operations. In other cases operational considerations tend to dictate the organisation's legal form, indicating that these are as much a cause of its legal status as a result of it – a point well illustrated by the workers' co-operative and the public corporation.

Organisational objectives

All business organisations pursue a range of objectives and these may vary to some degree over time. New private sector businesses, for example, are likely to be concerned initially with survival and with establishing a position in the marketplace, with profitability and growth seen as less important in the short term. In contrast, most well-established businesses will tend to regard profits and growth as key objectives and may see them as a means towards further ends, including market domination, maximising sales revenue and/or minimising operating costs.

Organisational objectives are also conditioned by the firm's legal structure. In sole traders, partnerships and some limited companies, control of the enterprise rests in the hands of the entrepreneur(s) and hence organisational goals will tend to coincide with the personal goals of the owner(s), whatever the point in the organisation's life cycle. In public companies, however – where ownership tends to be separated from control – the goals of the owners (shareholders) may not always correspond with those of the directors and senior managers who run the organisation, particularly when the latter are pursuing personal goals to enhance their own organisational position, status and/or rewards.

It is worth noting that the possibility of goal conflict also occurs where an individual company becomes a subsidiary of another organisation, whether by agreement or as a result of a takeover battle. This parent–subsidiary relationship may take the form of a holding company which is specially created to purchase a majority (sometimes all) of the shares in other companies, some of which may operate as holding companies themselves. Thus, while the individual subsidiaries may retain their legal and commercial identities and may operate as individual units, they will tend to be controlled by a central organisation which may exercise a considerable degree of influence over the objectives to be pursued by each of its subsidiaries. It is not inconceivable, for example, that some parts of the group may be required to make a loss on paper, particularly when there are tax advantages to be gained by the group as a whole from doing so.

Workers' co-operatives and public corporations provide further evidence of the relationship between an organisation's legal status and its primary objectives. In the case of the former, the establishment of the enterprise invariably reflects a desire on the part of its members to create an organisation which emphasises social goals (e.g. democracy, co-operation, job creation, mutual trust) rather than the pursuit of profits – hence the choice of the 'co-operative' form. Similarly in the case of the public corporation, a decision by government to establish an entity which operates in the interests of the public at large (or 'national interest') favours the creation of a state-owned-and-controlled organisation, with goals laid down by politicians and generally couched in social and financial terms (e.g. return on assets, reinvestment, job creation) rather than in terms of profit maximisation.

This apparent dichotomy between the profit motive of the private sector and the broader socio-economic goals of public bodies has, however, become less clear-cut over the last decade, as an increasing number of state-owned organisations have been 'prepared' for privatisation and successive governments have sought to bring private money into public projects by creating public/private partnerships. Equally, in other parts of the public sector – including the health service and local government – increasing stress is being laid on 'best value' and on operating within budgets – concepts which are familiar to businesses in the private sector. While it is not inconceivable that a change in government could reverse this trend, current evidence suggests that a shift in cultural attitudes has occurred and public bodies can no longer rely on unconditional government support for their activities. If this is the case, further convergence is likely to occur between state and privately owned bodies, with the former moving towards the latter rather than vice versa.

Finance

Business organisations finance their activities in a variety of ways and from a range of sources. Methods include reinvesting profits, borrowing, trade credit and issuing shares and debentures. Sources include the banks and other financial institutions, individual investors and governments, as well as contributions from the organisation's original owners (see Chapter 8).

In the context of this chapter it is appropriate to make a number of observations about the topic as it relates generally to the business environment:

1 All organisations tend to fund their activities from both internal (e.g. owner's capital, reinvested profits) and external sources (e.g. bank borrowing, sale of shares).
2 Financing may be short term, medium term or longer term, and the methods and sources of funding chosen will reflect the time period concerned (e.g. bank borrowing on overdraft tends to be short term and generally needed for immediate use).
3 Funds raised from external sources inevitably involve the organisation in certain obligations (e.g. repayment of loans with interest, personal guarantees, paying dividends) and these will act as a constraint on the organisation at some future date.

4   The relationship between owner's capital and borrowed funds – usually described as an organisation's gearing – can influence a firm's activities and prospects in a variety of ways (e.g. high-geared firms with a large element of borrowed funds will be adversely affected if interest rates are high).

5   Generally speaking, as organisations become larger many more external sources and methods of funding become available and utilising these can have implications for the structure, ownership and conduct of the organisation.

This latter point is perhaps best illustrated by comparing sole traders and partnerships with limited companies. In the case of the former, as unincorporated entities neither the sole trader nor the partnership can issue shares (or debentures) and hence their access to large amounts of external capital is restricted by law. Companies have no such restrictions – other than those which help to differentiate a private company from a public one – and consequently they are able to raise larger amounts by inviting individuals (and organisations) to subscribe for shares. Where a company is publicly quoted on the stock market, the amounts raised in this way can be very large indeed and the resultant organisation may have millions of owners who change on a regular basis as shares are traded on the second-hand market.

Organisations which decide to acquire corporate status in order to raise funds for expansion (or for some other purposes) become owned by their shareholders, who may be the original owners or may be individual and institutional investors holding equity predominantly as an investment and with little, if any, long-term commitment to the organisation they own. As indicated above, in the latter case, a separation tends to occur between the roles of owner (shareholder) and controller (director) and this can lead to the possibility of conflicting aims and objectives or differences in opinion over priorities within the enterprise – a problem discussed in more detail below under 'Stakeholders'.

A further illustration of the relationship between an organisation's legal structure and its ability to raise finance is provided by the public corporation. In this case, as a public body accountable to Parliament and the public via government, the public corporation is required to operate within a financial context largely controlled by government and normally conditioned by the government's overall fiscal policy, including its attitude to the size of the Public Sector Borrowing Requirement (PSBR). One aspect of this context in Britain has been the establishment of external financing limits (EFLs) for each nationalised industry, arrived at by negotiation between government and the board running the public corporation, and used as a means of restraining monetary growth and hence the size of the PSBR. Unfortunately this has also tended to prevent the more financially sound corporations, such as British Telecom before privatisation, from borrowing externally on a scale necessary to develop their business – a restriction which tends to disappear when the corporation becomes a fully fledged public company, either through privatisation or by some other means.

Stakeholders

All organisations have stakeholders; these are individuals and/or groups who are affected by or affect the performance of the organisation in which they have an interest. Typically they would include employees, managers, creditors, suppliers, shareholders (if appropriate) and society at large. As Table 7.2 illustrates, an organisation's stakeholders have a variety of interests which range from the pursuit of private gain to the more nebulous idea of achieving public benefit. Sometimes these interests will clash as, for example, when managers seek to improve the organisation's cash flow by refusing to pay suppliers' bills on time. On other occasions, the interests of different stakeholders may coincide, as when managers plan for growth in the organisation and in doing so provide greater job security for employees and enhanced dividends for investors.

The legal structure of an organisation has an impact not only on the type of stakeholders involved but also to a large degree on how their interests are represented. In sole traders, partnerships and smaller private companies, the coincidence of ownership and control limits the number of potential clashes of interest, given that objectives are set by and decisions taken by the firm's owner-manager(s). In larger companies, and, in particular, public limited companies, the division between ownership and control means that the controllers have the responsibility of representing the interests of the organisation's shareholders and creditors and, as suggested above, their priorities and goals may not always correspond.

A similar situation occurs in public sector organisations, where the interest of taxpayers (or ratepayers) is represented both by government and by those individuals chosen by government to run the organisation. In this case, it is worth recalling that the broader strategic objectives of the enterprise and the big decisions concerning policy, finance and investment tend to be taken by politicians, operating with advice from their officials (e.g. civil servants, local government officers) and within the context of the government's overall economic and social policies. The organisation's board of management and its senior executives and managers are mainly responsible for the day-to-day operations of the business, although the board and the person chairing it would normally play a key role in shaping overall objectives and decisions, through regular discussions with government and its officials.

One important way in which public sector organisations differ from their private sector counterparts is in the sanctions available to particular groups of stakeholders who feel that the organisation is not representing their best interests. Shareholders

Table 7.2   Organisational stakeholders and their interest

Types of stakeholder	Possible principal interests
Employees	Wage levels; working conditions; job security; personal development
Managers	Job security; status; personal power; organisational profitability; growth of the organisation
Shareholders	Market value of the investment; dividends; security of investment; liquidity of investment
Creditors	Security of loan; interest on loan; liquidity of investment
Suppliers	Security of contract; regular payment; growth of organisation; market development
Society	Safe products; environmental sensitivity; equal opportunities; avoidance of discrimination

in a company, for example, could withdraw financial support for a firm whose directors consistently disregard their interests or take decisions which threaten the security and/or value of their investment, and the possibility of such a reaction normally guarantees that the board pays due attention to the needs of this important group of stakeholders. The taxpayer and ratepayer have no equivalent sanction and in the short term must rely heavily on government and its agencies or, if possible, their power as consumers to represent their interest *vis-à-vis* the organisation. Longer term, of course, the public has the sanction of the ballot box, although it seems highly unlikely that the performance of state enterprises would be a key factor in determining the outcome of general or local elections.

The relative absence of market sanctions facing state-owned organisations has meant that the public has had to rely on a range of formal institutions (e.g. parliamentary scrutiny committees, consumer consultative bodies, the audit authorities) and on the media to protect its interest in areas such as funding, pricing and quality of service provided. As these organisations are returned to the private sector, the expectation is that the sanctions imposed by the free market will once again operate and shareholders in privatised utilities will be protected like any other group of shareholders in a privately owned enterprise. To what extent this will occur in practice, of course, is open to question, while the newly privatised public corporations face little, if any, competition. Government, it seems, prefers to hedge its bets on this question, at least in the short term – hence the establishment of 'regulators' with powers of investigation into performance and some degree of control over pricing.

Mini case   Big Mac gets bigger

Growth through franchising has become a preferred option for many organisations, typified by McDonald's, which is the world's biggest fast food chain. Established in 1955 when Raymond Croc opened his first burger restaurant, McDonald's was estimated to have had in excess of 20 000 outlets spread across the globe by the end of 1996. Contrary to popular predictions, the organisation has continued to expand at a significant rate and has benefited from the opening of new markets in eastern Europe and the Far East. In the mid-1990s, for example, it was estimated that at its current rate of growth, a new McDonald's was opening somewhere in the world every three hours.

When considering applicants for a coveted McDonald's franchise the company has always been concerned to ensure that its reputation for quality and service is maintained. Potential franchisees have to demonstrate not only a successful track record in a previous occupation, but also that they have the necessary financial resources and a willingness to commit themselves to the organisation. Individuals making the grade have traditionally been offered two kinds of franchise scheme. The conventional franchise involves a 20-year agreement between the franchisee and the company under which the latter buys and develops the site which the former takes over and operates for an agreed price, as well as paying McDonald's a royalty fee based on a pre-agreed percentage of turnover. Under the other option – the business facilities lease – the individual leases the restaurant normally for a three-year period, prior to being offered the opportunity to convert to a conventional franchise if funds permit.

As far as future expansion in parts of western Europe is concerned it remains to be seen how far the 'beef scare' will affect market demand in the medium to long term, and hence the opportunities available to aspiring franchisees. Elsewhere in the world, there appears to be ample scope for would-be entrepreneurs to trade under the McDonald's brand name and to take advantage of the seemingly inexorable global demand for Big Macs and associated products.

Postscript: In late October 2002 McDonald's announced its intention of sharply cutting back on its expansion plans and redirecting its efforts towards supporting its existing chain of restaurants (*see* the *Guardian* 23 October 2002).

 The website for McDonalds is *www.mcdonalds.com*

Franchising, licensing and joint ventures

To complete this review of the legal structure of business organisations, it is useful to consider three developments which have a legal aspect: franchising, licensing and joint ventures. All three may be seen as a means of carrying out a business venture in a way that reduces some of the risks normally faced by the entrepreneur.

Franchising

Franchising, which has grown significantly in recent years, is an arrangement where one party (the franchiser) sells the right to another party (the franchisee) to market its product or service. In terms of their legal status the parties involved could be any of the forms described above, but in practice it is usually the case that the franchiser is a company while the franchisee tends to be a sole trader or partnership. Both parties in law have a separate legal identity, but the nature of the contract between them makes their relationship interdependent and this has important implications for the operation of the franchise.

Franchise arrangements come in a variety of forms. Probably the best known is the 'business format franchise' (or 'trade name franchise') under which the franchiser agrees to allow the franchisee to sell the product or service with the help of a franchise package which contains all the elements needed to set up and run a business at a profit. These would typically include the brand name, any associated supplies, promotional material and other forms of support and assistance. In return the franchisee usually pays an initial sum or fee for the use of the service and its various elements, remits royalties based on sales and/or profits, agrees to make a contribution for consultancy, training and promotion, and undertakes to maintain standards. Wimpy, Kentucky Fried Chicken, Burger King, Prontaprint and Dynarod are examples of this type of franchise.

Other forms include manufacturer/retailer franchises (e.g. car dealers), manufacturer/wholesaler franchises (e.g. Coca-Cola, Pepsi) and wholesaler/retailer franchises (e.g. Spar and Mace) and it is estimated by the industry's trade body – the British Franchise Association – that in retailing alone franchising accounts for over 20 per cent of sales in the United Kingdom. One indication of its growing significance is the spread of franchising into further and higher education, with universities and other colleges of higher education franchising some of their courses to local further education colleges, which in turn may franchise some of their courses to schools and/or sixth-form colleges. Another indicator is the decision by many clearing banks and firms of accountants to establish franchise sections to help and advise individuals who want to open a franchise or who have already done so and are seeking further guidance.

 The British Franchise Association's main website is *www.british-franchise.org*

Undoubtedly the mutual benefits to be derived from a franchise arrangement help to explain its popularity as a way of doing business in both domestic and external markets and it has proved an attractive vehicle for some companies seeking rapid overseas expansion, without undertaking substantial direct investments – although this is sometimes necessary to support the operation (e.g. McDonald's had to invest in a plant to make hamburger buns in the United Kingdom). Equally, many would-be entrepreneurs find the security of a franchise more attractive than other methods of starting a business, especially as there is some evidence to suggest that franchises have better survival rates than the more conventional forms of independent enterprise (e.g. sole traders).

Current indications are that this popularity is likely to continue into the foreseeable future, although it is more likely that greater selectivity of potential franchisees will occur as the franchise industry becomes more mature and attempts to gain an increased degree of public respectability. Franchisees, too, are likely to become more particular about the businesses they agree to deal with, as they endeavour to join the enterprise culture. It is, after all, the franchisee who has to bear the financial risk of the business in return for a share in the profits; the franchiser has a reputation to think about.

Licensing

Licensing is another form of non-equity agreement under which a firm in one country (the licensor) authorises a firm in another country (the licensee) to use its intellectual property (e.g. patents, copyrights, trade names, know-how) in return for certain considerations, usually royalty payments. Licences may be granted to individuals, independent companies, subsidiaries of a multinational company or to government agencies and the rights granted may be exclusive or non-exclusive.

Companies invariably enter into licensing agreements to gain certain advantages. These might include:

- Reducing competition by sharing technology.
- Seeking overseas profits without direct foreign investment.
- Protecting an asset from potential 'pirates'.
- Avoiding restrictions on foreign investment or imports imposed by other countries.
- Recouping some research and development costs.
- Gaining a share of an overseas market.

Needless to say, most organisations granting licences tend to be based in the advanced industrial economies and are frequently multinationals which regard their trade marks and technologies as an integral part of their asset base. One problem of transferring the use of such assets to another firm is that the owner loses a degree of control over the asset, including the quality of production, and this may affect the product's image and sales elsewhere. Another is the possibility of the licensee dominating the market after the agreement ends, even to the extent of excluding the licensor from the marketplace by aggressive competition or the development of an alternative product.

Joint ventures

The term 'joint venture' tends to be used in two ways: to describe a contractual agreement involving two or more parties; or to describe a jointly owned and independently incorporated business venture involving more than one organisation. It is the latter usage which is mainly applied here.

Joint ventures – which are popular with international companies – can take a variety of legal forms and almost every conceivable type of partnership may exist, ranging from two companies joining together in the same domestic market (e.g. Sainsbury's and British Home Stores set up the Savacentre chain), to joint private/public sector ventures between participants from different countries. Sometimes numerous organisations may be involved and these may be based in one country or in several. Where this occurs the term 'consortium' is often used, as in the case of TransManche Link (TML), the international joint venture which built the Channel Tunnel.

As with licensing and franchising, joint ventures have increased in popularity in the last 25–30 years and have been one of the ways in which international companies have sought to develop an overseas market, particularly in the face of import restrictions, or heavy research and development costs. Multinational car companies have been active in this field – as evidenced by past links between General Motors and Toyota, Ford and Mazda – and these arrangements look likely to continue as markets become more global. For western companies wishing to exploit the gradual 'privatisation' of the former planned economies of eastern Europe, joint ventures with indigenous producers are likely to prove a safer bet than direct inward investment, particularly given the degree of economic and political uncertainty. They are also likely to prove more politically acceptable in states seeking to establish their own economic independence and identity after almost fifty years of regional domination.

Synopsis

Market-based economies throughout Europe and beyond have a range of business organisations with broadly similar legal structures. These legal structures help to determine not only the ownership and control of the enterprise, but also other aspects of its operations, including its objectives, its access to finance and its external relationships and obligations. Viewing businesses as legal entities provides a useful insight into a number of the external influences which impinge upon their daily existence and highlights some of the consequences faced by organisations which transfer from public (i.e. state) to private ownership. It also sheds light on other important developments in entrepreneurial activity, including franchising, licensing and joint ventures.

Summary of key points

- Business organisations have a legal structure.

- The three commonest forms of business in the private sector are sole traders, partnerships and limited companies.

- Whereas the owners of the first two types of business organisation face unlimited personal liability, in companies the legal separation of the firm from its owners affords the latter limited personal liability.

- Companies are normally run by directors who are appointed to represent the interest of the owners (the shareholders). In public companies this separation of ownership and control is a key distinguishing feature.

- Other forms of business organisation exist in the public sector (e.g. the public corporation) and the 'third sector' (e.g. the co-operative).

- Government-owned businesses are increasingly adopting private sector forms of organisation to provide for greater flexibility and freedom of action.

- The legal status of the organisation has implications for the objectives of the enterprise, how it is financed and for its stakeholder relationships.

- Franchising, licensing and joint ventures are significant developments in the operation of modern businesses.

CASE STUDY   The entrepreneurial spirit

Business studies textbooks teach us that new businesses invariably come into existence to satisfy the needs and ambitions of their owners. Once established, it is assumed that an enterprise will begin to grow and that the owner(s) will sanction this and take steps to bring it about. As the two case studies below illustrate, these assumptions may be correct or not, according to specific circumstances. Arguing from the particular to the general needs to be approached with caution in business, as in any other field of study.

T & S Stores PLC

Like many medium- to large-sized businesses, T & S Stores started from relatively modest origins and was the brainchild of one individual, Kevin Threlfall, a Wolverhampton entrepreneur.

A barrow boy by background, Threlfall received his early business training working from the age of 12 on his parents' pitch in West Midlands markets.

Despatched to public school, Threlfall soon found this market background was treated contemptuously by his fellow pupils and this made him determined to prove his worth in the business world. On leaving school he began providing pet-foods in bulk, before selling out his business and founding the Lo Cost food chain in 1972. This was subsequently bought for £1.5 million by Oriel Foods, later owned by the Argyll Group.

Threlfall's T & S Stores grew from the Wolverhampton market stalls and quickly expanded into retail outlets, with their emphasis on discount tobacco and convenience shopping. Using day-glo starbursts offering low-priced cigarettes, Threlfall cleverly attracted customers into his stores where they were tempted by the use of colourful confectionery gondolas and other techniques into impulse purchases of products carrying high margins. By keeping costs to a minimum, Threlfall was able to turn his company into a highly profitable enterprise with a stock market capitalisation of almost £140 million by 1991 and a chain of almost 600 stores.

In 1989, T & S acquired the Dillons and Preedy chains from Next for £54 million and subsequently purchased 22 stores from Johnson News Group for £4.25 million in February 1991, thus helping to increase the organisation's interest in convenience stores, which Threlfall believed would be the company's main area of future growth. Trading from outlets larger than most of the T & S shops and offering an extended range of grocery and frozen-food lines, Threlfall's One Stop convenience stores have generally achieved higher gross margins than the core tobacco shops and helped to contribute to the company's strong net cash position in the early 1990s. Despite these developments, Threlfall has maintained close contacts with what is happening on the ground and has attempted to maintain a degree of individual customer attention in a field of retailing which is rapidly changing.

Evidence suggests that Threlfall's entrepreneurial skills, coupled with the gains from introducing National Lottery and other facilities in many of the group's outlets, have continued to strengthen the organisation's financial and trading position. With hundreds of stores and increasing turnover and pre-tax profits, T & S has attracted outside investment from reputable fund managers who appear confident in the management's strategy of refocusing the business towards the growing convenience store market. Turnover by 2001 was recorded at £933 million; in 1995 it had been £445 million.

Postscript: T & S agreed on 30 October 2002 to sell its stores to Tesco for £530 million.

Dave Noble (Windsurfing)

Unlike Kevin Threlfall, Dave Noble came from a non-business background and had no ambitions as a child to seek a career in industry or commerce. Following A-levels at the local grammar school in Woking, Noble went to Aberystwyth University where he obtained a degree in philosophy, before continuing his studies at postgraduate level. After a brief spell doing research, he left university and worked on building sites, subsequently returning to study for a postgraduate certificate of education, a move which was to take him into teaching in Loughborough.

With the start of a family, Noble gave up his full-time teaching post to look after the children, continuing as a supply teacher as and when circumstances allowed. As a keen windsurfer, with an established reputation in the sport, he decided to use some of his time at home to make his own boards, buying the necessary fittings from suppliers to the trade. As requests from friends for similar equipment began to grow, Noble found himself dealing with suppliers on a larger scale and spending an increasing amount of his time making and equipping windsurfing boards. Before he had fully realised what was happening, Noble found himself in business as a sole trader, operating in the leisure industry, a growing sector in the UK economy.

With an initial injection of his own capital, supported by a weekly income from the government's Enterprise Allowance Scheme, Noble established his own venture in late 1986/early 1987, operating from home in Shepshed in Leicestershire. Despite only limited expenditure on advertising, the business began to grow quickly, allowing the venture to become totally self-financing. Before long, it became obvious that new premises would be needed and so in 1989 the Noble family (now five in total) moved to a Georgian house in the village of Wymeswold on the Leicestershire/Nottinghamshire border. Apart from providing adequate space for a growing family, the new house had numerous outbuildings suitable for making and selling equipment and for storing supplies and material. It was also sufficiently close to Shepshed to allow Noble to keep his existing customer and supplier bases which were fundamental to the success of the business.

Noble's initial enthusiasm at working from his village home – in a manner reminiscent of a traditional cottage industry – was soon to be dampened following complaints from neighbours who objected to the traffic from customers seeking boards and other equipment. Consequently, the business was forced to relocate to the nearby Wymeswold Airfield Industrial Estate, where Noble acquired two units from which to operate. Like other units on the estate, Noble's premises were relatively basic, but provided sufficient space for production, storage and sales and had more than adequate parking for customers and suppliers. Being in a rural location, with no houses in the immediate vicinity, complaints concerning disturbance ceased to be a problem for the business.

Despite the successive moves, Noble's business continued to grow, even in the recession years in the early 1990s. Part of this growth was manifestly attributable to the increased demand for leisure products, and the decision to add mountain bikes and ski equipment to the range of items on offer was clearly beneficial, although by no means part of a deliberate strategy of diversification. The most significant factor in the firm's success, however, and one which resulted in the need to hire additional staff to meet the increased demand, appears to have been Noble's deliberate policy of keeping customers and suppliers happy. By paying all his bills on time, Noble was able to strike good bargains with suppliers and to pass savings on to the customer in the form of highly competitive prices which other traders could not meet. In addition, Noble and his staff did their best to meet their customers' needs individually, even if it meant working extra hours and incurring some additional expense.

By the mid-1990s Dave Noble (Windsurfing) had become a formidable operator in the marketplace, with a dominant share of the market in the East Midlands and a loyal and extensive customer base. As the firm continued to prosper, Noble eventually decided to sell his business to the staff and to go into semi-retirement. He has, however, maintained an interest in the leisure industry, importing snowboards which he sells to the trade via mail order.

Case study questions

1 What characteristics have Threlfall and Noble in common which might help to explain their success as entrepreneurs?

2 Can you identify any changes in the external environment of either of the businesses in the case study which proved beneficial to their development?

For information on the T&S Stores Group see *www.tands.co.uk*
You can also find information on this and other companies at *www.hoovers.com/uk*

Review and discussion questions

1 Numerically, the sole proprietorship is the most popular form of business organisation throughout Europe. How would you account for this?

2 To what extent is corporate status an asset to a business organisation? Does it have any disadvantages?

3 Examine the implications of 'privatising' a public sector business organisation.

4 Discuss how the legal status of a business affects its objectives, its methods of finance and its stakeholders.

5 How would you explain the rise in the popularity of franchising in recent years?

Assignments

1 You have recently been made redundant and decide to set up your own small business, possibly with a friend. Assuming that you have £25 000 to invest in your new venture, draft a business plan which is to be presented to your bank manager in the hope of gaining financial support. Your plan should include a clear rationale for the legal form you wish your business to take, your chosen product(s) or service(s), evidence of market research, an indication of anticipated competition and supporting financial information.

2 You work in a local authority business advice centre. One of your clients wishes to start a business in some aspect of catering. Advise your client on the advantages and disadvantages of the various legal forms the proposed enterprise could take.

Notes and references

1 Liability may be extended where a company continues trading after insolvency.

2 It is also possible to have unlimited companies.

3 A similar growth occurred in the number of 'community businesses' in Scotland during this period. Though not strictly 'co-operatives', they are also part of the so-called third sector of business.

Further reading

Campbell, D. J., *Organizations and the Business Environment*, Butterworth-Heinemann, 1997.

Morrison, J., *The International Business Environment*, Palgrave, 2002.

Palmer, A. J. and Hartley, R., *The Business and Marketing Environment*, 3rd edition, McGraw-Hill, 1999.

Worthington, I., Britton, C. and Rees, A., *Economics for Business: Blending Theory and Practice*, Financial Times/Prentice Hall, 2001.

Web links and further questions are available on the website at:
www.booksites.net/worthington

8

Size structure of firms

Chris Britton

Businesses range in size from the single proprietor at one extreme to the large multinational at the other which employs thousands of people over several countries. The structure of these businesses will be very different and the problems they face will vary as a result of the differences in size. The size structure of business will depend on many factors which range from choice (the sole proprietor may choose to remain small) to external factors which are beyond the control of the firm.

Objectives

- To be aware of the size structure of UK industry.

- To understand the reasons why organisations grow in size.

- To understand the way in which organisations grow and the methods of finance.

- To recognise the limitations to growth.

- To survey the level of merger activity in the United Kingdom and the European Union.

- To be aware of the role and importance of the small-firm sector.

- To be aware of the role and importance of the multinationals.

Key terms

Capital market	External growth	Networking
Concentration	Flexible firm	Profit
Conglomerate merger	Gearing	Small firm
Cross-subsidisation	Globalisation	Stock Exchange
Debentures	Horizontal merger	Subcontracting
Diseconomies of scale	Industrial concentration	Takeover
Diversification	Internal growth	Transfer pricing
Dividends	Joint venture	Transnational corporation
Enterprise	Merger	Vertical integration
Equity	Money market	Virtual organisation
Establishment	Multinational corporation	

Introduction

There has been an increase in the level of industrial concentration in the United Kingdom over the last one hundred years. In 1909 the largest hundred companies produced 16 per cent of manufacturing output; by 1990 this had risen to around 30 per cent. Such an increase in the size of business organisations gives rise to worries about the concentration of power in the hands of a few producers and abuses of this power. If the companies are multinationals, they may be beyond the control even of national governments. More recently the trend towards greater concentration has been reversed, and there seems to be a movement towards employment in smaller units. This chapter will look at the size structure of British industry and the reasons for such a structure, with some international comparisons. It will consider the role of small and large firms in the economy. It will also examine the reasons for growth, the ways in which organisations grow, the financing of growth and the limits to growth. It will also consider the relatively more recent trend towards co-operation in production, rather than competition, through activities like joint ventures and networking.

The size structure of UK industry

When looking at the size of firms it is important to define the terms used in official data. The firm, or 'enterprise', is the organisation as a whole, and it might be comprised of several units or 'establishments'. Small firms like the corner shop will mostly be enterprises with only one establishment. Large firms like Sainsbury's will have many establishments as they have branches in most towns.

There are many different ways to measure the size of firms. Common measures used are turnover, the value of output, the capital employed or the level of employment. Such measurement is beset by problems, not least the difficulty of defining the small firm, as will be seen later in this chapter. The three measures mentioned above might give conflicting pictures, as an industry which is becoming increasingly mechanised will probably have rising levels of average capital employed and output but falling average levels of employment. Table 8.1 shows the 'top ten' companies in the United Kingdom using two of these measures and it illustrates the point that different measures of the size of a firm will give different rankings.

Some of these names will be familiar to the reader while others are less so. BAT Industries, for example, is a large tobacco company which has diversified into many other areas.

The most common measure of size used is the level of employment. Table 8.2 shows the size structure of units in manufacturing industry by the number of employees in the United Kingdom in 2000. The table shows that smaller firms predominate in terms of numbers, with 98.2 per cent of firms employing fewer than 100 employees. In terms of employment, however, these firms account for only 37.4 per cent of the total level of employment in manufacturing. At the other end of the scale establishments with over 500 employees account for only 0.3 per cent of the total number but 38.7 per cent of total employment. The pattern of size

Table 8.1   The ten largest companies in the UK, 2001

Ranking by turnover	Ranking by employment
1 CGNU plc	1 Anglo American plc
2 Unilever plc	2 Consignia plc
3 Shell International Petroleum Co Ltd	3 J Sainsbury plc
4 Glaxosmithkline plc	4 Tesco plc
5 Tesco plc	5 HSBC Holdings plc
6 British Telecommunications plc	6 Tesco Stores plc
7 J Sainsbury plc	7 Unilever plc
8 CGU International Insurance plc	8 BAT Industries plc
9 Tesco Stores plc	9 Kingfisher plc
10 Prudential plc	10 British Telecommunications plc

Source: *Key British Enterprises*, 2002.

Table 8.2   Size structure of UK manufacturing industry by employment, 2000

Employment size group	Number of units	% of total	Employment (000s)	% of total
1–9	292 340	88.0	619	14.8
10–19	17 705	5.3	247	5.9
20–49	11 235	3.4	353	8.4
50–99	4925	1.5	347	8.3
100–199	2870	0.9	402	9.6
200–499	1935	0.6	599	14.2
500 and over	1075	0.3	1623	38.7

Source: Adapted from www.statistics.gov.uk/statbase/tsdataset.asp?more=Y

structure varies across industries and over time. In the last twenty years there seems to have been an increase in the importance of small firms and a decline in the importance of large firms in their contribution to employment. In 1980 establishments with fewer than 200 employees accounted for 31.9 per cent of total employment in manufacturing and establishments with more than 500 employees accounted for 49.8 per cent. The comparable figures from Table 8.2 are 47 per cent and 38.7 per cent. Even the short period of time from 1991 to 2000 has seen a shift in the importance of small firms. There has been an increase of 188 968 in the number of units employing fewer than 20 people, while there has been a decrease of 13 332 in the number of units employing more than 20 employees. A similar pattern emerges with employment, with an increase in employment of 313 800 in the smaller units and a decrease in employment of 882 800 in the larger units.

Many of the large companies listed in Table 8.1 operate in more than one country and are therefore multinationals. **Multinational corporations** strictly defined are enterprises operating in a number of countries and having production or service facilities outside the country of their origin.[1] Multinationals pose particular problems for governments and economies because of their size. They are considered more fully later in this chapter.

Organisational growth

The reasons for organisational growth

Firms grow in size for many reasons; growth could be an explicit objective of management or could be necessary for the successful operation of the firm:

- Growth could be a managerial objective if it brings benefits to management such as greater security and higher remuneration.
- It could be that the market in which the business operates is expanding and growth is necessary to maintain market share. This is especially the case as markets become more international.
- Growth enables the organisation to reap the benefits of economies of scale (*see* Chapter 12).
- Growth enables firms to diversify into other markets, which means that risk can be spread further.
- Industries which are capital intensive will of necessity be comprised of large firms.
- In the area of product development it is possible that the necessary research and development could only be carried out by large companies.
- Growth could be pursued as a defensive strategy, as a reaction to the activities of competitors.

Table 8.3 shows how the stated objectives of EU firms for engaging in merger activity have changed over time and gives some indication of the reasons for growth. There has been a clear shift over time in reasons given for mergers. Much of this shift can be explained by changing market conditions which have resulted from the creation of the Single European Market in 1992. The relaxation of trade restrictions in the run-up to 1992 encouraged much greater competition, and hence expansion and strengthening of market position have assumed much greater importance since 1985, together accounting for nearly 75 per cent of mergers. It was expected that the increased competition would force companies to concentrate more upon their core activities and as a result diversification as a motive for merger fell from 17.6 per cent in 1985 to 2.1 per cent of cases in 1992.

Table 8.3   Main motives for mergers in Europe, 1985–1992

Motive	% of times mentioned			
	1985–86	1989–90	1990–91	1991–92
Expansion	17.1	26.9	27.7	32.4
Diversification	17.6	3.0	2.8	2.1
Strengthening market position	10.6	45.3	48.2	44.4
Rationalisation and synergies	46.5	17.7	13.3	16.2
Research and development	2.4	0.6	0	0
Other	5.9	6.4	8.0	5.0

Source: *European Economy*, no 57, 1994. Reproduced by permission of the Office for Official Publications of the European Communities.

In industrial economics firm size is seen as a function of growth. It is suggested that although there is no limit on the size of a firm there are limits on the rate of expansion. Growth rates are seen to depend on different things by different theorists, including the availability of finance, the level of consumer demand and the limitations of management. These theories, however, are primarily concerned with large firms and their development. Small firms are seen as potentially large firms that failed to grow for some reason or other. One interesting theory of growth is the stages model, where the firm is seen as passing through various stages in its development from small sole proprietor/partnership through the decision to expand into a large organisation. This again is a 'grow or fail' theory which does not apply well to industries which are dominated by successful small firms, as will be seen later in the chapter.

Mini case   Mergers in the energy industry in the UK

In April 2002, the UK saw a proposed merger between National Grid (the operator of the network of electricity pylons and transmission wires) and Lattice (the operator of the network of gas pipes). The agreed price was £6.3 billion and Lattice shareholders were to be offered 0.375 of a share in National Grid Group (NGG) for every one share owned in Lattice. The new company will be called National Grid Transco, it will have a market value of £30 billion and 30 000 employees. What are the motives for such a merger?

■ To form a new 'national champion'. The main argument put forward is that the new company will have the resources and power to expand overseas. The main target is the USA, as energy industries in the EU are protected by their governments. NGG has already taken over several similar providers on the East Coast of the USA.

■ To protect both companies from takeover (especially by foreign companies). In recent years both companies have been regarded as possible targets for takeover, Lattice had been without a Chief Executive since mid-2001. Many large foreign companies have already bought into the energy and water industries in the UK.

■ There will be economies of scale in operation. It is estimated that savings of £100 million per year will be made as a result of this merger.

The proposed merger will need the agreement of both the energy regulator and the Office of Fair Trading. Both companies are in favour of this merger and the regulator has made sympathetic noises but the merger might not get past the Office of Fair Trading. Both companies are monopolies in their own field and so the merger will concentrate monopoly power further in the hands of one company. It is possible that this will operate against the public interest, although the new company will still be under the control of the regulators. The economies of scale claimed for the merger will probably result in job losses, although initially these will be confined to the closure of one of the head offices in London, involving only a small number of redundancies. Safety issues are paramount and the two companies are at pains to stress that safety will not be compromised at all by the proposed merger. Lastly, as competition policy in the UK and the whole process of privatisation was designed to break up monopoly power in the energy industry, to allow this merger to happen would be a significant change in policy. We will have to wait and see.

For information on the UK energy industry see *www.nationalgrid.com* and *www.transco.uk.com*
For the gas and electricity regulator see *www.ofgem.gov.uk*

Methods of growth

Firms grow in size internally as part of normal business operation or externally through takeover and merger.

Internal growth

Growth is a natural process for many firms that start small, capture a segment of the market and then continue to expand either by producing more of the same goods or by extending their product lines. The advantage of internal growth over external growth is that the company grows within the existing structure of management; there are none of the problems of bringing together two different management systems. There might also be economies of scale from building a bigger plant that might not be available when companies merge and plant size does not change. Set against these, internal growth has certain disadvantages and this is why most of the growth in the size of organisations has occurred through external growth.

External growth

Growth by acquisition is called external growth and occurs through takeover or merger. A merger is the voluntary coming together of two companies with the agreement of the management of both companies, the result of which is the creation of a new legal identity. A takeover is where one company makes an offer to the shareholders of another. If the management of the threatened company resist it is called a hostile takeover, but if the price offered to shareholders is high enough they will accept. Takeover bids can be and have been successfully fought off by the management of the second firm. A holding company is a new company that is formed to acquire assets in other companies. The acquired companies retain their independent identities but are directed by the holding company.

External growth can be seen to have a number of advantages:

1 It is fast, so that productive capacity can be increased very quickly.
2 The acquiring firm has access to an established management team and system.
3 If the shares of the acquiring company have sufficiently high values relative to the acquired firm, there might be no need for additional cash to be raised.
4 The purchase of existing assets could be cheaper than building new productive capacity.

But set against these is the fact that the process might not be an easy one; it is a difficult job to merge two companies smoothly and successfully and there are likely to be many teething problems. Research by Coopers & Lybrand (now PriceWaterhouse Coopers) found that top executives regarded half of the takeovers in which they had been involved as failures. The main reasons for failure were lack of planning and managerial problems.

Although the definitions of merger and takeover are clear enough, it is often difficult to tell them apart in practice and they are usually put together in official publications under the heading of acquisitions. In order to understand fully the motivation for mergers and takeovers it is important to recognise that there are different types of mergers.

Horizontal mergers

A **horizontal merger** is where a combination between firms at the same stage in a production process takes place; for example, between two car manufacturers or between two brewers. The vast majority of mergers that take place are of this type and many of our largest companies have been formed through horizontal merger. Examples include mergers between banks and building societies. The motives for this type of merger are:

- *To benefit from economies of scale.* Horizontal mergers allow the merged firms a greater level of specialisation and the benefits of other economies of scale (*see* Chapter 12).
- *Greater market share.* When firms come together there will be a reduction in competition in the market and the resulting firm will have a much larger share of the market.
- *Rationalisation of output.* If the level of demand for a good is shrinking, merger between the producers could be necessary in order to rationalise output.
- *Reaction to competitors.* In markets where mergers are taking place, companies may feel that they have to do the same in order to maintain their market position.

Vertical mergers

A vertical merger involves firms at different stages of the same production process. It is vertical since it runs along the production process from extraction of raw materials to distribution. An example would be a merger between a car manufacturer and a metal-pressing company. **Vertical integration** can take place 'backwards' towards the beginning of the production process or 'forwards' towards the end of it and it can occur for several reasons:

1 In the case of backwards integration, to control the supplies of raw materials with respect to their quantity and quality. This brings greater security to the acquiring firm.
2 To restrict supplies of the raw materials to competitors.
3 In the case of forwards integration, to control the quality of the outlets for the finished product. Manufacturers finance the majority of advertising and they might well feel that a forwards merger would enable them to ensure that the good was being sold in the most appropriate setting.
4 In both cases, economies of scale are possible if different parts of the production process are brought together.
5 Again, vertical mergers can be carried out as a reaction to the activities of competitors.

Conglomerate mergers

These mergers are neither vertical nor horizontal but involve a merger between firms involved in producing different goods. An example would be the failed merger proposal between Kingfisher (general retailing) and Asda (grocery retailing) in 1999. The main motivation for this type of merger is diversification. It reduces the risk involved in producing for only one market and allows the firm to spread risk further. It can also provide the firm with another option if the original market declines in size.

As far as the economy is concerned, the main gains of mergers are in increased efficiency resulting from economies of scale and also the increased scope for research and development. A common view is that merger and takeover activity serves the purpose of rationalising business. The weak businesses go and the strong survive. Even when a takeover is carried out for the purpose of asset stripping this will be the case.

Growth by merger and takeover

Growth through merger and takeover first appeared in the USA over a hundred years ago and merger activity tends to come in waves (*see* the discussion later in this chapter). Four periods of heightened merger activity have been identified in the USA:[2]

- The period 1880 to 1905 – this coincided with the proliferation of the joint stock company and the international establishment of stock exchanges. This period was characterised by mergers of a horizontal nature.
- The 1920s – at this time the mergers were largely vertical in nature, as manufacturers took control of both suppliers and distributors.
- The 1960s – mergers in this period were mainly about diversification and the establishment of conglomerates.
- The post-1980 period – this wave of activity took place in a period of recession and was largely about cost-cutting and rationalisation.

The first two periods of heightened merger activity in the USA had little effect in Europe; however, there were waves of activity in Europe which coincided with the last two. The first wave of merger activity in Europe came in the 1960s after obstacles to trade were removed by the establishment of the EEC in 1957. The second wave of mergers came in the 1980s in the run-up to the establishment of the Single European Market in 1992. As yet there is little evidence of an increase in merger activity as a result of EMU in Europe.

The late 1990s saw another period of frantic merger and acquisition activity as companies in mature industries attempted to become global. In 1998 the total value of mergers and acquisitions worldwide was in excess of £1500 billion.

Finance for growth

Internal sources

As part of its operation the firm will generate income in the form of profit. Part of this profit will be distributed in the form of dividends to shareholders, the rest can be used for reinvestment and to finance growth. Although this is seen as a relatively easy and cheap source of finance, it does carry an opportunity cost and therefore should be judged on its rate of return like any other source of finance. Table 8.4 shows that internal funds were the largest single source of finance for industry in 1990, 1994 and 1997. It also shows that the totals available and the pattern of sources vary a great deal from year to year. (This data is no longer compiled by the Office for National Statistics.)

External sources

As the size and availability of retained earnings will be limited, most firms will also have to seek other sources of finance for expansion. There are many external sources of finance and a typical firm's capital structure will comprise a combination of these. The sources are as follows.

Banks

Banks provide short- and medium-term finance to companies in the form of loans or overdrafts. The relative cost of these depends upon how the firm wishes to use the funds. Loans carry a lower rate of interest but the interest is paid on the whole amount, while the interest on overdrafts is only paid on the amount drawn. British banks have been criticised by many for failing to provide longer-term finance for business, as banks do in other countries.

Table 8.4 Sources of funds for industry, 1990, 1994 and 1997; £ million

Source	1990	1994	1997
Internal funds	33 838	61 406	56 363
Banks and other short-term borrowing	19 911	−4841	6630
Loans and mortgages	9120	4557	4384
Ordinary shares	1880	8495	19 616
Debentures and preference shares	6367	1008	10 640
Other capital issues	7485	5067	10 526
Other overseas investment	11 233	−1400	25 938
Other	1444	3766	953
Total	91 278	78 056	135 050

Source: *Financial Statistics*, January 1993, 1996, and 1999. Crown copyright 1999. Reproduced by permission of the Controller of HMSO and of the Office for National Statistics, UK.

Capital market

The **capital market** is the place where stocks and shares are traded and is therefore a key provider of long-term finance to firms. The main institution in the capital market is the **Stock Exchange**. The capital market is made up of two parts: the primary part which involves the buying and selling of new stocks and shares; and the secondary part which involves the buying and selling of existing stocks and shares. It is therefore the primary part of the market that is the source of finance for firms. The secondary part of the market is, however, also important in this process as individuals and organisations are more likely to buy stocks and shares with the knowledge that there is a ready market on which they can be traded at a later date.

The main institutions that buy stocks and shares are the insurance companies, pension funds, investment trusts, unit trusts and other large financial institutions such as building societies.

A new issue of shares takes place when an existing company needs extra finance or when a company becomes a public limited company.

Types of stocks and shares

1 *Preference shares*. These are shares in a company which carry a fixed dividend. Holders have preference over other shareholders in the payment of dividends and on the liquidation of the firm. Preference shares usually carry no voting rights, and so holders have little influence over how the company is run.
2 *Ordinary shares*. Ordinary shares are called the '**equity**' of the company. They do not usually carry a fixed dividend; the company declares a dividend; depending upon its performance in that year. This means that in good years ordinary shareholders could receive high dividends, while in bad years possibly none at all. Ordinary shares are therefore more risky than preference shares, and in recognition of this they usually carry voting rights, so that holders can exercise some influence over how the company is run.
3 *Debentures*. **Debentures** or loan stock are bonds which are given in exchange for a loan to the company. The company agrees to repay the borrowed amount at some date in the future and to make annual payments of interest in the meantime. Interest on debentures is paid before payment of any dividends and the interest is allowable against tax. A debenture holder is a creditor of the company, a shareholder is an owner of the company.

New issue of shares

A company will go to an issuing house or merchant bank which will advise it on the type and number of shares to issue, the price at which they should be offered and other matters. They will often carry out the issue of shares on behalf of the firm. A new issue of shares is not a big source of finance for growth as it is fairly expensive; retained earnings are more convenient and cheaper. Also the amount of information that is required from companies which issue shares to the general public can act as a disincentive.

It is worth noting that in the UK the Stock Market essentially comprises three main elements: the main market, the Alternative Investment Market (AIM) and off-exchange share matching and trading facility (OFEX). The main market deals in the shares of the large and well-established companies. The Alternative Investment

Market provides an opportunity for growing smaller companies to raise capital and have their shares traded in a market without the considerable expense of a full market listing. OFEX tends to be used by companies seeking relatively small amounts of capital, mainly from private investors, and has to be seen as a stepping stone to a listing on a more senior market (e.g. the Official List, AIM, NASDAQ).

Money market

The money markets provide short-term finance for companies, often for as brief a period as overnight.

Government and other institutions

The government is a source of finance for firms. Through its regional policy it gives tax allowances, loans, grants and training allowances to firms in certain parts of the country (*see* Chapter 10). It has many schemes for helping business, particularly small businesses. This will be covered more fully later in this chapter.

Other sources

Other sources include trade credit and hire purchase (i.e. receiving assets now and paying later). This is only a small source of finance for companies. As Table 8.4 (on page 225) shows, industry draws a fairly high proportion of its funding from overseas. This includes finance from many different sources, including individuals, governments, financial institutions overseas and companies.

Firms will typically go for a mixture of different types of finance. The exact combination will depend upon many factors, including their relative costs, their availability and the desired capital structure of the firm. A firm's desired capital structure will largely depend upon the type of market in which it operates. The different types of finance are classified under the two headings of debt and equity. Debt refers to all types of capital on which payments have to made each year regardless of how the firm has performed; this would include loans and preference shares. Equity refers to ordinary shares where the payment of a dividend depends upon the performance of the firm. As a source of finance, debt is generally cheaper but it is also more risky since in bad years the firm will have to meet the interest payments. The ratio of debt to equity is called the gearing of the company. Debt is not well suited to firms in industries where profits fluctuate and such firms will have lower gearing than those in more stable markets.

Limits to growth

Several factors tend to act as a limit to organisational growth:

- To finance growth, excessive borrowing might have taken place and the firm may have trouble meeting debt repayments; therefore there is increased risk of bankruptcy.
- A serious constraint to growth might be the abilities of management. As organisations grow in size they may experience diseconomies of scale, which are mainly to do with managerial problems, like communication and control.

- If the size of the market for the product is stagnant or declining it may be both unnecessary and impossible for the firm to grow.
- Government policies, too, can have an important impact on growth. Every government has policies on competition which seek to limit anti-competitive practices and which normally regulate merger activity (*see* Chapter 14).

Merger activity in the United Kingdom

There are two common ways of measuring the level of merger activity – by the number of transactions or by the total value of the transactions. Figure 8.1 shows the level of merger activity in the UK according to the number of companies acquired in the UK by UK companies. It can be seen that there was a sharp rise in merger activity in the mid-1980s and a downturn in 1989. The cyclical pattern continues into the 1990s but the amplitude is reduced. This cyclical pattern is repeated in other countries and in the EU as a whole (*see* Figure 8.3 on page 230) and it implies that the level of mergers is in some way related to the state of the economy. The rise in the mid-1980s was due partly to an improvement in the state of the economy and partly to the liberalisation of the financial markets, which made finance for takeover bids more freely available. The fall in 1989 was due partly to the recession and partly to the problems that some companies subsequently experienced by overstretching themselves in the mid-1980s. The subsequent rise in the level of merger activity was due to the restructuring which took place in many diverse industries in the 1990s like the financial services sector and the public utilities.[3]

| Figure 8.1 | UK merger activity by number, 1983–2001 |

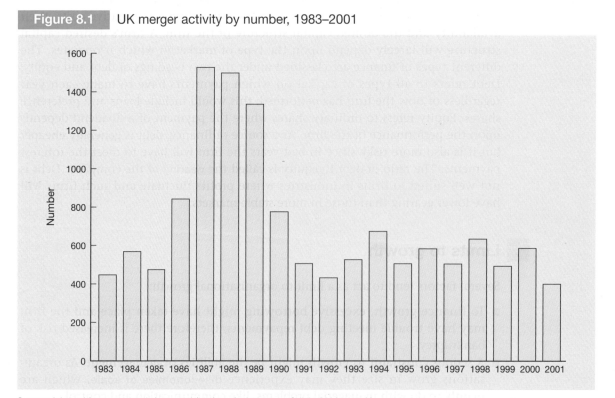

Source: Adapted from www.statistics.gov.uk/statbase/tsdataset.asp?vlink=933&more=Y

Figure 8.2 shows the level of merger activity in the UK according to the value of the transactions, and the same cyclical path can be discerned although the peaks and troughs do not exactly coincide with the number of transactions. The use of the value of the transactions as a measure of merger activity is problematic in that it will be distorted by any very high-value deals that take place, as in 1995–7 when the number of transactions fell but their value rose.

Merger activity in Europe

Figure 8.3 shows the level of merger activity in the EU between 1991 and 2001 as measured by the number of financial operations (the bars) and the value of operations (the line). The pattern for both is cyclical although there is usually greater variation in the value of operations because of the impact of large deals on the overall total. After four years of steady growth there was a sharp fall in the number of operations in 2001, while the value of operations fell a year earlier than that in 2000.

The most active country in the EU with respect to mergers and acquisitions in 2001 was the UK (which accounted for 31 per cent of operations) followed by Germany (16 per cent) and France (14 per cent). Three types of merger or acquisition can be identified depending upon geographical location of bidder and target – domestic (within each member state), community (within the EU) and international (involving non-members of the EU). Figure 8.4 shows that just over half of the operations between 2000 and 2001 were domestic, and this percentage did not change very much during the 1990s. Community and international operations mirror one another. Between 1998 and 2000 the percentage of community

Figure 8.2   UK merger activity by value, 1983–2001

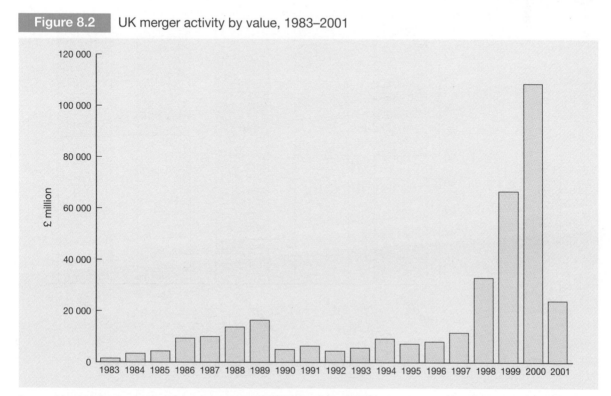

Source: Adapted from www.statistics.gov.uk/statbase/tsdataset.asp?vlink=933&more=Y

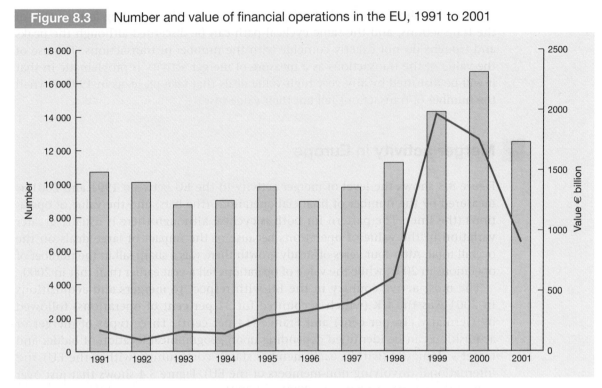

| Figure 8.3 | Number and value of financial operations in the EU, 1991 to 2001 |

Source: Adapted from Table 1 and Figure 3, of supplement to *European Economy*, December 2001

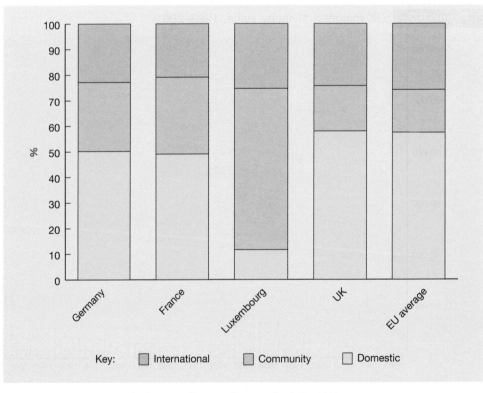

| Figure 8.4 | Geographical breakdown by member state, selected countries, 2000–2001 |

Source: Adapted from Table 5, supplement to *European Economy*, December 2001.

operations rose while the percentage of international operations fell. As Figure 8.4 shows there are differences between members of the EU.

The trends in the number of community operations and their value follows the same patterns shown in Figure 8.3. Between 1998 and 1999 there was an increase of 25 per cent in the number of operations but an increase of 257 per cent in the value of operations within the community. This demonstrates the impact of a small number of very large deals – in 1998 there was the Astra/Zeneca merger worth €29.4 billion and in 1999 there was the Vodafone/Mannerheim merger worth €204.8 billion. The pattern of inter-community mergers and acquisitions is captured in Table 8.5 which shows the target/bidder for selected countries.

This table shows that the important factors determining the pattern of inter-community mergers and acquisitions behaviour include the size of the economy, proximity between bidder and target and cultural ties between countries.

As far as international operations are concerned, at the beginning of the 1990s the EU was more often a target for mergers and acquisitions than a bidder but this has been reversed during the 1990s (*see* Figure 8.5).

The sector most affected by merger and acquisition behaviour in the period between 1991 and 2001 was the service sector (67 per cent of total) and within this hotels, personal and business services were the most targeted (27 per cent of total). A recent report[4] tried to ascertain whether EMU has had an impact upon the level of merger and acquisition behaviour in the EU. It compared the level of activity in the 11 members of EMU (Greece was excluded) with the other members of the EU. The evidence was not conclusive – the number of operations rose more slowly for the Eur11 until 1998 than for other members of the EU, then grew more quickly in 1999 and 2000 but experienced a steeper decline in 2001.

Table 8.5	Community operations, selected countries, 2000 to 2001, percentages

| | Acquired firm from | | | | |
Bidder firm from	Belgium	Germany	France	Italy	UK
Belgium	–	10.5	39.9	3.6	11.6
Germany	6.1	–	16.3	8.4	18.7
France	11.4	17.3	–	14	19.8
Italy	2.3	19.2	24.1	–	15.8
UK	4.1	21.1	20.5	7.6	–

Source: Adapted from Table 7, supplement to *European Economy*, December 2001

Small firms

There are serious problems in the analysis of the small-firm sector, including the lack of data over a long period of time and the problem of defining exactly what is a small firm. The Bolton Report,[5] published in 1971, was the report of a committee set up to look into the role of small firms in the UK economy. It used various

| Figure 8.5 | Number of international operations, 1991–2001 |

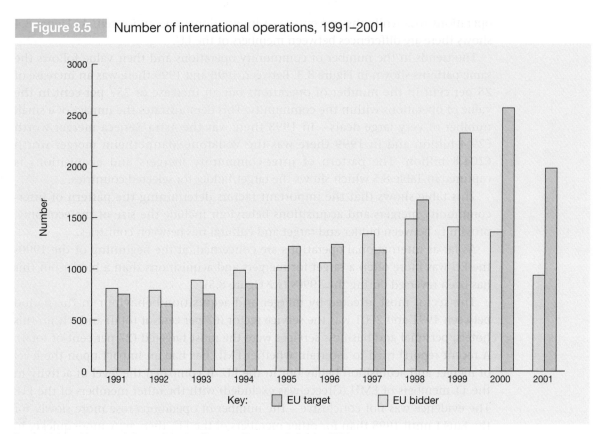

Source: Adapted from graph 9, supplement to *European Economy*, December 2001

definitions for statistical purposes, depending upon the industry being considered, on the grounds that what is small in one industry might be large in another. Table 8.6 shows the size distribution of firms based on their turnover for a selection of industries for 2000.

It is clear from Table 8.6 that the definition of 'big' will vary with the industry. In the Bolton Report the definition used for small firms in manufacturing was 'less

| Table 8.6 | Size of companies by turnover across different industries, 2000 (%) |

Industry	Turnover size ('000)		
	up to £250	£250–£500	over £500
Agriculture, forestry and fishing	89	7	4
Mining and quarrying and public utilities	40	10	50
Manufacturing	55	14	31
Construction	76	11	13
Wholesaling	52	13	35
Retailing	70	17	13
Financial services	58	8	34
Business services	80	8	12

Source: Adapted from Table 2 *Business Monitor* PA1003, 2000, Office for National Statistics, UK.

than 200 employees', while in construction it was 'less than 25 employees'. In some industries turnover limits were chosen while in others a mixture of employment and turnover was used. Although this is confusing and makes comparison between industries and countries difficult, it was accepted that there could not be a single definition which would apply to all sectors. The EU in 1994 recommended to its members that they use 'less than 250 employees' as the definition of a small to medium-sized enterprise (SME), in order to facilitate the easy comparison of data across member states. A further refinement of the definition used by Eurostat based on numbers employed is shown in Table 8.7.

Applying this definition to Table 8.2, it can be seen that 88 per cent of manufacturing firms in the UK are micro businesses, 10.2 per cent are small, 1.5 per cent are medium sized and 0.3 per cent are large. Although there are some national differences (the southern-most countries have relatively more micro businesses than the northern countries) the pattern of size structure is similar in the EU as a whole – 92 per cent of all enterprises are micro businesses, 7.4 per cent are small, 0.5 per cent are medium sized and 0.1 per cent are large.[6]

No matter how small firms are defined, they will suffer from similar problems, which are very different from those faced by larger companies.

Trends in the small-firm sector

Figure 8.6 shows the share of small establishments in total manufacturing employment from 1930 to 1990. The definition used is fewer than 200 employees. The establishment is the reporting unit. It can be seen that the small-firm sector was in decline up to the late 1960s and early 1970s, since when its importance has increased.

Table 8.2 showed that for manufacturing industries small firms are very important in terms of the numbers of companies, accounting for 99 per cent of total firms according to the Bolton Report definition. Even though they were less important in terms of employment they still accounted for 47 per cent of total employment. This tends to understate their importance because it does not include the service sector, many parts of which are heavily dominated by small firms due to the nature of the production process. Although there is a great deal of information available from official sources on the manufacturing sector, the same depth of information is not available for the service sector, so accurate information is difficult to obtain.

Table 8.7   Classification of firms by employment size

Number of employees	Type of firm
0–9	micro businesses
10–99	small enterprises
100–499	medium-sized enterprises
500+	large enterprises

Figure 8.6   Share of small establishments in total manufacturing employment, 1930–1990

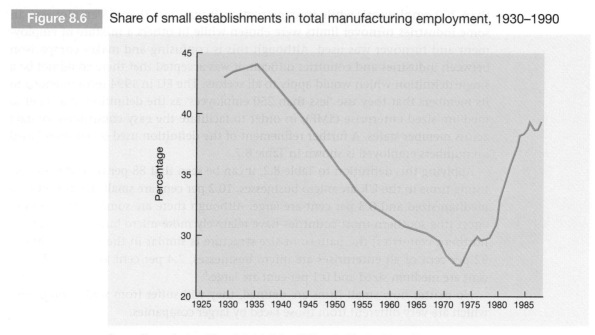

Source: Stanworth, J. and Gray, C. (eds.), *Bolton 20 Years On: The Small in the Firm in the 1990s*, Chapman 1991, table 1.1.

Reasons for the growth in the small-firm sector

There has clearly been a resurgence in the importance of the small-firm sector which appears to have been more pronounced in the United Kingdom than in other countries. Why? Some causal factors are as follows:

1 *The changing pattern of industry*. In Chapter 9 it is shown that there has been a change in the industrial structure of the United Kingdom away from manufacturing and towards services. Since many services are dominated by small firms, there will be a corresponding change in average firm size. However, this does not provide the full explanation as there has been a growth in the share of small firms even in the manufacturing sector. And it does not explain the international differences since there have been similar changes in industrial structure in other countries too.

2 *Changes in consumer spending habits*. A move from mass-produced goods to more specialised products puts small firms at an advantage as they can react more quickly to changes in demand and shorter product life cycles.

3 *Flexible specialisation and the growth of subcontracting*. A debate which started in the late 1980s centres round the idea of the 'flexible firm'.[7] As a result of the recession of the early 1980s there was a drive by firms to reduce their costs in order to remain competitive. One way of reducing overhead costs was to move to a flexible firm structure whereby the firm's activities are divided into core and peripheral activities. The core activities, which are central to the activities of the firm, would be kept 'in-house' and carried out by full-time permanent workers. The peripheral activities would be carried out by temporary workers or would be subcontracted. The firm has then reduced its overheads and can react to peaks in

demand by increasing the amount of temporary labour it uses or increasing the amount of subcontracting. This might also have had the effect of increasing the relative importance of the small-firm sector.

4 *Reorganisation and job reduction.* There has been an increase in the phenomenon of *downsizing* by organisations in an attempt to reduce costs. Ninety per cent of large companies have reorganised and cut jobs since 1985.

5 *Government policy.* After the Bolton Report there was a much greater interest in the role of the small firm in the regeneration of the economy and in the provision of jobs. But most of the initiatives designed to help the small firm came after the start of the resurgence of the small-firm sector in the early 1970s.

6 *The growth in self-employment.* A part of the growth in the small-firm sector has been due to the growth in the number of self-employed. The self-employed accounted for 9.8 per cent of the workforce in 1984 and 11.3 per cent in 2001 (*see* Table 8.8). This represents a 15 per cent increase in the number of those self-employed over this period.

The level of self-employment is likely to be related to the level of unemployment, so that as unemployment rose during the 1970s and 1980s there was an increase in the level of self-employment. This goes a long way to explaining the international differences as the growth in self-employment in the United Kingdom has far outstripped that in other countries. Again, however, it does not provide the full explanation as business births were growing in the late 1960s when unemployment was falling.

Table 8.8   Percentage of workforce self-employed, 1984–2001 (UK)

Year	% self-employed
1984	9.8
1985	10.0
1986	10.0
1987	10.9
1988	11.3
1989	12.1
1990	12.3
1991	11.9
1992	11.3
1993	11.2
1994	11.7
1995	11.6
1996	11.6
1997	11.5
1998	10.9
1999	10.8
2000	10.6
2001	11.3

Source: Adapted from Annual Abstract of Statistics (various), Office for National Statistics,UK.

7 *Technological change.* Changes in technology, particularly information technology and the miniaturisation of components, has made it possible for small firms to benefit to a similar extent to large firms. This has had the effect of reducing the importance of economies of scale and enabling small firms to compete more effectively with large ones.

8 *Competitive forces.* As far as the international differences are concerned, the Bolton Report found that industry in the United Kingdom was biased towards large size in comparison with other countries. So what may have happened as a result of competitive forces is that the balance of industry in the United Kingdom has moved towards the norm of other countries.

The role of the small-firm sector

The growing importance of the small-firm sector implies that small firms do have a valuable role in the economy apart from being a mere provider of employment. The areas in which the small firm has advantages over large firms are those where there are:

1 *Clearly defined small markets.* It is not worthwhile for large firms to enter such markets since there are no economies of scale and no scope for mass production.

2 *Specialist, quality, non-standardised products.* Again it would not be worth a large firm entering such a market as the benefits of large-scale production cannot be reaped.

3 *Geographically localised markets.* For example, the small corner shop.

4 *Development of new ideas.* It is often argued that the small firm is the 'seedbed' of ideas and that because of greater motivation and commitment on the part of the owner of the small firm, it is very conducive to invention and innovation.

Aid to the small-firm sector

The thinking on small firms has changed over time. Initially they were viewed favourably, but after the Second World War the dominant thinking was that large-scale production could take advantage of large economies of scale and that costs would be lower and production more efficient. It was not until more recently that the interest in the small-firm sector has increased again. The main reasons for the renewed interest are seen in the results of empirical studies which have shown that the role of the small firm is greater than previously thought in areas such as innovation, the balance of payments and employment.

The main argument for giving support to the small-firm sector is that it has a valuable role to play in the economy. In the 1980s and 1990s, for example, small firms were seen as a mechanism for reducing the very high levels of unemployment. Between 1983 and 1993 the small-firm sector created 2.5 million jobs. The basic premise for support is that small firms are at a disadvantage with respect to large businesses in areas such as raising capital, research and development and risk bearing. Two particular problems faced by small firms were highlighted in 1996: cash flow problems which stem from the late or non-payment of bills; and dealing with government red tape. These problems have been addressed by a number of recent developments. All public limited companies are now required by law to state in their annual reports the average length of time it takes them to pay their bills. The Federation of Small Businesses published a 'name and shame' list for the first time in April 1999 which should apply peer pressure which will encourage firms to pay bills on time. It also provides information to help small firms decide who to trade with. The Federation of Small Businesses estimates that 44 per cent of bills are paid more than 15 days after the normal 30-day credit period. The comparable figure is 35 per cent in the EU. It is estimated that about £20 million is tied up in late payment, with a half of this owed by large firms to small firms. The government also publishes 'league tables' of government departments which are slow in paying their bills, with the pledge that this will be improved. To reduce the amount of red tape faced by firms, the government has, over the years, relaxed many of the rules and regulations involved in running a business. For example, from 1996 there has only been a single form for registration for income tax, national insurance and VAT, from April 1999 small employers have been able to move from monthly to quarterly payment of PAYE and National Insurance contributions.

Government policy

Within the UK national policy for small firms has increasingly become a vital component of governmental attempts to create a competitive economy capable of achieving sustainable economic growth. To this end policy initiatives in recent years have become more focused and have tended to adopt a multi-agency approach, aimed at improving the environment in which small businesses emerge and grow, and at fostering enterprise and innovation. Key developments over the last decade have included:

- *Business Link* – a national network of 'one-stop shops' to provide information and support to small firms.
- *Direct Access Government* – a 'one-stop shop' on the Internet that provides businesses with access to regulatory guidance and forms.
- *The Enterprise Zone* – another Internet-based initiative to help firms with finding information on issues such as finance, exporting, technology, innovation and management.
- *The Teaching Company Scheme (TCS)* – the government's premier technology transfer mechanisms for linking UK higher education establishments and businesses.
- *The SMART Awards* – designed to promote technological development and innovation.

There have also been a number of legislative and fiscal changes aimed at reducing the burdens on small businesses (e.g. levels of corporation tax). Some of the most recent developments include the launch of the University for Industry (UfI), the Enterprise Fund, the University Challenge Fund, the Small Business Service (SBS) and the EU SME Initiative. The latter – introduced in December 1997 – aims to assist SMEs in rural areas or areas of industrial decline to become more competitive in overseas markets.

Networking between firms

A more recent trend in industry which is well documented is towards co-operation rather than competition.[8] This co-operation can take many forms: for example, subcontracting, networking (both formal and informal) and joint ventures. Such co-operation can be (and is) used by large as well as small- and medium-sized enterprises. For large companies it is a way to grow and diversify without risk. For smaller firms it allows them to stay small but at the same time to benefit from some of the advantages of large-scale production like specialisation.

Subcontracting

There has been an increase in the amount of subcontracting, where firms do not carry out the whole of the production process themselves but subcontract some of their activities to other firms. This represents a rejection of vertical integration and it is related to the notion of the flexible firm mentioned earlier. Subcontracting goes some way to explaining the phenomenal growth rate in 'business services' that occurred in the 1980s. It is increasingly common for businesses to subcontract specialist work in areas such as human resource management to outside consultancies. 'Partnering' between companies and consultancies is becoming more common where the consultancy is retained on a semi-permanent basis to give advice on a whole range of human resource matters from recruitment to planning for succession. This will obviously boost the small-firm sector. There has also been an increase in 'partnership sourcing' as large firms are developing long-term relationships between themselves and their suppliers. This phenomenon brings benefits to the large firms in the form of reducing stock levels and associated costs and facilitating just-in-time production methods. It also brings benefits to small firms, many of which are the suppliers, in the form of greater security.

Networking

Networking refers to the relationships that exist between organisations and the people within those organisations. These relationships can be of different types, both formal and informal, and there is increasing recognition of the importance of these relationships, especially to small firms (e.g. they may be based on the exchange of goods and services, like the relationship between a firm and its supplier or client). Subcontracting is an example of this kind of network but there are other links not based on exchange, like the relationship between a firm and the bank manager or other advisers. There are also informal links between the entrepreneur and family and friends, and between entrepreneurs in different organisations. There might also be co-operative links between firms. This can be seen in the market for executive recruitment where there has been a growth in the links between consultancies, particularly for international work. The creation of the Single European Market and the increased internationalisation of business left the smaller consultancies in a weak position relative to the large international recruitment firms like Korn Ferry International, which have branches in most European countries. The smaller consultancies have reacted by forming networks. There are basically two types of network:

1 Where firms are members of a network but where the network has a different name from the individual firms and the firms operate under their own name (i.e. the network has an identity of its own). The members are independent firms that co-operate in carrying out their business. There are 16 such groups in Europe including EMA Partners International and AMROP Heuer Group.
2 Where firms are part of a network of independent firms but where the network does not have a separate identity and the firms operate under their own names. There are ten such groups in Europe.

For information on companies mentioned see *www.kornferry.com*, *www.ema-partners.com* and *www.amrop.com*

The firm is seen as existing within a spider's web of relationships, as Figure 8.7 shows. It is possible for two firms to be linked in a variety of ways; in one market they may be competitors, in the next co-operators, customers in another and suppliers in another.

Networking has taken on greater significance because of changes that are taking place in the economy, which include the reversal of the trend towards higher industrial concentration, the adoption of Japanese methods of production, the decline of 'mass markets' and technological change that requires greater specialisation than previously. All of these changes favour the formation of networks.

The role of strategic alliances between firms has been recognised, especially in the small-firm sector where expansion through other means is often impossible and in the process of internationalisation.[9]

Figure 8.7   A typical network

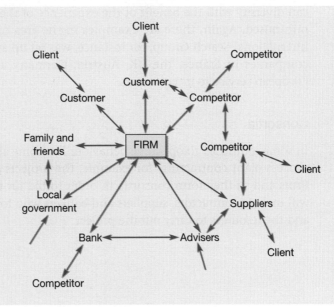

The virtual organisation

The virtual organisation is a network-based structure built on partnerships where a small core operating company outsources most of its processes. It is a network of small companies which specialise in various aspects of production. The organisation can be very big in trading terms but very small in the numbers of permanent staff. The process is typically mediated by information technology.

The main benefit of the virtual structure is that it helps organisations to deal with uncertainty. When virtual organisations are managed properly they can simultaneously increase efficiency, flexibility and responsiveness to changes in market conditions. The organisation is reaping the benefits of specialisation without having to develop those specialisms itself. Therefore overhead costs are minimised, as too are training costs and support costs. Information technology assumes many of the co-ordinating and managing roles that managers and committees carry out in large organisations. Information technology enables communication and the sharing of information across geographical boundaries. It is often the case, however, that the creation of a virtual organisation is driven solely by cost considerations rather than strategic considerations, in which case the benefits might not be realised. There will be a loss of control over outsourced activities and it may actually cost more to manage such activities. The organisation can become locked into contracts and specific relationships so that flexibility is reduced. There may be a lack of commitment of key resources (i.e. contractors) to the company and the loss of a contractor will be very serious.

There is some evidence that the incidence of virtual organisations is on the increase, facilitated by developments in information technology. It is a matter of 'wait and see' if this will become the dominant organisational structure in the future.

Joint ventures

As indicated earlier in this chapter, joint ventures are a good way for firms to diversify and enter other countries' markets. Joint ventures benefit both parties as each can diversify with the benefit of the experience of the other, and the level of risk is minimised. Again, there are examples in the area of executive recruitment. The International Search Group, for instance, was set up as a joint venture between five companies in France, the UK, Austria, Germany and Italy in order to offer a European service to its customers.

Consortia

In some industries co-operative behaviour has come about for particular reasons. In process plant contracting, for example, the projects are often too large for single firms and so they form consortia in order to bid for the contract. The consortium will include contractors, suppliers and bankers who together will have the expertise and the resources to carry out the project.

Multinationals

At the opposite end of the scale from the very small business are companies which have the capability to produce goods or services in more than one country but where control usually resides in a central location. Multinationals are often well-known household names, as the examples below illustrate:

- UK multinationals – BP, Glaxo SmithKline.
- European multinationals – Nestlé, Volkswagen.
- USA multinationals – General Motors, IBM.

These multinationals are huge organisations and their market values often exceed the GNP of many of the countries in which they operate. They are estimated to account for a quarter of the world's output.

The growth in the multinationals is due to relaxation of exchange controls making it easier to move money between countries, and the improvements in communication which make it possible to run a worldwide business from one country.

web link

For information on the companies mentioned on this page see: *www.bp.com*, *www.gsk.com*, *www.nestle.com*, *www.vw.com*, *www.gm.com* and *www.ibm.com*

The operation of multinationals (MNEs)

Multinationals can diversify operations across different countries. This brings them great benefits:

1 MNEs can locate their activities in the countries which are best suited for them. For example, production planning can be carried out in the parent country, the production itself can be carried out in one of the newly industrialised countries where labour is relatively cheap and marketing can be done in the parent country where such activities are well developed. The relocation of production may go some way to explaining the decline in the manufacturing sector in the developed nations.[10]

2 An MNE can cross-subsidise its operations. Profits from one market can be used to support operations in another one. The cross-subsidisation could take the form of price cutting, increasing productive capacity or heavy advertising.

3 The risk involved in production is spread, not just over different markets but also over different countries.

4 MNEs can avoid tax by negotiating special tax arrangements in one of their host countries (tax holidays) or through careful use of transfer pricing. Transfer prices are the prices at which internal transactions take place. These can be altered so that high profits can be shown in countries where the tax rate is lower. For example, in the USA in 1999 two-thirds of foreign-based multinationals paid no federal income tax. The loss to US taxpayers from this has been estimated as in excess of $40 billion per year in unpaid taxes.

5 MNEs can take advantage of subsidies and tax exemptions offered by governments to encourage start-ups in their country.

The very size of MNEs gives rise for concern as their operations can have a substantial impact upon the economy. For example, the activities of MNEs will affect the labour market of host countries and the balance of payments. If a subsidiary is started in one country there will be an inflow of capital to that country. Once it is up and running, however, there will be outflows of dividends and profits which will affect the invisible balance. Also there will be flows of goods within the company and therefore between countries, in the form of semi-finished goods and raw materials. These movements will affect the exchange rate as well as the balance of payments and it is likely that the effects will be greater for developing countries than for developed countries.

There is also the possibility of exploitation of less developed countries, and it is debatable whether such footloose industries form a viable basis for economic development. Added to this, MNEs take their decisions in terms of their overall operations rather than with any consideration of their effects on the host economy. There is therefore a loss of economic sovereignty for national governments.

The main problem with multinationals is the lack of control that can be exerted by national governments. In June 2000 the OECD updated its *Guidelines for Multinational Enterprises*, which are not legally binding but are promoted by OECD members' governments. These seek to provide a balanced framework for international investment that clarifies both the rights and responsibilities of the business community. It contains guidelines on business ethics, employment relations, information disclosure and taxation among other things. Against all this is the fact that without the presence of MNEs, output in host countries would be lower and there is little hard evidence that multinationals perform badly on labour market issues.

Mini case   Transnationality

Multinationals are huge organisations and their market values often exceed the GNP of many of the countries in which they operate. There are over 60 000 MNEs around the world and they are estimated to account for a quarter of the world's output. The growth in MNEs is due to relaxation of exchange controls making it easier to move money between countries, and the improvements in communication which make it possible to run a world-wide business from one country. These multinationals usually have their headquarters in a developed country – with three exceptions (Hutchison Whampoa Ltd (China), Petróleos de Venezuela and Cemex S.A. (Mexico)) the largest 100 MNEs are based in the developed world. Typically, MNEs still employ two-thirds of their workforce and produce two-thirds of their output in their home country. Multinationals are often well known household names, as Table 8.9 shows.

The transnationality index gives a measure of an MNE's involvement abroad by looking at three ratios – foreign asset/total asset, foreign sales/total sales and foreign employment/total employment. As such it captures the importance of foreign activities in its overall activities. In Table 8.9 BP has the highest index – this is because in all three ratios it has a high proportion of foreign involvement, but especially in employment. Since 1990 the average index of transnationality for the top 100 MNEs has increased from 51 per cent to 55 per cent in 1997 but fell back to 48 per cent by 1999 mainly reflecting a decline in the ratio of foreign to total assets.

Table 8.9	The world's largest 10 MNEs, ranked by foreign assets, 1999		
Rank	Company	Country	Transnationality index * %
1	General Electric	United States	25
2	Exxon Mobil Corporation	United States	78
3	Royal Dutch/Shell Group	Netherlands/UK	57
4	General Motors	United States	17
5	Ford Motor Company	United States	23
6	Toyota Motor Corporation	Japan	18
7	Daimler Chrysler AG	Germany	49
8	Total Fina SA	France	79
9	IBM	United States	50
10	BP	United Kingdom	82

* measured as the average of three ratios: foreign assets to total assets, foreign sales to total sales and foreign employment to total employment.

Source : UNCTAD, 2001.

For information on the operation of multinational organisations see
www.oecd.org or www.unctad.org

Globalisation

Globalisation is a term used to describe the process of integration on a world-wide scale of markets and production. The world is moving away from a system of national markets that are isolated from one another by trade barriers, distance or culture towards one where there is one huge global marketplace. This is certainly true for goods such as Coca-Cola or McDonald's although it is not true for all products. The globalisation of markets has been intensified by the globalisation of production where firms disperse parts of their production process to different parts of the world. It is not just the large multinational enterprises that are becoming global, many small and medium-sized enterprises are also engaged in global production and marketing.

The two main reasons for the increased globalisation of both markets and production are:

- The decline in barriers to trade and investment that has occurred over the last half century. Each day over $1.5 trillion is exchanged in foreign exchanges and international trade accounts for one third of the world's output. New markets that were formerly protected, like the Soviet bloc, have opened up for competition.
- The dramatic developments in communication and information technologies which not only facilitate global production through the transfer of information between different parts of a company, but also allow the transfer of ideas and beliefs around the world. The so-called 'global culture' makes it appear as if the

same trends occur in many parts of the world at the same time. Developments in transportation technology, such as the jet engine, have also served to make the world a smaller place.

Globalisation has meant that firms face an increasingly complex environment. For example, there are new markets to be captured, increased competition to be faced from abroad, an understanding needed of the workings of foreign exchange markets, and a knowledge of the differences which exist between countries. Despite what has been said about globalisation, there still remains a great diversity in the world – different countries have different cultures, political systems and legal systems. Global production and marketing require a knowledge of all of these.

Synopsis

This chapter has looked at the size structure of industry in the United Kingdom and Europe as a whole. It examined the motives for and the methods of growth, as well as the sources of finance for such growth. The role of the small firm was considered, as too was the role of the multinational. Although many industries are dominated by huge companies, the trend seems to be moving away from growth towards a process of disintegration for a variety of reasons. As a result of this trend there has been an upsurge in the small-firm sector, and an increase in the level of co-operative behaviour between firms.

Summary of key points

- The size structure of firms varies greatly within industries, within a country and between countries.

- Firms can grow internally through organic growth or externally through merger and takeover.

- There are many motivations for growth, including increased market share, the reaping of economies of scale, the diversification of risk.

- Growth can be financed internally through reinvested profits or externally through banks, the capital market and the money market.

- There are limits to organisational growth, such as diseconomies of scale.

- The level of merger activity in the UK and in Europe follows a cyclical pattern and is related to economic conditions.

- The small-firm sector is an important source of output and employment, and this importance has increased over time.

- Many factors have influenced the growth of the small-firm sector, including the changing pattern of industries, changes in demand, technological change, the trend towards increased subcontracting and government policy.

- At the other end of the size spectrum, multinational corporations have a massive impact on world output and employment through their activities.

Executive search

As this chapter shows, the size of firms within an industry depends upon many factors. The nature of the product and the production process are important in explaining why many service industries are dominated by small firms. Services have the following characteristics which differentiate them from goods and these characteristics have implications for the structure of the industry concerned:

- *Intangibility*. Services are intangible while goods are tangible. This means that it is impossible to sample a service before it is purchased.
- *Inseparability*. There is often no separation between consumption and production of services. Goods are produced, sold and then consumed. Services are sold, then production and consumption begin simultaneously.
- *Heterogeneity*. Given the nature of services, they are difficult to standardise; often each unit of a service sold is different. This stems from the central role that the buyer plays in service production.
- *Perishability*. Services are perishable, they are destroyed in the process of consumption and cannot be stored.
- *Irreversibility*. Many services are irreversible in that, once consumed, they cannot be returned nor can faults be rectified.

These characteristics have an important impact upon the shape of the industry and the firms that constitute the industry. This case study looks at one such service industry, executive search.

Executive search (or headhunting) is one part of the executive recruitment market. It refers to the recruitment of candidates through direct and personal contact by a specialist recruitment consultancy acting as an intermediary between employer and potential candidate(s). Although there are some large international consultancies, such as Korn Ferry and Egon Zehnder, the industry is one which is dominated by small firms (*see* Figure 8.8). Even the large international consultancies are small compared with firms in other industries. In 2000 the average number of consultants per firm was 5.4 and the most common firm size was 2 consultants. There are many reasons for this and some of these reasons apply equally to other services and are related to the services characteristics above. Some, however are specific to executive search and selection:

- There is a large personal element in the service provided which means that the production process will be labour intensive. The only scope for technological change is through the computerisation of records and processes. This is likely to be true for many services and means that there is no scope for mass production and the typical firm size will remain small. The average number of assignments per consultant in 2000 was eight.
- The perishable nature of services means that stocks cannot be kept, and given that the demand for services will fluctuate, firms with large numbers of consultants will have to bear the cost of excess capacity when demand is low. There is therefore a tendency towards small size.

| Figure 8.8 | Size distribution of search consultancies, 2000 |

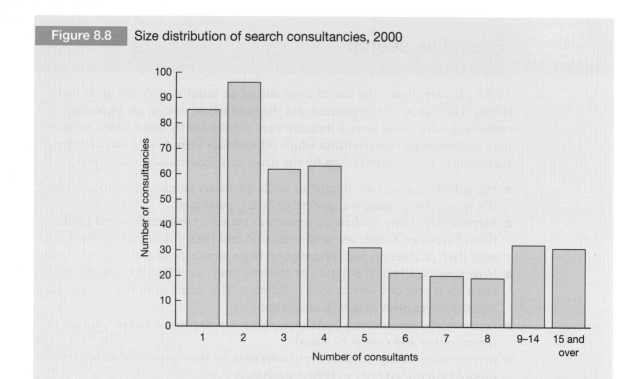

- The higher the number of consultants the greater the possibility of one or more leaving and starting a new consultancy in competition with the original, and taking their contacts with them. This is a fairly common method of entry for new firms in this industry. For this reason consultancies rarely have more than 14 consultants.
- Executive search is unique in that the greater the number of client companies, the smaller the pool of candidates. Most search firms offer an 'off-limits' guarantee – they will not approach someone they have placed for at least two years. Therefore the more people they place, the more restricted will be the pool of candidates.
- It could be that there is little scope for economies of scale – there are many firms with only one consultant surviving and performing well. Although the size of the firms in the industry is small, greater specialisation in the task can take place than in a personnel department. Many consultancies specialise by function or by industry, which may lead to reduced search times due to the consultants' easier access to candidates and data banks and better understanding of the industry. There is also the effect of repetition on the skills of the producer.
- Despite the fact that there may well be some scope for economies of scale in the industry, it is clear from the numbers of assignments involved that the minimum efficient scale of production is small. Firms can enter the industry and carry out a relatively small number of assignments and survive.
- Low barriers to entry and exit make the industry easy to enter and to leave. Because of the characteristics of services it is difficult for the quality of the service being provided to be ascertained. To overcome this lack of information, many service industries (accounting and law for example) have strong regulatory bodies which can enforce certain behaviour patterns upon the

firms in the industry. This, however, is not the case for executive search. There is no regulatory body, there are no pre-entry educational requirements and there are no legal limitations to entry, apart from the acquisition of a licence which can be obtained fairly easily for a small sum. Once a firm has entered there is little formal control over its operating methods; so legal barriers to entry are not high in executive search. The capital required to set up in business is small, since all that is required is a licence, a telephone, stationery, secretarial support and an office. The method of payment for assignments – which usually involves a part payment at the beginning of the assignment – reduces the 'break-in' period as loans can be quickly paid off. Consultancies become profitable after only a few assignments.

■ The service characteristic of inseparability of production and consumption often places a geographical limit on markets that can be served, and this will impact upon firm size. Many services involve 'direct sales' with no intermediaries, and so firms are likely to locate near to the demand for their services or near to where the decision is taken to use that service. Executive search is seen as an extension of the management division of labour since it is the externalisation of previous internal personnel functions. Hence, if the location of search consultancies is close to its demand, and the decision to use recruitment consultancies is taken in head offices, then the location of these head offices plays an important part in the location of consultancies. In Britain this partly explains the geographical concentration of search consultancies (77.5 per cent of consultancies) in London and the South East.

■ The inseparability of production and consumption in services means that the concept of vertical integration loses meaning when applied to services. Most services involve direct production, so the whole production process takes place when the service is performed. The existence of many business and other services represents a process of disintegration, as firms are increasingly shedding their peripheral functions and buying in these functions from external sources. Executive search is a good example of this process as recruitment and other personnel functions are increasingly being contracted out. Indeed there is further disintegration in the industry, as researchers are setting up their own firms and consultants are buying in their services. There is no obvious reason why horizontal mergers should not take place in service industries. The motivation for and incidence of horizontal mergers will vary between the very different services which exist. As far as services with large personal inputs are concerned, there will be limited scope for economies of scale, and so this reason for mergers is removed. Similarly services which are geographically localised are less likely to be horizontally integrated.

■ The particular nature of service production makes diversification into other areas more difficult than in other types of production. The obvious directions for diversification are into products either produced with common technology or through the development of existing technology, and into products that can be marketed though similar channels. Executive search consultancies diversify by offering other services to management, such as salary surveys or succession planning. The development of executive search itself has partly been through a process of diversification as large accountancy firms have moved into the area of management consultancy, including recruitment.

Conclusion

Executive search (like many other services) is characterised by small firm size. For such industries, the traditional theories on the growth of firms, which see development as a 'grow or fail' process are not very helpful. They are clearly not true when small firms not only survive but are successful. A more fruitful approach is to look at the constraints which might prevent the growth of the firm. In executive search, the internal constraints include the personal nature of the production process which means that consultants can only handle a small number of assignments per year. There is some evidence that an increase in support staff does increase the output of consultants but not by a significant amount – the range remains narrow. Another internal constraint might be a lack of individuals with the right skills. The skills required in a consultant are good interpersonal and communication skills, possibly some experience of recruitment work and, more importantly, contacts. An external constraint is that the service can be carried out by clients, which might well limit the extent of the market. Also, unique to executive search, is that consultants will not normally approach an individual they have placed for at least two years. Therefore as the number of consultants rise in a firm the possible pool of candidates shrinks. The bigger the consultancy, the higher is the probability that one or more of the consultants would leave to set up in competition against the original consultancy, taking all of their contacts with them. There have been examples of consultants doing this but taking with them researchers as well, leaving the original consultancy in a very weak position.

Case study questions

1 Why do you think that international expansion typically takes place through the formation of alliances in the executive search industry?

2 How might economic recession affect this industry?

web link

For information on executive search see
www.rec.uk.com (Recruitment and Employment Confederation)
www.executive-grapevine.co.uk

Review and discussion questions

1 Why is restructuring taking place in the airline industry?

2 Can you see any dangers in the creation of super utilities (large, diversified organisations which supply a range of utilities – gas, electricity and water)?

3 What advantages does networking bring to small firms and the economy as a whole?

4 How has the balance between large and small firms in manufacturing changed in the last ten years? Do you expect these trends to continue?

Assignments

1 You are an information officer at your local business advice centre and you have been given the job of designing and writing a leaflet aimed at the proprietors of small firms, outlining the government aid that is available to small businesses. Your brief is to keep the leaflet short and readable but with maximum information. (Information on government aid will be available at your local library or business advice centre.)

2 As part of 'Business Week' you have been asked to give a short talk to local sixth-formers doing Business Studies A-level on the size structure of UK industry. Prepare your talk by choosing two industries, describing and giving reasons for the typical size structure of the firms in those industries.

Notes and references

1 *Penguin Dictionary of Economics*.

2 'Mergers and acquisitions in Europe', *Panorama of EU Industry*, May 1997.

3 *See* case study in Chapter 8 of the 2nd edition of this book.

4 Supplement A, *European Economy*, no.12, December 2001.

5 *The Bolton Committee Report*, HMSO, 1971.

6 *Panorama of EU Industry*, 1994, European Commission.

7 Atkinson, J., 'Flexibility, uncertainty and manpower management', Report no. 89, Institute of Manpower Studies, 1984.

8 Pyke, F., 'Co-operative practices among small and medium-sized establishments', *Work, Employment and Society*, 2 (3), September 1988.

9 *See* case study at the end of Chapter 13 of the 2nd edition of this book.

10 *World Investment Report* 2001, United Nations.

Further reading

Griffiths, A. and Wall, S., *Applied Economics: An introductory course*, 9th edition, Financial Times/Prentice Hall. 2001.

Stanworth, J. and Gray, C., *Bolton 20 Years On: The Small Firm in the 1990s*, Chapman, 1991.

Web links and further questions are available on the website at:
www.booksites.net/worthington

9

Industrial structure

Chris Britton

Within any economy, there will be a whole range of industries that produce a variety of products for a variety of users. The particular combination of industries within a country is called the industrial structure of that country. There will be international differences in industrial structures, because of differences in the many factors that affect the determination of industrial structure.

Objectives

■ To understand what industrial structure is and how it is measured.

■ To examine the industrial structure of the United Kingdom and the European Union as a whole.

■ To identify the reasons for particular industrial structures and the factors which influence industrial structure.

■ To identify how and why the industrial structure of the United Kingdom and the European Union has changed over time.

Key terms

Crowding out	Manufacturing sector	Standard Industrial
Deindustrialisation	Primary sector	Classification (SIC)
Entrepreneurship	Productivity	Tertiary sector
Industrial structure	Secondary sector	
Life cycle model	Skill shortages	

Introduction

A country can produce many different and diverse types of goods and services ranging from the production of cars to the delivery of legal services to farming. The mix of these and the combination of industries that exist to produce them is called the industrial structure of a country. There are likely to be large differences in industrial structure between countries for many reasons. This chapter will look at the industrial structure of the European Union as a trading bloc and the United Kingdom in particular. There is a need for the industrial structure of a country to be measured in some way so that changes over time can be identified and international comparisons made. This chapter will look at the definitions of industries, the problems with such definitions and the official classification of industry used by the government in the United Kingdom. It will also identify the changes in industrial structure and the causes of these changes.

The structure of industry

The process of production

In Chapter 5 the three factors of production – labour, land and capital – were considered. Textbooks often add a fourth factor of production to this list, called 'entrepreneurship'. Entrepreneurship is the process of bringing together the other factors in order to produce goods and services. A firm produces goods and services because they are demanded and because a profit can be earned by selling them. Figure 9.1 shows a much simplified profit and loss account for a car manufacturer.

The items on the expenditure side represent the payments to the factors of production. Wages are payments to labour, raw materials and an element of overheads would be the payments to capital, and the payment for land would be included in overheads. The payment to the entrepreneur is in the form of profit.

Figure 9.1 A simplified profit and loss account

Revenues	£m.	Expenditures	£m.
Sales of cars	30.0	Raw materials	7.5
		Wages and salaries	10.0
		Overheads (rent, rates lighting, etc.)	2.5
			20.0
		Profit	10.0
	30.0		30.0

What has happened in this process is that the factors of production have been combined to make finished cars and in the process value has been added to the initial value of the raw materials.

The car manufacturer can be thought of as being in the centre of a process of production which links together raw materials at one end with the consumers at the other end. The raw materials are extracted and processed and then the finished goods are sold. In economic terminology, the extraction of raw materials is called *primary production*, the manufacture of cars is called *secondary production* and the distribution of the finished cars is called *tertiary production* (*see* Figure 9.2). Although this simple path from primary production through to tertiary production is the case for many industries, it is likely to be much more complicated in practice.

The discussion at present is confined to a single firm, but it can be moved to the *industry level*. The industries that deal with natural resources like farming and mining comprise the primary sector. Industries which process these natural resources comprise the secondary sector, which will include manufacturing, construction and energy suppliers. The service industries make up the tertiary sector. There are great difficulties involved in such a classification of industry, as will be seen later, but consideration will now be given to the official classification of industry in the United Kingdom.

The Standard Industrial Classification

The Standard Industrial Classification (SIC) of economic activity is the official classification of industries in the United Kingdom into different sectors. It was introduced in 1948 and has been updated and changed on occasions to take account of the development of new products and industries for producing those products. It was changed in 1980, mainly in order to bring the United Kingdom classification in line with the activity classification used by the Statistical Office of the European Communities (Eurostat) which is called Nomenclature générale des activités économiques dans les Communautés européennes (NACE).

Data on industrial structure in the UK is available from *www.statistics.gov.uk*
For the EU from *http://europa.eu.int/comm/eurostat*

| Figure 9.2 | A simplified production process |

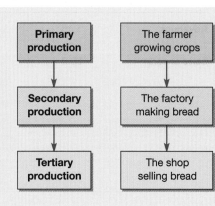

| Table 9.1 | SIC(80) |

Division	Industry
0	Agriculture, forestry and fishing
1	Energy and water supply industries
2	Extraction of minerals and ores other than fuels; manufacture of metals, mineral products and chemicals
3	Metal goods, engineering and vehicle industries
4	Other manufacturing industries
5	Construction
6	Distribution, hotels and catering; repairs
7	Transport and communication
8	Banking, finance, insurance, business services and leasing
9	Other services

The 1980 SIC is shown in Table 9.1. The 1980 classification has ten *divisions* (denoted by a single digit). Each of these is divided into *classes* (two digits), which in turn are divided into *groups* (three digits) and *activity headings* (four digits). In total there are ten divisions, 60 classes, 222 groups and 334 activity headings. Table 9.2 gives an example of these.

The term 'production industries' refers to divisions 1 to 4 of the above classification; the term 'manufacturing industries' refers to divisions 2 to 4. The SIC does not comply exactly with the broad classification of industry used in the last section. The primary sector of the economy is found in division 0 and parts of divisions 1 and 2; the secondary sector in parts of divisions 1 and 2 and all of divisions 3 to 5. The tertiary sector would be divisions 6 to 9.

The SIC is changed periodically to reflect changes taking place in industry, but this SIC has been used since 1980 as the basis for all officially collected data on industry. In 1990 the EC approved a new statistical classification of economic activities in the EC (NACE Rev. 1). This means that the United Kingdom had to introduce a new SIC in 1992. The standardisation of industrial classification across Europe will make interstate comparisons easier. The SIC(92) which has replaced SIC(80) is based on NACE Rev. 1, the only deviation being the addition of a fifth digit to further subdivide classes where it seemed necessary.

The SIC(92) has 17 sections instead of the ten divisions of SIC(80); each of these sections is denoted by a letter from A to Q. The sections are divided into subsections which are denoted by the addition of another letter. The subsections are then broken down into two-digit divisions and again into groups (three digits), into classes (four digits) and into subclasses (five digits). An example of this is given in Table 9.3.

| Table 9.2 | Division 4 of SIC(80) |

Division 4	Other manufacturing industries
Class 43	Textiles
Group 431	Woollen and worsted industry
Group 438	Carpets and other textile floor covering

Table 9.3	SIC(92)
Section D	*Manufacturing*
Subsection DE	Manufacture of pulp, paper and paper products; publishing and printing
Division 22	Publishing, printing and reproduction of recorded media
Group 22.1	Publishing
Class 22.11	Publishing of books
Class 22.12	Publishing of newspapers
Class 22.13	Publishing of journals and periodicals
Class 22.14	Publishing of sound recordings
Class 22.15	Other publishing

Note: There are no subclasses in this division.

There are 17 sections, 14 subsections, 60 divisions, 222 groups, 503 classes and 142 subclasses. The SIC(92) follows the NACE Rev. 1 exactly, except for the use of subclasses, which have been used for some industries in the United Kingdom.

The structure of the new SIC is given in the appendix to this chapter. It shows that not all of the sections are subdivided into subsections; some are broken down straight into divisions. Also some sections are subdivided more than others, the obvious example being section D where there are 14 subsections and 23 divisions. The level of detail depends upon the diversity of production included within the section.

Differences between SIC(92) and SIC(80)

First, there is the obvious change in the numbering system, but there are also some changes in the order in which industries appear. For example, electricity, gas and water have moved further down the list to appear after manufacturing in the SIC(92). There is also now a much more detailed breakdown of the service sector; the old division 9 has been broken up into eight different sections. This illustrates the increased acceptance of the importance of the service sector in the economy. There have also been changes in the classification within sections. Table 9.4 gives a comparison of the two Standard Industrial Classifications. The *Indexes to the SIC of Economic Activities 1992* (HMSO) gives detailed mapping between SIC(80) and SIC(92). Although the new SIC was introduced in 1992, many government statistics are still compiled using the 1980 categorisation.

Problems in classifying industries

The classification of industry is problematic. Firms could be grouped together according to similarities in what they produce but some firms produce a range of goods for quite different markets. Firms could be grouped together according to what they 'do', so that if their production processes are similar they could be considered as part of the same industry. The service industries are particularly problematic as they have traditionally been defined by the function they perform, but

Table 9.4	A comparison of SIC(92) and SIC(80)	
SIC(92)		*SIC(80)*
A	Agriculture, hunting and forestry	0
B	Fishing	0
C	Mining and quarrying	1 and 2
D	Manufacturing	1, 2, 3 and 4
E	Electricity, gas and water supply	1
F	Construction	5
G	Wholesale and retail trade; repair of motor vehicles, motor cycles and personal household goods	6
H	Hotels and restaurants	6
I	Transport, storage and communication	7 and 9
J	Financial intermediation	8
K	Real estate, renting and business activities	8 and 9
L	Public administration and defence; compulsory social security	9
M	Education	9
N	Health and social work	9
O	Other community, social and personal service activities	9
P	Private households with employed persons	9
Q	Extra-territorial organisations and bodies	9

developments in technology have led to these functions overlapping and therefore becoming more difficult to distinguish: for example, publishing and printing. All of this leads to industries that are seemingly very diverse being grouped together in the SIC. Although the SIC does not succeed in overcoming all of these problems, it does provide an accepted classification of industry which can be used for many purposes. The information collected provides a basis for comparing the structure of industry within a country over time and between countries.

Measuring industrial structure

The structure of industry in a country is not static, and it changes over time for a variety of reasons. For example:

- The development of new products means that new industries come into existence (e.g. the inventions and innovations in the field of electronic games).
- New patterns of demand mean that some industries will be declining while others become increasingly important.
- Changes in society will be reflected in industrial structure. For example, according to the Census in 1851, 22 per cent of the workforce in the United Kingdom was engaged in agriculture, forestry and fishing while in 2000 the figure was 1.5 per cent. This obviously reflects the movement away from an agriculturally based society to an industrial society.

Industrial structure is usually measured by the level of employment or output of the various sectors of the economy, and changes in industrial structure over time can be observed by looking at the changes in the employment and output levels in different industries. These will usually (but not always) paint the same picture; a sector in decline will have falling employment and output.

Industrial structure in the EU

Figure 9.3 shows the industrial structure of the EU as a whole as measured by employment in 1979 and 2000. During the 1980s there was a 20 per cent fall in the level of employment in agriculture, a 14 per cent fall in the level of manufacturing employment and a 15 per cent rise in employment in the service sector. In 2000, 5 per cent of the working population of the EU was employed in agriculture, 29 per cent in industry and 66 per cent in services. So there has been a gradual trend away from employment in the primary and industrial sectors in the EU as a whole and a gradual rise in employment in the service sector. Figure 9.4 indicates the changes in the relative sizes of the three sectors over the period 1980 to 2000.

The trends displayed in the EU are evident in other advanced industrial economies. Table 9.5 shows that while there are some differences in industrial structure between countries, the tertiary sector in all cases is predominant in

Figure 9.3   Percentage shares in employment in the three main sectors of the EU, 1979 and 2000

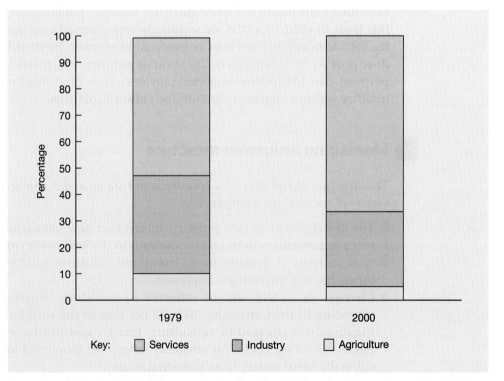

Source: *Eurostat Yearbook*, 2001. © European Communities. Eurostat. Reproduced by permission of the Publishers, the Office for Official Publications of the European Communities.

| Figure 9.4 | Employment by sector in the EU as a whole, 1980–2000 |

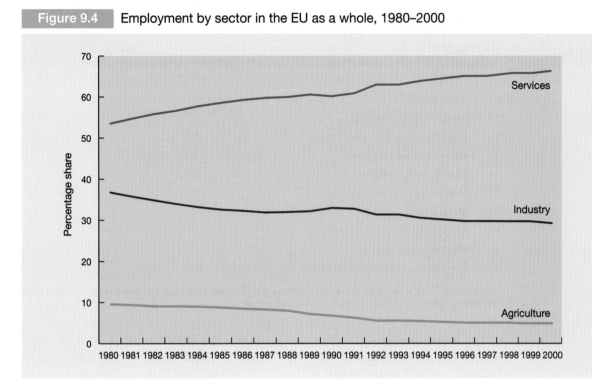

Source: *Eurostat Yearbook*, 2001. © European Communities. Eurostat. Reproduced by permission of the Publishers, the Office for Official Publications of the European Communities.

employment terms. Within the EU, the United Kingdom has a much smaller agricultural sector than other EU countries and the EU average while Germany has the largest production sector. Japan has a larger manufacturing sector than the EU average and the USA, and a smaller tertiary sector.

Industrial structure can also be gauged by looking at output figures. For both employment and output the figures tell the same story: the primary and secondary sectors of the main industrial countries have declined in importance, while the tertiary sectors have increased in importance. The reasons for these changes will be considered later in this chapter.

| Table 9.5 | Percentage employed in different sectors of selected countries (2000) |

	Agriculture	Production	Services
United Kingdom	1.5	26.0	72.0
Spain	7.0	31.0	62.0
Italy	5.0	32.0	62.0
Germany	3.0	34.0	63.0
France	4.0	26.0	69.0
EU	5.0	29.0	66.0
Japan	5.2	31.6	63.2
USA	2.6	23.1	74.4

Source: *Eurostat Yearbook*, 2001. © European Communities. Eurostat. Reproduced by permission of the Publishers, the Office for Official Publications of the European Communicaties.

| Table 9.6 | The ranking of major EU sectors by employment and output, 2000 |

NACE code		Rank by	
		Output	Employment
64	Retail trade	1	1
41	Food, drink and tobacco	2	3
26	Chemicals and man-made fibres	3	7
35	Motor vehicles and parts	4	6
34	Electrical engineering	5	2
32	Mechanical engineering	6	5
31	Metal articles	7	4
47	Paper, printing and publishing	8	8
14	Mineral oil refining	9	17
22	Preliminary processing of metals	10	13

Source: *Eurostat Yearbook*, 2001, © European Communities. Eurostat. Reproduced by permission of the Publishers, the Office for Official Publications of the European Communities.

The broad averages hide differences between the industries in each sector. Table 9.6 shows the rankings of major EU sectors by output and employment in 2000. Industries which were forecast by the EU to grow faster than the average between 1995 and 1999 included hotels and restaurants, other market services, air transport, auxiliary transport services and motor vehicles. Industries which were expected to yield negative growth included iron and steel, textiles and clothing and pharmaceuticals.

In the EU there are three main reasons for the restructuring of manufacturing that has taken place over the past 20 years: first, deregulation, which has led to greater internal competition; second, greater competition both internally and externally from third-party countries, especially the less developed, low-wage countries; and third, the creation of the Single European Market and the resulting increases in competition brought about by the elimination of barriers to trade. There are a great variety of ways in which companies have reacted to these changes but the *Panorama of EU Industry* identifies several 'typical' responses, some of which will have contradictory effects. These include:

- Increased investment for the prime purpose of increasing productivity. This has led to an increase in the level of unemployment in the EU as machinery has replaced relatively expensive labour in the production process.
- A tendency towards greater concentration in industry both vertically and horizontally through merger and acquisition, in order to benefit from economies of scale and to be in a position to benefit from the increased competition (*see* Chapter 8).
- Greater specialisation in production. Many companies in quite diverse industries (window frames, chemicals, clothing and textiles) have decided to reduce product lines and concentrate on particular market segments.
- Greater flexibility in the production process. This has been achieved by greater automation in production processes, the externalisation of certain activities, subcontracting and increased use of part-time and temporary workers.

Industrial structure in the UK

The United Kingdom does not fare well in international comparisons, as the trend is the same as in the EU but the decline in the manufacturing sector has been more pronounced in the United Kingdom and the jobs lost in manufacturing have not been offset by jobs created in the service sector. It is also true that while there has been a relative decline in the output of manufacturing in all countries, it is only in the case of the United Kingdom that there has been an absolute decline.

Figure 9.5 shows a graph of employment in manufacturing in four countries over the period 1974 to 2000. It is clear from this graph that the decline in employment in manufacturing has been much greater in the United Kingdom than the others. The United Kingdom started from a much higher base in 1974 and in 2000 had the lowest level of employment in manufacturing except for Japan, which has experienced a sharp economic slump.

Table 9.7 gives an indication of the change in industrial structure in Great Britain between 1969 and 2000. It shows the total numbers employed in various industries for 1969, 1995 and 2000. It is important to realise that when different years are compared the figures will be affected by the state of the economy in each of those years, but nevertheless the comparison will give an indication of changes in the relative importance of the three sectors of the economy. The change in the Standard Industrial Classification that occurred during this period would have had a minimal effect on the figures and has been corrected as far as possible.

Figure 9.5 Index of employment in manufacturing industry in selected countries (1995 = 100)

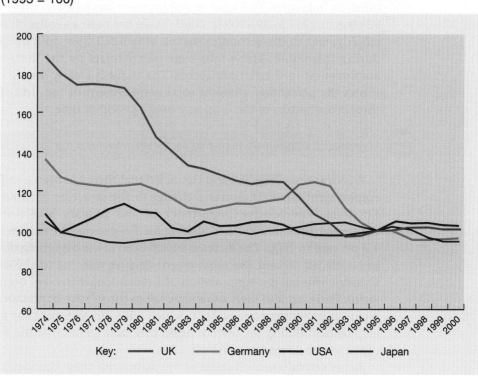

Source: *Quarterly Labour Force Statistics*, 2001, OECD

| Table 9.7 | Total numbers in employment mid-June 1969, 1995 and 2000 (Great Britain) |

SIC(92) Sections	1969 (000s)	1995 (000s)	2000 (000s)
A/B	492	294	327
C	437	68	66
Total primary	**929**	**362**	**393**
D	8355	3840	3855
E	406	399	261
F	1459	814	1156
Total secondary	**10220**	**5053**	**5272**
G	2711	3564	3995
H	710	1257	1378
I	1561	1272	1425
J		930	973
K	3742	2630	3475
L		1315	1409
M	2749	1790	1881
N		2417	2469
O-Q		984	1146
Total tertiary	**11 473**	**16 159**	**18 151**
Total employment	**22 622**	**21 574**	**23 816**

Source: Adapted from Table 7.5. *Annual Abstract of Statistics*, 2001, Office for National Statistics, UK.

There has been a slight increase in the level of total employment during this period but a substantial change in the pattern of employment between the different industries. The level of employment has fallen in the primary sector from 929 000 in 1969 to 393 000 in 2000. There has been a similar change in the level of employment in the secondary sector, which fell from 10.2 million to 5.3 million during the period. These falls were partly offset by the increase in the level of employment in the tertiary sector. The trend is clearly seen in Table 9.8, which shows the percentage share of total employment in the United Kingdom in the three broad sectors of the economy over a period of time.

For data on employment/output by sector see *www.oecd.org*

It is clear from Table 9.8 and Figure 9.6 that there has been a shift in the pattern of employment which indicates a change in the structure of industry in the United Kingdom. The relative importance of the primary sector has declined over the period 1969 to 2000, accounting for 3.6 per cent of employment in 1969 and 1.7 per cent in 2000. The increase experienced at the beginning of the 1980s was due to North Sea oil and the most recent decline was due to the decline of the coal industry. This fall is a continuation of a much longer trend of decline in the primary sector. There has also been a dramatic fall in the relative importance of the secondary sector in providing employment, which fell from 46.8 per cent to 22.1 per cent of employment during the period. Again this table shows that the relative importance of the service sector has increased.

Before consideration is given to the reasons for these changes, the other key indicator of changes in industrial structure will be considered – the level of output. These figures show a similar pattern to those on employment. There has been a fall

Table 9.8	Percentage share of total employment of primary, secondary and tertiary sectors (UK), 1969–2000

Year	Sector		
	Primary	Secondary	Tertiary
1969	3.6	46.8	49.3
1973	3.5	42.1	54.3
1979	3.1	38.2	58.7
1984	3.8	31.1	65.1
1985	3.6	30.5	65.8
1986	3.3	29.9	66.3
1987	3.0	29.5	67.6
1988	2.7	29.0	68.3
1989	2.4	28.5	68.9
1990	2.5	28.1	69.1
1991	2.4	26.4	71.2
1992	1.6	27.4	71.0
1993	2.1	25.0	72.9
1994	1.9	24.6	73.5
1995	1.7	23.6	74.9
1996	1.8	22.6	75.6
1997	1.7	22.4	75.9
1998	1.7	22.3	76.0
1999	1.6	22.5	76.0
2000	1.7	22.1	76.2

Source: Adapted from Table 7.5. *Annual Abstract of Statistics*, 2001, Office for National Statistics, UK.

Figure 9.6	Percentage share of total employment of the secondary and tertiary sectors of the UK economy

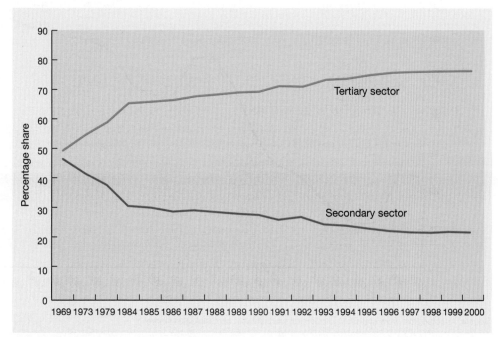

Source: Adapted from Table 7.5, *Annual Abstract of Statistics*, various editions, Office for National Statistics, UK.

in the relative importance of the secondary sector and an increase in the importance of the tertiary sector. There was an increase in the importance of the oil and natural gas industries in the late 1970s and early 1980s because of the production of North Sea oil and gas; this trend, however, has now been reversed. The broad classification used in Table 9.9 hides the fact that there are differences within the sectors, where some industries grow while others decline in importance.

The changes in relative sizes of the different sectors of the economy in the United Kingdom are the same as in other countries. It is only in the United Kingdom that there have been periods of absolute decline in the output of manufacturing industries, as Figure 9.7 shows. This decline in manufacturing is regarded by many as relatively unimportant; it is seen as a natural process of change which started with the Industrial Revolution and the movement from the land. To some extent this natural growth argument is supported by Table 9.5 (on page 259). Spain, which is the least developed of those in the table, has the highest level of employment in the agricultural sector.

Table 9.9   Output by industry 1987–1998 (% of total GDP)

Industry	1987	1988	1989	1990	1991	1992	1993	1994	1995	1996	1997	1998
Agriculture, forestry and fishing	1.9	1.7	1.8	1.8	1.7	1.8	1.9	1.9	1.9	1.8	1.5	1.3
Energy and water supply	6.2	5.0	4.7	4.3	4.8	4.6	4.7	4.7	3.8	2.7	2.3	2.1
Manufacturing	23.9	23.9	23.0	22.1	20.7	20.1	19.8	19.9	20.1	20.9	21.2	20.3
Construction	6.1	6.7	7.1	6.9	6.1	5.5	5.0	5.1	5.1	5.1	5.3	5.2
Services	61.9	62.7	63.4	64.9	66.7	68.0	68.6	68.4	69.1	69.5	69.7	71.1

Source: Adapted from Table 12.5, *Regional Trends* 36, 2001, Office for National Statistics, UK.

Figure 9.7   Output of manufacturing industry in the UK, 1979–2001 (1995 = 100)

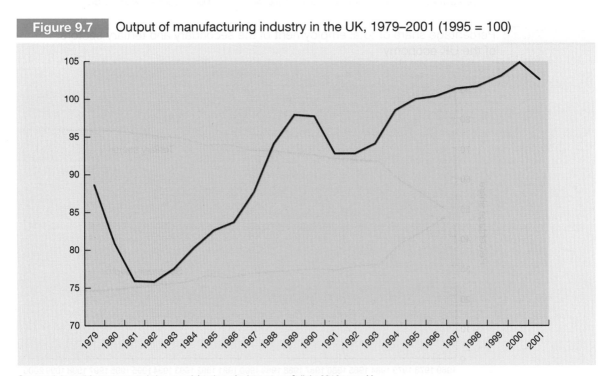

Source: Adapted from www.statistics.gov.uk/statbase/tsdataset.asp?vlink=631&more=Y

Mini case   The life cycle model

A common way of looking at a product and the organisation that produces it is through the use of the 'life cycle model', where the position of the product in its life cycle will have implications for such things as the marketing of that product. The life cycle model can be applied equally to a market, an industry or even an industrial sector, where the position in its life cycle will have implications for industrial structure, market structure (*see* Chapter 12) and for the strategic choices which will confront the organisation in that industry.

The four phases in a life cycle – development, growth, maturity and decline – are shown in Figure 9.8.

The first phase is the development, birth or entry phase of the life cycle when the industry is in its infancy and growth is still very low. The growth phase is where there is rapid growth in sales and profitability. Firms are likely to have larger market shares and there will be lower costs due to economies of scale and the experience effects. The maturity phase, where growth has stabilised, is the most common state of the majority of industries and it could last a very long time.

The decline phase is where the growth rate starts to fall for many possible reasons, for example technological change which has made the industry obsolete or changing patterns of demand by consumers, to mention two. There is likely to be cost cutting and the market can be 'niched', possibly looking to overseas markets.

Figure 9.8   A life cycle

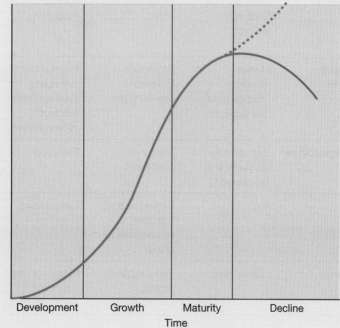

Development   Growth   Maturity   Decline
Time

Various points can be made about this life cycle. First, a product or an industry may not go through all of these stages; for example, an industry may not make it past the development stage for a variety of reasons, as in the case of the disc cameras which never found popularity with the public. Second, the length of each of the stages of the life cycle is not uniform and is likely to vary a great deal between industries – this can be seen by applying the model to the agricultural sector, where the growth phase lasted for several hundreds of years. Third, it is possible to miss the decline phase altogether, through diversification and innovation, in which case the growth path runs along the dotted line in the figure and the organisation has embarked upon another life cycle.

The implications of the stage in the life cycle for various factors are summarised in Table 9.10.

It is important to note that the behaviour of organisations will affect the shape of the life cycle of the product and the industry. Porter[1] looks at the strategic possibilities which confront a firm at various stages in its life, depending upon its position in the market – a leader or a follower. One important factor is that a product might be at a different stage in its life cycle at different geographical locations, so an industry which is saturated in the West might be able to extend its life by expanding into other countries.

Table 9.10 Implications of the different stages of the life cycle

Stage	Development	Growth	Maturity	Decline
Market growth	Low	Very rapid	Slowing or constant	Negative
Degree of competition	Low because there are few firms in the industry	Increasing as new firms enter	High Market stabilising	Declining Tendency towards oligopoly or monopoly
Marketing activities	Market research Promotion of new product	Promotion Increasing market share	Maintaining or increasing market share Product differentiation	Depends on strategy
R&D expenditure	High on new products and processes	Mainly on processes	Fairly low	Depends on strategy
Costs	High	Slower rate of increase (economies of scale)	Cost cutting	Depends on strategy
Profits	Low or zero	Growing fairly rapidly	Margin of profit squeezed by competition	Falling

This change in industrial structure is a trend which is evident in other countries. It might also be the case that some of the growth in the service sector is illusory. For example, if firms are externalising services that they once carried out themselves, there is actually not an increase in the amount of work done but a change in where it is done. It is not surprising that employment levels in manufacturing should fall, given the expansion of services and increases in productivity. What is more disturbing is that the absolute value of output in manufacturing has fallen and while similar patterns can be observed in other countries, the United Kingdom does not fare very well in international comparisons.

Causes of changes in industrial structure

There are several explanations put forward for the changes that take place in industrial structure. Broadly speaking these can be classified into demand and supply factors.

Demand factors

Changing patterns of demand will cause changes in the structure of industry. Demand will change as a result of changes in tastes and fashions, changes in the structure of the population, and changes in the levels of income. As income increases there is normally an increase in total spending on goods and services but there will be differences between different types of goods. There will be relatively large increases in expenditure on goods which have high income elasticities of demand[2] and relatively small increases or even falls in demand for other goods. Goods with low income elasticities are necessities like food, fuel, clothing and footwear. Luxury items have high income elasticities of demand; these would include things like durable goods, alcohol and services like tourism and leisure activities. Naturally what constitutes a necessity and luxury would change over the years. Figures 9.9 and 9.10 show the trend in expenditure on selected goods and services over a period of time in the United Kingdom.

Figure 9.9 shows that the expenditure on food and clothing has remained fairly constant over time, as expected. The expenditure on durable goods is much more affected by movements in the trade cycle and the level of income. Expenditure grew over the 1980s but fell back again during the recession of the late 1980s and early 1990s. The expenditure on tobacco fell steadily over the 1980s, probably as a result of increased health awareness but has risen again more recently. Figure 9.10 reinforces the findings above that services are like durables in that their demand is closely linked to the level of income. The pattern of expenditure is very similar to that for durables. It should also be remembered that suppliers have an impact upon the level of demand for products as they can manipulate demand through advertising and other forms of promotion.

The differential effects of rising income on demand for goods and services would in part explain the growth in the size of the service sector over the years. The change in industrial structure can then be seen as a natural process of change. During the Industrial Revolution there was a movement from agriculture to industry, in the same way as there is now a movement from manufacturing towards services. Changes in demand, however, cannot explain all of this change. Growth

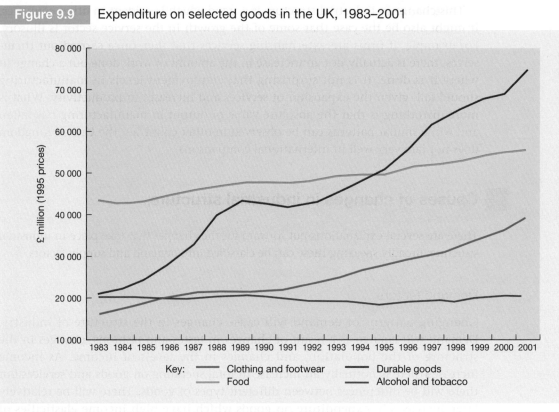

Figure 9.9   Expenditure on selected goods in the UK, 1983–2001

Key: —— Clothing and footwear   —— Durable goods
       —— Food   —— Alcohol and tobacco

Source: Adapted from www.statistics.gov.uk/statbase/tsdataset.asp?vlink=631&more=Y

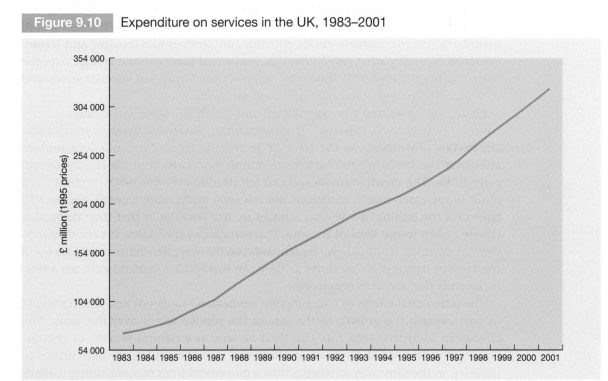

Figure 9.10   Expenditure on services in the UK, 1983–2001

Source: Adapted from www.statistics.gov.uk/statbase/tsdataset.asp?vlink=631&more=Y

in the service sector does not necessarily mean that there should be a decline in the size of the manufacturing sector when there are high levels of unemployment in the economy. Labour can be drawn from the unemployed rather than from manufacturing industry. During the time period under consideration there have been periods of high unemployment. It is also the case that the import of manufactured goods has not fallen, so it is not that demand has fallen for those goods but that we are buying them from abroad.

Supply factors

Changes in industrial structure can also be triggered by changes in supply conditions. The oil crisis of the 1970s is a good example of this. As a result of the massive increase in oil prices, there was a concerted campaign to reduce the consumption of oil and a search for other forms of energy. Technological change gives rise to new products and/or new processes of production. Different industries will vary in the scope for technological change and for increases in productivity (this is considered more fully later in this chapter).

Demand and supply forces are interlinked so it is often difficult to separate their effects as new products will generate new demands or could be developed to meet new demands.

Added to these internal factors is the fact that the United Kingdom is part of an international economy and competition from abroad will have an impact on the structure of industry through both demand and supply factors.

Deindustrialisation

The decline in the importance of manufacturing has been termed 'deindustrialisation' by many economists. The following causes are put forward for deindustrialisation.

'Crowding out'

The argument here is that the growth in the size of the public sector has been at the expense of the private sector. The resources that could have been used to expand the private sector have instead been used in the public sector, so that the public sector has 'crowded out' the private sector. This was a popular argument used in the 1980s to call for reductions in public spending. With higher levels of unemployment the argument loses its validity because it is not just a matter of using resources in the private or public sector – they are lying idle. As a result the 'crowding out' argument is less popular now. It is also argued that the higher rates of interest which might accompany higher spending on the public sector discourage private spending. Again, there is little concrete evidence that lower investment results from higher rates of interest. It could be that investment falls because of lower returns on that investment, and the returns on capital employed have been lower in the United Kingdom than in other countries.

Productivity

In terms of productivity the UK has not performed as well as other countries, as the mini case study shows. Low productivity has implications for international competitiveness. It can be offset by lower wages in order to stop costs from rising which might be passed on in the form of higher prices. Although the UK wages are relatively low compared with those of many of its competitors, they are not low enough to offset the low productivity levels completely. Alternatively the exchange rate could fall so that prices remain competitive internationally. Although this happened after the UK left the ERM, for long periods during the 1970s, 1980s and 1990s the UK exchange rate was high, and hence its international competitiveness was adversely affected.

Mini case | **Productivity**

There are a number of ways of measuring productivity. The productivity of labour can be measured by output per person employed or by output per hour worked. Neither of these are perfect measures because they will both be affected by the amount of capital employed and the productivity of this capital, but as there are great problems involved in measuring the productivity of capital this problem will be ignored for the time being. Table 9.11 shows output per person employed in selected countries in 2000.

Table 9.11 | Output per person employed, selected countries, 2000 (1994 = 100)

USA	114.3
France	106.9
Germany	107.2
Italy	108.1
UK	109.8

Source: Adapted from Table 13, *National Institute Economic Review*, no. 180, April 2002. Reproduced with permission.

These figures show that the UK has performed well compared with the other European countries listed, however it is the case that in both the USA and the UK workers work longer hours. It is therefore better to look at output per hour worked, (*see* Table 9.12).

Table 9.12 | Comparative output per hour worked, selected countries, 1999

USA	125
France	123
Germany	111
Italy	123
UK	100

Source: Adapted from Table 1, 'Productivity and Convergence in the EU', Mary O'Mahony, *National Institute Economic Review*, April 2002. Reproduced with permission.

This table shows a different picture for both the UK and the USA. The paper that Table 9.12 draws on divides EU countries into three groups according to their productivity rates: the first group, which has productivity levels similar to the USA, includes France, Italy, Belgium and the Netherlands; the second group includes Austria, Denmark, Finland, Germany, Ireland, Sweden and the UK; the third group, where productivity is lowest includes Spain, Greece and Portugal.

Measures of labour productivity (and capital productivity) are difficult to compare because they do not take into account the quantity or quality of the capital (or labour) used in the production process. A measure which takes into account both of these is 'total factor productivity' which measures the efficiency of both labour and capital. Table 9.13 shows the survey results for the same countries. As can be seen the UK does rather better on this measure of productivity.

Many reasons have been put forward for the relatively low productivity levels in the UK, including the educational system, the activities of trade unions, the high value of the pound, low levels of investment and low levels of research and development spending. As many of these have already been considered elsewhere in this book, only a few will be discussed here.

Low productivity has serious implications for international competitiveness (see text of chapter) and growth rates. The CBI estimates that an increase in the UK's productivity rates to the French and German level would increase GDP by £60 billion per year.

Table 9.13 Comparative total factor productivity, selected countries, 1999

USA	113
France	104
Germany	102
Italy	109
UK	100

Source: Adapted from Table 4, 'Productivity and Convergence in the EU', Mary O'Mahony, *National Institute Economic Review*, April 2002.

International competition

Because of competition from both the developed world and the developing world, where wage rates are lower than the UK rates, the United Kingdom has lost markets. At home much demand for goods and services is met by imports. Internationally the United Kingdom has lost markets too, as the level of its exports has fallen. There is evidence of this from the UK balance of payments. For example, in the mid-1980s the United Kingdom started to import more manufactured goods than it exported for the first time since the Industrial Revolution, and there was a widening deficit on the balance of payments in manufactured goods. High exchange rates have not helped the situation and have contributed to the decline. It is argued that the United Kingdom competes badly in both price and quality.

Specialisation

The United Kingdom tends to specialise in sectors which do not have great export potential; its percentage shares in sectors like electrical equipment, computers and transport equipment are less than the EU averages. The energy sector is of great importance to the United Kingdom economy.

Research and development

In the United Kingdom the proportion of spending on research and development has not changed very much over the last 20 years. This is not the case for other countries. It is also true that in the United Kingdom a much greater percentage of R&D is financed by government rather than private industry (*see* Chapter 5).

The educational system

The educational system in the United Kingdom is said to be biased towards the arts and pure sciences rather than applied scientific, engineering and business-type subjects. In the United Kingdom, 30 per cent of engineers have a professional quali-fication, while in Germany the figure is 70 per cent. Five per cent of UK retail workers have received training similar to an apprenticeship; in Germany the corres-ponding figure is 75 per cent. As far as international trade is concerned the United Kingdom also lags behind other European countries in its language training.

Level and type of investment

The level of investment in the United Kingdom is low. This means that the stock of capital may be too low and that it will be relatively 'old' (*see* Chapter 5).

Non-price factors

Non-price factors include quality, design and after-sales service. The United Kingdom is late compared to other countries to take up total quality management. These techniques were started in the West but then taken up and honed by the Japanese and are now being used worldwide. Quality management schemes can only be successful if other conditions are right, like a well-trained and qualified and highly motivated workforce.

Skills shortages in manufacturing

Even in times of high unemployment, there are still skill shortages. In the UK, a survey by Reed Personnel Services in 1999 found that 70 per cent of manufacturing organisations had difficulty recruiting suitably skilled employees. This problem is not confined to the UK or to manufacturing. TMP Worldwide carried out a survey of 350 European managers in 2001. Around half said that skills shortages were having a major impact on their operations and 80 per cent thought that the situa-tion would worsen. Shortages exist within sectors as diverse as IT and construction and metalworking. EU countries are not training enough people to meet demand or to replace those who are retiring.

 For TMP Worldwide see *www.tmp.com*

The financial system

It is often argued that the UK banks are less supportive of business than banks in other countries. In the United Kingdom, banks tend to offer only short-term to medium-term finance for industry; the only long-term finance would be in the form of mortgages. In other countries banks are large providers of long-term finance to industry through the purchase of stocks and shares.

Lack of qualified managers

It is argued that manufacturing has not recruited the best-qualified candidates for management, although management training can overcome this to some extent.

North Sea oil

The existence of North Sea oil has had a mixed effect on the United Kingdom. On the one hand it has led to an inflow of cash which has helped the balance of payments, but it has also served to keep the exchange rate of the pound higher than it would have been in its absence. A higher exchange rate has the effect of making United Kingdom goods more expensive abroad and foreign goods cheaper in the United Kingdom. Thus there is a corresponding deterioration in the balance of payments. The high exchange rate makes the United Kingdom less competitive in international markets, and as the biggest part of what we export is industrial goods, this sector will be most affected.

Government policy

During the 1980s the United Kingdom government repeated the argument that the decline in manufacturing was not important. It was seen as the working of the market mechanism, and would be replaced by services. The government therefore took a relaxed view of the decline. In the early 1980s the adherence to a strict monetarist policy of high interest rates and cut-backs in government expenditure all contributed to the decline in manufacturing.

Synopsis

Industrial structure refers to the relative sizes of the different industries in the economy. Firms are grouped together into industries and industries are grouped together into sectors in some way, although this is often difficult to do. The government has an official Standard Industrial Classification which has been changed to bring it in line with the EU classification.

The size of industries and sectors of the economy is measured by looking at the level of employment or the level of output. In the United Kingdom the primary sector is small and declining, although there was an increase in its importance in the 1980s due to the discovery and extraction of North Sea oil and gas. The secondary sector has also been declining in importance, in terms of both employment and output. The biggest sector of the economy at present is the tertiary sector. This pattern is similar to what is happening in other industrialised countries, although the detail varies slightly between countries. The industrial structure of a country and the way it changes depend upon many factors, most of which have been considered in this chapter.

Summary of key points

- Each country has a particular mix of primary, secondary and tertiary sectors which make up its industrial structure.

- Over the last 100 years there has been a shift in industrial structure in all countries, firstly from agriculture to manufacturing and then from manufacturing to services.

- This shift has taken place both in terms of employment and output.

- Changes in demand are one of the major causes of changes in industrial structure, as evidenced by the case study.

- Supply factors like technological change are also important in the process of change.

- The decline in manufacturing has been termed deindustrialisation and this process has been particularly pronounced in the UK.

- Reasons put forward for this include 'crowding-out', productivity, investment, research and development, the educational system and the high value of the pound.

CASE STUDY   Spending on leisure services

The growth of the service sector has been partly due to changes in the spending patterns of consumers. Many services have high income elasticities of demand and as income has increased over time so has spending on services. Figure 9.10 (on page 266) illustrates this point and the cyclical pattern in spending is further evidence of the link between spending on services and income. This case study will look at spending on leisure services in general and then go on to look at theme parks in particular to investigate factors which influence industrial structure.

The relationship between income and spending can also be illustrated with cross-sectional data, where households are broken into deciles, or tenths, according to their income levels. The first income decile represents the lowest tenth of income earners and the highest decile indicates the highest tenth of income earners. Figure 9.11 shows that spending on food falls steadily as a percentage of their total spending as income increases. Figure 9.12 shows that the percentage spent on all services and leisure services within that rises as income rises.

Theme parks in the UK

The USA is the market leader in theme parks, with 450 of them, the UK has 85 and Germany has 52. On average every American visits a theme park once a year, in the UK the figure is once every three years while in Europe the average is once every five years. The European market is therefore seen as having great growth potential. Theme parks make an important contribution to the level of employment, GDP and the balance of payments through tourism, but there is little official information available.

Demand factors

Within the sector there are differences. The popularity of zoos for example has declined over the last twenty years – many have closed or diversified. Windsor Safari Park was rescued from receivership by Legoland in the 1990s. Such diversification can be seen as a way of avoiding the decline phase of the life cycle (see mini case). The number of admissions to theme parks in the UK increased between 1995 and 2000 by 12 per cent but revenue increased by over 40 per cent because of higher admission prices and increased in-park spending.

Figure 9.11   Percentage of spending on food by income decile, 2000–2001

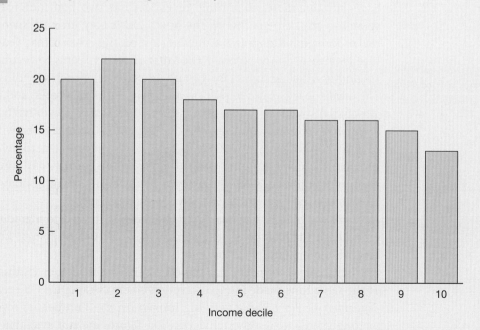

Source: Adapted from Table 3, *Family Spending*, 2001, Office for National Statistics, UK.

Figure 9.12   Percentage of spending on services by income decile, 2000–2001

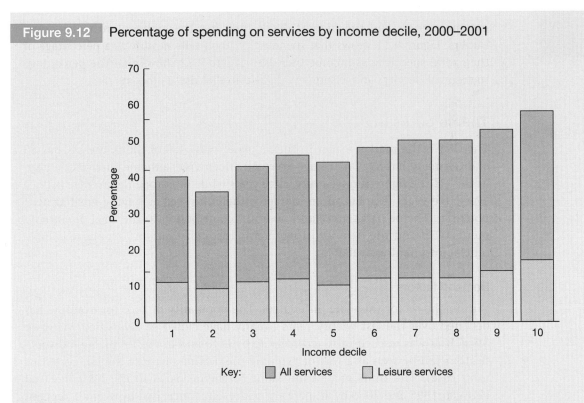

Source: Adapted from Table 3, *Family Spending*, 2001, Office for National Statistics, UK.

Factors which influence demand are:

■ *Economic conditions*. Economic recession has two contradictory effects on spending on theme parks: on the one hand it may increase spending since it makes foreign holidays less attractive and on the other it may reduce expenditure because of lower income. The latter certainly seems to be true for in-park spending, which accounts for around 46 per cent of such spending.

■ *The weather* has a major impact on attendance at theme parks, and explains why although demand has grown over the last 10 years this growth has been cyclical.

■ *Location*. The catchment area of a theme park is thought to be within a radius of 150–200 kilometres. Many theme parks have tried to overcome this problem by extending the use of the parks beyond the 'day trip' by offering accommodation on site. The growth in the short break holiday has helped, and some parks offer a discount on a two-day ticket.

■ *Demographic change*. The ageing of populations has led to a gradual change of emphasis in theme parks away from the high profile 'white knuckle' rides towards a more family atmosphere

■ *The high value of the pound* has put off foreign visitors from visiting the UK and at the same time made foreign travel relatively cheaper for UK travellers.

■ *September 11 2001* had a very big impact on the numbers of foreign tourists visiting the UK and although admission figures are not available yet for 2002 they are expected to be lower (*see* Case study Chapter 1).

Supply factors

In the UK there are 85 theme parks of varying size. The biggest is Alton Towers which had 2.65 million visitors in 1999, followed by Legoland which had 1.62 million visitors in 1999. Most of the theme parks are independently owned, the main exception being Tussauds which owns Alton Towers (number 1), Chessington World of Adventure (number 3) and Thorpe Park (number 6).

Factors which influence supply are:

- *Extended season*. The traditional season for the theme parks is the summer and school holidays. Many parks have extended their opening periods – sometimes to include Christmas. Opening hours have been extended into the evening, even though the entrance fee covers the whole day, this might well lead to increased in-park spending. Marketing has been aimed at attracting groups (school trips or corporate customers) in the weekdays during term time.
- *Diversification*. Theme parks have started to offer special events out of season, like fireworks displays, classical music concerts and Halloween parties to boost attendance. Given demographic changes, the parks have started to offer other attractions as well as the white knuckle rides to appeal to the whole family – like puppet shows or magic shows. Some are even offering children's birthday parties.
- *Cost considerations*. Theme parks employ a high number of temporary and part-time employees and so any legislation which affects the employment of these types of workers will impact upon costs. Tickets are now available on the Internet – this cuts administrative costs and gives the theme park more control over its own marketing.
- *Competition*. There is much greater competition than in the past. Many attractions were opened to coincide with the Millennium – the Dome and the London Eye are two examples.

The future

Two recent reports[3] both predict that demand will continue to rise along the same trend as in the past but point to the opening of a gap between the popular theme parks with money to upgrade attractions and the smaller, less well off parks that will not be able to do this. Possible micro factors which might impact upon the market include proposed changes to the school year and the Disability Discrimination Act which from 2004 requires that 'reasonable adjustments be made to premises to overcome physical barriers to access'. This will have important implications for cost.

This case study has shown that the major impetus for the growth of this sector has come through the demand factors, most of the items considered as supply factors have merely been reactions to the demand characteristics. It therefore shows how important demand is in the determination of and changes to industrial structure.

See *www.BALPA,org* (British Association of Leisure Parks, Piers and Attractions); *www.ALVA.org.uk* (Association of Leading Visitor Attractions); *www.alton-towers.co.uk*; *www.lego.com*

Case study questions

1 Assuming that virtual reality machines become really popular, what are the implications for the recreation park providers?

2 How might they avoid the decline phase of their life cycle?

Review and discussion questions

1 Select industries in various stages of their life cycles. How closely do the observed characteristics of these industries correspond with the expected characteristics summarised in Table 9.10 in the mini case (page 264)?

2 On what basis could you judge whether manufacturing was more important to an economy than services?

3 What would be the effect on the industrial structure of a country of the discovery of large supplies of oil?

4 What is the difference between an industry and a market?

5 What policies can governments introduce to increase productivity?

Assignments

1 You are the research assistant for an MP who is to participate in a debate on the importance of the manufacturing sector to the economy. You have been asked to produce a list of the arguments that are likely to be used by both sides in the debate: that is, reasons why the decline does matter and the set of counter-arguments. Provide a suitable list.

2 You work for an organisation which provides European intelligence to local businesses and the media. Your line manager has to give a presentation at an international conference on the likely effects that enlargement of the EU will have on industrial structure and has asked you to research the topic. You are required to:
- collect the necessary information on the industrial structures of the potential new entrants;
- assess the impact that the accession of these countries would have on the industrial structure of the EU;
- assess the likely impact of membership on the industrial structures of the countries themselves.

(Sources: see the case study at the end of Chapter 13 and for information on these countries see the OECD *Quarterly Labour Force Statistics* at your local library.)

Notes and references

1 Porter, M., *Competitive Advantage: Creating and Sustaining Superior Performance*, The Free Press, New York, 1985.

2 See Chapter 11.

3 See Mintel report, *UK Theme Parks*, July 2000 and Keynote report, *Tourist Attractions*, 2001.

Further reading

Cook, G., *Economics and Business Studies Update: A Student Guide*, Hidcote Press, 2002.

Donaldson, P., *Understanding the British Economy*, Penguin, 1991.

Jones, T. T. and Cockerill, T. A. J., *Structure and Performance of Industries*, Philip Allan, 1984.

Indexes to the SIC of Economic Activities, HMSO, 1992.

Worthington, I., Britton, C. and Rees, A., *Business Economics: Blending Theory and Practice*, Financial Times/Prentice Hall, 2001.

Web links and further questions are available on the website at:
www.booksites.net/worthington

Appendix 9.1 The Standard Industrial Classification (SIC), 1992

Division	Industry
Section A	**Agriculture, hunting and forestry**
Section B	**Fishing**
Section C	**Mining and quarrying**
Subsection CA	Mining and quarrying of energy producing materials
Subsection CB	Mining and quarrying except energy producing materials
Section D	**Manufacturing**
Subsection DA	Manufacture of food products; Beverages and tobacco
Subsection DB	Manufacture of textiles and textile products
Subsection DC	Manufacture of leather and leather products
Subsection DD	Manufacture of wood and wood products
Subsection DE	Manufacture of pulp, paper and paper products; Publishing and printing
Subsection DF	Manufacture of coke, refined petroleum products and nuclear fuel
Subsection DG	Manufacture of chemicals, chemical products and man-made fibres
Subsection DH	Manufacture of rubber and plastic products
Subsection DI	Manufacture of other non-metallic mineral products
Subsection DJ	Manufacture of basic metals and fabricated metal products
Subsection DK	Manufacture of machinery and equipment not elsewhere classified
Subsection DL	Manufacture of electrical and optical equipment
Subsection DM	Manufacture of transport equipment
Subsection DN	Manufacturing not elsewhere classified
Section E	**Electricity, gas and water supply**
Section F	**Construction**
Section G	**Wholesale and retail trade; repair of motor vehicles, motor-cycles and personal and household goods**
Section H	**Hotels and restaurants**
Section I	**Transport, storage and communication**
Section J	**Financial intermediation**
Section K	**Real estate, renting and business activities**
Section L	**Public administration and defence; compulsory social security**
Section M	**Education**
Section N	**Health and social work**
Section O	**Other community, social and personal service activities**
Section P	**Private households with employed persons**
Section Q	**Extra-territorial organisations and bodies**

10

Government and business

Ian Worthington

In any society multiple interactions exist between government and business and these occur at a variety of spatial levels and in a wide range of contexts. One such interaction stems from the government's attempts to alleviate the problems of regional and/or local economic decay and decline and these tend to be the focus of governmental policies at local, regional, national and even supranational level. While such measures are formulated and administered by governmental agencies, business organisations in market economies often exercise considerable influence on government decisions. This influence can be enhanced if the views of the business community are expressed through powerful and persuasive representative organisations.

Objectives

- To consider the rationale for government involvement in the economy.

- To investigate the nature and scope of United Kingdom government regional policy.

- To survey government policy initiatives at sub-regional level, including the role of local government in economic development.

- To examine the notion of corporate community involvement.

- To consider the role of business as an influence on government.

Key terms

Assisted Area
Business angels
Business Link
Chambers of Commerce
City Action Teams
City Challenge
City Grant
Community initiatives
Confederation of British
  Industry
English Partnerships
Enterprise grants

Enterprise zones
European Structural Funds
Externalities
Industrial policies
Inner City Task Forces
Local Enterprise Agencies
Market failure
Merit goods
Negotiated environment
Public goods
Region
Regional chambers

Regional Development
  Agencies
Regional government offices
Regional Selective
  Assistance
Single Regeneration Budget
Trade Associations
Urban Development
  Corporations
Urban Regeneration
  Companies

Introduction

All democratic market-based economies accept the need for government involvement in the day-to-day workings of the economy. The critical question, therefore, is not whether a role for government should exist, but *what* that role should be and *where* the boundaries should be drawn between private and public (i.e. collective) action. Governments of a 'socialist' persuasion normally favour a substantial role for the state as both producer and regulator, whereas non-socialist administrations tend to prefer limited state influence that is directed towards improving the operation of the free market. Either way, the actions of the state in the economy can be influential at both the macro and the micro level and this has important implications for the conduct of business in the non-state sector.

In examining the role of government in the macroeconomy, Chapter 4 emphasised how changes in fiscal and monetary policy could be used to influence aggregrate levels of income, output and employment in the economy and how attempts to regulate the overall level of economic activity were related to a government's macroeconomic policy objectives. By way of contrast, in this and a number of subsequent chapters (especially Chapter 14) the focus is on the ways in which government actions impinge upon the operations of firms and markets and the rationale underlying the decisions by the state to intervene at the micro level. Such interventions may take place at the request of the business community or despite its opposition, but it is rare for them to occur without business expressing an opinion which it expects government to take into consideration. This role of business as an important influence on government policy is examined in the concluding section of this chapter.

Government and business: an overview

In considering reasons for government intervention in the economy, economists have traditionally pointed to the problem of 'market failure'. This is the notion that if left entirely to their own devices, markets can operate in a way which is not always economically or socially desirable. To this extent interventionist policies can be portrayed as an attempt by governments of all political complexions to deal with the problems inherent in the operation of free markets.

The key areas of 'market failure' are well known. Primary concerns include:

1 The unwillingness of markets to produce goods and services which are either unprofitable or which it is not practical to provide through private means (i.e. 'public goods' such as defence, social services and so on).
2 The likely under-provision of certain goods and services felt to be of general benefit to the community (i.e. 'merit goods' such as education, libraries and so on).
3 The failure to take into account the external costs and benefits of production or consumption (i.e. 'externalities' such as pollution, congestion and so on).
4 The danger of monopoly power if businesses can be freely bought and sold.

5 The under-utilisation of economic resources (e.g. unemployment resulting from demand deficiency, new technology or structural or frictional problems).

6 The tendency for output to be determined and distributed on the ability to pay rather than on the basis of need or equity.

Government responses to these problems have normally taken a number of forms, including public ownership, legislation and administrative or fiscal regulation, and examples of all these approaches can be found to a greater or lesser extent in all countries. In recent years, however, under the influence of economists of the 'new right', governments have begun to take steps to disengage the state from some of its activities (e.g. public ownership) and have increasingly turned to market solutions to problems emanating primarily from the operation of the market system itself (e.g. schemes to charge for the use of roads which are heavily congested).

While all forms of government intervention in the economy invariably have direct or indirect consequences for businesses, it is possible to distinguish certain policies which are designed specifically to influence the industrial and commercial environment – sometimes described as 'industrial policies'. In the United Kingdom and elsewhere, these have typically included:

■ attempts at direct industrial intervention (e.g. the establishment of the National Enterprise Board);
■ privatisation policies;
■ policies relating to competition and monopoly control; and
■ policies designed to influence industrial location and to encourage economic regeneration at different spatial levels.

Though it cannot be claimed that such measures amount to a single and coherent policy for business, nevertheless they indicate that successive governments accept they have an important role to play in shaping the environment in which private businesses function. Competition and privatisation policy – discussed in detail in Chapter 14 – tend to focus on the operation of markets and on the benefits which derive from private provision under a competitive market structure. Government spatial policies – the subject-matter of this chapter – are mainly concerned with addressing the problems of regional disparities in income, employment and output, and the associated problem of localised economic decline as businesses fail or decide to relocate their premises.

Regional policy

Regions

A region is a geographical area which possesses certain characteristics (e.g. political, economic, physical) which give it a measure of unity that allows boundaries to be drawn round it, thus differentiating it from surrounding areas. In the United Kingdom the standard planning regions have traditionally been the North, North West, Yorkshire/Humberside, East Midlands, West Midlands, South West, East

Anglia, South East, Wales, Scotland and Northern Ireland, with each of these further divided into sub-regions based on administrative counties and on designated metropolitan areas. These planning regions and sub-regions historically have formed the units of classification for a wide range of official government statistics (*see* Chapter 17).

With the establishment of the regional government offices and the setting up of the Regional Development Agencies (RDAs) the regional map of the UK has become influenced by these structures. Moreover, outside London, regional chambers have been established in each of the eight current English regions (the North West, North East, Yorkshire and the Humber, West Midlands, East Midlands, East of England, South East, South West) to represent the various regional interests in relation to the work of the region's RDA. The membership of the regional Chambers – mostly called 'Assemblies' – includes representatives of the local authorities, employer and employee groups, the small business sector, the health service, educational establishments, rural and environmental groups and other regional stakeholders. At the time of writing there are no directly elected regional assemblies in England (excluding London) of the kind found in many other European states, although the government has recently (May 2002) signalled its intention to allow referendums on the issue of regional government.

> **web link**
>
> Further information on regional aspects of government in the UK can be found on the websites of the Department for Transport, Local Government and the Regions, *www.regions.dtlr.gov.uk* and the Department of Trade and Industry, *www.dti.gov.uk*
> On Regional Chambers, see for example, *www.regions.dtlr.gov.uk/chambers/index*

The basis of regional policy

Many countries have a recognisable 'regional policy' of one kind or another. Such policies are generally designed to identify and demarcate those geographical areas which are experiencing substantial economic and/or social problems and which are felt to require government assistance. Using a range of socio-economic indicators – such as unemployment levels, population density, economic activity rates, income – governments tend to distinguish those regions which depart significantly from the national average and designate these regions 'assisted areas'. These areas then become the focus of government assistance and tend to be given priority in the provision of financial aid for capital projects and for measures designed to increase employment and growth. Such aid generally comes in a variety of forms and may include assistance from international and supranational sources, as in the case of EU regional policy (*see* below).

UK regional policy

The origins of UK regional policy can be traced back to the 1930s when the government first began to provide help to a number of depressed areas in the form of low-interest loans, subsidised rents and the establishment of government trading estates. By the closing decades of the twentieth century the system had evolved into one in which the government designated three types of assisted area that became eligible for regional aid. These were:

1 Development areas (DAs);
2 Intermediate areas (IAs);
3 Northern Ireland – which received special regional help owing to the problems it was experiencing in attracting investment in industrial and commercial projects.

The areas qualifying for government regional assistance under this scheme underwent some revision in 1993. Subsequently, following new European Commission rules on regional aid in March 1998, all EU member states were required to further revise their Assisted Areas maps by 1 January 2000 in preparation for the enlargement of the EU. The UK's initial response – which was submitted to the Commission in July 1999 – was rejected and the proposed regional aid map had to be adjusted following consultation with the various interested parties. The revised proposals for a new Assisted Areas map for the UK were published on 10 April 2000.

Information on the new Assisted Areas proposals is available at *www.dti.gov.uk/regional/assistedareas*.
The annex to this site also contains a map of areas for assistance under the revised proposals.

Under this current scheme regional aid is available in those areas covered by existing EU law (e.g. Amsterdam Treaty Articles 87[3]a and 87[3]c). These areas, designated Tiers 1 and 2, remain in force until the end of 2006, subject to adjustments to reflect any significant socio-economic changes which occur during the period. Should any additions be made to the agreed regional aid map, these have to be offset by exclusions in other areas to maintain the overall population ceiling.

The UK government has also designated a new Tier 3 which extends outside Tiers 1 and 2 and where the emphasis is on aid to small and medium-sized enterprises in the form of enterprise grants. This decision is designed to complement other measures to encourage smaller businesses, including the establishment of the Small Business Service (SBS) and the creation of the Enterprise Fund (*see* Chapter 8).

Within the designated areas Regional Selective Assistance (RSA) is the main form of discretionary grant aid, now administered by the Regional Development Agencies and designed to secure employment opportunities and increase regional competitiveness and prosperity. In order to qualify, businesses must be investing in fixed capital items, with minimum fixed costs over £500 000, and must demonstrate that a project meets a number of predetermined criteria, including creating/safeguarding jobs and contributing positive benefits to both the regional and the national economy. Grants are available to firms of all sizes in Tier 1 and Tier 2 Assisted Areas, with the regional aid guidelines allowing higher maximum grant levels in areas designated Tier 1 (e.g. Cornwall).

In Tier 2 and 3 areas Enterprise Grants are also available to SMEs investing in fixed capital items. The maximum fixed costs must be no more than £500 000 and the grant ceiling is 15 per cent of those costs, up to a maximum grant of £75 000. Currently this grant is specifically, though not exclusively, targeted at high growth businesses seeking to maximise value added projects with demonstrable quality outputs and it aims to support projects in these areas that would not otherwise have gone ahead without grant aid.

web link The Regional Government Offices are a useful source of information on what grants are available for businesses in particular regions of the UK. See, for example, *www.go-nw.gov.uk/business/financial* and *www.go-wm.gov.uk/rsa/enterprisegrant* which contains information on Enterprise Grants.

It is worth noting that in the UK the extent of regional assistance provided by government under the various schemes has been significantly reduced over several decades, both in terms of the amount of resources committed to the regional aid budget and the geographical areas receiving assistance. While the new guidelines issued by the European Commission in 1998 were evidently designed to promote greater transparency and comparability in the regional aid system across member states, they were also part of a drive to reduce the overall level of aid to industry within the EU prior to the enlargement of the Community.

Regional aid within the European Union

In addition to any funding provided by the national government, businesses in the member states of the European Union can also benefit from grant aid under agreed European programmes that have been designed to tackle national and regional disparities within the EU. The majority of this aid is provided from European Structural Funds which are used to assist those areas that compare unfavourably with the EU's average levels of prosperity. The EU's four structural instruments are:

1 The European Regional Development Fund (ERDF);
2 The European Social Fund (ESF);
3 The European Agricultural Guidance and Guarantee Fund (EAGGF);
4 The Financial Instrument for Fisheries Guidance (FIFG).

For the period 2000–2006 it is estimated that around €195 billion will be spent by these four sources of funding, with a further €18 billion provided through the Cohesion Fund (*see* Table 10.1).

Under new Structural Fund Regulations which came into effect on 1 January 2000, the EU has identified three priorities or 'objectives' for grant aid. These are:

- Objective 1 – promoting the development and structural adjustment of regions whose development is lagging behind.
- Objective 2 – supporting the economic and social conversion of industrial, rural, urban and fisheries areas facing structural difficulties.
- Objective 3 – supporting the adaptation and modernisation of policies, systems of education, training and employment.

In the period 2000–2006 it is estimated that Objective 1 areas will cover around 22 per cent of the EU population and will probably command around 70 per cent

Table 10.1	European Structural Funds

Fund	Main focus
European Regional Development Fund	Designed to redress the main regional imbalances within the EU through the development and structural adjustment of regions whose development is lagging behind. Funding supports investment in sites and facilities for business, infrastructure, local economic development initiatives, environmental protection and improvement, tourism and cultural projects etc.
European Social Fund	Aimed primarily at improving employment opportunities and reducing social exclusion by promoting employability and equal opportunities and by investing in human resources, particularly through education and training initiatives.
European Agricultural Guidance and Guarantee Fund	Designed to support rural development and encourage rural restructuring and diversification in order to promote economic prosperity and social inclusion, while protecting and maintaining the environment and rural heritage.
Financial Instrument for Fisheries Guidance	Aims to contribute to achieving a sustainable balance between fishery resources and their exploitation. Funds projects to modernise the structure of the fisheries sector and related industries and to encourage diversification of the workforce and the industry into other sectors.

web link

Information on European Structural Funds can be found on the websites of the Regional Government Offices and the DTLR (see weblinks above). The EU's own website also contains substantial amounts of information on funding and on policy.
See *europa.eu.int/comm/regional_policy*

of the designated funding, with 11.5 per cent going to Objective 2 Areas and 12.3 per cent to support Objective 3 in areas not accorded Objective 1 status. In the UK, Tier 1 and Objective 1 Areas currently coincide, though changes are likely after 2006. The main aims and focus of funding in the three areas is shown in Table 10.2.

Alongside the three key objectives, the EU has also designated a number of community initiatives which focus on finding common solutions to specific problems and which will account for around 5 per cent of spending from the Structural Funds over the same period. Interreg III, for example, focuses on cross-border, transnational and international co-operation and is funded under the ERDF. Urban II seeks to promote sustainable development in the troubled urban districts of the EU through the design and implementation of innovative models of development for economic and social regeneration, again funded under the ERDF. Leader+ promotes rural development through local initiatives using funds from the EAGGF.

Smaller amounts of funding are also provided under schemes to promote innovative actions and for the adjustment of fisheries structures outside the Objective regions, with the former designed to encourage the testing of new ideas and practices that might not be funded under the traditional programmes of the Structural Funds.

| Table 10.2 | Objectives areas and funding |

Main funding instruments	EU Objective Areas	Main aims of funding	Main focus of funding	Eligible areas within EU
ERDF/ESF/ EAGGF/FIFG	Objective 1	To support development in the less prosperous regions of the EU so as to narrow the gap between development levels in the various regions.	Funding for take-off of economic activities by supporting projects concerning infrastructure, human resources, and aid for production sectors.	Regions where GDP per head is at or below 75 per cent of EU average (e.g. Saxony, Western Greece, Galicia, Sicily, Algarve, West Wales and the Valleys, Merseyside, South Yorkshire, Cornwall and the Isles of Scilly).
ERDF/ESF	Objective 2	To revitalise areas facing structural difficulties whether industrial, rural, urban, or dependent on fishery.	Funding for economic and social conversion.	Eligible areas must meet specified criteria related to structural decline. Covers 18 per cent of EU population.
ESF	Objective 3	To support national efforts to modernise policies and systems of education, training and employment.	Funding aimed at combating unemployment and developing human resources.	All areas have Objective 3 status outside Objective 1 regions.

Mini case   Attracting foreign inward investment

Though not the only factor explaining the destination of direct inward investment, government grant aid and other forms of assistance are clearly important in determining where multinational enterprises decide to locate new factories and offices. In 1994, for example, the South Korean electronics company, Samsung, announced a £450 million investment in a new complex on Teesside which was expected to bring up to 3000 jobs to the area by the turn of the century. As an incentive to the company, the British government offered nearly £60 million in regional selective assistance and further contributions were promised by the local county council, the TEC and English Partnerships, the government-backed development agency. Sadly for the North East, Samsung subsequently cancelled its planned investment in the wake of the global economic crisis (see Mini case in Chapter 4).

Other announcements of further multi-billion pound investments in Britain by huge Korean conglomerates (*chaebol*) seem to confirm the importance of regional incentives in locational decisions. Not that the Far East is the only source of such inward investment. In August 1995, the German industrial giant Siemens indicated its intention to build a £1.1 billion semi-conductor factory on Tyneside near the site of the Swan Hunter shipyard. All the indications were that this decision was heavily influenced by the personal intervention of the then Prime Minister, John Major, and his deputy, Michael Heseltine, in a deal which included a substantial package of state aid. As in the Samsung case, Siemens qualified for contributions from the DTI in the form of regional selective assistance, together with funding from local authorities and other agencies, and help from English Partnerships to develop the site.

While for both Tyneside and Britain, Siemens' decision was something of a triumph, economic events – particularly the collapse of prices of semi-conductors – undermined Siemens' overseas investment plans. In 1998 the company announced the closure of its plant on Tyneside.

UK urban policy

The urban 'problem'

The progressive decline and decay of urban areas – with its associated unemployment amongst the low paid, unskilled and ethnic members of the population – first came to prominence in the 1960s and gave rise to an Urban Programme aimed predominantly at funding capital projects and education schemes in deprived inner-city locations. Implicit in this programme was the view that the urban 'problem' was largely one of physical decline coupled with failings on the part of individuals which could be corrected by selected government intervention, designed to improve the prospects and environment faced by local citizens. This largely 'pathological' perspective was ultimately exposed by both academic research and community projects undertaken in the 1970s, with the result that government came to see the problem as one of economic and social change, and its impact on the local environment. This 'structuralist' view suggested that policy should be directed towards economic development through partnership between the centre, the localities and the private sector, with the emphasis on schemes to overcome structural weaknesses. Riots in several large UK cities in the 1980s served to emphasise that the problem was particularly acute in those inner-city core areas that had suffered a significant loss of industry and population over a number of years.

The focus of policy implementation

Whereas regional policy is managed centrally through a single government department, urban policy has traditionally operated through a variety of agencies including local authorities, voluntary organisations, quangos and a number of independent bodies set up by central government. The relative importance of these agencies in implementing government policy has changed significantly over time.

The initial focus of policy implementation under the Urban Programme was the local authorities which acted as a channel for central government funds into projects designed to regenerate economic activity (e.g. by providing premises), to improve the physical environment (e.g. by clearing land or renovating buildings) and to meet social needs (e.g. by providing community facilities for deprived groups). This role was further enhanced by the Inner Urban Areas Act 1978 which conferred wide powers on certain designated local authorities to assist industry wherever a need was felt to exist and where government help was seen to be appropriate. Central to the government's strategy was its attempt to regenerate inner-city areas through capital investment and through environmental improvement, some of which was to be funded from the private sector. To encourage private sector investment, local authorities in the designated areas were allowed to declare industrial and commercial improvement areas and to give financial assistance to companies which located in such areas.

With the election of the Conservative government in 1979, a number of new initiatives were introduced which indicated a move towards an even more spatially selective policy for urban areas. These initiatives – which included Enterprise Zones, Urban Development Corporations, freeports and City Action Teams (*see* below) – frequently by-passed local authorities or reduced their powers over the allocation of resources and/or land use, and were seen by many commentators as a vote of no confidence in local government's ability to stimulate urban regeneration. At the heart of the new approach lay an attempt by central government to turn inner-city areas into investment opportunities for the private sector by clearing dereliction and improving infrastructure. The basic idea, as the *Financial Times* (30 October 1990) pointed out, was to reduce downside risk to a level where private investors would see enough potential to develop in cities rather than take softer profits elsewhere.

In March 1988 the government launched its 'Action for Cities' initiative which covered a range of programmes administered by different government departments that were designed to promote industrial and commercial investment and hence create employment in the inner-city areas. Programmes under this initiative were co-ordinated by a special unit located at the Department of the Environment and local co-ordination occurred through City Action Teams. After 1994, in an attempt to achieve greater co-ordination in policy and to introduce competition for resources, the government began to amalgamate a wide range of inner-city programmes under the Single Regeneration Budget (SRB), with the funds initially being administered by the newly integrated regional government offices which brought together the existing regional offices of a number of major government departments (e.g. Environment, Trade and Industry, Transport, Employment). It also established a new development agency (English Partnerships) that was to draw its public funding from the SRB. From April 1999 English Partnerships' regional functions and the SRB Challenge Fund became the responsibility of the newly established Regional Development Agencies. The latter have been set up to take the lead in delivering more effective and integrated regeneration programmes which promote sustainable economic, social and physical regeneration within the regions. They are seen as a key actor in developing and delivering partnership-based regeneration strategies at sub-national level.

Recent urban policy instruments

The Urban Programme

Historically the Urban Programme, which was designed to help combat the economic, social and environmental problems of urban areas, was the main mechanism for allocating funds to those inner-city areas facing the greatest need. Of the 57 designated local authority areas which fell into this category, 9 were 'partnership authorities', where the government formed a close partnership with local authority agencies to tackle the problem of urban decay (e.g. Hackney, Liverpool, Manchester, Salford). The remaining 48 'programme authorities' (including Barnsley, Bolton, Sandwell, Wrekin) had no such partnership, but were eligible for government assistance for projects which contribute to the economic development of the inner area. In both cases, requests for funds had to be submitted from or via the local authorities which assessed the application and paid the grant for projects receiving official approval.

With the advent of the Single Regeneration Budget, the Urban Programme has gradually been phased out and in future all cities, towns and rural areas will be brought within the remit of government regeneration policy. Since the new regime is designed to be competitive, towns and cities within an area will inevitably be competing for funding against each other.

Urban Development Corporations (UDCs)

Urban Development Corporations were independent development agencies, established by central government to oversee inner-city development within designated areas. The first two such areas were London Docklands and Merseyside which gained UDCs in 1980. Subsequently, UDCs were established in Trafford Park (Manchester), the Black Country (Birmingham and surrounding districts), Teesside, Tyne and Wear, Cardiff Bay, Central Manchester, Leeds, Sheffield and Bristol. These ten agencies – whose powers of development within their designated areas superseded those of the local authorities in their area – ceased operations in 1998.

Using funds mainly provided by central government and employing around 500 permanent staff in total, the UDCs had the following objectives:

1 To bring land and buildings into effective use.
2 To encourage the development of industry and commerce.
3 To ensure housing and other social facilities are available in order to encourage people to live and work in the designated area.

To achieve these aims, corporations were given wide powers to acquire, reclaim, assemble, develop, sell or lease land and to provide the necessary infrastructure. In addition they had powers to build houses for rent or sale and to renovate and reuse existing buildings. In short, they were the development control authorities for their areas.

A fundamental aspect of the UDC's role as an agency for urban regeneration was its ability to act as a catalyst for encouraging private sector investment. Using public money to bring about environmental improvement and infrastructural development, corporations sought to attract private investors by removing some of the abnormal costs of development such as land clearance and servicing. This 'pump-priming' role cost the taxpayer over £500 million in the early 1990s, with the lion's share of the funds going to the London Docklands Development Corporation (LDDC), whose fortunes were considerably affected by the collapse in property prices in the late 1980s and early 1990s.

Enterprise Zones (EZs)

Like UDCs, Enterprise Zones were first established in the early 1980s, with the first batch of 11 EZs being designated in 1981 with a planned lifespan of 10 years. By the late 1980s the number of EZs had risen to 27, though the number has fluctuated over time as some of the original EZs (e.g. Corby) were wound up and new ones announced in the wake of the closure of a large number of pits in the United Kingdom coal industry.

In essence, Enterprise Zones were small areas of territory within a locality where the government was seeking to encourage industrial and commercial activity by the removal of certain tax burdens and other impediments to enterprise (e.g. bureaucratic procedures). Among the principal benefits for firms located or locating in an EZ were:

- Exemption from rates on industrial and commercial property.
- Allowances of 100 per cent for corporation and income tax purposes on all capital expenditure related to industrial and commercial development.
- A greatly simplified planning regime.

In addition, businesses normally faced fewer requests from public bodies for statistical information and were often exempt from other administrative procedures.

Whether EZs were successful in attracting enterprise and in creating significant numbers of jobs in inner-urban areas is open to dispute. Some evidence exists to suggest that the net job-creation effect has been relatively small and that many of the 'new' jobs are simply relocations by local businesses moving to take advantage of the benefits offered to firms within an EZ. However, according to an evaluation of EZs in the later 1990s it is estimated that the experiment helped to create over 50 000 net new jobs at a cost in the region of £1700 per year (see e.g. *www.regeneration.dtlr.gov.uk/rs/00495*).

City Action Teams (CATs)

City Action Teams were designed to bring together government departments, local authorities, local community groups, voluntary organisations and businesses working in inner-city areas. In addition to providing information and advice to any business working in or moving to an inner-city area, a CAT could help with funding for schemes which safeguarded or created jobs, improved the environment, provided training places or encouraged enterprise and the growth of business. It also funded feasibility studies and assisted with consultancy fees for local projects. With the recent change in emphasis of government regeneration policy, funding for CATs has steadily fallen and was a mere £1 million by 1995/6. Like UDCs, City Action Teams have been phased out.

City Challenge

City Challenge was designed to concentrate resources on key areas in the 1990s. Under the initiative, local authorities in partnership with the private sector, local organisations and the local community were asked to draw up detailed plans for solving the problems of their area and special government funds were allocated to acceptable projects. The first 11 partnerships completed their five-year programmes to bring self-sustaining economic regeneration in deprived areas by March 1997. Nineteen Round 2 partnerships finished their programmes the following year.

City Grant

City Grant is the descendant of the Urban Development Grant – an idea copied from the United States after the Toxteth and Brixton riots in the early 1980s. The aim of the grant is to support private sector capital projects which benefit local areas (e.g. bringing derelict land and buildings into use) by bridging any adverse gap between the estimated costs of a project and its expected market value, thus allowing a developer to make a reasonable profit on the venture. Large-scale projects that give rise to new jobs or housing and which improve the environment have been the focus of the grant aid, and priority generally has been given to schemes within City Challenge areas before those from the 57 local authorities that are part of the old Urban Programme. In recent years, City Grant has been administered by English Partnerships (*www.englishpartnerships.co.uk*).

Inner-City Task Forces

Task Forces were composed of small teams of civil servants from various government departments and people on secondment from the private sector who worked directly with local authorities and local businesses to stimulate economic development in inner-city areas. Their role was to co-ordinate and monitor the whole range of government initiatives within the designated area. The Task Force programme ceased on 31 March 1998.

Current developments in urban policy

With the change of government in 1997, urban policy in the UK has taken on a more targeted and focused approach, with funding increasingly being directed towards a range of economic, social and environmental initiatives. Key developments have included:

- *The New Deal for Communities programme* – designed to combat social exclusion through focused and intensive neighbourhood renewal projects in the most deprived neighbourhoods.
- *SRB Challenge Round 5* – with a more regional focus and an increased emphasis on partnership capacity building, with eighty per cent of new resources concentrated in the most deprived areas.
- *Housing estate regeneration* – through Housing Action Trusts and Estate Action.
- *Coalfields initiatives* – especially the Coalfields Regeneration Trust and the Enterprise Fund.
- Initiatives to tackle problems such as education, drugs, health and crime.

In 1998 the government established an Urban Task Force chaired by Lord Rogers to examine the causes of urban decline and to recomend solutions to bring people back into towns and cities. In its report in June 1999 the Task Force made 105 recomendations, including the establishment of Urban Regeneration Companies (URCs) to lead and coordinate redevelopment and new investment in declining areas. This suggestion was subsequently endorsed in a White Paper on Urban Renaissance published in 2000 which also underlined the need to create local strategic partnerships in order to develop a co-ordinated approach to strategy formulation and implementation.

To emphasise the increased importance being attached to tackling urban issues and problems the current government has established a Cabinet Committee on Urban Affairs and an Urban Policy Unit within the DETR. It has also announced a review of the work of English Partnerships, the discontinuation of the national rounds of the SRB (after Round 6) and an Urban Summit to discuss the whole area of urban regeneration policy. This meeting is scheduled to take place in Autumn 2002.

For further information on the different aspects of the UK urban regeneration policy you should consult *www.regeneration.detr.gov.uk*

Local government and business in the UK

The basis of local economic development

As a major service provider, consumer, employer and landowner, local government has always played an important role in the economy and its influence on business activity at local level remains considerable. Large local authorities annually spend hundreds of millions of pounds, employ tens of thousands of workers and support many thousand additional jobs through the placement of contracts with local businesses. Further employment is also created through the 'multiplier effect', as local authority employees spend their income in the local economy and local citizens consume local authority services such as transport and leisure.

Not content with local economic conditions, many local authorities have actively intervened in the local economy by establishing economic development programmes which are designed to alleviate the familiar problems of unemployment, industrial decline and environmental decay. These programmes – often co-ordinated through an economic development unit within the local authority – normally comprise a range of initiatives designed to create or safeguard local jobs by supporting local businesses and encouraging enterprise in a variety of ways (see below). While the origins of such initiatives can be traced back to the nineteenth century, the majority of measures have been introduced in the last 25 years and represent a move from a reactive to a proactive role by local authorities in local economic development.

The basis for such local authority intervention is partly legal and partly political. Under the law, local authorities in the United Kingdom can only engage in activities for which they have statutory authority, whether granted by public statute (i.e. applying to all authorities) or by private Act (i.e. applying to a specific authority). These statutes not only impose specific duties on local authorities to provide certain services (e.g. education, special housing, care in the community), but also may grant both general and permissive powers which allow local government to engage in different forms of development activity such as the purchase and sale of land and other assets, the granting of financial assistance to industry, and the provision of promotional and advisory services. It is worth noting that the 1989 Local Government and Housing Act introduced, for the first time, a clear statutory basis for local authorities' economic development activities. Under subsequent legislation (i.e. The Local Government Act 2000) local authorities in England and Wales now have a duty to prepare 'community strategies' which improve the economic, social and environmental well-being of their area and its inhabitants and contribute to the achievement of sustainable development in the UK.

Funds for local economic development come from local, national and supranational sources, though not all authorities qualify for all three. By far the largest contribution has come normally from locally generated income, which includes the council tax, local authority reserves and revenue derived from charging for local authority services. Central funding includes the government's block grant to support local authority services, income from other centrally funded programmes (e.g. environment) and from the various initiatives which are part of the government's regional and urban policy. In the case of the latter, these have traditionally been available to authorities within the assisted areas and/or the Urban Programme areas, though some funds have been channelled through other agencies (e.g. the Scottish and Welsh Development Agencies).

Supranational support from the European Union has come mainly from the ERDF and has been used in the assisted and Urban Programme areas to fund infrastructural projects (e.g. Tyne and Wear Metro, Liverpool Ring Road). In addition, further funding may also be available under certain circumstances from the European Social Fund (e.g. for training), the European Coal and Steel Community (e.g. for support for declining steel and coal areas), the European Investment Bank (e.g. low-interest loans for infrastructural investment) and a number of other sources. More often than not, these funds have been directed at those areas identified by the national government as areas of greatest need – hence the decision by the United Kingdom government in the 1980s to extend the number of authorities covered by its Urban Programme, thus qualifying those added to the list for EU financial aid (see discussion above). As with other funds from non-local sources, EU funding has increasingly required the provision of match funding and the establishment of cross-community partnerships before funds can be accessed for economic development purposes.

Types of intervention

Local authority aid to industry and commerce takes a wide variety of forms, but three areas in particular are worth noting: help with land and buildings; financial assistance; and the provision of information, advice and other support services. These were three of the major priorities identified by local authorities in a survey carried out in the late 1980s by the chartered accountants Deloitte, Haskins & Sells.[1]

As far as land and buildings are concerned, local councils as planning authorities, landowners and site developers clearly have an important role to play in industrial development, and despite some attempts by central government to reduce their influence, their involvement in the local property market has remained significant over time. Among the key activities undertaken by local government in this area have been:

1 The identification of land available for industrial use (e.g. local authority registers of vacant land and land use), including services connected with attracting inward investment.
2 The provision of local-authority-owned land for industrial and commercial development.
3 The supply of on-site infrastructure (e.g. roads, drainage).
4 Land reclamation and site assembly.
5 Environmental improvement (including derelict land).
6 Advice and help to private sector developers.

In addition, local authorities have often been involved in the provision and/or conversion of premises for business use (including starter units, workshops and small factories) and have encouraged the development of a number of science parks, usually working in conjunction with private companies and institutions of higher education.

Financial assistance has also been important in encouraging business activity, with local authorities sometimes providing grants to firms seeking to move to new premises or to expand and/or convert existing buildings, particularly if additional jobs are likely to be created. Funds – mainly in the form of grants or loans – have also been made available to firms wishing to purchase new equipment or to establish certain types of enterprise (e.g. co-operatives) or to meet some of the costs of creating jobs for the unemployed or to cover rental charges. Added to this, some councils established Enterprise Boards, which were essentially trading companies concerned with the provision of long-term development capital for investment in local businesses and property. Using funds from local sources, the boards invested in local companies – usually by taking an equity stake – and managed their portfolio of investments through a specially created company which was independent of the local authority. Through such investments the boards sought to attract additional funds from financial institutions such as pension funds, thus creating a financial leverage which was designed to multiply the impact of the support from the public sector.[2]

To complement these direct forms of intervention, all local authorities have sought to encourage local economic development through their promotional and advisory activities which are aimed at both existing and would-be entrepreneurs. Many councils, for example, produce publicity material, booklets, leaflets, information packs and other types of promotional literature, extolling the advantages of their area for tourism or for industrial and commercial use; this can be one of the factors encouraging investment, including direct inward investment by multinational companies, particularly if it is supported by financial and/or other incentives offered by the local authority (e.g. the Toyota development at Burnaston near Derby) or under regional or urban assistance programmes (e.g. the Nissan plant near Sunderland).

Similarly, as active providers of information to businesses on matters such as vacant premises and sites, local labour market conditions, housing availability and sources of finance, local councils deliberately promote their respective areas and many make use of trade fairs or trade delegations to ensure that the 'message' is not restricted to a domestic audience but also reaches potential overseas investors. For the most part, these activities tend to be co-ordinated through the economic development unit or some other agency operating under the purview of an authority's chief executive officer. Significantly, however, an increasing number of authorities have established specialist marketing departments in an effort to 'sell' their area to organisations and individuals who are likely to contribute to the regeneration of the local economy through investment in capital assets and through job creation.

Partnership with the private sector

While local authorities acting alone can be an important agency for local economic development, their support for local businesses often occurs through some form of partnership with the private sector and, increasingly, with a range of other agencies (e.g. local authorities have been asked by central government to set up 'strategic partnerships' to tackle cross-sector issues within the local community). Such partnerships – including the establishment of Local Enterprise Agencies – are increasingly seen as a vital element in effective economic regeneration in the SME sector at both local and regional level.

Local Enterprise Agencies (known as Enterprise Trusts in Scotland) date back to the early 1970s, but their main period of growth began a decade later, with the number of agencies reaching around 300 by the end of the 1980s. Using funds provided by industry and commerce and by central and local government, LEAs act essentially as business development organisations assisting both new and existing enterprises. Their core activity is to provide information and business counselling (often referred to as 'signposting') which points individuals wishing to start a business to sources of help or assists those already running a business with specific problems. In addition most LEAs provide a number of other services, including business training, workspace, help with the preparation of business plans, provision of *ad hoc* services (e.g. solicitors), advice on marketing, taxation, personnel matters and help in locating premises. In recent years LEAs have worked increasingly in partnership with other support organisations, particularly through the Business Link network.

Unlike Enterprise Boards which were essentially interventionist bodies established by Labour local authorities, Enterprise Agencies are independent organisations which are either private sector initiatives or more regularly a partnership between the public and private sectors, operating through a board which is private sector led. Increasingly, LEAs have tended to work together to provide a more effective service to small businesses, as exemplified by the formation of the Local Investment Networking Company (LINC) in 1987. LINC – which was run jointly by a number of LEAs located throughout the United Kingdom and sponsored by several large companies including BP and Lloyds Bank – was established to help small businesses seeking funding and additional managerial input to find suitable investors. The aim of the organisation was to help both small start-up and growing firms whose financial requirements tended to fall into an 'equity gap' (below £250 000) which was often difficult to bridge through conventional sources. It did this by bringing together private investors willing to invest in new or expanding small businesses and companies looking for such investment and/or additional management skills to aid their development. LINC was replaced in 1999 by the National Business Angels Network – a network of informal investors ('business angels') willing to invest time and money in supporting cash-starved entrepreneurs.

Further encouragement to the creation of public and private sector partnerships comes from organisations such as Business in the Community (BITC), which also operates as an umbrella organisation for local enterprise agencies. BITC's main role is to encourage the involvement of the business community in a wide range of issues affecting local areas and, in particular, in economic development at local, sub-regional and regional levels. The assumption is not only that the business sector has a responsibility to the local community but also that it has the skills, experience, expertise, contacts and other resources which help to increase the chances of such economic development initiatives being successful.

Within the area of economic development and enterprise, BITC has been particularly active in encouraging community-based partnerships between businesses, government, local groups and individuals aimed at regenerating urban and rural communities, and in this it often works alongside national organisations such as the Action Resource Centre and the Civic Trust. In addition, through a range of initiatives on community enterprise, customised training, business support, innovation and partnership sourcing, the organisation has sought to develop closer links between firms and their local communities in the belief that such community involvement is a natural part of successful business practice, as well as a key influence on the quality and quantity of business activity at local level.

The growth of corporate community involvement

The active involvement of business in the development of local communities has been a growing feature of entrepreneurial activity over the last decade or so. From a simple concern with the interests of traditional 'stakeholders' (e.g. employees, shareholders, customers), many businesses have come to recognise that policies which enhance the well-being of the wider community (e.g. job creation, pollution control, welfare provision) can also benefit the organisation and increase its chances of success. This fundamental change in British corporate culture stems from a growing acceptance that corporate community involvement helps to contribute to local economic and social development, thus creating a more stable and prosperous environment within which firms operate. According to David Grayson – managing director of BITC's business strategy group – such involvement is one of the strategic management tools that is essential to any company which wants to thrive in the current environment.[3]

Increased community involvement clearly benefits businesses in a variety of ways (*see* also Chapter 16). Firms participating in community projects and campaigns can enhance their reputation and create goodwill in the local area, as well as increasing public awareness of their products and developing more effective networks with local individuals and organisations. Where these initiatives involve supporting education and training projects, improvements tend to occur in the quality of the workforce and in its attitude towards the organisation and its products. Similarly, through support for local economic development, businesses help to improve the physical environment and stimulate the growth of new businesses, thus helping to attract further financial investment and to boost the local economy upon which many of them depend for their long-term survival.

While most of the initiatives in this area have tended to be associated with US businesses which have traditionally been community-minded, a growing number of UK-owned or based companies have embraced corporate community involvement. BAT Industries, for example, supported the Southampton Enterprise Agency as long ago as 1981 and has subsequently assisted the Brunswick Small Business Centre in Liverpool, Brixton Small Business Centre and the South London Business Initiative. In addition, BAT subsidiaries, such as Eagle Star, have been active in other areas of community support – including the Church Urban Fund which raises money for community projects in disadvantaged urban areas and in a project on local crime prevention in Gloucestershire.

All the signs are that such community involvement will increase substantially in the coming years as a combination of economic, social, political and consumer pressures force firms into becoming more socially aware and responsible and not simply concerned with increasing market share and profit margins. Moreover, with the development of global markets and the growth in overseas investment, the successful firms are likely to be those which accept that community concerns have an international content. Toyota, for example, claims that its activities are designed to meet local needs and to contribute to the economies and communities of the countries in which it operates. Accordingly the organisation has been involved in a range of cultural, educational, social and environmental projects in an effort to promote itself as a good corporate citizen.[4]

Business as influence on government

Both individually and collectively, business organisations in a market economy are an important influence on government decision making; they are an essential part of what has been termed the 'negotiated environment' in which individuals and groups bargain with one another and with governments over the form of regulation of the environment that a government may be seeking to impose.[5]

At an individual level, it tends to be large companies – and in particular multinational corporations – that are in the strongest position to influence government thinking, by dint of their economic and political power, and many of them have direct contacts with government ministers and officials for a variety of reasons (e.g. large defence contractors supply equipment to the Ministry of Defence). In addition, many large businesses use professional lobbyists, or create their own specialist units, whose role is to liaise directly with government agencies and to represent the interest of the organisation at national and/or supranational level (e.g. in Brussels), using the kind of techniques described in Chapter 3. While such activities do not ensure that governments will abandon or amend their proposals or will pursue policies favourable to a particular company's position, they normally guarantee that the views of the organisation are considered alongside those of the other vested interests. Added weight tends to be given to these views when they are supported by all the leading firms in an industry (e.g. the tobacco lobby's fight against a complete ban on tobacco advertising).

The voice of business is also heard in political circles through various voluntary representative organisations such as Chambers of Commerce, employers' associations, trade associations and the Confederation of British Industry (CBI). Chambers of Commerce, for example, largely represent the views and interests of small businesses at local level, but also have a national organisation that lobbies in Whitehall and Brussels. In contrast, trade associations – which are sometimes combined with employers' associations – are usually organised on an industry basis (e.g. the Society of Motor Manufacturers and Traders) and handle consultations with appropriate government agencies, as well as providing information and advice to members about legislation and administration pertinent to the industry concerned.

Mini case   Oiling the wheels?

Lobbying government is a legitimate activity in democratic countries; in some cases pressure groups may help to push a government towards a particular policy decision, in others they may cause it to abandon a course of action it had originally intended to take. Either way, governments usually deny that lobbying has any effect on their decisions.

The UK Labour government's proposals to impose a tax on the use of superstore car parks provides an interesting example of lobbying activity. According to a report in the *Observer* (26 July 1998) the supermarket chain Tesco received prior notice of the government's plans for a car park tax. The information on government thinking appears to have been provided by a firm of lobbyists which had close links with the Labour leadership when in opposition. The firm told undercover reporters from the newspaper that advance knowledge of the proposal had been useful in planning Tesco's campaign against the tax.

The evidence seems to suggest that as late as May 1998 the government still intended to go ahead with the charge for car parking and that it was to be included in a forthcoming Department of Transport White Paper. Following a meeting in late May between Tesco and the minister responsible for transport affairs, the plan was shelved and an alternative arrangement involving corporate support for subsidised community transport was subsequently announced in the delayed White Paper. Both the government and Tesco deny that any deal was done over the car park tax, although the company admits that lobbying did take place and that it had made a £12 million donation to the Millennium Dome project earlier that year. As the *Observer* points out, there is of course no suggestion that the Dome donation and the outcome of the car park tax issue were in any way related.

The Confederation of British Industry (CBI)

The largest employers' association overall, representing thousands of companies employing millions of workers, is the CBI, whose members are drawn from businesses of all types and sizes and from all sectors, but especially manufacturing. Through its director-general and council – and supported by a permanent staff which has representation in Brussels – the organisation promotes the interests of the business community in discussions with governments and with national and international organisations, as well as seeking to shape public opinion. Part of its influence stems from its regular contacts with politicians, the media and leading academics and from the encouragement it gives to businesses to take a proactive approach to government legislation and policy. Additionally, through its authoritative publications – including the Industrial Trends Surveys and reports – the CBI has become an important part of the debate on government economic policy generally, as well as a central influence on legislation affecting the interests of its members.

A good example of its more proactive approach in recent years was its attempt to shape government thinking on environmental policy in the 1990s and to harmonise the work of both government and businesses in this area by promoting its own 'Action Plan'. To this end the CBI established a group of staff dedicated especially to work on environmental issues of interest to business and set up a policy unit and a management unit to provide information, contacts and advice to the various parties involved. The policy unit's role was to monitor developments in legislation, liaise with government departments and enforcement agencies (e.g. the former National Rivers Authority), lobby government and other organisations, provide information and advice, and help to formulate CBI policy on vital environmental issues. The management unit produced promotional literature for businesses, organised conferences and seminars on specific topics, conducted surveys and provided advice on financial and other assistance available to its members to help them develop good environmental management practices within their organisation.

In a report published in late 1998, entitled 'Worth the risk – Improving Environmental Legislation', the CBI launched an attack on what it called an over-prescriptive approach to environmental laws. It called upon government to listen to industry and to concentrate pollution control on the biggest risk areas. According to the chairman of the CBI's environmental protection panel, the existing approach to legislation did not take account of the cost of regulation and its impact on the competitiveness of industry. By using a risk-based approach, the CBI argued that the government could achieve a better system of regulation without compromising business competitiveness.

In the last few years the CBI's views and position on environmental issues – and a host of matters from transport to taxation – have become more widely articulated through its comprehensive website (www.cbi.org.uk) and through its information and research services. The easily accessible policy briefs on topics of interest and concern to the CBI are a useful resource for students of business, as are its 'issue statements', which summarise the CBI's policy positions on key business topics.

While it is impossible to say with any degree of certainty how influential industry is in shaping government policy in this or other areas, there is little doubt that the views of leading industrialists and their representative bodies and associations have received increased attention, particularly under recent Conservative administrations. Regular pronouncements by senior government ministers, including the former Prime Minister and Chancellor of the Exchequer, frequently refer to the fact that a particular policy or piece of legislation has been framed 'with industry in mind' and there are clear signs that the current Labour government under Tony Blair has sympathies in the same direction. It is not without just cause that the CBI claims that it has 'unparalleled access to decision-makers in Whitehall, Westminster and Brussels' and that it is often consulted informally before new proposals are published for full public debate.

Synopsis

State involvement in business activity takes many forms and can be seen as an attempt by government to tackle the problems caused by the operation of the free market. One such problem – regional imbalance – is normally the focus of a government's regional policy that seeks to correct economic disparities through spatially selective forms of assistance. Similarly, the adverse consequences associated with urbanisation and localised economic decay and decline have generally given rise to a range of government initiatives, often in partnership with the private sector, and involving different forms of state intervention at local, national and supranational level.

Local government, too, has been active in this sphere and has used a variety of means to encourage local economic development and to support the local business community, both as agent for central government and as sponsor in its own right. Many of its activities have involved direct collaboration with businesses and with the voluntary organisations which represent them, and the private sector has remained a key influence on government policy at all spatial levels. Given the increasing emphasis on free market activity, the voice of business is destined to remain a key input into the process of economic decision making in Britain and elsewhere for the foreseeable future.

Summary of key points

- Government involvement in the workings of market-based economies is often rationalised on the grounds of 'market failure'.

- Market failure is the notion that if left entirely to their own devices markets do not always deliver economically or socially desirable outcomes.

- Different forms of government intervention occur, some of which are designed specifically to influence the industrial and commercial environment and can be loosely called 'industrial policies'.

- Regional policy seeks to reduce disparities in the economic and social performance of different areas of a country, predominantly through different systems of grant aid for business and for other projects.

- Funds for such projects may be available from local, national, international and/or supranational agencies.

- Urban policy is targeted at problems in urban areas including unemployment, social exclusion, physical decline and environmental degradation.

- Over the years governments have experimented with a range of policies and schemes to regenerate urban locations.

- Local authorities are normally involved in the implementation of the various centrally devised schemes and also support local businesses through their own programmes of local economic development as well as through their various roles in the local community.

- Increasingly many of the current schemes require the establishment of multi-sector partnerships involving government, business and other agencies.

- Business involvement in the development of local communities can bring certain commercial benefits.

- Businesses can also gain influence in the policy sphere through their actions and through their representative organisations.

CASE STUDY
Government and business – friend or foe?

As we have seen, governments intervene in the day-to-day working of the economy in a variety of ways in the hope of improving the environment in which industrial and commercial activity takes place. How far they are successful in achieving this goal is open to question. Businesses, for example, frequently complain of over-interference by governments and of the burdens imposed upon them by government legislation and regulation. Ministers, in contrast, tend to stress how they have helped to create an environment conducive to entrepreneurial activity through the different policy initiatives and through a supportive legal and fiscal regime. Who is right?

While there is no simple answer to this question, it is instructive to examine the different surveys which are regularly undertaken of business attitudes and conditions in different countries. One such survey by the European Commission – and reported by Andrew Osborn in the *Guardian* on 20 November 2001 – claimed that whereas countries such as Finland, Luxembourg, Portugal and the Netherlands tended to be regarded as business-friendly, the United Kingdom was perceived as the most difficult and complicated country to do business with in the whole of Europe. Foreign firms evidently claimed that the UK was harder to trade with than other countries owing to its bureaucratic procedures and its tendency to rigidly enforce business regulations. EU officials singled out Britain's complex tax formalities, employment regulations and product conformity rules as particular problems for foreign companies – criticisms which echo those of the CBI and other representative bodies who have been complaining of the cost of over-regulation to UK firms over a considerable number of years.

The news, however, is not all bad. The Competitive Alternatives study (2002) by KPMG of costs in various cities in the G7 countries, Austria and the Netherlands indicated that Britain is the second cheapest place in which to do business in the nine industrial countries (see *www.competitivealternatives.com*). The survey, which looks at a range of business costs – especially labour costs and taxation – placed the UK second behind Canada world-wide and in first place within Europe. The country's strong showing largely reflected its competitive labour costs, with manufacturing costs estimated to be 12.5 per cent lower than in Germany and 20 per cent lower than many other countries in continental Europe. Since firms frequently use this survey to identify the best places to locate their business, the data on relative costs are likely to provide the UK with a competitive advantage in the battle for foreign inward investment (see mini case above).

Case study questions

1 How would you account for the difference in perspective between firms who often complain of government over-interference in business matters and ministers who claim that they have the interests of business at heart when taking decisions?

2 To what extent do you think that relative costs are the critical factor in determining inward investment decisions?

Review and discussion questions

1 Why should a government committed to the free market intervene in the working of the economy?

2 Explain the connection between 'market failure' and the need for some form of government regional policy.

3 Why are some local authorities more interventionist than others?

4 Why have cross-sector partnerships to tackle social and economic problems become so fashionable in recent years?

Assignments

1 You are employed in the publicity and promotion unit of a local authority. Part of your work involves promoting the area as a suitable location for industrial and commercial activity. Your task is to produce a leaflet – for distribution to potential clients – indicating the advantages of locating within the area and the forms of assistance available.

2 You are the chairperson of the local Chamber of Commerce. The local authority has written to you concerning its plans to pedestrianise the town (or city) centre and asking for the reaction of local businesses. Your task is to produce a short report, for the next meeting of the Chamber, outlining the benefits and disadvantages to the local business community of such a scheme and indicating how the Chamber of Commerce could make its views known in political circles.

Notes and references

1 Deloitte, Haskins & Sells, *Local Authority Assistance to Growing Businesses*, London, 1989.

2 Many Enterprise Boards were set up by Metropolitan County Councils. Their activities have generally continued, despite the abolition of these councils.

3 *Guardian*, 14 April 1993, p. 14.

4 *Toyota Factfile*, April 1992.

5 *See* Thomas, R.E., *The Government of Business*, 3rd edition, Philip Allan, 1987.

Further reading

Griffiths, A. and Wall, S. (eds), *Applied Economics: An Introductory Course*, 9th edition, Financial Times/Prentice Hall, 2001, esp. ch. 11.

Hare, P. and Simpson, L. (eds), *British Economic Policy: A Modern Introduction*, Harvester, 1993.

Hornby, W., Gammie, R. and Wall, S. *Business Economics*, 2nd edition, Financial Times/Prentice Hall, 2001.

McKeown, P., 'Regional Policy' in Atkinson, B., Livesey, F. and Milward, B., *Applied Economics*, Macmillan, 1998.

Williams, R. H., *European Spatial Policy and Planning*, Paul Chapman Publishing, 1996.

Worthington, I., Britton, C. and Rees, A., *Economics for Business: Blending Theory and Practice*, Financial Times/Prentice Hall, 2001, chapter 11.

Web links and further questions are available on the website at:
www.booksites.net/worthington

Part 4

MARKETS

11

The market system

Chris Britton

As part of their normal production activity, businesses are involved in buying (inputs – like labour and raw materials) and selling (outputs – the finished product). Buying and selling take place in markets and although there are many different types of markets the basic analysis remains the same.

Objectives

- To understand the working of the market system.

- To apply the theory to the real world.

- To understand the importance of key concepts like elasticity to business.

- To understand the wider economic effects of changes in market forces.

Key terms

Buyers' market	Equilibrium quantity	Market system
Complements	Excess demand	Normal goods
Cross-price elasticity	Excess supply	Price ceiling
Demand	Factor market	Price controls
Demand curve	Free market	Price elasticity
Effective demand	Income elasticity	Price floor
Effective supply	Inelasticity	Product market
Elasticity	Inferior goods	Sellers' market
Elasticity of demand	'Law of demand'	Substitutes
Elasticity of supply	'Law of supply'	Supply
Equilibrium price	Market	Supply curve

Introduction

As indicated in Chapter 4, the market system is an economy in which all of the basic economic choices are made through the market. The market is a place where buyers and sellers of a product are brought together. The nature and location of the market depends on the product. For example, within your local town there is likely to be a vegetable market where you would go to buy vegetables. Here, buyers and sellers meet face to face in the same location, but this is not always the case. The market for used cars might be the local newspaper classified section; the sale of stocks and shares passes through a broker so that the buyer never meets the seller. There are many different types of market, involving different buyers and sellers. Firms sell the goods and services they produce to households on the product markets, while in the factor markets firms are buying resources such as labour and raw materials. The discussion in this chapter will concentrate on the product markets but much of the analysis could also be applied to the factor markets.

A free market system is one in which the basic economic choices are made through the market, without any intervention by the government. In reality, markets are not completely free; governments intervene in markets for many reasons and in many different ways (*see* Chapter 14), but in this chapter such intervention will be ignored.

The market mechanism

In every market there will be a buyer and a seller, and somehow they have to be brought together so that a sale can take place. The market mechanism is the way in which this takes place in a market economy. In the product market, the buyer is the household and the seller is the firm. In economic language the household demands the good or service and the firm supplies the good or service. Each of these will be considered separately first and then brought together.

Demand

The quantity demanded refers to the quantity of a good or service that households are willing and able to purchase at a particular price. This definition shows that it is effective demand that is important; although many people would like to own a Rolls-Royce they could not afford it and so their demand is not effective on the market. The demand for a good or service depends on a number of factors, the most important of which are:

■ the price of the good;
■ the prices of other goods;
■ disposable income; and
■ tastes.

Table 11.1   The demand for 'Real Brew' draught beer

Price (£ per pint)	Quantity demanded (000s of pints/week)
0.90	83
1.00	70
1.10	58
1.20	48
1.30	40
1.40	35
1.50	32

To begin with, the relationship between quantity demanded and price will be looked at, assuming that the other factors above remain the same. This assumption will be relaxed in the subsequent analysis.

Table 11.1 shows what happens to the quantity demanded of beer as the price per pint goes up. Note that demand is measured over some period of time. The information is then presented in a graphical form in Figure 11.1; the line joining the various combinations of price and quantity demanded is called a demand curve. The demand curve shows that if all of the other factors which influence demand are constant then as price goes up, quantity demanded goes down. This is commonly referred to as 'the law of demand'. What happens when price rises is that some individuals will cut down their consumption of beer and others may switch to other types of beer. There are some goods where this relationship might not hold:[1] for example, in the stock market where a rise in share prices might lead to the expectation of further price rises and therefore an increase in demand on the part of those wishing to make a capital gain. However, these exceptions are rare and it is therefore safe to assume that the law of demand holds.

Figure 11.1   A demand curve for 'Real Brew' draught beer

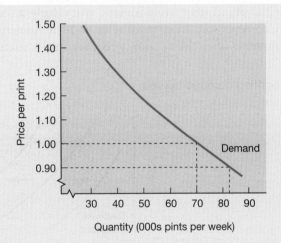

If the price of beer changes, there is a movement along the demand curve. For example, if the price of beer goes up from 90p a pint to £1.00 a pint, the quantity demanded goes down from 83 000 pints per week to 70 000 pints per week. In drawing the demand curve the assumption was made that other factors affecting demand are constant. If this assumption is relaxed, what happens to the demand curve?

Price of other goods

The quantity of beer consumed will be affected by the prices of other goods. These other goods are likely to be substitutes or complements. A substitute for beer may be lager, and if the price of lager goes down, some individuals may switch from beer to lager; thus the demand for beer goes down. What happens to the demand curve is that at all price levels, the demand for beer is now lower. Thus the demand curve shifts to the left, indicating that at £1.00 per pint only 60 000 pints of beer are demanded per week. If the price of a substitute goes up, there will be an increase in the demand for beer. The demand curve moves to the right. These movements are shown in Figure 11.2. The closer the goods are as substitutes and the greater the change in the price of the substitute, the greater will be the shift in the demand curve.

A complementary good is one which tends to be consumed with another good. For beer, it is possible that individuals eat crisps or smoke cigarettes at the same time as drinking beer. The relationship is the opposite of that for substitutes. If the price of a complement goes up, individuals might be less likely to drink beer, and demand will fall. The demand curve moves to the left. If the price of a complement goes down, the demand for beer will rise. Again the closer the goods are as complements, and the greater the price change of that complement, the greater will be the shift in the demand curve.

Disposable income

Changes in disposable income will clearly affect demand. If the economy moves into recession, then retail sales and the housing market might suffer. As incomes increase once the economy recovers, then such sectors will pick up again. Higher

Figure 11.2   Shifting demand curves

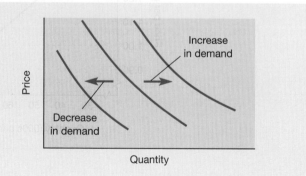

incomes will lead to increased consumption of most goods. If your income is boosted, how will this affect your consumption? You might buy more textbooks, and probably spend more money on leisure activities and clothes. Most students might also drink an extra pint of beer per week. Thus an increase in disposable income will lead to an increase in demand for these goods, indicated by a rightward shift in the demand curve. As incomes fall the demand for these goods will fall, indicated by a leftward shift in the demand curve. These types of goods are called **normal goods**.

There are goods, however, that experience a fall in demand as a result of income increases. These goods are called **inferior goods**. A good example is hard toilet paper; as individuals become richer, they are likely to substitute more expensive soft toilet paper, and thus the demand for hard toilet paper will fall.

Tastes

Taste includes attitudes and preferences of consumers, and will be affected by such things as fashion, and advertising campaigns by producers or by governments. For example, a successful advertising campaign by the government pointing out the effects of smoking would cause tastes to change and demand for cigarettes to fall.

The demand curve, then, is downward sloping, indicating that as the price of the good rises the quantity demanded by households falls, shown by a *movement along the demand curve*. Changes in the other determining factors lead to *movements of the demand curve*.

Supply

The other side of the market is the supply side. In the market for goods and services it is the firm that is the supplier. The quantity supplied of a good is defined as the quantity that firms are willing and able to supply to the market at a particular price. Again notice the wording of the definition is such that it only includes **effective supply** and, as with demand, it is measured over a specific time period.

The quantity supplied to the market depends on a number of factors, the most important of which are:

- the price of the good;
- the prices of other goods;
- the prices of the resources used to produce the good;
- technology;
- expectations; and
- number of suppliers.

In the same way as for demand, all factors other than price will be assumed to be constant and the relationship between quantity supplied and price will be considered first.

Table 11.2 provides some information on price and quantity supplied of beer. The same information is represented graphically in Figure 11.3; the line joining the

Table 11.2	The supply of 'Real Brew' draught beer	

Price (£ per pint)	Quantity supplied (000s of units/week)
0.90	0
1.00	35
1.10	43
1.20	48
1.30	55
1.40	60
1.50	68

Figure 11.3	The supply of 'Real Brew' draught beer

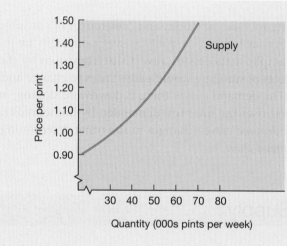

points together is called the supply curve. The upwards-sloping curve illustrates 'the law of supply'. This states that, as the price of a good rises, the quantity that firms are willing to supply also rises. This is because if costs are constant as we have assumed, then higher prices must mean higher profits to the firm.

Note that there is no supply at a price below 90p per pint; this is the minimum price required by the producer to produce the beer. If the price per pint changes there is a movement along the supply curve in the same way as for demand. If any of the other factors listed above change there will be a movement of the supply curve.

Other prices

The supply of one good can be influenced by the price of another. For example, if the brewery in which Real Brew beer is brewed is also producing lager, then an increase in the price of lager (with the price of beer remaining the same) will encourage the firm to produce less beer and more lager, as lager is now more

Figure 11.4   Shifting supply curves

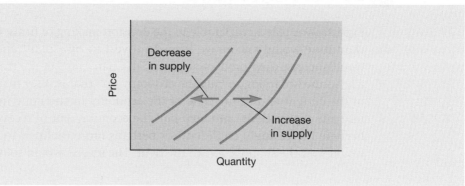

profitable to produce. The supply curve for beer would shift to the left, indicating that at every possible price, less is now supplied than before. If the price of lager fell, the supply of beer would increase. This is shown by a rightward shift of the supply curve. The size of the shift would depend upon the degree to which the goods could be substituted for each other in production, and the size of the price change. These shifts are illustrated in Figure 11.4.

Goods can also be complements in their production process; for example, beef and leather hides. An increase in the price of beef would increase not only the supply of beef but also the supply of hides. There would be a corresponding shift in the supply curve for hides.

The prices of the resources used in the production of the good

If any of the costs of production (wages, rent, rate of interest, and so on) increased, then the profitability of that good at each price would fall and there would be a tendency for supply to be reduced. The supply curve would move to the left. If costs of production fell there would be an increase in supply and a rightward movement of the supply curve. The extent of the shift depends upon the size of the price change, the significance of that factor in production, and the degree to which the factor could be substituted for another factor.

Technology

As illustrated in Chapter 5, technical development in all aspects of production has led to great improvements in output per worker (*see also* Chapter 15). Such improvements generally result in either more being produced with the same resources, or the same being produced with fewer. In most cases it would also lead to a substitution of one factor of production for another. For example, car production becomes less labour intensive as robotic techniques take over. Even such a product as traditional British beer has benefited from significant technical improvements in production. The effect of such advances would result in increased supply at each price level and hence a movement of the supply curve to the right.

Business expectations

Expectations play a crucial role in the decision making of firms. Good expectations of the future would encourage firms to invest in new plant and machinery, which would increase their productive potential. Chancellors of the Exchequer are occasionally accused of trying to 'talk the economy up': that is, they may paint a rosy picture of the current and future state of the economy in the hope that this will enhance business expectations, and help pull the economy out of recession. If business does become increasingly confident, or perhaps more inclined to take risks, then this would shift the supply curve to the right. The reverse would shift it to the left.

The number of suppliers

As the number of suppliers in a market increases the supply will rise; the supply curve shifts to the right. If suppliers leave the market, supply will fall and the supply curve moves to the left.

Price determination

The market is the place where buyers and sellers meet and where demand and supply are brought together. The information on demand and supply is combined in Table 11.3 and presented graphically in Figure 11.5.

The equilibrium price

At a price of £1.20, the quantity demanded is the same as the quantity supplied at 48 000 pints per week. At this price the amount that consumers wish to buy is the same as the amount that producers wish to sell. This price is called the equilibrium price and the quantity being bought and sold is called the equilibrium quantity. The

Table 11.3 The supply and demand for 'Real Brew' draught beer

Price (£ per pint)	Quantity demanded (000s/wk)	Quantity supplied (000s/wk)
0.90	83	0
1.00	70	35
1.10	58	43
1.20	48	48
1.30	40	55
1.40	35	60
1.50	32	68

Figure 11.5   The market for 'Real Brew' draught beer

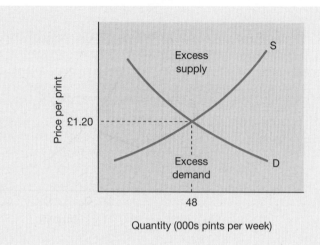

point of equilibrium can be seen on the diagram at the point where the demand and supply curves cross.

At price levels above £1.20 the quantity that producers wish to supply is greater than the quantity consumers wish to buy. There is excess supply and the market is a 'buyers' market'. At prices less than £1.20 consumers wish to buy more than producers wish to supply. There is excess demand and the market is a 'sellers' market'.

In competitive markets, situations of excess demand or supply should not exist for long as forces are put into motion to move the market towards equilibrium. For example, if the price level is £1.30 per pint, there is excess supply and producers will be forced to reduce the price in order to sell their beer. Consumers may be aware that they are in a buyers' market and offer lower prices, which firms might accept. For one or both of these reasons, there will be a tendency for prices to be pushed back towards the equilibrium price. The opposite occurs at prices below equilibrium and price is pushed upwards towards equilibrium.

Shifts in demand and supply

So long as the demand and supply curves in any market remain stationary, the equilibrium price should be maintained. However, there are numerous factors that could shift either or both of these curves. If this were to happen, then the old equilibrium would be destroyed and the market should work to a new equilibrium. How does this happen?

In Figure 11.6 the original equilibrium price for Real Brew draught beer is P_1. Assume that the demand curve moves from D_1 to D_2. This increase in demand could be due to a variety of factors already mentioned. For example, the price of a rival drink may have increased; disposable income could have risen; or sales may have benefited from a successful advertising campaign. In any event, at the old equilibrium price there now exists an excess of demand over supply of Q_1Q_3. It is likely that price will be bid upwards in order to ration the shortage in supply. As price rises, demand is choked off and supply exhausted. Eventually, there is a

Figure 11.6   A shift in the demand curve

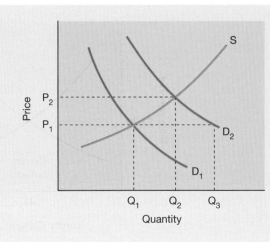

movement to a new equilibrium of P_2. At this new price both supply and demand at Q_2 are higher than they were at the previous equilibrium. If, alternatively, the demand curve had shifted to the left, then the process would have been reversed and the new equilibrium would have been at a level of demand and supply less than Q_1, with a price below P_1. Illustrate this process diagrammatically for yourself.

In Figure 11.7 there is a shift in the supply curve from S_1 to S_2. Refer back in this chapter to envisage specific reasons for such a shift. At the original equilibrium price of P_1 there would now be an excess supply over demand of Q_1Q_3. Price would therefore fall in a free market. As it does, demand will be encouraged and supply diminished. Eventually there will be a new equilibrium at P_2 with a higher quantity demanded and supplied than at the previous equilibrium. If the supply curve had instead shifted to the left, then market forces would have resulted in a lower quantity supplied and demanded than before. Once again, illustrate this diagrammatically for yourself.

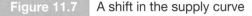

Figure 11.7   A shift in the supply curve

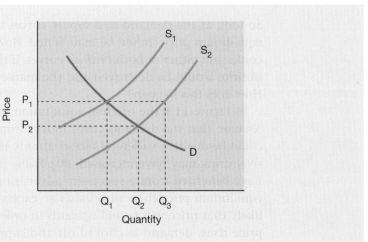

Mini case   House prices

One market where the operation of demand and supply can be easily seen is the housing market. According to the Nationwide Building Society average house prices in the UK jumped by over 10 per cent in the year up to May 2002. A recent report[3] estimated that house prices in London would treble by the year 2020 if present trends continue. The increase in house prices is causing particular problems for first-time buyers, in low-paid occupations particularly in the South. Many public sector organisations like schools are looking at their own house building schemes in order to attract new teachers. Why should this situation have arisen?

Demand for houses is buoyant: in the UK there is a high propensity for owner occupation (69 per cent of households) and first-time buyers are desperate to get onto the first step of the property ladder. The rate of interest is low so the cost of borrowing for house purchase is low. Recent population growth estimates from the government have shown higher than expected population growth especially in the South. All of these factors have kept demand high. On the supply side there is a shortage of housing. The UK comes twelfth out of fifteen EU countries in new housing completions; the Joseph Rowntree Trust estimates that there will be a shortage of 1 million houses by 2020. One of the main reasons for this is that the planning process in the UK is very slow. These factors can be illustrated using demand and supply diagram (Figure 11.8). The supply curve (S) is shown as relatively inelastic, indicating the difficulty of building new homes. The demand curve (D) for 2020 is much higher than the demand curve for 2002, indicating the increase in demand. The result is a massive increase in house prices.

It is important to remember however that forecasting forward 18 years in itself is problematic; there are many other factors which affect the housing market. An increase in the rate of interest (which is expected in late 2002) will have the effect of pushing up the cost of borrowing which could in turn lead to a bursting of the bubble. It could be that there will be a repeat of the slump in house prices seen in the early 1990s in the UK.

Figure 11.8   The housing market

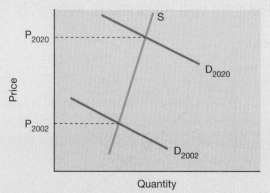

Nationwide Building Society produce commentary and information on house prices in the UK – see e.g. *www.nationwide.co.uk/hpi*

The analysis so far has been relatively straightforward; it has been assumed that either the demand or the supply curve moves alone. However, it is likely that in any given time period both curves could move in any direction and perhaps even more than once.

Given the many factors that may shift both the demand and the supply curves, it is easy to imagine that markets can be in a constant state of flux. Just as the market is moving towards a new equilibrium, some other factor may change, necessitating an adjustment in an opposite direction. Given that such adjustment is not immediate, and that market conditions are constantly changing, it may be the case that equilibrium is never actually attained. It is even possible that the very process of market adjustment can be destabilising.[2] The constant movement of price implied by the analysis may also be detrimental to business. The firm might prefer to keep price constant in the face of minor changes in demand and supply.

Price controls

Governments occasionally take the view that a particular equilibrium price is politically, socially or economically unacceptable. In such circumstances, one course of action is the imposition of price controls. This involves the institutional setting of prices at either above or below the true market equilibrium. For example, if it was felt that the equilibrium price of a good was too high, then the government might try to impose a lower price on the market. This would now be the maximum acceptable price or price ceiling. Price may not rise above this ceiling. Alternatively, the equilibrium price could be seen as too low. In this case, a higher price, or price floor is imposed, below which price should not fall.

Figure 11.9 illustrates the market for a basic foodstuff. Imagine that it is wartime and the disruption has shifted the supply curve to the left. This could be largely due to a movement of resources away from the production of this good and towards munitions. The free market price at P_1 is seen to be unacceptably high relative to the pre-war price, and the decision is made to impose a price ceiling of P_2. It is hoped that such a ceiling will alleviate the problems of consumers who could not afford the free market price. The problem now is that at the price ceiling only Q_3 units will be supplied, whereas

Figure 11.9   Imposition of a price ceiling

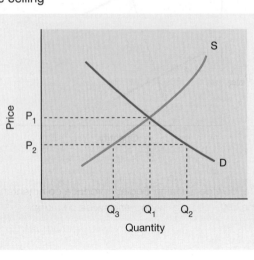

demand is for Q_2. The volume of output Q_3Q_2 therefore represents an excess of demand over supply. Many customers are frustrated in their desire to purchase that good. To help bring order to the situation, a system of rationing might be introduced. This could allocate the limited output between the many customers in a more orderly fashion than 'first come, first served'. For example, one unit could be allocated per person and priority could be given to the old and the sick. This does not solve the problem of excess demand. It is commonly found in such situations that illegal trading starts to emerge at a price above the ceiling. To obtain the good many would be willing to pay a higher price. This is commonly referred to as black market trading.

Figure 11.10 illustrates the market for a specific type of labour. The downward-sloping demand curve indicates that, at lower wages, employers will wish to take on additional workers. The supply curve shows how more people will offer themselves for work as wage rates increase. At the intersection of the curves, the market is in equilibrium. Imagine that this equilibrium wage is seen to be too low, and the authorities seek to impose a minimum wage of W_2. Employers are not permitted to pay any less than this amount. It is hoped that the policy will improve the welfare of workers by raising their living standards to some acceptable level.

At this minimum wage, employment becomes more attractive, and Q_3 persons seek employment. On the other hand, employers only wish to take on Q_2 workers. There is now a situation of excess supply. Only Q_2 find work, the remainder Q_2Q_3 are unsuccessful. The policy has actually reduced the level of employment from Q_1 to Q_2. In such a situation, there will be a temptation to flout the legislation. For example, unscrupulous employers observing the ranks of unemployed would realise that many would willingly work at less than the minimum wage.

The above examples illustrate the problems that arise once price is imposed away from its equilibrium. Further examples of such price controls would include the guaranteed minimum prices to farmers within the Common Agricultural Policy (CAP) of the European Union (*see* case study at end of this chapter), and various post-war attempts to control the cost of rented accommodation at a price affordable to the low paid. The former has been associated with overproduction and the need to control the mountains of excess supply, while the latter tended to result in landlords taking their properties off the rental market in order to seek more profitable returns. The success of such policies requires careful control and monitoring. In many circumstances, it might be better to consider alternative ways of achieving the policy goals.

Figure 11.10 Imposition of a price floor

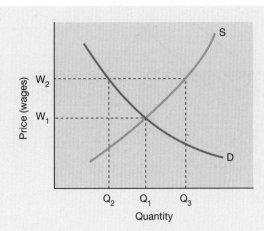

Mini case   Pollution

An issue which has been hotly debated over recent years is the emission of greenhouse gases and global warming.[4] The main greenhouse gas contributing to global warming is carbon dioxide. Carbon dioxide mainly comes from the burning of fossil fuels like coal and oil and the burning of forests. Economists have put forward two main policies to deal with this problem – taxes and targets – both of which can be analysed using simple demand and supply diagrams.

One way of reducing the amount of carbon dioxide released into the atmosphere is to place a tax on the products that cause the release of carbon dioxide. This is the nature of the 'carbon tax' where tax is levied on the three fossil fuels – coal, oil and gas – in proportion to their carbon content. This results in an increase in the costs of using these fuels and therefore (according to simple demand and supply analysis) a reduction in the quantity being consumed and a resultant reduction in the amount of carbon dioxide being released into the atmosphere. The taxation on the input is an additional cost of production, therefore the supply curve moves upwards (S_1) and to the left and causes equilibrium quantity to fall (see Figure 11.11).

The other method of dealing with pollution is the use of targets or quantitative restrictions. This could range from a ban on polluting activities to the introduction of minimum or maximum standards or the use of pollution permits. The use of pollution permits has gained popularity recently and they were a cornerstone of the Kyoto Protocol's (1997) attempts to reduce greenhouse gases world-wide. Tradable carbon credits were issued to countries which were then rewarded for introducing energy-saving measures by being able to sell their 'spare' carbon credits to other countries. There is some evidence that a similar scheme in the USA to reduce emissions of sulphur dioxide has been successful.

Test your understanding of demand and supply by drawing a diagram to show how pollution permits work.

Figure 11.11   The effect of taxation on the market

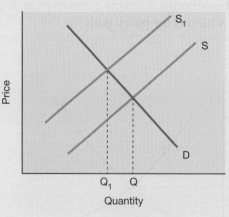

Elasticity of demand

It has been shown that as long as other factors affecting demand remain constant, a decrease in price would be expected to increase the quantity demanded by consumers. This knowledge is obviously of importance to business, in that it implies that sales will expand as the good becomes more price competitive. It does not, however, say anything about the degree to which sales might increase. As prices change, will demand change by a large or a small amount? At the end of the day, will the extra sales bring in more or less total revenue? In short, a measure is needed of the responsiveness of demand to price changes. In the same way the responsiveness of quantity demanded to other factors like income or other prices can also be measured. It is also important to be aware of the responsiveness of supply to changes in prices. All of these are measured by the concept of elasticity.

Price elasticity of demand

Figure 11.12 illustrates two different-shaped demand curves and shows the effect of a price increase from 40p to 60p in each case. On the left-hand diagram, the increase in price causes demand to fall from 25 to 20 units. Total revenue received by the producer (i.e. price multiplied by the number of units sold) changes from £10.00 (40p × 25 units) to £12.00 (60p × 20 units). As illustrated, the area A represents the gain in revenue as a result of the price change, while B shows the loss of revenue. In this case there is a clear net gain. The reason for this is that the significance of the price rise is greater than the fall in demand. Compare this with the right-hand diagram. The same price rise now causes total revenue to fall from £20.00 (40p × 50 units) to £6.00 (60p × 10 units). The loss of revenue, area B^1, is clearly greater than the gain in revenue, area A^1. There is a net loss of revenue. This is a situation where the decrease in demand is of greater significance than the increase in price.

Figure 11.12 Responsiveness of demand to a price change

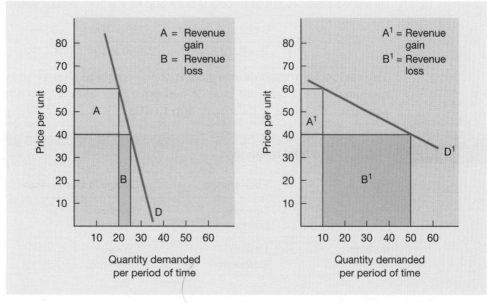

The traditional way of measuring the responsiveness of demand to a change in price is via the concept of price elasticity, the formula being:

$$\text{Price elasticity of demand (Ep)} = \frac{\text{Percentage change in quantity demanded}}{\text{Percentage change in price}}$$

$$\text{Ep} = \frac{\% \text{ change QD}}{\% \text{ change P}}$$

The significance of this formula lies in whether the value of price elasticity is greater or less than 1. If it is greater, then the percentage change in quantity demanded is greater than the percentage change in price. Demand is referred to as being relatively elastic, or responsive to price changes. If, on the other hand, the percentage change in quantity demanded is less than the percentage change in price, then price elasticity will be less than 1. Demand is now referred to as being relatively inelastic, and demand is not very responsive to price changes.

The higher or lower the value of price elasticity, the greater or lesser the responsiveness of demand to the price change. Table 11.4 demonstrates the connection between price elasticity and total revenue. It will be observed that if price elasticity is greater than 1, then there is a negative relationship between price changes and total revenue. For example, an increase in price results in a decrease in total revenue. Whereas, if elasticity is less than 1, then there is a positive relationship.

Calculating elasticity

From the information portrayed in Figure 11.12 (page 321), in the left-hand diagram price rose from 40p to 60p and demand fell from 25 to 20 units; thus:

$$\text{Ep} = \frac{\% \text{ change QD}}{\% \text{ change P}} = \frac{5/25 \times 100}{20/40 \times 100} = \frac{20\%}{50\%} = 0.4$$

This shows that demand is inelastic. One problem with this measurement is that if you measured elasticity when price fell from 60p to 40p the answer would be different:

$$\text{Ep} = \frac{\% \text{ change in QD}}{\% \text{ change in P}} = \frac{5/20 \times 100}{20/60 \times 100} = \frac{25\%}{33.3\%} = 0.75$$

The reason for this variation is that the percentage change in each case is being measured from a different base. When price rises from 20p to 40p, this is a 50 per cent rise. Yet when it falls from 60p to 40p this is only a 33.3 per cent fall. The

Table 11.4	Elasticity and total revenue	
Elasticity	Price change	Change in total revenue
Elastic	Upward Downward	Downward Upward
Inelastic	Upward Downward	Upward Downward

value of elasticity therefore varies. To avoid this ambiguity, elasticity is measured as the percentage change from the average value of price and quantity before and after the change, that is:

$$\% \text{ change} = \frac{\text{Change in value} \times 100}{\text{Average value}}$$

The value of elasticity for the price increase and decrease must now be identical:

$$\text{Ep} = \frac{\% \text{ change QD}}{\% \text{ change P}} = \frac{5/22.5 \times 100}{20/50 \times 100} = \frac{22.2\%}{40\%} = 0.55$$

The determinants of elasticity

There are a number of factors which determine how responsive quantity demanded is to price changes. First, the nature of the good and how it is viewed by consumers. A good which is a necessity will have a low value of elasticity, as an increase in price will not have a very big impact on the quantity consumed. Goods like cigarettes will have inelastic demand because they are habit forming. The tastes of consumers will be important: whether they view a television, for example, as a necessity or a luxury will determine the value of elasticity. Another factor is whether substitutes are available for the good or not. If there is no substitute for a particular good and the household wishes to continue to consume it, an increase in price will have little effect on the level of demand. Other factors include the importance of the good in the household's total expenditure. The smaller the proportion of the household's budget which is spent on a particular good, the smaller will be the effect on demand of any change in price.

Income elasticity of demand

Income elasticity of demand is a measure of the responsiveness of quantity demanded to changes in income. It can be negative in the case of inferior goods, where an increase in income leads to a fall in the demand for a good, or positive in the case of a normal good, where an increase in income leads to an increase in demand. There is also a difference between luxuries and necessities. Luxuries will have positive income elasticities with values over 1. This means that an increase in income will cause an increase in demand for that good and that a 1 per cent increase in income will cause a more than 1 per cent increase in demand. A necessity on the other hand will also have a positive income elasticity but its value will lie somewhere between 0 and 1, showing that an increase in income of 1 per cent causes an increase in demand by less than 1 per cent.

Income elasticity is calculated in a similar way to price elasticity except that it is income which is changing rather than the price of the good:

$$\text{Income elasticity} = \frac{\% \text{ change in quantity demanded}}{\% \text{ change in income}}$$

The effect of changes in income on the overall level of expenditure depends upon the type of the good being considered, as Table 11.5 shows.

| Table 11.5 | Income elasticity and total expenditure |

Type of good	Income elasticity	Change in total expenditure brought about by an increase in income of 1%
Inferior	Negative	Downward
Normal	Positive	Upward
Luxury	Positive and above 1	Upward by more than 1%
Necessity	Positive between 0 and 1	Upward by less than 1%

Cross-price elasticity of demand

Cross-price elasticity of demand is a measure of how the demand for one good is affected by changes in the prices of other goods. It is calculated with the formula:

$$\text{Cross-price elasticity} = \frac{\% \text{ change in quantity demanded of good X}}{\% \text{ change in the price of good Y}}$$

Like income elasticity it can be positive or negative depending this time upon the nature of the relationship between the goods. If the goods are substitutes for one another, as the price of Y goes up, the quantity demanded of X will also rise, as consumers substitute the relatively cheaper good (e.g. margarine for butter). Therefore cross-price elasticity will be positive. If the goods are complements, as the price of Y rises the demand for X will fall and cross-price elasticity will be a negative value. The size will depend upon how closely the goods are related, either as substitutes or complements.

Elasticity of supply

The concept of elasticity can be applied to supply as well as demand, and is a measurement of how responsive quantity supplied is to changes in the price of a good. Figure 11.13 illustrates two differently shaped supply curves and the effect of the same price change in each case.

Elasticity of supply is measured with the following formula:

$$\text{Elasticity of supply} = \frac{\% \text{ change in quantity supplied}}{\% \text{ change in price}}$$

The higher the numerical value, the more responsive is supply to changes in price.

The main determinants of the elasticity of supply for a good are the nature of the production process and the time-scale in question. It may well be easier to increase the supply of manufactured goods than agricultural goods, given the nature of the production processes involved. Even agricultural goods can be increased in supply, given time to replant stock, so supply is more responsive to price changes in the longer time period.

| Figure 11.13 | Responsiveness of supply to a price change |

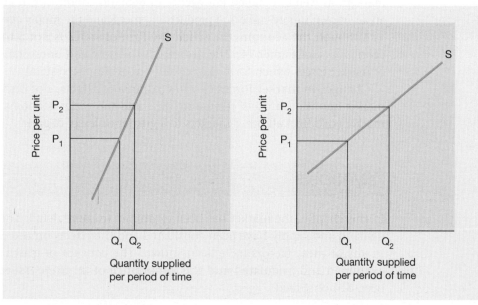

The importance of the market to business

All firms operate in markets, whether they are localised, national or international. Although firms might be able to influence the market conditions that face them, they need a knowledge of their own markets and how markets fit together in the market economy. Firms often have a range of products and they need to be aware of the differing conditions in each of their markets. They need a knowledge of the shape and position of the demand curve they face, including knowledge of the following aspects:

- The nature of the good they produce.
- The way in which it is viewed by consumers.
- The factors which affect the demand for their good.
- Any changes likely in the future which will affect the market.
- Any likely government intervention in the market.

Only through this information can the firm hope to retain markets, expand existing markets and move into new ones.

An understanding is also needed of the concept of elasticity of demand. Knowing how the demand for its product responds to changes in its price will help the firm in its pricing policy. Measures of income elasticity help the firm in forecasting the effects of changes in income on the demand for its products. Economic growth will affect markets with high income elasticities much more than markets with low income elasticities. This knowledge will also help the firm in developing its marketing strategy. For example, goods with low income elasticities could be marketed as 'economical', thus hopefully increasing the market share.

If the firm wishes to be successful in existing markets and to expand into new markets, as well as detailed knowledge of demand conditions, it also needs to know about its own supply curve and production process and the supply curves of other firms.

Although the economy in which the firm operates is not a totally free market economy (*see* Chapter 14), the firm needs to know and understand the importance of market forces which form the basis of our economic system.

Changes in market forces can have dramatic effects, not only on the affected market but also on other related markets and the wider economy. Changes in one market will affect all other markets to a greater or lesser degree.

Synopsis

In this chapter, the market has been examined in some detail. The determinants of demand and supply have been considered and the effects on the market of changes in any of these factors have been shown. The concept of elasticity has also been examined and calculated and the importance of all these issues to business has been demonstrated.

Summary of key points

- In a free market both the quantity being traded and the price of a product are determined by the forces of demand and supply.

- The demand for a good or service depends upon a number of factors, including price, the price of other goods, the income of consumers, tastes and so on.

- The supply of a good or service also depends upon a range of influences, including price, the costs of production, technology and the number of suppliers.

- Changes in demand and supply cause changes in the price of the product and the quantity being traded.

- Where demand and supply are equal, the market is said to be in equilibrium.

- Where this occurs, equilibrium price and quantity result.

- Intervention in the market mechanism can take the form of minimum or maximum prices, taxation or subsidy.

- Elasticity is a measure of the responsiveness of demand or supply to various factors, including price, income and the price of other goods.

- It is important for businesses to be aware of the demand and supply characteristics of the good or service they are producing.

CASE
STUDY The Common Agricultural Policy of the
European Union

The Common Agricultural Policy (CAP) of the European Union (EU) demonstrates well the working of price controls in the market place. In order to support the agricultural sector in the EU and to ensure an adequate supply of food, a variety of policies have been used. The guaranteed minimum price was one such control.

One characteristic of agricultural goods is that price fluctuates a great deal from year to year depending upon weather conditions and the size of harvests. This means that the incomes of farmers cannot be predicted from one year to the next. By guaranteeing a minimum price for agricultural goods, this problem can be avoided, and a supply of agricultural goods can be assured.

In Figure 11.14, if a minimum guaranteed price is set at or below the market price, there is no impact on the market and the good will be sold at the market price. If, however, the guaranteed minimum price is set above equilibrium as was the case in the CAP, a situation of excess supply will exist at that price. Over-production occurs and this excess supply was the wine lakes and the food mountains of the 1980s. At times during the 1980s there was large-scale destruction of the excess supplies of agricultural goods – a politically unacceptable solution.

The CAP has long been a subject for heated debate within the EU. It accounts for over 50 per cent of the EU budget and supports a sector which accounts for only 2 per cent of the EU electorate. It is also the source of arguments about equity as some countries are net contributors to the CAP budget while others are net recipients (*see* Figure 11.15).

There has been an acceptance within the EU that the policies used by the CAP have not worked in the way they were designed – they have created inefficiencies by encouraging over-production rather than cost cutting – and in the process have produced a dependency culture among farmers. The OECD estimates that the EU paid out on average $17 000 to every farmer in the EU compared with an average of $11 000 in countries belonging to the OECD. It also estimates that families in the EU pay an extra $1200 a year on food as a direct result of EU policies.

Figure 11.14   The operation of guaranteed minimum prices

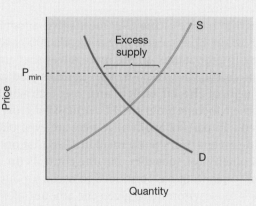

| Figure 11.15 | Recipients of CAP aid, 2000, Euros billion |

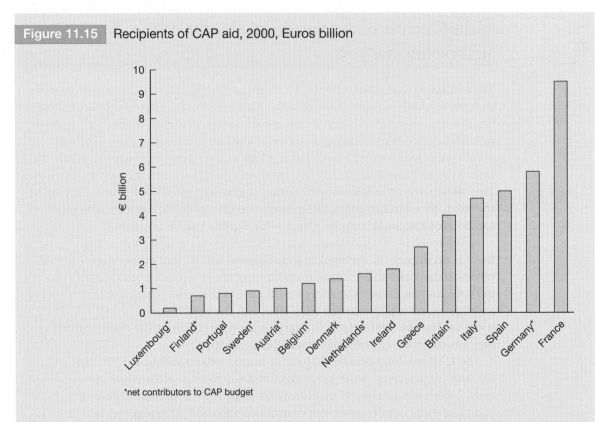

*net contributors to CAP budget

Source: Eurostat, 2002. © European Comunities. Eurostat. Reproduced by permission of the Publishers, the Office for Official Publications of the European Communities.

Reforms to the CAP were introduced in 1999 under the heading of Agenda 2000. They are designed to cap CAP until 2006 and to change the direction of agricultural policy. First, guaranteed prices were to be brought down towards world levels, which at the time would have entailed a 20 per cent cut in the price of cereals, 30 per cent cut in the price of beef and 15 per cent cut in the price of milk. Second, there was to be a movement to a system of direct payments to farmers which are unrelated to production – this should have the effect of reducing the incentive to over-produce. More recently, there has been a movement to shift subsidies to environmental conservation, and the use of subsidies to encourage greener agriculture.

Despite these policies, the nature of the CAP means that anomalies still occur. The production of olives in the EU is subject to the Agenda 2000 reforms. They are still subsidised according to production, so the more olives that are produced the higher is the payment from the CAP. In 2001, the subsidies paid to olive farmers accounted for 2.5 per cent of the EU budget and it is estimated that Spanish farmers receive half of their income from the EU. A massive programme of olive tree planting has resulted – in parts of Spain olive trees are even planted on traffic islands. In an attempt to prevent this, the EU ruled in 1998 that only trees planted before that year would qualify for subsidies, but the controls on this have been almost non-existent and so planting has continued to occur. Production on such a level has implications for the environment, given the amount of water needed to sustain it, and it encourages desertification and soil erosion.

The main reason that olives have not been subject to the same controls as other agricultural goods is that the olive farmers have a powerful lobbying presence within the EU. The main beneficiaries have not been the small-scale olive growers but the large-scale intensive agricultural producers, many of which are owned by banks and insurance companies.

The problems of the CAP are likely to worsen with the enlargement of the EU. Most of the potential entrants have much larger agricultural sectors; in Poland, for example, 20 per cent of the population is engaged in agricultural production. The EU estimates that the accession of these countries would cost a net total of €25 billion in subsidies between 2004 and 2006. It would also turn many existing members, like Ireland and Spain, into net contributors to the budget. To circumvent this, the EU announced in 2002 that new members would only be entitled to 25 per cent of the level of subsidy received by existing EU farmers, although that will rise to 100 per cent within ten years. This will hopefully keep the cost of accession down while at the same time producing a policy which is not too unfair to the newcomers.

The guaranteed minimum price of the CAP is an example of the use of minimum price controls which worked against the market rather than with the market. Although the motivation for this policy was sound, the effect was not. Many of the policies introduced since by the EU have been attempts to alleviate the problems caused by guaranteed minimum prices.

Case study questions

1 Other policies used by the CAP have been the use of quotas on production and 'set aside', where the farmer is paid not to cultivate land. Illustrate these policies by using demand and supply diagrams.

2 There have been calls by many for the complete removal of guaranteed minimum prices and the payment of subsidies. What is the likely effect of such a strategy?

Data is available from *www.europa.eu.int/comm*/agriculture. For a summary of the discussion on the future of CAP see *www.eu-cap.net*

Review and discussion questions

1 Show the effects on the market for houses of the following:
   (a) a fall in income levels;
   (b) a rise in the rate of interest;
   (c) the lack of a 'feel good factor' in the economy.

2 Considering the market for CDs, show the effects of the following changes using demand and supply diagrams:
   (a) an increase in the number of people owning CD players;
   (b) a fall in the cost of producing CDs; and
   (c) a movement away from releasing music on LP and towards releasing music on CD.

3 Have the changes you predicted in your answers to questions 1 and 2 actually happened in the real world? If not, why not?

Assignments

1 You are a journalist on a local newspaper and have been asked to write an article on the current state of the housing market in your locality. You should identify factors which influence house prices in general and more specifically in your region. The following information from the Nationwide house price index may help (www.nationwide.co.uk/hpi).

Region	Average house prices, quarter 1, 2002	% change since quarter 1, 2001
East Anglia	£102 395	+18.0
East Midlands	£82 226	+16.4
Greater London	£171 169	+16.0
North	£59 504	+8.7
North West	£76 465	+12.6
South East	£119 896	+15.2
South West	£110 306	+17.6
Scotland	£69 591	+8.5
Wales	£70 109	+10.5
West Midlands	£90 632	+14.6
Yorkshire and Humberside	£70 166	+11.9
UK	£95 356	+13.6

2 You work in the marketing department of a company that produces light bulbs. The company is considering increasing the price of its light bulbs by 20 per cent. At present a 100 watt light bulb costs 80p. The only information that is available is a study carried out in the previous year on the sensitivity of sales to price, the results of which are shown below:

Price	Sales (million)
80p	5800
100p	4000

Write a report for your manager on the likely effects of the proposed price increase, explaining the concept of elasticity of demand and the factors which are likely to affect it for this product.

Notes and references

1   In such cases the demand curve would be upward sloping, indicating that as price rises demand rises. Other examples include 'snob goods', which are consumed *because* their price is high and everyone knows that. Also antiques and valuable works of art may have upward-sloping demand curves.

2   In the markets described in this chapter there is an automatic tendency for the market to move back towards equilibrium once it is disturbed. However, it is possible for the demand and supply curves to be so shaped that once the market is disturbed it tends to move away from equilibrium rather than towards it. This is called the cobweb model. The interested reader should look at R. Lipsey, *An Introduction to Positive Economics*, Weidenfeld & Nicolson, 1989.

3   Centre for Economics and Business Research, April 2002. see *www.cebr.co.uk*

4   See the case study at the end of chapter 11 of the third edition of this book for a more detailed discussion.

Further reading

Begg, D., Fischer, S. and Dornbusch, R., *Economics*, 6th edition, McGraw-Hill, 2000.

Griffiths, A. and Wall, S., *Applied Economics: An Introductory Course*, 9th edition, Financial Times Prentice Hall, 2001.

Lipsey, R. and Chrystal, A., *An Introduction to Positive Economics*, 8th edition, Oxford University Press, 1995.

Worthington, I., Britton, C., and Rees, A., *Economics for Business: Blending Theory and Practice*, Financial Times/Prentice Hall, 2001.

 Web links and further questions are available on the website at:
www.booksites.net/worthington

12

Market structure

Chris Britton

All businesses operate in a market which will be peculiar to that industry. Each market will have its own particular characteristics which depend upon many factors, and although it is not possible to have a model which describes every market, there are some economic models which provide some guidance to the kind of characteristics and behaviour that will be found in individual markets.

Objectives

- To understand the market structures of perfect competition, monopoly, oligopoly and monopolistic competition and their implications for the behaviour of firms.

- To appreciate the applicability of these predictions to the real world.

- To introduce Porter's five-forces model to analyse the structure of industries.

- To understand the measurement of competition by concentration ratios.

- To survey differences in industrial concentration between industries, countries and over time.

- To recognise what determines market structure and what determines the behaviour of firms.

Key terms

Abnormal profits	Interdependence	Perfect mobility
Average costs of production	Market structure	Price competition
Barriers to entry	Minimum efficient scale of production (MES)	Price discrimination
Barriers to exit		Price leadership
Cartel	Monopolistic competition	Price maker
Collusion	Monopoly	Price taker
Concentration ratio	Monopsony	Price war
Contestable market	Natural monopoly	Sticky prices
Differentiation	Non-price competition	Structure–conduct– performance model (S–C–P)
Economies of scale	Normal profits	
Five-forces model	Oligopoly	
Homogeneous products	Perfect competition	Transaction cost economics
	Perfect knowledge	

Introduction

In economics the behaviour and the performance of firms in an industry are thought to depend upon some basic structural characteristics. This view is exemplified by the structure–conduct–performance model, where structure determines conduct, which in turn determines performance. The basic elements included under these headings are given in Table 12.1.

The structure–conduct–performance model provides a good framework for classifying and analysing an industry. A simple example of the process can be seen in the soap powder industry. Here the market is dominated by two large producers, Unilever and Procter & Gamble. This apparent lack of competition gives rise to certain behavioural characteristics like the massive amount of advertising, the existence of many brand names and fairly uniform prices. This process will be considered in more detail later in the chapter, but the example serves to indicate the relationship between the structure of the market and the behaviour and ultimately the performance of firms in an industry.

web
link

For more information on these companies see *www.unilever.com* and *www.proctorandgamble.com*

'Market structure' refers to the amount of competition that exists in a market between producers. The degree of competition can be thought of as lying along a continuum with very competitive markets at one end and markets in which no competition exists at all at the other end. This chapter looks at the two extremes (perfect competition and monopoly), and the market structures which exist between. The theory predicts the effects of market structure on behaviour and performance in those markets. However, as with the working of the market

Table 12.1	Structure–conduct–performance model

Structural factors

- Amount of actual competition: (a) seller concentration; and (b) buyer concentration.
- Existence of potential competition.
- Cost conditions.
- Demand conditions.
- Existence of barriers to entry.

Conduct factors

- Pricing policy.
- Amount of advertising.
- Merger behaviour.
- Product differentiation.

Performance factors

- Profitability.
- Technological innovation.

mechanism, the real world is often different from the theory and therefore this chapter will look at real markets and the relevance of the theory to the real world. The structure–conduct–performance model is open to criticism[1] since it says little about what determines structure in the first place. It also tends to view the firm as passive in the face of market structure, accepting the implications for conduct and performance, rather than actively trying to change and mould market structure. Michael Porter's 'five-forces model'[2] will be used to broaden out the analysis.

Market structure is important not only because of the implications it has for conduct and performance but also because it has an impact upon the strategic possibilities which face the organisation, its ability to act strategically and the likely effects of such strategic behaviour (*see* Chapter 17).

In addition, this chapter will examine how the level of competition is measured in a market, how the level of competition varies between industries and countries, and how and why this has changed over time.

Market structures – in theory and practice

As mentioned above, market structures can be thought of as lying along a continuum with perfect competition at one end and monopoly at the other (*see* Figure 12.1). Both of these market structures are unrealistic representations of the real world, but are useful as benchmarks in assessing the degree of competition in a market. Between these two extremes lie other market structures, which are more realistic. Two will be described, oligopoly and monopolistic competition.

Perfect competition

This is the most competitive market structure. A number of conditions need to be fulfilled before perfect competition is said to exist. These conditions are as follows:

1 There are so many buyers and sellers in the market that no *one* of them can influence price through its activities.
2 The good being sold in the market is homogeneous (i.e. all units of the good are identical).
3 Perfect knowledge exists in the market. This means that producers have perfect knowledge of prices and costs of other producers and that consumers know the prices charged by all firms.

Figure 12.1 Market structures

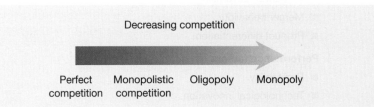

Decreasing competition

Perfect competition   Monopolistic competition   Oligopoly   Monopoly

4 There exists perfect mobility of both the factors of production and consumers. This means that people, machines and land can be used for any purpose, and that consumers are free to purchase the good from any of the producers.

5 There are no barriers to entry or exit in the industry. There is nothing to prevent a new firm setting up production in the industry.

Naturally, this is a highly theoretical model and these conditions are unlikely to be all met in reality, but if they did, and the theory is followed through, the conclusion is that there will only be one price in the market for the good being sold. For example, if one firm is charging a higher price for the good than other firms, everyone in the market will know (because of perfect knowledge), and because the good is homogeneous and because of perfect mobility on the part of consumers, consumers will simply purchase the good from another firm. The firm that was charging a higher price will be forced to reduce the price of the good in order to sell it, or face mounting stocks of the good. There is therefore only one price for the good and this will be determined by *market* demand and supply – that is, total demand and total supply, no one consumer or producer having enough market power to influence the price. Accordingly, the firm is said to be a 'price taker'.

Price determination in perfect competition

Firms need to cover costs of production and to earn a certain level of profits in order to stay in business. This minimum level of profits is called 'normal profit', and profits over and above this level are called 'abnormal profits'. If the firm is trying to maximise its profits it will decide what level of output to produce by setting the cost of producing the last unit of the good equal to the revenue gained from selling the last unit: in economic terminology, where marginal cost equals marginal revenue. Included in cost would be elements of wages, rent, rates, interest, raw materials *and* normal profits. If these costs are not being covered the firm will be making a loss.

As there is only one price in perfect competition, the revenue derived from selling the last unit must be equal to its price. Therefore, the price of the good depends on the level of marginal cost.

In the short run, individual firms can earn abnormal profits, but these are not sustainable in the longer term. If one firm is earning abnormal profits, given the assumption of perfect knowledge, everyone will know and, since freedom of entry exists, other firms will enter the market in order to earn abnormal profits. This means that there is an increase in market supply and price will fall back to a level where abnormal profits have been competed away. Similarly when losses are being made, freedom of exit means that supply will be reduced and price will rise again until normal profits have been regained.

The implications of perfect competition for market behaviour and performance are summarised in Table 12.2. Perfect competition involves very restrictive assumptions, which will rarely be fulfilled in the real world. The usefulness of the model lies in its role as an *ideal market* in which competition is at a maximum, rather than in its applicability to the real world.

Table 12.2	Implications of perfect competition for conduct and performance of firms in an industry
Extent of market power	The firm has no market power at all.
Price	There will only be one price for the good. The firm will be a 'price taker'.
Advertising	There will be no advertising, as all units of the good are the same and everyone knows this.
Profitability	There can be no abnormal profits, except possibly in the very short run if a producer reduces price and captures a larger share of the market.

An example of perfect competition?

The nearest example to perfect competition is probably the fruit and vegetable market in the centre of a large town. The goods will be fairly homogeneous, with perhaps slight variation in the quality. Knowledge will be almost perfect with respect to prices charged, as consumers could quickly walk around the market and ascertain the price of tomatoes, for example. Mobility of consumers is also high because the sellers are located in the same place. Thus the conditions for perfect competition nearly hold. The prediction is that there will be only one price for a particular good. Again this prediction is nearly fulfilled; the price of tomatoes tends to be rather similar across such a market, and when one trader reduces the price towards the end of the day, others tend to follow suit. Another market which is said to be close to perfect competition is the stock exchange, although with the increasing use of computers this is less likely to be true in the future.

Monopoly

Monopoly lies at the opposite end of the spectrum of competition. In its purest form a monopolistic market is one in which there is no competition at all; there is a single producer supplying the whole market. The monopolist has considerable market power and can determine price or quantity sold, but not both because he or she cannot control demand. The power of the monopolist depends on the availability of substitutes, and on the existence and height of barriers to entry. If there are no close substitutes for the good being produced, or if there are high barriers to entry, the power of the monopolist will be high and abnormal profits can be earned in the long run.

A monopolist could also be a group of producers acting together to control supply to the market: for example, a cartel such as OPEC (Organisation of Petroleum Exporting Countries).

web link For information on OPEC see *www.opec.org*

In monopolistic markets the producer might be able to charge different prices for the same good: for example, on an aeroplane it is quite likely that there will be passengers sitting in the same class of seat having paid very different prices, depending upon where and when the tickets were bought. Essentially they are paying different prices for the same service, and the producer is said to be exercising price discrimination. Why is this possible? There are certain conditions that must hold for this type of price discrimination to occur. First, the market must be monopolistic and the producer must be able to control supply. Second, there must be groups of consumers with different demand conditions. For example, the demand for train travel by the commuter who works in London will be more inelastic than the demand of a student going to London for the day, who could use alternative forms of transport or even not go. This means that the willingness to pay among consumers will vary. The final condition necessary is that it must be possible to separate these groups in some way. For example, telephone companies are able to separate markets by time so that it is cheaper to phone after a certain time; British Rail used to separate groups by age for certain of its railcards.

The monopolist will maximise its profits by charging different prices in different markets. Price discrimination is often thought of as a bad thing as the monopolist is exploiting the consumer by charging different prices for the same good. But there are some advantages, in that it makes for better use of resources if cheap airline tickets are offered to fill an aeroplane which would otherwise have flown half-full. It can also lead to a more equitable solution in that higher-income users pay a higher price than lower-income users. The main problems with the notion of price discrimination is not that it is always a bad thing, but that it is the monopolist who has the power to decide who is charged what price.

Again the effects of monopoly on the behaviour and performance of the firm can be predicted (*see* Table 12.3). Like perfect competition, this is a highly theoretical model and is mainly used as a comparison with perfect competition to show the effects of the lack of competition.

Table 12.3   Implications of monopoly for the conduct and performance of firms in an industry

Extent of market power	The firm has absolute market power.
Price	There will only be one price for the good, except in the case of price discrimination. The firm is a 'price maker'.
Advertising	There will be no need for advertising, as there is only one firm producing the good.
Profitability	Abnormal profits can exist in the long run as there is no competition which might erode them away.

A comparison of perfect competition and monopoly

- It would be expected that price would be higher under monopoly than under perfect competition because of the absence of competition in the monopolistic market. It is argued, for example, that the large telephone companies (including BT) are overcharging the consumer. The benefits of the considerable technological advances that have been made in this area have not been passed on fully to the consumer. This can only be sustained by virtue of the monopolistic power of the companies. *But*, to counter this it could be argued that a monopolist is in a better position to reap the benefits of economies of scale, therefore it is possible that price might be lower.
- There might be less choice under monopoly since firms do not have to continually update their products in order to stay in business. *But*, it is also possible to think of examples where monopolies provide greater choice (e.g. in the case of radio stations), where under perfect competition all radio stations would cater for the biggest market, which would be for pop music. A monopolist, however, would be able to cover all tastes with a variety of stations.
- There is less incentive to innovate under monopoly, since the monopolist is subject to less competition. *But*, equally, a monopolist might have more incentive to innovate as it can reap the benefits in terms of higher profits. It may also have more resources to devote to innovation.

As can be seen there is not a clear set of arguments that imply that perfect competition is better than monopoly, and, as will be seen in Chapter 14, this is taken into account in UK competition policy.

An example of monopoly?

Although it is easy to think of examples of industries where the dominant firm has a great deal of monopoly power, there is no such thing as a pure monopoly, as substitutes exist for most goods. For example, British Rail used to have monopoly power in the market for rail travel, but there are many alternative forms of travel. This point highlights the difficulties of defining markets and industries discussed in Chapter 9. The nearest examples of monopolies are the old public utilities, like gas, electricity, water and so on, many of which have been privatised.

The government, in determining whether monopoly power exists in a market, has a working definition of what constitutes a monopoly. It is when 25 per cent of the market is accounted for by one firm or firms acting together. This would form grounds for investigation by the Competition Commission. The process of UK competition policy is discussed in Chapter 14 in more detail. The sources of monopoly power are the existence of barriers to entry and exit and the availability of substitutes (these will be discussed later in this chapter).

For information on the the operation of the Competition Commission see *www.competition-commission.org.uk*

Oligopoly

In both perfect competition and monopoly firms make independent decisions. In the case of monopoly there are no other firms in the industry to consider; in the case of perfect competition the firm has no power to affect the market at all. So for different reasons they act as though they have no rivals. This is not true in the case of oligopoly. Oligopoly is where a small number of producers supply a market in which the product is differentiated in some way. The characteristics of oligopoly are:

- A great deal of interdependence between the firms; each firm has to consider the likely actions of other firms when making its decisions.
- A lack of price competition in the market; firms are reluctant to increase their prices in case their competitors do not and they might lose market share. Firms are also reluctant to reduce their prices, in case other firms do the same and a price war results which reduces prices but leaves market share unchanged and so everyone is left worse off.[3]
- The lack of price competition means that different forms of non-price competition take place, such as branding or advertising. Oligopolists will sell their products not by reducing the price but through heavy advertising, brand names or special offers. The Premier points scheme was a good example of such non-price competition. The purchase of petrol from certain outlets gave the customer points which were accumulated on their Premier points card and then redeemed for money-off vouchers to be spent at Argos. Table 12.4 shows the implications of oligopoly for conduct and performance of firms in an industry.

The way in which price is determined in an oligopolistic market is through either price leadership or some sort of collusion. Price leadership is where one firm takes the lead in setting prices and the others follow suit. The price leader is not necessarily the firm with the lowest cost, as it depends upon the power of the firm. So price could be set at a higher level than in a competitive market. Collusion is an explicit or implicit agreement between firms on price, which serves to reduce the amount of competition between firms. Collusion is illegal in most countries as it is seen as a form of restrictive practice, but this does not mean that collusion does not take place. A cartel is a form of collusion where firms come together to exercise joint market power. Cartels are now illegal in most countries, but the most famous of all is OPEC which has had a dramatic effect on the oil industry over the last 30 years. Collusive agreements, as well as possibly being harmful to the consumer, tend to be unstable as there is great temptation on the part of individual firms/countries to cheat. What is clear in the case of oligopoly is that once price is set there is a reluctance to change it. Therefore price competition is replaced by non-price competition of the sort mentioned above.

Table 12.4   Implications of oligopoly for conduct and performance of firms in an industry

Extent of market power	A great deal of market power.
Price	A stable price level. Prices set by price leadership or collusion.
Advertising	Much advertising and branding. Non-price competition is common.
Profitability	Abnormal profits can exist, their extent depends on the strength of competitors.

Mini case · Price wars in the newspaper industry

The newspaper industry in the UK had a very bad winter in 2001. Sales were down, advertising revenue had fallen and redundancies had taken place. Table 12.5 shows the change in circulation for selected publications between April 2001 and April 2002.

The only positive note was the fact that the price wars in the industry seemed to be over.[4] That is until 1 May 2002, when the *Express* reduced the cover price of both its weekday and weekend papers. The weekday price was reduced to 20p. The *Mirror* was the first to respond, having just relaunched itself as the *Daily Mirror*, by also reducing its weekday price to 20p from 10 May. The *Sun* then matched the price cut penny for penny. Neither the *Sun* nor the *Daily Mirror* reduced the price of their weekend issues. The *Daily Star* then reduced its weekday price to 10p

Although it is too early to judge the effects of this price war, in the first week the *Daily Mirror* claims that sales were up 8 per cent by 160 000, the *Sun* claims that sales were up 5 per cent by 200 000, but the biggest winner seems to be the *Express* which claims that weekday sales have risen 14 per cent by 200 000. It is important to remember, however, that these are circulation figures and this says little about revenues. The costs of production will remain the same during this price war so lower prices will result in a squeeze on profits. It then comes down to which newspaper can withstand this squeeze for longest.

The price wars that are seen periodically in the newspaper industry often give the newspapers a short-term boost in circulation figures, but usually the effect does not continue once prices are put back up again. Undoubtedly prices will rise again, as only News International (the *Sun*) has the resources to sustain a prolonged price war.

Table 12.5 National daily newspaper circulation, percentage change between April 2001 and April 2002, UK

	Percentage
Sun	− 4.0
Mirror	− 4.33
Daily Star	+ 12.61
Daily Record	− 4.64
Daily Mail	+ 0.21
Express	− 3.75
Daily Telegraph	− 1.78
The Times	+ 1.89
The Financial Times	+ 2.63
Guardian	+ 0.79
Independent	+ 0.61

Table 12.6	The top firms' share of the market in the UK (percentages)	
Industry		*Percentages*
Cigarettes[a]		91*
Brewing[b]		90**
Ice cream (impulse purchase)[c]		87*
Sugar and artificial sweeteners[d]		80*
Jeans[e]		39**

* top 3 firms in the industry, ** top 5 firms.
Sources: [a] Keynote Report, 1998; [b] Keynote Report, 2001; [c] Mintel Report, 2002;
[d] Mintel Report, 2000; [e] Mintel Report, 2001.

The most often quoted examples of oligopoly are the market for tobacco and the market for soap powder. Both of these markets are dominated by a very small number of producers and both exhibit the predicted characteristics. There is little price competition and price is fairly uniform in both markets. There is a high degree of non-price competition in both markets – high advertising, strong brand names and images, and the use of special offers or gifts at times in order to sell the goods.

Compared with monopoly and perfect competition, oligopoly is a much more realistic market structure, with many markets exhibiting the characteristics stated above. Table 12.6 gives a few examples.

web link For information and reports on specific industries see *www.mintel.co.uk* and *www.hybrid.keynote.co.uk*

Monopolistic competition

A market structure of monopolistic competition exists when all of the conditions for perfect competition are met except for the existence of a homogeneous good, so that each firm has a monopoly over its own good but there is a great deal of competition in the market from other suppliers producing very similar products. In monopolistic competition the good is slightly differentiated in some way, either by advertising and branding or by local production. There does not have to be a technical difference between the two goods, which could be identical in composition, but there must be an 'economic difference' – that is, a difference in the way the goods are perceived by consumers. There is also some degree of consumer loyalty, so that if one firm reduces price, consumers might not necessarily move to that firm if they believe that the difference between the brands justifies the higher price. Abnormal profits can exist in the short run but cannot persist since new firms are free to enter the industry and compete away abnormal profit (*see* Table 12.7).

| Table 12.7 | Implications of monopolistic competition for the conduct and performance of firms in an industry |

Extent of market power	The firm has little market power.
Price	There will be small differences in price.
Advertising	There will be heavy advertising and branding.
Profitability	Small abnormal profits can exist in the short run but will be competed away in the longer run.

An example of monopolistic competition?

There are many examples of this type of industry: for example, the paint industry where ICI is the only producer of Dulux but there are many other types of paint on the market.

How accurate is the theory?

The implications of the theory of market structures for the behaviour and performance of firms are summarised in Table 12.8.

As argued above, both perfect competition and pure monopoly tend to be based on assumptions that are somewhat unrealistic and should be regarded as 'ideal types' of market structure, in the sense that they establish the boundaries within which true markets exist and operate, and against which they can be analysed. In contrast, oligopoly and monopolistic competition are much nearer to the types of market structure which can be found in the real world, and economic theory does appear to explain and predict behaviour in these markets to a certain extent. In oligopolistic markets, for example, price tends to be 'sticky' and much of the competition between firms occurs in non-price ways, particularly branding, advertising and sales promotion (*see* Table 12.9). Occasionally, however, price wars do occur – as in the petrol market in the 1980s and more recently between the four biggest supermarkets.

Table 12.9 shows the top advertisers in the United Kingdom ranked for 2000; their ranks in 1995 are also given. The names in the list are familiar and largely

| Table 12.8 | Implications of theory for behaviour of firms |

	Market power	Price	Advertising	Profitability
Perfect competition	None	One price	None	Only normal profits
Monopoly	Absolute	Price discrimination possible	None	Abnormal profits
Oligopoly	High	One price	High	Abnormal profits
Monopolistic competition	Little	Small differences in price	High	Only normal profits in long run

Table 12.9	Top advertisers in the UK in 2000		
Rank		Advertiser	Total adspend (£000)
2000	1995		
1	5	Procter & Gamble	121,151
2	1	BT	107,546
3	6	Central Office of Information	102,704
4	8	Renault	70,667
5	15	L'Oréal	59,767
6	3	Vauxhall Motors	57,083
7	2	Ford Motor Co	55,775
8	12	Van den Bergh Foods	51,724
9	28	British Sky Broadcasting	47,875
10	35	Vodafone	47,802

Source: *Advertising Statistics Yearbook*, 2001, Advertising Association, NTC Publications.

expected from the predictions: for example, Procter & Gamble is one of the two companies which together with Unilever account for around 90 per cent of the market for washing powder.

For information on advertising see *www.adassoc.org.uk*

It is much more difficult to judge how accurate the behavioural implications are. Lack of data is one problem, as is the fact that only one structural characteristic has been considered here – the level of competition between producers. The other structural factors listed in Table 12.1 (on page 333) will also have an effect, like the level of demand, the degree of competition between the buyers and the degree of potential competition. Profitability, price and advertising, for instance, will be affected by the level of demand in the market.

Porter's five-forces model

Porter's model[5] says that the structure of an industry and the ability of firms in that industry to act strategically depend upon the relative strengths of five forces: current competition, potential competition, the threat of substitute products, the power of buyers and the power of suppliers. Each of these five forces will be examined in turn.

Current competition

Current competition has already been considered under the heading of market structure but the important point to remember is that by acting strategically firms can change the structure of the industry. Firms in a highly competitive market might be unhappy with the lack of power they have over various factors like pricing and may through their strategic actions try to change the situation. If they are successful there will be a change in the level of current competition and therefore in market structure.

Potential competition (or threat of new entry)

It has been shown that market structure or current competition affects the behaviour of firms in an industry. However, looking at the number of firms in an industry does not provide the whole picture. It is possible that firms in an oligopolistic market might act in a way consistent with perfect competition because of the threat of potential competition. This threat can affect the behaviour of firms even if it does not happen. The degree of potential competition depends upon the existence and height of barriers to entry and exit.

Barriers to entry

Barriers to entry are any barriers which prevent or inhibit the entry of firms into the industry. There are several sources of barriers to entry.

Some industries are what are called 'natural monopolies' in that the production process is such that competition would be wasteful. The old public utilities are good examples of these, as it would be very wasteful for there to be two national grid systems in the electricity industry.

Some production processes are subject to economies of scale. As firms grow in size, or as the scale of production increases, certain economies occur which serve to reduce the average cost of production. The scale of production can be increased in many ways, for example by increasing the capacity of the existing plant, by increasing the number of plants or by increasing the product range. Figure 12.2 shows how the average *cost* of production changes as the *scale* of production changes.

The downward-sloping part of the curve shows falling average cost or economies of scale. The upward-sloping part shows rising average cost or diseconomies of scale. Economies of scale reduce average cost and therefore benefit the producer and also the consumer if they are passed on in lower prices.

 Figure 12.2 A firm's average cost curve

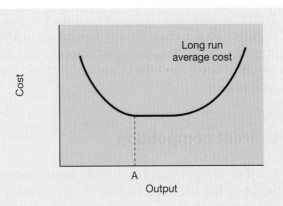

The sources of economies of scale are usually classified under three headings: technical; marketing; and financial.

Technical economies come from increased specialisation and indivisibilities. The larger the scale of production the more the production process can be broken down into its component parts and the greater the gain from specialisation. There are certain indivisibilities involved in production, which only large firms can benefit from. For example, a small firm cannot have half a production line as that is meaningless, but might not be big enough to use a whole production line. Another type of indivisibility is involved in the notion of fixed costs. Fixed costs like the cost of rates or the fees of an accountant, for example, remain the same irrespective of the level of production. Therefore the greater the level of production, the lower will be the average cost of items as it is being spread over a larger output.

Marketing economies come from spreading marketing costs over a larger output, so that average costs will be lower. The company can also take advantage of bulk buying, and will probably have a specialised department devoted to marketing.

Financial economies come from the fact that larger companies find it easier and often cheaper to borrow capital.

Added to these is *risk diversification* which is possible with larger companies as they may well have interests in other industries. All of these economies of scale give rise to falling average cost and therefore explain the downward-sloping part of the cost curve in Figure 12.2. Economies of scale are a very effective barrier to entry. If the incumbent firm in an industry has lower average cost as a result of economies of scale, it will be hard for a newcomer to compete effectively at a smaller scale of production. Gas, electricity and water are examples of this. The production processes of these goods are subject to economies of scale and it is therefore difficult for others to come into the market in competition with established firms. This is why such industries are called 'natural monopolies'.

Barriers to entry can be legal ones, as in the case of patents and franchises which serve to restrict competition and prevent new firms from entering an industry. Advertising and branding can also be barriers, in that industries where brand names are well established are difficult to enter without massive expenditure on advertising. Some industries require a high initial capital investment to enter, for example, dry cleaning, where the machinery is very expensive. Switching costs can also be regarded as a barrier to entry. If the consumer has to bear a cost in switching from one good to another that might be enough to deter the consumer from doing so and therefore serve as a barrier to entry. The recent practice of the building societies and banks of offering low fixed-rate mortgages with penalties for early withdrawal can be seen as an example of the introduction of switching costs into the market.

A contestable market[6] is one in which there are no barriers to entry or exit. This means that all firms (even potential entrants) have access to the same technology and there are therefore no cost barriers to entry. It also means that there are no sunk or unrecoverable costs which would prevent a firm leaving the industry. It follows that it is possible to ensure that firms behave in a competitive way, even if the market structure they operate in is imperfectly competitive, by ensuring that the market is contestable. What is regulating market behaviour then is not *actual* competition but *potential* competition.

Barriers to exit

Exit barriers are those which prevent or deter exit from an industry; they are mainly related to the cost of leaving the industry. The cost of exit depends upon how industry-specific the assets of the firm are. If we take physical assets as an example, a printing press is highly specific to the printing industry and could not be used for anything other than printing. There will be a second-hand market for printing presses but it would probably have to be sold at a loss, therefore incurring a high cost. A van, however, would be different, as it is still a physical asset but one that would not be specific to a particular industry, therefore the loss involved in selling would be less. Generally speaking, the more industry-specific an asset is the lower will be the second-hand value and the higher the cost of exit. An intangible asset like knowledge of the market or expenditure on research and development cannot be resold and must be left in the market, and therefore is a sunk cost – a non-recoverable cost.

Barriers to entry and exit can be 'innocent' or can be deliberately erected. Economies of scale can be regarded as innocent barriers to entry since they are inherent in the production process. Advertising and branding can be thought of as deliberately erected barriers to entry since they increase the expense of any firm entering the market. Similarly, the introduction of penalty clauses on mortgages is a deliberately erected barrier since it incurs switching costs for the consumer.

Where innocent barriers to entry or exit are low, potential competition will be high and firms within such a market are faced with the choice of accepting the situation or deliberately erecting some barriers. This is an example of strategic behaviour on the part of firms; whether it is attempted or not depends on the likelihood of success and the relative costs and benefits. It is another area where game theory is used to formulate strategic possibilities.[7]

The threat of substitute products

The threat from substitute products largely depends upon the nature of the good being traded in the market and the extent of product differentiation. It has a clear impact upon market structure, because if there are no substitutes for a good the producer of that good will face little competition and have a great deal of market power. However, as was seen earlier, even industries which appear to be pure monopolies like the former British Rail face competition from substitutes since there are other ways to travel. Much of the expenditure by firms to differentiate their products is designed to reduce the threat from substitute products.

The power of buyers

So far this chapter has concentrated on the competition between producers in a market, but the amount of competition between buyers will also have an impact on an industry. Markets will range from those where there are many buyers, as in the case of retailing, through markets where there are a small number of buyers, as in the case of car and parts manufacturers, to markets where there is only one buyer.

This latter type of market is called a monopsony, and it is the buyer who has a great deal of market power rather than the seller. An example of this is the coal industry, where the majority of output goes to the electricity producers. Increasingly in retailing the giant retailers are exerting a great deal of power over the manufacturers. TOYS 'R' US, the world's largest toy retailer, is involved very early on by manufacturers in the design process for new toys and as a result gets many exclusives that are not available in other toy shops.

The level of buyer power could be measured in the same way as seller power (*see* later in this chapter), but no data are collected centrally on the level of buyer concentration. It is clear, however, that there are many markets in which powerful buyers can and do exert a great deal of control over suppliers, and this power is an important source of marketing economies of scale. It is possible to put together the level of competition between producers and consumers in order to predict behaviour. For example, a market which consists of a single buyer and a single seller will have quite different characteristics from a market which has many buyers and sellers. The existence of strong buyers might have beneficial effects on the market as they could offset the power of strong producers or it could lead to higher seller concentration as sellers come together to counteract the power of the buyer.

In markets where there are strong sellers and weak buyers the producers' power can be offset by, for example, consumer advice centres or watch-dog bodies, as in the case of the former public utilities.

A distinction can be made between existing and potential customers. Existing customers are particularly significant to firms in industries where repeat orders are important or where goods are supplied on a regular basis, as in grocery retailing. It is no surprise that the large grocery retailers are using loyalty cards to increase the loyalty of existing customers. The power of existing customers is much lower where the firm supplies goods on a one-off basis, although the firm cannot disregard existing customers as this will affect its reputation and the ability to attract potential customers. Potential customers might be new to the market or can be buying from an existing competitor at present.

Power of suppliers

The power of suppliers over the firm is likely to be extremely important in certain markets, depending upon the nature of the product being supplied. For example: Is the product highly specialised? Is the same or similar product available from elsewhere? How important is the product in the production process? The importance of good and reliable supplies has assumed greater significance since firms have started to adopt just-in-time production methods. Reducing stock levels to reduce costs can only be effective if firms can depend upon their suppliers; hence there has been the development of partnership sourcing as firms develop long-term relationships with their suppliers.

Another important factor here is whether or not the firm itself can produce the components it needs in the production process. If it can the power of suppliers is greatly reduced. The decision as to whether to produce or to buy from a supplier is the subject of a relatively new area of economics called transaction cost economics.[8]

Measuring the degree of actual competition in the market

In industrial economics the level of competition in a market is measured by concentration ratios. These measure the percentage of value added, total output or employment that is produced by a stated number of the largest firms in the industry. The common numbers are three or five. The five-firm concentration ratio measures the percentage of employment or output accounted for by the five largest firms in the industry, and was reported in the *Annual Census of Production* produced by the UK government until 1992. Publication of concentration ratios was discontinued in 1992.

Although Table 12.10 shows only a small selection of industries, it does indicate that there is great variation in the degree of concentration across industries. Only one service industry is listed because of the unavailability of data relating to the services; most official data refer to manufacturing industry because of its relative historical importance. Generally services are less concentrated than manufacturing industries because of the nature of the production process and the fact that there is less scope for economies of scale.

Although it is relatively easy to compare the level of concentration in particular industries over time it is more difficult to make any conclusion about the 'average' level of concentration (*see* mini case: Concentration in this chapter). Table 12.11 gives the percentage share of total employment and sales of the largest 100 private firms in the United Kingdom from 1979 to 1992. Although these are not concentration ratios as such, the data do provide an indication of how concentration has changed over time in aggregate. The change in the Standard Industrial Classification during this period has only a small impact on the figures. Note how the level of 'average' concentration decreased slightly during the first part of the period, reversing the trend of the first half of this century where industrial concentration increased. The reason for the decrease is largely the process of privatisation and the growth in the small-firm sector during the 1970s and 1980s. In the later part of the period concentration started to rise again, mainly due to the industrial restructuring taking place and the increased level of merger activity identified in

Table 12.10 Five-firm concentration ratios for selected industries in the UK (1992)

Industry	Employment (%)	Output (%)
Sugar and sugar by-products	100.0	100.0
Tobacco	97.7	99.5
Iron and steel industry	90.9	95.3
Asbestos goods	90.5	89.8
Mineral, oil processing	52.2	61.9
Footwear	44.3	48.2
Pharmaceutical products	31.5	43.5
Leather goods	12.4	16.1
Executive recruitment industry*	6.0	11.0

* Note: An eight-firm concentration ratio.[9]

Source: *Census of Production*, 1992. Crown copyright 1992. Reproduced by permission of the Controller of HMSO and of Office for National Statistics, UK.

Table 12.11	100 largest private enterprise groups

| Year | Percentage share of total | |
	Employment	Sales
SIC(68)		
1979	12	18
SIC(80)		
1980	13	15
1981	13	16
1982	12	15
1983	12	16
1984	15	19
1985	9.5	14
1986	9.7	15.4
1987	10.8	17.1
1988	9.4	17.6
1989	12.1	21.6
1990	14.6	23.6
1991	14.9	21.2
1992	16.9	24.9

Source: *Census of production*, various. Crown copyright. Reproduced by permission of the Controller of HMSO and of the Office for National Statistics, UK.

Chapter 8. Again the UK government ceased publication of these figures in 1992 which makes it difficult to assess what has happened to concentration more recently. There are two industries common to Tables 12.10 and 12.6 – sugar and tobacco – and in both cases concentration has fallen between 1992 and 1998/2000, although it cannot be assumed that this is a general trend.

It is difficult to make comparisons between different countries because of this problem of 'averaging' concentration and because of national differences in the way in which data are collected and reported. Moreover official EU publications on industry have changed the way in which they report data, so comparisons over time are impossible. Available evidence[10] suggests, however, that in the 1960s concentration increased in Europe and stabilised by the 1970s before declining in the 1980s, as in the United Kingdom.

One of the main arguments for the creation of the Single European Market was that the bigger market would allow greater economies of scale through the growth in the size of firms. Chapter 8 has already identified an increase in merger activity in the EU in the late 1980s in the run-up to 1992 and Table 12.12 shows the change in the five-firm concentration ratios according to value added in selected sectors in the EU between 1986 and 1991.

Most sectors experienced an increase in concentration levels, although there are differences between the sectors. Aerospace is one sector where concentration increased by 20 per cent, mainly due to the growth of British Aerospace and Rolls-Royce. The level of concentration in the EU has risen as a result of increased merger

Table 12.12 Five-firm concentration ratios on a value-added basis (%) for selected sectors in the EU

Sector	1986	1991	% change
Tobacco	58.39	59.16	0.76
Chemicals	42.25	41.48	−0.77
Rubber and plastic products	14.78	21.71	6.93
Iron and steel	47.21	82.31	35.10
Aerospace	51.24	71.97	20.72
Computers	34.08	33.17	−0.91
Drink	39.73	43.24	3.50
Food	16.92	20.37	3.45
Printing and publishing	19.20	19.34	0.14

Source: Commission of the European Communities, *European Economy*, no. 57, 1994. Reproduced by permission of the Office for Official Publications of the European Communities.

activity and a competition policy which is torn between promoting competition by preventing market domination and the need to establish European competitiveness by encouraging it.

Despite the difficulties in comparing concentration ratios, the general view of industrial economists is that concentration is greater in the United Kingdom than in other member states.

Mini case   Concentration

Although it is difficult to talk about the 'average' level of concentration in a country, the government in the UK produced data on the percentage share of the largest 100 enterprises in employment and output up to 1992 (*see* Table 12.11 on page 349). These data show that concentration increased in the first half of this century but has stabilised and even fallen at times. It is also true that the relative importance of the small firm to both output and employment has increased over recent years at the expense of larger organisations. What are the reasons for these changes?

The main benefits to result from increased size and concentration are the economies of scale discussed in the text. The techniques of mass production which produced standardised goods at low cost rely upon the economies of specialisation and division of labour. Although there are many industries which are still dominated by very large organisations, the recent trends in firm size and concentration indicate that smaller firms are increasingly able to compete with large firms. In unsegmented markets where the product is standardised the techniques of mass production are still appropriate, but increasingly there is a movement to a more flexible approach to manufacturing. This has been called the 'Japanisation' of industry.

■ Changes in consumer demand have led to a demand for a bigger range of products so that markets are increasingly segmented and there is greater product differentiation. Under such conditions the benefits of economies of large-scale production have little significance, and large-scale organisations are less responsive to changes in demand than small firms. The use of 'flexible manufacturing systems' gives much greater flexibility in production and enables firms to produce a wider range of products at lower cost than traditional methods of production.

■ Developments in information technology like Computer Aided Design (CAD) and Computer Aided Manufacturing (CAM) have exacerbated this trend since they serve to reduce the minimum efficient scale of production and make economies of scale possible at lower levels of output. Thus small firms can benefit from economies of scale in the same way as large firms. CAD and CAM make possible the manufacture of different products so that the product mix can be altered quickly.

■ Economies of scope exist where a firm can produce two or more products at a lower per unit cost than if it produced each product separately. They result where related activities use similar labour and equipment and where producing related goods is a way of using up excess capacity. The economies stem from the spreading of fixed costs over larger output. Since economies of scope are not due to increased scale of production they can be realised by large and small firms alike. One small firm industry which has benefited from economies of scope is executive recruitment consultancy, where firms increasingly offer a range of related services like training audits and succession planning.

■ Techniques like just-in-time production are more accessible to small firms since they eradicate the need for keeping large inventories and the associated costs of storage.

Reasons for high concentration

Many industries in the United Kingdom are highly concentrated and it is believed that the United Kingdom has higher concentration ratios than other large industrial countries. Why are there different market structures between industries?

Referring back to Figure 12.2 (page 344), the point at which the curve becomes horizontal (A in diagram) is called the minimum efficient scale of production or MES. It is the point at which all economies of scale have been reaped by the firm, and the point at which firms that wish to maximise their efficiency must operate.

The higher the MES relative to the total output of the industry, the fewer will be the number of firms operating in an industry and therefore the higher will be the level of concentration. For example, if the MES in an industry is half of the industry output, the industry could only support two firms, as smaller firms could not achieve low enough costs to compete with the large firms.

As the scale of production continues to increase, average costs eventually start to rise. This is due to diseconomies of scale, which are mostly attributed to managerial inefficiencies. These are the difficulties faced by management in controlling, co-ordinating and communicating in a large organisation.

Firms in every industry will face differing average cost curves and therefore market structures will be different. In services, for example, because of the nature of the product, the scope for economies of scale is small and, accordingly, the MES is small relative to the size of the total market and the industries tend to be unconcentrated. The level of concentration in manufacturing tends to be much higher because of the nature of the production process and the scope for economies of scale.

The size of the MES is not the only explanation of why there are different market structures. If it was, one might expect that the same industry would have similar levels of concentration in different countries, but this is not the case, as indicated above. The strength of the five forces will differ greatly between industries and will therefore give many different structures. Obviously government policy can influence the type of market structure, and this will differ between countries. It is also true that the significance of barriers to entry varies between countries. Empirical results from West Germany and the United Kingdom show that in both countries barriers to entry are high, but that in the United Kingdom advertising is the most important barrier, while in West Germany it is economies of scale.

Synopsis

In this chapter, four different market structures were considered that embraced the whole spectrum of competition: perfect competition; monopoly; oligopoly; and monopolistic competition. Each of these market structures gives predictions about the behaviour of firms in those markets. Generally the more realistic of these market structures predict well what happens in the real world. This analysis was then incorporated into Porter's five-forces model which includes further factors largely ignored by traditional economic theory. Nevertheless, these factors are particularly important in certain industries, like the power of the giant retailers as buyers and the importance of potential customers to industries where the level of repeat business is high.

The amount of competition in a market is measured using concentration ratios and evidence on concentration was examined both within the United Kingdom and between countries as far as that was possible.

Summary of key points

- There are four different market structures identified by business economists. These are (arranged with most competitive first): perfect competition, monopolistic competition, oligopoly and monopoly.

- Perfect competition is a market structure which is very competitive and where the producers are 'price takers'.

- Pure monopoly is a market structure with a single producer that is a 'price maker'.

- Monopolistic competition is a market structure where there is a great deal of competition but where the product is slightly differentiated, so producers have a little market power.

- Oligopoly is a market structure where there is a small number of large producers, interdependent in their decision making. This is a common market structure.

- The determinants of market structure include the existence and height of barriers to entry and exit and the existence of economies of scale.

- Knowledge of market structure gives some indication of likely behaviour of firms with respect to factors like pricing and advertising.

Structure–Conduct–Performance analysis of the airline industry

The pressures on the global airline industry have been severe in 2002 after the catastrophic events on 11 September 2001. There were pressures on the industry prior to that but these have been greatly exacerbated. The airline industry is one where the level of fixed costs is very high – the airlines have to buy and maintain a fleet of aeroplanes, they have to pay to land at airports. These costs do not fall if aeroplanes are half empty, which means that the fortunes of the airline companies are highly dependent upon fluctuations in demand, and after 'September 11' demand fell very sharply. Since then there has been major restructuring in the industry. 2002 has seen major redundancies by the mainstream airlines, the collapse of Sabena Airlines and the merger between easyJet and Go. This case study uses the S–C–P approach to try to understand why this is happening.

Structure

Demand factors

- There are two main reasons for travel on aeroplanes – leisure and business. It is estimated that business travel accounts for around 22 per cent of air travel and leisure 78 per cent.
- It is generally believed that the demand for leisure travel is price elastic: as prices go down travel increases sharply.
- It is also generally believed that business travel is price inelastic, that business travellers are less concerned about what they pay as someone else picks up the bill. (However, this is questioned by the extent to which the low-cost, no-frills airlines have expanded in the business market.)
- Both travel for leisure and travel for business are cyclical and will depend upon economic growth.
- Over the last 50 years the demand for air travel has increased greatly. Demographic factors, like increased life expectancy, and better health have meant that all ages travel more than before. The average growth rate in air travel over the last 20 years is around 5 per cent per annum.[11]
- This demand, however, is highly susceptible to external forces. The Gulf War in the early 1990s, for example, led to a massive fall in demand for air travel as travellers feared acts of terrorism (*see* Figure 12.3).
- Most recently of course, the events of 11 September 2001 also led to a massive fall in demand which by April 2002 had not yet recovered (*see* Table 12.13).

Supply characteristics

- There are three types of airline company in the world – the large mainstream airlines like British Airways and American Airways, the small low-cost airlines like easyJet and Ryanair and the medium-sized companies like SWISS International Air Lines and Pan Am.

Figure 12.3 Annual percentage change in IATA members' traffic, 1990–94

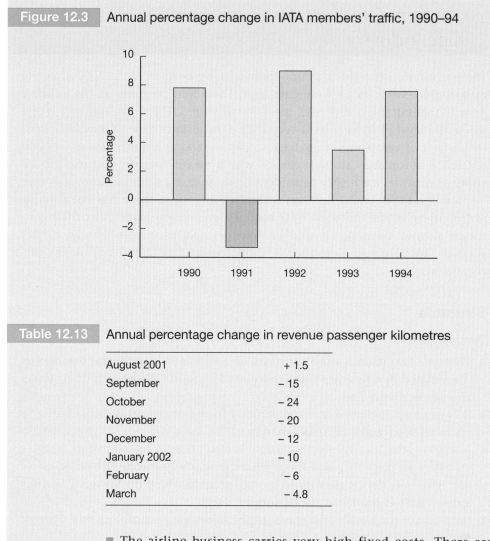

Table 12.13 Annual percentage change in revenue passenger kilometres

August 2001	+ 1.5
September	– 15
October	– 24
November	– 20
December	– 12
January 2002	– 10
February	– 6
March	– 4.8

■ The airline business carries very high fixed costs. There are the costs of purchasing and maintaining the aeroplanes and the cost of landing at airports. All of these are fixed costs in that they will not change if an aircraft is half-empty.

■ There is not much of an alternative to air travel for international travel. Domestically, the airlines are in competition with all other sorts of travel but there is evidence from the UK that the low-cost airlines are cheaper than other methods of travel and of course much faster. The fact that in Europe countries are joined and the rail network is more developed may in part explain why the low-cost airlines do not yet have much of the market (5 per cent) compared with the UK (20 per cent) and the USA (22 per cent).

■ Airspace was deregulated in the 1970s in the USA and in the 1990s in Europe, such that any qualified airline can fly anywhere in the EU without government agreement. This increased the level of competition and allowed the smaller low-cost airlines to establish themselves. Deregulation in the USA led to increased concentration in the airline industry.

■ Technological change has helped the low-cost airlines – it is estimated that 90 per cent of easyJet's tickets are sold over the Internet.

■ In addition to all of these there are other costs to be taken into account – the cost of labour, fuel and the new safety procedures introduced post-September 11. Increasingly environmental groups are concerned by the fact that air transport is the fastest-growing source of greenhouse gases and pressure is being applied for increases in the taxation on aircraft fuel.

Conduct

Pricing

■ There are two different strategies for pricing within the airline industry. The large mainstream airlines mainly depend upon their business passengers, who are willing to pay more for more luxurious amenities in the airport and on the aircraft. The economy seats are sold off, discounting if necessary right up to the day of the flight. The low-cost airlines, however, adopt a different strategy. They sell off a number of seats at a very low price and then sell off groups or 'buckets' of seats increasing in price until the day of the flight. On any one flight there could be up to 10 different prices but even the most expensive will be cheaper than the mainstream airlines.

■ Prices are kept low on the low-cost flights by the lack of food or drink served on the flights. The aeroplanes are cleaned by the flight team and the airlines use less well known airports, sometimes a little way from large conurbations, where they are often paid for landing there because of the trade they bring in. In addition, the use of the Internet for ticket booking keeps down the administrative costs to the low-cost airlines.

■ The response of the low-cost airline Ryanair after September 11 was to cut prices further in order to stimulate demand and to keep people travelling. The large airlines cut capacity.

Merger activity

There are several possibilities for growth within the airline industry:

■ The airlines could grow organically – the airlines can expand by buying more aeroplanes and expanding the number of airports they fly to. This has been the most common form of growth in the low-cost sector – for example, easyJet grew by increasing the frequency of its flights and Ryanair grew by adding extra routes.

■ The airlines could grow through merger and acquisition – this has always been fairly commonplace among the large providers – the British Airways purchase of British Caledonian in 1988 and the merger between American Airlines and TWA in 2001, for example. The relevant competition authority disallows many proposed mergers. This type of growth spread to the low-cost sector in 2002 with the takeover of Go by easyJet.

■ The third method of expansion popular in the airline industry is the formation of strategic alliances – there are three main alliances (see Table 12.14). The main aim is to provide 'seamless travel' to customers.

Table 12.14	Major airline alliances, 2002

Airline alliance	Airline companies
oneworld Alliance	Aer Lingus, American Airlines, British Airways, Cathay Pacific, Finnair, Iberia, LanChile, Quantas Airways
Star Alliance	Air Canada, Air New Zealand, ANA, Austrian Airlines, bmi british midland, Lauda, Lufthansa, Mexicana, Scandinavian Airlines, Singapore Airlines, Thai Airways International, Tyrolean, United Airlines, Varig Brazilian Airlines
SkyTeam	Air France, Aeromexico, Czech Airlines, Delta, Italia, Korean Air

Since the events of September 11, the global airline industry has shrunk in size. By November 2001 airline carriers had reduced the available seats per kilometre by more than 10 per cent on 2000 levels and between 1 September 2001 and 1 March 2002, 140 000 seats had been withdrawn.

Performance

- By any measure of performance things were bad for the airline industry in 2002. It is estimated that the world's airlines lost $11 billion in 2001 and although losses are expected to be lower in 2002, they could still be up to $7.5 billion.
- Performance in 2002, however, has varied between the different types of airline company. The large airlines have cut capacity – they have made redundancies and retired aeroplanes. Some (Sabena) have even been forced out of business and many in the middle of 2002 are still in severe financial difficulty. The low-cost providers, however, continue to do well. In the first quarter of 2002, Southwest Airlines (the first of the low-cost airlines) was the only American carrier to make a profit. The growth of the low-cost airlines is running at 25 per cent per annum, despite the crisis.

The future

The is some evidence in mid-2002 that the travelling public is beginning to return to air travel, the effect looks similar to that experienced after the Gulf War, where demand had returned within a year. This however rests on the assumption that nothing else similar to 'September 11' takes place again. Restructuring in the industry is likely to continue as some airline companies (United Airlines and US Airways, for example) are still in severe difficulties. There are signs that the mainstream airlines have recognised the threat posed by the low-cost airlines and are trying to match their low prices. In the low-cost sector, the merger between easyJet and Go reduces the level of competition and could lead to higher prices, especially as the merged company is the only low-cost airline on seven routes. At the time of writing the new company denies any intention of doing this.

Other factors which might impact upon the industry include proposed increases in aviation fuel tax to be introduced in the EU in 2003 and the impact on the price of fuel brought about by any action by the USA in the Middle East. If demand in the future rises at pre-2001 rates there will be increased problems of congestion in the air.

What is undoubtedly true is that the airline industry is one which is still undergoing changes in its structure.

Case study questions

1 What are the advantages and disadvantages of the different method of growth detailed in the case study? (*See* Chapter 8)

2 Why is there unlikely to be a price war between the low-cost providers in the airline industry?

web link

For information on the airline industry see
www.IATA.org (International Air Transport Association)
www.AEA.org (Association of European Airlines)
www.CAA.org (Civil Aviation Authority)

Review and discussion questions

1 Use Porter's five-forces model to analyse two industries of your choice. Try to choose industries which have contrasting market structures.

2 What economies of scale are likely to exist in retailing?

3 Think of examples of a market which is very competitive and a market which is not very competitive. Does the behaviour of the firms in these markets comply with the predictions in Table 12.8 on page 342?

4 Why are goods like washing powders and coffee advertised more heavily than goods like matches or bread?

Assignments

1 You are working in the strategic planning department of a large recorded music producer and have been asked to write a briefing document for a board meeting on the structure of the industry. Use either the S–C–P model or Porter's five-forces model as a framework for this briefing. (Sources of information: Competition Commission reports, the previous editions of this book, media and local libraries, Mintel and Keynote).

2 You are working in the local consumer advice centre which each week produces an information sheet giving the prices of a typical 'basket of goods' in local shops. Choose ten branded items (like Nescafé, for example) to constitute your basket of goods and survey three types of retail outlet: a small corner shop, a mini-market on a local main road and a large supermarket. Design an information sheet and present the information you have gathered in the form of a table. Include a list of bullet points which might explain any differences in price.

Notes and references

1   *See* Hay, D. A. and Morris, D. J., *Industrial Economics: Theory and Evidence*, Oxford University Press 1979, for a summary of the criticisms which are beyond the scope of this book.

2   Porter, M., *Competitive Strategy: Techniques for Analyzing Industries and Competitors*, The Free Press, New York, 1980.

3   For a full discussion of this, *see* Begg, D., Fischer, S. and Dornbusch, R., *Economics*, 6th edition, McGraw-Hill, 2000.

4   See case study at end of chapter 12, second edition of this book

5   Porter, M., *Competitive Strategy: Techniques for Analyzing Industries and Competitors*, The Free Press, New York, 1980.

6   Baumol, W. J., Panzar, J. C. and Willig, R. D., *Contestable Markets and the Theory of Industry Structure*, Harcourt Brace Jovanovich, 1988.

7   In this context students should note the use of game theory to model and predict the behaviour of firms in oligopolistic markets. For a simple introduction to this area, see Griffiths, A. and Wall, S., *Applied Economics: An Introductory Course*, 9th edition, Financial Times/Prentice Hall, 2001.

8   Williamson, O. E., 'The Economics of Organisation: The Transaction Cost Approach', *American Journal of Sociology*, 87, 3 (1981), pp. 548–77.

9   Britton, L. C., Doherty, C. M. and Ball, D. F., 'Networking and Small Firms – the example of executive search and selection', published in the proceedings of the Small Business and Enterprise Development Conference, Leeds, March 1996.

10   *18th EC Competition Policy Report*, 1989.

11   See *www.IATA.org*

Further reading

Begg, D., Fischer, S. and Dornbusch, R., *Economics*, 6th edition, McGraw-Hill, 2000.

Griffiths, A. and Wall, S., *Applied Economics: An Introductory Course*, 9th edition, Financial Times/Prentice Hall, 2001.

Jones, T. T. and Cockerill, T. A. J., *Structure and Performance of Industries*, Philip Allan, 1984.

Worthington, I., Britton, C. and Rees, A., *Economics for Business: Blending Theory and Practice*, Financial Times/Prentice Hall, 2001.

Web links and further questions are available on the website at:
www.booksites.net/worthington

13

International markets

Chris Britton

The importance of international markets will vary between firms and industries but most businesses do not operate solely within national boundaries. Businesses which operate in the export market will obviously need an understanding of international markets but even the sole proprietor producing for a small local market may well use imported raw materials in the production process and so will be affected by changes that take place internationally.

Objectives

- To understand why international trade takes place.

- To look at the international organisations which serve to promote free trade.

- To survey the balance of payments position in the United Kingdom.

- To understand the working of the foreign exchange markets.

Key terms

Balance of payments	European Economic Area	Invisible trade
Balance of trade	(EEA)	J-curve effect
Capital account	European Monetary System	Qualitative control
Common agricultural policy	Exchange control	Quota
(CAP)	Exchange rate	Single market
Common external tariff	Exchange rate mechanism	Specialisation
(CET)	(ERM)	Speculation
Common market	Financial account	Subsidy
Current account	Fixed exchange rate	Surplus
Current balance	Floating exchange rate	Tariff
Customs union	Free trade	Visible trade
Deficit	Import control	
Devaluation	Import penetration	

Introduction

International markets are important to most firms; even if they do not produce for the export market they may well be dependent upon raw materials which are imported and they will almost definitely be affected by movements in the exchange rate. Britain, like all other advanced industrial countries, is highly dependent upon international markets and that dependence has grown over the years. What makes international trade different from trade within a country is that the trade is taking place across national borders. Thus a system for international payments is needed. It is essential for students of business to have an understanding of international markets, exchange rates and the balance of payments.

International trade – why it takes place

Trade between countries takes place because resources are unevenly distributed through the world and the mobility of the factors of production is limited, consequently some countries are better at producing certain goods than others. Some countries could not actually produce a particular good: for example, Britain cannot produce minerals that are not indigenous or fruit that can only be grown in tropical weather conditions. If there is a demand for these goods in Britain, there are a number of possibilities: either the British could do without these goods; or an attempt could be made to grow them (in the case of the fruit) despite the climatic conditions; or Britain could buy the goods from other countries that can produce them. In other words it can trade for them.

It is easy to see that if country A can produce video cameras more cheaply than country B and B can produce wheat more cheaply than A, specialisation should occur and A should produce video cameras and B should produce wheat and they should trade with one another. Complete specialisation is, however, unlikely, for strategic reasons. It is also true that even if country A can produce both goods more cheaply than country B there is scope for benefits from trade. As this may not be so easy to imagine, Table 13.1 gives a numerical example. Country A can produce 100 video cameras or 100 units of wheat using 100 workers. Country B can produce 20 video cameras or 40 units of wheat with the same number of workers. Country A can therefore produce both goods at lower cost than country B. To show that even in this situation trade will benefit the world, assume that both countries produce both goods and that they each devote half of their workforce to each good.

Table 13.1   Production of video cameras and wheat

	Number of units that 100 workers can produce	
	Video cameras	Wheat
Country A	100	100
Country B	20	40

Table 13.2   Production of video cameras and wheat

	Video cameras	Wheat
Country A	50	50
Country B	10	20
	60	70

Table 13.3   Production of video cameras and wheat

	Video cameras	Wheat
Country A	65	35
Country B	0	40
	65	75

The total output of video cameras is 60 units and of wheat is 70 units. Country A is 5 times more efficient at producing video cameras than country B, but only 2.5 times more efficient than B in producing wheat (*see* Table 13.2). It would therefore benefit both countries if production was rearranged. If B specialised completely in wheat and A produced 35 units of wheat and 65 video cameras, world output would be as indicated in Table 13.3.

In short, world output has been increased and everyone is better off provided that trade takes place. This simplified example illustrates the basic argument for free trade. Free trade brings the advantages of higher world output and higher standards of living. Countries will produce the goods in which they have a cost advantage and trade with other countries for other goods. So countries can buy goods at lower prices than they could be produced for at home. Where economies of scale are present, the savings as a result of specialisation can be immense.

Theoretically, free trade brings most benefit; however, there are often restrictions to such trade and it is unlikely that complete specialisation will take place. Most countries would regard being totally dependent on another country for a particular good as a risky proposition.

Restrictions to international trade

There are a number of things that governments do to restrict international trade. These restrictions include:

- **Quotas** A physical limitation on the import of certain goods into a country, sometimes by mutual agreement (e.g. voluntary export restraints).
- **Tariffs** A tax placed on imported goods.
- **Exchange controls** A limit to the amount of a currency that can be bought, which will limit the import of goods.

- **Subsidies** Payments made to domestic producers to reduce their costs and therefore make them more competitive on world markets.
- **Qualitative controls** Controls on the quality of goods rather than on quantity or price.

All of these serve to restrict international trade, and therefore reduce specialisation on a world level. They invite retaliation and could lead to inefficiencies. **Import controls** have a wide effect on industry. The 200 per cent tariffs, that the Americans threatened to impose on French cheeses and wines at the end of 1992 if the GATT talks were not successful, would have impacted on many other industries like the bottle-making industry or the insurance industry. But there are powerful arguments used in support of import controls. For example, they can be used to protect industries, whether these industries are 'infant' industries or strategic industries. In the 1999 debate within the EU on bananas, it was argued by the African, Caribbean and Pacific countries which receive preferential treatment in the EU for their bananas that the relaxation of these preferential terms might lead to the complete devastation of their economies. Import controls can also be used to improve the balance of payments position in the case where a deficit exists.

The United Kingdom is a member of a number of international organisations that serve to promote free trade and control the restrictions to free trade, like the World Trade Organisation (*see* Chapter 4).

Mini case   Trade wars in steel

In March 2002, the USA delivered another blow to the struggle for free trade and increased the probability of another trade war. It announced tariffs on imported steel of up to 30 per cent for a period of three years to allow the steel industry in the US to recover from the effect of cheap imports of steel from the EU and Asia. Several countries immediately lodged complaints with the World Trade Organisation and the EU proposed measures which would protect its steel industry from an influx of the steel turned away from America. Brussels will impose tariffs of between 15 per cent and 26 per cent on steel imports over a certain quota. These measures are to be introduced initially for 200 days but if the US sanctions are still in place by that time they will apply to make them permanent. Under WTO rules tariffs are acceptable as a 'safeguard' measure, but it is alleged that the American tariffs were imposed at a time when steel imports to the US were falling anyway. There are calls from EU members for the introduction of tit-for-tat sanctions on particular products like Florida orange juice, although there is no general agreement on these. In addition to these sanctions, the EU has demanded compensation from the USA for the value of lost imports.

It is argued that the American action has jeopardised efforts to liberalise world trade as agreed at the WTO meeting in Doha in November 2001. The introduction of tariffs was in sharp contrast to the rosy atmosphere at the Doha meeting. The world economic outlook at that time was very gloomy in the wake of September 11 and an agreement was reached to launch new multilateral talks on international trade culminating in January 2005. There was agreement between the two biggest trading blocs in the world – the

USA and the EU and several bilateral trade disputes (such as bananas) seemed to have faded. Since then it has become clear that the effects of September 11 were not as catastrophic as at first thought and the economic outlook is brighter. Opponents of the American action argue that President Bush's main motivation in imposing these tariffs was to buy votes from certain key seats in the mid-term elections in November 2002.

It is further argued that the American action has jeopardised the very existence of the WTO. It has exempted Mexico and Canada who are both free trade partners of the USA. This therefore suggests that the USA regards bilateral trade agreements as more important than the multilateral agreements sought by the WTO. This sends a very worrying message to the rest of the world.

There is unlikely to be a swift resolution to this problem as at the time of writing, there was a bill about to be signed by President Bush which will give new subsidies to American farmers. This is problematic as liberalisation of agricultural products is one of the central themes of the Doha talks.

 For information on the work of the World Trade Organisation see *www.wto.org*

The European Union (EU)

The EU was established in 1958 by the Treaty of Rome. The six original members, France, West Germany, Italy, Holland, Belgium and Luxembourg, were joined in 1972 by the United Kingdom, Ireland and Denmark. Greece joined in 1981, followed by Spain and Portugal in 1986 and Austria, Finland and Sweden on 1 January 1995. These countries, along with the former East Germany, currently constitute the 15 member states of the Union, a number which is likely to grow further by the end of the decade. Many of the former Eastern bloc countries have applied to join, and negotiations were started in November 1998 over the formal accession of the first six of these – Poland, Hungary, Slovenia, Estonia, the Czech Republic and Cyprus. Other countries which are waiting to join could bring the number of member states to 27. The accession of these countries will bring fundamental changes to the nature of Europe (*see* case study at the end of this chapter).

 For information on the European commission see *http://europa.eu.int/comm/index_en.htm*
For European statistics see *http://europa.eu.int/comm/eurostat*

The primary aim of the Treaty of Rome was to create a 'common market' in which member states were encouraged to trade freely and to bring their economies closer together, ultimately culminating in the creation of a 'single market' within the Union. To bring this about, a protected free trade area or 'customs union' was established, which involved the removal of tariff barriers between member states and the institution of a common external tariff (CET) on goods from outside the Union. Institutional structures (*see* Chapter 3) and Union policies – most notably the common agricultural policy (CAP) – also contributed to this end and to the creation of a trading bloc of immense proportions. Within this bloc, member states were expected to gain numerous advantages, including increased trade and investment, huge economies of scale and improvements in productivity and cost reductions. To support the goal of increased trade and co-operation between community members, a European monetary system was established in 1979 in which a majority of member states undertook to fix their exchange rates within agreed limits (*see* below).

A significant step towards the creation of a single market – capable of competing effectively with the United States and Japan – was taken in 1986 when the then 12 community members signed the Single European Act. This Act established 31 December 1992 as the target date for the creation of a Single European market: an area (comprising the 12 EU countries) without internal frontiers, in which the free movement of goods, services, people and capital was to be ensured within the provisions contained in the Treaty. Among the measures for making the single market a reality were agreements on the following issues:

■ the removal or reduction in obstacles to cross-border travel and trade (e.g. customs checks);
■ the harmonisation or approximation of technical and safety standards on a large number of products;
■ closer approximation of excise duties and other fiscal barriers (e.g. VAT);
■ the removal of legal obstacles to trade (e.g. discriminatory purchasing policies);
■ the mutual recognition of qualifications.

In all, the overall programme has involved hundreds of changes to each country's national laws – a majority of which have now been introduced, though not always exactly as originally envisaged.

The benefits expected to flow from the creation of the single market can be viewed in both macro and micro terms. At the macro level, for instance, it was suggested by the Cecchini report that, at the worst, the new measures would increase the EU's gross domestic product by 4.5 per cent and would create 1.8 million jobs – a prediction, which, given the economic climate in the early 1990s, was rather ambitious.[1]

In micro terms, it is generally accepted that despite some additional costs for firms which have to implement the new requirements (e.g. safety standards), many businesses are likely to gain from increased trade and efficiency (e.g. through greater economies of scale), although this will vary between firms and across sectors within and between member states. Likely beneficiaries are those larger firms which have adopted a European approach to business development and have put in place structures and procedures to cope with the threats as well as the opportunities of the single market (e.g. by establishing joint ventures; by modifying personnel policies; by adapting marketing strategies; by modifying products). The sectors which arguably have the greatest potential are those where technical barriers are high or where a company has a distinct cost advantage over its rivals. In the United Kingdom, these would include the food and drink industry, pharmaceuticals, insurance and a number of other service industries.

Further steps in the development of the EU have come with the decision to establish a European Economic Area (EEA) – which permits members of the European Free Trade Area (EFTA) to benefit from many of the single market measures – and, in particular, from the Treaty on European Union, agreed by the 12 member states in December 1991 at Maastricht. Apart from the institutional changes mentioned in Chapter 3, the Maastricht Treaty contained provisions for:

- increased economic and monetary union between member states;
- a single currency;
- a social charter to protect workers' rights;
- a common foreign and security policy;
- community citizenship.

These various measures were scheduled to be introduced over a number of years, although in some cases – most notably the United Kingdom – specially negotiated 'opt-out' clauses have meant that some provisions have not been implemented simultaneously by all member states (e.g. the single currency; the social charter). Maastricht set out a three-stage plan towards Economic and Monetary Union (EMU):

Stage 1 – the creation of the single European market by January 1993.
Stage 2 – by January 1994, exchange rates to be fixed within narrow bands, inflation rates to be matched and targets set for government budget deficits and interest rates.
Stage 3 – an intergovernmental conference to be set for 1996 to review progress towards EMU and towards a single European currency.

European monetary union was finally achieved on 1 January 1999 with the creation of 'Euroland'. Eleven members of the EU are included – the UK, Denmark and Sweden chose not to participate, while Greece failed the convergence criteria for membership but has since joined in 2001. Euroland is effectively a single economic zone since it operates with a single currency – the Euro (*see* the text later in this chapter) and members have given up sovereignty over monetary policy, which is now to be determined by the European Central Bank. National sovereignty over fiscal policy has been retained, so there can be some differences in tax rates and government spending, but this is to operate in a framework of 'harmonisation'. The creation of Euroland enables increased specialisation across the whole of Europe and bigger economies of scale. Euroland embraces more than 300 million people and is responsible for one-fifth of the world's output and as such comes a close second to the USA as an economic superpower.

The UK has chosen not to join Euroland and the single currency until a referendum has been held. In 1997 the Chancellor of the Exchequer set out five economic tests of whether the UK should join Euroland or not. These are:

1 Are business cycles and economic structures of the UK and Euroland compatible and *sustainable*?
2 If problems emerge, is there sufficient flexibility to deal with them?
3 Would joining EMU encourage long-term investment in the UK?
4 What impact would it have on the competitive position of the UK's financial services industry?
5 Will joining EMU promote higher growth, stability and employment?

There is speculation among government sources that there will be a referendum in the UK in 2003. The Treasury has already embarked upon a thorough assessment of the five economic tests, which will be completed by the summer of 2003.

The balance of payments

The balance of payments is a record of the United Kingdom's international trade with other countries over a period of time, usually a year. It records the flows of money rather than goods, so that an import will be recorded as a negative amount since the money is flowing out of the country to pay for the good, and an export is recorded as a positive amount. Money flows into and out of the United Kingdom for two basic reasons: first, in exchange for goods and services (current transactions), and second, for investment purposes (capital transactions). These two flows are recorded separately in the UK balance of payments accounts which are produced by the government. Since 1992, when customs posts were abolished, balance of payment figures have been collected through Intrastat and are based on VAT returns.

For information on the balance of payments in the UK *see www.statistics.gov.uk*
For information on international trade see *www.oecd.org and www.wto.org*

Current transactions

The current account records the flows of money received and paid out in exchange for goods and services. It is subdivided into visible trade (the import and export of goods) and invisible trade (the import and export of services). Invisible trade includes:

1 Services like banking, insurance, tourism.
2 Interest, profits and dividends.
3 Transfers, which include grants to developing countries, payments to international bodies like the EU and private transfers such as gifts.

The balance of these flows on visible trade is called the balance of trade and the balance on the current account overall is called the current balance. It is to one of these balances that journalists and politicians are usually referring when they talk about the balance of payments. Table 13.4 shows the balance of payments for the United Kingdom in 2001. It can be seen that the balance of trade was –£33 048 million, the invisible balance was +£15 608 million and the current balance was –£17 440 million. More will be said later about the history of the balance of payments in the United Kingdom.

Capital transactions

As well as these current transactions there are flows of money for investment purposes. These include funds from both the public and private sectors and long-term and short-term monetary movements.

Long-term capital transactions include:

■ Overseas investment in the United Kingdom (e.g. purchase of shares, acquisition of real assets, purchase of government securities by non-residents).

The balance of payments 367

Table 13.4	**UK balance of payments, 2001 (£m)**	

Visible balance		−33 048
Invisible trade		
Services	11 703	
Interest, profits and dividends	11 151	
Transfers	−7246	
Invisible trade balance		15 608
Current account balance		−17 440
Capital account balance		1439
Financial account		
Direct investment	9960	
Equity capital		
Reinvested earnings		
Other capital transactions		
Portfolio investment	−51 214	
Equity securities		
Debt securities		
Financial derivatives	8432	
Other investments	49 592	
Reserve assets	3085	
Net transactions on financial account		19 855
Balancing item		−3854

Source: Adapted from www.statistics.gov.uk/statbase/tsdatset/asp?vlink=210&more=Y

- UK private investment overseas, where UK residents buy shares, acquire real assets, and so on, in overseas countries. The capital account does not include interest, dividends or profits but only flows of money for investment purposes. A capital transaction can give rise to a current flow in the future. If a non-resident bought shares in a UK company the initial amount would appear on the capital account. The resulting flow of dividends paid in the future would be recorded as a flow on the invisible account.
- Official long-term capital (i.e. loans from the UK government to other governments).

Short-term transactions include:

- Trade credit – as goods are often not paid for as they are received the physical export and import of goods is not matched with an inflow or outflow of money. In order that the balance of payments balances, these amounts would be included here as trade credit.
- Foreign currency borrowing and lending abroad by UK banks.
- Exchange reserves held by other countries and other organisations in sterling.
- Other external banking and money market liabilities in sterling.

These capital transactions are recorded in the UK balance of payments as changes from the previous year; they are not a record of all the transactions that have taken place over time. If money is flowing into the United Kingdom for investment purposes there is an increase in the UK liabilities and these are shown as positive amounts on the balance of payments. If money is flowing out of the country there is an increase in the UK assets and these are shown as negative amounts in the balance of payments.

Until 1986, capital flows to/from the private sector and capital flows to/from the public sector were shown in two separate accounts. In 1986 the format of the balance of payments was changed to show all capital transactions in one account under the heading of 'UK transactions in external assets and liabilities'. In 1998 the format of the balance of payments was changed once more to bring it into line with the standards published in the fifth edition of the IMF *Balance of Payments Manual*. The UK balance of payments now comprises three sections:

- the current account, as before;
- the capital account, which records capital transfers and transfers of non-financial assets into and out of the UK. As Table 13.4 shows, the balance on this account was £1439 million in 2001;
- the financial account, which gives the balance of trade in financial assets. This section of the balance of payments is itself subdivided between direct investment, portfolio investment, other investments and reserve assets. The balance on the financial account for 2001 was +£19 855 million.

Speculative flows of currencies would appear in the financial account of the balance of payments. Portfolio investment is the purchasing of shares in companies while direct investment is the setting up of subsidiaries. Reserve assets shows the change in official reserves – an increase in official reserves is shown as a negative amount and a decrease is shown as a positive amount.

The balance of payments overall should balance as negative flows will be balanced by positive flows. As this is often hard to understand two examples will be given.

Example 1

If a UK resident buys foreign goods there will be a negative entry in the current account equal to the value of those goods. That individual has to pay for those goods in foreign currency and could do this by using money from a foreign currency bank account if he or she has one, or by borrowing the foreign currency from a bank in that country. Either way there is an increase in the amount of liabilities and the same amount would be shown as a positive amount in the capital account.

Example 2

If a foreign investor purchased shares in a UK company, there would be a positive amount recorded in the capital account. The investor might pay for these shares by using sterling from a sterling bank account and so there would be an equal negative amount shown in the capital account.

The balance of payments should therefore always balance but invariably fails to do so, owing to errors and omissions in the recording process, and so a balancing item is included to ensure that it does. As can be seen from Tables 13.4 and 13.5, the balancing item can be very large, and this calls into question the accuracy of the figures.

Equilibrium in the balance of payments

If the balance of payments always balances how can there be a deficit on the balance of payments? The answer is that the media and politicians are referring to the current balance or the balance of trade rather than the overall balance of payments position. A balance of payments surplus on the current account is where the value of exports exceeds the value of imports. A deficit is where the value of imports exceeds the value of exports. As explained above, if there is a surplus on the current account, this will be matched by an outflow in the capital account, for example a reduction in the size of sterling bank balances, or an increase in official reserves. The opposite is true for a deficit. This implies that there cannot be a balance of payments problem; however, persistent surpluses or deficits on the current account are considered to be problematic. A persistent deficit has to be financed in some way, either through borrowing, to increase the external liabilities or by selling more of its assets. A deficit will also lead to pressure on the exchange rate, as will be shown later. A continued surplus is also a problem, since one country's surplus must mean that other countries are experiencing a deficit, and they will be faced with the problem of financing the deficit. Political pressure will be brought to bear, and there is the possibility of the introduction of tariffs or other import controls in order to reduce a deficit.

Methods of correcting balance of payments deficits

Since surpluses are not regarded as being such a problem as deficits, this section will concentrate on action needed to overcome a deficit, although the actions would be reversed for a surplus. When there is a current account deficit, the outflow of funds is greater than the inflow of funds from international trade. The authorities need to increase exports and/or reduce imports. Thus:

1 A fall in the exchange rate will have the double effect of making exports cheaper abroad and imports dearer at home, thus encouraging exports and discouraging imports. This will be explained fully later.
2 To increase exports British companies that produce for the export market could be subsidised. This would have the effect of reducing the price of UK goods abroad, making them more competitive.
3 Import controls could be imposed to restrict the level of imports coming in to the country.
4 A rise in the rate of interest would make Britain more attractive to investors and therefore increase capital flows into Britain and help offset the current account deficit.

The history of the balance of payments in the United Kingdom

Table 13.5 gives a summary of the balance of payments in the United Kingdom over the last ten years. The table shows that the current account was in deficit from 1991 until 1997, when it went into surplus for two years, and then went back into deficit in 1999. The weaknesses on the current account pre-date this and are somewhat hidden in the overall figures. The current account deficits started in 1987, the visible balance has been in deficit since 1983 (and still is) and within this the non-oil balance has been in deficit since 1982. This did not show in the overall current account figures until 1987 because of the offsetting effect of invisibles and oil. The

Table 13.5		UK balance of payments, 1991–2001 (£m)									
	1991	*1992*	*1993*	*1994*	*1995*	*1996*	*1997*	*1998*	*1999*	*2000*	*2001*
Visible balance	–10 223	–13 050	–13 319	–11 091	–11 724	–13 086	–11 910	–20 598	–27 524	–30 023	–33 048
Invisible balance	1849	2968	2701	9633	7979	12 486	18 213	22 072	8433	13 018	15 608
Current account	–8374	–10 082	–10 618	–1458	–3745	–600	6303	1474	–19 091	–17 005	–17 440
Capital account	290	421	309	33	534	736	837	438	808	1976	1439
Financial account	9990	5716	9447	–6082	937	1781	–8620	–9094	21 462	16 505	19 855
Balancing item	–1906	3945	862	7507	2274	–1917	1480	7182	–3179	–1476	–3854
Drawings on (+) or additions to (–) official reserves	–2679	1407	–698	–1045	200	510	2380	165	639	–3915	3085

Source: Adapted from www.statistics.gov.uk/statbase/tsdataset.asp?vlink=210&more=Y

United Kingdom's underlying weaknesses on the current account come from several sources:

1 Exports have risen but imports have risen faster. In the United Kingdom there is a high propensity to import goods.

2 The collapse of oil prices has reduced the value of the United Kingdom's oil exports.

3 The recession of the early 1980s left the UK manufacturing base in an extremely weak position. This means that it is difficult to produce enough goods for export or even to meet domestic demand, so the balance of payments has been hit from both directions. The changes in the structure of industry in the United Kingdom described in Chapter 9 have implications for the balance of payments, as services are less exportable than goods.

4 The consumer boom that occurred in the late 1980s after the Lawson budget of 1986 led to an increase in the level of imports.

5 The impact of oil has been twofold. First, as the United Kingdom is now an oil-exporting country it brings in revenue which will improve the balance of payments. Second, it has kept the exchange rate higher than it would have been, as will be shown in the next section, which makes UK goods less competitive in world markets and will therefore lead to a worsening of the balance of payments.

6 The high value of the pound in the late 1990s has hit the UK's export market.

7 The most recent deterioration is due to a fall in the level of non-European exports, especially to Asia and Russia.

The surpluses on the current account in 1997 and 1998 stemmed from good performances on invisibles – services and income on investments (interest, profits and dividends). Figure 13.1 shows the breakdown of the current account between the balance in goods, services and interest, profits and dividends. It is clear that in recent years the invisible balance has compensated for weak trade in goods and also that interest, profits and dividends have increased in importance within the invisible balance. According to the Office for National Statistics the surpluses in 1997 and 1998 were largely due to the huge losses made by foreign-owned banks in the City of London because of global financial turmoil. This had the effect of reducing the profits they sent out of the country compared with previous years. At the same time the overseas profits of British companies increased. Again this serves to hide in the overall figures a further deterioration in the visible balance which worsened to –£30 023 million in 2000.

Figure 13.1 Components of the current account, UK, 1990–2001

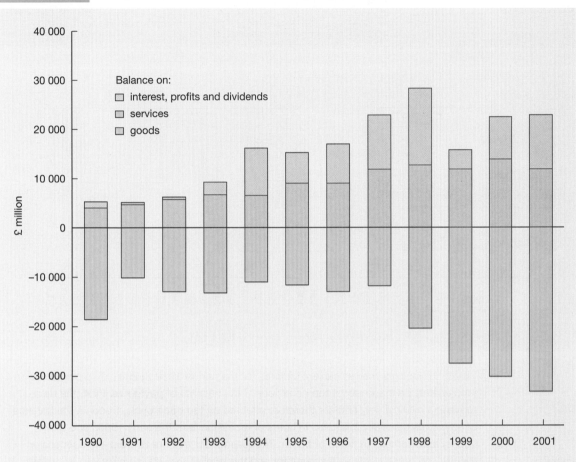

Source: Adapted from www.statistics.gov.uk/statbase/tsdataset.asp?vlink=210&more=Y

Mini case   The current account of the balance of payments

Figures on the balance of payments are produced every month by the government in the UK and are often seized upon by commentators as indications of either an improvement in the UK's economic performance or a deterioration, depending upon the details of the figures. There are a number of reasons why their observation is incorrect. First, balance of payments figures are notoriously unreliable, and are often revised by very large amounts. In June 1996, for example, the estimated deficit on the balance of payments for 1995 was revised from £6.7 billion to £2.9 billion because of the discovery of large investment flows. Second – and this applies to all short-term economic indicators – there are very short-term changes in economic variables which are not translated into long-term trends. So the balance of payments can vary quite dramatically each month due to short-term factors which are evened out over the course of the year. In addition, the balance of payments, like other indicators, often does not behave as expected. As late as December 1998, the Treasury was predicting a current account deficit of £1.75 billion, but higher than average investment income flows resulted in a surplus overall of £1.5 billion.

Figure 13.2 UK current balance, 1970–2001 (£ million)

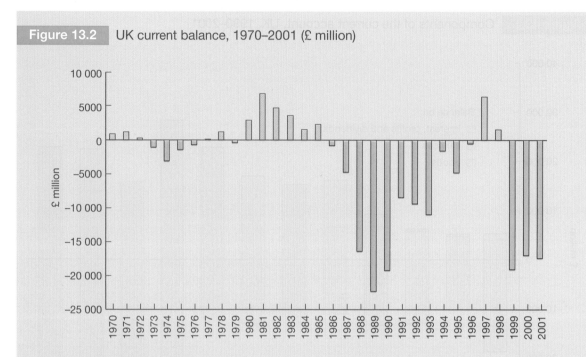

Source: Adapted from www.statistics.gov.uk/statbase/tsdataset.asp?vlink=210&more=Y

Figure 13.2 shows the UK current balance for the period 1970 to 2001. Two points can immediately be made about the behaviour of the balance of payments. First, the data move in a cyclical way and are therefore affected by the trade cycle. Second, the balance of payments generally improves in times of recession (e.g. the early 1980s and early 1990s) and worsens in times of boom. The reasons for this are twofold – in a recession the level of imports falls as income falls and the level of exports is unlikely to fall unless other countries are experiencing the same level of economic downturn. The balance of payments therefore improves. Usually the balance of payments improves enough in a recession to push it into surplus, although this did not happen in the early 1990s when the UK's current account remained in the red.

The unpredictability of the balance of payments is very evident in the figures for the 1990s. In 1994 the balance of payments improved, despite the recovery in economic conditions which would have been expected to worsen the balance of payments. This improvement continued in the late 1990s despite economic conditions which implied the opposite. The balance of payments should have suffered as a result of the high value of the pound and the economic turmoil in Asia and Russia. One possible explanation for the apparently contrary behaviour of the balance of payments is the J-curve effect (see Figure 13.7 on page 379). It could be that the improvement in the balance of payments in the mid-1990s was caused by the fall in the value of the pound after the UK left the ERM, even though that happened in 1992, because of the time lags involved. Similarly, the effects of the high value of the pound were not evident until 1999 onwards.

The deficit on the balance of payments in the UK in the last quarter of 2001 was the worst ever, mainly due to the global economic downturn after September 11. The two main contributors were the collapse in investment income abroad and the increase in direct payments to the EU. Commentators were surprised at the speed with which the balance of payments had been affected, although the UK was not as badly affected as other countries. If this trend continues into 2002 there will be pressure on the high value of the pound.

The multitude of factors which impact upon the balance of payments and the difficulties involved in accurate data collection make the balance of payments figures unreliable and very difficult to predict. The use of one month's figures by commentators to prove either that recovery is under way or that a recession is imminent is unsound.

Patterns of trade

Over time, patterns of trade change, for many reasons, Table 13.6 shows UK patterns of trade by destination/source and Table 13.7 shows UK trade by type of good. From these tables it is possible to look at how the country's patterns of trade have changed.

The most obvious change, as can be seen in Table 13.6, is that trade with the EU has become more important over the last 30 years while trade with the rest of western Europe has declined. In 2000 54 per cent of Britain's imports came from the EU and nearly 60 per cent of exports went to the EU. Despite this, the USA has remained important to Britain and has become more important both for imports and exports since 1990. There has been a decline in Britain's trade with other OECD countries over the whole period, although the importance of Japan within that group has increased, particularly with respect to imports. Britain's trade with the oil-exporting countries has declined in importance, as too has trade with the rest of the world, although this increased between 1990 and 2000. The rest of the world includes many of the old Commonwealth countries, which at one time were Britain's biggest markets.

Table 13.6 UK's imports and exports of goods by destination/source (%)

	1970		1980		1990		2000	
	Exports	Imports	Exports	Imports	Exports	Imports	Exports	Imports
European Union	32	32	46	44	53	52	59	54
Other W. Europe	13	12	12	12	9	13	4	6
United States	12	11	10	12	13	11	17	15
Other OECD countries of	11	10	6	7	5	7	6	8
which Japan	2	2	1	4	2	6	2	5
Oil-exporting countries	6	11	10	9	6	2	3	2
Rest of the world	18	14	12	11	10	10	12	16

Source: Adapted from Tables 18.5, 18.6, *Annual Abstract of Statistics*, various, Office for National Statistics, UK.

Table 13.7 Pattern of trade by type of good (%)

	1970		1990		2000	
	Exports	Imports	Exports	Imports	Exports	Imports
Food and animals	3	20	4	8	4	7
Beverages and tobacco	3	2	3	1	2	2
Crude materials except fuels	3	12	2	5	1	3
Minerals, fuels	3	14	8	7	6	3
Chemicals and related products	9	6	13	9	14	10
Manufactured goods	24	20	15	17	12	14
Machinery	43	19	41	38	48	46
Miscellaneous manufacturing	9	7	13	15	12	15
Total manufacturing	76	46	69	70	72	75
Others	3	2	2	1	1	1

Source: Adapted from Tables 18.4, 18.3, *Annual Abstract of Statistics*, various, Office for National Statistics, UK

Since 1970 the United Kingdom has been importing less food and fewer animals for consumption. The impact of oil can be seen in Table 13.7, as the quantities of oil-related products imported into the United Kingdom have fallen over the period. Manufacturing is clearly the most important category of good as far as the balance of payments is concerned. Manufacturing has retained its importance for exports, accounting for 76 per cent of exports in 1970 and 72 per cent in 2000. As far as imports are concerned, the percentage has increased a great deal over the last 30 years. The United Kingdom is now a net importer of manufactured goods. In 2000 the value of imported manufactured goods was £144 265 million, whereas the value of exported manufactured goods was £119 051 million. One reason for this is the increased import penetration in the United Kingdom. Table 13.8 shows import penetration in UK manufacturing for 1970, 1980, 1990, 1994 and 1996, from which it can be seen that the penetration has increased over this time period.

Table 13.8 Import penetration[a] in manufacturing in UK (%)

1970	1980	1990	1994	1996
16.6	26.2	36.7	50[b]	56

Notes: [a]Measured as $\dfrac{\text{import value}}{\text{home demand}} \times 100$

[b]New SIC definition

Source: *Annual Abstract of Statistics*, 1972, 1982, 1992, 1996, 1999.
Crown copyright. Reproduced by permission of the Controller of HMSO and of the Office for National Statistics, UK.

Exchange rates

The exchange rate of a currency is the price of that currency in terms of other currencies. If each country has its own currency and international trade is to take place an exchange of currencies needs to occur. When a UK resident buys goods from France, these must be paid for in euros. The individual will probably purchase euros from a bank in exchange for sterling in order to carry out the transaction. There must therefore be an exchange rate between sterling and euros. Likewise there will be exchange rates between sterling and all other currencies.

Basically, there are two types of exchange rate: the floating exchange rate; and the fixed exchange rate. There are also hybrid exchange rate systems which combine the characteristics of the two main types.

The floating exchange rate

A floating exchange rate is one that is determined within a free market, where there is no government intervention, and the exchange rate is free to fluctuate according to market conditions. The exchange rate is determined by the demand for and the supply of the currency in question.

As far as sterling is concerned, the demand for the currency comes from exports – that is, overseas residents buying pounds either to buy British goods and services or for investment purposes. The supply of pounds comes from imports – that is, UK residents who are buying foreign currencies to purchase goods and services or for investment purposes and who are therefore at the same time supplying pounds to the market.

The market for sterling can then be drawn using simple demand and supply diagrams. In Figure 13.3, the price axis shows the price of £1 in terms of US dollars and the quantity axis shows the quantity of pounds being bought and sold. The equilibrium exchange rate is determined by the intersection of demand and supply at £1 = $2. As this is a totally free market, if any of the conditions in the market change the exchange rate will also change.

Figure 13.3 The determination of the exchange rate of £ for $

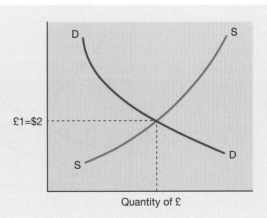

Quantity of £

The demand for and supply of sterling, and therefore the exchange rate, is affected by:

1 Changes in the balance of payments.
2 Changes in investment flows.
3 Speculation in the foreign exchange markets.

Changes in the balance of payments

Figure 13.4 shows the effect on the exchange rate of changes in the balance of payments. The original demand curve is DD and the original supply curve is SS. At the equilibrium exchange rate of £1 = $2 the demand for pounds is equal to the supply of pounds. In other words, if the demand for pounds comes from exports and the supply of pounds comes from imports, imports and exports are equal and the balance of payments is in equilibrium. Now it is assumed that a balance of payments deficit appears, caused by the level of imports rising while the level of exports stays the same. If exports remain the same there will be no change in the demand curve for pounds. As imports rise there will be a rise in the supply of pounds to the market; the supply curve moves to the right to S^1S^1. At the old exchange rate of £1 = $2, there is now excess supply of pounds, and as this is a free market there will be downward pressure on the value of the pound until equilibrium is re-established at the new lower exchange rate of £1 = $1. At this exchange rate the demand for pounds is again equal to the increased supply of pounds and the balance between imports and exports is re-established.

How does this happen? When the value of the pound falls two things happen: the price of imports rises and the price of exports falls. Thus the level of imports falls and the level of exports rises and the deficit is eradicated. A simple numerical example illustrates this point:

At old exchange rate £1 = $2:

An American car which costs $20 000 in USA costs £10 000 in UK.
A British car which costs £10 000 in UK costs $20 000 in USA.

| Figure 13.4 | The effect of changes in the balance of payments on the exchange rate |

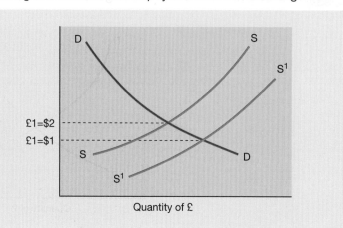

If the exchange rate falls to £1 = $1:

> The American car still costs $20 000 in USA but now costs £20 000 in UK.
> The British car still costs £10 000 in UK but now costs $10 000 in USA.

Therefore a depreciation in the exchange rate has made imports dearer (the American car) and exports cheaper (the British car). Thus a fall in the value of the pound helps to re-establish equilibrium in the balance of payments.

In the case of a surplus on the balance of payments, the exchange rate will rise, making exports more expensive and imports cheaper and thereby re-establishing equilibrium in the balance of payments. You should test your understanding of the working of the foreign exchange markets by working through what happens if a surplus develops.

A fall in the value of the pound in a free market is called a 'depreciation' in the value of the pound, a rise in its value is called an 'appreciation'.

Changes in investment flows

In Figure 13.5, the original equilibrium exchange rate is £1 = $2. If there is an increase in the level of investment in the UK from overseas, there will be an increase in the demand for pounds. The demand curve moves to the right (to D^1D^1), and the exchange rate rises to £1 = $2.5.

The effect of speculation

If the exchange rate of sterling is expected to rise, speculators will buy sterling in order to make a capital gain by selling the currency later at a higher exchange rate. There will be an increase in the demand for pounds and the exchange rate will rise. If the exchange rate is expected to fall, speculators will sell sterling in order to avoid a capital loss, there will be an increase in the supply of sterling and therefore a fall in the exchange rate. Illustrate these changes yourself using demand and supply diagrams.

Figure 13.5   The effect of changes in the investment flows on the exchange rate

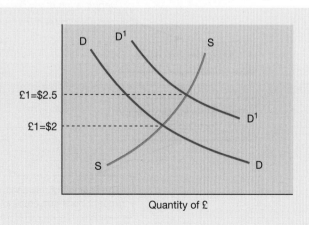

The important thing about speculation is that it tends to be self-fulfilling. If enough people believe that the exchange rate is going to rise and act accordingly, the exchange rate will rise.

The main advantage of the floating exchange rate is the automatic mechanism it provides to overcome a balance of payments deficit or surplus. Theoretically, if a deficit develops, the exchange rate will fall and the balance of payments is brought back into equilibrium. The opposite occurs in the case of a surplus. Of course in reality it does not work as smoothly or as quickly as the theory suggests. A depreciation is supposed to work as demonstrated in Figure 13.6.

There are, however, a number of problems which may occur to prevent this self-correcting mechanism working properly. First, if in the United Kingdom the goods which are imported are necessities that cannot be produced at home, then even if their price goes up as a result of a depreciation, they will continue to be demanded. Thus, not only will the balance of payments deficit not be automatically rectified, another economic problem will result, that of inflation. The United Kingdom will continue to buy the imported goods at the new higher price. A second problem occurs on the other side of the equation. It is assumed above that, as the price of exports falls, more exports are sold. This presupposes that in the United Kingdom the capacity is there to meet this increased demand, but this may not be the case, especially if the economy is fully employed already or if the export-producing industries are not in a healthy enough state to produce more.

These problems give rise to what is called the 'J-curve effect'. A fall in the exchange rate may well lead to a deterioration in the balance of payments in the short term, until domestic production can be increased to meet the extra demand for exports and as substitutes for imported goods. Once this can be done there will be an improvement in the balance of payments, hence the J-curve effect pictured in Figure 13.7. The effect of a fall in the exchange rate is limited and the curve levels off after a certain time period. The depreciation in the value of the pound seen

Figure 13.6   The effect of depreciation

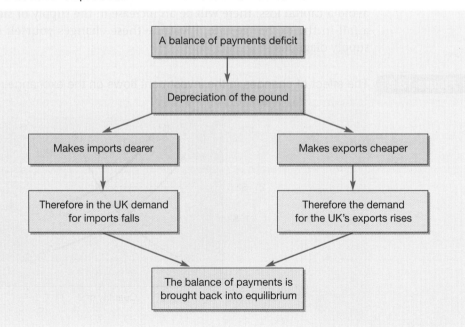

Figure 13.7   J–curve

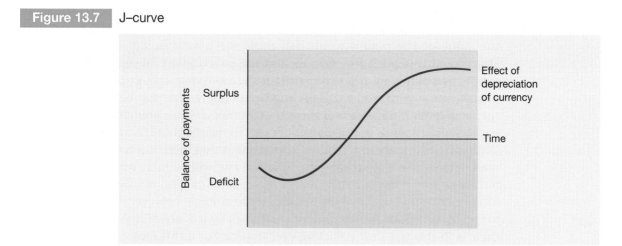

when Britain left the ERM did not have an immediate effect on the balance of payments and many argued that this was due to the J-curve effect.

One big disadvantage of the floating exchange rate is that it introduces uncertainty into the market, and for firms that operate internationally, this is another variable which needs to be considered when planning. Moreover, since the possibility of speculation exists with the floating exchange rate, this can be destabilising and unsettling to markets, something which businesses do not welcome.

The fixed exchange rate

The fixed exchange rate is one that is fixed and maintained by the government. An exchange rate can be fixed in terms of other currencies, gold or a basket of other currencies. In order to maintain a fixed exchange rate the government has actively to intervene in the market, either buying or selling currencies.

Figure 13.8 shows the action needed by the UK authorities in the case of downward pressure on the value of the pound. The exchange rate is fixed at £1 = $2, and the government wants to maintain that rate. If a balance of payments deficit

Figure 13.8   The effect of changes in the balance of payments on a fixed exchange rate

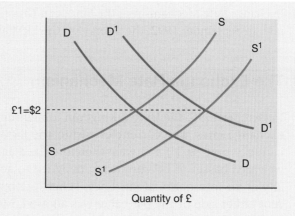

develops, brought about by an increase in imports, exports remaining the same, there will be excess supply of pounds at the fixed exchange rate. In a free market the value of the pound would fall until the excess supply had disappeared. However, this is not a free market, and the government must buy up the excess supply of pounds in order to maintain the exchange rate at £1 = $2. Thus the demand curve moves to the right and the exchange rate has been maintained at the same level. Alternatively if there is excess demand for pounds, the government has to supply pounds to the market in order to maintain the fixed exchange rate.

A prime advantage of a fixed exchange rate is that there is less uncertainty in the market; everyone knows what the exchange rate will be in a year's time, and long-term planning is made easier. It also reduces the likelihood of speculation in the foreign exchange markets. One serious disadvantage, however, is that there is no longer an automatic mechanism for rectifying any balance of payments problems as there is in the case of the floating exchange rate and this means that government intervention is necessary not just to support the exchange rate, but also to overcome any balance of payments problems. Added to this, a fixed exchange rate is not sustainable in the case of persistent deficits or surpluses. In the event of a surplus, the government must supply pounds to the market and if the surplus persists then eventually the government will exhaust its reserves and might well have to revalue the pound (i.e. increase the exchange rate of the pound). In the case of a persistent deficit, the size of the government's reserves will be increasing over time and the government may have to devalue the pound to correct the problem.

There are, then, advantages and disadvantages to both types of exchange rate and there have been hybrid exchange rate systems which serve to combine the advantages of both systems. In such an exchange rate system the exchange rate is basically fixed but is allowed to fluctuate by a small amount either side of the central value. The Exchange Rate Mechanism (ERM) of the European Union was an example of this. When the United Kingdom entered the ERM the exchange rate was fixed against other member currencies but allowed to vary by 6 per cent either side of the central value before action was needed.

Over the years the United Kingdom has had a variety of different types of exchange rate. Before the First World War and for some time between the wars, the exchange rate was fixed in terms of gold – the gold standard. From the Second World War until 1972, the United Kingdom was part of the Bretton Woods system of fixed exchange rates, where the pound was fixed in terms of dollars. Then from 1972 to 1990, there was a floating exchange rate. In 1990, however, Britain joined the Exchange Rate Mechanism of the European Union, which was again a fixed exchange rate. In September 1992, the pound left the ERM and was allowed to float once more.

The Exchange Rate Mechanism

In October 1990, the United Kingdom joined the ERM, which was a system of fixed exchange rates. The currencies within the ERM were fixed against the European currency unit (ECU) and were therefore fixed against one another. The ECU was a weighted basket of EU currencies, designed to act as a unit of account and eventually as an international currency. When the pound entered, a variation of 6 per cent either side of the par value was allowed. Most other European countries were allowed only a 2.25 per cent fluctuation either side of their central values. The understanding was that the United Kingdom would eventually go to 2.25 per cent fluctuation and in the end all European currencies would be completely fixed against one another. Table 13.9 shows the central exchange rates of the pound against other ERM currencies at the time Britain joined the ERM.

The essence of the ERM was that it provided a means of stabilising the exchange rates of participating member states. If the pound, for instance, strayed too far from its central rate the Bank of England and other central banks of ERM members would buy or sell currencies in order to stabilise the exchange rate. Each member held reserves in the European Co-operation Fund in order to settle debts between countries, and these funds could be used to stabilise currencies. Another thing that could be done to help an ailing currency was to change the domestic rate of interest. If the pound's exchange rate fell towards its lower limit, an increase in the rate of interest would make the United Kingdom a more attractive place for investors and therefore increase the demand for pounds. If both of these approaches failed, there could be a realignment of the currencies within the ERM. This happened from time to time, but such realignments were against the spirit of the fixed exchange rate, and countries were expected to avoid this if possible.

Britain's reasons for entering the ERM in 1990 were as follows:

- To enjoy the benefits of fixed exchange rates and, in particular, less uncertainty and reduced speculation.
- As part of the government's anti-inflationary stance, since the discipline of the ERM would force the United Kingdom's rate of inflation towards the lower European average.
- As part of Britain's commitment to Europe, the Maastricht Treaty and the Delors plan called for economic and monetary union between the countries of the EU.

Figure 13.9 shows the fluctuations in sterling's exchange rate since joining the ERM. The exchange rate of the pound was much more stable while the UK was a member of the ERM, but sterling ran into problems in mid-1992, mainly as a result of speculation against the pound. The Bank of England intervened in the market but was unable to stop the fall in the value of the currency. An increase in interest

Table 13.9 Central exchange rates of the pound against other ERM currencies, October 1990

	Exchange rate
Belgian franc	60.85
Danish kroner	11.25
French franc	9.89
German Deutschmark	2.95
Irish punt	1.10
Italian lira	2,207.25
Luxembourg franc	60.85
Dutch guilder	3.32
Spanish peseta	191.75

Note: Estimate of the pound's effective limits against the Deutschmark: 2.77–3.13 DM.

Figure 13.9   Exchange rate of sterling with the Deutschmark

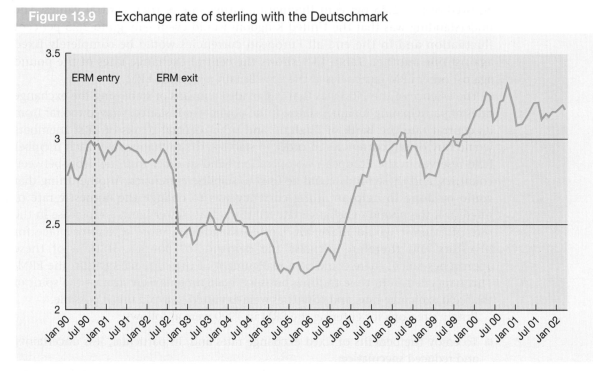

Source: Adapted from: www.statistics.gov.uk/statbase/tsdataset.asp?vlink=210&more=Y

rates was announced but then withdrawn very quickly because of political pressures and the effect such a move would have on UK industry in the midst of recession. In the end the pound was suspended from the ERM and allowed to float, and has since fallen in value sharply.

Since mid-1996 there has been a fairly dramatic rise in the value of sterling against the Deutschmark. This has been attributed to two main factors:

- The impending European Economic and Monetary Union and the introduction of the Euro have produced a great deal of uncertainty on the markets. This has resulted in an increase in the demand for sterling as a relatively safe and known currency.
- Short-term interest rates have been higher in the UK than elsewhere and this has resulted in increased capital flows into the UK.

 For information on exchange rates see *www.bankofengland.co.uk*

The single European currency

On 1 January 1999 the single European currency – the euro – was introduced. In order to qualify for membership of the single currency, EU members had to fulfil strict convergence criteria with respect to inflation rates, budget deficits and the rates of interest.[2] In the end all countries qualified except Greece, where there were problems with high inflation rates. The UK, Denmark and Sweden decided not to join the single currency, so Euroland comprised 11 members. Greece has since joined. Each of the currencies of these members is fixed to the euro at a specified rate, but each is a sub-unit of the euro rather than a separate currency.

Initially the euro was only a paper and electronic currency. Financial and government transactions took place in the new currency, but the only currency in circulation was national currencies. Although UK membership is still in abeyance, it is already possible to open euro bank accounts, and UK banks and building societies are offering euro savings accounts and mortgages. Euro notes and coins were put into circulation on 1 January 2002 and circulated alongside national currencies until 28 February 2002, after which national currencies ceased to be legal tender. There are euro-cent coins in 1, 2, 10, 20 and 50-cent denominations, plus 1 and 2 euro coins. Notes are currently in denominations of 5, 10, 20, 50, 100, 200 and 500 euros.

The changeover on 1 January 2002 was remarkably smooth, given the scale of the operation – €132 billion worth of notes and €37.5 billion worth of coins were put into circulation. Banks only dispensed euros and shops only gave change in euros, so that while only euros were being put into circulation national currencies were being withdrawn. There were a few glitches, for example in Gran Canaria in March 2002 there was still a shortage of small change and many tourist amenities like coin-operated TVs and pool tables were still accepting only pesetas. There was little evidence of the expected increase in inflation brought about by some organisations trying to profit out of the changeover by increasing prices, although there have been some examples of this. In fact, the shortage of small change in Gran Canaria led to many shops and supermarkets offering a discount for payment by cheque or card.

The smoothness of the transition was made possible by the gradual phasing in of the euro over the three years prior to 2002. Companies had already started to publish their accounts in euros and have been trading in euros for some time, share prices have been quoted in euros for the past three years and prices in shops have been shown in local currencies and euros. The euro had already been in existence for three years prior to its introduction into circulation.

Even though the UK has not joined the single currency, many businesses in the UK have already adapted to its existence. Many large companies are using the euro for accounting purposes – Marks and Spencer stores are fully equipped to accept the euro. Even without entry, preparation is necessary for practical reasons, since many large companies have started to invoice and pay bills in euros – computer systems will have to be adapted to allow for this. There will also be a cost involved in the UK as banks are charging fairly high commission for converting euros, particularly for small users. Preparation is also a strategic issue for business. First, EMU will result in greater competition, as price differences will be more obvious to consumers. The cost of converting currencies serves to increase the costs of UK businesses and make them less competitive. Second, EMU will probably result in more mergers and acquisitions across Europe and this will have dramatic effects on the structures of industries.

In the UK the debate over the single European currency continues. The pro single currency camp claims that the UK will be further marginalised in Europe if it does not join in the single currency. It also argues that there are great benefits to membership – a reduction in transaction costs like the cost of currency exchange, a reduction in the uncertainty caused by changing exchange rates, lower interest rates and the continuance of London as a financial centre in currencies. The anti camp argues just as vociferously that all of this would be at the expense of the loss of sovereignty – the UK would be unable to change its exchange rate in order to boost the competitiveness of UK goods. In addition to this, there is also the high value of the pound against the euro to consider. In March 2002, €1 was worth 62p, which represents a 13 per cent fall in the value of the euro since January 1999. Many commentators believe entry into the single currency at the current exchange rate would be disastrous and that until the value of the pound falls entry should not be contemplated.

The performance of the euro since its birth has not been very impressive. Figure 13.10 shows the value of the euro against sterling since January 1999 when €1 was worth 70p. The fall in the value of the euro is mainly down to the widespread gloom about the performance of the European economy. In addition, it is felt by many that the ECB has made some dubious decisions regarding rate of interest changes.

There are a number of problems brewing in Europe. First, many economic commentators have identified the imposition of a single interest rate across Europe as a problem – the growing Irish economy, for example, could bear a higher interest rate while the shrinking German economy could not. Second, member countries have to act to reduce the size of their budget deficit if it exceeds 3 per cent of GDP. Again this might be acceptable in a booming economy but not in an economy heading for recession. The members most likely to have problems with this policy in the future are France, Germany, Italy and Portugal. Third, the accession of new countries to the EU (*see* case study) might have unforeseen effects on the EMU.

Figure 13.10 Exchange rate of the euro with sterling

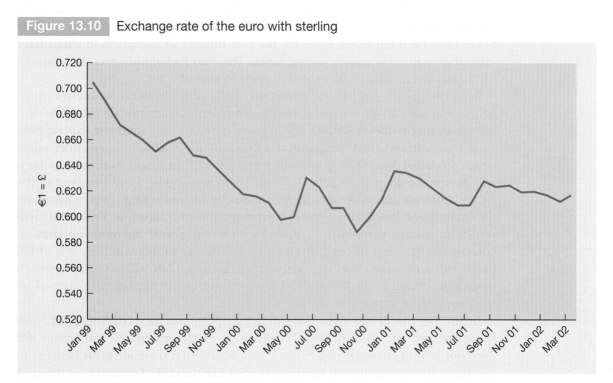

Source: Adapted from www.bankofengland.co.uk/Links/setframe.html

Exchange rates and business

Reference has already been made to the fact that changes in exchange rates can affect businesses in several ways. These would include:

- making it easier or harder to export (as prices change);
- making it easier or harder for foreign competitors to penetrate the domestic market (again through the price effect);
- causing uncertainty in both trading and investment terms;
- adding to or reducing the cost of imported raw materials and component parts.

In addition, if a falling exchange rate causes inflationary pressures within the economy, this could add to a firm's production costs (e.g. through higher wage bills) and could encourage the government to introduce counter-inflationary policies which might subsequently depress demand in the home market.

For businesses regularly involved in currency dealing and/or multinational activities, changing currency values can also bring other gains or losses. Shell and Allied Lyons, for example, lost over £100 million each on currency gambles in the early 1990s by entering into deals when the exchange rate between currencies was not fixed in advance. In contrast, Unilever's record profits for the financial year 1992/93 included substantial overseas earnings, some of which were the direct result of a weaker pound, which in turn, meant that remitted profits increased when converted back into sterling. Clearly the introduction of a single European currency will impact upon such gains or losses.

Synopsis

This chapter has looked at the international marketplace and, in particular, the benefits that derive from international trade. Consideration has also been given to some of the restrictions that exist to free trade and the organisations that are active in promoting it. Patterns of trade in the United Kingdom have been examined, as well as a recent history of the balance of payments position. Finally, exchange rates were covered, including an analysis of how businesses are affected by changes in the value of currencies.

Summary of key points

- International trade takes place because it increases the output of the whole world.

- Despite this there are restrictions to international trade which include tariffs and quotas, but there are international organisations which seek to limit these and promote free trade.

- The balance of payments is a record of one country's trade with other countries.

- A balance of payments deficit is a situation where imports are greater than exports, a balance of payments surplus is the opposite, where exports are greater than imports.

- The exchange rate is the price of one currency in terms of another.

- A floating exchange rate is determined by the free market, a fixed exchange rate is determined by the government or some other authority.

- The euro is a single currency introduced into circulation in January 2002 by the members of Euroland.

- The EU is currently involved in negotiations with 13 possible new members.

CASE STUDY   European Union enlargement

The European Union has gone through four enlargements, increasing its initial membership of six countries in 1957 to fifteen members in 1999. The reasons for the establishment of the EU are well documented in this chapter and they provide the rationale for the enlargement of the EU. When communism collapsed in 1989 the EU pledged to allow the countries of Eastern Europe to join – to spread peace, prosperity and stability. It looks as though fulfilment of that pledge is near.

In 1997 the European Commission recommended that entry talks should be started early in 1998 with the first tranche of countries wishing to join the EU. The applicants were divided into two groups, depending on their ability to meet the conditions set down for entry. The 'early joiners' comprise ten countries – Cyprus, the Czech Republic, Estonia, Hungary, Latvia, Lithuania, Malta, Poland, Slovakia and Slovenia. The 'lagging group', who were deemed to need more information and time to meet the conditions of entry, include Bulgaria, Romania and Turkey. Turkey has been acknowledged as an applicant but negotiations have not yet started because of concerns about its human rights record. Discussions started in March 1998 and initially the date of 2002 was put forward as a likely date for accession of the first wave of countries. However, the earliest date now regarded as possible is 2004.

The benefits arising from the enlargement of the EU include:

1 *Political stability*. Expansion of the EU gives European leaders the chance to bring political stability to Europe and end the divisions which twice during the twentieth century ended in war. Membership of the EU will help to entrench the new-found democracies of the former communist countries in Eastern Europe.

2 *Economic benefits*. The admission of the first wave of ten countries will increase the size of the population of the EU by about 30 per cent. This will enhance the EU's position as a major trading bloc in the world.

Figure 13.11   A map of Europe

The admission of new members will fundamentally change the EU. Figure 13.12 shows the GDP per person of the new applicants and existing members of the EU.

GDP per head in all of the applicants is lower than the EU average, and it is estimated that admission of the first ten will increase the size of GDP in the EU by only 5 per cent. The average GDP per head will fall by around 16 per cent in terms of purchasing power. Accession of these countries to the EU will lead to changes in the distribution of both regional and agricultural aid, which together account for around 80 per cent of the EU's budget. Given that the newcomers are mostly poorer than existing members and have large agricultural sectors, there are important financial implications.

The distribution of regional aid

This has implications for both richer and poorer members alike. On present EU rules nearly all of the new Eastern European members would qualify for regional aid. This will either mean a huge increase in the EU budget or a redistribution of

Figure 13.12 GDP per head for selected countries, ECU, 2000

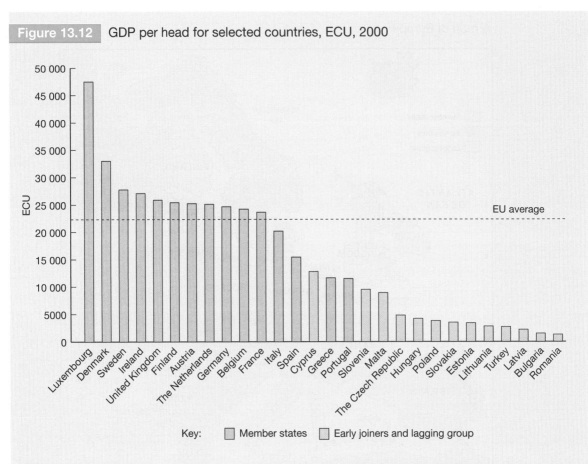

Key: ☐ Member states ☐ Early joiners and lagging group

Source: Adapted from www.oecd.ord/EN/document/O,,EN-document-O-nodirectorate-no-1-9066-o,oo.html#title1

the existing budget away from the poor areas in the west. For net contributors to the EU budget, like Germany and the UK, it might mean increased payments to the EU and for net beneficiaries, like Spain and Portugal, it might lead to a reduction in their share of regional aid or result in them becoming net contributors. To address this, the EU has ruled that members will not receive regional aid in excess of 4 per cent of their GDP. For the Eastern European countries this severely curtails the amount of aid they can receive and means that poorer areas of Western Europe can still receive aid.

The Common Agricultural Policy

The proposed expansion of the EU would bring in countries with large, inefficient agricultural sectors – for example in Poland 20 per cent of the population is engaged in agricultural production. Proposals announced in 2002 attempt to deal with this problem by entitling new members to only 25 per cent of the subsidies received by existing members, although the figure will rise to 100 per cent within 10 years. It is hoped that when a new budget is set by the EU in 2006 this problem can be resolved. As can be imagined, these proposals have not been well accepted by the potential entrants.

These changes are seen as necessary steps to keep down the costs of accession but are seen as unfair by many of the potential entrants. They argue that the spirit of the EU requires that there should be one rule which applies to all and that the new proposals discriminate against newcomers. Although these are the two main problems brought up by accession, there are others under discussion, like how these countries can introduce and oversee changes in their laws required by membership of the EU, whether and when they should join the euro and relations with Russia (especially important to the Baltic states).

The discussions so far

Negotiations have started with all countries except Turkey. Many of the potential entrants have done well in working towards the entrance criteria but glitches remain. Malta and Estonia, for example, have progressed well in their discussions but both countries have Euro-sceptic populations. Poland, although a large and important applicant, has too large an agricultural sector and there is disquiet among farmers about the changes in EU rules. Discussions with Cyprus have been hampered by the division of the island – it does not seem possible that the Greek half of the island could be admitted without the Turkish half and so that will cause problems with Turkey. Nevertheless, discussions continue and although the EU is not being specific about the date of accession it talks about a 'big bang' increase in membership when all ten early joiners will join at the same time. It is possible this might take place in 2004 although many still regard 2005 as the likely date.

Questions on the case study

1 What are the main *economic* benefits to existing members of enlarging the EU?

2 What are the main economic benefits to the applicants of joining the EU?

For information on the enlargement of the European Union see
http://europa.eu.int/comm/enlargement/index.htm

Review and discussion questions

1 For a business considering expansion into Europe, what methods of expansion are available?

2 Using demand and supply diagrams, show the effect on the market for foreign exchange of the following:
   (a) a decreased level of imports;
   (b) a fall in the rate of interest; and
   (c) the development of a balance of payments surplus.

▶

3 What is the likely effect on a system of fixed exchange rates of continued speculation in one of the member currencies?

4 Explain why businesses generally prefer fixed rather than floating rates of exchange.

5 How might the US government help its ailing steel industry without resorting to trade sanctions?

Assignments

1 You work in a local chamber of commerce and have been asked to make a presentation to its members on the arguments for and against UK membership of the single European currency. The audience is likely to be mixed in its attitude to the single European currency. Prepare the presentation, anticipating and answering any possible questions the audience might have.

2 You work for a trade union in the hosiery industry which strongly supports the use of import restrictions to protect its workers from competition from countries where wage rates are much lower. You have been asked to take part in a debate on the issue by the local Conservative MP, who is a champion of the free market. Present a set of arguments that will counter any points that your opponent is likely to make.

Notes and references

1 Cecchini, P., *The European Challenge 1992: The Benefits of a Single Market*, Widwood House, Aldershot, 1988.

2 See the 2nd edition of this book, Chapter 13.

Further reading

Ellis, J. and Williams, D., *International Business Strategy*, Pitman Publishing, 1995.

Griffiths, A. and Wall, S., *Applied Economics: An Introductory Course*, 9th edition, Financial Times/Prentice Hall, 2001.

Worthington, I., Britton, C. and Rees, A., *Business Economics: Blending Theory and Practice*, Financial Times/Prentice Hall, 2001.

Web links and further questions are available on the website at:
www.booksites.net/worthington

14

Governments and markets

Ian Worthington

The central role played by government in the operation of the economy and
its markets has been a recurrent theme of this book. Paradoxically, many of
the government's interventionist policies have been designed to remove
existing barriers to the operations of free markets and to promote greater
competition and choice. In some cases, the government's strategy has
been to disengage the state from some of its involvement in the economy –
as in the case of 'privatisation'. In other cases, policy changes and legislation have been deemed the appropriate course of action – as in the
government's approach to competition policy and to the operation of the
labour market.

Objectives

- To outline the rationale underlying the government's approach to markets.

- To analyse UK privatisation policy and give examples of privatisation in
  other countries.

- To examine the changing nature of UK competition policy, including the
  legislative and institutional framework within which it operates.

- To survey government initiatives on the labour market and, in particular,
  its approach to employment and trade union power.

Key terms

Competition Act 1998	Keynesianism	Office of Fair Trading
Competition Commission	Labour market	Privatisation
Competition policy	Labour market flexibility	Third way
Director General of Fair	Learning and Skills Council	Training and Enterprise
Trading	Monetarism	Councils
Economic efficiency	New Deal	

Introduction

A belief in the virtue of competition and in the need to develop competitive markets remains a central tenet of government economic policy in capitalist states. At the heart of this belief lies the widely accepted view that competition provides the best means of improving economic efficiency and of encouraging wealth creation. Proponents of this view argue that competition:

■ ensures an efficient allocation of resources between competing uses, through the operation of the price system;
■ puts pressure on firms to perform as efficiently as possible;
■ provides a mechanism for flexible adjustment to change, whether in consumption or in the conditions of supply;
■ protects consumers from potential exploitation by producers, by offering alternative sources of purchase.

It follows that an absence or lack of competition in either the factor or product markets is seen as detrimental to the well-being of the economy as a whole and that governments have a responsibility for ensuring wherever possible that markets operate freely, with a minimum of state interference.

Much of the philosophical basis for this perspective can be traced to the 'monetarists' who have tended to dominate official thinking in Britain and elsewhere for much of the last two decades. Broadly speaking, monetarists argue that levels of output and employment in the economy are supply-determined, in contrast to the 'Keynesian' view which emphasises the importance of demand in shaping economic activity. Accordingly, supply-side policies seek to improve the output responsiveness of the economy, by focusing on the workings of markets and in particular on removing the obstacles which prevent markets from functioning efficiently.

The influence of the supply-side approach to economic management can be seen in a number of key areas, and in particular, in the UK government's policy of privatisation and in the reforms in the labour market in the 1980s. Concerns over competition and potential abuses of market power also figure prominently in governmental approaches to monopolies and mergers. These three aspects of government intervention in markets – privatisation, competition policy and labour market reforms – are considered separately below and illustrate how state involvement can be a key influence in the environment of individual business organisations on both the input and output side.

Privatisation policy

On privatisation

In its broadest sense, 'privatisation' involves the transfer of assets or different forms of economic activity from the public sector to the private sector. In the United Kingdom such transfers occurred throughout the 1980s and 1990s under different

Conservative administrations. Although the current Labour government has continued the process to some degree (e.g. with the partial privatisation of the National Air Traffic Services), the heyday of huge state sell-offs in Britain has probably passed. In government circles the talk is now of public/private partnerships as a mechanism for increasing private sector investment in the public services – part of what has become known as the 'third way' in British politics.

In practice, the term 'privatisation' has been applied to a range of activities that involve a measure of state disengagement from economic activity. Typically these have included:

- The sale of government-owned assets, especially nationalised industries (e.g. British Telecom, British Gas) or industries in which the government had a substantial shareholding (e.g. BP).
- The contracting out of services normally provided by the public sector (e.g. school meals, hospital cleaning).
- The deregulation or liberalisation of activities over which the state had previously placed some restriction (e.g. the deregulation of bus routes or postal services).
- The injection of private capital into areas traditionally financed by the public sector (e.g. the road system).
- The sale of local authority-owned property to private citizens or organisations (e.g. council houses, school playing fields).
- The privatisation of government agencies (e.g. Her Majesty's Inspectors for Education).

Of these, the sale of state assets – especially the public corporations and nationalised industries – has been the main plank of UK privatisation policy and the one which has captured the most public and media attention. For this reason, in the discussion below attention is focused on this aspect of the privatisation programme.

The scope of government asset sales in the period 1979–96 is indicated in Table 14.1. In the first phase, between 1979 and 1983, these tended to generate relatively small sums of money compared with what was realised in later years and generally involved the sale of government shares in companies such as British Aerospace, Britoil, BP, ICL and Ferranti. Between 1983 and 1988, the government disposed of a

Table 14.1   Major asset sales, 1979–1996

Amersham International	British Telecom	National Grid
Associated British Ports	Britoil	Railtrack
British Aerospace	Cable & Wireless	Rolls-Royce
British Airports Authority	Electricity industry	Rover Group
British Airways	Enterprise Oil	Royal Ordnance
British Coal	Fairey Aviation	Sealink (British Rail)
British Energy	Ferranti	Short Brothers
British Gas	Forestry Commission	Unipart (Rover)
British Petroleum	Istel (Rover)	Water authorities
British Rail Hotels	Jaguar (British Leyland)	Wytch Farm onshore oil (British Gas)
British Steel	National Bus Company	
British Sugar Corporation	National Enterprise Board Holding	

number of its largest industrial and commercial undertakings, including British Telecom, British Gas and British Airways, along with Rolls-Royce and Jaguar. These were followed by the sale of British Steel, the Rover Group, the National Bus Company and, more significantly, by the regional water authorities and the electricity industry in the late 1980s and early 1990s.[1] In the most recent phase, major sales have included British Coal, Railtrack, the flotation of the National Grid, and the privatisation of the nuclear industry. It is worth noting that Railtrack has recently gone through a period of administration and has subsequently been turned into a not-for-profit organisation.

In disposing of national assets governments have used a number of different methods, including selling shares to a single buyer, usually another company (e.g. the sale of Rover), selling shares to the company's management and workers (e.g. the management buyout of the National Freight Corporation), and selling shares on the open market for purchase by individuals and institutions (e.g. the stock market flotation of British Telecom). In some cases the process took place in several stages, as a proportion of shares was released on to the market over several years (e.g. BP); in other cases a one-off sale occurred, with investors invited to subscribe for the whole of the equity (e.g. British Steel). As Figure 14.1 indicates, proceeds from privatisation sales between 1979 and 1991 exceeded £34 billion, with the majority of the revenue being raised in the mid- to late 1980s. Estimates for the period 1991–4 suggest that privatisation yielded a further £25–£30 billion for the Exchequer. According to the Office of National Statistics, between 1984 and 1996 privatisation revenues were equal to around 1–2 per cent per annum of GDP.

Figure 14.1 Proceeds from privatisation

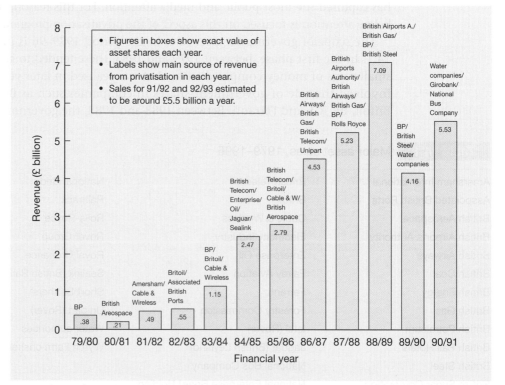

Source: Cook, G. C., *Privatisation in the 1980s and 1990s*, Hidcote Press, 1992.

Rationale

The roots of privatisation policy lie in the attempt by the Conservative government, then under the leadership of Margaret Thatcher (1979–90), to tackle the perceived deficiencies in the supply side of the UK economy. Central to the government's philosophy was the belief that the free market was a superior method of allocating economic resources and that large-scale state involvement in business activity hampered economic progress. 'Rolling back the frontiers of the state' – by reducing the size of the public sector – was consequently seen as a key component in improving the country's economic performance at both national and international level.

The government's case for privatisation centred round the claim that the sale of state-owned businesses would improve their efficiency and general performance, and would give rise to increased competition that would broaden consumer choice. Under state control, it was argued that businesses had no incentive to strive for efficiency or to respond to consumer preferences, since many of them lacked any direct competition and all of them could turn to government for financial support, if revenue was insufficient to meet operating costs. In contrast, firms which were exposed to the 'test' of the market would have to satisfy both the consumer and the financial markets if they were to survive or to avoid takeover by more efficient and competitive organisations.[2]

Allied to this argument was the proposition that privatisation would improve the performance of an organisation's management and workers. Freed from the need to meet objectives laid down by government, management could concentrate on commercial goals such as profitability, improved productivity and cost reduction, and on encouraging greater flexibility and technical innovation within the organisation. Implicit in these claims was the acceptance that a considerable degree of restructuring would need to occur within each privatised company and that this was likely to act as an incentive to the workforce to improve its performance. Additional encouragement was also expected to derive from the use of employee share-ownership schemes, under which current employees within a newly privatised company were offered a proportion of the equity, thus giving them a vested interest in the organisation's fortunes.

The sale of shares to employees and to the public generally was also presented as a benefit of privatisation in that it helped to encourage wider share ownership and to create a 'share-owning democracy', with increased sympathies towards capitalist modes of production (and possibly the Conservative party). Concomitantly, the sale of state assets also served to reduce the size of the public sector borrowing requirement (PSBR) – since revenue from sales was counted as negative public expenditure – and this helped to reduce the government's debt burden and to take some of the pressure off interest rates, as well as releasing funds for use by the private sector.

Criticisms of privatisation

Opponents of privatisation have likened the process to 'selling the family silver' – disposing of important national assets for short-term financial gains. Under privatisation, these assets, once owned by the general public, pass into the hands of those individuals and organisations able and willing to buy shares and this includes overseas buyers who could ultimately gain control of important parts of British industry, unless prevented from doing so by government action (e.g. through a 'golden share'). To add to this criticism, some observers claim that valuable assets, bought over many years by public funds, have been sold off too cheaply to private investors who have reaped the benefit at the expense of the general public. Only industries which are not attractive to the stock market are likely to remain in public ownership and this will mean that the taxpayer has to pay the bill to support their continued existence.

Further criticisms include the loss of future government revenue from the sale of profitable state-owned businesses and the problem of ensuring that commercial goals are not allowed to displace completely the broader economic goals once pursued by nationalised industries (e.g. the possible closure of unprofitable rural telephone boxes or railway lines under privatisation). In essence, the fear is that once freed from government regulation, privatised companies will tend to replace the loss-making 'public service' element of their former activities with products or services that offer the greatest levels of profit. While this will benefit some consumers, the cost is likely to be borne by other buyers who have limited market power and, in some cases, no alternative product to turn to.

This problem of lack of choice is particularly acute where the privatisation of a state monopoly gives rise to a private monopoly, as initially was the case with many of the privatised utilities. Despite the establishment of 'regulators' to oversee the operations of some of the newly privatised concerns (*see* Table 14.2) and to act as a kind of proxy for true competition, some opponents still feel that the interest of consumers is not fully protected under the current arrangements. They also feel that exploitation through higher prices or other abuses of market power remains possible. Evidence from investigations by the former Monopolies and Mergers Commission (*see* below) and from the regulatory authorities suggests that this view is not without foundation. This evidence has also conveniently provided the current government with a justification for levying windfall taxes on the profits of the privatised utilities as a means of boosting Exchequer revenues.

 Regulatory body websites include *www.oftel.gov.uk, www.ofwat.gov.uk, www.ofgem.gov.uk*

Table 14.2   Key regulatory bodies for selected privatised utilities

Name	Date established	Main activities
Office of Tele-communications (OFTEL)	1984	Regulator of the UK telecommunications industry. Its duties include promoting the interest of consumers, maintaining effective competition and ensuring that services in the UK meet all reasonable demands.
Office of Water Services (OFWAT)	1989	Regulates domestic and non-domestic supply by water and sewerage companies. Regulates price increases to customers.
Office of Gas and Electricity Markets (OFGEM)	2000	Regulates the gas and electricity industries in England, Scotland and Wales with the aim of enhancing customer choice and value by promoting competition and controlling monopolies.

Privatisation overseas

Before offering an assessment of privatisation in the United Kingdom, it is worth noting that most other states have embarked on similar experiments in economic liberalisation, irrespective of their size, ideology or level of economic development. At the end of the 1980s it was estimated that worldwide sales of state assets to the private sector exceeded $25 billion or about £14 000 million and this figure has continued to grow with the ongoing privatisation process in eastern Europe and else-where. According to *The Economist* (23 November 1996), in the period 1985–95 the combined revenues from privatisation in France, Germany, Italy, the Netherlands and Spain alone were in excess of $70 billion, with France having the lion's share of $34 billion. For the same period the United Kingdom's receipts were estimated at $85 billion, making it the most significant privatisation programme within the OECD.

As the following examples of overseas privatisation indicate, a wide range of state assets from different sectors of the economy have been sold by governments of different political complexions and have often involved a significant measure of foreign participation:

- In Portugal major privatisations between 1989 and 1997 included banks, insur-ance companies, public utilities and businesses producing cement, oil, paper products, tobacco and beer.
- In the Netherlands privatisations have included the national airline (KLM) and the water, gas and electricity utilities.
- In Brazil part of the country's rail network has been sold off; in Jamaica privatisa-tion has included the National Commercial Bank and the Caribbean Cement Company.
- In France privatisations range from chemicals and oil to insurance, banking and vehicles.
- In India plans to divest a significant proportion of public sector enterprises is well under way, with sales including businesses involved with steel, zinc and petrochemicals.

Arguably the most dramatic and exciting experiments in privatisation are currently taking place in eastern Europe, particularly among the transition economies which are moving from a planned economic system towards private enterprise. In the newly unified Germany, for instance, the federal government appointed a special privatisation agency (Treuhand) to oversee and assist in the large-scale privatisation of former East German state industries and firms, and other governments (including those in Hungary, the Czech Republic and Poland) have committed themselves to similar programmes of rolling privatisation and have undertaken legal and institutional changes to speed up the process. While progress has varied in the different states and has generally been influenced by questions of economic and political stability (e.g. in the Russian Federation), the large-scale sell-off of public assets by the former communist states looks set to continue in the foreseeable future. Current evidence suggests that the transition in these countries is proving a significantly more painful experience than that encountered in states already possessing a market-based economic system (see e.g. the article by Nick Potts in the Further Reading at the end of the chapter).

Mini case | Privatising electricity in Poland and Portugal

The privatisation of electricity utilities has proved fashionable. Following Britain's successful sale of the various elements of its electricity industry, a number of other countries decided to follow suit. In Poland, for example, plans for selling off the electricity generating and distribution sector were announced in a government white paper (March 1996) which recognised the need to modernise the country's energy supply and distribution system. Broadly modelled on the UK approach to electricity privatisation, the white paper called for the formation and privatisation of between five and ten groups of power producers augmented by smaller local generating businesses drawn from existing suppliers. These companies would sell power to regional distributors and directly to large customers under a scheme which also involved the privatisation of the country's national grid.

Portugal, too, had ambitious plans for its electricity industry. The government's scheme involved inviting a global offering for Electricidade de Portugal, the holding company for the country's national power production, transport and distribution utilities. Starting with an initial public offering of 10–20 per cent, the government anticipated having privatised almost half of the group by late 1998. This approach – which superseded a plan proposed by the previous administration – aimed to raise over one billion escudos for the government, thus helping it to reduce the burden of its public debt.

While the privatisation of Poland's electricity industry might appear something of a risk for potential investors, in Portugal's case the prospects could be said to be more favourable. With high levels of turnover and profitability and significant internal improvements, the company should prove a 'safe' investment. As with any commodity traded in a free market, whether it be video recorders or a country's electricity supplies, ownership will ultimately be determined by the willingness and ability to pay the price.

Assessment

Measured against some of the UK government's stated objectives, privatisation appears to have been successful, and has involved a transfer of ownership of over 7 per cent of GDP from the public to the private sector. Apart from the fact that many other national governments have sought to emulate Britain's approach to asset sales, the privatisation programme has been cited as an important component of the improvement in the supply side of the economy after 1979. It has also been a critical element in promoting the free market approach which has come to dominate governmental thinking in Britain and elsewhere for over two decades. All of this has evidently been achieved with the support of the British public (although some opinion polls have indicated a decline in the popularity of privatisation). In 1979, for instance, only 7 per cent of adults owned shares in public companies. By the early 1990s this figure had risen to 25 per cent, or 11 million shareholders, many of whom had bought shares for the first time in the 1980s with the sale of the big public utilities.

This significant growth in the number of ordinary shareholders can be explained in a number of ways. For a start, most stock market flotations were accompanied by extensive and costly advertising campaigns which helped to raise public awareness and to attract investors (e.g. British Gas's 'Tell Sid' campaign). Added to this, investors in public utilities were often offered special incentives to buy shares in businesses they dealt with on a regular basis (e.g. cheaper telephone bills) or in which some of them worked and therefore had a vested interest. Perhaps most importantly, and with the benefit of hindsight, some privatisation stock appears to have been sold at substantially lower prices than the market would bear and this guaranteed quick profits for people who bought and then sold immediately as prices rose. In the circumstances it is not surprising that many flotations were hugely oversubscribed – a fact which led to criticism that some privatisation stock had been considerably undervalued.

Many shareholders who invested for longer-term capital gains also benefited from underpricing of share issues and in some cases received free additional shares and other benefits (including annual dividends) by holding on to their investment. An analysis by Gary Cook of the share performance of privatised companies shows that some of the earlier privatisations have produced spectacular long-term gains, though some privatised company shares performed less well.[3] Cable & Wireless shares, for example, were issued at an average price of 56p in the early 1980s and were trading at 588p by August 1991. Similarly, BT's initial issue price of 130p in 1984/5 had risen to 391p by the same date, a threefold increase despite the stock market crash in 1987.

Whatever the reason for the growth in share ownership, it is clear that privatisation, along with the sale of council houses, has helped the government to claim that it has encouraged the growth of a 'property-owning democracy' in which an increasing number of citizens have a stake in the success of the economy and therefore in the performance of the private sector. That said, it is still the case that the majority of shares in public companies are held by individuals in better-paid professional and managerial occupations and that overall the percentage of *all* UK shares owned by individuals has fallen dramatically over the last thirty years. In contrast, the holdings of institutional investors (such as insurance companies and pension funds) have risen rapidly – a fact which not only gives them significant influence over the future of many public companies, but which also suggests that the claim of wider share ownership has to be treated with a degree of caution.[4]

Notwithstanding this latter point, the government's relative success in selling state assets also helped it initially to achieve another one of its objectives – that of reducing the size of the PSBR. From the early 1980s onwards, public expenditure as a percentage of GDP fell substantially – partly as a result of the revenues from the privatisation programme – and by the latter part of the decade the government had a budget surplus (or public sector debt repayment) as revenue exceeded spending. Once again, however, this apparent benefit needs to be seen in context. For a start, much of the improvement in public finances during this period was a result of the government's restraint on public spending, rather than the effects of privatisation, though the receipts clearly helped the government to balance its books. Added to this, by the early 1990s, as the recession took hold, public spending rapidly began to outstrip the amounts raised in revenue, causing a dramatic growth in the size of government borrowing, despite a decade of privatisation receipts. Understandably, some critics have asked whether the sale of valuable state assets was in vain and distracted the incumbent government from addressing some of the underlying structural weaknesses in the British economy.

With regard to privatisation as a spur to greater organisational efficiency and performance, this is an area in which assessment is particularly problematical. Part of the difficulty arises from the fact that direct comparisons between state and privatised companies are often impossible, since some goods and services have not normally been provided by both the public and private sectors simultaneously (e.g. railways). In addition, even where such provision occurs (e.g. the health service), the public sector usually has to pursue a number of non-commercial objectives laid down by politicians and this makes direct comparisons somewhat unfair, particularly if profitability alone is taken as a measure of performance.

One way of approaching some of these 'problems' is to attempt a comparison between the performance of an organisation before privatisation and its performance after it has become part of the private sector – using measures such as relative profitability, productivity or levels of service. Yet, once again, significant methodological difficulties exist which call into question the validity of many of the conclusions. Industries such as British Gas and British Telecom, for instance, have always been profitable and profits have tended to grow since privatisation; but this could as easily reflect the benefits of monopoly price rises as improvements in efficiency resulting from a change in ownership. Conversely, the decline in the fortunes of the once publicly owned steel industry could be interpreted as a decline in efficiency and/or performance under privatisation, when in fact a combination of overcapacity in the world steel industry and the impact of the recession have clearly been the main culprits.

Comparisons of productivity can also be misleading and usually fail to take into account the substantial 'economic' costs of privatisation (e.g. large-scale redundancies). Many state industries were substantially restructured prior to flotation in order to attract investors, and the resulting job losses – invariably at the taxpayer's expense – helped many newly privatised businesses to claim substantial productivity gains in their first few years of trading. Perhaps ironically, the greatest improvements in productivity in the period 1984–91 often occurred within industries nationalised at the time – such as British Coal and British Rail – whose massive redundancy programmes helped them to outpace the productivity gains of manufacturing industry by anything up to three times, according to Treasury figures. In such circumstances, it would be easy – though probably unreasonable – to conclude that while being privatised was good for productivity, it was not as good as not being privatised!

Further complications arise when one compares the performance of privatised companies which have remained monopolies with the performance of those which have consistently operated under competitive market conditions. Writing in the *Guardian* on 3 March 1993, Victor Keegan argued that the fortunes of companies such as British Steel, Rolls-Royce and Rover had been seriously affected by the sort of violent cyclical disturbances which had previously driven them into the public sector and that this had significantly influenced their attractiveness to private investors. In comparison, businesses which had faced little effective competition in some areas of the market (e.g. Cable & Wireless, British Airways) and those facing none (e.g. the water companies, British Gas) had invariably performed well for their shareholders; though the price of this success had frequently been paid by customers (in the form of inflated charges) and workers (in the form of redundancy).

Keegan's conclusion, that it is competition rather than ownership which acts as a spur to increased efficiency, is one that is widely held and underlies some of the recent attempts by government and by the regulatory bodies to identify ways of reducing the monopoly power of the privatised public utilities. The proposition is that under a more competitive market structure the commercial pressures of the marketplace force management to seek ways of improving organisational efficiency and performance, for fear of the consequences if they fail to meet the needs of the consumer and the investor. If left to their own devices, the large utilities are unlikely to put themselves to such 'tests' voluntarily, and this approach would presumably find favour with shareholders who have a vested interest in maximising revenue. Paradoxically, in order to improve the position of the consumer, government may be forced to intervene more aggressively and imaginatively in the marketplace, in order to promote greater competition among producers and increased choice for the consumer. Such intervention could easily be justified under current competition policy.

Competition policy

Whereas privatisation has focused on the balance between public and private provision within the overall economy, UK government competition policy has largely been concerned with regulating market behaviour and in particular with controlling potential abuses of market power by firms acting singly or in concert in specific markets. To achieve these aims, successive British governments have relied mainly on legislation, as well as on a measure of self-regulation and persuasion, and have generally taken a more liberal view of market structures than that taken in the United States, where monopolies have been deemed illegal for over a century. This legislative framework to regulate market activity, and the institutional arrangements established to support it, are considered immediately below.

There are lots of useful websites relating to UK competition policy. A good starting point is the Office of Fair Trading (OFT) which is at *www.oft.gov.uk*
You could also try the Competition Commision at *www.competition-commision.org.uk*
and the Department of Trade and Industry at *www.dti.gov.uk*

The evolving legislative framework

Official attempts to control market behaviour through statutory means date back to the late 1940s with the passage of the Monopolies and Restrictive Practices Act 1948. This Act, which established the Monopolies Commission (later the Monopolies and Mergers Commission), empowered it to investigate industries in which any single firm (a unitary monopoly), or a group of firms acting together, could restrict competition by controlling at least one-third of the market. Following such an investigation, the Commission would publish a report which was either factual or advisory and it was then the responsibility of the relevant government department to decide what course of action, if any, to take to remove practices regarded as contrary to the public interest. In the event, the majority of the Commission's recommendations tended to be ignored, though it did have some success in highlighting the extent of monopoly power in the United Kingdom in the early post-war period.

In 1956 investigations into unitary monopolies were separated from those into restrictive practices operated by a group of firms, with the enactment of the Restrictive Trade Practices Act. This Act, which outlawed the widespread custom of manufacturers jointly enforcing the retail prices at which their products could be sold, also required firms to register any form of restrictive agreement that they were operating (e.g. concerning prices, sales, production) with the Registrar of Restrictive Practices. It was the latter's responsibility to bring such agreements before the Restrictive Practices Court and they were automatically deemed 'against the public interest', unless they could be justified in one of a number of ways (e.g. benefiting consumers, employment, exports). Further extensions to the Act in 1968 (to cover 'information agreements') and in 1973 (to cover services) were ultimately consolidated in the Restrictive Trade Practices Act 1976. This new Act vested the responsibility for bringing restrictive practices before the court in the recently established Director General of Fair Trading (*see* below).

A further extension of legislative control came with the passage of the Monopolies and Mergers Act 1965. The Act allowed the Monopolies Commission to investigate actual or proposed mergers or acquisitions which looked likely to enhance monopoly power and which involved at that time the takeover of assets in excess of £5 million. The aim of this Act was to provide a means of regulating activities which threatened to be contrary to the public interest, by permitting government to decide which mergers and acquisitions should be prohibited and which should be allowed to proceed and, if necessary, under what terms. Additional steps in this direction were taken with the passage of the Fair Trading Act 1973 and the Competition Act 1980, the main provisions of which are summarised below:

1 A scale monopoly exists where at least 25 per cent of a market is controlled by a single buyer or seller; this can be applied to sales at local as well as national level and can include monopolies resulting from nationalisation.
2 Investigations can occur when two related companies (e.g. a parent and a subsidiary) control 25 per cent of a market or when separate companies operate to restrict competition even without a formal agreement (e.g. tacit collusion).
3 Mergers involving gross worldwide assets of over £70 million or a market share of over 25 per cent can be investigated.
4 Responsibility for overseeing consumer affairs, and competition policy generally, lies with the Director General of Fair Trading (DGFT), operating from the Office of Fair Trading (OFT). The DGFT has the power to make monopoly references to the renamed Monopolies and Mergers Commission (MMC) and to advise the relevant government minister on whether merger proposals should be investigated by the MMC.

In the latter context, it is worth noting that while there was no legal obligation on companies to inform the OFT of their merger plans, the Companies Act 1989 introduced a formal procedure enabling them to pre-notify the DGFT of merger proposals, in the expectation that such pre-notification would enhance the prospects for rapid clearance in cases which were deemed straightforward.

While the question of market share still remains an important influence on official attitudes to proposed mergers or takeovers, there is no doubt that in recent years increasing attention has focused on anti-competitive practices and under the Competition Act 1980 such practices by individuals or firms – as opposed to whole markets – could be referred to the MMC for investigation. In addition the Act allowed the Commission to scrutinise the work of certain public sector agencies and to consider the efficiency and costs of the service they provided and any possible abuses of monopoly power, and similar references could also be made in the case of public utilities which had been privatised (e.g. under the Telecommunication Act 1984, the Gas Act 1986, the Water Industry Act 1991).

Additional statutory control also comes in the form of EU legislation governing activities which have cross-border implications. Article 81 (formerly Article 85) of the Treaty of Rome prohibits agreements between enterprises which result in a restriction or distortion in competition within the Union (e.g. price fixing, market sharing). Article 82 (formerly Article 86) prohibits a dominant firm, or group of firms, from using their market power to exploit consumers; while further Articles prohibit the provision of government subsidies if they distort, or threaten to distort, competition between industries or individual firms.

Moreover, under Regulation 4064/89 which came into force in September 1990, concentrations or mergers which have a 'Community dimension' have become the subject of exclusive jurisdiction by the European Commission. Broadly speaking, this means that mergers involving firms with a combined worldwide turnover of more than €5 billion are subject to Commission control, provided that the EU turnover of each of at least two companies involved exceeds €250 million and the companies concerned do not have more than two-thirds of their EU turnover within one and the same member state. Mergers which do not qualify under the regulation remain, of course, subject to national competition law. This regulation is currently under review.

Since previous editions of this book were published the UK government has acted to bring UK competition policy into line with EU law. Under the Competition Act 1998 – which came into force on 1 March 2000 – two basic prohibitions have been introduced:

1 A prohibition on anti-competitive agreements, based closely on Article 85 of the Treaty of Rome (now Article 81).
2 A prohibition of abuse of dominant position in a market, based on Article 86 (now Article 82).

These prohibitions, which replace a number of other pieces of legislation (e.g. the Restrictive Trade Practices Act 1976; the Resale Prices Act 1976; the majority of the Competition Act 1980), are enforced primarily by the DGFT, together with the utility regulators, who have concurrent powers in their own sphere of operations. Companies breaching either or both of the prohibitions are liable to fines and may be required to pay compensation to third parties affected by their anti-competitive behaviour.

Mini case   The ice cream war hots up

Anti-competitive practices can take many forms and are not always easy to detect or prevent. Official attempts to reduce or remove such practices can in part be hampered by problems of information and interpretation.

In 1994 an MMC investigation into the UK market for wrapped ice cream bought for immediate consumption concluded that Walls, a subsidiary of Unilever, had not abused its dominant position in the ice cream market. Competitors such as Mars and Nestlé had complained that Walls was lending freezer cabinets to retailers on condition that they were used to stock only its own ice cream and that this acted as an unfair barrier to new entrants into the market. Despite accepting that 'freezer exclusivity' did exist, the MMC decided that this practice did not operate against the public interest, after having apparently received assurances from the company that retailers were free to purchase ice cream from any supplier (i.e. there was no 'wholesaler exclusivity').

Doubts as to the accuracy of the company's claims on 'wholesaler exclusivity' led the Office of Fair Trading (OFT) to launch an investigation in 1995. Following a nine-month inquiry, the OFT apparently concluded that a prima facie case existed that the company's executives had deliberately misled the MMC in the early 1990s (see, for example, The Economist, 6 January 1996). In part this conclusion seems to have been based on documentary evidence which allegedly shows that retailers were under pressure to buy supplies exclusively from concessionaires. The existence of such evidence clearly calls into question the rigour with which the MMC undertook its original investigation into the ice cream market.

Far from dying down, the issue of Walls' behaviour has continued to come under official scrutiny. Following the 1996 investigations into the ice cream industry, the company was ordered to make a number of changes to its distribution arrangements by March 1999. Despite promising to abide by the MMC's ruling, the company was subsequently accused of breaking this undertaking. A number of independent wholesalers claimed that some retailers had been offered incentives which were unavailable to buyers from independent suppliers (see Guardian, 4 March 1999). This complaint came as the MMC was in the midst of yet another inquiry into competition between leading suppliers – the third into the industry in five years – and which ultimately called for changes in the ice cream market in order to prevent further monopoly abuse (see e.g. www.competition-commission.org.uk/reports/436ice).

With the publication of the competition White Paper in July 2001 (Productivity and Enterprise: A World Class Competition Regime), the government has signalled its intention to reform the merger and monopoly regimes. Future changes – announced in the Enterprise Bill in March/April 2002 – will include a move to decisions taken by independent competition authorities, new duties for OFT to promote competition, and criminal penalties for those involved in cartels. The idea, in effect, is to modernise the current system and to provide a strong legal basis for the competition authorities to actively promote competition rather than just responding to anti-competitive practices.

The institutional framework

The formulation and implementation of UK competition policy involves a variety of agencies, including the Department of Trade and Industry, the Office of Fair Trading, the Monopolies and Mergers Commission and the Mergers Panel. Of these, the MMC (now the Competition Commission) and the OFT deserve special attention.

From its foundation in 1948 until its replacement in 1999, the Monopolies and Mergers Commission remained a statutory body, independent of government both in the conduct of its inquiries and in its conclusions which were published in report form. Funded by the DTI, the Commission had a full-time chairperson, and around 35 other part-time members, three of whom were deputy chairpeople and all of whom were appointed by the Secretary of State for Trade and Industry. Such appointments normally lasted for three years at the outset and included individuals drawn from business, the professions, the trade unions and the universities. To support the work of the appointed members, the Commission had a staff of about 80 officials, two-thirds of whom it employed directly, with the remainder being on loan from government departments (especially the DTI) and increasingly from the private sector.

It is important to note that the Commission had no legal power to initiate its own investigations; instead, references – requests for it to carry out particular inquiries – came either from the Secretary of State for Trade and Industry or the Director General of Fair Trading, or from the appropriate regulator in the case of privatised industries and the broadcasting media. Where a possible merger reference was concerned, the initial evaluation of a proposal was made by a panel of civil servants (the Mergers Panel) who considered whether the merger should be referred to the MMC for further consideration. The decision then rested with the Secretary of State, who took advice from the Director General of Fair Trading before deciding whether the proposal should be investigated or should be allowed to proceed.

Under the legislation, references to the Commission could be made on a number of grounds. As indicated above, these included not only monopoly and merger references but also references concerned with the performance of public sector bodies and privatised industries and with anti-competitive practices by individual firms (i.e. competition references). In addition, the Commission was empowered to consider general references (involving practices in industry), restrictive labour practices and references under the Broadcasting Act 1990, as well as questions of proposed newspaper mergers, where special provisions apply.

On receipt of a reference, the Commission's chairperson appointed a small group of members to carry out the relevant inquiry and to report on whether the company (or companies) concerned was operating – or could be expected to operate – against the public interest. Supported by a team of officials, and in some cases including members appointed to specialist panels (e.g. newspaper, telecommunications, water and electricity), the investigating group gathered a wide range of written and oral evidence from both the party (parties) concerned and from others likely to have an interest in the outcome of the inquiry. In reaching its conclusions, which tended to take several months or more, the group had to take into account the 'public interest', as defined under section 84 of the Fair Trading Act 1973, which stressed the importance of competition, the protection of consumer interests and the need to consider issues related to employment, trade and the overall industrial structure. While in most references, issues relating to competition were the primary concern, the Commission was able to take wider public interest issues into account and could rule in favour of a proposal on these grounds, even if the measure appeared anti-competitive.

The culmination of the Commission's inquiry was its report which, in most cases, was submitted to the Secretary of State for consideration and was normally laid before Parliament, where it often formed the basis of a debate or parliamentary questions. In the case of monopoly references judged to be against the public interest, the Secretary of State – with the advice of the DGFT – decided on an appropriate course of action, which could involve an order to prevent or remedy the particular adverse effects identified by the Commission. In the case of merger references, a similar procedure occurred in the event of an adverse judgement by the Commission. The Secretary of State, however, was not bound to accept the Commission's recommendations; nor was he or she able to overrule the conclusion that a merger does not operate, or may be expected not to operate, against the public interest.

It is important to note that at all stages of this multi-stage process, a considerable degree of lobbying occurred by the various interested parties, in an attempt to influence either the outcome of the investigations or the subsequent course of action decided upon. Moreover, considerable pressure tended to occur, even before a decision was taken as to whether or not to make a reference to the MMC. As a number of recent cases have shown, lobbying *against* a reference can represent a key step in justifying a proposed merger. By the same token, lobbying *for* a reference has tended to become an important weapon used by companies wishing to resist an unwelcome takeover, particularly where matters of public interest appear paramount.

Following the passage of the Competition Act 1998, the MMC was replaced (on 1 April 1999) by the Competition Commission, a public body that has taken on the MMC's former reporting role. The Competition Commission also hears appeals against decisions made under the prohibition provisions of the new legislation. The chairperson (full-time) and members (part-time) of the Commission are appointed by the Secretary of State for Trade and Industry following an open competition and – as in the case of the MMC – are drawn from a variety of backgrounds and initially serve for a period of three years. Organised into a series of panels, the Commission is supported by a staff of about 90, which includes administrators, specialists and individuals engaged in support services. Most of these are direct employees; the remainder are seconded from government departments.

The Office of Fair Trading is a non-ministerial government department headed by a Director General, who is appointed by the Secretary of State for Trade and Industry. Under the Fair Trading Act 1973, the DGFT was given the responsibility of overseeing consumer affairs as well as competition policy and this includes administering various pieces of consumer legislation, such as the Consumer Credit Act 1974 and the Estate Agents Act 1979. In carrying out his or her responsibilities in both these areas, the Director General is supported by a team of administrative, legal, economic and accountancy staff and has a Mergers Secretariat to co-ordinate the Office's work in this field.

With regard to competition policy, the OFT's duties were originally governed primarily by the Fair Trading Act and the Competition Act 1980; in addition, under the Restrictive Trade Practices Act 1976 the Director General had responsibility for bringing cases of restrictive practices before the Restrictive Practices Court. With the passage of the Competition Act 1998, the new prohibition regime is to be applied and enforced by the DGFT, and the OFT is to be given additional resources to root out cartels and restrictive behaviour. The legislation gives the Director General considerable powers to investigate if he/she has a reasonable suspicion that either of the prohibitions is being infringed. Under certain circumstances the DGFT can also grant exemptions from the scope of the two prohibitions and may be called upon to defend her/his decisions before the Competition Commission. As indicated above, the role of the OFT is currently under reform and looks likely to be strengthened in the future.

Some recent cases

Since it was established in 1948, the MMC/Competition Commission has produced hundreds of reports, covering a wide range of issues and affecting firms of different sizes in a variety of markets. At the outset most of its inquiries concerned monopolies – reflecting its initial role as the Monopolies Commission. In more recent years, its work has embraced not only mergers, which have tended to be its major preoccupation, but also nationalised industries and, more recently, the work of the privatised large utilities. These changes are indicated by Figure 14.2 which shows the distribution of the Commission's work up to the mid-1990s.

The examples below provide a good insight into the Commission's role in competition policy and its relationship with the Office of Fair Trading. Students wishing to investigate a particular case in more detail should consult the appropriate report, a full list of which can be obtained from the Commission's library in London or via its website (www.competition-commission.org.uk).

Nestlé, 1991

This concerned the claim that the Swiss-based foods group was using its monopoly on the supply of instant coffee in the United Kingdom to keep prices high. Concerned that the company was being slow to pass on to consumers the benefits of a fall in the price of raw coffee beans, the DGFT asked the MMC to investigate the instant coffee market. Following a nine-month investigation, the Commission concluded that, while the company supplied more than 47 per cent (by volume) of the United Kingdom's instant coffee, there was still effective competition in the market and a wide degree of consumer choice, with more than 200 brands available (in 1989) and the leading supermarkets stocking on average 30 brands. Despite the facts that Nestlé had higher levels of profitability than its main competitors, and that there was a tendency for branded coffees generally to respond less quickly than own brands to reductions in input prices, the Commission concluded that Nestlé's monopoly did not operate against the public interest. The DGFT indicated, however, that the operation of the soluble coffee market should be kept under review to ensure that it remained competitive.

Figure 14.2 MMC reports published

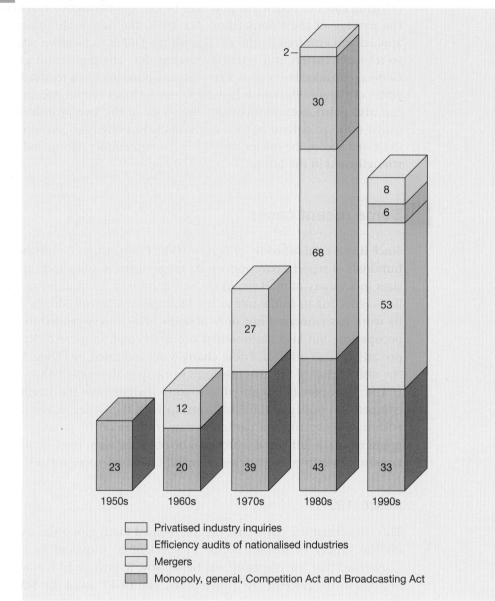

Source: Monopolies and Mergers Commission.

British Gas, 1992

This involved two parallel references to the Commission by both the President of the Board of Trade (under the terms of the Fair Trading Act) and the Director General of Gas Supply (under the Gas Act 1986). The first asked the Commission to investigate the supply of gas through pipes to both tariff and non-tariff customers; the second to investigate the supply of gas conveyance and gas storage facilities. According to the Office of Fair Trading, very little competition existed in the gas industry, since 17 million domestic household customers had no alternative source of supply and BG's control over storage and transmission facilities inhibited true competition in the industrial market where, theoretically, industrial customers could buy from other suppliers. In the Commission's report published in August 1993, the MMC called for British Gas to lose its monopoly of supply to domestic households by no later than 2002 and for the privatised utility to be split into two separately owned companies.

Midland Bank, 1992

This concerned two bids for the Midland Bank, made by Lloyds Bank and the Hong Kong and Shanghai Banking Corporation, and illustrates the question of split jurisdiction between the United Kingdom and the EU. Lloyds' bid fell within the United Kingdom's jurisdiction and was referred to the MMC as raising potential competition issues – a course of action which caused Lloyds to abandon its proposed merger. In contrast, the HSBC bid was deemed to be of wider concern and was referred to the competition authorities in Brussels. Following clearance by the EU, the HSBC proceeded with its bid and this was accepted by Midland's shareholders.

Video games, 1995

This investigation concerned the supply of video games to the UK market which was dominated by two Japanese companies, Nintendo and Sega. The Commission found the existence of a monopoly situation which affected pricing and entry by new firms. It recommended the abolition of licence controls which allowed the two suppliers to charge excessive prices and the removal of restrictions on rental of games.

UK car prices, 1999–2002

After persistent claims that UK car prices were higher on average than prices in other European countries, the OFT called for a full-scale monopolies investigation into the relationship between car makers and dealerships. In its most recent report the Competition Commission found that the existing system operated against the public interest, particularly with regard to prices, choice and innovation (see e.g. www.competition-commission.org.uk/reports/439cars). It highlighted, in particular, the adverse effects of the selective and exclusive distribution system permitted by the Block Exemption within the EU (see case study below).

Government and the labour market

Government involvement in the labour market takes a variety of forms and its influence on market conditions can be direct or indirect and can operate at different spatial levels. Many of the government initiatives mentioned in Chapter 10, for example, seek to affect employment prospects in the regions or in local economies and thus clearly have labour market implications. Similarly, in its general management of the economy through fiscal and monetary means (*see* Chapter 4), the government will influence the overall demand for labour, which is derived from the demand for the products that labour produces. Some of that demand, of course, will come from the government itself, as a central provider of goods and services and hence a key employer of labour, and its attitude to pay settlements will affect wage levels throughout the public sector. This, in turn, can spill over to the wage bargaining process in the private sector and on occasions may even involve the use of statutory or voluntary restrictions on wage rises that invariably interfere with the operations of the free market (e.g. incomes policies).

While all of these areas would need to be considered in any detailed analysis of labour market policies, in the brief discussion below attention is focused on government initiatives to improve employment prospects and training opportunities for the unemployed, and on the government's efforts to curb the power of the trade unions. Both of these approaches are particularly pertinent to the discussion on how government has sought to improve the efficiency of markets as part of its supply-side approach to economic management – using, in this case, a combination of policy and legislation to achieve its objectives.

Curbing trade union power

As a major force in the labour market, representing the interests of millions of workers, trade unions have been seen as an obstacle to the operation of market forces and as a cause of high wage costs and low labour productivity in the United Kingdom. For almost twenty years after 1979, Conservative governments sought to curb the influence of the trade unions through legislative means, in the belief that more labour market flexibility would develop and that this would benefit businesses seeking to respond to competition and change. To assist further in this direction, the government – with the general support of industry – abolished the Wages Councils (which were set up to protect the interests of the lower-paid) and originally refused to participate in the Social Chapter of the Maastricht Treaty (which included a provision for works' councils and the principle of equal pay for male and female workers for equal work).

The government's step-by-step approach to reducing the influence of trade unions is demonstrated by the following legislative measures, enacted in the period 1980–93.

The Employment Act 1980

This Act gave employers legal remedies against secondary picketing and most other types of secondary action. It also provided for all new 'closed shops' to be approved by four-fifths of the workforce and for public funds to be made available to encourage unions to hold postal ballots.

The Employment Act 1982

This Act further tightened the law on closed shops and outlawed union-labour-only contracts. Employers were given legal remedies against 'political' strikes and trade unions were made liable for damages, if they instigated unlawful industrial action (e.g. 'secondary' action).

The Trade Union Act 1984

This Act sought to strengthen internal union democracy. Unions were required to hold a secret ballot every ten years if they wished to keep a political fund and union executives had to submit themselves for re-election by secret ballot every five years. In addition, pre-strike ballots were required if unions wished to retain their immunity from civil action for damages in the event of a strike.

The Employment Act 1988

This Act strengthened the rights of individual union members. Unions were banned from disciplining members who refused to support strike action; all senior union officials had to be elected by secret ballot; workers were permitted to apply for court orders instructing unions to repudiate industrial action organised without a secret ballot. Moreover strikes in defence of the closed shop lost all legal protection.

The Employment Act 1990

This Act made unions legally liable for 'wildcat' strikes called by shop stewards without a proper ballot. Pre-entry closed shops were banned and so individuals could not be refused a job for not belonging to a trade union prior to appointment.

Trade Union and Labour Relations (Consolidation) Act 1992

This Act consolidated previous legislation in the field of labour relations.

The Trade Union Reform and Employment Rights Act 1993

This Act essentially had two main purposes: first, to impose further restrictions on trade unions and trade union activity; second, to enact certain employment rights as a consequence of EU directives and case law. Under section 13, for example, employers are permitted to provide inducements to employees to opt out of collective bargaining or to leave a union, while section 17 introduces a requirement for industrial action ballots to be conducted fully by postal voting.

While there is no doubt that such legislation has altered the balance of power between employee and employer and has significantly weakened the power of the trade unions, this has been only one influence, and arguably not the most important. Apart from the fact that union membership has fallen significantly over the last decade, weakening their financial position and making them less able to sustain union action, the unions have had to operate in a market severely affected by changes in the economic cycle. Gone are the days when governments aspired to full employment and were willing to use fiscal and monetary means to achieve this objective. In the new climate of less than full employment, the influence of organised labour in the economy has inevitably been reduced and has been replaced, to some degree, by the pursuit of individual self-interest.

As a postscript it is worth noting that since the election of a Labour government in 1997 there has been a kind of rehabilitation of the trade unions and an attempt by government to enshrine certain employment rights in law. Following the Employment Rights Act of 1996, other significant pieces of legislation have included the Employment Rights (Dispute Reduction) Act 1998, the National Minimum Wage Act 1998, the Working Time Regulations 1998, the Human Rights Act 1998 and the Employment Relations Act. For students wishing to examine this legislation in more detail the Institute of Employment Research is a useful starting point (www.ier.org.uk/tu_law).

Employment policies

Employment policies are targeted specifically at the unemployed and have included a wide range of measures aimed at assisting individuals to prepare themselves for employment and to gain a job. Many of the schemes have been designed to give a limited amount of work experience and/or to improve vocational training, and in recent years increasing emphasis has been given to the problem of skills shortages in the economy and to matching the needs of labour with the requirements of firms. Additionally, as the following examples illustrate, governments have sought to promote the idea of 'self-help' among the unemployed and to encourage the growth of self-employment, in the hope that an expanding small firms sector will generate a large number of jobs, to replace those lost in medium and larger-sized enterprises.

- *Restart* – introduced in 1986 and requiring anyone drawing unemployment benefit for over six months to see a specialist counsellor to try to identify possible routes back into employment.
- *Youth Training (YT)* – replaced the Youth Training Scheme in 1990. Under this scheme any person under 18 who was unemployed was guaranteed a YT place (with some exceptions, e.g. students). It has been used to combine training and education and to allow individuals to acquire nationally recognised qualifications (e.g. NVQs).
- *Employment Training (ET)* – introduced in 1988 for long-term unemployed people and others with specific needs, including those returning to the labour market. It aimed to provide training in order to help individuals to acquire the skills needed to get jobs and vocational qualifications (or credits towards them).
- *Employment Action (EA)* – introduced in 1991 and designed to help the unemployed to maintain their skills and find employment. It provided opportunities for individuals to undertake community work and offered structured jobsearch support.
- *Training for Work (TfW)* – started in 1993 to replace ET and EA, combining the characteristics of both programmes.
- *Work Trials* – designed to give long-term unemployed people a chance to prove themselves to employers by working on a trial basis while receiving benefit.

The change in government in 1997 saw the introduction of the New Deal, a flagship scheme designed to get individuals claiming unemployment benefits off welfare and into work. Targeted initially at 18–24 year olds, the scheme has now been extended to other categories of person (e.g. those over 25 and those over 50, lone parents, the disabled and partners) and further reforms are currently under way. Funded from the windfall tax levied on the privatised utility companies, the New Deal is an attempt to reduce reliance on state benefits and to make work more attractive to groups often excluded from the labour force. Like other measures, including working families' tax credits and efforts to increase the numbers going into further and higher education, it is part of an attempt by government to improve the supply side of the economy.

Local schemes

Local schemes have taken a variety of forms, including interest-free loans for individuals wishing to set up a local business (e.g. Sir Thomas Whyte Charity in Leicester), local training awards to stimulate interest among local employers or individuals (e.g. Bedfordshire TEC), programmes for groups with specific training needs such as women returners (e.g. Calderdale and Kirklees TEC) and partnerships with local companies to part-fund new training initiatives (e.g. Birmingham TEC's Skills Investment Programme). As a final comment it is important to note that the government's national training programme was initially run by a system of local Training and Enterprise Councils (TECs) which were responsible for providing training schemes for the unemployed and school leavers and for administering various business enterprise schemes. Funded by central government and run by a board of directors drawn predominantly from industry, the TECs (known as Local Enterprise Councils in Scotland) had control of the training funds for existing training programmes and were given the wider role of encouraging training and enterprise in the economy, including supporting initiatives aimed at promoting local economic development. To this end the TECs were expected to work closely with local employers in both the public and private sector and to improve the quality and effectiveness of training in their locality, by identifying priorities and needs within the local community. TECs were replaced by the Learning and Skills Council (LSC) in April 2001 which became responsible for all post-16 education and training, excluding higher education. The LSC operates through a network of local LSCs which deliver national priorities at a local level (n.b. LECs in Scotland still exist).

Synopsis

In market-based economies, governments exercise considerable influence over the structure and functioning of markets, not only through their own economic activities but also through their legislative and policy preferences. Privatisation policy seeks to reduce the role of the state in the workings of the economy through the sale of government-owned assets, in the belief that this will improve the operation of the free market. Competition policy tends to focus on the use of legal and institutional changes to curb the growth of monopoly power and to regulate market behaviour in a manner felt to be conducive to the public interest.

In both these areas the focus of government attention is essentially on the supply side of the economy and this parallels its approach to the operation of the labour market. Through a variety of legislative and administrative changes, the government has sought to create a more 'flexible' market for labour through the introduction of initiatives on training and employment and through its attempts to curb the power of the trade unions through statutory means.

Summary of key points

- Competitive markets are thought to provide major advantages, particularly with regard to enhancing wealth creation, economic efficiency and consumer choice.

- Governments, through policy and legislation, can promote increased competition within the economy and its markets.

- Privatisation has become a global phenomenon and reflects the belief in official circles that competitive, private markets are a superior method of allocating economic resources.

- Privatisation in practice has both advantages and disadvantages.

- Competition policy is basically concerned with regulating market behaviour and with controlling potential abuses of market power.

- Governments in the UK and elsewhere use legislation and regulation to promote competition and have established institutional arrangements to implement and oversee their chosen policies.

- Through its membership of the EU, the UK is influenced by competition laws that have been adopted at Community level.

- Other forms of government intervention in markets include steps taken to improve the workings of the labour market and, in particular, to promote greater labour market flexibility.

- Key approaches in this area in the UK have included legislation to curb the power of the trade unions and the use of targeted employment policies designed to boost employment opportunities and generally improve the supply side of the economy.

CASE STUDY — 'Wither the block exemption?'

As we have seen in the chapter, governments frequently use laws and regulations to promote competition within the marketplace in the belief that this has significant benefits for the consumer and for the economy generally. Such interventions occur not only at national level, but also in situations where governments work together to provide mutual benefits, as in the European Union's attempts to set up a 'single market' across the Member states of the EU.

While few would deny that competitive markets have many benefits, the search for increased competition at national level and beyond can sometimes be restrained by the political realities of the situation, a point underlined by the decision of the EU authorities to allow a block exemption from the normal rules of competition in the EU car market. Under this system, motor manufacturers operating within the EU have been permitted to create networks of selective and exclusive dealerships and to engage in certain other activities normally outlawed under the competition provisions of the single market. It was argued that the system of selective and exclusive distribution (SED) benefited consumers by providing them with a cradle-to-grave service, alongside what was said to be a highly competitive supply situation within the heavily branded global car market.

Introduced in 1995, and extended until the end of September 2002, the block exemption has been highly criticised in recent years for its impact on the operation of the car market in Europe. Following a critical report by the UK competition authorities in April 2000, the EU published a review (in November 2000) of the workings of the current arrangement for distributing and servicing cars, highlighting its adverse consequences for both consumers and retailers and signalling the need for change. Despite intensive lobbying by the major car manufacturers, and by some national governments, to maintain the current rules largely intact, the European Commission announced its intention of replacing the block exemption regulation when it expired in September, subject of course to consultation with interested parties.

In essence the Commission's proposals aim to give dealers far more independence from suppliers by allowing them to solicit for business anywhere in the EU and to open showrooms wherever they want; they will also be able to sell cars supplied by different manufacturers under the same roof. The plan also seeks to open up the aftersales market by breaking the tie which exists between sales and servicing. In future it is proposed that independent repairers will get greater access to the necessary spare parts and technology, thereby encouraging new entrants to join the market with reduced initial investment costs.

While these proposals have been broadly welcomed by groups representing consumers (e.g. the Consumer Association in the UK), some observers feel that the planned reforms do not go far enough to weaken the power of the suppliers over the market (*see* e.g. the editorial in the *Financial Times* 11 January 2002). For instance it appears to be the case that while manufacturers will be able to supply cars to supermarkets and other new retailers, they will not be required by law to do so, suggesting that a market free-for-all is highly unlikely in the foreseeable future (*see* mini case in Chapter 3, 'Cars off the shelf'). Equally the Commission's plans appear to do little to protect dealers from threats to terminate their franchises should there be a dispute with the supplier.

To what extent the proposed new regulations will ultimately improve the lot of the consumer (e.g. by lower prices and/or better choice) still remains to be seen, but it is reasonable to speculate that the car lobby has been relatively successful in limiting the damage to its current position. According to one EU spokesperson (quoted in the *Guardian* 6 February 2002), it was wrong to see the plans as either a maintenance of the status quo or a wholesale deregulation of car distribution arrangements and to imagine that there would be a sudden shift to supermarket or Internet sales, given that cars were not seen by the Commission as commodities that could be sold like yoghurts. In short, the proposals represent a compromise, something we have come to expect from the bureaucrats and politicians in Brussels.

Postscript

Just as this manuscript was going to the publishers, a report appeared in the *Guardian* (22 May 2002) that the European Commission had signalled its intention of delaying some of the proposed reforms, following intensive lobbying from the German car industry. According to the article, the plan to allow car dealers the freedom to solicit and open for business anywhere in the EU had alarmed Europe's powerful car lobby and had upset the German Chancellor, Herr Schröder, who was due to face an election later in the year and who was anxious not to upset Volkswagen and BMW executives. While it still remains unclear what the final outcome will be, it seems likely that the Commission is willing to be more flexible on the introduction of the new system than it had originally indicated. For UK consumers, hopes that car prices will fall in the near future appear to be on hold for the moment.

Case study questions

1 Can you suggest any reasons why the European Commission was willing to grant the block exemption in the first place, given that it ran counter to its proposals for a single market?

2 Why might the planned reforms make cars cheaper for European consumers?

Review and discussion questions

1 Explain the paradox that government needs to intervene in the economy to allow markets to work more freely. What forms does this intervention take?

2 Why is privatisation felt to be a spur to greater efficiency in the major utilities? How would you measure such efficiency 'gains'?

3 In what ways might a government's policy on privatisation be related to its policy on competition?

4 Examine the basis of the previous government's attempts to reform the labour market. How far do you think its reforms have been successful?

Assignments

1 Draft a press release on behalf of the government explaining why it favoured turning Railtrack into a not-for-profit company. Indicate in your statement why the option to renationalise the company was rejected.

2 You are employed by a firm of professional lobbyists which has been commissioned by a group representing European consumer interests to lobby the European Commission over its scheme to reform the European car market. Produce a reasoned case for extending the Commission's current proposals regarding the ending of the block exemption (*see* case study).

Notes and references

1 Numerous books and articles exist on privatisation within the United Kingdom. An excellent starting-point for students wishing to study UK policy is G. C. Cook's *Privatisation in the 1980s and 1990s*, Hidcote Press, 1992.

2 The concept of 'market testing' has increasingly been applied to all parts of the public service, including the civil service, with some civil servants being required to compete with the private sector for their jobs.

3 Cook, *op. cit.*, pp. 23–4.

4 In a sense, however, individuals invest indirectly in shares through their pension funds, insurance policies, unit trusts and bank accounts.

Further reading

Cook, G. C., *Privatisation in the 1980s and 1990s*, Hidcote Press, 1992.

Cook, M. and Farquharson, C., *Business Economics*, Pitman Publishing, 1998, esp. chs. 22 and 24.

Curwen, P. (ed.), *Understanding the UK Economy*, 4th edition, Macmillan, 1997.

Griffiths, A. and Wall, S. (eds), *Applied Economics*, 9th edition, Financial Times/Prentice Hall, 2001.

Livesey, F., 'Competition Policy' in Atkinson, B., Livesey, F. and Milward, B., *Applied Economics*, Macmillan, 1998.

Martin, S., and Parker, S., *The Impact of Privatisation: Ownership and Corporate Performance in the UK*, Routledge, 1997.

Potts, N., 'Privatisation: a false hope', *International Journal of Public Sector Management*, Vol. 12(5), pp. 388–409, 1999.

Worthington, I., Britton, C. and Rees, A., *Economics for Business: Blending Theory and Practice*, Financial Times/Prentice Hall, 2001.

Web links and further questions are available on the website at:
www.booksites.net/worthington

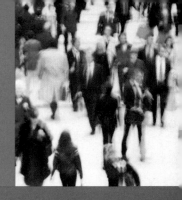

Part Five

ISSUES

15

The technological environment: e-business

Martyn Kendrick

Thus far the development of Internet technology and the emergence of electronic marketplaces and electronic networks have complemented rather than simply replaced existing industry value systems and market structures. That said, technology is starting to revolutionise the way that some businesses operate, and we are seeing new business models emerge. Undoubtedly the emergence of e-business will have a significant global economic impact over the next 10–20 years.

Objectives

- To identify, describe and define e-business and its sub-categories.

- To examine emerging business models, such as business-to-business (B2B) and business-to-consumer (B2C).

- To highlight the key theoretical benefits, opportunities and limitations of e-business with respect to businesses, consumers and society.

- To consider the impact of technology on industry value systems and market structures.

Key terms

Business-to-business (B2B) commerce
Business-to-consumer (B2C) commerce
Buy-side marketplace
Demand chain management (DCM)
Electronic business (e-business)
Electronic commerce (e-commerce)
Electronic customer relationship management (eCRM)

Electronic data interchange (EDI)
Electronic fund transfer (EFT)
Electronic markets (e-markets)
Electronic point-of-sale (EPOS)
Extranet
First-mover advantage
Internet
Intranet
Knowledge management system

Mass customisation
One-to-one database marketing
Sell-side marketplace
Smart cards
Supply chain management (SCM)
Value system

Introduction

We are on the verge of a revolution that is just as profound as the change in the economy that came with the industrial revolution. Soon electronic networks will allow people to transcend the barriers of time and distance and take advantage of global markets and business opportunities not even imaginable today, opening up a new world of economic possibility and progress. (USA Vice-President, Al Gore Jnr, July 1998)

This is undoubtedly an exciting time to be considering developments in the technological environment, with the emergence of new business terms and concepts such as electronic markets (e-markets), electronic business (e-business), and electronic commerce (e-commerce). In the so-called 'new economy' digital networking and communication infrastructures provide a global platform through which enterprises and people interact, collaborate, communicate and search for information.

The potential growth for electronic business worldwide is impressive. A wealth of complementary digital technologies, including digital communications networks (Internet, intranets, extranets), computer hardware and software, and other related networks, databases and information systems, distribution and supply chains, knowledge management and procurement are being merged into a powerful combination for business change using the World Wide Web (WWW) as the driving force. Starting more or less from zero in 1995, total electronic business for 1997 was estimated at $26 billion, and it has been forecast to grow to $330 billion for 2002, and $1 trillion by 2005.[1] Predicting the future growth of e-business is fraught with difficulty, but given that it has the potential to deliver a low-cost, universal, interactive and global medium that provides a simple and secure method for exchanging information instantaneously, the business case appears compelling.

In addition, we might speculate that an Internet-based society will also notice a dramatic change to other aspects of people's lives, outside of the workplace. For instance, changes such as new distance-learning methods and material are starting to emerge in education and many other areas of daily life are increasingly being affected by technological developments.

However, we should also remember that while terms such as e-business and e-commerce are relatively new, they are part of an evolutionary technology process dating back over 30 years. The concept of e-business has actually emerged from a fusion of various separate technologies, such as electronic data interchange (EDI), electronic fund transfer (EFT), electronic point-of-sale (EPOS) and smart cards that had previously struggled in isolation to achieve mass acceptance.

Indeed, the terms 'electronic business' and 'electronic commerce' have no universally accepted definitions, and confusingly are often used interchangeably. However, for our purposes there is a significant difference between the two terms.

Broadly, e-business means doing any element of business over the Internet, and embraces activities such as servicing customers and collaborating with partners, in addition to buying goods, services and information. E-business can be formally defined as the exchange of products, services or information, whether paid or unpaid, across electronic networks, at any stage within the value system, including the supply chain, the value chain and the distribution chain (*see* Figure 15.1). There are a number of potential sub-sets within the general term 'e-business'.

Figure 15.1 The value system

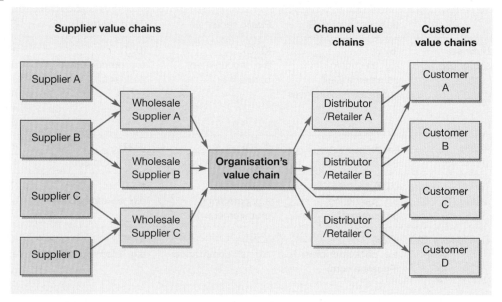

E-commerce covers a narrower sphere of activities than e-business, and refers in particular to the process of electronic transactions involved in the exchange of products, services and information between buyer and seller. The activities of e-retailers such as Amazon would fall under this category.

web link You can access Amazon at *www.amazon.com*

Within an organisation, there are several activities (for example, information and knowledge management, resource co-ordination etc.) that might be more effectively achieved through use of an intranet. Table 15.1 provides a common classification of e-business by nature of transaction. For the purposes of analysis, business organisations have been sub-divided into private sector (B), public sector (G), and third sector (T) organisations. There is also a column for consumers (C).

It can be seen from Table 15.1 that e-business encompasses a wide spectrum of potential external commercial and information exchanges and applications. However, the classifications business-to-business (B2B) and business-to-consumer (B2C) represent the core of electronic commerce and these are the areas that have received the most interest and development to date. These classifications are now considered below in some detail

Table 15.1   Broad spectrum of e-business applications

	Business sector (B)	Public sector (G)	Third sector (T)	Consumers (C)
Business sector (B)	(B2B) e.g. electronic commerce (Dell), business marketplaces	(B2G) e.g. procurement partnering	(B2T) e.g. procurement partnering	(B2C) e.g. electronic commerce (Dell, Amazon), consumer marketplaces (Shopsmart.com)
Public sector (G)	(G2B) e.g. information	(G2G) e.g. co-ordination	(G2T) e.g. information	(G2C) e.g. information
Third sector (T)	(T2B) e.g. partnering procurement	(T2G) e.g. partnering procurement	(T2T) e.g. co-ordination	(T2C) e.g. services information
Consumers (C)	(C2B) e.g. consumer bids (Priceline.com)	(C2G) e.g. tax compliance	(C2T) e.g. Information	(C2C) e.g. auction models (EBay, QXL), consumer reviews (Deja.com)

Source: Adapted from OECD (2000).

Business applications 1: business-to-business (B2B) commerce

Features of B2B

Business-to-business (B2B) transactions account for, in terms of value, about 80 per cent of all Internet transactions. Both the buyer and seller are business organisations. The technological and legal aspects of B2B commerce tend to be more complex than business-to-consumer (B2C) commerce, and it often requires sophisticated software. It can be arranged through either inter-organisational systems (IOS) or electronic markets.

B2B commerce is characterised by a number of key features, many of which differentiate it from B2C commerce. Turban and colleagues[2] suggest that the following are some of its salient aspects:

- an automated trading process;
- high volumes of goods traded;
- high net value of goods traded;
- multiple forms of electronic payment and funds transfer are permitted, unlike B2C commerce, which tends to be restricted to credit cards and smart cards;
- high level of information exchange, including shared databases, between the different trading partners. This often involves the use of extranets;
- prior agreements or contracts between the business partners requiring a higher level of documentation;

- different types of legal and taxation regimes depending on where the two parties are based, and what type of goods or services are the subject of the transaction;
- multiple levels of authorisation of purchases, each level having its own limits on expenditure or types of goods.

Benefits of B2B

On examination there appear to be a number of potential benefits and drivers of B2B commerce. The first of these is that it encourages the adoption of an Internet electronic data interchange (EDI) system to improve the efficiency of business processes. The DTI describes EDI as 'the computer-to-computer exchange of structured data, sent in a form that allows for automatic processing with no manual intervention. This is usually carried out over specialist EDI networks'.[3]

Using EDI to streamline business processes has a number of discernible benefits. These would include the following:

- A safe, secure and verifiable electronic environment that allows manufacturers or retailers to link their stock databases directly to suppliers. This reduces lead times by reducing the time taken in placing and receiving orders.
- Lower costs in creating, processing, distributing, storing, retrieving and destroying paper-based information; fewer errors in data entry; improved inventory control, and reduced staff time involved in the process.
- Improved warehouse logistics, and improved co-ordination for moving goods to the appropriate place, at the defined time and in the correct quantities.
- Better and more efficient integration of support functions such as human resources, inventory control, order processing, accounting and payment processing.
- More efficient strategic alliances and partnering with suppliers, customers and competitors. For instance, in the motor industry, leading firms such as General Motors, Ford and Chrysler have set up a joint extranet with suppliers.

It should be recognised that EDI has been around since the 1960s, but before the development of an integrated Internet EDI system, it was seen to have some serious shortcomings that undermined the potential benefits. Two in particular are worth noting:

- It required an expensive private dedicated network connection between two established trading partners. According to Forrester Research (*www.forrester.research.com*) only 100 000 of the 2 million companies in the USA employing 10 or more employees chose to deploy traditional EDI. The rest felt that it was too expensive, was not interactive enough, and did not enable them to access or negotiate with their suppliers and other partners.
- The lack of agreed international standards for document formats meant that early EDI was based on proprietary technologies such as value added networks (VANs). Each EDI tended to be set up specifically for a single buyer and supplier, and consequently became heavily embedded deep within the organisation's IT systems. This served to inhibit change within the organisation, making it difficult and expensive to change suppliers because of the difficulties of switching the existing system to a new supplier. It also meant that where a firm was multisourcing, a separate EDI might be needed for each supplier.

However, Internet-based EDI overcomes most of these shortcomings. Rather than using proprietary technology (VANs) it makes use of the public Internet. Therefore, Internet EDI, unlike traditional EDI, is ubiquitous, global, cheap, easy to use, and readily available and accessible both within (intranet) and outside (extranet) the company.

In addition, Internet EDI standards are becoming increasingly compatible with eXtensible Mark-up Language (XML). XML is already the key international standard for transferring structured data, and has wide acceptance, having been championed by organisations such as Microsoft, Netscape and Sun Microsystems, as well as by the WorldWideWeb consortium. The widespread adoption of XML means that most companies are now able to use Internet-based EDI to exchange documents cheaply and quickly. The International Data Corporation (IDC) has predicted that Internet EDI's share of EDI revenues will rise from 12 per cent to 41 per cent over the period 1999–2003, with this trend to continue into the future.[4]

A further potential benefit and driver of B2B commerce is that it provides for expansion from a local or national market to a global electronic market (e-market). For a relatively minimal capital outlay, a business can access a wider range of (better and/or cheaper) suppliers, and contact a larger potential customer base.

B2B activities vary from firm to firm, and industry to industry, but as well as global electronic markets, where many buyers and sellers meet for the purposes of trading electronically together, other common types of markets include a sell-side marketplace (where one company does all the selling), and a buy-side marketplace (where one company does all the buying).

Other benefits and drivers of B2B commerce include the following:

- That it provides an opportunity to market, sell and distribute goods and services to other businesses for 24 hours a day, 365 days a year, the so-called 'martini effect'.
- That it can sometimes significantly reduce fixed costs, perhaps through savings on premises, where a website has effectively become the organisation's showroom.
- That it also has the potential to improve pull-type supply chain management, such as JIT manufacture and delivery, based on integrated and fully-automatic supply chain management (SCM), and demand chain management (DCM) systems.
- That it can encourage organisations to adopt a more customer-centric approach, in which the business tracks consumers' preferences and re-engineers itself quickly to meet consumer needs. This might involve developing a mass customisation business model such as that adopted by Dell Computers, and discussed in the case study below.
- That it can facilitate the development of an integrated electronic customer relationship management (eCRM) system, based on customer information gathering, data warehousing and other market intelligence.
- That it may improve knowledge management systems within the organisation as employees use the company intranet system to access organisation-wide know-how.

Many of these potential advantages of B2B can be illustrated by looking at the following case study, based on Dell Computers. To facilitate your understanding of the issues discussed in the text an extended case study has been used in this chapter rather than two mini cases and there are additional questions at the end of the case study which you might like to attempt.

 The web address for Dell computers is *www.dell.com*

Dell Computers

Dell Computers was developed in the early 1980s by Michael Dell; by 1990 Dell was assembling its own brand personal computers and sales were over $500 million, with an established reputation for both laptops and desktop computers. Sales efforts were focused on selling directly to business customers, including educational and government agencies.

In the early 1990s Michael Dell developed a small team to explore using the Internet as a way of communicating with customers, and selling products on-line. This team increasingly became convinced that the Internet was an ideal channel for Dell products. There were a number of reasons for this:

- The number of Internet users was 20 million in 1996, and this was expected to double every year.
- Dell's major customers – business users – were already involved in the Internet, both in their use of the Internet, and the development of intranets.

Dell Computer launched its on-line website in July 1996, selling computers direct to customers. Company sales at this point had reached $7.8 billion, with an operating income in excess of $710 million. After six months Internet sales had reached about $1 million per day, and by autumn 1999, Internet sales accounted for 27 per cent of total revenue, at $15 million per day.

Dell is now the world's number one PC maker, having overtaken Compaq in July 2001, with a 13 per cent share of the market, and in the near future expects to see 50 per cent of its revenue come from Internet selling. So what are the critical success factors behind Dell's use of the Internet to grow its business, and why have rivals struggled to copy its business model?

First, Dell now sells all the items it produces via the Internet: desktops, workstations, notebooks, network servers and storage devices, software, and add-ons (e.g., zip drive, printer, etc.). These items are also sold by telephone, fax and mail, with an additional call centre service that can complement the Internet home page. Service, support and an introduction to the company are also presented on the home page.

Second, Dell has achieved high price competitiveness, because its business model centres on having the lowest costs in the industry. For instance, its sales representatives need fewer calls to close a sale generated from an Internet lead, and achieve higher sales than the industry average. Furthermore, order processing via the Internet is more efficient. Each quarter Dell receives 200 000 visits to its website to check order status, 500 000 technical service visits and 400 000 library downloads. Each of these transactions would have cost between $5 and $15 in time if handled over the telephone. In addition, technical manuals are available on-line, instead of Dell having to print these out and mail them.

Third, Dell was the first Web-based computer seller, and already had significant experience in direct marketing. Some commentators suggest that this has given it a significant **first-mover advantage** over its rivals.

Fourth, Dell is a relatively young company, which was built on a business model based on direct telemarketing, so there was no need for Dell to change its business strategy to adopt Internet commerce. The Internet is simply another medium for contacting distant customers interactively. However, for other rival companies this was not the case. For them, changing business strategy fundamentally was difficult, expensive, and time-consuming. Dell is also predominantly a one-product company, unlike many others in the electronics and computer industry.

Fifth, Dell has readily invested in the most advanced technology available, to provide a fully integrated value network, linking end consumers all the way back through the supply chain. In 1999, Dell invested in i2 Technologies software. The software enables it to monitor practically every part, every day. Dell also uses the Web thoroughly and creatively. Dell allows business buyers to download Premier Pages, enabling customers to configure what information their employees can see, and even which employees can see it.

Sixth, Dell has pioneered the concept of **mass customisation**, with its adaptive build-to-order fashion manufacturing system. To keep the price competitive without longer delivery time, efficient procurement of small numbers of parts from vendors, flexible manufacturing systems, and economical distribution to customers are essential. Dell computers can be assembled to order in about four minutes, with a further 90 minutes needed to load the software. They are delivered, on average, within three days of order.

Seventh, Dell uses the Internet effectively to manage and enhance its relationships with its suppliers, as well as with its customers. It has a fully integrated supply chain management system, and consequently Dell has relatively few suppliers, fewer than 200 in total. Many of its main rivals have at least 2000 suppliers.

Eighth, Dell's direct relationship with all of its customers makes **one-to-one database marketing** more effective. Dell learns about its customers by monitoring how they use the website, and is able to identify new market trends through analysing changes it notes in new build-to-order specifications over time.

Ninth, Dell provides global reach and value-added services as a single contact point. It currently sells computers in more than 170 countries. Dell has more than 10 000 service providers around the world who provide technology planning and acquisition, system deployment, network and product maintenance. The Internet can provide an efficient single point of contact for these services backed by corporate-level accountability for their products and services. The Internet makes it easier and reduces costs for customers to do business with Dell. Because the customers spend their own time to obtain service from the Internet, which previously required human agents in the call centre, the Internet has also reduced Dell's cost.

Finally, Dell has worked hard to establish a high reputation for quality and reliability. For instance, Dell products such as OptiPlex and Dell Dimension Desktop computer have picked up over 174 industry awards for performance, reliability and service. Internet customers in particular will hesitate to order expensive and complicated items without a trial, unless they are satisfied by the prior reputation of the company concerned.

Case study questions

1 Identify all the key elements of Dell's successful business model. Using a rating scale of 1–5 for each element identified (where 1 denotes the most important factor), summarise these into a single table.

2 Critically examine the four most important (highest rated) elements that you believe explain Dell's success. Explain your rationale for selecting those particular factors.

3 In your opinion, to what extent are other businesses (not just in the computer industry, but in any sector of the economy) able to successfully replicate Dell's business model? Illustrate your answer with appropriate examples.

Potential problems and limitations of B2B

As we have illustrated, there are a number of significant advantages to the widespread adoption of B2B commerce. However, it should be noted that there are also some potential limitations or barriers that may serve to delay or hamper the growth in B2B commerce. These include:

- Internet technology is continually developing, encouraging some organisations to postpone investment in the short term;
- technical limitations such as lack of system security, reliability and protocols – there are also currently some problems with telecommunications bandwidth and speed;
- the cost and difficulty of integrating existing (legacy) IT applications and databases with Internet and related software;
- the slow progress made in achieving universal international standards for the electronic transfer of information documentation;
- many legal, taxation and regulatory issues remain unresolved.

Nevertheless, on balance the clear benefits of B2B commerce are likely to outweigh the disadvantages, and we should expect to see continued dynamic growth in this area for some years to come.

Business applications 2: business-to-consumer (B2C) commerce

Key features

The business-to-consumer (B2C) model was the first to mature on the Internet, and has generated the most publicity. It involves a simple, singular retailing transaction between a business and a consumer. About one-fifth of e-business is between businesses and consumers. One example of the successful development and use of a B2C business model is by the e-retailer Amazon.com, which we will look at in more detail later.

It has been estimated that about 75 million individual Internet users participated in some form of on-line shopping in 2001.[5] The total amount of worldwide B2C revenue is highly contentious, with huge variations in estimates, but realistically is likely to exceed £500 billion per year by 2004.

B2C commerce can be characterised by a number of key features, including:

- Goods or services are offered for sale and purchased over the Internet; these may include both *digitised* products, such as music, airline tickets, or computer software that can be delivered *virtually* direct on the Internet, or physical products such as books, flowers and groceries that are delivered by post or courier.
- Transactions are typically quick and interactive.
- There are no pre-established business agreements.
- Security is primarily an issue for the buyer, rather than the seller.
- Low volume between each individual purchaser and supplier, often for relatively inexpensive items and/or frequently purchased items such as groceries.
- Well known packaged items, which have standard specifications.
- Items backed by a security guarantee and/or high brand recognition. The remoteness from the customer means that a strong reputation may be required to establish consumer confidence.
- Items whose operating procedures can be most effectively demonstrated by animation or video.
- Well designed websites, which are attractive and easy to use, are essential.

Emerging B2C and e-retailing business models

There are a number of ways of classifying the various B2C business models that are emerging:

- Direct marketing product websites – where manufacturers advertise and distribute their own products to customers via Internet-based stores, bypassing the use of intermediaries. Examples include Dell Computers, Nike, Cisco, The Gap and Sony.
- Pure electronic retailers (e-retailers) that have no physical stores, being purely cyber-based, such as Amazon.com.
- Traditional retailers with websites – sometimes called brick-and-click organisations – where the Internet provides an additional distribution channel for an existing business. Examples include Wal-Mart, Tesco, and Barnes & Noble.
- Best price searching agents – intermediaries, such as BestBuyBooks.com and Buy.com, that use software to search for the lowest prices available on the Net.
- Buyer sets the price – the customer nominates a price which they are willing to pay for certain goods or services, and the intermediary then tries to find a seller willing to sell at that price or lower. An example is Priceline.com.
- Electronic (on-line) auctions – host sites, such as E-Bay act like brokers, offering website services where sellers post their goods for sale, thereby allowing buyers to bid on those items.

Benefits of B2C commerce

There are a number of potential benefits and drivers of B2C commerce. Some of the more important are as follows:

1 For existing business organisations, many of the benefits are similar to B2B commerce, in that B2C commerce can expand the marketplace, lower costs, and improve management support systems, internal communications and knowledge sharing. It can also allow firms to focus more effectively on customer relationships. However, it might also promote more competition.

2 For new businesses, the Internet can reduce barriers to entry, and thus make it easier to enter new markets. One example would be Amazon.com, which did not need to incur the expense of opening up high street shops in order to successfully enter the retail book industry.

3 For customers, B2C on average provides faster and more complete information, a wider choice, and cheaper products and services. It also allows greater interaction with other customers.

4 For the wider community, an increase in B2C commerce may well have an impact in employment patterns, perhaps with an increase in home-working.

Possible limitations

While B2C commerce has some obvious benefits for the parties involved in transactions of this kind, as one might anticipate there are a number of potential limitations to its future growth and development. These include:

- lack of trust and consumer resistance;
- unresolved security, legal and privacy issues;
- insufficient buyers and sellers on-line;
- technical issues such as poor reliability, insufficient bandwidth, and speed;
- hardware and software tools are rapidly evolving and changing;
- the very expensive off-line marketing costs involved in building brand recognition for new on-line companies;
- lower barriers to entry will increase competition, and potentially increase rather than decrease consumer search and selection costs, as well as possible reduced industry profits overall;
- there are still significant distribution and storage costs involved for the sale of physical goods;
- existing bricks-and-mortar companies will not go away, and will continue to compete hard to maintain existing market share.

Many of the potential advantages and disadvantages of B2C can be illustrated by looking at the case study below, based on Amazon.com. As with the previous case study, you are encouraged to attempt at least some of the questions at the end of the text.

Synopsis

Technology plays an important role in all areas of business operation and is increasingly providing opportunities for businesses to interact with their customers and suppliers. With the development of the Internet there has been a revolution in the way in which business transactions are taking place and an increasing number of firms have begun to engage in electronic business-to-business and business-to-customer relationships alongside their traditional methods of doing business. We have even seen the emergence of some new businesses which have only an electronic existence. While such electronic relationships can have their problems and limitations, this is an area of the business environment in which there is likely to be significant developments in the coming years.

Summary of key points

- Technological developments have revolutionised the global marketplace and have spawned a whole new business vocabulary including the notion of e-business.

- The concept of e-business relates to the different aspects of doing business over the Internet and embraces a whole range of activities concerned with the exchange of products, services or information across electronic networks.

- E-commerce denotes a narrower range of activities related to the process of electronic transactions between buyer and seller.

- B2B and B2C represent the core of the notion of electronic commerce and provide a number of potential benefits for the parties involved in the transaction process.

- Both B2B and B2C, however, have their limitations which may hamper the growth of these two types of commerce.

- In the field of retailing a number of B2C business models have begun to emerge.

- Developments in this field have implications for both the demand side and supply side of markets.

- Technological advancement is a never-ending process that continues to shape the business environment.

Amazon.com

Bookselling over the Internet is one of the most sophisticated and successful B2C e-business sectors to have developed. The global cyber book market is expected to have grown beyond $1.1 billion by 2002.

Amazon is one of the most famous websites on the Internet, with 50 per cent of the cyber book market share. Amazon officially opened in July 1995, and had a turnover of $600 million by 1998, with an average monthly growth rate of 34 per cent.

As a pioneer, Amazon enjoyed considerable first-mover advantage, generating enormous publicity, which created awareness and established its brand name among the book buying public. Jeff Bezos, Amazon's founder, was convinced that consumers would enjoy the experience of browsing books electronically, reading reviews and excerpts from a particular book, and having it delivered a few days later. Bezos also felt that Amazon should be more profitable than traditional retailers in the longer term, on the basis that: 'We're short on real estate and long on technology. Technology gets cheaper every year and real estate more expensive.'

After initially gaining a reputation as a cyber bookstore, Amazon has gradually expanded its range of offerings into areas such as music, video, gifts and auctions. However, while Amazon has an impressive customer base, with over $1 billion in cash, and expanding sales, it has yet to make a profit. So far it has raised over $2 billion from the stock market, and spent roughly the same amount.

In fact, Amazon has found that it faces many of the problems of traditional retailers. For instance it has had to build a vast infrastructure of warehouse and distribution centres to house its burgeoning inventories of product lines, and has needed to spend heavily on off-line marketing to attract new customers.

Competition in the cyber book industry is also now very fierce with new competitors entering the market all the time. Barnes & Noble started to counterattack in 1997, and it quickly reached 15 per cent of the cyber book market share. Amazon also faces competition from software agents, such as BestBuyBooks.com and Buy.com, which offer to find the lowest prices available anywhere on the Net.

Nevertheless, Amazon still has many supporters. These argue that the lack of profits so far have arisen simply because the company has striven to build up a dominant position in e-commerce, and that triple-digit growth rates, and expansion into new product lines will produce the increased sales needed to cross over into profitability. Also its rival on-line retailers lack scale. For instance, Barnes & Noble, Amazon's nearest rival, only attracts a third of Amazon's 14 million unique visitors a month.

Amazon has always shown an incredible ability to innovate and to diversify its product range. It has introduced ideas such as allowing customers to review books on its website, and publish rankings that assign a chart position to every book in print based on its sales. These ideas are now commonplace on other sites.

Amazon has also successfully patented its Associates programme that allows an on-line merchant to sell products through other websites by paying commissions for customer referrals. For instance, if you run a website selling rare coins, you can publish a website listing the best books available on rare coins. When visitors click on these titles they are transported (one-click) to the Amazon website, which will pay the referring website a commission, if the visitor buys a book. It is estimated that about $1 billion of Amazon's future sales (out of a total of $3.4 billion) per year could arise through this affiliate system.

To attract customers Amazon is also increasingly making special offers, such as free shipping, or further discounted prices, although critics claim this is financially unsound given the current lack of profitability.

Amazon though does have a number of opportunities to diversify and expand further. For instance, it has created partnerships with companies such as Toy 'R' Us, and Borders Groups Inc., which have found it difficult to operate their own on-line operations. What these companies are seeking is to share and benefit from Amazon's expertise in delivery. Bezos has made the point that while the distribution centres of traditional retailers are good at shipping containers of products to stores, they are not designed to deliver single items direct to customers, something which requires very different capabilities, and in which Amazon specialises.

Second, there are a number of economic opportunities to expand the selling of additional higher-priced (if lower-margin) items on-line. Amazon is currently able to offer a selection of 25 000 electronic items on its site, compared with say 5000 in a big electronic store. Although gross margins in electronics are smaller than books, at only 10–15 per cent, the costs of storage, packing and shipping are roughly the same for a £300 digital camera as for a book. So overall the net profit per unit for these goods is actually higher.

Case study questions

1 Have a look at the websites of Amazon (*www.amazon.com* or *www.amazon.co.uk*) and its biggest American rival Barnes & Noble (www.bn.com) and compare what they do, and how their websites are structured.

2 Carry out a SWOT analysis of Amazon.com Inc. Using a rating scale of 1–5 for each factor identified (where 1 represents the most salient factor), summarise these into a single table.

3 Identify, in your opinion, the most important (highest-rated) factor for each category (strength, weakness, opportunity and threat), and explain your rationale for selecting those particular factors.

4 Try searching the WWW, using a search engine such as Google or Yahoo, for 'booksellers'. How many hits do you get? What do these results suggest?

5 In the light of question 4, and using Porter's five-forces model as a framework, consider the impact that Amazon.com. Inc. has had on the book selling industry.

6 Consider whether the strategy pursued by Amazon (cyber-based only) or that of Barnes & Noble (traditional bricks and mortar plus cyber space) will be the more successful in the longer term. Explain your reasons.

Review and discussion questions

1 Do you expect to see faster growth in B2C or B2B commerce in future? Explain your answer.

2 Which items (goods and services) are likely to be sold successfully on-line? Which type of items would you never consider buying on-line? Why?

3 What is eCRM? Why is it important for on-line businesses?

4 What is EDI? In relative terms, large companies have adopted EDI in greater numbers than smaller companies. Why do you think this is?

5 What is a brick-and-click business? Do these businesses have advantages or disadvantages compared with bricks-and-mortar businesses? If so, what are they? Do these businesses have advantages or disadvantages over cyber- only based businesses? If so, what are they?

Assignments

1 You have been commissioned to identify a new B2B business model. Write a report explaining how your proposed business model will generate income.

2 Many web-based businesses have failed. Search the Web, and identify such a business. Prepare a 10-minute PowerPoint presentation explaining what happened, and why you believe the business failed. In your conclusion, consider whether the same business concept might work in future, once the e-business environment has developed further.

Notes and references

1 OECD Information Technology Outlook, 2000. This is available at www.oecd.org

2 Turban, E., Lee, J., King, D. and Chung, M.H., *Information Technology for Management*, 3rd edition, John Wiley, 2000.

3 DTI, *Business in the Information Age – International Benchmarking Study 2000*, UK Department of Trade and Industry, 2000. Available on-line at: www.ukonlineforbusiness.gov.uk.

4 IDC, *Reinventing EDI: Electronic Data Interchange Services Market Review and Forecast*, 1998–2003, International Data Corporation, 1999.

5 emarketer.com, July 2001.

Further reading

Chaffey, D., *E-Business and E-Commerce Management*, Prentice Hall, 2002.

Chen, S., *Strategic Management of e-Business*, John Wiley, 2001.

DTI, *Business in The Information Age – International Benchmarking Study 2000*, UK Department of Trade and Industry, 2000.

IDC, *Reinventing EDI: Electronic Data Interchange Services Market Review and Forecast, 1998–2003*, International Data Corporation, 1999.

Rayport, J. and Jaworski, B., *Introduction to E-commerce*, McGraw Hill, 2001.

Shapiro, C. and Varian, H., *Information Rules*, Harvard Business School Press, 1999.

Turban, E., Lee, J., King, D. and Chung, M.H., *Electronic Commerce 2002: A Managerial Perspective*, Prentice Hall, 2002.

Whinston, A.B., Choi, S-Y. and Stahl, D.O., *The Economics of Electronic Commerce*, Macmillan Technical Publishing 1997.

Web links and further questions are available on the website at:
www.booksites.net/worthington

16

Corporate responsibility and the environment

Dean Patton

There is a growing body of opinion that businesses have a duty to fulfil objectives that stretch beyond the simple well-being of the organisation to the promotion of greater corporate social responsibility, particularly with regard to the natural environment. This chapter looks at the reasons which lie behind this perspective and speculates on how businesses can be encouraged to accommodate environmental policies into their strategic management techniques.

Objectives

- To investigate the involvement that business has with other elements of society.

- To identify a corporation's primary and secondary stakeholders.

- To define the meaning of corporate social responsibility and determine the actions business needs to undertake in order to be considered socially responsible.

- To estimate the benefits that are available to business from following a strategy of corporate social responsibility.

Key terms

Business culture
Competitive advantage
Corporate image
Corporate social
  responsibility
Cost-benefit analysis
Eco-label

Eco-Management and Audit
  Scheme (EMAS)
Environmental management
  systems
Genetically modified foods
Investment appraisal
Learning curve effect

Life-cycle analysis
Market niche
Polluter pays principle
Self-regulation
Social costs and benefits
Sustainable development
Top-down approaches

Introduction

Corporate social responsibility means that a corporation should be held accountable for any of its actions that affect people, their communities and their environment. It implies that negative business impacts on people and society should be acknowledged and corrected if at all possible. Corporate responsibility, however, does not preclude organisations from making profits, nor does it mean that firms acting in a responsible manner cannot be as profitable as other firms that are less responsible. The concept requires organisations to balance the benefits to be gained against the costs of achieving those benefits. An organisation that sought to act in a responsible way would need to compromise and take into account the secondary effects, i.e. the externalities of business practice when undertaking work. These responsibilities are directly linked to the essential functions the organisation performs for society and the influence it has upon the lives of individuals. The term 'corporate social responsibility' encompasses a variety of subjects which would include business ethics, corporate governance, business and the environment, and corporate citizenship or business in the community (*see* also Chapter 10).

The issue of corporate responsibility has been pushed up the management agenda; driven to a degree by society's growing doubts over previously held implicit assumptions about ethical business behaviour. This response acknowledges that the way in which much of business now operates makes it impossible to assume that those involved in it instinctively know how to 'do the right thing'. The business community has slowly come to terms with this perception and many business leaders now appear to accept that management has a wider remit and that its decisions must involve and be transparent to a variety of bodies that include governments, citizens, shareholders, customers and employees. As a result, the issues which companies must address have broadened well beyond financial performance, to embrace corporate, ethical and environmental governance. This viewpoint is supported by a survey of European companies conducted by Harris Research (1997) which indicated that 70 per cent of companies reported corporate responsibility to be a very important issue; that 88 per cent regarded corporate reputation as exerting a big influence on corporate value; and that 25 per cent saw greater expectations of social responsibility as the main reason that 'reputation management' was rising in importance.

web link The Corporate Social Responsibility Forum has a website at *www.csrforum.com* You might also like to consult *www.ebbf.org* for a paper on CSR and business success and the Business for Social Responsibility forum at *www.bsr.org* for a helpful definition.

Historically actions that have led to improvements in corporate social responsibility have been viewed as having the potential to deflect attention away from the classical organisational aims of profit maximisation and increased shareholder value. The above survey indicates a growing realisation that changes in societal values mean that such actions are integral to an organisation's ability to achieve these classical aims. Nevertheless, there is still some discussion on the extent to which it is appropriate for organisations to pursue policies that create greater corporate responsibility. The debate revolves around the purpose of business and the knowledge/abilities of those that run the organisation. If the sole responsibility of business is to the provider of capital, then all the resources of such an organisation should be devoted to making profit and any deviation from this by the managers of a firm's resources is contrary to the objectives of the organisation. Furthermore it can be argued that individuals who are given the task of running a business are not equipped to decide what actions are of a corporately responsible nature, and as such should simply operate within the rules established by the elected representatives of the people.[1] This is not, however, a view that is shared by all, and although most commentators would agree that business will not generally behave in a socially responsible manner out of altruism, it is acknowledged that there are benefits to be gained by business by at least making some efforts towards corporate responsibility.[2]

Entrepreneurs and industrialists are increasingly taking the view that a change in **business culture** may be a more successful strategy. Roddick, of Body Shop, Carey, of Lucas Industries, and others may have started this trend but it has now moved into mainstream business. In the BT publication 'Changing Values' (1998) for instance, Sir Ian Vallance indicated that the 'pursuit of sustainable development is not an option ... it is nothing more or less than a necessity for economic survival'. This sets out an alternative perception to the environmental responsibility of business, whereby business can make a contribution by facing up to moral choices concerning profits as opposed to social responsibilities. Roddick has commented that Body Shop continues to espouse its values in the hope that one day the cosmetics industry will wake up and realise that the potential threat of Body Shop is not so much economic as simply the threat of good example. Body Shop, for many, represents an alternative view of how business might be run. This alternative view, however, has become more accepted and it is interesting to note that the Institute of Directors (IoD) in an attempt to raise personal and corporate ethical standards has recently devised its own code of professional ethics to which it expects its 54 000 members to adhere. The code goes further than any existing code of professional conduct, focusing on personal responsibility towards employees, customers, suppliers and the wider community.

web link

Most large companies now refer to corporate responsibility in their annual reports and other literature. For useful examples see *inter alia* the websites of companies such as Ford (*www.ford.com*); Shell (*www.shell.com*); BP (*www.bp.com*); The Co-operative Bank (*www.co-operative.bank.co.uk*); and Body Shop (*www.bodyshop.com*).

To summarise, there is a range of opinions over how business should interact with its environment and therefore how best to incorporate concern for the environment within corporate policy. However, if the majority of firms do not perceive the sea change necessary in business culture to promote sustainable development, then external influences must ensure the protection of wider interests. Indeed one school of thought would argue that such control is the prerogative of elected representatives and that the attempts of business to develop social programmes independent of this would be to undermine the democratic process.

In essence, the stimulus behind organisational developments in the environmental management of business process and practice lies on some continuum between the need to operate in the confines of what is legally acceptable and the desire to create a business that is sustainable.

Stakeholder theory

As indicated in Chapter 7, stakeholders are all the groups affected by a corporation's decisions, policies and operations. The number of stakeholders and the variety of interests that a company's management must consider when setting its aims and objectives can make decision making a complex process. The amount of influence would depend upon the amount of power each group of stakeholders could wield and this will tend to vary over time.

Stakeholder theory suggests that there is a number of groups to which a business is answerable when pursuing stated aims and objectives. Traditionally it has been held that these will be the shareholders, customers and employees of the business – a very narrow definition that concentrates on those groups involved directly with the organisation. This assumption is being called increasingly into question and the incidents at Shell (Brent Spar, or its activities in Nigeria), or Perrier, or more recently with Monsanto (with the introduction of GM foods) have shown the influence that the wider society can bring to business practice.[3] It is often argued that businesses and organisations should be seen as tools for providing goods and services to satisfy the wants and needs of society. Such a view deals with the purpose of business as a servant to society rather than simply a servant to a narrow set of groups involved directly with the business. This represents an important distinction. Organisations pervade all our lives to an ever-increasing extent; if they are to accept responsibility for the environment, then there is a need to integrate an 'environmental perspective' into the formulation and implementation of corporate policies. This is a necessary step in converting concern into actual behaviour. Accordingly, it could be suggested that the extension of stakeholders to include groups that are not directly involved in the business induces a more corporately responsible business culture.

To illustrate this point the Co-operative Bank, in 1998, published alongside its annual results what it called a partnership report – essentially an audit of the impact of its activities on society, the environment and its 'partners' or stakeholders. The partnership report was based on the bank's acknowledgement that it has relationships with such groups as customers, staff and their families, suppliers and the wider community as well as its only shareholder, the Co-operative Wholesale Society. In general, businesses have become increasingly aware of the need to manage organisational reputation and many business leaders take the view that reputation is best achieved via a more inclusive approach which pays due recognition to all stakeholders. This standpoint has enabled the more indirect stakeholders to generate greater levels of power and therefore control over the actions of organisations.

It would appear that the growing unease that society has displayed over the degree to which business will operate from an ethical standpoint has led to a greater democratisation of organisational decisions and a codification of desired standards and attitudes. In 1987 only 18 per cent of large UK companies were known to have codes of business ethics, but by 1997 that figure had trebled to 57 per cent. The Institute of Business Ethics' 1998 report shows that 271 of the UK's 500 largest companies now have a code. As indicated previously, the IoD has devised its own code of professional ethics to which all its members are expected to subscribe.

Environmental management: an issue of corporate responsibility

Organisations accepting responsibility for the impacts of business process upon air, land and water is just one of the issues to be addressed within the debate on business attitudes towards corporate responsibility. It is, however, the one area where governments, communities and business have worked most closely to improve their understanding of the issues and resolve the identified problems; in particular, to reconcile the perceived need for economic growth with the demand for greater environmental protection and reduced levels of ecological degradation.

Historically, economic development and growth through business activity have been portrayed as beneficial to the well-being of a society and as an important influence on the quality of life of its citizens. Accordingly, organisational practices and processes designed to increase production and consumption have generally been encouraged and welcomed, even though their detrimental effects on the natural environment have been recognised for some time.[4]

While growth invariably remains an objective of governments, its environmental impact has become part of the political agenda at both national and international level, where particular concern has been expressed about the extent of ecological degradation, the rate at which limited resources are being depleted, and the frequency and scale of accidents caused as a result of business practice. Pessimists have argued that in the pursuit of growth many countries may have already surpassed levels of usage of essential resources and sustainable levels of pollution, and have blighted future generations for the sake of present consumption. The more optimistic view is that individual and collective action can give rise to sustainable development which allows for present requirements to be met without compromising the ability of successive generations to meet their own needs. The concept of scarcity and choice is not new, but the way in which human needs are to be met while seeking not to compromise the future is the practical challenge that will face society and therefore all business organisations.

It is the philosophy of sustainable development that many argue is the only way forward for the world economy. The problem of environmental degradation is closely related to the issue of economic growth, and both industry and society need to balance environmental protection with economic development. The difficulties in finding an appropriate balance lie not just in the need to reconcile a range of conflicting interests but also in the relative lack of information on the relationship between economic development and its long-term impact on the natural environment.

The seriousness of the situation and its potentially disastrous consequences suggest that an environmental revolution is needed which may require a dramatic change in the behaviour of society and industry as both consumers and producers. Much attention has, of course, been focused on political initiatives which are testimony to the widely accepted view that environmental policy needs to be formalised and co-ordinated at international level if it is to be effective in tackling the salient issues. 'Top-down' approaches, however, can only be part of the overall solution and much depends on the actions of firms and individuals in the marketplace and on their willingness to accept responsibility for their own behaviour and its consequences. In short, concern for the environment needs to be expressed through the actions of a myriad of actors, and for a revolution in environmental responsibility to be successful it must permeate all levels of society.

Business response to environmental concerns

Corporately responsible actions and/or expenditures have a trade-off cost: the alternatives that the money, resources, time and effort could have been used for if they had not been devoted to more socially oriented goals. As indicated previously, this is generally known as the 'opportunity cost', the notion that in a world of finite resources, whatever a business chooses to do, it does at the expense of something else, the opportunity forgone. As a result, the timing of returns is a critical factor in the decision-making process. The returns to investment in greater environmental responsibility are, however, likely to be of a long-term nature, a situation which may offer little comfort to firms, particularly small businesses that are fighting for survival and need short-term returns. Thus while businesses, in general, may want to provide a more environmentally responsible policy – particularly if their stakeholders are forcing them to look to the wider concerns of business practice and process – the implementation of such a policy may only occur if it is deemed to be in the best interests of the business: that is, where the resources are used in an optimum way to provide sufficient reward for the hierarchy of stakeholders.

Business culture at present is still largely driven by short-term profit and the stakeholders that generally hold the most influence are the providers of financial capital, the shareholders or owners of the business. In order to develop greater environmental awareness in business it is necessary to review the way objectives are prioritised to take account of the viewpoints of indirect stakeholders, thus ensuring that the issue of sustainable development is brought on to the corporate agenda. The willingness and/or ability of a firm to be corporately responsible for its own sake has little, if any, precedent in current business practice; organisational policy is far more dependent upon the business environment in which the organisation works. All business activity, by definition, involves some environmental damage and the best a business can achieve is to clear up its own mess while searching hard for ways to reduce its impact on the environment.

It is, therefore, impossible to expect the type of business environment not to influence the level of corporate responsibility, and the degree of change, the intensity of competition and the scale of complexity will all be factors in the creation of policy, whether this be to increase market share or to reduce the levels of air emissions.

If firms are to provide a greater level of corporate responsibility, does society have to resort to the use of laws and government regulation, or will business perceive the change in societal expectations and decide voluntarily to act more responsibly towards the general environment? The answer probably lies somewhere between the two, but there is obviously a close association between the level of legislative impact upon a firm and the degree of perceived impact the organisation would expect to have upon the environment that may lead to the implementation of environmental management systems. Sethi puts forward a threefold typology:[5]

1 *Social obligation.* A situation where the organisation uses legal and economic criteria to control corporate behaviour. The strategy is, therefore, reactive and dependent upon change instigated by the market or through legislation. The organisation exhibits an exploitative strategy, giving in to environmental concerns only when it can obtain direct benefit. The principal stakeholder in this type of organisation is the shareholder and the pursuit of profit the primary objective.

2 *Social responsibility.* This type of organisation tries to go beyond the requirements prescribed by law and instead seeks to conform to the current values and norms of society. The organisation will, therefore, accept responsibility for solving current environmental problems and will attempt to maintain current standards of both the social and physical environment. In order to achieve this the organisation must be accountable to a range of stakeholders and this assumes that profit, although the dominant motive, is not the only one.

3 *Social responsiveness.* This organisation exhibits a proactive strategy, actively seeking future social change. The policies of the organisation are followed with a fervent zeal, the business seeks to lead the field in terms of promoting a corporately responsible attitude. It accepts public evaluation of its policies and procedures and is prepared to impinge upon profit to maintain the high profile it has established through its corporately responsible actions.

The concept that business will be purely socially responsible must come from an ethical position, a standpoint which is difficult to envisage within the British economy but one to which Body Shop must offer a close approximation. Businesses, however, may actually follow a socially responsible approach as a result of the possible advantages it might afford the organisation. In general the hypothesis can be supported that a better society produces a better environment for business. Further, it often makes sound investment sense, leading to increases in market share, a lowering of costs through energy and material savings and finally an improvement in the 'corporate image'.[6] Provision for responsible behaviour is therefore financially good for the business. A further possible impetus for implementing environmental management systems could come from political rather than economic sources. In simple terms, organisations that instigate their own environmental policies and/or regulations tend to face a reduced threat from external regulatory bodies and this improves company image while reducing possible checks upon corporate practices and processes.

web link   Body Shop's website address is *www.bodyshop.com*

In essence, the conclusions reached highlight the fact that organisations will not normally pursue a proactive role in the development of environmentally responsible policies. The initial short-run costs are prohibitive when the payback is generally assumed to be over the long term. What might be required is a re-education of those involved in the decision-making process so that they understand the benefit of a longer-term view and can identify policies that offer a sustainable competitive advantage over time. This is true for all strategy and is therefore applicable to the implementation of environmental policies.

| Mini case | Environmental performance in the small firms' sector |

Approximately 97 per cent of firms in the UK have fewer than 50 employees. These firms account for 50 per cent of the total working population and nearly one-third of the country's GDP. The economic importance of the sector has grown since 1979 and as a consequence the environmental impact of the sector has also become more significant.

The small-firm sector has not, however, kept pace with the general environmental awareness of business. Small firms have continually underperformed in the use of environmental audits, knowledge of environmental legislation and the publication of environmental reports.

A number of reasons have been put forward for the perceived failure of small firms to become environmentally aware:

1 *Cost.* Small firms have limited resources and in general do not perceive an economic gain from implementing environmental policies.

2 *Lack of expertise.* Small firms simply do not have the human or physical resources for developing improved environmental practices. In addition they are very sceptical of inviting expensive outside consultants to investigate their existing practices.

3 *Ignorance of legislation.* The plethora of small firms limits the ability of any agency to monitor the whole sector. As a consequence many small firms rely upon the fact that 'what they do not know cannot hurt them'. Small firms are notoriously 'ignorant' of their environmental responsibilities and rely to some extent upon the problems of scale that monitoring agencies face.

4 *Scale advantages.* Small firms cannot spread the cost of any environmental initiatives over a large product range. Nor can they benefit significantly from the improved public relations often generated by environmental good practice.

These factors may have led to a market imperfection in the development of environmental responsibility within business. As a result, new and imaginative initiatives are needed to create greater interest within the small-firm sector and to improve its environmental practices.

The interaction of business and society

In assuming that business needs to be more aware of its environmental impacts, society as a whole is expressing a dissatisfaction with existing performance. The method by which a group or individual may come to this decision could be very subjective, based upon value judgements and experience. The Institute of Chartered Accountants of Scotland published a report that suggests that, in spite of increasing evidence that environmental issues have a potential impact on the numbers reported in financial statements, UK financial statements only rarely make explicit reference to such matters. The report identifies a small group of leading-edge companies that is carefully monitoring environmental developments and, as a matter of policy, seeking to respond in advance of anticipated developments in the environmental area. It is in these leading-edge businesses where accountants are actively responsive, putting a focus on formal assessment of risks and liabilities, active provisioning and identification of environmental costs in their accounts. A number of bodies, including the Association of Certified and Corporate Accounts (ACCA), has recommended that company annual reports and accounts should contain an 'environmental review section' that would detail their environmental policies and contain a summary of their legal compliance status and a review of their actual environmental performance. To add weight to any argument there needs to be a more scientific measurement of performance that is based upon criteria other than those that can be easily assigned a monetary value.

Cost-benefit analysis is one technique which attempts to set out and evaluate the social cost and benefits of an action. The essential difference between cost-benefit analysis and ordinary **investment appraisal** methods used by firms is the stress on the **social costs and benefits**, and such an approach can prove problematical. Two specific difficulties arise:

1 The measurement of physical units such as improvements or otherwise in the quality of life.
2 The complexity involved in reducing all costs and benefits to some common unit of account in order to offer a degree of comparison. Since the unit of account most commonly used is money, this means that values must be attached to environmental degradation, resource usage and in some instances human life.

The main reasons why it is important to place a monetary valuation on environmental gains and losses is that it offers a measurement of society's preference. Placing a value upon environmental degradation allows ordinal ranking of preferences between the desire to have goods and services against the desire to maintain the environment and reduce the use of scarce resources. Monetary values offer a direct and more tangible comparison. Cost-benefit analysis, therefore, allows careful itemisation of all relevant classes of costs and benefits, the exclusion of irrelevant transfer payments, quantification of what can reasonably be quantified and a full specification of the complete set of alternatives to the action under consideration. This is said to provide a sounder basis for the decision and, most importantly, to permit an estimate of the implicit money values that must be attached to particular non-monetary benefits and costs in order to justify a particular action. Thus cost-benefit analysis can be viewed as a means of making the best possible information available to the decision makers.

Methods of encouraging environmental concern within business

The quality of the existing environment and improvements in it would be regarded by economists as a form of public good. This is a good for which the principle of exclusion does not apply; it can be jointly consumed by many individuals simultaneously, at no additional cost and with no reduction in the quality or quantity of the public good consumed by any citizen.

The fact that the principle of exclusion does not apply creates the 'free-rider' problem because some groups will believe that others will take on the burden of paying for the public good: in this case the extra cost incurred to improve the quality of the environment. Historically, the government has taken charge of public goods (e.g. the fire and police services or the provision of street lighting) in order to ensure that they are provided and not left to the vagaries of the market. Recent events suggest, however, that state intervention in the future cannot be taken for granted, particularly in areas where market solutions appear possible.

Government intervention

Direct action by government within the business sector has not led to improved environmental responsibility. Nationalised industries have not been the bastions of the ecological environment and in some instances in the United Kingdom (e.g. the 'tall stacks' policy) have appeared to disregard the environmental degradation that they created. Indirect action through regulation or legislation may be more effective, but this is not in keeping with the general policy of *laissez-faire* which operated in the United Kingdom under the Conservative government throughout the 1980s and in the 1990s and has been largely followed by the Labour government post-1997.

Furthermore, there is a number of dangers associated with a reliance solely upon a regulatory system as a means of control. Laws tend to be reactive and there may be significant differences between the letter and the spirit of the law. Industry may hold a monopoly of expertise, making government regulation ineffective. Finally, transnational issues (e.g. leaks from nuclear power stations, global warming, acid rain) are far too multifarious and intricate to resolve through regulation. This is not to say that the legal system is always ineffectual, but simply that it is not a precise means of control, often providing the unscrupulous with scope to act as they please.

Indeed, regulation has become an increasingly complex tool to control business practice.[7] The globalisation of business means that organisations are having to deal with different legislative controls and requirements in different countries. In some instances, company policies change from country to country to meet the lowest standards possible. The tragedy at Bhopal, in India, illustrated how the multinational organisation Union Carbide was willing to accept lower standards of safety in a Third World plant than would have been deemed appropriate for a domestic plant in the United States. It pursued a policy of satisfying the law or regulatory frameworks of the individual host country. Similar arguments can be made for the many shipping organisations registering under flags of convenience which allow cost reductions.

Alternatively, to sell in all markets may require working to the highest common denominator. Not all countries operate the same environmental standards and, although the EU has attempted to standardise some legislation there are still differences in what environmental requirements organisations must fulfil in different countries. Conforming to the stringent requirements of certain markets may improve the competitive position of firms in other markets.

Proposed or possible regulation may also persuade organisations to consider the impact of their activities, particularly if in future more stringent legislation looks likely as governments accept the principle of the **polluter paying** for any environmental damage caused. To judge by recent American experience, it is possible that retrospective action may be taken, with companies being penalised for decisions taken years previously.[8]

For some organisations legal compliance is an end in itself, for others regulations form a minimum standard of behaviour. The culture of the organisation, within obvious cost constraints, will determine the level of behaviour above the law. For the organisation that sees its responsibilities over and above the law, there may be some additional benefits. Those organisations that develop environmentally sensitive processes and systems first will have greater experience than those slower to react, who may find themselves overtaken by the quickening rate of new legislation. It may also be the case that those firms that undertake environmental initiatives first are able to develop a **competitive advantage** over other businesses in the same sector because they are able to take advantage of benefits associated with experience and **learning curve effects**. There is, however, a danger that organisations view the use of environmental management tools as a one-off measure. Like any business plan, such a process must be regularly reviewed in order to take account of our increasing knowledge of this subject and the changing needs of the organisation.

To summarise, legislation and regulation do have an important role to play in improving the environmental performance of business overall; this is most evident when governments have the relevant information concerning business practice and process. Frequently, however, business possesses the necessary information and the government has to incur a significant resource cost to acquire the relevant knowledge; suggesting that other tools of control are necessary to instil within business the required corporate responsibility. A strong argument can be made for providing greater information concerning products to the consumer, thereby offering the opportunity to individuals to make more informed decisions about which products to consume. Such a policy would reduce the level of government involvement and help to educate individuals as to the part they play in creating environmental hazards and damage.

Market mechanisms

The increased level of environmental awareness among the population – owing to the easier availability of information – has already led to more informed choices being made by various stakeholder groups that interact with business.[9] Customers, suppliers, employees and investors are all more aware of their responsibilities to the environment, and there are various ways in which their considered decisions can influence the overall objectives of business and ensure that the organisation is corporately responsible for its actions. Increasingly, discerning consumers offer a powerful inducement to firms and despite the lack of perfect information some product switching is already occurring. Firms seeking to maintain current market share, or looking for new opportunities, must be aware of these changes. There has been a number of eco-labelling schemes that have been developed which have assisted consumers in identifying products which are thought to have the least impact upon the environment in their particular class.

An EU **eco-label** was launched in 1993, but take-up has been slow across EU members and only around 200 products have been successfully introduced and certified under the scheme. In the UK the Department of the Environment, Transport and the Regions (DETR) decided in 1998 no longer to continue with the scheme and called upon the EU member states to push for an 'integrated product policy'.

Well-labelled eco-friendly products are far more prevalent in Europe, where there is a much broader view of nature rather than a focus upon particular issues, such as animal rights or certified forestry schemes. This has led to better-regulated and publicised initiatives on encouraging and labelling eco-friendly products. For example, nine national eco-labels are currently operated in seven EU member states (The Netherlands and Spain each have two) and eco-label schemes in Europe are generally well respected, with certification controlled by independent bodies.

The forerunner of these various labels was established in Germany in 1978 and was colloquially known as the 'Blue Angel'. The label has been adopted by more than 4300 products and 90 product groups; and it is claimed that the majority of households look out for the Blue Angel when choosing environmentally friendly products. Other labels include, in the Netherlands, Stichting Milieukeur; in France, NF Environnement; in Finland, Norway and Sweden, the Nordic White Swan. Most importantly, businesses that wish to apply for these labels will have to provide proof of environmental performance from their suppliers to qualify. In this way products will be evaluated using **life-cycle analysis**, a cradle-to-grave assessment of a product's impact upon the environment.

Further emphasis upon the environment has been created with the introduction of a number of **environmental management systems (EMS)** standards. The UK developed the first EMS (British Standard 7750) but this has subsequently been replaced by ISO 14001 to allow the introduction of a common international EMS standard. There is, however, a European Union EMS standard known as the **Eco-Management and Audit Scheme (EMAS)** which is generally regarded as the most demanding EMS standard. EMS standards have followed the same basic approach as the quality standards and it is hoped that these EMS standards will be able to enjoy the same level of success as the quality standards (BS 5750/ISO 9001). This theme is highlighted by the actions of Body Shop which demanded that Peter Lane, the organisation chosen to distribute its stock, had satisfactorily to pass an environmental audit before being given the contract. The point is further supported by the actions of B&Q, a UK chain of hardware stores, which has audited not only its own products but those of its suppliers. These audits were the precursor of implemented 'environmental' policies, including the delisting of a large peat supplier who refused to desist from sourcing from Sites of Special Scientific Interest. It seems safe to argue that business will in future face greater pressures to meet new demands from the more discerning customer, be they individuals or other businesses.

It is interesting to note that premiums paid to insurance companies have increased in line with losses incurred for environmental damage caused by normal business activity. In the same way that householders who can demonstrate increased security measures in their homes are rewarded with lower premiums, companies which demonstrate evidence of environmental safeguards may also reap such rewards. More critically, failure to demonstrate extensive environmental management systems may lead to a refusal to offer insurance cover. Moreover, lending institutions may not wish to be associated with 'poorly safeguarded' organisations.

In the United States, a further development in legislation means that lending institutions may be held liable for environmental damage caused by plant held as collateral for loans. As a result there has been a significant tightening in the flow of funds to polluting industries such as scrap merchants, businesses dealing with hazardous waste, pulp and paper mills and petrol filling stations. Similar trends are evident in the United Kingdom, where banks have become increasingly careful about loans made to small businesses that have any conceivable environmental risk potential. Therefore, finance that is already limited is being further reduced not because of the viability of the business but because of the environmental liability hanging over them. Thus, while the United Kingdom is yet to see this type of legislation, banks and other lending institutions are already very aware of their environmental responsibilities and this is increasingly encapsulated in their lending policies.

External pressure

There has been a considerable amount of pressure from external groups upon business; these have ranged from *ad hoc* groups formed in local communities to large transnational organisations like Greenpeace. The size and scale of the groups may differ but their objectives are similar: to use whatever power they have at their disposal to influence the decision-making process, and there have been a number of notable successes. For many groups, however, this does not go far enough and accordingly the calls for increased democratisation of the decision-making process to include wider stakeholder groups are becoming more frequent and vociferous.

Effective democratisation assumes greater stakeholder access, with attendant changes in structure and culture; the depth of access and the magnitude of change depends upon the degree to which democratisation is embraced. Participatory democracy may be the most effective form, if yet a largely untested philosophy; however, the success of such an approach will require not only involvement in the decision-making processes, but also access to information and expert knowledge which provide the basis for effective power and influence. Significantly, this approach has still to be culturally accepted by the majority of businesses in the United Kingdom.

Finally, there are the dangers of companies burying their heads in the sand in the hope that the 'new environmentalism' is the latest management fad. The costs, however, of a late response and the possible threat of legal action as well as punitive fines could be critical for those that are slow to develop environmentally sensitive policies. Organisations must realise that the stakes are high and that the costs of getting it wrong (e.g. a serious incident causing environmental damage) are significant in terms of company image, fines, lost production, lost sales, insurance premiums and customer loyalty.

Self-regulation

As noted previously, industry is frequently the holder of the information and expertise required for the effective and efficient implementation of regulation. To regulate, the government has to acquire that information and this can be an expensive process.

However, if industry were to **self-regulate** and adopt environmental controls without waiting for the government, then this process of information gathering could be avoided. There are obvious drawbacks to this type of approach. Mintzberg has pointed out that often the implementation of self-regulation is a response by business to attempt to offset on-coming regulation. This has two very positive outcomes for the business sector. First, it offers credibility with society that as a sector it has the interests of the environment in mind when conducting business. Second, it provides a convenient smokescreen for practices which may be regarded as dubious by an external body. It is, therefore, inherent in the idea of self-regulation that the organisation can be trusted to fulfil the environmental requirements of the rest of society.

Growing public awareness of environmental issues and the subsequent regulation of business activities have demonstrated that society is not prepared to allow business to be conducted without restriction or without consideration of its impact upon the environment. The assumption that organisations will abide by the rules and norms of their society has been seen to be misplaced. If society is to trust managers of businesses, it must ask by whose social norms they are controlling their organisations. The growing trend for annual environmental reports is a positive step in this direction; nearly one in four FTSE 100 companies publishes a separate 'green' report which recognises the impact that business has on the environment. Body Shop has gone one stage further with the publication of a 'values' report (*see* mini case), a wide-ranging, independently verified audit of the company's track record on the issues of the environment, animal protection and human relationships within the business. Most reports, however, provide little in the way of substantive statements and disclosures of what remains very sensitive information and, not being covered by any regulation or standard, they tend to lack consistency. Governments are, therefore, likely to be forced to continue to monitor self-regulatory systems and to retain the power to enforce environmental objectives.

Mini case   Body Shop values report

In 1996 Body Shop introduced a 'values' report. The company has suggested that this provides an independently verified audit of its track record on the environment, animal protection and human relations within the business. The report covers a wide range of issues, and aims to measure 'performance against policies, internal management systems, programmes and targets, shareholder expectations and external benchmarks'.

The diverse nature of the audit is reflected in a statement made by D. Wheeler, general manager of the company's ethical audit department: 'At a time when lots of people are talking about the stakeholder economy, this is a way of identifying how a company acts upon its own stakeholders – anyone we impact upon or anyone who impacts upon us – and using the information to improve the company.'

The report is derived from a number of attitude surveys to the company's activities among customers, suppliers, employees, franchisees and shareholders. The surveys were undertaken by an audit committee and sought to obtain an independent evaluation of how well the organisation had met its stated objectives. The outcome of these surveys has been the establishment by Body Shop of clear targets for improvements in business planning and/or providing more communication and support for suppliers. How well the company achieves these targets will be assessed in subsequent reports.

The values report may have taken the concept of an environmental audit a stage further than the majority of companies would wish to undertake. It does, however, indicate a growing trend by companies in general to take greater account of the secondary effects of business. It is estimated that by the mid-1990s two-thirds of the UK's top companies had some kind of environmental evaluation in their annual reports, and that around a quarter of FTSE 100 companies had published a separate green report. This provides clear evidence that the stakeholder concept is gaining increased credibility within the business decision-making process.

The benefits to business from the implementation of environmental policies

The previous section has indicated that industry is being driven to develop more environmentally friendly policies; the implication is that organisations would revert to previous policies if the forces driving environmentalism were negated. This assumption, however, fails to take account of the benefits that the implementation of corporately responsible policies has brought some organisations. The drive for greater corporate responsibility has emanated from North America where companies are increasingly expected to draw up their own plans for meeting environmental obligations, putting a premium on having accurate knowledge about their own performance. Business strategists within North America have suggested that in the coming years environmentalism will be at the cutting edge of social reform and therefore one of the most important areas that business must consider. The commitment of industry, however, lags behind the rhetoric and this is particularly true within business in the UK. In order to improve environmental performance there needs to be an increase in information and training, not simply about the environmental consequences, but also concerning the benefits that are being obtained by organisations that are adopting greater corporate responsibility.

Efficiency of factor inputs

Business strategists as well as organisations have already generated a considerable amount of pro-environmental jargon; PPP (Pollution Prevention Pays), WOW (Wipe Out Waste) and WRAP (Waste Reduction Always Pays) are some of the better-known acronyms. The obvious message is that more efficient use of materials and energy will reduce cost, provide a positive effect on the company's accounts and improve the 'bottom line'. 3M, for example, announced savings of approximately £200 million in 1986 mainly due to energy and material cost reductions under its PPP policy. Barclays Bank has had an energy efficiency audit operating since 1979, during which time it estimates it has saved the bank millions of pounds. Body Shop also commissioned an energy audit, where savings of £23 000 per annum were realised immediately through 'small investments' and further potential savings of £28 700 per annum were also identified as available with further investment. The message that businesses are beginning to receive is that too much attention has been extended to labour and capital costs at the expense of material and energy costs and the new environmental management systems are highlighting this issue.

web link   3M can be accessed at *www.3m.com*
The main website for Monsanto (*see* below) is *www.monsanto.com*

Improved market image

The image that organisations portray to the rest of society is increasingly important, owing to the development of rapid information flows. Creating this image can be expensive and resources may be wasted as a result of a careless action or remark. A good example of this would be the aggressive marketing campaign used by Monsanto to introduce genetically modified (GM) foods into the European market. This campaign had not taken account of the specific market conditions in Europe and the acute concerns of the consumer towards food products. As a result the campaign has backfired. In a similar vein a chance remark by a BP representative concerning the oil spillage from the tanker *Braer* in the Shetlands (*see* case study) was used in an advertising campaign by Greenpeace to illustrate the lack of responsibility shown by large corporations. BP spent an undisclosed sum promoting and implementing a green strategy in order to project the image of an organisation that cares. It can be assumed that the Greenpeace advertisement will have at the very least reduced the effectiveness of this campaign.

Given the current climate of public opinion, organisations which are seen to be improving their levels of corporate responsibility and are able to communicate this to the consumer are likely to improve their market share and to develop customer loyalty (e.g. Varta's development of technology which reduced the heavy metal content of its consumer batteries). The image that a company portrays could also affect the quality of human resources available. Increasingly employees are taking into account an organisation's record on corporate responsibility when deciding upon future employment. The claims of companies must, however, be supported by actions that can be readily communicated and understood by the consumer. Initiatives such as the eco-label and ISO 14001/EMAS will assist in providing clear statements of intent that provide better information for a more informed purchase.

Providing new market niches

The clear message from the market is that there is a growing number of consumers who are prepared to be more discerning about the type of goods they buy, thereby taking into account the impact their purchases have upon the environment. As a result, a number of market niches has developed and this has proved attractive to business, given that consumers are prepared to pay extra for a product that is less harmful to the environment. In many cases this means that margins can be increased, a factor which is contrary to current market trends.

In addition to this, there are other market opportunities that result from the need to take action to improve the degree of environmental responsibility. Levels of environmental expenditure are increasing, and this extra expenditure must be generating revenue for those organisations providing the right type of product or service. There are significant market opportunities available, for example, in pollution reduction, energy saving and waste control technologies, and if it is assumed that the push towards more sustainable development will continue, then there will be further opportunities for firms in the field of product and process design.

Proactive legislative compliance

The legislative framework within which businesses operate involves a growing number of regulatory bodies. As indicated in previous chapters, legislation from the UK government is supported and often surpassed by EU directives, and organisations seeking to operate successfully in the Single Market must demonstrate compliance if they wish to compete. Regulations which were once confined to product and process now often extend to the way in which decisions are made within organisations and it seems more likely that the Cadbury Report on corporate governance has started a process of increased democratisation of the decision-making process which businesses will have difficulty in preventing. Past organisational performance on environmental issues has not instilled confidence and trust, and it is unlikely that mere rhetoric will calm the calls for more accountability. In future it seems more likely that the demand will be for a socially responsive organisation that accepts full public evaluation of its activities and makes itself accountable to all interested parties; in short, an organisation which is proactive in developing greater corporate responsibility and which is committed in practice as well as in principle to the concept of sustainable development.

Corporate responsibility without intervention?

Many businesses at present appear to be taking up the challenge of corporate responsibility if only out of the slow realisation that it is in their own interest – that is, to avoid regulation, to increase market share and/or to reduce costs. In its purest form, corporate responsibility could be supported for its own sake as representing a noble way for corporations to behave and such a stance can be closely associated with a business attitude of social responsiveness. Since this approach can conflict with a key objective of business – namely, profit maximisation – the question is whether the two are mutually exclusive or if a way can be found to combine profitability and corporate responsibility. Many observers believe that a business environment which is allowed to operate without government intervention seems unlikely to engender corporately responsible organisations. By the same token, legislation on its own cannot be expected to oversee all aspects of business, including the impact that firms have on the natural environment.

Arguably what is required is that a tone is set, through both legislation and societal norms and values, that provides clear signals to businesses; it will then be up to organisations to interpret these signals and to transmit them into policies which provide for the wants of society and at the same time satisfy the requirements of legislation. In this way corporate responsibility will tend to be seen as essential to competitive advantage and will become an integral part of the strategic management process. In short, the pursuit of a philosophy of sustainable development can be instilled into business practice without the excessive use of intervention that so often impinges upon the entrepreneurial flair of organisations. Businesses, however, need to play their part.

Synopsis

Organisational change is one of the most important themes to have come out of the study of business policy in the later twentieth century, and the failure of business, especially in the United Kingdom, to respond to increasingly dynamic and complex markets is often given as a reason for the country's poor industrial performance and its relatively low record of economic growth. One of the most significant areas of change in recent years has been the growing demand for businesses to behave in a socially responsible manner, and this has become an important aspect of the strategic decision-making process in a growing number of organisations. Corporate social responsibility can be defined as the obligation on a business to seek socially beneficial results along with the economically beneficial results from its actions. This obligation may be imposed on firms by outside pressures or it may result from decisions within the organisation. Either way, it seems likely that businesses which accept it will find that the benefits ultimately outweigh the costs.

Summary of key points

- Corporate social responsibility (CSR) is the idea that organisations should be held accountable for the effects of their actions on people, their communities and the environment.

- CSR has become an important consideration for modern businesses, alongside traditional concerns with profitability and growth.

- Being socially responsible as a business does not preclude being profitable.

- Increasingly, business organisations have to take account of the views of their stakeholders on questions of social responsibility.

- One area where this has become particularly significant is with regard to the impact of business operations and decisions on the natural environment.

- Different businesses respond in different ways, ranging from reactive stances through to more proactive environmental approaches which go beyond compliance with regulatory demands.

■ The key 'drivers' of corporate environmental responsiveness include government intervention, market forces, external pressures and self-regulation by organisations.

■ Firms which implement environmental policies can find they benefit from improved resource efficiency, enhanced market image, new market opportunities, increased competitive advantage and anticipatory reaction.

CASE STUDY   # The *Braer* oil tanker disaster

Introduction

The *Braer* was built by Oshima Shipbuilding in Nagasaki in 1975; it was a single-engined vessel, 241.5 m long, with a dead weight of 89 730 tons. It was registered with the Norwegian classification society Det Norske Veritas (DNV) in 1985 and according to that particular institution had an exceptional record. The ship was required to undergo rigorous surveys every five years and an annual inspection; the last periodic survey was carried out in July 1989 while the last annual inspection occurred in May 1992. Records show that neither of these inspections found anything that could improve seaworthiness and DNV regarded the *Braer* as a very good ship. The vessel itself had not previously been involved in a shipping casualty and Skuld Protection and Indemnity, the insurers of the ship, stated that in their opinion it was a sound ship managed by a sound and responsible company.

The emergency began at about 5.30 a.m. on 5 January 1993 when the tanker, carrying 85 000 tons of light crude oil from Norway to Quebec was passing through the 22-mile gap between Shetland and Fair Isle. The storm force seas had somehow managed to drive seawater into the fuel tank and by 6 a.m. the *Braer* was without power and drifting sideways towards Shetland. The first tug was dispatched from Lerwick harbour, 30 miles from the incident, at approximately 7.30 a.m., a crucial delay of at least 90 minutes from the time the engines failed. Despite the efforts of the salvage crews, the tanker hit the rocks at 11.30 a.m.; by 3 p.m. there were already reports of large oil slicks, with their subsequent effects on wildlife in the area.

Consequences of the oil spillage

The environmental impact of the wrecked *Braer* oil tanker near Sumburgh Head in Shetland was described by the World Wide Fund for Nature as 'potentially catastrophic'. The site of the disaster is a region of high cliffs and sheltered coves teeming with wildlife all year round. At the time Sumburgh Head was due to be designated a special protection area under the European Community birds directive. The oil coating the rocks settled on plants and fish in the intertidal zone and moved through the food chain, poisoning the feeding sea birds and threatening both the otter and seal population which had a stronghold in the area. A spokesperson for the Wildfowl and Wetlands Trust stated that they were particularly worried about the spillage, in light of a previous incident in 1979 when the *Esso Bernicia* spilled 1174 tonnes of fuel oil at Sullem Voe. This spillage had been fatal for all the ducks in the immediate area and the general population declined by 25 to 30 per cent.

While many Shetlanders were dismayed by the threat to the birds and sea life caused by the pollution, their main concern was the economic threat to the fishing and fish farming industries. In spite of oil wealth, Shetland still earned much of its living from fish. Almost a third of the islands' 10 000-strong labour force worked in the fish industry, including fishermen, fish processors and salmon farmers. A spokesperson for the Shetlands Fishermen Association stated that 'the Shetlands were more dependent on fish than any other part of the EC'. Without fishing, the future of the community appeared doubtful. The Shetland salmon industry alone was worth approximately £35 million of the £80 million turnover of the islands' fishing industry. Although the ship's cargo was largely harmless to fish because the oil floats upon the surface, the chemical dispersants employed against oil slicks produce an oily emulsion that can kill fish as it sinks to the sea bed. The combination of dispersant and oil was known to be more toxic than oil alone.

Historical precedent

The *Braer* disaster was yet another example of oil tankers which have come to grief on the seas. In 1967 the *Torrey Canyon* disaster released 30 000 tons of oil in a 35-mile-long slick off Cornwall. It was the first and remains the largest oil disaster in the United Kingdom. At the time one senior government official claimed that it had created 'an oil pollution problem of unparalleled magnitude'. There has been a regular stream of similar occurrences since this date, including:

1970	*Pacific Glory*, 3500 tons of oil	
1978	*Eleni V*, 5000 tons of oil	
	Amoco Cadiz, 223 000 tons of oil	
1979	*Atlantic Empress* and *Aegean Captain*, 1.2 million barrels of oil	
1987	*Exxon Valdez*, 240 000 barrels of oil	
1990	*American Trader*, 7600 barrels of oil	
1992	*Aegean Sea*, 24 million gallons of oil	

From July 1993, under anti-pollution rules negotiated by the International Maritime Organisation (IMO), all new tankers had to be constructed with a double-skinned hull. Since 1995 existing vessels also have to meet more stringent standards. In practice, this has sometimes meant sending many older ships to the scrapyard because they are not worth the cost of rebuilding to meet these standards. However, as a spokesperson for the IMO indicated at the time, ships built in the 1970s were regarded as technically out of date, but, needed to be retained to meet the demand for oil. With 136 governments involved during that period and a world tanker fleet of 2900 ships, it was accepted that change could not happen overnight.

The issues of corporate responsibility

The ship's course

Environmental experts initially found it difficult to understand why the captain of the *Braer* had followed a course that took it so close to the Shetland coastline. The waters around the Shetland Isles are classified as 'an area to be avoided' and this was confirmed by the IMO. Furthermore, International Collision Regulations say a ten-mile protection zone is necessary to avoid the risk of oil pollution and severe damage to the environment and the economy of Shetland. The regulations stipulated that all shipping of more than 5000 gross tons should avoid the area. The main reason offered for the presence of the *Braer* in the area was the extreme bad weather, which may have led the captain to put the safety of the crew before any risk to the environment. Weather forecasts can, however, be brought into the equation, since the vast majority of crews usually relied on three-day forecasts rather than the longer ten-day forecasts that were available. In effect the dependence on the shorter prediction means that the crew was committed to a route as soon as a vessel left port. Paul Roberts, a representative of Oceanroutes, which advised the shipping industry on weather conditions along prime trading routes, stated that oil tankers did not have standard routes: 'From Norway it is fairly natural for tankers to go around the top of Britain. If conditions are horrendous we might recommend the Channel, but extra miles means extra days means lots of bucks.'

Safety standards and flags of convenience

There has been a gradual increase over the years in the number of owners cutting costs by registering ships under overseas 'flags of convenience'. At times of worldwide recession, some owners burdened by ageing fleets have adopted the lower safety standards of countries such as Cyprus, Panama and Liberia, whose flag was carried by the *Braer*. The Merchant Navy Officers' union, NUMAST, said it had warned the government about the dangers of allowing so-called coffin ships to carry dangerous goods around Britain's coast. More than 60 per cent of foreign ships checked in British ports in 1991 were found to have defects. The union's then general secretary, John Newman, said a disaster was inevitable given the increasing amounts of hazardous cargoes being carried by vessels with 'safety records up to 100 times worse than British vessels'.

The structure of the ship's hull

US legislation, in response to the *Exxon Valdez* disaster, had concentrated on the gradual introduction of double-hulled tankers and the phasing out of the older oil carriers with a single-skinned hull. This stance was subsequently incorporated into new international law which required all new tankers to be constructed using the double-hull technique. This belated response hides a number of issues. First, the legislation does not indicate what should happen to the vessels built before 1993 but which were still very much in use. Second, it has been cogently argued by Joe Nichols, technical manager at the International Tanker Owners' Pollution Federation, that the double hull would not necessarily have prevented either the *Braer* or the *Exxon Valdez* disaster. Moreover the double-hull design itself can cause problems through the build-up of gases and new so-called mid-deck designs may yet prove superior. Legislation, in other words, may not be sufficiently flexible to accommodate all the necessary safety requirements.

The level and quality of training offered to the crew

The concentration upon the technical and safety requirements of the tanker could have meant that an important issue had been overlooked. Approximately 80 per cent of oil spills are caused by human error, which indicates an urgent need to harmonise training procedures throughout the seafaring world. Although tanker crew members must have internationally recognised certificates of training, it is notoriously difficult to obtain uniformity within the awarding bodies. Possibly of more concern is the incidence of such certificates being purchased from markets in the Far East. According to a director of the International Shipping Federation 'there are indications that the overall world training standards have diminished'.

The depressed costs of chartering vessels

Training problems may be a symptom of the very low charter rates for oil tankers caused by over-capacity in the industry. A company which during that period invested in an up-to-date tanker with the necessary pollution control measures needed to make approximately $60 000 a day on charter rates. This compared to the $15 000 a day offered by the hard-bargaining oil companies. In effect charterers were not prepared to pay for quality shipping and could be said to have indirectly sponsored the continuation of substandard shipping.

The delayed request for assistance

Comparison has been made between the *Braer* and the *Amoco Cadiz* (1978) disasters, given the critical delay by the *Braer's* captain in acknowledging the fact that the tanker was in extreme danger and in need of salvage under Lloyd's 'open form'. The *Braer's* captain may have felt in no imminent danger as the ship was lying roughly midway between the islands when the power failed, and he may have assumed that the tanker had a good chance of making it through the channel to relative safety. With the benefit of hindsight, it is difficult to understand how someone in such a position could make a rational decision based upon some form of cost-benefit analysis, given that the intangible costs of ecological and environmental damage and the secondary effects of lost income and quality of life would at the time be unquantifiable.

Conclusion

The *Braer*, built in 1975, was owned by B & H Ship Management of New York. The pollution protection held by the company was in keeping with that of other businesses with interests in shipping: B & H had contributed to a 'protection and indemnity' club under the management of Skuld in Oslo. These clubs are groups of like-minded shipowners which were formed at the turn of the century to provide for areas not covered by conventional policies. The cover they offer is compulsory for ships carrying 2000 tonnes or more of crude oil to or from UK ports. If this was not enough, the state-supported International Oil Pollution Compensation Fund, administered by the IMO, came into force, providing a ceiling of £662 per tonne of ship. In the case of the Braer this would be £54.63 million. Both schemes come under UK law. In effect, shipowners become liable for damage caused by the spillage itself, for the clean-up costs, and any damage caused by the clean-up measures. Skuld provided a standard $500 million-worth of coverage which in this case was never going to be enough once the full scale of the disaster was known, and this has led to renewed calls for raising minimum levels of compensation paid on oil spills. These calls have been consistently thwarted by tanker owners who face rising premiums and other costs. It is widely accepted that the compensation levels are set too low now and that delays in paying out compensation are far too long

Case study questions

1 In the Braer case who are the stakeholders, what are their interests and how might they influence future decisions to avoid further environmental incidents such as the tanker disaster?

2 What part do you think that environmental organisations can play in reducing the likelihood of future environmental disasters of this kind?

Review and discussion questions

1 To what extent are governments responsible for establishing the parameters by which organisations conduct business? Should a business be free to decide its own level of corporate responsibility?

2 Consider the case for greater democracy in the decision process of firms. To what extent is it feasible for businesses to implement the recommendations of the Cadbury Report?

3 Writers have argued that the only objective of business is to make profit, within the boundaries established by government. Do you agree?

Assignments

1 As a group, select an environmental issue (e.g. business or natural feature) and write a report to the leader of a local pressure group which details an environmental impact assessment of the issue. The report should make clear reference to:
   (a) a cost-benefit analysis, carried out by the group, of the salient factors;
   (b) any legislation/regulation that concerns the case; and
   (c) the provision of a stakeholder map that illustrates who the stakeholders are, their importance to the case and their ability to affect future decisions.

2 As a newly appointed trainee manager you have been asked to look afresh at the business, with particular reference to the implementation of an environmental management system. Your immediate superior has asked you to write a report. Accordingly, you are required to:
   (a) consult the available literature and identify what you consider to be the necessary processes and procedures that would comprise an environmental management system;
   (b) indicate the areas within the organisation that need to be addressed; and
   (c) explain how such a policy should be implemented within the organisation.

Notes and references

1 Friedman, M., 'The social responsibility of business is to increase its profits', *New York Times Magazine*, 13 September 1970, pp. 7–13.

2 Mintzberg, H., 'Who should control the organisation?', *California Management Review*, Autumn 1984.

3 This refers to the problems that have faced the companies named as a result of wider stakeholder groups drawing attention to aspects of their environmental management systems. In the case of Perrier it was the problem of small amounts of benzene occurring in the natural spring water source. At Shell it was the proposed dumping at sea of the Brent Spar oil platform, with the possible risk of marine contamination.

4 For a fuller discussion of the issues involved see Worthington, I., Britton, C. and Rees, A., *Business Economics: Blending Theory and Practice*, Financial Times/Prentice Hall, 2001, Chapter 14.

5 Sethi, S. P., 'Dimensions of corporate social performance: an analytical framework', *California Management Review*, Spring 1975.

6 Mintzberg, *op. cit*.

7 The complexity associated with implementing environmental policy is illustrated by the setting up of the Environment Agency in the UK. This is a new 'quango' which has taken over the functions of the National Rivers Authority, Her Majesty's Inspectorate of Pollution and the local authority waste regulators, and has the task of regulating the water, air and land environment in an integrated way.

8 Simon, B., 'Sharks in the water', *Financial Times*, 27 November 1991.

9 Peattie, K., *Green Marketing*, Pitman Publishing, 1992.

Further reading

Bansal, P. and Roth, K., 'Why Companies Go Green: A Model of Ecological Responsiveness', *Academy of Management Journal*, 43(4) pp.717–36, 2000.

Cannon, T., *Corporate Responsibility: A Textbook on Business Ethics, Governance, Environment*, Pitman, 1994.

Frederick, W.C., Post, J.E. and Davis, K., *Business and Society: Corporate Strategy, Public Policy, Ethics*, 7th edition, McGraw-Hill, 1992.

Griffiths, A. and Wall, S., *Applied Economics*, 9th edition, Financial Times/Prentice Hall, 2001, Chapter 10.

Mercado, S., Welford, R. and Prescott, K. *European Business*, 4th edition, Financial Times/Prentice Hall, 2001, Chapter 11.

Pearce, D.W. and Turner, R.K., *Economics of Natural Resources and the Environment*, Harvester Wheatsheaf, 1990.

Roberts, P., *Environmentally Sustainable Business: A Local and Regional Perspective*, Paul Chapman Publishing, 1995.

Smith, D., *Business Strategy in the Environment*, Chapman, 1993.

Welford, R., *Corporate Environmental Management: Systems and Strategies*, Earthscan Publications, 1996.

Welford, R. and Gouldson, A., *Environmental Management and Business Strategy*, Pitman Publishing, 1993.

Welford, R. and Starkey, R. (eds), *Business and the Environment*, Earthscan Publications, 1996.

Worthington, I., Britton, C. and Rees, A., *Economics for Business: Blending Theory and Practice*, Financial Times/Prentice Hall, 2001, Chapter 14.

Web links and further questions are available on the website at:
www.booksites.net/worthington

17

Monitoring change

Ian Worthington

Business organisations operate within a changing and often uncertain environment. To ensure that corporate resources are used effectively in pursuit of organisational objectives, firms need ideally to examine the external influences upon them and, where possible, to anticipate the nature and extent of environmental change. The study and practice of strategic management and decision making has provided a number of useful approaches in this area and has generated a variety of techniques for analysing the business environment. These techniques rely on the generation of data and information, much of which is in the public domain. Accessing this information has become significantly easier with improvements in computer technology and in collecting and collating material from both national and international sources.

Objectives

- To demonstrate the need to monitor the changing business environment.

- To examine broad approaches to environmental analysis.

- To analyse a range of qualitative and quantitative techniques used by business organisations as an aid to decision making.

- To provide a comprehensive review of national and international sources of information and data useful to both students and practitioners of business.

Key terms

Brainstorming
Cross-impact matrix
Environmental analysis
Environmental scanning
PESTLE analysis

Porter's five-forces model of
    competition
Scenario writing
Strategic fit
Strategic management

SWOT (or TOWS) analysis
The Delphi method
Trend extrapolation
Trend–impact analysis

Introduction

Few companies have been so universally admired as International Business Machines (IBM) – nicknamed 'Big Blue' after the colour of its packaging. For most of the second half of the twentieth century it completely dominated the world computer industry, becoming market leader in mainframe computers and the widely accepted industry standard in its field of technology. Investing huge sums in research and development, IBM had grown into the largest high-tech company in America and Europe and one of the biggest in Japan, and had served as a model for other global firms. Its reputation for protecting the interests of its stakeholders – including its employees, who had been offered lifetime employment and opportunities for education and training – was legendary and had helped to enhance its reputation not only in business circles, but also in the wider community, where it had been an important sponsor of sporting and cultural events.

In its quest for excellence, IBM had traditionally been a customer-driven organisation with a marketing and sales orientation in every part of the company and this had been a critical factor in its success. With a worldwide workforce of over 400 000 in the mid-1980s, IBM achieved operating profits of more than $10 billion. Buoyed by a booming world economy and a seemingly inexorable demand for its products, including its personal computers, IBM recorded the largest earnings in its history and this boosted its share price to record levels. At the time, senior executives confidently predicted that by 1990 sales would reach $100 billion and would stand at $185 billion by 1994 – figures which few inside or outside the industry dared challenge given the company's performance and apparently invincible position.

In the event these predictions proved woefully inaccurate. Pre-tax losses in 1992 amounted to $9 billion (about £5.84 billion) – the biggest loss in American corporate history – and this followed a net loss the previous year of almost $3 billion, the first loss in the company's history, on sales that had fallen for the first time since 1946. By mid-January 1993, IBM's stock market value stood at only $27 billion and its shares were worth less than a third of their peak price in 1987. On the employment side, the company proposed a 25 000 cut in the workforce in 1993, and this came on top of the 40 000 jobs axed the previous year, which had reduced the number of employees to 300 000 and which had involved the company in huge restructuring costs that had helped to plunge it into the red. The announcement by John Akers, the company chairman, that IBM might have to abandon two of its most cherished principles – no compulsory redundancies and no dividend cuts – only served to emphasise the depth to which the organisation had descended in such a relatively short time.

What went wrong? The answer in simple terms is that IBM failed to pay sufficient heed to the technological and commercial trends in the business environment in which it was operating. Improvements in 'chip' technology had given rise to the development of ever more powerful and flexible personal computers and IBM's decision to enter this market helped to legitimise the product. Unfortunately for the company, it also opened the doors to a multitude of new competitors who made use of the same off-the-shelf technology to build machines to the same standards and capable of running the same software, but at a fraction of the prices charged by IBM. At first this did little to affect IBM's mainframe business and the company continued to keep faith with its 'cash cow'. But as technological improvements occurred, mainframes came increasingly to be challenged by a new variety of extra-powerful desktop machines called 'workstations' which could be linked together in 'networks' and could be designed to customer specifications at highly competitive prices.

The twin threats of technological change and vigorous competition seem to have been largely ignored at first by IBM's senior executives, whose minds seemed set on the belief that success in the industry was related to selling large pieces of hardware to corporate customers. Rapidly changing market conditions, however, brought about by technological advances and the aggressive behaviour of the cheap clone-makers, and further exacerbated by a world recession, caused the company to reconsider its position and to institute a series of organisational and other changes designed to overcome its difficulties. While these changes – which included the replacement of senior executives, a restructuring of the organisation, a reduction in the workforce and a shift of resources from mainframes to the growth segments of the computer market – were largely welcomed by investors, they clearly illustrate the problems which can be faced by businesses which take a reactive rather than a proactive approach to changes in the business environment and which fail to ask critical questions about markets and competitors until a crisis occurs.

 IBM's website address is *www.ibm.com*

The need to monitor change

IBM's experiences underline the need for business organisations to consider the environment in which they are operating and, wherever possible, to anticipate changes that can affect their position. Ideally, a firm's management should regularly monitor the external context in order to identify the potential threats and opportunities it poses for the enterprise and should fashion its decisions accordingly. As the previous chapters have indicated, this context comprises not only those groups and individuals affected directly by the organisation's primary operations, such as its customers, competitors and other stakeholders, but also the broader societal environment in which these operations take place.

Undertaking some form of environmental analysis or scanning (*see* below) inevitably implies the need to commit human and financial resources, which some organisations may be unable or unwilling to contemplate, particularly when the returns in terms of opportunities gained or threats avoided are difficult to calculate. While such a view might be understandable, especially among smaller organisations operating in markets which appear relatively stable (e.g. undertakers), it may be misguided for at least two basic reasons. First, the resource cost of such an analysis need not necessarily be prohibitive, since a considerable amount of relevant data and information is available within both the organisation and the public domain at little or no cost to the enterprise. Second, the price paid for not investing resources in even a rudimentary form of environmental scanning may prove substantial and can range from lost opportunities to the ultimate failure of the organisation or its demise as an independent enterprise.

Problems of environmental complexity, uncertainty and the large number of external variables may prove a further disincentive to organisations seeking to monitor actual or potential changes in the business environment, and undoubtedly help to explain why many firms adopt either a 'do nothing' or a reactive approach. Alternatively, the existence of these problems may be used as a convenient excuse by managers, who for one reason or another prefer to focus their attention on the day-to-day operations of the enterprise and to treat environmental influences as either irrelevant or peripheral to the processes of production. While such a view may be sustainable in the short term, as a strategic approach it can prove highly risky, particularly if one's competitors take a more enlightened stance. It also indicates a lack of appreciation of the extent to which the internal and external environments are interdependent and of the need for management to achieve a 'strategic fit' between what the environment requires and the organisation can offer, as well as what the enterprise needs and the environment can provide.

Analysing the business environment: broad approaches

Environmental analysis or scanning should be seen as part of the process of strategic management and a prerequisite to the formulation and implementation of organisational strategies (*see* Figure 17.1).[1] It involves the monitoring and evaluation of information from the firm's internal and external environments and the dissemination of this information to key individuals within the enterprise for whom the internal strengths and weaknesses and external opportunities and threats are of critical significance in decision making. As implied above, accurate forecasting of changing elements in a firm's environment not only reduces the danger that it will be taken by surprise by environment changes, but also may give the firm a competitive advantage within its industry, especially if its rivals are less proactive in this sphere.

Much of the process of environmental scanning can, of course, be undertaken on an informal and individual basis and the information can be gleaned from a variety of sources, including suppliers, customers, consultants, financial institutions, pressure groups, local organisations (e.g. Chambers of Commerce) and government. Larger organisations, however, may feel the need to supplement this

Figure 17.1   The strategic management process

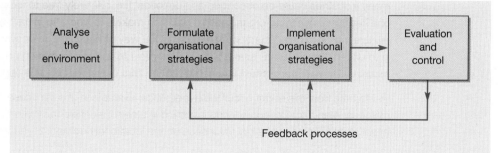

Feedback processes

approach by a more formalised system of information gathering and analysis, involving the use of a range of techniques – some of which are described below.

In broad terms, these more deliberate approaches to environmental scanning tend to focus on the firm's societal and task environments. As indicated in Chapter 1, PESTLE or PEST analysis looks at likely changes in political, economic, socio-cultural and technological factors and seeks to predict the extent to which change is likely to occur and its possible consequences for the organisation (e.g. as more women returned to work in the United States, Avon shifted its emphasis from selling its cosmetics at home to selling them at the office during the lunch break). In contrast, industry-based approaches focus on firms producing the same or similar products and on the key features of their competitive environment, including the relative power of buyers and suppliers and the actual or potential threats from rival organisations.

In this context, Porter's five-forces model of competition provides a useful framework for analysis (*see* Chapter 12). In essence Porter argues that an organisation's environment is predominantly conditioned by the intensity of competition in the industry, or industries, within which it is operating and that this is a critical influence not only on the competitive rules of the game, but also on the strategies potentially available to the firm. This competition is determined by five basic competitive forces – referred to above – and it is the collective strength of these forces which determines the ultimate profit potential in the industry, measured in terms of long-run return on capital invested.

While not denying that a range of short-term factors may influence a firm's profitability (e.g. strikes, sudden increases in demand), Porter's contention is that any meaningful structural analysis must be based on an identification of the underlying characteristics of an industry which are rooted in its economics and technology, and it is these which are critical to the strengths of each competitive force. Foremost among these characteristics would be entry barriers to new firms, the intensity of rivalry among existing competitors, the pressure from substitute products, the relative bargaining power of buyers and suppliers and the importance of government in influencing competition.

Mini case   Multinational inward investment: a PESTLE analysis

In highly competitive markets businesses must be constantly alert to the challenges they face and ideally should attempt to gain some form of advantage over their main rivals. For some organisations this might mean investing in production and/or service facilities in other countries, either as a means of reducing costs (e.g. by exploiting cheaper sources of labour) or as a strategy for boosting demand (e.g. by developing new markets). Given that many industries could be described as 'footloose' (i.e. relatively free to locate anywhere), one key question facing organisational decision makers is *where* to invest: what are the relative merits of one country over another? One way of beginning to answer this question is to undertake a PESTLE analysis in order to provide useful information about the broad macro-environmental context against which the final decision has to be taken.

To illustrate how this might occur the hypothetical example in this mini case looks at how a major car manufacturer considering investing in a new greenfield facility in Eastern Europe might identify some of the key influences on the locational decision. Given that there is no definitive way in which to undertake an analysis of this kind, the approach adopted here is to highlight some of the key questions that are likely to be considered by those charged with the final decision on where to invest. For convenience these questions are presented in tabular form (Table 17.1). You should note that the allocation of questions to categories can be a matter of personal choice (e.g. is a government tax law *political* or *legal* or *economic*?); the important point is that the questions are asked, not which category they go in.

Table 17.1 Locating a car plant: a PESTLE approach

Political

- How stable is the government now and in the future?
- Is the political regime favourable to foreign investment?
- Is membership of the EU planned and likely in the near future?

Economic

- Is there a favourable economic framework within which to engage in business?
- Is the economy likely to remain stable over the longer term?
- Is there a favourable business infrastructure?

Social

- How will the structure of the population impact upon the demand for the product and/or the supply of labour?
- Are economic conditions likely to provide increased market opportunities?
- What skills currently exist within the labour force?
- Are the welfare and educational systems supportive of the planned investment?

Technological

- What is the current state of technological advance?
- Is technology transfer feasible?
- Will the current (or future) infrastructure help or hinder the investment process?
- What facilities exist for technological training?

Legal

- Is the current legal framework likely to support or hinder business operations?
- Do the current (or planned) employment laws provide an advantage or disadvantage to the business?
- Do the current tax laws favour the organisation?

Ethical

- Are the ethical standards in a chosen location likely to affect the operations of the business favourably or unfavourably and/or the company's image?
- How will the organisation be affected by current (or planned) environmental standards and regulations?

As Table 17.1 illustrates, a PESTLE analysis can provide a valuable insight into some of the potential risks and uncertainties of a locational decision and can encourage corporate decision makers to examine future as well as current circumstances in each of the alternative locations. By adding weightings to reflect the relative importance of the different factors to the final decision and building in some allowance for the perceived degree of risk, the analysis can become more sophisticated and hence a more useful tool that can be used by the organisation. While it is likely that an approach of this kind will often be used negatively (i.e. to rule out certain locations), the fact that a particular country looks a less favourable location than the alternatives does not necessarily mean it will not be chosen. It could be, for example, that other factors weigh heavily in the final choice of location and that the PESTLE analysis has more influence on the level and nature of the investment undertaken (e.g. a joint venture might be seen as preferable to a direct commitment of funds) rather than where it occurs.

Techniques

To assist in an analysis of the business environment, organisations can make use of a wide variety of techniques, ranging from those involving quantitative measurements and predictions to the more qualitative approaches involving judgement and associated with opinion canvassing. In practice the choice of technique(s) used will tend to be conditioned by a variety of factors, including the type of information required, the extent and accuracy of data available, the time factor, resource constraints and the perceived importance of the forecast to the process of organisational decision making.

 If you would like more details of the various techniques referred to in this section (e.g. SWOT, the cross-impact matrix, the Delphi technique) try typing these terms into Yahoo. You will get numerous references such as *www.icehouse.net* and *www.mindtools.com* and so on.

Trend extrapolation

As its name suggests, trend extrapolation is essentially a technique for predicting the future based on an analysis of the past. Implicit in this is the assumption that, in the short run at least, most factors tend to remain fairly constant and critical changes in the key variables are unlikely to occur. Accordingly, extending present trends into the future is seen as a useful means of anticipating forthcoming events and tends to be one of the techniques most frequently used by business organisations seeking a relatively simple and inexpensive means of forecasting.

At its simplest level, trend analysis tends to be used to predict changes over time (e.g. in the likely demand for a product), a process which can sometimes prove relatively accurate where there are sufficient historical data to allow seasonal and cyclical fluctuations to be taken into consideration. The analysis can also be refined to examine an observed relationship between one factor (e.g. sales) and another (e.g. levels of disposable income) and can even be extended to the simultaneous consideration of several variables felt to influence the subject under consideration (e.g. by using multiple regression techniques). In addition, techniques also exist to investigate causal or explanatory factors that link two or more time series together (e.g. statistical modelling techniques) and to consider the likely impact on forecasted trends of a range of factors, identified by analysts as likely both to occur and to have an effect on the predicted outcome. The latter technique is generally known as 'trend–impact analysis' and is sometimes used by large companies in conjunction with other methods of forecasting, including the Delphi approach and opinion canvassing (*see* below).

The fundamental drawback in the use of trend analysis as a forecasting tool is that there is no guarantee that the trends identified from historic patterns will continue in the future; sudden discontinuities – such as the United Kingdom's decision to leave the ERM – can invalidate or undermine the existing assumptions on which a trend was predicted. In a majority of cases, trends are based on a series of patterns or relationships among a wide range of variables, a change in any one of which can drastically alter the future course of events. These variables are not always easy to identify and the interactions between them are not necessarily fully understood. Attempts to link a simple cause with a simple effect run the danger of underestimating the complexities of the business environment.

Scenario writing

Scenario writing is essentially an attempt to paint a picture of the future; it is designed to provide a realistic description of possible future developments within the environment and/or an industry and to consider their likely impact on the organisation should they occur. This technique – which often includes 'best case', 'worst case', 'most likely case' predictions – helps organisational decision makers to anticipate potential changes in the environment and to consider appropriate responses should such changes occur; as such it can be a useful stimulus to risk analysis and contingency planning in a corporate context.

In practical terms, organisational approaches to scenario writing can vary quite considerably. In some cases the technique – if used at all – is likely to be no more than a general prediction of the future based on relatively informal discussions between senior management, and will accordingly tend to be conditioned by the subjective judgements of the individuals concerned and by the influences upon them. In other cases, a more complex analysis of the future may occur, using a range of techniques which may include canvassing the views of individuals outside the organisation with no vested interest in its fortunes (*see* below).

Mini case	Scenario forecasting at Shell

In seeking to anticipate changes in the business environment, organisations have a range of analytical techniques that they can utilise. One such technique is scenario forecasting. This is generally associated with larger organisations and tends to be used as an aid to long-range planning and strategy development.

The multinational oil giant Royal Dutch Shell has been one of the world's leading commercial users of scenario forecasting. Traditionally, the company's planners used to forecast future trends in the oil market by extrapolating from current demand. In the early 1970s, however, the decision was taken to develop a range of possible future scenarios which managers could use as a starting-point for decision planning under different conditions. This approach to forecasting proved particularly beneficial in the mid-1980s when a rapid fall in oil prices sent shock waves through the world oil market. Shell planners had envisaged such a possibility and its managers had planned responses in the event of such a scenario happening. As a result, effects on the company appear to have been minimal, whereas some of its competitors were less fortunate.

Shell's use of scenarios as an aid to planning has continued in recent years and it helped the company to overcome the difficulties caused by the disruption to oil supplies during the Gulf War. Shell's current approach to forecasting appears much more streamlined than in the 1970s and it now uses relatively simple techniques to create its scenarios. Under the Shell approach, planners normally reduce the number of anticipated futures to two likely scenarios and these are used as a basis for strategic planning and decision making. It is important to remember that scenario forecasting is only a means to an end rather than an end in itself, but it can be a useful technique in the search for robust corporate strategies. Organisations can use scenarios to examine and address the long-term threats and opportunities they face. As Shell's experience has demonstrated, an awareness of possible alternative future situations can help organisations not only to respond to changing market conditions but also to capitalise on them.

While scenario building is appropriate to all types and sizes of organisations and at all stages of their existence, Porter has argued that it is a particularly useful tool for emerging industries, where uncertainty tends to be considerable and where the only certainty is that change will occur. Through a structured analysis of possible developments in product/technology, markets and competition and their likely consequences, Porter claims that firms in an emergent industry will be in a position to examine where they stand and how they can behave strategically should one or other predicted scenario occur. For some firms, such an analysis will provide a means of establishing the key events which will signal whether one scenario or another is actually occurring, and this can guide their actions. For others, with sufficient resources, it may encourage them to direct their efforts towards causing the most advantageous scenario to occur and, in doing so, it will strengthen their ultimate position within the industry.

Expert opinion: the Delphi method

To predict future developments or to build likely scenarios, some organisations turn to experts, an increasing number of whom work as consultants. These experts often operate as a group to produce an analysis which is presented to management in the form of a report or which emanates from a discursive technique known as 'brainstorming'. Alternatively, the organisation may prefer to canvass the views of an anonymous panel of experts, using a technique known as the Delphi method, which was originally developed by the Rank Corporation in the United States to forecast likely military events.

In essence the Delphi approach involves eliciting opinions from a group of experts who operate individually, and anonymously, unaware of the other members of the group. Each expert is asked to respond to an initial set of questions and the answers are clarified and tabulated by a neutral investigator who uses them to generate a more refined set of questions that are then put to the experts. Following their replies, further revisions may occur and the respondents may be asked again to provide another set of predictions that take into account the information provided in the earlier replies. This process may continue for several rounds until a measure of convergence occurs between the views of the panel and a form of consensus is reached on likely future developments. As a technique the Delphi method tends to be expensive and time-consuming and there is no guarantee that a clear view will emerge. It can, however, be used to investigate any aspect of a firm's environment and to identify not only the effects of predicted changes, but also their causes, and this information may be incorporated into other forms of environmental analysis of both a qualitative and quantitative kind.

Cross-impact matrices

The cross-impact matrix provides a more complex means of assessing and forecasting environmental change than some of the other methods previously described. Under this approach, analysts identify a set of events that are forecast to occur within a given time period, and specify not only the expected timing of each event but also its probability of occurrence. Arranging these events in anticipated chronological order in rows and columns of a matrix (*see* Figure 17.2) permits attention to be focused on the interaction between the events and, in particular, on the extent to which one may influence the timing or likely occurrence of another.

As a means of predicting likely interactions between anticipated future developments, cross-impact analysis serves at least two significant purposes. First, it can be used to check the consistency of the various forecasts which go into it – such as the prediction of events and their relationships – given that inconsistencies will become apparent from an analysis of the results. Second, it provides a means of identifying events and trends that will have the greatest impact on subsequent developments, whether they be in individual segments of the environment or across a range of segments, as in the case of interactions between economic, technological, social and political factors.

'SWOT' or 'TOWS' analysis

It is widely accepted that corporate performance is influenced by a combination of internal and external factors. These factors can be characterised as the organisation's internal 'strengths' and 'weaknesses' and its external 'opportunities' and 'threats'. Systematically analysing these factors as an aid to strategic decision making represents a form of situational analysis known commonly by the acronym 'SWOT' (or 'TOWS').

The starting-point for a SWOT analysis is usually a review of the organisation's internal strengths and weaknesses, which may be undertaken by management or

Figure 17.2 A simple cross-impact matrix

Probability and timing	Event 1	Event 2	Event 3	Event 4	Event 5
Event 1 (probability/timing)					
Event 2 (probability/timing)					
Event 3 (probability/timing)					
Event 4 (probability/timing)					
Event 5 (probability/timing)					

by external consultants brought in to provide a more objective view. The identified factors which have been listed may then be given scores to indicate their importance, with the more significant issues receiving a larger score. This process is then repeated for the firm's external opportunities and threats in order to highlight those external factors which are likely to occur and which are expected to have an impact on the organisation's future position. The resultant SWOT grid can then be used to focus attention on the key environmental influences faced by the organisation and to consider how far current strategy is relevant to the changes taking place in the business environment.

It is worth pointing out that the analysis of opportunities and threats cannot be absolute, since what might at first appear to be an opportunity may not be so when viewed against the organisation's resources or its culture or the expectations of its stakeholders. Moreover, the true value of the SWOT approach lies not in the listing of influences but in their contribution to the formulation of appropriate organisation strategies. One means of focusing attention on the latter is to produce a SWOT (TOWS) matrix which matches the firm's opportunities and threats against its internal strengths and weaknesses (*see* Figure 17.3). The result is four sets of possible strategic alternatives – termed SO, ST, WO and WT strategies – which range from the positive exploitation of strengths in order to take advantage of opportunities to the essentially defensive strategy of minimising weaknesses and avoiding anticipated threats.

Figure 17.3   A SWOT matrix

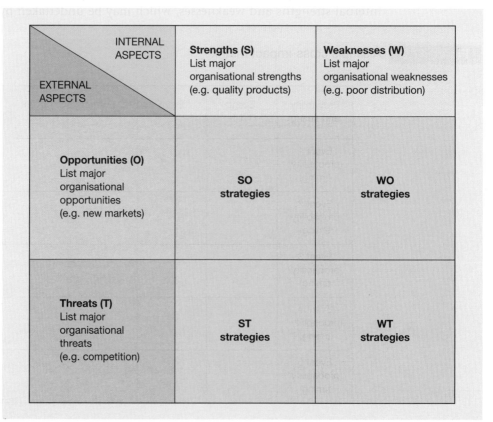

INTERNAL ASPECTS / EXTERNAL ASPECTS	**Strengths (S)** List major organisational strengths (e.g. quality products)	**Weaknesses (W)** List major organisational weaknesses (e.g. poor distribution)
Opportunities (O) List major organisational opportunities (e.g. new markets)	**SO strategies**	**WO strategies**
Threats (T) List major organisational threats (e.g. competition)	**ST strategies**	**WT strategies**

Limitations to environmental analysis

The techniques described above represent some of the ways in which organisations can examine the changing business environment in an attempt to understand what changes are likely to occur, how these may affect the organisation and what responses would be appropriate in the circumstances. In short, the value of such analysis lies not only in the information provided but also in the process of gathering and evaluating it and in applying it to the task of strategic management.

Despite its potential value as a tool of decision making, environmental analysis is not without its limitations and these need to be taken into account. For a start, analysing the business environment is not a precise science and does not eliminate uncertainty for an organisation, caused, for instance, by unanticipated events which do not follow the normal pattern. Nor should it be regarded by managers as a means of foretelling the future, allowing them to avoid their responsibilities as strategic planners and decision makers by blaming problems on a deficiency in the application of a particular technique or on inaccuracies in the data provided.

Added to this, environmental analysis of itself is by no means a guarantee of organisational effectiveness, and can sometimes complicate the decision-making process by providing information which calls into question the intuitive feeling of experienced managers. The danger is that the analysis may become an end in itself and may obscure information and data coming from other sources, rather than being used in conjunction with them. Accordingly, its value in strategic thinking and strategic decision making may not be exploited to its full potential and this may represent a lost opportunity to the organisation, as well as an inefficient and ineffective use of resources.

Information sources

Researching the business environment can be a daunting task, given the extensive amount of information and statistical data available. To help in this direction the final section of this chapter outlines some of the key national and international information sources which are readily accessible to both students and businesses. While the list is by no means exhaustive, it gives a good indication of the wide range of assistance available to researchers and of the different formats in which information is published by government and non-government sources for different purposes. Much of this information is available in an electronic as well as a print format, with the latter a particularly good starting point for students of business. The development of the Internet is also of key significance for research purposes.

Statistical sources

Statistical information is an important component of business research and students need to be aware of what is available, particularly as some data turn up in the most unexpected places. Three key guides in locating statistical information are:

1 *National Statistics – the official UK statistics site*. A portal to UK officially produced statistics. Some information is available on-line, at other times you will be referred to print publications, including the ones listed below (*http://www.statistics.gov.uk/*).

2 *Sources of Unofficial UK Statistics*. Provides details of a large number of unofficial statistical publications from a wide variety of organisations (e.g. pressure groups, trade unions, professional associations).

3 *World Directory of Non-Official Statistical Sources*. Published by Euromonitor and a key guide to non-official sources in selected countries outside western Europe, the latter being covered by the *European Directory of Non-Official Statistical Sources*. The *Directory* concentrates particularly on sources dealing with consumer goods, consumer trends, key industries and national economic and business trends. It has a subject and a geographical index. Also available on the GMID web service.

Some of the main statistical sources, arranged in alphabetical order, are discussed below:

4 *Annual Abstract of Statistics*. Published by the ONS, this is an authoritative source of official statistics arranged under various headings, which include population, production, energy, transport, trade and public services. Figures usually cover a ten-year period and are presented in tabulated form. There is a detailed alphabetical index at the end.

5 *Consumer Europe*. Produced by Euromonitor and available on CD-ROM and via the Internet. This is a pan-European source of marketing statistics with the emphasis on consumer goods and consumer trends. The information examines the main product groups and includes predictions on future levels of consumption.

6 *Datastream*. A finance and economics on-line database, produced by Primark International. Accounts for public companies around the world, as well as share prices and stock market indices are available. The economics databases cover a vast range of current and historical international economic series, including money supply, inflation and interest rates for 150 countries. Data are taken from many statistical sources, including OECD and the UK government, central banks and unofficial statistical sources.

7 *Economic Survey of Europe*. Published annually by the United Nations (UN). The survey includes data in various forms on individual countries and on geographical groupings in Europe and identifies trends in areas such as agriculture, industry, investment and trade. Tables and charts include written commentary.

8 *Economic Trends*. A monthly publication by the ONS and a key guide to the current economic indicators (e.g. prices, unemployment, trade, interest rates, exchange rates). The figures span several years, as well as the latest month or quarter, and tables and charts are provided. A quarterly supplement covering the balance of payments and the national accounts was added in March 1993.

9 *Economist Intelligence Unit country reports*. Reviews the business environment for countries, and is divided into six major regions of the world. Quarterly reports summarise major events, issues and trends and provide key statistics. These are available on paper, CD-ROM or the Internet.

10 *Employment in Europe.* Contains an excellent overview of employment issues in Europe. Published annually by the European Commission, with a different focus in each issue.

11 *Europa world year book.* Published by Europa, London. An annual book which has an A–Z listing of all countries. Each entry contains a political and historical overview of a country, key statistics, contact details and basic facts about leading organisations, political parties, the media, diplomatic representation, etc.

12 *Europe in figures.* An overview of Europe, with lots of graphs and tables. A simple introduction, but published irregularly.

13 *European Economy.* Published by the European Commission and concerned with the economic situation and other developments. The journal includes data on economic trends and business indicators and provides a statistical appendix on long-term macroeconomic indicators within Europe. There are two issues and three reports per year.

14 *European Marketing Data and Statistics.* An annual publication by Euromonitor providing statistical information on the countries of western and eastern Europe. The data cover a wide range of market aspects – including demographic trends, economic indicators, trade, consumer expenditure, retailing – and often show trends over a 21-year period. The information is provided primarily in a spreadsheet format and there is an alphabetical index.

15 *Family Expenditure Survey.* A comprehensive breakdown of data on households, including income, expenditure and other aspects of finance. The survey has very detailed tables and charts – mostly for the latest year – and some regional analysis is provided. Published by The Stationery Office (TSO).

16 *Financial Statistics.* A monthly publication by the ONS on a wide range of financial aspects including the accounts of the public and non-public sectors of the economy. Figures cover the latest month or quarter together with those of previous years. Data are available on floppy disk from ONS. *See also www.statistics.gov.uk/statbase/mainmenu.asp.*

17 *General Household Survey.* A continuous sample survey produced by the ONS, based on the financial year of the general population. The survey spans a wide range of household-related aspects – including housing, health, education and employment – and is widely used as a source of background information for central government decisions on resource allocation. Since 1994 it has been renamed 'Living in Britain: Results of the General Household Survey'.

18 *International Marketing Data and Statistics (IMDAS).* An international compendium of statistical information on the Americas, Asia, Africa and Oceania published annually by Euromonitor. Information on demographics, economic trends, finance, trade, consumer expenditure and many other areas usually covers a 21-year trend period, and an alphabetical index is provided. Available on CD-ROM – 'World Marketing Data and Statistics'. *See also www.euromonitor. com/Imdas.html.*

19 *Labour Market Trends.* Formerly the *Employment Gazette*, this is a monthly publication by the ONS that contains labour market data and a number of feature articles.

20 *Labour Market Quarterly Report.* Published by the Department for Education and Employment (DfEE), and containing information and data on labour market trends and other issues such as training.

21 *Marketing Pocket Book*. Published by NTC Publications. An essential source of statistics and information. Published annually. Sister publications include *European Marketing Pocket Book* and *Retail Pocket Book*.

22 *Monthly Digest of Statistics*. The key source of current information on national income, output and expenditure, population, employment, trade, prices and a range of other areas. Previous as well as current data are provided. Published by ONS.

23 *New Earnings Survey*. An annual publication in parts by ONS. It contains detailed statistical information on earnings by industry, occupation, region, country and age group. Available on-line via NOMIS.

24 *National Income and Expenditure*. Now known as the *United Kingdom National Accounts* (or 'Blue Book'). Published annually by ONS, it contains data on domestic and national output, income and expenditure, and includes a sector-by-sector analysis. Figures often cover ten years or more and an alphabetical index is provided. Available on CD-ROM and on-line.

25 *OECD Economic Outlook*. A periodic assessment of economic trends, policies and prospects in OECD and non-member countries. Published twice a year, the *Outlook* includes articles as well as figures, tables, charts and short-term projections, and looks at developments on a country-by-country basis. Available for subscribers on the Internet (*www.oecd.org/eco/out/eo.htm*).

26 *OECD Economic Surveys*. An annual publication by the OECD providing individual country reports of the world's advanced industrial economies. Very useful. Available on CD-ROM.

27 *Overseas Trade Statistics with Countries outside the European Community*. Published quarterly by TSO and containing statistical information on trade with non-EU countries. Available on the Internet via *www.tso-online.co.uk*.

28 *Panorama of EU Industry*. Produced by the Office for Official Publications of the European Communities. Provides an overview of industries in Europe, with statistics, analysis and company information. Published irregularly.

29 *Quest Economics*. A collection of macroeconomic and country risk data from a variety of sources. Available as an on-line, Internet or CD-ROM database.

30 *Regional Trends*. An annual ONS publication providing a wide range of information on social, demographic and economic aspects of the United Kingdom's standard planning regions, together with some data on the sub-regions and on the EU. The guide includes a subject index. Available on the Internet via *www.ons.gov.uk*.

31 *Social Trends*. Another annual ONS publication, in this case looking at different aspects of British society, including population, education, environment, housing, leisure and transport. It provides a more detailed analysis of data produced for the *Annual Abstract of Statistics* and includes a large number of charts and diagrams. Information often spans a 15–20-year period and an alphabetical subject index is included. Available on the Internet via *www.ons.gov.uk*.

32 *United Kingdom Balance of Payments*. Known as the Pink Book. It is a comprehensive guide to the United Kingdom's external trade performance and contains a wide range of statistics covering a ten-year period. Available on the Internet (*see Social Trends*)

33 *United Nations Statistical Yearbook.* Written in both English and French, the *Yearbook* is a detailed international comparative analysis of UN member countries. Data cover a wide variety of topics, including international finance, transport and communications, population, trade and wages, and a World Statistical Summary is provided at the beginning.

34 *World Economic Outlook.* Published twice a year by the IMF in various languages. It is an analysis of global economic developments in the short and medium terms. It gives an overview of the world economy and looks at current global issues.

Other useful statistical sources

1 Many government departments publish statistics on their own websites. They include:

(a) *Department for Education and Skills – Statistics.* Good starting point for statistics on lifelong learning, education and training (*see http://www.dfes.gov.uk/statistics/*)

(b) *DFEE Datasphere.* Datasphere is a gateway maintained by the DFEE. It provides links to information on the UK labour market, including statistics, national and regional trends (*see http://www.dfes.gov.uk/datasphere/*).

(c) *Bank of England* Includes information, news and fulltext publications (*see http://www.bankofengland.co.uk*).

(d) You might also wish to look at: Department of Transport, Local Government and the Regions local government finance, planning, transport and housing statistics (*http://www.dtlr.gov.uk/statistics.index.htm*); Department of Trade and Industry – includes SME statistics and regional competitive indicators (see *http://www.dti.gov.uk/statistics/index.htm*); Office of the e-Envoy – e-commerce and internet access statistics (*http:///www.e-envoy.gov.uk/*).

2 *Europa.* The European Union on-line with links to statistics and publications, including the Eurostat site (*see http://europa.eu.int/index_en.htm*).

3 *The Data Archive.* The Data Archive (University of Essex) – is a specialist national resource containing the largest collection of accessible computer-readable data in the social sciences and humanities in the UK. Users must register; minimal charges apply for data delivery. Most of the large survey data can be accessed on-line free by academic researchers via MIMAS (*see http://www.data-archive.ac.uk/*).

4 *MIMAS.* Based at the University of Manchester, this is another data centre which provides on-line access to census information, international data and large-scale survey information (e.g. OECD, IMF).

5 *Sources of further information.* By selecting a gateway site, you will often find links to just the information you need much more quickly than by just using Google.

(a) *Business information on the Internet.* A gateway maintained by Karen Blakeman, including links to websites covering most aspects of business (*see http://www.rba.co.uk/sources/index.htm*).

(b) *Useful UK Statistics sites from the University of Glasgow Library.* Very thorough summary (*see http://www.lib.gla.ac.uk/D..ts/MOPS/Stats/useful.html*).

(c) *Subject guide to statistics at Warwick.* Although this listing also includes specialist databases (which may not be available without payment) it is a very clear and comprehensive list (*see http://www.warwick.ac.uk/services/library/subjects/ officialpublications/officialpublications_stats_er.html*).

Information sources

Information on the different aspects of the business environment can be found in a variety of sources, including books, newspapers and periodicals. These often provide a wealth of contemporary data and commentary which can be located relatively easily in most cases, using specialist databases designed to assist the researcher. While an increasing amount of information is available on the Internet, the fastest and most reliable way of finding what you want tends to be to use newspapers and magazines, which are often available electronically (and which are loved by librarians!). In the last few years more and more abstracting databases have moved over to the Web, and now also offer the full text of articles, thereby reducing the amount of time it takes to research a topic. ProQuest Direct (*see* below) can be used to trace information, but there are other alternatives (e.g. Lexis and Nexis). It is even possible to customise your business databases to cover the most popular titles in a particular library. But remember, the situation tends to change on a regular basis, so you need to keep up to date. Some key sources in this area are discussed below:

1 *Business and Industry*. Covers trade and business news titles worldwide and is available as an on-line, subscription web database.

2 *Business Source Premier*. Covers over 2500 full-text titles and abstracts many others in all areas of business, economics and management.

3 *Clover Newspaper Index*. Now known as *Newspaper Index*, a fortnightly publication covering all the main quality dailies as well as the Sunday papers. The list of articles is arranged in alphabetical order by subject and provides a readily accessible means of tracing topics of current interest. *See* www.cloverweb.co.uk.

4 *Emerald*. An Internet version of all the journals published by MCB University Press; includes some keys titles like the *European Journal of Marketing*. Also includes abstracts from many other journals in the *Emerald* reviews section.

5 *FT McCarthy*. Available as a CD-ROM, on-line or Web database, McCarthy covers business and management articles from over 50 newspapers and trade publications in the UK, Europe and further afield. Its business focus make it an excellent starting-point for any research, since it usually contains relevant key stories.

6 *General BusinessFile International*. Available as a web database (under the name Infotrac General Businessfile) this database covers a wide range of academic and trade journals.

7 *IMID/MICWeb*. Based on the holdings of the Institute of Management's book and journal article databases which form part of the largest collection of resources on management in Europe, focusing on all aspects of management theory and practice. MICWeb is updated monthly, as is the IMID CD-ROM. Business students can join the Institute of Management and have access to the library services.

8 *PROMT*. Another database available on-line, on the Web or on CD-ROM. Covers trade and business news sources worldwide.

9 *ProQuest Direct* (also known as *ABI/Inform*). One of the best business databases because of its range and the quality of its abstracting and information retrieval. Many businesses now have access to the full text of many articles as well as summaries.

10 *Scimp*. The selective co-operative index to management periodicals (hence 'scimp'), published ten times a year and a useful source of information on European publications on management issues.

11 *The Times*. The text of the newspaper is available on CD-ROM, on the web and from specialist databases.

Other useful sources

1 *Bank of England Quarterly Bulletin*. An assessment of economic developments in the United Kingdom and the rest of the world. It includes articles and speeches, together with general commentary on the economy and is available from The Bank of England site.

2 *Bank Reviews*. Quarterly publications by some of the leading clearing banks and often available free on request. These include *Barclays Economic Review and Lloyds Economic Bulletin*.

3 *Business Studies Update*. Published annually by Hidcote Press and a very useful source of discussion on contemporary business issues.

4 *CBI Industrial Trends Survey*. A quarterly guide to the state of UK manufacturing industry based on questionnaire responses by businesses. It provides a useful insight into business prospects and an indicator to future changes.

5 *Company Annual Reports*. Available on request from all public companies and some private ones. Many are available on-line through company websites or from the following sites:
   (a) *Annual reports of the world's biggest companies*. Provides links to the annual reports of the largest companies worldwide (*see http://www.areport.com*).
   (b) *Carol World*. Good source of free company reports, international in scope (*see http://carol.co.uk/reports/europe/index.html*).
   (c) *Corporate information*. Gateway providing international coverage of company information including industry sector profiles, economic data and country and regional-specific searches (*see http://www.corporateinformation.com/ukcorp.html*).
   (d) *UK Company researcher*. UK company information. Has Chamber of Commerce directories so is particularly good for regional information. Also includes industry profiles and links to company websites (*see http://www.ukcompanyresearcher.com*).
   (e) *Vrisko*. This site includes a searchable database listing the Home Pages of all UK PLCs with an Internet presence (*see http://www.vrisko.com*).
   (f) *Wright research centre*. This site includes information on 18 000 companies in fifty countries. In many cases it includes ten years of financial data (*see http://profiles.wisi.com/profiles/Comsrch.htm*).

6 *Consumer Goods Europe*. Replaces *Marketing in Europe*. It is a monthly publication by Corporate Intelligence on Retailing and contains detailed studies of the markets for consumer products in leading European countries.

7 *Economics Update*. Another annual publication by Hidcote Press and designed to provide a review and discussion of contemporary issues relevant to students of economics and business.

8 *Ernst and Young's International Business Series*. Entitled 'Doing business in ...', it contains a wide range of information on business conditions in different countries and is a very useful reference source. The information is updated fairly regularly. PriceWaterhouse Cooper has a rival publication that is also very informative.

9 *European Business Review*. A pan-European journal published by MCB University Press. It includes articles, editorial comment, news reports and a discussion of recent publications. The journal also incorporates the *New European* which looks at the more cultural, political and environmental developments within Europe. Has CD-ROM and on-line facilities.

10 *European Journal of Marketing*. Another publication by MCB University Press, relevant particularly to students of international marketing. It includes abstracts in French, German and Spanish and offers an on-line service.

11 *European Policy Analyst Quarterly*. Formerly *European Trends*. Published by the EIU, it is a quarterly review of key issues and business developments in a European context.

12 *Income Data Services*. A regular series of studies and reports on pay and other labour-market issues (e.g. teamworking, child care, redundancy), containing valuable up-to-date information and some statistical analysis. Available on the Internet via *www.incomesdata.co.uk*.

13 *Journal of Marketing*. A quarterly publication by the American Marketing Association and comprising articles together with recent book reviews in the field of marketing. *See www.ama.org*.

14 *Kelly's Business Directory*. A substantial volume giving details of the addresses and main products of UK businesses. Available via *www.kellys.co.uk* and on CD-ROM.

15 *Key British Enterprises*. A multi-volume compendium from Dun and Bradstreet giving details of Britain's top 50 000 companies. Companies are listed alphabetically and are also indexed by trade, product and geographical location. Available on the Internet via *www.dunandbrad.co.uk*; also on CD-ROM.

16 *Kompass UK*. A multi-volume directory produced in association with the CBI and providing details on UK companies, including names, addresses, products, number of employees, and so forth. Directories for other countries are also available. See *www.reedbusiness.com* and CD-ROM 'Kompass CD plus'.

17 *Lloyds Bank Economic Bulletin*. A bi-monthly publication covering a topic of current interest in an easily accessible form. Internet site currently being changed.

18 *Management Decision*. Published ten times a year by MCB University Press. Looks at management strategy and issues. Available on CD-ROM and on-line.

19 *Marketing*. A weekly source of facts and articles on various aspects of marketing, presented in a journalistic style. Available on the Internet via *www.marketing.haynet.com*.

20 *Marketing Intelligence*. Also known as *Mintel Marketing Intelligence* and an invaluable source of information and statistics on a wide range of products. Reports cover market factors, trends, market share, the supply structure and consumer characteristics, and frequently include forecasts of future prospects. Available on-line via *www.mintel.co.uk*.

21 *Retail Price Index – Headline Rate.* A site maintained by Devon County Council giving a table with the RPI (headline rate), month by month for the last thirty years. Available at *www.devon.gov.uk/dris/economic/retprice.*

22 *Sell's Product and Services Directory.* A useful directory in a number of sections listing products and services, company details and trade names. Produced in two volumes and available on CD-ROM.

23 *The Economist.* A standard reference source, published weekly and examining economic and political events throughout the world. It is an invaluable publication for business students and regularly contains features on specific business-related topics. It has a useful update on basic economic indicators. Available on the Internet via *www.economist.co.uk/* or *www.economist.com/.*

24 *The Times 1000.* Essentially a league table of UK top companies, with information on profitability, capital employed and other matters. Additional information is also provided on the monetary sector and on leading companies in other countries. Published annually and available on CD-ROM.

25 *UK Online.* The gateway to all UK government information on-line. Available at *www.ukonline.gov.uk.*

26 *WARC Advertising and Marketing Knowledge.* The World Advertising Research Centre's Advertising and Marketing Knowledge database is a vast collection of case studies and articles from authoritative sources. It covers all areas of advertising, marketing and media activity. The database also contains demographic information on a wide range of countries. Available at *www.warc.com/.*

27 *Who Owns Whom.* An annual publication which identifies parent companies and their subsidiaries. It is a very useful source of information for examining the pattern of corporate ownership in the United Kingdom. Companion volumes are also available covering other parts of the world.

A final comment

When researching a business topic you are particularly recommended to use library catalogue sites, especially the British Library catalogue (BLPC) and COPAC, which is the combined catalogue of major British academic libraries. You might also want to check references on the Internet bookshop sites such as Heffers (www.heffers.co.uk), the Internet bookshop (www.bookshop.co.uk) or the Book Place (www.thebookplace.co.uk), as well as Amazon.co.uk (which most people know about).

Synopsis

IBM's experiences graphically illustrate the need for business organisations to monitor the environment in which they exist and operate and, where possible, to anticipate changes which are likely to affect the enterprise. Rather than being an optional extra, environmental analysis or scanning should be seen as an intrinsic part of strategic management and should ideally provide data and information that are used to guide the decision-making process. Many of these data and much of the information already exist in published form and/or can be easily gathered from both literary and electronic sources on a national and international basis.

Analysing them is also possible, using a range of techniques which have been developed by businesses and academics over a considerable number of years.

Summary of key points

■ A firm's business environment changes over time.

■ Firms need to consider and anticipate potential changes in their general and operational environments in order to take advantage of opportunities and/or minimise possible threats.

■ Environmental analysis should be seen as a key part of the strategic management process; ideally it should form part of the basis on which corporate decisions are taken.

■ Such analysis can occur at both a societal level (e.g. through PESTLE analysis) and at a task level (e.g. through industry-based approaches) and can involve the use of a wide variety of established techniques.

■ Key techniques include trend extrapolation, scenario writing, the Delphi approach, cross-impact matrices and SWOT analysis.

■ In researching the business environment, students and practitioners can utilise a wide range of information sources, many of which are relatively inexpensive and readily accessible.

■ Accessing this information has been made considerably easier with improvements in information technology, especially the Internet.

CASE STUDY   ## Scanning the environment: East Midlands Electricity Plc

The privatisation of the electricity industry in the United Kingdom led to the formation of a number of private companies responsible for the generation and distribution of electricity. As far as distribution was concerned, this was placed in the hands of 12 regional electricity companies (RECs) which were the successors to the old electricity boards that had operated under the system of public ownership. In the East Midlands area – covering all of Leicestershire, most of Derbyshire, Lincolnshire, Northamptonshire, Nottinghamshire and Warwickshire, and parts of Bedfordshire, Buckinghamshire, Cambridgeshire, South Yorkshire, Oxfordshire and Staffordshire – distribution to commercial, industrial and domestic users was vested in East Midlands Electricity Plc (EME), operating from its headquarters in Nottingham. Like all other RECs, EME also retained the right to retail electrical appliances through its own shops and to provide electrical contracting services to its various customers.

Like many other large private sector companies, EME immediately recognised the importance of gathering information about the changing environment in which it was operating. In pursuit of its mission to be 'simply the best electricity company in the United Kingdom', EME developed a marketing plan which was used to examine the market environment in which the Electricity Division of the organisation operated. This marketing plan moved via a step-by-step approach from consideration of the company's corporate objectives, through an audit of the internal and external factors likely to affect the organisation's performance in the coming year, to the formulation of marketing plans and their subsequent evaluation and review (*see* Figure 17.4). This plan was then used to direct the activities of the company's marketing and sales teams in the year ahead.

A key step in the process was the use of a SWOT analysis which drew on information and data collected during the market audit. As Figure 17.5 illustrates, the focus of attention was on both internal and external factors and these provided a valuable input into the formulation of marketing objectives and strategies. The aim of such an analysis, in essence, was to identify ways in which to exploit the organisation's strengths or capabilities and to maximise the opportunities offered

Figure 17.4   EME's marketing plan, 1992/3

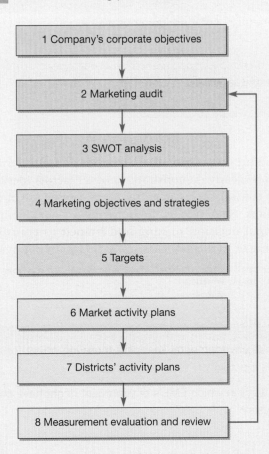

Figure 17.5   A SWOT analysis of the domestic electricity market, 1992/3

INTERNAL TO THE COMPANY	
Strengths	**Weaknesses**
• Tariff development	• Low profitability of certain tariff
• New product development	• Perceived high cost of electricity
• Dedicated sales force	• Customers perceive vulnerability in single fuel source
• Capital cost advantage	

EXTERNAL TO THE COMPANY	
Opportunities	**Threats**
• Net increase in population	• Slow recovery from recession predicted
• Possible Building Regulations review 1993/94	• Aggressive competitive activity
• Growing 1–2 bed house sector	• Gas dominance in home heating systems

by the market, while addressing corporate weaknesses and minimising external threats.* As this example clearly demonstrates, not all factors identified by the analysis are within the control of the organisation and some are of more immediate concern than others. Nevertheless they provide a valuable input into the process of organisational decision making and helped to contribute to the company's understanding of its marketplace in the aftermath of privatisation.

*In late 1996 EME was taken over by the US-based Dominion Resources. Was this a threat or an opportunity? It was subsequently sold to PowerGen.

Case study questions

1 Did 'privatisation' make environmental scanning more important for an organisation like East Midlands Electricity?

2 Can you think of any ways in which EME's environment might have changed since it undertook this analysis?

web link   East Midlands Electricity website can be accessed at *www.eme.co.uk*

Review and discussion questions

1 Discuss the costs and benefits to businesses of the introduction of a system for monitoring and analysing the changing external environment in which they operate.

2 To what extent do you agree with the proposition that only large firms should or can make use of the various techniques of environmental analysis?

3 Using a firm or organisation of your choice, attempt a 'SWOT' analysis. For example, can you apply such an analysis to the organisation in which you work or study?

4 Using the information sources discussed in the text, and any others with which you are familiar, provide a comparative analysis of consumer markets in at least eight leading European countries (including eastern Europe).

Assignments

1 You work for a medium-sized private company in the UK fashion industry (it can be on either the production or the retailing side). As a personal assistant to the managing director, your brief is to provide help and advice on various aspects of the firm's operations. You have recently become concerned about the lack of a system for monitoring changes in the business environment and have agreed to produce a report on the issue for the board of directors. In producing this report, you are required to identify both the costs and the benefits to the business of implementing a system of environmental scanning.

2 As a librarian in a college (or university) library, with responsibility for help and advice to students on business studies courses, you are frequently asked for guidance on how to access information and data on a particular company. Choosing any well-known company you wish, produce a diagrammatic representation (e.g. flow chart) of the steps you would advise students to undertake to get the information they require. At each step, indicate what type of information is available and how and from where it can be obtained.

Note and reference

1 For a useful introduction to the subject *see* Fahey, L. and Narayanan, V.K., *Macroenvironmental Analysis for Strategic Management*, West Publishing, 1986.

Further reading

Cook, M. and Farquharson, C., *Business Economics : Strategy and Applications*, Pitman, 1998.

Cooke, S. and Slack, N., *Making Management Decisions*, 2nd edition, Prentice Hall, 1991.

Fahey, L. and Narayanan, V. K., *Macroenvironmental Analysis for Strategic Management*, West Publishing, 1986.

Finlay, Paul. N., *Strategic Management: An Introduction to Business and Corporate Strategy*, Financial Times/Prentice Hall, 2000.

Grant, R.M., *Contemporary Strategy Analysis: Concepts, Techniques, Applications*, 4th edition, Blackwell Business, 2002.

Johnson, G. and Scholes, K., *Exploring Corporate Strategy*, 6th edition, Financial Times/Prentice Hall, 2002.

Ringland, G., *Scenario Planning : Managing for the Future*, Wiley, 1998.

Weihrich, H., 'Daimler-Benz's move towards the next century with the TOWS matrix', *European Business Review*, 93(1), 1993, pp. 4–11.

Wheelen, T.L., *Strategic Management and Business Policy : Entering 21st-century Global Society*, Addison-Wesley, 6th edition, 1998.

Worthington, I., Britton, C. and Rees, A., *Business Economics : Blending Theory and Practice*, Financial Times/Prentice Hall, 2001, esp. Chapter 15.

Web links and further questions are available on the website at:
www.booksites.net/worthington

Glossary

Abnormal profits: profits over and above normal profits.

Accelerator effect: increases in investment spending as a result of changes in output or sales.

Acceptance: under contract law acceptance is the notion of legally agreeing to an offer that is made.

Age structure: the proportions of a population in different age band.

Ageing population: the increase in the average age of a population.

Agent: a person or organisation who is authorised by another person or organisation to act on behalf of the latter.

Aggregate monetary demand: the total demand for goods and services in the economy.

Articles of Association: a document regulating the internal administration of a company including the rights of shareholders, the qualifications required of directors and rules relating to company rules etc.

Assisted Area: an area qualifying for state aid under government regional policy.

Authoritarianism: the disposition to settle disputes through the enforcement of rules, regulations and orders by an established authority

Average cost of production: total costs per unit of output.

Backbench MPs: ordinary members of Parliament who do not occupy a role in government or on the Opposition front bench.

Balance of payments: a record of the transactions between one country and the other countries with which it trades.

Balance of trade: the balance of the import and export of goods.

Barriers to entry: any barriers which prevent or inhibit the entry of firms into an industry or market.

Barriers to exit: any barriers which prevent or inhibit the exit of firms out of an industry or market.

Black economy: unofficial economic activity beyond the gaze of the tax authorities.

Brainstorming: is normally taken to mean a discursive activity designed to generate ideas and solutions to problems.

Bureaucracy: an organisational form associated with hierarchy and a system of rules and procedures.

Bureaucrats: in government those who are official and permanent advisers to elected decision-makers e.g. civil servants.

Business angels: informal investors in business organisations, especially smaller enterprises.

Business culture: the underlying attitudes and values of business organisations which affect their decisions and operations.

Business Link: an agency which provides advice and information to UK small businesses.

Business-to-Business (B2B) Commerce: The full spectrum of e-commerce that can occur between two business organisations, including supply management, procurement and purchasing, sale activities, payments, and service and support.

Business-to-Consumer (B2C) Commerce: The full spectrum of e-commerce business models, in which businesses sell to consumers.

Buyers' market: a market where there is excess supply of the product. This affords the buyer greater market power.

Buy-Side Marketplace: a marketplace where one organisation does all the buying.

Cabinet: in UK central government the core decision-making body comprising the Prime Minister and the other senior ministers responsible for formulating government policy and overseeing its implementation.

CAD: the use of computers in the design of products and processes.

Capacity: under contract law, capacity is the notion that a party to an offer is legally able to enter into a binding contract

Capital: man-made assets which are capable of producing goods and services.

Capital account: a record of the international flows of money for investment purposes.

Capital market: the market for longer term loanable funds.

Capitalist economy: a politico-economic system based upon private property and the pursuit of private profit through entrepreneurial activity.

Cartel: a collection of firms acting together as one producer to exercise market power.

Case law: law established by previous judicial decisions i.e. judicial precedent.

Central bank: a country's state or national bank, usually responsible for exercising control over the country's monetary system.

Centrally planned economy: an economy in which the state makes the major decisions over resource allocation.

Chambers of Commerce: a body representing the interests of smaller firms in a particular locality.

Checks and balances: in a democratic system the existence of social, economic and political arrangements which act as a constraint on the power of government.

Circular flow of income model: a simplified model of the economy which portrays economic activity as a flow of income and expenditures passing between households and firms in a circular motion.

City Action Teams: teams of individuals drawn from government, voluntary organisations, local community groups and businesses to tackle problems in inner city areas.

City Challenge: a scheme designed to concentrate resources in areas experiencing urban problems by establish cross-sector partnerships to bid for project funding.

City Grant: a system of grant-aid that was designed to support private sector capital projects in urban areas.

Civil servants: permanent officials appointed to advise government ministers and to implement government decisions. Also called bureaucrats.

Classical theories of organisation: theories of organisation which essentially focus on organisations as formal structures established to achieve certain objectives under the direction of management.

Coalition government: a government formed by representatives of two or more parties either by choice or following an election in which no single party wins a majority of the seats being contested.

Codes of practice: a code of conduct, usually drawn up voluntarily with the aid of a professional or trade association, which members of the trade or profession are expected to follow.

Collusion: co-operation between independent firms to modify their behaviour.

Common Agricultural Policy: a policy set up by the European Union to help the agricultural sector in Europe.

Common external tariff: a tariff payable on goods entering the European Union from non-member countries.

Common Market: a group of countries acting as one in terms of trade – there are no barriers to trade between members and a common external tariff for non-members.

Company: a corporate body recognised by law as having a legal identity separate from that of its members (i.e. shareholders).

Company directors: individuals appointed or elected by a company's shareholders to run the company and to represent their interest.

Competition Act 1998: a major piece of UK competition policy designed to bring UK law in line with EU law on issues of anti-competitive agreements and abuse of dominant market position.

Competition Commission: a public body replacing the UK Monopolies and Mergers Commission with responsibilities in the field of competition policy.

Competition policy: government policy aimed at promoting competition in the market place by regulating market behaviour and controlling potential abuses of market power by firms acting singly or in concert.

Competitive advantage: the sources of superior performance by an organisation.

Complements: products which are related to each other such that as the price of one goes up the demand for the other goes down, CD players and CDs as an example.

Concentration: a measure of the level of competition in an industry or market. Concentration can be measured by sales or employment.

Concentration ratio: a ratio which calculates the percentage of the total market accounted for by the largest firms.

Confederation of British Industry: a body formed to promote the interests of British industry and to represent its views in government circles in an attempt to influence government decisions.

Conglomerate integration: a merger or take-over between firms in different, unrelated industries.

Consideration: under contract law some right, interest, profit or benefit accruing to one party or some forbearance, detriment, loss or responsibility given, suffered, or undertaken by the other.

Consortium: an association or syndicate of business organisations normally established in order to undertake a major enterprise by polling resources and/or expertise.

Consumer societies: a form of 'self-help' organisation set up to serve its members.

Consumer sovereignty: the notion that the pattern of supply and hence the allocation of resources in the economy is dictated by the demands of consumers.

Contestable market: a market where there are no barriers to entry or exit.

Contingency approaches: in organisational theory the idea that organisational design and management should adapt to the situation confronting an organisation.

Corporate image: essentially how an organisation is seen by its customers and other interested parties.

Corporate social responsibility: the idea that an organisation should be responsible for the effect its actions might have on the broader society.

Cost-benefit analysis: a technique which seeks to evaluate the social costs and benefits of an investment project as an aid to decision-making.

Council: in local government, the central elected decision-making body.

Criminal law: that branch of law which relates to a legal wrong, a breach of public duty punishable by the state on behalf of society.

Cross price elasticity: the responsiveness of quantity demanded of one product to changes in the price of other products.

Cross subsidisation: where profits from one market can be used to keep prices down in another market – common in multinationals.

Cross-impact matrix: a technique for evaluating and assessing environmental change based on an identification of events thought likely to occur including an indication of their sequencing and probability of occurrence.

Crowding out: the thesis that the use of funds by government for public expenditure denies the private sector access to those funds for entrepreneurial activity.

Current account (Balance of Payments): a record of the international flows of money in exchange for goods and services.

Current balance (Balance of Payments): the balance of payments on the current account.

Customs: particular forms of behaviour which have come to be accepted as social norms within a specific community.

Customs Union: a union of countries which constitute a single customs territory (see common market above).

Cyclical unemployment: unemployment which results from downswings in the trade cycle.

Debentures: long term bonds or loans to the company on which it pays interest.

Deficit (Balance of Payments): a situation where imports are greater than exports, so that there is an outflow of money from a country.

De-industrialisation: a decline in the importance of manufacturing industry in the economy.

Delegated legislation: law made by a person or body to which Parliament has given limited powers of law-making.

Demand: the quantity of a product that buyers are willing and able to buy at every conceivable price level.

Demand Chain Management (DCM): the management of the organisation's activities related to its customers, distribution channels, and markets.

Demand curve: a graph which shows the relationship between the price of a product and the quantity demanded of that product.

Democracy: literally government by the people. In practice democracy refers to the idea of elected government, based upon universal suffrage and regular, free and fair elections.

Demographic time bomb: the shortage of young people entering the labour force as a result of low birth rates 16 years earlier.

Derived demand: a demand for a product which is not required for its own sake but because it is used to produce another product.

Devaluation: a deliberate reduction in the exchange rate of a currency.

Differentiation: making a product different in the minds of consumers – these difference may be real or imagined.

Digital products (services): products that are transformed to information that can be expressed digitally. Music, computer software, and movies are examples of products that can be digitised and delivered electronically to buyers.

Direct controls: government policies designed to tackle specific economic problems such as the control of imports or wage inflation.

Direct democracy: where government decisions are based upon the expressed preference of the people, usually through a referendum.

Direct taxation: taxes imposed on income and wealth.

Director General of Fair Trading: in the UK the person responsible for overseeing consumer affairs and competition policy on behalf of the government.

Diseconomies of scale: increases in average costs of production which occur when an organisation grows in size (or scale). These mainly stem from the problems of managing large organisations.

Diversification: extending production into unrelated areas through development of new products or entry into unrelated markets.

Dividends: the distribution of part of the company's profit to its shareholders.

Divisional structure: an organisational form involving the splitting up of an organisation into a number of self-contained units or divisions, each of which operates as a profit centre.

Downsizing: a reduction in the size of the firm, normally through redundancy and/or delayering.

Eco-label: a system of labelling products so as to identify those which have a reduced impact on the environment.

Eco-Management and Audit Scheme (EMAS): a voluntary EU standard indicating a participating firm's level of environmental management.

Economic efficiency: efficiency in the use and allocation of resources.

Economic growth: a country's increase in national income (national output) over time.

Economic scarcity: a situation in which there are insufficient resources to satisfy all the actual and potential demands for those resources.

Economics: a social science concerned primarily with the production, distribution and consumption of goods and services under conditions of relative economic scarcity.

Economies of scale: reductions in average costs of production which occur when an organisation grows in size (or scale). These can stem from a variety of sources including technical, marketing and financial.

Educated workforce: a workforce which has the necessary level of education and training for a modern economy.

Elasticity of demand: the responsiveness of quantity demanded of a product to changes in its price.

Elasticity of supply: the responsiveness of quantity supplied of a product to changes in its price.

Electoral system: a system for electing a country's or area's governing authority.

Electronic Business (*E-Business*): The exchange of products, services, or information, whether paid or unpaid, across electronic networks, at any stage within the value system (including the supply chain, the value chain, and the distribution chain). The term embraces activities such as servicing customers, and collaboration with partners.

Electronic Commerce (*E-Commerce*): *E-Commerce* covers a narrower sphere of activities than *E-Business*, and refers in particular to the process of electronic transactions involved in the exchange of products, services, and information between a buyer and seller.

Electronic Customer Relationship Management (eCRM): software and management practices designed to serve the customer from order through delivery and after-sales service.

Electronic Data Interchange (EDI): the computer-to-computer exchange of structured data, sent in a form that allows for automatic processing with no manual intervention. This is usually carried out over specialist EDI networks.

Electronic Enterprise (*E-Enterprise*): An organisation that uses the Internet and/or WWW to execute some, or all, of its main business processes.

Electronic Fund Transfer (EFT): the process of exchanging account information electronically over private communications networks.

Electronic Markets (*E-Markets*): The business centre, where business transactions take place, is a network-based location, and not a physical location. This is sometimes referred to as the *marketspace*. The buyers, sellers, and intermediaries are all situated at different locations. The electronic market handles all the necessary transactions, including the transfer of payments.

English Partnerships: a government development agency involved in reclaiming industrial sites for economic purposes.

Enterprise: the business unit or organisation as a whole.

Entrepreneurship: often added as a fourth factor of production, it is the act of bringing together land, labour and capital in the production of goods and services.

Environmental analysis: the process of monitoring and evaluating the nature and direction of change in the business environment.

Environmental change: the predisposition of the business environment to undergo change rather than to remain static.

Environmental Management System: a formalised set of procedures designed to guide an organisation on how to control its impact on the natural environment.

Environmental scanning: see environmental analysis.

Equilibrium price: the price at which demand and supply are equal. It is the market clearing price.

Equity: the ordinary share capital of the company.

Establishment: parts or branches of an enterprise. Large enterprises like supermarkets are likely to have a number of branches or establishments.

European Commission: the EUs major bureaucratic arm responsible for implementing EUdecisions, for proposing policies and legislation and for acting as guardian of the Treaties.

European Economic Area: an organisation which consists of members of the EU and members of the European Free Trade Association.

European Monetary System: a system of fixed exchange rates for members of the EU.

European Parliament: the EUs elected decision-making body.

Excess demand: where market price is below equilibrium price and as a result demand exceeds supply.

Excess supply: where market price is above equilibrium price and as a result supply exceeds demand.

Exchange control: a limit on the quantity of currency that can be purchased.

Exchange rate: the price at which one currency exchanges for another currency.

Exchange rate mechanism: a system of fixed exchange rates.

Executive directors: company directors with responsibility for a division or functional area within an organisation.

Export subsidy: a payment made to the producers of goods and services for export.

External environment: the external context within which an organisation exists and operates.

External growth: growth in firm size which takes place through merger or take-over.

Externalities: the spill-over effects of economic activity that are over and above the private costs and benefits that occur.

Extranet: a Web-based network that connects an organisation's network to the networks of its business partners, selected customers, or suppliers.

Factor market: the market where factors of production are bought and sold.

Factor of production: a resource used in the production of goods and services in an economy – land, labour, capital and entrepreneurship.

Factory gate prices: literally the price of goods leaving an organisation which can be used as an indication of possible future inflationary pressures in the economy.

Federal system of government: a system of government in which decision-making authority is split between a central (i.e. federal) government and government at sub-national level.

Financial account (Balance of Payments): a record of the international flows from trade in financial assets.

Financial intermediaries: individuals or institutions which help to link borrowers to lenders in the financial system.

First Mover Advantage: in the context of E-Business, an assumption that the deployment of the internet would increase switching costs and create strong network effects, which would provide first movers with competitive advantages and robust profitability.

First-past-the-post system: a system of elections in which the winner in a given constituency is the person with a simple majority of the vote cast. Also called a plurality system.

Fiscal policy: government policy concerned with the taxing and spending decisions of government.

Five forces model: an economic model used to characterise industries and markets. It says that these are formed by five forces acting upon them – current competition, potential competition, the power of buyers, the power of sellers and the power of suppliers.

Fixed capital: the investment in fixed physical assets within a firm – buildings, plant and machinery are examples.

Fixed exchange rate: where the exchange rate is determined by the government or some other authority.

Flexible firm: a firm which is organised in such a way that it distinguishes between core and peripheral activities as a cost saving measure.

Floating exchange rate: where the exchange rate is determined by the free market.

Formal structures: the intended or official structure within an organisation that represents the way it is intended to function.

Franchising: an agreement between two parties in which the one permits the other to market something in its possession according to an agreed format and under certain contractual conditions.

Free market economy: an economic system in which resource allocation is determined by market forces.

Full employment: when all or virtually all the labour force in a country is employed in paid work.

Functional organisation: an organisational form based on the grouping of individuals by common purpose or function.

Functional specialisation: where individuals within an organisation specialise in particular tasks associated with a specific function such as marketing or production.

G7 nations: the Group of Seven leading industrial nations namely USA, Japan, UK, France, Germany, Canada, Italy. The G8 incorporates Russia

Gearing: the proportional relationship between a firm's debt capital and its equity capital.

General (or Contextual) environment: the broad external context in which an organisation exists and operates. It comprises the PESTLE factors.

Genetically modified foods: food products which have undergone some element of genetic modification.

Geographical immobility: the inability to move between geographical locations.

Globalisation: the internationalisation of products and markets.

Golden share: a special retained share holding by government when privatising a state owned organisation that permits the government to exercise some control over future developments.

Government: the structures and processes within a given territory by which laws are made and put into effect.

Government departments: large, state bureaucratic agencies which play a key role in shaping and implementing government policy within their sphere of competence.

Government spending: spending by government on public goods and services. Also called public spending or public expenditure.

Gross domestic product: the value of total economic activity within an economy over a particular period of time.

Gross investment: the total amount of capital goods purchased by firms.

Headline inflation: the rate of inflation in the UK including the effect of mortgage interest payments. Known as RPI.

Holding company: a company set up to maintain or gain control of one or more other companies by holding a majority of shares of these subsidiaries.

Homogeneous products: products which are regarded by consumers as identical to each other and therefore perfect substitutes.

Horizontal integration: a merger or take-over between competitor firms at the same stage of the production process.

House of Commons: the lower house of the UK Parliament with major responsibility for discussing and deciding on laws proposed by the government.

House of Lords: the upper house of the UK Parliament, currently with limited powers.

Human relations approach: an approach to the study of organisation and management which emphasises the importance of social and psychological factors in the workplace.

Human Resource Management: the management of people within an organisation, including the processes of selection, recruitment, performance evaluation, rewards and compensation and training and development.

Immediate (or Operational) environment: the more immediate external influences on an organisation from its customers, competitors, suppliers and other stakeholder groups.

Immobility of labour: the inability of labour to move between geographical locations, jobs or occupations.

Import control: a control placed on the import of goods and services into a country. This could be in the form of a quota, a tariff or exchange controls.

Income elasticity: the responsiveness of quantity demanded to changes in household income.

Income flows: flows of income or expenditure in the economy between its constituent parts as a result of economic activity.

Indirect taxation: taxation imposed on consumption or spending.

Industrial concentration: the proportion of an industry which is dominated by large firms.

Industrial policies: loosely speaking any government policy designed to improve the performance of a country's industries.

Industrial structure: the combination of industries and sectors in an economy.

Inferior goods: goods where, as income rises, demand falls.

Inflation: an increase in the general level of prices within the economy which results in a fall in the value of money (i.e. in the purchasing power of a given nominal sum of money).

Information technology: the use of computer systems for storing, retrieving and communicating information.

Infrastructure: services considered to be essential to a developed economy, such as power and transport systems.

Injections: in the circular flow of income model, those major increases in spending over and above consumption which increase the level of income in the economy (e.g. export spending, investment spending, government spending).

Inner City Task Forces: small teams of civil servants and others established to promote economic development in inner city urban locations.

Innovation: the use of new ideas, methods or approaches.

Inputs: the resources which flow into the production process in order to produce outputs.

Intention to create legal relations: under contract law, the notion of an intent to enter into a contract that is recognised in law as being legally binding.

Interdependence: the idea of the interconnectedness of firm behaviour in an oligopoly market.

Interest rates: the price(s) of borrowed money.

Internal growth: growth in the firm which takes place from within.

Internet: a global network of computer networks that use a common protocol (TCP/IP) for communication.

Intranet: a network within a single organisation that enables access to company information using internet technology such as web browsers and email.

Investment: spending by firms on capital goods – physical productive assets.

Investment appraisal: the analysis of the costs and benefits of possible new investment projects with a view to deciding on the desirability of committing resources to them.

Invisible trade: the import and export of services.

J-curve effect: a curve which describes the effect of a devaluation of a currency on the balance of payments over time.

Joint venture: a jointly owned and independently incorporated business venture involving more than one organisation.

Judicial precedent: see case law.

Judiciary: the legal institutions within a country responsible for enacting and interpreting the law.

Keynesianism: broadly speaking the view that economic activity is predominantly shaped by demand.

Knowledge Management infrastructure: an infrastructure that provides an organisation with a framework for making knowledge available where it is required internally.

Labour: human resources.

Labour market: the market(s) in which wage levels are theoretically determined by the supply and demand for labour.

Labour market flexibility: the degree to which individuals in the labour market are able to respond to changing market demands.

Land: natural resources; resources which are not man-made including the soil, air, seas, minerals etc.

Law of demand: as the price of a product rises the quantity demanded will normally fall.

Law of supply: as the price of a product rises the quantity supplied will normally rise.

Leakages: in the circular flow of income model, those activities which potentially cause a reduction in spending on domestically produced products and hence on income flows in the economy (e.g. taxation, import spending, saving).

Learning curve effect: the idea that performance can be improved as a result of experience in carrying out a procedure or action.

Learning and Skills Council: a newly established body responsible for funding and planning education and training for over 16 year olds in England.

Legislation: laws made by the elected decision-makers. Also called statute law and (in the UK) Acts of Parliament.

Legislature: a country's law-making body.

Licensing: a form of non-equity agreement in which one party (e.g. a firm) grants another party or parties (e.g. another firm) the right to use its intellectual property (e.g. patent, trade name) in return for certain considerations (e.g. royalty payments).

Life cycle analysis: a technique for assessing the environmental impact of a product throughout its life cycle. Sometimes called 'cradle-to-grave' analysis.

Life cycle model: a model of the changes in sales and profitability of a product over time. There are four phases – development, growth, maturity and decline.

Lobbies: groups of individuals actively seeking to influence decision-makers.

Local Enterprise Agencies: companies limited by guarantee, typically set up as partnerships between the private sector and local authorities, to deliver business support services to clients.

Macroeconomic analysis: economic analysis concerned with interactions within the economy as a whole.

Macroeconomic environment: the broad economic influences which are part of the external environment within which firms exist and operate.

Management: the structures and processes involved in directing an organisation towards the achievement of its objectives.

Managing Director: the chief administrative or executive officer within a company who is responsible for ensuring that Board decisions are put into effect and who forms the key link between the Board of directors and the management team of senior executives.

Manifesto: a document setting out a political party's views and policy preferences when seeking election to government.

Manufacturing sector: the sector of the economy which produces manufactured products.

Market: a place where buyers and sellers are brought together.

Market failure: the notion that free markets sometimes deliver solutions which are not always socially or economically desirable.

Market mechanism: the interaction of demand and supply.

Market niche: a gap in a market which can be exploited by a firm by satisfying a need that is not currently being met.

Market structure: the amount of competition that exists between producers in a market.

Marketing: essentially those processes involved in finding out what customers want and supplying them with the product in a way which is profitable to the organisation.

Marketing concept: the idea that organisations should seek to satisfy consumer wants by adopting a customer-focused orientation.

Marketing mix: the set of controllable variables which a firm can use to try to influence the consumer's response.

Marketspace: the digital equivalent of a physical-world marketplace.

Mass Customisation: the ability to provide tailored products or services for individual customers or a group of similar customers, but retains the economies of scope and the capacity of mass marketing or production.

Matrix structure: an organisational form based on both functional specialisation and structures built round products, projects or programmes.

Memorandum of Association: a document setting out the name of a company, its legal status, the address of its registered office, its objects, the amount of nominal share capital and a number of other aspects of the firm's operations.

MEPs: directly elected members of the European Parliament.

Merger: the voluntary combination of two or more separate companies into one.

Merit goods: goods/services which the government feels to be of general benefit to the community and which are therefore often funded by the state (e.g. education).

Microeconomic analysis: economic analysis which focuses on economic decisions by both individuals and firms.

Minimum efficient scale: the level of production where all economies of scale have been reached by the firm.

Minimum wage: the specification of a minimum level for wage rates.

Ministers: individuals who occupy senior decision-making roles in government.

Monetarism: broadly speaking the view that the level of output and employment in the economy are supply determined.

Monetary aggregates: the different measures used to calculate the money stock.

Monetary policies: government policies concerned with the availability and/ or price of credit within the economy.

Money market: the market for short-term funds.

Money stock: the quantity of money in existence in an economy as determined by which monetary aggregates are included in the calculation.

Monopolistic competition: a market structure where there are a large number of sellers producing a differentiated product.

Monopoly: a market structure where there is one dominant producer.

Monopsony: a market where there is a single buyer.

Multinational corporation: an enterprise that operates in a number of countries and which has production or service capabilities outside the country of origin.

Multiplier effect: a measure of the effect on total national income of some component change in aggregate monetary demand.

National debt: the accumulated debt from borrowings by past and present governments.

Nationalised industry: a state owned and controlled industry.

Natural monopoly: a industry where production conditions (e.g. large economies of scale) mean that the least wasteful market structure is monopoly.

Natural resources: resources which are not man-made (see land above).

Negotiated environment: the idea that the policy making environment in a democratic country is characterised by a bargaining process involving individuals, groups and government in shaping decisions.

Net investment: the level of investment after replacement investment has been taken out – it represents net additions to the capital stock.

Networking: the relationships that exist between organisations and the people within those organisations.

New Deal: a UK government programme aimed at tackling the problem of social exclusion.

Non-executive directors: directors in a company (usually part-time) without functional responsibility.

Non-price competition: the use of non-price factors to sell a product e.g. advertising, branding or special offers.

Non-renewable resources: resources which cannot be replenished after use, such as oil and coal.

Normal goods: goods where, as income rises, demand falls.

Normal profits: the minimum profit required by the entrepreneur to stay in production.

Occupational immobility: the inability of workers to move between different occupations.

Occupational structure: the proportions of the workforce in different occupational groups.

Offer: under contract law a declaration by the offeror that they intend to be legally bound by the terms stated in an offer if it is accepted by the offeree.

Office of Fair Trading: a non-ministerial government department responsible for consumer affairs in the UK.

Oligopoly: a market structure where there are a small number of large producers and a great deal of interdependence of decision making.

One-to-One marketing: a unique dialogue that occurs directly between an organisation and individual customers.

Open system: a system in interaction with the external environment.

Opportunity cost: the real cost of a decision expressed in terms of the value of the alternative courses of action which have been sacrificed.

Ordinary shares: or 'equity' are shares in a company which do not carry a fixed dividend. Dividends paid depend upon the performance of the company.

Organisation by product: an organisational form in which the division of work is determined by the product or service being provided.

Organisation chart: a diagram which seeks to portray the responsibilities and relationships within an organisation or part of an organisation.

Outputs: the goods or services or other results that derive from the production process.

Parliament: in the UK the supreme law-making body.

Parliamentary system of government: a system of government based on election to a parliament from whom the senior members of the political executive are chosen.

Participation rate: the proportion of the population that works.

Partnership: an unincorporated form of business organisation comprising two or more individuals working together for mutual benefit.

People: human resources or labour.

Perfect competition: a market structure in which there are many buyers and sellers all producing an identical product and where the degree of competition is very high.

Perfect knowledge: where all actors in a market have complete knowledge of everything in the market.

Perfect mobility: a situation where there are no barriers to movement – it can be applied to firms, consumers and workers.

PESTLE Analysis: analysis of the business environment which focuses on the political, economic, social, technological, legal and ethical influences on the firm.

Plebiscites: see referendums.

Political accountability: the idea that elected politicians are ultimately accountable for their actions and decisions to the people who elected them.

Political executive: the key elected decision-making part of government responsible for the formulation and implementation of government policy and legislation.

Political parties: voluntary groups of like-minded individuals who organise themselves to contest elections and to seek formal political office.

Political sovereignty: the legitimate authority given to an individual or group to make decisions affecting large numbers of people.

Politics: the processes which help to determine how conflicts are contained, modified, postponed or settled.

Polluter pays principle: the idea that the responsibility for resolving environmental problems rests with the person causing them.

Porter's Five Forces model: see 'Five forces model'.

Preference shares: shares in a company which carry a fixed dividend.

Presidential system of government: a system of government in which the head of government or chief executive is elected separately by the people and is not normally part of the elected legislature.

Pressure groups: voluntary groups of like-minded people who join together in order to seek to influence government decision-makers. See also 'lobbies'.

Price ceiling: a maximum price above which the price of the product is not allowed to rise.

Price competition: the use of changing prices to sell products.

Price controls: a control exercised over price which prevents the working of the market mechanism.

Price discrimination: the charging of different prices to different users for the same product.

Price elasticity of demand: the responsiveness of quantity demanded of a product to changes in its price.

Price floor: a minimum price below which the price of the product is not allowed to fall.

Price leadership: where one firm in an industry takes the lead in setting prices and other firms follow.

Price maker: a producer that has enough market power to influence price.

Price taker: a producer that has no power over price, as in perfect competition.

Price war: a situation where a reduction in price by one company is followed by reductions in price by other companies.

Primary sector: the part of an economy that deals with the extraction of raw materials, including agriculture and mining.

Prime Minister: the head of government and of the majority party in the UK Parliament.

Principal: under agency law, a person or organisation hiring an agent to act on their behalf.

Private law: law governing the relationship between individuals.

Private Limited Company: an incorporated business organisation restricted by its Articles of Association from any invitation to the general public to subscribe for its shares or debentures.

Privatisation: the process of transferring the ownership of state assets to the private sector.

Process innovation: the development of new approaches in the production process.

Product innovation: the development of new products.

Product market: the market where products are bought and sold.

Productivity: the relationship between input and output, for example labour productivity measures output per worker.

Professional lobbyist: a person or organisation paid to lobby on behalf of another person or organisation.

Profit: the payment or reward to the entrepreneur for bringing together the other factors of production.

Profit centre: a section or area of an organisation to which revenue can be traced and costs attributed so that profits (or losses) can be ascribed to that area.

Project team: a temporary form of organisational structure set up to carry out a particular task.

Proportional representation: a form of voting system in which the final result of a ballot more closely approximates the number of votes cast for a candidate or candidates than under a first-past-the-post system of voting.

Public corporation: a state owned and controlled organisation set up to run a publicly owned enterprise.

Public goods: goods which must be supplied communally because they cannot be withheld from one individual without withholding them from all (e.g. national defence).

Public law: laws relating to the relationship between individuals and the state.

Public Limited Company (PLC): an incorporated form of business organisation which can invite the general public to subscribe for its shares and debentures.

Public sector net borrowing: the extent to which a government's annual expenditure on public goods and services exceeds it revenue from taxation and other sources of income.

Public sector organisations: organisations in the state sector of the economy.

Qualified majority vote (qmv): a voting system in which the outcome of a vote is determined by a previously agreed proportion of votes cast by the majority of voters.

Quality of people: the quality of labour in a country, which is largely determined by the level of education and training.

Quota: a physical limitation on the level of imports.

Real cost: see 'opportunity cost'.

Real flows: flows of good and services and resources in the economy as a result of economic activity.

Real interest rates: the true cost of borrowing allowing for inflation.

Real national income: the value of the national income having allowed for price inflation.

Recession: a downturn in economic activity, currently defined in the UK as two successive quarters of negative economic growth.

Re-engineering: radical redesign of business processes.

Referendums: an example of direct democracy in which individuals are able to cast their vote for or against a proposal with the expectation that the majority view will prevail. Also called plebiscites.

Region: a geographical area possessing certain characteristics which help to differentiate it from surrounding areas thus permitting boundaries to be drawn around it.

Regional Development Agencies: recently established agencies in the UK regions for designing and delivering integrated programmes of regional regeneration.

Regional Selective Assistance: a discretionary form of government assistance to businesses under UK regional policy.

Renewable resources: resources that can be replenished after use, such as fishing stocks and solar power.

Replacement investment: spending on capital goods which replace old and worn out capital goods.

Representative government: government chosen to represent the people through a system of democratic election.

Research and development: the introduction of and the development of new ideas.

Resources: scarce inputs into the production process used to produce goods and services.

Retail Prices Index (RPI): a weighted index of a 'basket of consumer goods and services' used in the UK to calculate the rate of inflation.

Revaluation: a deliberate increase in the exchange rate of a currency.

Scenario writing: a technique of environmental analysis based on imagined future developments in the business environment.

Scientific management: an approach to organisation and management which essentially believes that scientific methods can be used to improve performance in the work place.

Secondary sector: the part of an economy that includes industries which process raw materials, like manufacturing and construction.

Secretary of State: in UK government, the political head of a major government department.

Self-regulation: where the state allows organisations (e.g. businesses) to regulate themselves in certain areas (e.g. environmental performance).

Sellers' market: a market where there is excess demand for the product. This affords the seller greater market power.

Sell-Side Marketplace: a marketplace where one organisation does all the selling.

Separation of powers: where the three major functions of government are held by separate authorities.

Sex distribution of population: the balance of men and women in a population.

Shareholders: the owners (or members) of a limited company.

Single Market: a common market (see above). Often applied to the European Union.

Single Regeneration Budget: a scheme to bring together a number of programmes from different government departments aimed at simplifying and streamlining the assistance available for local regeneration.

Skill shortages: shortages which exists in certain skills (e.g. IT skills) and which at times can co-exist with unemployment.

Small firm: a firm which is small in terms of the number of people it employs or its turnover.

Smart Cards: physical cards that contain a memory chip that can be inserted into a smartcard reader before items can be purchased.

Social capital: capital that is owned by the community such as hospitals and schools.

Social costs and benefits: the costs and benefits to society associated with production and consumption decisions.

Sole trader: an unincorporated form of business organisation owned by one individual. Also called a sole proprietorship.

Speculation: the buying and selling of currencies in order to make a capital gain on any movements in exchange rates.

Stakeholders: anyone with an interest in an organisation and who is affected by and can affect its performance.

Standard Industrial Classification (SIC): the official classification of industries in the UK, it is based on the European classification – Nomenclature générale des activités économiquees dans les Communautés européennes (NACE).

State bank: see 'central bank'.

Statute law: see 'legislation'.

Sticky prices: this describes the phenomenon of rigid prices commonly found in oligopolistic markets.

Stock: the capital of a business entity.

Stock exchange: a market for second-hand securities.

Strategic fit: the notion of achieving a match or fit between the organisation's internal and external environments in pursuit of its objectives.

Strategic management: the management of the organisation as a whole through strategic analysis, choice and implementation.

Structural unemployment: unemployment caused by a decline in a particular industry as a result of a long term change in demand or technological conditions.

Structure-conduct-performance model: an economic model used to characterise industries and markets. It says that the structure of the market determines conduct which in turn determines performance.

Subcontracting: the outsourcing of part of the production process to another firm.

Substitutes: products which are related to each other such that as the price of one goes up the demand for the other goes up e.g. different brands of petrol.

Sub-systems: the component parts of a system.

Supply: the quantity of a product that sellers are willing and able to sell at every conceivable price level.

Supply Chain Management (SCM): the management of the organisation's activities related to its suppliers, and supply channels.

Supply curve: a graph which shows the relationship between the price of and the quantity supplied of a product.

Supreme Court: the ultimate judicial authority in interpreting the law under a written constitution.

Surplus (balance of payments): a situation where the value of exports is greater than the value of imports, so that there is an inflow of money into a country.

Sustainable development: an approach to economic growth and development which takes account of the social and environmental consequences.

SWOT (or TOWS) analysis: a technique for analysing a firm's internal strengths and weaknesses and its external opportunities and threats.

Systems approach: an approach to organisational analysis which portrays organisations as socio-technical systems interacting with their external environment.

Takeover: the acquisition of one company by another.

Tariff: a tax imposed on imported products.

Technological change: changes in the technology used in production – automation and computerisation are examples.

Technological unemployment: unemployment resulting from the replacement of labour by technology (e.g. robotics).

Technology: the sum of knowledge of the means and methods of producing goods and services.

Tertiary sector: the part of the economy devoted to the production of services.

The Delphi method: a technique of environmental analysis involving several iterations by expert observers of the business environment. Also called expert opinion.

Theory X and Y: the idea that management sees individuals in the workplace as either inherently lazy or committed to the organisation and seeking responsibility.

Theory Z: an approach to management which gives individuals a positive orientation towards an organisation as a result being of provided with a number of discernible benefits.

Third way: broadly speaking the notion of new progressivism in politics based on the traditions of social democracy as applied to the modern world.

Top-down approaches: the tendency for decisions to be determined by those in formal positions of authority.

Tort: a civil wrong other than a breach of contract or a breach of trust; a duty fixed by law on all persons.

Trade Associations: bodies formed to protect and assist members in the same industry.

Trade Union: organisations of workers which are designed to counteract and protect their members from the power of the employer.

Training and Enterprise Councils: a system set up by the UK government to run its national training programme. Now replaced by the Learning and Skills Council.

Transfer pricing: internal pricing used in large organisations to transfer products (raw materials for example) between divisions.

Transformation system: a system by which inputs are converted into outputs.

Transnational corporation: an international organisation that does not have a national base.

Trend extrapolation: a technique for predicting the future based on an analysis of the past.

Trend-impact analysis: a technique of environmental analysis designed to examine the likely impact on forecasted trends of a range of variables.

Trust: an equitable obligation imposing on one or more persons a duty of dealing with property, over which they have no control, for the benefit of other persons who may enforce the obligation.

Trusted control protocol/Internet protocol (TCP/IP): the standard for passing of data packets on the Internet.

Underlying inflation: the rate of inflation excluding the effect of mortgage interest payments. In the UK known as RPIX.

Unitary system of government: a system of government in which sovereign power is vested in a single central authority.

Unlimited personal liability: in unincorporated business organisations the legal liability of the owner of the business for all the debts of the business.

Urban Development Corporations: independent government development agencies set up to oversee inner-city regeneration in designated areas.

Value System: an interconnection of processes and activities within and among organisations that create benefits for intermediaries and end consumers.

Vertical integration: a merger or take-over between firms at different stages of the production process.

Virtual organisation: broadly speaking a loose web of freelance individuals or businesses who organise themselves to produce a specific consumer product. Also an organisation where the core operating company outsources most of its processes to a network of other companies.

Visible trade: the import and export of goods.

Wage rate: earnings per hour or per standard working week excluding overtime payments.

Wages: the payment made to people for their labour services.

Wages/prices inflationary spiral: a situation in which wage increases fuel inflation which in turn fuels further wage demands causing further inflation and so on.

Withdrawals: see 'leakages'.

Workers' co-operatives: a business owned and controlled by the people who work in it and who co-operate for mutual benefit.

Workforce: the number of people able and eligible to work and offering themselves for work.

Working capital: the investment in a firm in capital used on a day-to-day basis such as raw materials; often called circulating capital.

Working week: the number of hours spent in work per week.

Index